THE HISTORY OF THE
OLYMPICS

THE HISTORY OF THE
OLYMPICS

Marshall Cavendish • London New York Sydney

Published by Marshall Cavendish Books Limited
58 Old Compton Street
London W1V 5PA

Some of this material has previously appeared in
the publication *The Game*

First printing 1975

Revised edition 1980

Printed in Great Britain

ISBN 0 85685 729 7

Introduction

In 1980 the world's premier sporting event breaks new ground. The Olympic Games takes its international appeal, its fervour of competition and its ideology into Eastern Europe. Moscow is the setting for the XXII Olympiad. It falls to Russia to ensure the continuing success of this unique sporting extravaganza, the purity of which has been threatened by devastatingly high costs of organization, by political overtones and by professionalism.

The History of the Olympics previews the Moscow Games, the next chapter in the saga of this outstanding occasion in sport. How will it compare with the lavish, western opulence of the two Olympiads of the 70s, in Munich and Montreal? Can the Olympics of the 80s retain its hold on its simple, original philosophy that taking part is more important than winning?

That was certainly the ideal of the first 285 all-male entrants who began the tradition of the Modern Olympics in Athens in 1896. *The History of the Olympics* relives those formative times, and through the colour of words, photographs and statistics examines each subsequent staging of the event up to the multi-sport spectacular of today. From St. Louis to Stockholm, from London to Los Angeles, from Melbourne to Montreal . . . and now to Moscow. A truly world-wide circus that on its travels has uncovered performers who have become legends . . . Emil Zatopek, Fanny Blankers-Koen, Mark Spitz, Olga Korbut and Cassius Clay.

The History of the Olympics also recreates for you the story of the Winter Games, from its first separation from the summer event in 1924. Then, in Chamonix, there were just 14 gold medals, and in the women's figure skating an 11-year-old from Norway finished last. But the Winter Olympics had found its first heroine, for young Sonja Henie was to win gold in each of the next three Winter Olympiads. By 1968 this section of the Games had expanded five-fold.

The history, the pageantry, the raw competitiveness and the friendliness of the Olympic Games are all brought to life in the following pages. It is a tale of sporting heroism which excites and thrills. Today's pressures on the Games are enormous, both financial and political. But when the torch is lit for the first time on Russian soil in July 1980, the quality of the sport will once again surely provide the justification.

One of the truly outstanding sports photos captures the power and determination that won America's Willie Davenport his gold medal in the 110 metres hurdles at Mexico City.

Contents

Foundation and Growth

No sporting event grips the world's imagination like the Olympic Games. The World Cup can fascinate the television viewers of Europe and South America—the baseball World Series transfixes the population of the United States—and the Melbourne Cup brings the state of Victoria to a dead stop. But the Olympics belong to the whole world. Participation in the Games is looked on not only as an achievement, but as an honour. Little-known Africans become household names all over the world . . . American sprinters are offered huge fees to play professional football . . . and Russian soldiers gain promotion . . . simply because they win a small medal in the Olympic Games.

Various legends purport to account for the inception of the Olympic Games in ancient Greece. Pindar tells of how Hercules initiated the Games after cleansing the Augean stables. Augeas, ruler of Elis, made Hercules clean out his enormous stables in a single day. Hercules extracted a promise from the king that if he did so he would be given a tenth of the king's herds. Unwisely, the king did not keep to his side of the bargain, and Hercules promptly killed Augeas and his family, made himself a present of the entire stock of cattle, and instituted the Olympic Games to mark the occasion. This is only a legend, but the Greeks did hold religious Games as a part of everyday life. Homer, in the *Iliad*, describes the ritual Games at the funeral of Patroclus, in about 1100 BC.

The Olympic Games were only one of a number of similar celebrations in Greece, but they became the most important, and a list of champions from the year 776 BC exists. At first the Games occupied only one day, and consisted of a single event—a running race for one length of the stadium (about 210 yards). In time they were extended, lasting five days (with two more days devoted to religious observances). The programme eventually included four running events—the one-stadium-length dash, a race over two lengths of the stadium, a long-distance race (the *dolichos*) of about 2¾ miles, and a race in armour. Combat sports included boxing and the *pankration*—a no-holds-barred event in which only gouging and biting were forbidden. Further elaborations of the programme included a chariot race for *quadrigas*—chariots drawn by four horses—and a pentathlon. As its name implies, the pentathlon consisted of five events, but it was, by some accounts, an elimination contest. The order of the first four events,

the long jump, javelin, discus, and a sprint, is uncertain, but it is generally accepted that wrestling was the fifth event, and was resorted to only if the competition was not already decided.

But the Olympics were essentially religious affairs, and the Greeks always proclaimed a sacred truce—the *hieromenia*—for the duration of the Games, and for the people travelling to and from Olympia. The competitors and spectators had to be male free-born Greeks, though the circumscription on women spectators was later lifted. To the Greeks it was important to win well, and any competitor found guilty of an unfair practice had to pay a fine which was used to build a statue of Zeus at the entrance to the stadium. In all the history of the ancient Games, only 13 of these were erected.

Gradually, the Games lost their reputation, especially after the

Roman Emperor, Nero, entered and was allowed to win the chariot race in AD 66. Finally, in AD 393, the Olympic Games were abolished by a decree from the emperor Theodosius, and in the 5th century the once sacred buildings were demolished. In time, earthquakes and floods buried the site beneath about 20 feet of soil.

The modern Olympics

Happily, the memory and ideals of the Greeks' Olympic organization did not crumble with the ruins of Olympia. In the 19th century, archaeologists began excavating the site of the temple of Zeus, and between 1875 and 1881 most of the Olympia complex was uncovered. With the growing interest in sports of all kinds in the 19th century, it was, perhaps, inevitable that the ideals of the Greek Olympic Games should be revived. The credit for this belongs to the Frenchman Baron Pierre de Coubertin (1863-1937). He thought that at least one reason for the flowering of Greece during the 'Golden Age' was sport and the ideals of the Olympic Games. He also saw a parallel in the stature of 19th-century Britain in the games played at the famous public schools. Furthermore, nothing could be lost—and a great deal gained—by bringing together the youth of the world in friendly competition. The new Olympic Games would be a period of concord in which all differences of status, religion, politics, and race would be forgotten. It was with these thoughts in mind that he summoned an international meeting at the Sorbonne in Paris in 1894, and two years later his

ideas took a concrete form at the first celebration of the modern Olympic Games, in Athens.

In 1894, de Coubertin also founded the International Olympic Committee, which consisted of members chosen by him for their devotion to the Olympic movement. This body has seen the Olympics grow from a small gathering of enthusiasts (285 strong in 1896) to vast gatherings: 5,215 men and 844 women competed at Mexico City in 1968. The IOC awards the Games to a city, rather than a country, some six years before they are due to be held. And because of the commercial gains to be made from hosting the Games, city councils will go to great lengths to impress the IOC. At a special IOC meeting all the cities applying for the Games state their cases with the help of films, models, and press hand-outs. The stadiums are normally built especially for the Olympics, and they remain as amenities for the population afterwards.

The Olympics are held in the first year of an Olympiad, which is a period of four years beginning in a year divisible by four (ie 1896 or 1968). It is a rule of the IOC that the Games must be celebrated in the first year of an Olympiad, and they cannot be postponed. The first modern Olympics were, therefore, held in the first year of the first modern Olympiad—1896 —and so on The Games were to be universal, and so they are held all over the world. Thus, as early as 1904, the Games went to America—St Louis. The Greeks wanted to keep the Olympics in Greece, and in 1906 an Interim Games was held in Athens. But this was the only such 'intercal-

Radio Times Hulton Picture Library

1 The first Olympic torch relay, part of the **1936** celebrations, passed through eastern Europe on its way from Olympia to Berlin. **2** Baron Pierre de Coubertin, the founder of the modern Olympic Games, saw his brain-child grow from a small gathering at Athens in **1896** to world-wide meetings of the world's best sportsmen. **3** De Coubertin's words, the ideal underlying the Olympic movement, are displayed on the scoreboard at the opening ceremony of every Olympic Games. **4** The Olympic torch begins its journey from the host city of Olympia, and is carried in a relay until **5** it burns throughout the Games in the stadium.

London Express News & Feature Service

Mark Shearman

ated' celebration.

The Games of 1900 and 1904 were subordinate to concurrently held trade fairs, and this detracted from their importance. Such unfortunate treatment was amended at the 1908 Games in London, which can justifiably by regarded as the prototype for all subsequent Games.

The first women to compete in the Olympic Games were entrants to the tennis and golf events in 1900. But it was not until 1912 at Stockholm that women's swimming events were included in the Games; and athletics events for women formed part of the programme for the first time at Amsterdam in 1928. Meanwhile, in 1924, a separate Winter Olympic Games had been established, the first of them being held at Chamonix. Before 1932, the Games had been outside Europe only once, but that year both Games were held in the United States—the Winter Games at Lake Placid in New York State and the full Games in Los Angeles. An Olympic Village was established for the first time at the

Los Angeles Games.

As communications became easier more people were able to compete in and visit the Olympics wherever they were held. And as the Games became more important, the host cities endeavoured to outdo the previous hosts. The apotheosis of such one-upmanship came at the Berlin Games of 1936 which were used by the Nazis as a shop-window. Later, nobody wanted to be compared with Germany under the Nazis, and after 1936 the Olympics tried to remain as free from politics as possible. But as the Games have grown as the major international spectacle, receiving unprecedented exposure, they have become more vulnerable to political pressure groups seeking maximum exploitation to further their claims. The threatened boycott by the Africans, and the taking hostage of Israeli team members by Palestinian guerrillas, both at Munich, served as unwanted reminders that politics and sport were linked more than ever before.

World War II necessitated the cancellation of two Olympic Games—the 1940 Games first scheduled for Tokyo and in 1938 awarded to Helsinki, and the 1944 Games scheduled for London. But after 12 years the 1948 Games were held—at short notice—in London. No new sports arenas were built for these Games, but London already had a number of suitable venues.

In 1956 the Olympics were held in Melbourne, the first time they had not been celebrated in Europe or America. But because of the strict Australian quarantine laws the equestrian events had to be held separately, in Stockholm. This remains the only instance of one sport being held in a different country from the main Games.

Tokyo was the host city for the 1964 Games, the first to be held in Asia. The Japanese organized their Games with amazing efficiency and flair, while the hospitality of the people won them many friends. More than £200,000,000 was spent on providing suitable facilities for the Games, including a vast programme of new roads.

There was no more controversial choice of venue for the Olympics than Mexico in 1968. The main criticism was that the rarefied air of the city put 'sea-level' athletes at a grave disadvantage. Though this was a valid point, the Games proved a splendid success. What shocked many, however, was the enormous cost of staging the Games when, it was pointed out, the Mexicans might have put the money to far better use by building decent homes for the thousands of poorly paid and unemployed who are forced to live in a squalor which compares badly with Mexico City's superficial affluence.

The Olympic Games are confined to amateurs. Any amateur sport widely practised—in 40 countries in 3 continents in the case of men's sports and 20 countries in 2 continents in the case of women's (according to the 1970 regulations)—can be considered for inclusion in the Games. Entry standards have been laid down in athletics, although every country is entitled to enter one competitor in every event. In team events, only one team is allowed from any country, but reserves can be used.

The opening and closing ceremonies follow the same basic pattern from one Games to another, although minor changes are made. At the opening ceremony, the words of Baron Pierre de Coubertin are displayed on the scoreboard : 'The important thing in the Olympic Games is not winning, but taking part. The essential thing in life is not conquering but fighting well.' The head of state of the host country enters with the president of the IOC and the president of the organizing committee, and they take their places. The scoreboard then displays the words 'Citius, Altius, Fortius'—faster, higher, stronger. The teams enter, and in accordance with tradition the Greek team leads and the host country brings up the rear. The others march in alphabetical order.

This completed, the president of the organizing committee requests the president of the IOC to ask the head of state or his representative to open the Games. The Olympic flag is raised to the strains of the Olympic hymn, and the official flag of the Games (presented by the Belgian Olympic Committee at the Antwerp Games of 1920) is handed over to the mayor of the host city who keeps the flag until the next celebration. Thousands of pigeons are released, a salute of three guns is fired, and then the final runner in the torch relay from Olympia enters—a feature of the Games which was introduced in 1936. The flame is lit, and the Olympic oath is taken by a competitor of the host country. It reads : 'In the name of all competitors I promise that we will take part in these Olympic Games, respecting and abiding by the rules which govern them, in the true spirit of sportsmanship, for the glory of sport and the honour of our teams.' The Olympic Games have begun.

The closing ceremony is shorter. The central feature is a march of representatives of the competing nations in a single body regardless of their nationality. The name of the host country is displayed on the scoreboard, the Olympic flame is allowed to go out, and the Olympics are over for another four years.

The Olympic opening ceremony is one of the most colourful pageants to be seen anywhere. 1 The Olympic flag is borne into the stadium. 2 Some teams parade in their national dress—Mongolia's flag bearer at the 1968 Games. 3 The host country's team always brings up the rear of the procession—Mexico's team at Mexico City in 1968.

International Olympic Committee

The International Olympic Committee (IOC) is the body responsible for the most important amateur sporting festival in the world, the Olympic Games. It was established in 1894 by the founder of the modern Olympics, Baron Pierre de Coubertin, and the members were chosen personally by him for their devotion to the Olympic movement.

The IOC was, and is, a self-perpetuating body, and its members are considered not as delegates from their countries, but as ambassadors from the IOC. This system has engendered much censure, but the IOC's success is seen in each Olympic Games, and its independence from national influences has much to commend it.

Successive strong presidents have given the IOC its authority, none more so than Avery Brundage, who became president in 1952. His idealistic views have been the subject of much criticism and ridicule, but his uncompromising attitude may have saved the IOC from the worst aspects of commercialism.

Members must speak French or English, and are elected by the IOC themselves, and in general no country has more than one member on the 60-70-strong body. Members are elected for life, but as a rule must retire at 72 years of age. On election, the new member is welcomed by the president and then undertakes to safeguard the Olympic ideals. All members must be free from political, sectarian, and commercial influences.

Every detail of the Olympic Games is controlled by the IOC, and it is the IOC's responsibility to decide, some six years ahead, the venue of both summer and winter celebrations. Regular meetings, and conferences with the representatives of national Olympic committees and international sporting organizations, ensure that the views of every sport and national body are known at first hand to the men who are the most important members of the international amateur sporting fraternity.

Transworld

Above: **Avery Brundage, the president of the IOC from 1952 to 1972 and probably the staunchest defender of the amateur faith in sport.**
Right: **The skiers, with their brand-carrying equipment and star image, often bore the brunt of Brundage's anti-commercialism attitudes.**
Below: **The opening of the Mexico City Olympics—the culmination of many years of planning by the IOC.**

PRESIDENTS OF THE INTERNATIONAL OLYMPIC COMMITTEE	
1894-1896	Dimitrios Vikelas (Greece)
1896-1925	Baron Pierre de Coubertin (France)
1925-1942	Count Henri de Baillet Latour (Belgium)
1946-1952	Sigfrid Edstrom (Sweden)
1952-1972	Avery Brundage (USA)
1972-	Lord Killanin (Ireland)

Ed Lacey

Ed Lacey

Ed Lacey

Mark Shearman

A myriad of sports, and disciplines within those sports, comprise the 'summer' Olympic Games. Athletics, or track and field, is the sport that holds the public more than most, thanks to extensive television coverage and the obvious drama and explosive talent it provides. Swimming, too, has the ability to throw up the instant super-star for the media to exploit. Yet the Olympic Games is much more: in 1972, for example, some 21 sports were contested.

Away from the glare of the main Olympic arena, boxers, weightlifters, gymnasts and others draw the spectators indoors; often well away from the Olympic village, rowers, canoeists, cyclists, yachtsmen, and horsemen (and women) draw their own adherents.

The horse is involved in another event apart from the three equestrian disciplines. This is the modern pentathlon, which requires the courage of the horseman, the steady hand of the marksman, the élan of the fencer, and the durability of the runner and swimmer.

The Summer Olympic Games

Athens Olympic Games (1896)

The first modern Olympic Games, revived about 1,500 years after the original Games died, produced moments of drama and periods of sheer farce—but, mostly the latter. The epic victory of Greek shepherd Spiridon Louis in the marathon, and the high jump won at a shade under 6 ft, cannot be denied as genuine athletic achievements. But then there was the dapper Frenchman who ran his 100-metre heat in white kid gloves . . . the American 100-metre swimmer who dived into the icy sea water, screamed 'I'm freezing!' and hastily climbed out . . . the English tourist who casually entered the tennis tournament—and won it.

It all started in the mind of a French nobleman, Baron Pierre de Coubertin. His great interest was public education, and he believed strongly (and heretically for those days) that you could not separate mental and physical development. He became increasingly despondent about commercialism in sport, and eventually dreamed up an antidote—a revival of the ancient Olympic Games. He envisaged amateur athletes from all parts of the world meeting every four years to compete in a selected number of sports.

In 1894 the baron presided over a congress of 13 nations at the Sorbonne, in Paris. Twenty-one other nations wrote in, also pledging their support. The assembled nations unanimously resolved that: 'in order to maintain and promote physical culture, and particularly to bring about a friendly intercourse between the nations, sports competitions should be held every fourth year on the lines of the Greek Olympic Games and every nation should be invited to participate.'

De Coubertin had planned to hold the first of these modern Games in Paris, in 1900, as part of the Paris International Exposition. But the Greek delegates put in an eloquent plea, based on tradition and history, for Athens as the inaugural seat of the Games. This was agreed, and the date fixed for 1896.

With a scant two years to prepare, the Greek authorities were suddenly faced with a fund-raising problem. They eventually prevailed upon George Averoff, a wealthy Greek philanthropist living in Alexandria, to foot the bill for a million drachmas (nearly £40,000 in those days). With this windfall, plus the money from commemorative stamps and public appeals, the Greeks proceeded to restore the Pan-Athenaic Stadium of Herodis. The 2,000-year-old ruins were rebuilt in marble, with a capacity of about 70,000 spectators. The stadium was about 200 yards long, and the 400-metre track had corners that were impossible to negotiate at speed.

Thirteen nations sent representatives (most of them unofficial) to compete in nine sports: cycling, fencing, gymnastics, lawn tennis, shooting, swimming, athletics, weight-lifting, and wrestling. Rowing had also been on the agenda, but was cancelled because of bad weather. Total entries for all sports were under 500.

The unofficial 13-man American team (five of whom came from the Boston Athletic Association) were unaware that Greece was still using the Julian calendar (which differed from the Gregorian by some 11 days). They did not arrive in Athens until the eve of the Games. To add to their troubles, they had barely recovered from a long and tedious journey by boat and train before they were paraded in front of a hospitable Greek crowd and persuaded to drink innumerable toasts late into the night.

The Panathenaic Stadium, splendidly restored in glistening white marble, formed an apt setting for the first modern Olympic Games.

The opening ceremony of the first modern Olympic Games took place on Easter Monday, April 6, 1896—the 75th anniversary of Greece's independence from Turkey—before 80,000 spectators. In the presence of Queen Olga, Crown Prince Constantine, Baron de Coubertin, and a throng of other VIPs, King George announced: 'I hereby proclaim the opening of the First International Olympic Games in Athens.' The opening ceremony closed with a cantata, and a bugle-call announced the first event.

There were 12 events in the athletics programme. Performances were disappointing, even for those days, even allowing for the horseshoe track and the horribly loose cinders. American athletes won nine of the events; two—the 800 and 1,500 metres—went to a former Australian mile champion then resident in England; and one —the marathon, the last and greatest event of the programme —was won by a Greek.

The first Olympic champion was James B. Connolly, from Boston who won the triple jump with a distance of 44 ft 11¾ in. A Greek came second, more than a yard behind. In those days the event was hardly known outside Greece, and competitors were allowed to take two hops and a jump—today's rules specify a hop, a step, and a jump. The world record of 48 ft 6 in had been set by an American three years before.

Throwing the discus followed. This was another event hardly known outside Greece but, in spite of this, three Greeks, three Danes, an Englishman, an American, a Frenchman, a Swede, and a German took part. Bob Garrett, the American, had never even seen a proper discus before reaching Athens, and was relieved to discover that the real thing was much easier to handle than the crude imitation he had been hurling across the Princeton campus. In the event, the Greeks took full marks for grace, but Garrett led the field by 8 inches. The American later added the shot to his discus triumph.

On the second day, the Americans continued to dominate the track and field events. Ellery Clark won both the long jump and the high jump, and sprinter Tom Burke easily took the 400-metre title in 54.2 sec. Burke had been American champion in 1895 and a few months after the Games clocked a time almost 6 seconds faster for the event—an indication of the atrocious running conditions in Athens. Burke also won the 100-metre final.

The fourth double victor was the Australian Edwin Flack, a member of the London Athletic Club. He beat Arthur Blake of Boston by a yard in the 1,500 metres, easily won the 800 metres on the third day, and soon afterwards departed for Marathon to try his luck in the long-distance race.

This final athletics event was the highlight of the Games. When the programme was being discussed, Michel Bréal, a French student of Greek mythology, suggested the idea of commemorating the feat of a legendary Greek hero with a long-distance race. In 490 B.C. on the plains of Marathon, nearly 25 miles from Athens, the heavily outnumbered Athenians repelled a Persian invasion. According to the legend, Pheidippides, a Greek soldier and champion Olympic runner, was entrusted to carry the good news to the capital. Exhausted after the battle, Pheidippides nevertheless loped off towards Athens and finally staggered into the market place there. He delivered his message, collapsed, and died.

The idea of commemorating the event caught on, and a race was arranged to start on the plains of Marathon over the route that Pheidippides had allegedly covered —a distance of about 40 kilometres (nearly 25 miles) to the stadium in Athens. The host nation had come

nowhere in the track and field events. If they were to salvage anything from the Games, it was now or never.

Among the 25 starters, all of whom had spent the previous night at Marathon, was a 25-year-old, handsome, moustachioed Greek shepherd called Spiridon Louis. During army service he had shown great stamina and all Greece pinned high hopes on him. The competitors started to the sound of a pistol shot from the bridge of Marathon at 2 p.m. precisely. They were accompanied

by a troop of soldiers, acting as marshals; a posse of doctors trundled behind in carts.

After 30 minutes the leader, Lermusiaux of France, reached the village of Pikarni. With rather an optimistic sense of pace he had already surged more than a mile ahead of Flack, in second place. Louis was nowhere, but still supremely confident. At the half-way stage the order was France, Australia, United States. Lermusiaux was so far ahead at Karvati that he was prematurely crowned by the villagers with a victor's gar-

land. But after 32 km he had had enough and dropped out of the race, exhausted. Louis, who had steadily been working his way through the field, came up to Flack's shoulder. At the 36th kilometre Flack suddenly collapsed.

As Louis jogged on, approaching the stadium, the murmur from the crowd swelled to a roar. Hundreds of doves were released. Prince George and Crown Prince Constantine rushed to the entrance, and when the shepherd hero trotted in, a full seven minutes ahead of his nearest rival, they ran round the track beside him on his final lap. Gifts of all kinds were pressed on the victor. As it happened, five of the first six men were Greeks, so honour was saved. Louis had been promised, if he won, a number of 'fringe benefits', such as free haircuts for life, free groceries, free transport, and similar attractions.

The scenes of jubilation had interrupted the pole vault, which was going on in the stadium. Americans took first and second places in the event, helped by poles of extraordinary length which enabled them to jump the (then) fabulous height of 3.30 metres (10 ft 9¾ in).

There were 10 weight-lifters

1 Today, the rebuilt Panathenaic Stadium is preserved as a perpetual monument to the Olympic Games. As a tribute to athletics in general, the closing ceremony of the 1969 European championships was held in the stadium. 2 The start of the 110 metres hurdles manifests a variety of styles, with US winner Tom Curtis getting down on four points. 3 Spiridon Louis, marathon champion, poses after the victory ceremony. In addition to the gold medal and olive branch, awarded to each winner, Louis was also presented with a silver cup and an ancient vase. 4 Baron Pierre de Coubertin, whose vision and untiring efforts led to the world-wide revival of the ancient Olympic Games.

tinidis, the eventual winner, not only had the handicap of a lengthy signature, but managed to break his bicycle shortly after the turn. He borrowed the starter's machine and soon regained his lead. But again he fell off, wrecked the second bicycle, and was overtaken once more. Bloody, but nothing daunted, he jumped onto a friend's bike and pedalled home to victory a good 20 minutes ahead of the second man.

The tennis tournament was a somewhat light-hearted affair held in a shed on the shores of the Illissos. It was won by an English tourist called Boland, who entered because he happened to be there at the time. Sir George Stuart Robertson, the Greek scholar and hammer-throwing Oxford Blue, also entered the tennis tournament —because it was the only way he could get the use of a court. He also took part in the shot-put and discus, and composed and recited the valedictory Greek ode.

Of the 160 entrants for the 200-metre shooting event, 150 were Greeks. The six gymnastics events included an item labelled 'arm exercises with smooth cord', more easily recognizable, perhaps, as rope-climbing. Fencing consisted of a foils contest (in which Frenchmen came first and second), sabres (won by a Greek), and a special foils contest for 'fencing masters'—that is, professionals!

For the record, although the figures are quite without significance, the United States won 11 firsts, Greece 8, Germany 6½, France 5, Britain 2½, Australia, Austria, and Hungary 2 each, and Denmark and Switzerland 1 apiece.

The presentation of prizes, on the tenth and final day, took place in pouring rain. King George of Greece presented each winner with a gold medal and an olive branch. Runners up received a bronze medal and a laurel branch. The specially composed Greek ode was recited, and the winners paraded slowly round the stadium. As the band played and the crowd cheered, a special ovation was reserved for Spiridon Louis, marching proudly and happily in the front row of the champions of the First Olympiad.

competing. Launceston Elliott, from England, won the single-handed lift, but he seems to have attracted more attention for the beauty of his person than for his prowess with the weights. After the contest, a servant who was ordered to remove the weights, found the task beyond him. Prince George came to his aid and, picking up the heaviest weight with ease, threw it a considerable distance.

Launceston Elliott's good looks were of no help to him in the wrestling, in which there were no weight limits. Herr Schumann of Germany, who won the event, seized him round the middle and 'threw him to the ground in the twinkling of an eye', according to a contemporary report.

The swimming events were somewhat parochial. Some were held in the ice-cold water of the Bay of Zea, to the consternation of swimmers who had trained in heated pools. Only 3 of the 29 entries for the 500-metre race took part, and three Greeks were the only swimmers to compete in the race 'for sailors of the Royal Navy'.

Cycling consisted of six events. Three of them, all won by Frenchman Paul Masson, were short—the longest being the 10,000 metres, which Masson narrowly won from his compatriot Léon Flamaud. The latter gained some consolation by winning the 100 km (one of the three long events), consisting of some 300 dizzying laps of the Velodrome. The cycling marathon started in Athens, wended its way to Marathon, where the six competitors had to sign their names on a parchment in the presence of a special commissioner, and returned to the Velodrome in Athens. A. Konstan-

1 Three marathon runners of the 1896 Games get down to a spot of road work with not a horseless carriage in sight.
2 A proud victor receives his olive branch from King George of Greece. **3** The Games are over, and the winners parade slowly round the stadium for the last time.

ATHENS OLYMPIC GAMES, 1896 (Gold Medallists)			
Athletics			
100 metres	Thomas Burke	USA	12.0 sec
400 metres	Thomas Burke	USA	54.2 sec
800 metres	Edwin Flack	Australia	2 min 11.0 sec
1,500 metres	Edwin Flack	Australia	4 min 33.2 sec
Marathon	Spiridion Louis	Greece	2 hr 58 min 50.0 sec
Hurdles	Thomas Curtis	USA	17.6 sec
High Jump	Ellery Clark	USA	5 ft 11¼ in
Pole Vault	William Hoyt	USA	10 ft 10 in
Long Jump	Ellery Clark	USA	20 ft 10 in
Triple Jump	James Connolly	USA	44 ft 11¾ in
Shot	Robert Garrett	USA	36 ft 9¾ in
Discus	Robert Garrett	USA	95 ft 7½ in
Cycling			
333⅓ metres	Paul Masson	France	24. 0 sec
2,000 metres	Paul Masson	France	4 min 56.0 sec
10,000 metres	Paul Masson	France	17 min 54.2 sec
100 km	Leon Flamand	France	3 hr 08 min 19.2 sec
12 hours race	Felix Schmal	Austria	195¾ miles
Marathon (50 miles)	A. Konstantinidis	Greece	3 hr 22 min 31.0 sec
Fencing			
Foil	E. Gravelotte	France	
Foil (for fencing masters)	Leon Pyrgos	Greece	
Sabre	Jean Georgiadis	Greece	
Gymnastics			
Parallel Bars (individual)	Alfred Flatow	Germany	
Horizontal Bars	Hermann Weingartner	Germany	
Pommelled Horse	Louis Zutter	Switzerland	
Long Horse	Karl Schumann	Germany	
Rings	Jean Mitropoulos	Greece	
Rope Climbing	Nicolaos Andriakoupolos	Greece	23.4 sec
Team Events		Germany	
Lawn Tennis			
Men's Singles	P. Boland	GB	
Doubles	P. Boland (GB), Fritz Thraun (Germany)		
Shooting			
Rifle Match 300 metres	Georges Orphanidhis	Greece	
Rifle Match 200 metres	Pantelis Karasseudas	Greece	
Revolver 25 metres	John Paine	USA	
Revolver 30 metres	Sommer Paine	USA	
Pistol 25 metres	Jean Phrangoudis	Greece	
Swimming			
100 metres	Alfred Guttmann	Hungary	1 min 22.2 sec
500 metres	Paul Neumann	Austria	8 min 12.6 sec
1,200 metres	Alfred Guttmann	Hungary	18 min 22.2 sec
100 metres (sailors' race)	Jean Malokinis	Greece	2 min 20.4 sec
Weight Lifting			
One Hand	Launceston Elliot	GB	156 lb (71.0 kg)
Two Hands	Viggo Jensen	Denmark	245 lb (111.5 kg)
Wrestling	Karl Schumann	Germany	

Paris Olympic Games (1900)

In conjunction with the Paris International Exhibition of 1900, various sporting events were held in the French capital from May 14 to October 28. Exactly which of these sports, 15 altogether, can be termed 'Olympic' in the true sense of the word is debatable. A realistic view would seem to be that a number of sports were promoted, and it is a matter of choice which of them should be regarded as official. For instance, there were 23 shooting events with all kinds of weapons: the fencing embraced amateurs and professionals: the swimming competitions—listed in the FINA handbook—included an underwater swim for distance and an obstacle race. There was a tug-of-war in which a joint Danish and Swedish contingent beat the United States, and a tennis tournament in which the Doherty brothers were prominent.

The athletics events—at least some of them—may be regarded as Olympic, although the programme was headed 'Republique Francaise, Exposition Universelle de 1900, Championnats Internationaux'. Even so, the events were haphazardly arranged, and included some contentious handicaps. They were scheduled to take place over two days on a 500-metre grass track laid out in the Bois de Boulogne. The turf was very thick, and was heavily watered. The sprint course and the long jump run-up were said to be downhill, and as part of the course was among trees it was impossible for the timekeepers to see the starter from the winning post. The competitions, such as they were, were marred by the scratching of some Americans who refused to compete on a Sunday.

The star of the athletics was Alvin Kraenzlein of Pennsylvania, who won four events—the 60 metres dash, the 110 and 200 metres hurdles, and the long jump. Another American, Ray Ewry, won three titles—the standing high jump, long jump, and triple jump.

The double-champions in athletics included John Tewksbury, who took the 200 metres and the 400 metres hurdles, and was second in the 100 metres, third in the 200 metres hurdles, and fourth in the 60 metres. Irving Baxter won the high jump and the pole vault, rather luckily in each case because his more favoured rivals refused to compete in the Sunday's finals; Baxter was also second in the standing high and long jumps.

British entries had a field day in the middle-distance events. Alfred Tysoe took the 800 metres in 2 min 1.2 sec, Charles Bennett the 1,500 metres in 4 min 6.2 sec, and in a British clean-sweep of the

1 Irving Baxter—winner of high jump and pole vault at the 1900 Olympic Games.
2 The first great all-rounder in the modern Olympic Games was Alvin Kraenzlein who won the long jump, 60 metres, and both hurdles events.
3 Britain's Charles Bennett won the 1,500 metres and was a member of Britain's winning 5,000 metres team.
4 The great Irish-American hammer thrower John Flanagan won the first of three successive Olympic titles.

4,000 metres steeplechase J. T. Rimmer edged out Bennett for first place. Tysoe, Bennett, and Rimmer all ran for Britain in the 5,000 metres team race in which they defeated a French team. Some idea of the comic opera nature of these 'Games' can be gathered from the fact that another member of Britain's team, Stan Rowley, was an Australian who had previously come third in the 60, 100, and 200 metres sprints.

In the throwing events America won all three titles. Robert Garrett, defending his shot and discus titles, had an unhappy time. In the shot he improved on his Athens performance by nearly 4 ft. but was still beaten into third place by his team-mates Richard Sheldon and Josiah McCracken. In the discus throw, he had trouble throwing the implement straight down a lane of trees, and was unplaced. John Flanagan won the first Olympic hammer title with a respectable 163 ft. 2 in.

The arrangements for the marathon typified the whole proceedings. The race was run on July 19, and the course of 25 miles followed the old Parisian fortifications. As soon as the runners left the Bois and entered the city through the Passy Gate, they were mobbed by a crowd of cyclists and early cars. Only 7 men of the 19 starters finished, and the winner by over 5 minutes was Michel Theato, a Parisian baker's roundsman said to be fully familiar with the course—and the short cuts.

The swimming was held in the River Seine. Britain's John Jarvis

won the 1,000 and 4,000 metres events by considerable margins, and Australia's Freddy Lane the 200 metres freestyle and a 200 metres obstacle race. His prize for the 200 metres was a replica of the Louvre, weighing more than 50 pounds, and for the obstacle race a similar sized bronze of a peasant girl.

PARIS OLYMPIC GAMES, 1900 Champions

Athletics

Event	Name	Country	Result
60 metres	Alvin Kraenzlein	USA	7.0 sec
100 metres	Frank Jarvis	USA	11.0 sec
200 metres	John Tewksbury	USA	22.2 sec
400 metres	Maxwell Long	USA	49.4 sec
800 metres	Alfred Tysoe	Great Britain	2 min 1.2 sec
1,500 metres	Charles Bennett	Great Britain	4 min 6.2 sec
Marathon	Michel Theato	France	2 hr 59 min 45.0 sec
5,000 metres team race		Great Britain	26 points
2,500 metres steeplechase	George Orton	USA	7 min 34.4 sec
4,000 metres steeplechase	John Rimmer	Great Britain	12 min 58.4 sec
110 metres hurdles	Alvin Kraenzlein	USA	15.4 sec
200 metres hurdles	Alvin Kraenzlein	USA	25.4 sec
400 metres hurdles	John Tewksbury	USA	57.6 sec
High jump	Irving Baxter	USA	6 ft 2¾ in
Pole vault	Irving Baxter	USA	10 ft 10 in
Long jump	Alvin Kraenzlein	USA	23 ft 6¾ in
Triple jump	Myer Prinstein	USA	47 ft 5¾ in
Standing high jump	Ray Ewry	USA	5 ft 5 in
Standing long jump	Ray Ewry	USA	10 ft 6½ in
Standing triple jump	Ray Ewry	USA	34 ft 8¼ in
Shot	Richard Sheldon	USA	46 ft 3 in
Discus	Rudolf Bauer	Hungary	118 ft 3 in
Hammer	John Flanagan	USA	163 ft 2 in
Tug-of-war		Denmark-Sweden	

Swimming

Event	Name	Country	Result
200 metres freestyle	Freddie Lane	Australia	2 min 25.2 sec
1,000 metres freestyle	John Jarvis	Great Britain	13 min 40.0 sec
4,000 metres freestyle	John Jarvis	Great Britain	58 min 24.0 sec
5 x 40 metres relay		Germany	—
Underwater swim	M. de Vaudeville	France	60 metres
200 metres obstacle race	Freddie Lane	Australia	2 min 38.4 sec

Photographic Library of Australia

St Louis Olympic Games (1904)

The International Olympic Committee's official figures for participation at the 1904 Olympics is a mere 496 men from 10 nations, and no women. Other sources claim as many as 9,000 competitors. All that is certain is that some sort of Olympic celebrations were held in St Louis between May and September 1904. The Games were first scheduled to take place in Chicago, but were later handed over to the Louisiana Purchase Exposition of St Louis, and as a result the Games were in reality of very little importance compared with the exhibition itself. 'All sports', the semi-official report runs, 'given under the auspices of the Exposition must bear the name "Olympic",' and under this banner were held all sorts of events: interscholastic events open only to schoolboys from the state of Missouri, open handicaps for residents of Missouri, YMCA championships, and so on. It is quite impossible to tell which events were truly Olympic and which were not.

The vast majority of gold medals went to the United States, and in track and field athletics there was only one non-US winner—Etienne Desmarteau of Canada, a policeman from Montreal, who won the 56-lb weight throw. Indeed, the only non-American medallists of any kind were John Daly of Ireland (second in the steeplechase), Paul Weinstein of Germany (third in the high jump), and Nicolaos Georgantas of Greece (third in the discus). The United States made a clean sweep of seven boxing events, with O. L. Kirk winning the bantamweight and featherweight titles, cycling (Marcus Hurley won four events), and rowing (11 events in all), and won all but one gymnastics event. Only in fencing, where Cuba won five out of six contests, and in swimming, where Hungarians and Germans took six events to the

1 Freddie Lane, who at Paris in 1900, won Australia's first swimming titles, beating Hungary's Zoltan Halmay by 5.8 seconds in the 200 metres freestyle and also winning the 200 metres 'obstacle' race. The obstacle race, sometimes called 'hurdle swimming', was an amusing affair, but it is not surprising that this was the only time it was in the Olympic programme. The competitors had to struggle through barrels every 50 metres in this 200 metres race. Lane, from Sydney, won by 1.6 seconds from Otto Wahle of Austria, and it was probably his size—he weighed only 9½ stone—that helped him to victory. Lane used a double overarm stroke, similar to the trudgen but with a narrow kick, which was considered too strenuous until this rugged little man won the New South Wales title in 1899.

2 Alvin Kraenzlein, the first man to win four gold medals in one Olympic Games: in the 60 metres, 110 metres hurdles, 200 metres hurdles, and long jump at Paris. In 1898 and 1899, he had set world best performances in three different events.

ST LOUIS OLYMPIC GAMES, 1904 Gold Medallists			
Athletics			
60 metres	Archie Hahn	USA	7.0 sec
100 metres	Archie Hahn	USA	11.0 sec
200 metres	Archie Hahn	USA	21.6 sec
400 metres	Harry Hillman	USA	49.2 sec
800 metres	James Lightbody	USA	1 min 56.0 sec
1,500 metres	James Lightbody	USA	4 min 5.4 sec
Marathon	Thomas Hicks	USA	3 hr 28 min 53 sec
2,500 metres steeplechase	James Lightbody	USA	7 min 39.6 sec
4 mile team race	New York AC	USA	
110 metres hurdles	Fred Schule	USA	16.0 sec
200 metres hurdles	Harry Hillman	USA	24.6 sec
400 metres hurdles	Harry Hillman	USA	53.0 sec
High jump	Samuel Jones	USA	5 ft 11 in
Pole vault	Charles Dvorak	USA	11 ft 6 in
Long jump	Myer Prinstein	USA	24 ft 1 in
Triple jump	Myer Prinstein	USA	47 ft 0 in
Standing high jump	Ray Ewry	USA	4 ft 11 in
Standing long jump	Ray Ewry	USA	11 ft 4¾ in
Standing triple jump	Ray Ewry	USA	34 ft 7¼ in
Shot	Ralph Rose	USA	48 ft 7 in
Discus	Martin Sheridan	USA	128 ft 10½ in
Hammer	John Flanagan	USA	168 ft 1 in
56 lb weight	Etienne Desmarteau	Canada	34 ft 4 in

United States' five, was there anything that could be described as serious foreign competiton.

In the track and field events, held over six days from August 29 to September 3, there were four triple winners—Archie Hahn in the 60, 100, and 200 metres, James Lightbody (800 metres, 1,500 metres, and steeplechase), Harry Hillman (400 metres flat and 200 and 400 metres hurdles), and Ray Ewry, who repeated his 1900 hat-trick of winning the three standing jumps—high, long, and triple. The best performances came from Hahn, who won the 200 metres over a straight course in 21.6 sec, and Hillman, who ran the 200 metres hurdles in 24.6 sec.

The marathon event, run over 40 kilometres, provided the Games with an element of drama. Run on a hot day on roads deep in dust, the race caused 17 of the 31 starters to retire, including one Fred Lorz. He gave up at 9 miles, but having had a lift in a car he ran the last 5 miles into the stadium, where he was hailed as the winner. His prank was soon discovered, and Lorz was suspended for life, although he did compete in, and win, the Boston Marathon the following year. The actual winner, Thomas Hicks, finished 6 minutes in front of the next man. His spirits were kept up in the closing stages by ministrations of strychnine, raw eggs, and brandy.

The swimming events were held in an ornamental lake with the swimmers starting from a raft. Hungary's Zoltan Halmay won the 50 and 100 yards, not without having to compete in a swim-off for the 50 yards title after the judges had failed to agree and passions had been inflamed to fighting pitch. New York AC won the 4 x 50 yards relay and the water polo in these Games, the only time that individual club sides have contested an Olympic swimming competition. But then this was no ordinary Olympics.

1 Harry Hillman soars over the final hurdle in the 200 metres event. Hillman, of New York AC, also won the 400 metres hurdles and the 400 metres dash on the track.
2 James D. Lightbody of the Chicago AA won the 800 and 1,500 metres, and the 2,500 metres steeplechase, and thus gained the award for amassing most individual points.
3 Etienne Desmarteau, a Montreal policeman, stopped the United States winning all the events by coming out on top in the 56-lb weight throw.
4 Standing jump expert Ray Ewry won the high, long, and triple jumps, retaining all the titles he had won four years previously at the Olympic meeting in the Bois de Boulogne.

Interim Olympic Games

(Athens, 1906)

The first modern Olympic Games, held in Athens in 1896, proved such a success that the Greek organizers asked to keep the Games permanently in their country. Baron de Coubertin, the acknowledged resuscitator of the Olympics, believed that they should be fully international in character, and not the preserve of one country. Had he not received the full support of the International Olympic Committee, it is doubtful that the Olympics would have secured the status they now possess. But the Greeks, though bitterly disap-

1 The start of the 1906 84 km cycle race, an event which ended in a tie between two French competitors. **2** Prince George applauds the winner of the marathon, William Sherring.

pointed at the IOC's decision, obtained permission to stage a Games in Athens on the tenth anniversary of their revival. They planned that there should be a Games in Athens every ten years, but the 1906 venture was in fact unique.

Known variously as the 'Intercalated' or 'Interim' Games, the 1906 Games were opened on April 22 by King George of Greece in the presence of other

A rather fancifully posed shot of Georgantas, winner of the stone putting event. He threw the 14 lb weight an impressive 65 ft. 4 in.

INTERIM OLYMPIC GAMES, 1906 Gold Medallists

Athletics

Event	Name	Country	Result
100 metres	Archie Hahn	USA	11.2 sec
400 metres	Paul Pilgrim	USA	53.2 sec
800 metres	Paul Pilgrim	USA	2 min 1.2 sec
1,500 metres	Jim Lightbody	USA	4 min 12.0 sec
5 miles	H. Hawtrey	Great Britain	26 min 26.2 sec
Marathon	William Sherring	Canada	2 hr 51 min 23.6 sec
1,500 metres walk	George Bonhag	USA	7 min 12.6 sec
110 metres hurdles	R. Leavitt	USA	16.2 sec
High jump	Con Leahy	Great Britain	5 ft 9¾ in
Pole vault	Fernand Gonder	France	11 ft 6 in
Long jump	Myer Prinstein	USA	23 ft 7½ in
Triple jump	Peter O'Connor	Great Britain	46 ft 2 in
Standing high jump	Ray Ewry	USA	5 ft 1½ in
Standing long jump	Ray Ewry	USA	10 ft 10 in
Shot	Martin Sheridan	USA	40 ft 5 in
Discus	Martin Sheridan	USA	136 ft 0 in
Discus (Greek style)	Werner Jarvinen	Finland	115 ft 5 in
Javelin	Erik Lemming	Sweden	175 ft 6 in
Pentathlon	H. Mellander	Sweden	
Tug-of-War		Germany	
Rope climb (10 metres)	D. Aliprantis	Greece	11.4 sec
Lifting the bar bell (both hands)			
	D. Tofalos	Greece	317.6 lb
Lifting the bar bell (each hand separately)			
	H. Steinbach	Austria	168 lb
Throwing the stone (14 lb)			
	G. Georgantas	Greece	65 ft 4 in

Cycling

Event	Name	Country	Result
333⅓ metres time trial	Francesco Verri	Italy	22.8 sec
1,000 metres scratch	Francesco Verri	Italy	1 min 42.2 sec
5,000 metres	Francesco Verri	Italy	8 min 35.0 sec
2,000 metres tandem	J. Matthews & A. Rushen	Great Britain	
20 km paced race	W. J. Pett	Great Britain	29 min 0 sec
Road race (84 km)	Vast / Bardonneau	France / France	2 hr 41 min 28.0 sec

Fencing

Foil—individual	M. Dillon-Cavanagh	France
Epee—individual	Comte de la Falaise	France
Epee—team		France
Sabre—individual	Jean Georgiadis	Greece
Sabre—team		Germany
Football		Denmark

Gymnastics

Team competition		Norway

Lawn Tennis

Men's singles	Max Decugis	France
Men's doubles	Max Decugis & M. Germot	France
Ladies' singles	Miss Semyriotou	Greece
Mixed doubles	Max & Mme Decugis	France

Rowing

Canoe race	Delaplane	France
Coxed pairs (1,000 m)	E. Brunna, E. Fontanella, G. Cerana (cox)	Italy
Coxed pairs (1,600 m)	E. Brunna, E. Fontanella, G. Cerana (cox)	Italy
Coxed fours (2,000 m)		Italy

Shooting

There were 15 shooting contests. Norway and Switzerland each won five, France three, Great Britain one, and Greece one.

Swimming

Event	Name	Country	Result
100 metres freestyle	Charles Daniels	USA	1 min 13.0 sec
400 metres freestyle	Otto Scheff	Austria	6 min 23.8 sec
1,600 metres freestyle	Henry Taylor	Great Britain	28 min 28.0 sec
1,000 metres team		Hungary	16 min 52.4 sec
High diving	Gottlob Walz	Germany	156.00 pts

assorted royal persons and a packed crowd of 60,000 in the Panathenaic stadium built for the 1896 celebrations. The track, the surface of which was soft and invited some criticisms, was quite unsuited to stern competitions: it had straights some 200 yards long, and the turns were sharp. In addition, the races were run in a clockwise direction.

Athletics contests were held in some 24 events, including rope-climbing, tug-of-war, and weight-lifting. The United States, with a team selected for the first time as the result of special 'tryouts', was most formidable, winning 11 events. Archie Hahn, the 1904 victor over 60, 100, and 200 metres, was restricted to winning the 100 metres, the only sprint on the programme, and Jim Lightbody repeated his 1,500 metres victory. But Lightbody could not duplicate his 800 metres success of 1904, losing to Paul Pilgrim, a late addition to the United States team who was also successful in the 400 metres. Great Britain gained three wins: H. Hawtrey in the 5 miles, Con Leahy (an Irishman) in the high jump, and Peter O'Connor (another Irishman) in the triple jump. O'Connor, the world record holder, was runner-up in his speciality, the long jump, to the American Myer Prinstein, who had set his final world record of 24 ft. 7¼ in. in 1898. Olympic champion Ray Ewry won the standing high and long jumps, while Martin Sheridan, the 1904 discus champion, won the shot and the discus. The Greek-style discus throw, however, went to the first of the great Jarvinen family, Werner, who beat the Greek hero George Georgantos. Greece failed to win any of the regular track and field events, but excelled in the more esoteric competitions —the rope climb, 'lifting-the-bar-bell-with-both-hands', and throwing the 14-lb stone.

Paul Pilgrim just beats Jim Lightbody to the tape in the 800 metres. Pilgrim was also successful in the 400 metres.

Charles Daniels, the American who had won two swimming events at St Louis, won the 100 metres freestyle in a slow time of 1 min. 13.0 sec. This was understandable as the event was held in the sea at Phaleron. Otto Scheff won the 400 metres and Henry Taylor the mile—both in times well in excess of their best.

French players dominated the lawn tennis, with Max Decugis winning three events, the singles, doubles (with M. Germot), and the mixed doubles with his wife.

The Greeks, the ancient founders of the Olympics, succeeded in fulfilling a great need at the beginning of the 20th century. The disorganised competition at Paris in 1900 and the cumbersome arrangements for the 1904 Games in St Louis—both of which were run concurrently with and subordinate to a trade fair—had, despite their shortcomings, shown that international competitions were wanted by sportsmen and public alike. The 1906 Games saw the beginning of the Olympics in a form which has persisted, roughly, ever since.

London Olympic Games (1908)

Two of the strangest sights in all sporting history were seen in the the new Shepherd's Bush stadium built especially for the Olympic Games of 1908. The first was the British Lieutenant Wyndham Halswelle 'running over' to win the 400 metres, and the second was the Italian candy-maker Dorando Pietri collapsing in the stadium at the end of the marathon.

There were a number of Olympic celebrations in London that year. The summer sports were held in July, and so-called autumn sports —boxing, football, lacrosse, and skating—later in the year. The 1908 Games were the last at which the host country had full jurisdiction over the sports. There were so many protests from the visitors that international bodies were soon formed to iron out various problems of rule-interpretation and amateurism.

The athletics, swimming, wrestling, gymnastics, and cycling events were held in the stadium; the rowing over the 1½-mile course at Henley; shooting at Bisley and Uxendon; and other sports at local venues more suited to them. But motor-boat racing was held on the Solent, and the 12-metre yachting on the Clyde.

A strong American team dominated the athletics events on the newly laid ⅓-mile track. Their most successful competitor was Melvin Sheppard who won the 800 metres and 1,500 metres. His 800 metres time, 1 min 52.8 sec, was a world record, and in the 1,500 metres he beat the British world record

holder, Harold Wilson, by a couple of yards, with another Briton, Norman Hallowes, third. And in the 1,600 metres relay (200+200+400+800 metres), Sheppard anchored the United States team, to win his third gold medal of the Games.

Americans won most of the more 'technical' events. Forrest Smithson in the 110 metres hurdles and Charles Bacon in the 400

metres hurdles set world records in winning. Ray Ewry gained his customary double in the standing jumps; John Flanagan won his third hammer gold medal; and Martin Sheridan walked off with both discus titles. Only Sweden's Erik Lemming (in the two javelin events) and Ireland's Timothy Ahearne who was competing for Britain in the triple jump broke the American stranglehold in the

**1 Harold Blackstaffe wins the 1908 Olympic single sculls.
2 The start of the 100-kilometre cycle race in the new stadium.
3 John Flanagan won his third consecutive hammer title with a throw of 170 ft. 4¼ in. Other Americans were second and third.**

field events.

The British Empire supplied the winners of the shorter sprints, through South Africa's Reggie Walker in the 100 metres and Canada's Bobbie Kerr in the 200 metres. But the big talking point of the track races was the victory of Halswelle in the 400 metres. In the final he was opposed by three Americans. The race was not run in lanes, and one of the Americans, J. C. Carpenter, appears to have edged Halswelle wide as they entered the finishing straight. A shout of 'Foul' went up, and the British officials broke the tape before the finish. Carpenter was disqualified and a re-run was ordered, but when the time for the re-run arrived the other two Americans, W. C. Robbins and J. B. Taylor, refused to take part. So Halswelle ran over—the only instance of such an occurrence in the history of the Games.

Despite the controversy of the 400 metres, the most famous race was the marathon. Run from Windsor Great Park along the roads of West London to the stadium in hot, windless weather, the race was attempted by 56 men of whom only 27 finished. The little Italian, Dorando Pietri, did not follow the initial fast pace, and after 15 miles the South African Charles Hefferon was in the lead. He held this advantage until the 24th mile, when first Pietri and then the American John Hayes passed him. But the Italian's effort had so exhausted him that he was almost unconscious when he entered the stadium. He collapsed on the track, officials put him back on the right course (an act which immediately disqualified him), and the brave man struggled on and was helped to the tape. Hayes, who had run a sensible race in the heat, was just over half-a-minute behind Pietri at the finish, and he was awarded the gold medal. Pietri's heroic effort so affected the British queen that she presented him with a special gold cup.

British athletes, out of contention in the marathon, had a field day in the other distance events. Emil Voigt won the 5 miles, Arthur Russell the 3,200 metres steeplechase, and George Larner the 3,500 metres and 10 miles walks. And the British team in the 3-mile team race packed five men into the first seven places to win comfortably.

Second in importance to the athletics was the swimming, where Britain's Henry Taylor from Chadderton in Lancashire won three gold medals. In the 100-metre pool he won the 400 and 1,500 metres events in world record times, and anchored Britain to a fine 4 by 200 metres relay win. Fred Holman of Britain won the 200 metres breaststroke from his team-mate 38-year-old W. W. Robinson. But probably the best swimmer on display was the American sprinter Charles Daniels, who won the

100 metres in a world best time. Britain won the water polo, and in the team was Paul Radmilovic, who also won a gold in the relay—the only man ever to win golds in both swimming and water polo.

A collapsible tower had been built for the diving events, and European divers won six of the seven medals awarded, there being a tie for third place in the fancy diving. Swedes, headed by Hjalmar Johansson, made a clean sweep of the plain diving, and Albert Zurner led a German assault in the fancy diving—Kurt Behrens was second and Gottlob Walz third, tying with America's George Gaidzik.

A 660-yard cycle track, built round the running track, completed the new arena, but the events were marred by continual rain and a large number of punctures. British cyclists took every gold medal except the tandem—won by France—and the 1,000 metres sprint which was declared void after the riders had exceeded the time limit.

Outside the stadium, British sportsmen were no less successful, winning all the lawn tennis championships, rowing, and yachting, as well as the polo, racquets, six of the shooting events, and two of the three motor-boat titles. For the eights at Henley a veteran Leander crew had been in training to beat the Belgian European champions. With a magnificently histrionic gesture, the Belgians tossed their cigar butts into the Thames before embarking, but they went down narrowly to Leander in one of the greatest races seen at any regatta.

Of the 'autumn' sports, the boxing was a clean sweep for the home country. Future England cricket captain, Johnny Douglas, won the middleweight gold. Britain also won the soccer, hockey, and ladies figure skating. But in the rugby final a visiting Australian team beat the English county champions, Cornwall, 32-3, while Canada not surprisingly beat Britain 14-10 at lacrosse.

The summer sports ended with a ceremonial prizegiving by Queen Alexandra. Gold, silver, and bronze medals, and diplomas of merit were awarded. Lord Desborough, who had organized the Games with tremendous flair, called for three cheers for the Queen, and the Games of the Fourth Olympiad passed into history.

1 Reggie Walker (right) won the 100 metres in 10.8 sec.
2 John Hayes, the eventual winner of the marathon, passes through Willesden. He finished 32 sec behind the disqualified Pietri.
3 Ulrich Salchow won the first ever Olympic figure skating title, which was held as part of the London Games.
4 12-metre yachts contested their event on the river Clyde in Scotland.

Official Report of 1908 Olympics

5 J. C. Carpenter crosses the finishing line in the 400 metres final as British officials break the tape and signal a 'no race'.
6 Carpenter was disqualified as a result of an examination of the runners' footprints. The race was not run in lanes.

Mansell

LONDON OLYMPIC GAMES, 1908 Gold Medallists

Archery			
York round (men)	W. Dod	Great Britain	
National round (women)	Q. Newall	Great Britain	
50 metres Continental	E. G. Grisot	France	
Athletics			
100 metres	Reginald Walker	South Africa	10.8 sec
200 metres	Robert Kerr	Canada	22.6 sec
400 metres	Wyndham Halswelle	Great Britain	50.0 sec
800 metres	Melvin Sheppard	USA	1 min 52.8 sec
1,500 metres	Melvin Sheppard	USA	4 min 3.4 sec
5 miles	Emil Voigt	Great Britain	25 min 11.2 sec
Marathon	John Hayes	USA	2 hr 55 min 46.4 sec
Relay (2 x 200 +1 x 400 + 1 x 800 metres)		USA	3 min 29.4 sec
110 metres hurdles	Forrest Smithson	USA	15.0 sec
400 metres hurdles	Charles Bacon	USA	55.0 sec.
3,200 metres steeplechase	Arthur Russell	Great Britain	10 min 47.8 sec
3 miles team race		Great Britain	
3,500 metres walk	George Larner	Great Britain	14 min 55 sec
10 miles walk	George Larner	Great Britain	1 hr 15 min 57.4 sec
Standing high jump	Ray Ewry	USA	5 ft 2 in
Standing long jump	Ray Ewry	USA	10 ft 11¼ in
High jump	Harry Porter	USA	6 ft 3 in
Pole vault	Edward Cooke	USA	} 12 ft 2 in
	Alfred Gilbert	USA	
Long jump	Frank Irons	USA	24 ft 6½ in
Triple jump	Timothy Ahearne	Great Britain	48 ft 11¼ in
Shot	Ralph Rose	USA	46 ft 7½ in
Discus (free style)	Martin Sheridan	USA	134 ft 2 in
Discus (Greek style)	Martin Sheridan	USA	124 ft 8 in
Hammer	John Flanagan	USA	170 ft 4¼ in
Javelin (free style)	Erik Lemming	Sweden	178 ft 7½ in
Javelin (conventional)	Erik Lemming	Sweden	179 ft 10½ in
Tug of War		Great Britain	
Boxing			
Bantamweight	H. Thomas	Great Britain	
Featherweight	R. K. Gunn	Great Britain	
Lightweight	F. Grace	Great Britain	
Middleweight	John Douglas	Great Britain	
Heavyweight	A. L. Oldham	Great Britain	
Cycling			
One lap (660 yards)	Victor Johnson	Great Britain	
1,000 metres sprint	final declared void		
5,000 metres	Ben Jones	Great Britain	8 min 36.2 sec
20 kilometres	C. B. Kingsbury	Great Britain	34 min 13.6 sec
100 kilometres	C. H. Bartlett	Great Britain	2 hr 41 min 48.6 sec
Team pursuit (3 laps)		Great Britain	2 min 18.6 sec
2,000 metres tandem	Maurice Schilles	} France	
	Andre Auffray		
Fencing			
Epee—individual	Gaston Alibert	France	
Epee—team		France	
Sabre—individual	Jeno Fuchs	Hungary	
Sabre—team		Hungary	
Football—Association		Great Britain	
Football—Rugby		Australia	
Gymnastics			
Combined exercises	Alberto Braglia	Italy	317 pts
Team		Sweden	438 pts
Hockey	England team	Great Britain	
Lacrosse		Canada	
Lawn Tennis—Grass courts			
Singles—men	M. J. G. Ritchie	Great Britain	
Singles—women	Dorothea Lambert Chambers	Great Britain	
Doubles—men	George Hillyard	} Great Britain	
	Reginald Doherty		
Lawn Tennis—Covered courts			
Singles—men	Arthur Gore	Great Britain	
Singles—women	G. Eastlake Smith	Great Britain	

Doubles—men	Arthur Gore	} Great Britain	
	Herbert Roper-Barrett		
Motor Boats			
Unrestricted	E. B. Thubron	France	(in *Camille*)
Under 60 ft long	Tom Thornycroft	Great Britain	(in *Gyrinus*)
6½-8 metre racing cruisers	Tom Thornycroft	Great Britain	(in *Gyrinus*)
Polo		Great Britain	
Racquets			
Singles—men	E. B. Noel	Great Britain	
Doubles—men	V. H. Pennell &	} Great Britain	
	J. J. Astor		
Rowing (course 1½ miles)			
Single sculls	Harry Blackstaffe	Great Britain	9 min 26 sec
Coxless pairs	J. Fenning	} Great Britain	9 min 41 sec
	Gordon Thomson		
Coxless fours		Great Britain	8 min 34 sec
Eights		Great Britain	7 min 52 sec
Shooting			
National rifle teams		USA	
Individual rifle, 1,000 yards	J. K. Millner	Great Britain	
Open rifle teams		Norway	
Open rifle, 300 metres	A. Helgerud	Norway	
Miniature rifle teams		Great Britain	
Miniature rifle—individual	A. A. Carnell	Great Britain	
Miniature rifle— disappearing target	W. K. Styles	Great Britain	
Miniature rifle— moving target	A. F. Fleming	Great Britain	
Revolver—team		USA	
Revolver—individual	P. van Asbroek	Belgium	
Running deer—team		Sweden	
Running deer—individual	Oscar Swahn	Sweden	
Running deer—double shot	W. Winans	USA	
Clay pigeon—individual	W. H. Ewing	Canada	
Clay pigeon—team		Great Britain	
Skating			
Figures—men	Ulrich Salchow	Sweden	
Figures—women	Madge Syers	Great Britain	
Pairs	Anna Hubler	} Germany	
	Heinrich Burger		
Special figures	N. Panin	Russia	
Swimming			
100 metres freestyle	Charles Daniels	USA	1 min 5.6 sec
400 metres freestyle	Henry Taylor	Great Britain	5 min 36.8 sec
1,500 metres freestyle	Henry Taylor	Great Britain	22 min 48.4 sec
200 metres breaststroke	Frederick Holman	Great Britain	3 min 9.2 sec
100 metres backstroke	Arno Bieberstein	Germany	1 min 24.6 sec
4 x 200 metres relay		Great Britain	10 min 55.6 sec
Plain high diving	Hjalmar Johansson	Sweden	83.76 pts
Fancy diving	Albert Zurner	Germany	85.5 pts
Water Polo		Great Britain	
Tennis (Jeu de Paume)	Jay Gould	United States	
Wrestling—Catch as catch can			
Bantamweight	George Mehnert	USA	
Featherweight	George Dole	USA	
Lightweight	G. de Relwyskow	Great Britain	
Middleweight	Stanley Bacon	Great Britain	
Heavyweight	G. C. O'Kelly	Great Britain	
Wrestling—Greco-Roman			
Lightweight	Enrico Porro	Italy	
Middleweight	Fritjof Martensson	Sweden	
Light-heavyweight	Werner Weckman	Finland	
Heavyweight	Richard Weisz	Hungary	
Yachting			
6-metre class	G. U. Laws	Great Britain	(in *Dormy*)
7-metre class	C. J. Rivett-Carnac	Great Britain	(in *Heroine*)
8-metre class	Blair Cochrane	Great Britain	(in *Cobweb*)
12-metre class	T. C. Glen-Coats	Great Britain	(in *Hera*)

Official Report of the 1912 Olympics

Official Report of 1912 Olympics

Official Report of 1912 Olympics

Official Report of the 1912 Olympics

Stockholm Olympic Games (1912)

The 1912 Olympic Games surpassed the previous three promotions in organization, participation, and performance. Held with typical Scandinavian flair in the Swedish capital, the Games attracted 2,484 men and 57 women competitors who took part in a programme that included no fewer than 18 shooting events, 3 gymnastic team events, and indoor and outdoor tennis. Women's swimming events were included in the Olympics for the first time, and there was a new sport—the modern pentathlon—which was designed to find the best all-round athlete in the world.

This last event was the brainchild of Baron Pierre de Coubertin, the founder of the Games, and he was doubtless pleased at the way in which the new sport caught on. Swedes gained the first four places, with the gold medal going to Gustaf Lilliehook. The first foreign finisher was G. S. Patton, Jr, of the United States, later famous as General 'Blood and Guts' Patton of World War II. The inclusion of women's swimming events was a break-through for female emancipation in athletic sports, although women's events had previously been held in archery, tennis, and skating.

The outstanding features of the track and field athletics were the all-round excellence of the Ameri-

1 Already garlanded, Ken McArthur wins the Stockholm marathon for South Africa. **2** The modern pentathlon gold medallist, Gustaf Lilliehook of Sweden. **3** The great Jim Thorpe, who was stripped of his two titles. **4** Eventual gold medallist Ted Meredith wins his 800 metres semi-final from Hanns Braun of Germany. **5** The tall Englishman, Arnold Jackson, wins the 1,500 metres in a blanket finish. **6** Hannes Kolehmainen beats Jean Bouin for the 5,000 metres gold. **7** Double sprint champion Ralph Craig grits his teeth as he wins the 200 metres. **8** Hawaiian Duke Kahanamoku began his reign with a convincing 100 metres freestyle victory at Stockholm. **9** First and second for Australia in the women's 100 metres: Fanny Durack (right) set a world record in the heats; Wilhelmina Wylie got the silver.

can team and the emergence of Finland as a strong nation of runners. Americans won 16 of the athletics events, although later two were rescinded. Individually, the stars of the Games were Hannes Kolehmainen of Finland and Jim Thorpe of the United States. Kolehmainen, nicknamed 'Hannes the Mighty' for his feats at the Games, won individual gold medals in the 5,000 metres (in a world record 14 min 36.6 sec), the 10,000 metres, and the cross-country race. He set a second world record in the heats of the 3,000 metres team race (8 min 36.8 sec), but the Finnish team failed to make the final. Kolehmainen gained a silver medal as well, as the Finnish team were narrowly beaten into second place in the cross-country.

But few people dispute that the best athlete—perhaps the greatest of all time—was America's Jim Thorpe. Yet his name does not even appear in the official records. In Stockholm he competed in four events, and won the track and field pentathlon and decathlon events with some ease. The following year, however, it was revealed that he had taken part in some professional baseball matches, and on the orders of the International Olympic Committee, Thorpe's name was struck from the records. But Thorpe is remembered: he won the 10-event decathlon by almost 700 points according to the tables then in use; he was first in all of the five events in the pentathlon, and in individual events came seventh in the long jump and equal-fourth in the high jump. In 1913, Thorpe became a professional footballer and made his mark in

this sport as surely as he had done in track and field.

America's other outstanding performer was 19-year-old James 'Ted' Meredith, who set two world records in the 800 metres final. His winning 800 metres time was 1 min 51.9 sec, and he ran on the extra 4.67 metres to set a world 880 yards record of 1 min 52.5 sec. Defending champion Mel Sheppard was relegated to second place, 0.1 sec behind Meredith, and was even less successful in defending his 1,500 metres crown two days later, being unplaced. This race resulted in an unexpected victory for Britain's Arnold Jackson after a remarkably severe sprint down the home straight, with only 0.8 sec separating first from fifth.

In addition to Thorpe and Kolehmainen, two other men won two gold medals. Finland's Armas Taipale won the discus and the 'discus throw—two hands' which was the only time this event featured in the Games (as was the case with the shot and javelin two-handed aggregate events). The American Ralph Craig won the 100 and 200 metres sprints. In the 100 metres, five of the six finalists were Americans, and this race was notable for there being no fewer than eight false starts.

Elsewhere, honours were fairly evenly divided. South Africa's Ken McArthur won the marathon from his team-mate Chris Gitsham; Canada's George Goulding won the 10,000 metres walk; Gustaf Lindblom won the triple jump to give Sweden a gold medal; and Constantin Tsiclitiras won a rare gold medal for Greece, in the standing long jump.

The Leander eight retained their Olympic title in 1912.

Outside the newly constructed athletics stadium, the swimming was being held in a pool built in an inlet of Stockholm harbour. But the water was perfectly calm, and a number of world records were set. Duke Kahanamoku of Hawaii made his first Olympic appearance, winning the 100 metres freestyle. Canada's George Hodgson set a world 1,500 metres record and won that event and the 400 metres. Germany's Walter Bathe won both breaststroke events in most impressive style, and an Australasian team won the 4 by 200 metres relay. This team comprised three Australians and one New Zealander, Malcolm Champion—the first and for at least 60 years the only New Zealander to win an Olympic swimming gold medal. The new women's events were a great success. Australia's Fanny Durack won the 100 metres freestyle from her team-mate Wilhelmina Wylie, and Great Britain won the free-style relay. Domestic honour was satisfied when Greta Johansson

won the high diving for Sweden.

Britain had a successful time in the rowing. William Kinnear won the single sculls, and the Leander Club crew won the eights from a New College VIII. The second Olympic soccer tournament resulted in a second victory for the Great Britain team, who beat Denmark 4-2 in the final. This game was played in burning heat, and Britain were perhaps lucky to win as a number of the Danes had been injured in their semi-final match with the Netherlands.

It was fortunate for the Olympic movement in general that these Games had been so well organized. Apart from the Thorpe incident—which in any case did not arise until months after the Games were over—and the tragic death of a Portuguese marathon runner named Lazaro, the Games passed without any of the acrimony that had been so typical of the London Games four years previously. It was for this reason that they were so promptly revived after the 'war to end wars', which put paid to the 1916 Games scheduled to be held in Berlin.

Above: Ralph Rose, here winning the shot at London, retained his Olympic title in Stockholm. *Left:* 'Mighty' Matt McGrath, Tipperary-born but a gold medallist for the United States.

Antwerp Olympic Games (1920) [1]

'Firsts'—quite apart from those that won gold medals—were the order of the day at the VIIth Olympic Games held in the Belgian city of Antwerp in 1920. It was the first stumbling attempt at a global get-together in a world recently shattered. The Olympic flag was unfurled for the first time, and the Olympic oath was first introduced. Most exciting of all, perhaps, Paavo Nurmi, the 'Phantom Finn', made his Olympic debut.

The disappointingly sparse attendances betrayed the haste with which the Games had been organized. Belgium had had but one year's notice in which to prepare, and her war-weary people were in no mood for games of any kind. In spite of a new 30,000-seat stadium and a nominal admission fee, the crowds did not much exceed 20,000.

The Belgians did not invite any of the Central Powers (Austria, Bulgaria, Germany, Hungary, or Turkey), but the the new countries of Czechoslovakia and Estonia, and newly independent Finland took part. There were 29 countries represented in 22 sports, and the total number of contestants was something under 3,000.

The Games proper were opened on August 14 by King Albert of the Belgians, in the presence of Baron de Coubertin, founder of the modern Olympic Games. Fifteen nations shared the 150 gold medals, the United States claiming 41 of them, followed by Sweden with 19 and Finland with 15. Belgium, Britain, Italy, and Norway reached double figures. Tiny Finland, spearheaded by the redoubtable Nurmi, dug deep into her track and field talent to produce nine gold medals for those events. The Finns tied with the United States, the first and only time the Americans have been equalled in track and field.

In athletics Paavo Nurmi was incomparably the man of the Games. Although he stood only on the threshold of his glittering career, Nurmi won two individual gold medals and one silver—after inexperience had cost him his first race (the 5,000 metres) to Joseph Guillemot of France. During the next 10 years the Finn was to compete successfully in two more Olympic Games and set world records at every event from 1,500 metres to 1 hour.

Hannes Kolehmainen, the first

Press Association

ANTWERP OLYMPIC GAMES, 1920 Gold Medallists

Archery

Fixed Bird Target—Men

Individual	(Small Bird)	E. Van Meer	Belgium
	(Large Bird)	E. Clostens	Belgium
Team	(Small Bird)		Belgium
Team	(Large Bird)		Belgium

Moving Bird Target—Men

	(28 metres)	H. Van Innis	Belgium
	(33 metres)	H. Van Innis	Belgium
	(50 metres)	Louis Brule	France
Team	(28 metres)		Netherlands
	(33 metres)		Belgium
	(50 metres)		Belgium
60- and 50-yard Individual —Women		Miss Q. Newall	GB

Association Football

Belgium

Athletics

Track and Field events

100 metres	Charles W. Paddock	USA	10.8 sec
200 metres	Allan Woodring	USA	22.0 sec
400 metres	Bevil G. D. Rudd	S Africa	49.6 sec
800 metres	Albert G. Hill	GB	1 min 53.4 sec
1,500 metres	Albert G. Hill	GB	4 min 01.8 sec
3,000 metres team race		USA	
5,000 metres	Joseph Guillemot	France	14 min 55.6 sec
10,000 metres	Paavo Nurmi	Finland	31 min 45.8 sec
Marathon	Hannes Kolehmainen	Finland	2 hr 32 min 35.8 sec
110 metres Hurdles	Earl J. Thompson	Canada	14.8 sec
400 metres Hurdles	Frank F. Loomis	USA	54.0 sec
3,000 metres Steeplechase	Percy Hodge	GB	10 min 00.4 sec
Cross Country (10,000 metres)			
Individual	Paavo Nurmi	Finland	27 min 15 sec
Team		Finland	
3,000 metres Walk	Ugo Frigerio	Italy	14 min 55 sec
10,000 metres Walk	Ugo Frigerio	Italy	48 min 06.2 sec
4x100 metres Relay		USA	42.2 sec
4x400 metres Relay		GB	3 min 22.2 sec
High Jump	Richard W. Landon	USA	6 ft 4¼ in
Pole Vault	Frank K. Foss	USA	13 ft 5 in
Long Jump	William Pettersson	Sweden	23 ft 5½ in
Triple Jump	Vilho Tuulos	Finland	47 ft 7 in
Shot	Ville Porhola	Finland	48 ft 7 in
Discus	Elmer Niklander	Finland	146 ft 7¼ in
Hammer	Patrick Ryan	USA	173 ft 5½ in
Javelin	Jonni Myyra	Finland	215 ft 9¾ in
Pentathlon	Eero Lehtonen	Finland	
Decathlon	Helge Lovland	Norway	
Tug of War		GB	

Boxing

Flyweight	Frank De Genaro	USA
Bantamweight	Clarence Walker	S Africa
Featherweight	Paul Fritsch	France
Lightweight	Samuel Mosberg	USA
Welterweight	T. Schneider	Canada
Middleweight	Harry Mallin	GB
Light-Heavyweight	Edward Eagan	USA
Heavyweight	R. Rawson	GB

Cycling

1,000 metres Sprint	Maurice Peeters	Netherlands	1 min 38.3 sec
2,000 metres Tandem	Harry Ryan, Thomas Lance	GB	2 min 49.4 sec
4,000 metres Team Pursuit		Italy	5 min 20 sec
Road Race—Individual	Harry Stenquist	Sweden	4 hr 40 min 01.8 sec
—Team		France	19 hr 16 min 43.2 sec

Equestrian Sports

Grand Prix (Jumping)		
Individual	Tommaso Lequio	Italy
Team		Sweden
Grand Prix (Dressage)	Janne Lundblad	Sweden
Three Day Event—Individual	Helmer Morner	Sweden
—Team		Sweden

Fencing

Foil —Individual	Nedo Nadi	Italy
—Team		Italy
Epee —Individual	Armand Massard	France
—Team		Italy
Sabre—Individual	Nedo Nadi	Italy
—Team		Italy

Gymnastics

Combined Exercises —Individual	Giorgio Zampori	Italy

Hockey

GB

Ice Hockey

Canada

Lawn Tennis

Men's Singles	Louis Raymond	S Africa
Ladies' Singles	Mlle Suzanne Lenglen	France
Men's Doubles	O. G. Turnbull & Max Woosnam	GB
Ladies' Doubles	Mrs J. McNair & Miss Kitty McKane	GB
Mixed Doubles	Max Decugis & Mlle S. Lenglen	France

Modern Pentathlon

	Gustaf Dyrssen	Sweden

Polo

GB

2

3

4

5

1 (overleaf) US high flyer Frank Ross soared to a world record of 13 ft 5$\frac{9}{16}$ in. in the pole vault, in spite of a waterlogged track. He left his nearest rival 13 inches below him.

2 Britain's Percy Hodge, with a wealth of cross-country experience behind him, won the steeplechase in a fraction over 10 min. It was at Antwerp that this event was finally standardized at its present length of 3,000 metres.

3 Pat Ryan, one of a succession of Irish-American 'whales', tossed the hammer a little over 173 ft for the gold medal and a new world record. He later established a mark of 189 ft 6½ in that stood unbeaten for nearly a quarter of a century—a lengthy record period for any event.

4 Iron man Frank Loomis of America also broke a world record—he skimmed over the 400-metre hurdles in a time of 54 sec dead. He had previously won the American championship in the same event, and also held the 220-yard low hurdles title.

5 Earl 'Tommy' Thomson, the Canadian hurdler, brought a tinge of gold to the maple leaf when he captured the 110 metres high hurdles for his country in world record time. Thomson had more than a little American help in his great win—he had trained for many years in the US.

of the flying Finns, who had thrilled the fans at the 1912 Olympics with his three gold medals in the middle distance events, won a sensational marathon at Antwerp by 13.2 seconds—the closest Olympic marathon ever. In addition to Nurmi's and Kolehmainen's contributions, Finland won four field events and the track and field pentathlon.

The United States took the two sprints and the sprint relay. The spectacular Charley Paddock, the first of many to be dubbed 'the world's fastest human', collected a gold for the 100 metres, but in the 200 metres ran out of steam 20 metres before reaching the tape. Canada won the 110 metres hurdles through the efforts of Earl 'Tommy' Thomson who, in spite of a leg injury, broke the Olympic record. English-born Bevil Rudd won the 400 metres for South Africa, and Britain won the 4x400 metres relay to add to her victories in the 800 and 1,500 metres, the steeplechase, and the tug-of-war.

In the swimming, the United States made almost a clean sweep, winning seven out of ten of the men's events and four out of five of the women's. Sweden collected the remaining three men's events and a Danish girl won the women's high diving. The Hawaiian, Duke Kahanamoku, swimming for the United States, won the 100 metres freestyle in a new world record time and picked up a second gold medal as a member of the record-breaking 4x200 metres relay team. Another mem-

---

ANTWERP OLYMPIC GAMES, 1920 Gold Medallists *(continued)*

Rowing			
Single Sculls	John Kelly	USA	7 min 35.0 sec
Double Sculls	John Kelly, Paul Costello	USA	7 min 09.0 sec
Coxless Pairs	E. Olgeni, G. Scatturin	Italy	7 min 56.0 sec
Coxed Fours		Switzerland	6 min 54.0 sec
Eights		USA	6 min 05.0 sec
Rugby Football		USA	
Shooting			
Pistol and revolver (50 metres)			
—Individual	Carl Frederick	USA	
—Team		USA	
Pistol and revolver (30 metres)			
—Individual	Guilherme Paraense	Brazil	
—Team		USA	
Running Deer			
—Individual singles	Otto Olsen	Norway	
—Individual doubles	Ole Lilloe-Olsen	Norway	
—Team doubles		Norway	
Small Bore (Miniature) Rifle			
—Individual	Lawrence Nuesslein	USA	
—Team		USA	
Military Rifle (300 metres)			
2 positions —Individual	Morris Fisher	USA	
—Team		USA	
Standing —Individual	Carl Osburn	USA	
—Team		Denmark	
Prone —Individual	Otto Olsen	Norway	
—Team		USA	
Military Rifle (300 and 600 metres)			
Prone —Team		USA	
Military Rifle (600 metres)			
Prone —Individual	Hugo Johansson	Sweden	
—Team		USA	
Clay Pigeon—Individual	Mark Arie	USA	
—Team		USA	
Skating			
Figure—Men	Gillis Grafstrom	Sweden	
—Women	Magda Julin-Mauroy	Sweden	
Pairs	Ludovika Jakobsson & Walter Jakobsson	Finland	
Swimming and Diving—Men			
100 metres Freestyle	Duke Kahanamoku	USA	1 min 00.4 sec
400 metres Freestyle	Norman Ross	USA	5 min 26.8 sec
1500 metres Freestyle	Norman Ross	USA	22 min 23.2 sec
100 metres Backstroke	Warren Kealoha	USA	1 min 15.2 sec

200 metres Breaststroke	Haken Malmroth	Sweden	3 min 04.4 sec
400 metres Breaststroke	Haken Malmroth	Sweden	6 min 31.8 sec
4x200 metres Relay		USA	10 min 04.4 sec
Platform Diving	Clarence Pinkston	USA	
Plain High Diving	Arvid Wallman	Sweden	
Springboard Diving	Louis Kuehn	USA	
Swimming and Diving—Women			
100 metres Freestyle	Ethelda Bleibtrey	USA	1 min 13.6 sec
300 metres Freestyle	Ethelda Bleibtrey	USA	4 min 34.0 sec
4x100 metres Relay		USA	5 min 11.6 sec
Platform Diving	Stefani Fryland-Clausen	Denmark	
Springboard Diving	Aileen Riggin	USA	
Water-Polo		GB	
Weight lifting			
Featherweight	F. de Haes	Belgium	485 lb
Lightweight	Alfred Neyland	Estonia	567 lb
Middleweight	B. Gance	France	540 lb
Light-Heavyweight	E. Cadine	France	639 lb
Heavyweight	Filippo Bottini	Italy	595 lb
Wrestling			
Freestyle			
Featherweight	Charles Ackerley	USA	
Lightweight	Kalle Antilla	Finland	
Middleweight	Eino Leino	Finland	
Light-Heavyweight	Anders Larsson	Sweden	
Heavyweight	Robert Roth	Switzerland	
Graeco-Roman Style			
Featherweight	Oskari Friman	Finland	
Lightweight	Emil Ware	Finland	
Middleweight	Carl Westergren	Sweden	
Light-Heavyweight	Claes Johansson	Sweden	
Heavyweight	Adolf Lindfors	Finland	
Yachting			
12-metre class (old type)		Norway	
(new type)		Norway	
10-metre class (old type)		Norway	
(new type)		Norway	
8-metre class (old type)		Norway	
(new type)		Norway	
7-metre class (old type)		GB	
6-metre class (old type)		Belgium	
(new type)		Norway	
6·5-metre class		Netherlands	
40-metre class		Sweden	
30-metre class		Sweden	
12 ft centreboard boat		Netherlands	
18 ft centreboard boat		Netherlands	

ber of that renowned team was Norman Ross, who also won the 400 and 1,500 metres freestyle races.

Among the women, three gold medals went to the American girl Ethelda Bleibtrey, all with new Olympic records, in the 100 and 300 metres freestyle and the 4x100 metres freestyle relay. The American Aileen Riggin was just 13 years old when she won the springboard diving competition.

Largely through the prowess of John Kelly, a young bricklayer from Philadelphia, the United States won three of the five rowing events. Kelly, father of Princess Grace of Monaco, was probably the greatest individual oarsman in history. In 1919 and 1920 he won 26 consecutive races. At Antwerp he beat Britain's Jack Beresford in the single sculls by 1 second and, half an hour later, teamed with his cousin Paul Costello to take the double sculls. They repeated this victory in 1924 at Paris. Beresford eventually competed in five Olympics, winning three gold and two silver medals.

The 14 yachting events were held at Ostend in very rough seas. Norway had by far the largest entry of the six nations taking part and won seven of the events. The Netherlands took three, Sweden two, and Belgium and Britain one apiece. The solitary British victory was in the 7-metre (old type) class, with Dorothy Winifred acting as helmswoman. After these Games it was decided that conditions of entry in the yachting events should be standardized, and the whole programme was put under the control of the International Yachting Federation.

Fifteen teams took part in the football. Britain was hustled out by Norway in the first round, and the final was fought between Belgium and Czechoslovakia. On their way to the final, the Belgians had beaten Spain (3–1) and the Netherlands (3–0). The Czechs had beaten Yugoslavia (9–0), Norway (4–0), and France (4–1).

The final itself was a debacle. The referee weakened before a large Belgian crowd, and when he sent a Czech player off in the second half there was trouble. The Czech's furious team-mates joined him off the field, and the jury awarded the match to Belgium.

The boxing titles were fairly evenly distributed. The United States won three, Britain two, and France, Canada, and South Africa one each. Edward Eagan, who won the light-heavyweight title, gained a bobsleigh gold medal 12 years later at Lake Placid, New York, the only competitor ever to win golds at both summer and winter Games. He later became chairman of the New York State Boxing Commission. The American Frank de Genaro, who took the flyweight crown, later became professional flyweight champion of the world. Harry Mallin, who won the middle-

weight title for Britain, repeated his success four years later in Paris.

The Scandinavian countries scooped all 15 places in the five wrestling events. Finland was most successful with five victories in the two classes. Finnish grapplers won two gold medals in the freestyle, and three gold, four silver, and a bronze in the graeco-roman.

Italians won five of the six fencing events, but the individual epée gold medal went to Armand Massard of France, who in 1946 was to become a member of the International Olympic Committee. A Belgian fencer, Victor Boin, had the honour of taking the Olympic oath, for the first time, on behalf of the assembled athletes.

The star of the tennis competitions was Suzanne Lenglen, pride of France and, according to many

1 Jonni Myrrä, the Finnish javelin champion, took the gold medal for this event at Antwerp with a throw of 215 ft 9¾ in. Scandinavian athletes have had a long tradition of success in the javelin, and Myrrä enhanced this reputation by repeating his success four years later at the Paris Olympics, but this time with a throw that was more than 9 ft shorter.
2 American ace sprinter Charley Paddock, first of the 'world's fastest humans', was renowned for his flying leap at the tape. Here he hurls himself through the air to win the 100 metre title in 10.8 sec. He collected a second gold medal for anchoring the victorious US 4 x 100 metre relay team.

experts, the greatest-ever woman tennis player. She swept up the singles and, with her partner Max Decugis, the mixed doubles titles, and was a finalist in the women's doubles. The veteran Decugis had won the singles and, with his wife, the mixed doubles, 14 years earlier in the interim Games at Athens.

Belgium, France, and the Netherlands were the only countries to enter the archery competitions. They had been held once before, in 1908, but after Antwerp they were dropped. In the cycling events the 4,000 metres team pursuit race was held for the first time, and in the equestrian competitions figure riding was included for the first and last time. The British polo team won the gold medal, beating Spain 13—11 in the final. Polo had been included in the 1908 Games and was to make its final appearance in the Berlin Olympics of 1936.

There were only four events in the gymnastics, and only four nations—Denmark, Italy, Norway, and Sweden—competed, with Italy winning two gold medals. But there were no less than 21 competitions in the shooting programme, including pistol and revolver, military rifles, and miniature rifles. The United States took the lion's share of medals, with Norway coming a poor second. Ice hockey was first introduced at the Antwerp Games, and the Canadians started as they meant to continue by winning the first championship.

Finally, it should be added for the record that the United States walked off with the rugby championship, and to prove that it was no fluke, repeated the victory four years later in Paris—an oddity equalled only by their humiliation of the England soccer team in the 1950 World Cup.

Paris Olympic Games (1924)

The second Olympics to be held in Paris were a great contrast to the chaotic sports meeting of 1900. The Olympic celebrations began at Chamonix at the end of January 1924 with the first ever Winter Olympic Games, and in May and June continued with rugby and association football competitions. In the rugby, only three teams took part: France, the United States, and Romania. The games involving Romania were a formality, France winning 61-3 and the United States 37-0. But in the deciding match the United States beat France 17-3. Twenty-three teams competed in the soccer, and in the final Uruguay beat Switzerland 3-0. The South Americans—whose team included such future stars of the World Cup as Scarone, Cea, and Petrone—scored 17 goals and conceded only 2 throughout the five rounds.

Athletics

The Games proper began on July 5, and the athletics events saw one of the greatest exhibitions of middle-distance running ever. The man responsible was the Finn Paavo Nurmi, who won five gold medals. Over six consecutive days he took part in seven races, and won them all. First he won his heats of the 5,000 and 1,500 metres on two consecutive days, and then on the third day within the space of 1½ hours he won the 1,500 metres in an Olympic record time of 3 min 53.6 sec, and the 5,000 in 14 min 31.2 sec—another Olympic record. The day after this double triumph, Nurmi led his team home in the heat of the 3,000 metres team race and without even a day's rest won the 10,000 metres cross-country event. The day was extremely hot, and of the 39 starters only 15 completed the course. The other 24 had collapsed, overcome by the heat and exhaustion, but Nurmi entered the stadium at the end hardly perspiring. On the next day he led the Finnish team to victory in the 3,000 metres team race, coming home first in 8 min 32.0 sec, less than 2 seconds outside his own world record.

The small Finnish contingent won a further five gold medals. Ville Ritola, runner-up to Nurmi in the 5,000 metres and the cross-country and second man home in the 3,000 metres team event, took the 10,000 metres and the 3,000 metres steeplechase. Albin Stenroos, who was 35 years old and had been third in the 10,000 metres at Stockholm in 1912, finished almost six minutes ahead of the field in the marathon. Jonni Myrra, the world record holder, retained his javelin title with a modest 206 ft. 7 in., and in the track and field pentathlon Eero

Lehtonen also won his second Olympic gold medal.

The most successful athletics nation, in terms of gold medals, was the United States with 12 titles. Jackson Scholz beat his team-mate Charley Paddock (the world record holder) in the 200 metres. In the 110 metre hurdles three Americans reached the final, where Dan Kinsey just edged out South Africa's Syd Atkinson for the gold medal. And in the 400 metres hurdles Morgan Taylor won by over a second from the Finn Erik Vilen. Taylor's time— 52.6 sec—beat the existing world record by 1.4 seconds, but as he knocked a hurdle over it was not accepted under the existing rules. Taylor reached two more Olympic finals in this event, finishing third at Amsterdam in 1928 and Los Angeles in 1932.

In the high jump, Harold Osborn won with an Olympic record leap of 6 ft. 6 in., and later gained a unique double victory with a win in the decathlon.

1 The innocence of the early Olympics—the Austrian standard bearer gives the Olympic salute later adopted by the Nazis.
2 Paavo Nurmi breaks the tape to win the 1,500 metres title and
3 leads the field in the tough 10,000 metres cross-country race.
4 An American victory in the 200 metres: Jackson Scholz beats leaping Charley Paddock (left) to the line to win in 21.6 sec.
5 Harold Osborn clears 6 ft. 6 in. to win the high jump gold.
6 The great inter-war walker Ugo Frigerio added the 1924 10,000 metres title to his previous wins at 3,000 and 10,000 in 1920.
7 William DeHart Hubbard wins the long jump with 24 ft. 5 in.
8 Gold for Britain—Harold Abrahams wins the 100 metres dash.
9 Triple swimming champion Johnny Weissmuller won gold medals in the 100 and 400 metres freestyle, and the 4 by 200 metres team.
10 Australia's 'Boy' Charlton was a sensation in the 1,500 metres, breaking the world record by over a minute.

Americans continued their unbroken run of success in the pole vault, winning all three medals. Glenn Graham and Lee Barnes tied with 12 ft. 11½ in., but the 17-year-old Barnes won the jump-off and the gold medal. Another American 1-2 came in the long jump, with William DeHart Hubbard clearing 24 ft. 5 in. to beat Ed Gourdin, the world record holder, whose best was 23 ft. 10½ in. As it turned out, the world's best long jumper was not competing. This was Robert Le-Gendre, who had not qualified for the long jump in the American trials but excelled himself to clear 25 ft. 5¾ in.—a new world record—during the pentathlon the day before the long jump was held.

Clarence Houser led an American clean sweep of the shot-put medals, and then won the gold medal in the discus. Another American triumph came in the hammer. Fred Tootell (174 ft. 10 in.) beat 46-year-old Matt McGrath (166 ft. 9½ in.) by 8 feet. McGrath thus gained his second Olympic silver—his first came in 1908—to add to the gold he won in 1912. His Olympic record of 179 ft. 7 in., set in 1912, was not beaten until 1936.

The other field event, the triple jump (then known as the 'hop,

step, and jump'), was won by Australia's 30-year-old Anthony Winter with a world record effort of 50 ft. 11¼ in., 4 inches more than the runner-up Luis Brunetto of Argentina.

Great Britain gained three victories on the track, in the 100, 400, and 800 metres. In the 100 metres Harold Abrahams equalled the Olympic record of 10.6 sec on three occasions. In the second round he returned his first 10.6, which equalled Willie Applegarth's 10-year-old British best, and though he was left badly at the start of his semi-final he still finished ahead of two Americans, defending 100 metres champion Charley Paddock and Chester Bowman. But there was no doubt about the final, which came four hours later. Abrahams led from start to finish to win by a clear yard from America's Jackson Scholz with New Zealand's Arthur Porritt third.

Abrahams also reached the final of the 200 metres, but his running lacked all inspiration and he finished sixth and last. Third was Britain's Eric Liddell, the British 100 yards record holder whose religious beliefs prevented his competing in the 100 metres (the first round of which was held on a Sunday). He did, however, take part in the 400 metres, and though he was not one of the pre-Games favourites he made the most of his proven speed when it came to the final. He set off at a seemingly suicidal speed, and was timed at 22.2 sec for the first 200 metres, most of which (the track was 500 metres round) was down the straight. He held on to his lead to win by 0.8 sec in 47.6 sec, which was an Olympic record and was also accepted as a world record, though it was inferior to Ted Meredith's 440 yards time set in 1916, and is no longer included in the official list.

Britain's third gold medal came through Douglas Lowe in the 800 metres. On form, the most likely winner was Hyla Stallard, Lowe's team-mate who has won the AAA title in a fast 1 min 54.6 sec. But in the final Stallard was suffering from an injured foot and faltered down the home straight, as Lowe and Switzerland's Paul Martin swept past him. Lowe beat Martin for first place by a fifth of a second, and Stallard just lost third place to Schuyler Enck of the United States on the line. Stallard had some small consolation two days later when he won the bronze medal in the 1,500 metres, with Lowe fourth. The United States teams won both relays, and set world records in each of them—41.0 sec for the 4 by 100 metres, in which Great Britain were second, and 3 min 16.0 sec for the 4 by 400 metres. None of the American 400 metres entries ran in their 4 by 400 metres team, and only one of the 100 metres men (Loren Murchison) in the 4 by 100.

Swimming

It was a vintage Olympic Games in the open-air swimming pool. Johnny Weissmuller won three gold medals, and Duke Kahanamoku appeared in his third Olympic Games—at the age of 33—and won the silver medal in the 100 metres. The men's 1,500 metres record was slashed by over a minute. The women's programme included backstroke and breaststroke events for the first time.

Weissmuller won the first three of his five Olympic golds—in the 100, 400, and 4 by 200 metres freestyle. He won the 100 metres by an enormous margin—2.4 sec —from Kahanamoku, the champion in 1912 and 1920. Weissmuller's second victory, in the 400 metres, was somewhat closer: he beat Sweden's Arne Borg by 1.4 sec. Third in the 400 metres was Andrew 'Boy' Charlton of Australia, at 16 the baby of the big boys in Paris, and his moment of glory was to come in the 1,500 metres. In the heats Arne Borg trimmed his own world record of 21 min 15.0 sec to 21 min 11.4 sec, but in the final two days later Charlton won by over half-a-minute from Borg in 20 min 6.6 sec. Third was Australia's Frank Beaurepaire—aged 33— who had also won the bronze in this event in 1908 and 1920. And fourth was Britain's Jack Hatfield, 31 years old, who 12 years earlier had been second in the 400 and 1,500 metres.

In the backstroke events, Warren Kealoha retained his men's title, and his American team-mate Sybil Bauer won the women's—4.2 seconds in front of the runner-up, Britain's Phyllis Harding. Aileen Riggin, who was third in this race, became the only competitor to win Olympic medals for swimming and diving when she came second in the springboard event.

After the United States, Britain were the next most successful team in the women's competitions. One Briton reached the first five of every event, the freestyle relay squad were runners-up to the United States, and Lucy Morton became Britain's first woman Olympic swimming champion by winning the 200 metres breaststroke, in which other British girls were third and fifth.

Other Sports

John B. Kelly, who had won the single sculls gold medal in Antwerp four years previously, did not defend his title, but he brought his tally of Olympic golds to three by partnering his cousin Paul Costello to their second victory in the double sculls. The single sculls title went to Britain's Jack Beresford, the Antwerp runner-up, who lost to America's William Garrett-Gilmore in his heat but won his way through the repechage to get his revenge in the final. A second gold came

Britain's way in the coxless fours: Trinity College, Cambridge, beat a Canadian crew by 1¼ lengths.

The Paris Games were the last at which lawn tennis featured as a championships event. The women's singles title went to the Californian Helen Wills, that year's Wimbledon runner-up. The Wimbledon champion, Britain's Kitty McKane, went out to France's Mlle Vlasto in the semi-finals. Miss Wills gained another gold medal by partnering Mrs Wightman—the instigator of the Britain v United States ladies match—in the doubles, in which they beat the British pair of Miss McKane and Mrs Covell. Frank Hunter and Vincent Richards, that year's Wimbledon doubles champions, beat the French idols Henri Cochet and Jacques Brugnon in the men's doubles.

The boxing events saw two countries winning two golds each in the eight events: the United States, with Fidel La Barba (flyweight) and John Fields (featherweight), and Great Britain, with Harry Mitchell (light-heavyweight) and Harry Mallin. Mallin became the first man to retain an Olympic boxing title, beating team-mate John Elliott in the middleweight final.

PARIS OLYMPIC GAMES, 1924 Gold Medallists

Athletics
Event	Name	Country	Result
100 metres	Harold Abrahams	Great Britain	10.6 sec
200 metres	Jackson Scholz	USA	21.6 sec
400 metres	Eric Liddell	Great Britain	47.6 sec
800 metres	Douglas Lowe	Great Britain	1 min 52.4 sec
1,500 metres	Paavo Nurmi	Finland	3 min 53.6 sec
5,000 metres	Paavo Nurmi	Finland	14 min 31.2 sec
10,000 metres	Ville Ritola	Finland	30 min 23.2 sec
Marathon	Albin Stenroos	Finland	2 hr 41 min 22.6 sec
3,000 metres team race		Finland	
110 metres hurdles	Dan Kinsey	USA	15.0 sec
400 metres hurdles	Morgan Taylor	USA	52.6 sec
3,000 metres steeplechase	Ville Ritola	Finland	9 min 33.6 sec
10,000 metres cross-country	Paavo Nurmi	Finland	32 min 54.8 sec
Cross-country team		Finland	
4 x 100 metres relay		USA	41.0 sec
4 x 400 metres relay		USA	3 min 16.0 sec
10 kilometres walk	Ugo Frigerio	Italy	47 min 49.0 sec
High jump	Harold Osborn	USA	6 ft 6 in
Pole vault	Lee Barnes	USA	12 ft 11½ in
Long jump	William DeHart Hubbard	USA	24 ft 5 in
Triple jump	Anthony Winter	Australia	50 ft 11¼ in
Shot	Clarence Houser	USA	49 ft 2¼ in
Discus	Clarence Houser	USA	151 ft 5 in
Hammer	Fred Tootell	USA	174 ft 10 in
Javelin	Jonni Myrra	Finland	206 ft 7 in
Pentathlon	Eero Lehtonen	Finland	14 points
Decathlon	Harold Osborn	USA	7,710.775 points

Boxing
Event	Name	Country
Flyweight	Fidel La Barba	USA
Bantamweight	William Smith	South Africa
Featherweight	John Fields	USA
Lightweight	Hans Nielsen	Denmark
Welterweight	Jean Delarge	Belgium
Middleweight	Harry Mallin	Great Britain
Light-heavyweight	Harry Mitchell	Great Britain
Heavyweight	Otto von Porat	Norway

Cycling
Event	Name	Country	Result
1,000 metres sprint	Lucien Michard	France	
2,000 metres tandem	Jean Cugnot, Lucien Choury	France	
50 kilometres track race	Jacobus Willems	Netherlands	1 hr 18 min 24 sec
4,000 metres team pursuit		Italy	5 min 12 sec
188-km Road Race			
—individual	Armand Blanchonnet	France	6 hr 20 min 48 sec
—team		France	

Equestrian
Event	Name	Country
Dressage	Ernst Linder	Sweden
Show jumping—individual	Alphons Gemuseus	Switzerland
—team		Sweden
Three day event—individual	Adolph van Zijp	Netherlands
—team		Netherlands

Fencing—Men
Foil —individual	Roger Ducret	France
—team		France
Epee —individual	Charles Delporte	Belgium
—team		France
Sabre—individual	Sandor Posta	Hungary
—team		Italy

Fencing—Women
Event	Name	Country
Foil—individual	Ellen Osiier	Denmark

Gymnastics
Event	Name	Country
Combined exercises		
—individual	Leon Stukelj	Yugoslavia
—team		Italy
Parallel bars	August Guttinger	Switzerland
Horizontal bar	Leon Stukelj	Yugoslavia
Pommel horse	Josef Wilhelm	Switzerland
Rings	Franco Martino	Italy
Vault—lengthwise	Frank Kriz	USA
—sideways	A. Seguin	France
Rope climbing	Bedrich Supcik	Czechoslovakia

Lawn Tennis
Event	Name	Country
Men's singles	Vincent Richards	USA
Ladies' singles	Helen Wills	USA
Men's doubles	Vincent Richards, Frank Hunter	USA
Ladies' doubles	Helen Wills, Hazel Wightman	USA
Mixed doubles	Hazel Wightman, R. N. Williams	USA

Modern Pentathlon
Event	Name	Country
	Bo Lindman	Sweden

Polo
Event	Name	Country
		Argentina

Rowing
Event	Name	Country	Result
Single sculls	Jack Beresford	Great Britain	7 min 49.2 sec
Double sculls	Paul Costello, John B. Kelly	USA	6 min 34.0 sec
Coxless pairs	E. Rosingh, A. Beynan	Netherlands	8 min 19.4 sec
Coxed pairs	Edouard Candeveau, Alfred Felber, Emil Lachapelle (cox)	Switzerland	8 min 39.0 sec
Coxless fours		Great Britain	7 min 8.6 sec
Coxed fours		Switzerland	7 min 18.4 sec
Eights		USA	6 min 33.4 sec

Rugby Football
Event	Name	Country
		USA

Shooting
Event	Name	Country
Optional rifle—team		USA
—individual	Morris Fisher	USA
Miniature rifle—team		France
—individual	Charles Coquelin de Lisle	France
Automatic pistol		
—team		USA
—individual	H. N. Bailey	USA
Running deer:		
single shot—team		Norway
—individual	John Boles	USA
double shot—team		Great Britain
—individual	Ole Lilloe Olsen	Norway
Clay pigeon—team		USA
—individual	Gyula Halasy	Hungary

Soccer
Event	Name	Country
		Uruguay

Swimming—Men
100 metres freestyle	Johnny Weissmuller	USA	59.0 sec
400 metres freestyle	Johnny Weissmuller	USA	5 min 4.2 sec
1,500 metres freestyle	Andrew Charlton	Australia	20 min 6.6 sec
200 metres breaststroke	Robert Skelton	USA	2 min 56.6 sec
100 metres backstroke	Warren Kealoha	USA	1 min 13.2 sec
4 x 200 metres freestyle relay		USA	9 min 53.4 sec
Springboard diving	Albert White	USA	
Plain high diving	Richmond Eve	Australia	
Fancy high diving	Albert White	USA	

Swimming—Women
Event	Name	Country	Result
100 metres freestyle	Ethel Lackie	USA	1 min 12.4 sec
400 metres freestyle	Martha Norelius	USA	6 min 2.2 sec
200 metres breaststroke	Lucy Morton	Great Britain	3 min 33.2 sec
100 metres backstroke	Sybil Bauer	USA	1 min 23.2 sec
4 x 100 metres freestyle relay		USA	4 min 58.8 sec
Springboard diving	Elisabeth Becker	USA	
Plain high diving	Caroline Smith	USA	

Water Polo
Event	Name	Country
		France

Weightlifting
Event	Name	Country	Result
Featherweight	Paolo Gabetti	Italy	887¼ lb
Lightweight	Edmond Decottignies	France	970 lb
Middleweight	Carlo Galimberti	Italy	1,085¾ lb
Light-heavyweight	Charles Rigoulot	France	1,107¾ lb
Heavyweight	Giuseppe Tonani	Italy	

Wrestling
Freestyle
Event	Name	Country
Bantamweight	Kustaa Pihlajamaki	Finland
Featherweight	Robin Reed	USA
Lightweight	Russel Vis	USA
Light-middleweight	Hermann Gehri	Switzerland
Middleweight	Fritz Haggmann	Switzerland
Light-heavyweight	John Spellman	USA
Heavyweight	Harry Steele	USA

Graeco-Roman
Bantamweight	Eduard Putsep	Estonia
Featherweight	Kalle Anttila	Finland
Lightweight	Oscari Friman	Finland
Middleweight	Edvard Vesterlund	Finland
Light-heavyweight	Carl Westergren	Sweden
Heavyweight	Henry Deglane	France

Yachting
Event	Name	Country
12-ft centreboard	Leon Huybrechts	Belgium
8-metre class	'Bera'	Norway
6-metre class	'Elisabeth V'	Norway

Amsterdam Olympic Games (1928)

The Games of the IXth Olympiad, held in July and August of 1928, were chiefly remarkable for the rather grudging inclusion of women track and field competitors for the first time—and a somewhat less grudging welcome to a 300-strong team of German athletes, the first since World War I. A total of 700,000 spectators flocked to the capital of the Netherlands to watch more than 3,900 competitors from 46 different countries take part. There were 109 separate competitions in the 17 sports.

A new stadium was built on marshy ground, to accommodate 40,000 spectators. The splendid 400-metre running track was surrounded by a 500-metre cycle track, with a football pitch in the centre. There was also a marathon tower, 150 ft high, bearing a bowl at the top in which a flame burnt throughout the period of the Games.

Prince Hendrick, the Prince Consort, acting for Queen Wilhelmina, performed the opening ceremony on July 28, and 35,000 sports fans were there to cheer the march past of the nations. They were unable to cheer the French contingent, who pointedly absented themselves from the parade because of alleged insults by a pro-German Dutch gatekeeper. In contrast to the enormous squads from Germany and the United States, Haiti, Cuba, and Panama each sent a solitary athlete.

Twenty-eight nations gained at least one gold medal each. As usual, the United States were way out in front with an impressive 22 gold medals, followed by Germany with 10, Sweden 9, and Finland 8. Britain won 3—two in track and field events and one in rowing; Canada had 4, and Australia, India, New Zealand, and South Africa one apiece.

Japan secured her first-ever gold medal through Mikio Oda, who won the triple jump with a leap of 15.21 metres (49 ft 10¾ in). Some 36 years later, at the Tokyo Olympics, Oda was a member of the organizing committee. His historic Japanese medal was commemorated in 1964 by a flagpole, bearing the Olympic flag and exactly 15.21 metres high.

With no hint of what lay in store for his boys in the prestigious track events, Major General Douglas MacArthur, president of the U.S. Olympic Committee, encouraged the folks back home with the following words: 'The opening of the Games finds the American team at the peak of form. We have assembled the greatest team in our athletic history.' Unfortunately for the General and his audience, the United States obtained only one gold medal in the 10 individual track events—the 400 metres being won by a star football player from Syracuse named Ray Barbuti. But they redeemed themselves by winning both the relay races, the high jump, long jump, pole vault, shot, and discus.

The solitary Haitian, Silvio Cator, distinguished himself by coming second in the long jump. He gained further fame four years later by becoming the world's first 26-ft long jumper. To this day he remains the only Haitian ever to win an Olympic medal.

Percy Williams, a curly-headed ex-waiter from Canada, achieved the coveted 'double' by winning both the 100 and 200 metre sprints, and Britain's Douglas Lowe repeated his Paris success in the 800 metres, the first man to do so at this distance. The powerful Finns won four track events and the decathlon. Paavo Nurmi, having won two gold medals in Antwerp and four in Paris, added another gold and two silver to his burgeoning collection. For most of the marathon two Japanese, a Finn, and an American battled grimly for the lead. But a few

1 The Amsterdam Olympics saw a member of the British peerage win a gold medal for a track event: Lord Burghley (later the Marquess of Exeter) took the 400 metres hurdles in 53.4 sec.
2 The Canadian team smashed the world record for the women's 4 x 100 metres relay, laying claim to their gold medals with a time of 48.4 sec. It was the first time that women had been allowed to compete in track and field events in the Olympic Games.
3 South African sprinter Sydney Atkinson (497) clocks a time of 14.8 sec to gain the coveted gold medal in the 110 metres hurdles.

miles from the tape, El Abdel Ouafi, a 29-year-old Arab, strode through the pack to win the gold for France by 150 yards.

The Irish Free State gained her first win as an independent country through the mighty Patrick O'Callaghan, appropriately throwing the hammer, an event in which Irish-Americans had excelled for many years. Altogether, nine new Olympic records (four of them also world records) were set in the men's track and field events.

The women had to content themselves with three track and two field events: 100 metres, 800 metres, sprint relay, high jump, and discus. Canada won the high jump through Ethel Catherwood, and the Canadian team also gained golds in the sprint relay. In the 800 metres, won by Germany's Linda Radke, many of the competitors (some of whom had never run the distance before) showed signs of distress. The organizers were so disturbed that the event was subsequently dropped; the distance, they concluded, was too great for the weaker sex. Nearly a quarter of a century elapsed before it was reintroduced into the Games.

Thirty-three competitors from 11 countries were eager to display their talents in the modern pentathlon. The competition consists of five events—shooting, swimming, fencing, cross-country running, and cross-country riding. At these Olympics, the points awarded for each event corresponded to the position in which the competitor finished, and the competitor with the lowest total was the overall winner. Sweden gained her fourth successive victory in this event through Sven Thofelt.

There were eight swimming events for men and seven for women. The United States won 10 of these, the remaining five each going to a different country. The American Johnny Weismuller, who subsequently created the film role of Tarzan, gained gold medals

in the 100-metres freestyle and in the relay. These he added to the three golds already won in the Paris Olympics for the 100 metres and 400 metres freestyle, and the relay.

Arne Borg of Sweden maintained his swimming reputation in the 400 metres and 1,500 metres. In 1924 he had taken a silver medal in the 400 metres; this time, he had to be content with a bronze. But in the 1,500 metres, for which four years earlier he had won a silver medal, he came home with a gold. Similarly with Australian Andrew 'Boy' Charlton. In Paris he had swum his way to a bronze medal in the 400 metres; in Amsterdam he turned it into a silver. He won a second silver in the 1,500 metres—the event that he had won in 1924.

After a tremendous struggle in the platform diving event, Pete Desjardins of the United States snatched victory from the American-trained Egyptian, Farid Simaika, by 0.16 of a point. Desjardins also took first place in the springboard diving. Altogether, nine world records were set up in the swimming and diving events.

Eighteen teams competed in the association football championships, but Britain was a notable absentee. It was alleged that many of the competing countries were paying their players for 'broken time' (time lost from their ordinary jobs) and Britain opted out in protest at this breach of amateurism. The holders, Uruguay, met near neighbours Argentina in the final. The pitch resembled a battlefield at times, and with the score at 1–1 after 15 minutes of extra time both teams were happy to lick their wounds in preparation for the replay. In the second final Argentina scored first with a disputed goal. Uruguay equalised, and eventually retained the championship 2–1.

The eight boxing divisions attracted nearly 150 fighters from 29 countries. Italy came off best with three gold medals, but it was

Sport in Beeld

1 Paavo Nurmi, perhaps the best known name in the history of athletics, won the 10,000 metres crown and came second in the 5,000 metres and 3,000 m steeplechase.
2 Master French swordsman Lucien Gaudin took the foils and epée title.
3 Germany's Linda Radke sets a world record of 2 min 16.8 sec for the 800 metres, leaving Miss Hitomi (265) trailing in second place.
4 French Arab El Abdel Ouefi jogs home an easy winner in the 1928 marathon.
5 Norway's entry *Norna* took the gold medal in the 6-metre class at Amsterdam.
6 American footballer Ray Barbuti powers his way to the tape in the 400 metres, in a shade over 47 sec.

AMSTERDAM OLYMPIC GAMES, 1928 Gold Medallists

Association Football
Uruguay

Athletics—Men
100 metres	Percy Williams	Canada	10.8 sec
200 metres	Percy Williams	Canada	21.8 sec
400 metres	Ray Barbuti	USA	47.8 sec
800 metres	Douglas G. A. Lowe	GB	1 min 51.8 sec
1500 metres	Harry E. Larva	Finland	3 min 53.2 sec
5000 metres	Ville Ritola	Finland	14 min 38 sec
10000 metres	Paavo Nurmi	Finland	30 min 18.8 sec
Marathon	A. El Ouafi	France	2 hr 32 min 57 sec
4x100 metres relay		USA	41.0 sec
4x400 metres relay		USA	3 min 14.2 sec
110 metres hurdles	Sydney Atkinson	S Africa	14.8 sec
400 metres hurdles	Lord David Burghley	GB	53.4 sec
3000 metres steeplechase	Toivo A. Loukala	Finland	9 min 21.8 sec
High Jump	Robert W. King	USA	6 ft 4⅜ in
Long Jump	Edward Hamm	USA	25 ft 4¾ in
Triple Jump	Mikio Oda	Japan	49 ft 10¾ in
Pole Vault	Sabin W. Carr	USA	13 ft 9¼ in
Shot	John Kuck	USA	52 ft 0¾ in
Discus	Clarence Houser	USA	155 ft 3 in
Hammer	Patrick O'Callaghan	Ireland	168 ft 7 in
Javelin	Erik Lundqvist	Sweden	218 ft 6 in
Decathlon	Paavo Yrjola	Finland	8053.29 pts

Athletics—Women
100 metres	Elizabeth Robinson	USA	12.2 sec
800 metres	Linda Radke	Germany	2 min 16.8 sec
4x100 metres relay		Canada	48.4 sec
High Jump	Ethel Catherwood	Canada	5 ft 2⅜ in
Discus	Helena Konopacka	Poland	129 ft 11¾ in

Boxing
Flyweight	Anton Kocsis	Hungary
Bantamweight	Vittorio Tamagnini	Italy
Featherweight	L. van Klaveren	Netherlands
Lightweight	Carlo Orlandez	Italy
Welterweight	Edward Morgan	New Zealand
Middleweight	Piero Toscani	Italy
Light-Heavyweight	Victorio Avendano	Argentina
Heavyweight	Rodriguez Juvado	Argentina

Cycling
1000 metres	R. Beaufrand	France	
1000 metres time trial	Willy Falk-Hansen	Denmark	1 min 14.4 sec
2000 metres tandem	B. Leene, D. van Dijk	Netherlands	
4000 metres team pursuit		Italy	5 min 01.8 sec
Road Race—Individual	Henry Hansen	Denmark	4 hr 47 min 18.0 sec
Team		Denmark	15 hr 9 min 14.0 sec

Equestrian Events
Dressage—		
Individual	Carl von Langen	Germany
Team		Germany
Show Jumping—		
Individual	F. Ventura	Czechoslovakia
Team		Spain
Three Day Event—		
Individual	Lt. Ferdinand Pahud de Mortanges	Netherlands
Team		Netherlands

Fencing—Men
Foil—Individual	Lucien Gandin	France
Team		Italy
Epee—Individual	Lucien Gandin	France
Team		Italy
Sabre—Individual	Odon Terszyansky	Hungary
Team		Hungary

Fencing—Women
Foil—Individual	Helene Mayer	Germany

Gymnastics—Men
Vaulting Horse	Eugen Mack	Switzerland
Pommelled Horse	Hermann Hanggi	Switzerland
Horizontal Bar	George Miex	Switzerland
Parallel Bars	Ladislav Vacha	Czechoslovakia
Rings	Leon Stukelji	Yugoslavia
Combined Individual	George Miex	Switzerland
Combined Team		Switzerland
Women's Team		Netherlands

Hockey
British India

Lacrosse
USA

Modern Pentathlon
	Sven Thofelt	Sweden

Rowing
Single Sculls	Henry Pearce	Australia	7 min 11 sec
Double Sculls	Paul Costello, Charles McIlraine	USA	6 min 41.4 sec
Coxwainless Pairs	K. Moeschler, B. Muller	Germany	7 min 6.4 sec
Coxed Pairs	H. Schochlin, C. Schochlin, H. Bourquin (cox)	Switzerland	7 min 42.6 sec
Coxwainless Fours		GB	6 min 36.0 sec
Coxed Fours		Italy	6 min 47.8 sec
Eights		USA	6 min 3.2 sec

Swimming—Men
100 metres freestyle	John Weismuller	USA	58.6 sec
400 metres freestyle	Albert Zorilla	Argentina	5 min 1.6 sec
1500 metres freestyle	Arne Borg	Sweden	19 min 51.8 sec
100 metres backstroke	George Kojac	USA	1 min 8.2 sec
200 metres breaststroke	Yoshiyuki Tsurata	Japan	2 min 48.8 sec
4x200 metres freestyle relay		USA	9 min 36.2 sec
Springboard Diving	Pete Desjardins	USA	
Highboard Diving	Pete Desjardins	USA	

Swimming—Women
100 metres freestyle	Albina Osipovich	USA	1 min 11.0 sec
400 metres freestyle	Martha Norelius	USA	5 min 42.8 sec
100 metres backstroke	Marie Braun	Netherlands	1 min 22.0 sec
200 metres breaststroke	Hilde Schrader	Germany	3 min 12.6 sec
4x100 metres freestyle relay		USA	4 min 47.6 sec
Springboard Diving	Helen Meany	USA	
Highboard Diving	Elizabeth Pinkston	USA	

Water-Polo
Germany

Weightlifting
Featherweight	Franz Andrysek	Austria	634 lb
Lightweight	Kurt Helbig*	Germany	711 lb
	Hans Haas	Austria	
Middleweight	Francois Roger	France	738 lb
Light-Heavyweight	Said Nosseir	Egypt	782 lb
Heavyweight	Josef Strassberger	Germany	810 lb

*Results and bodyweights being equal Helbig and Haas were declared joint champions.

Wrestling

Freestyle
Bantamweight	Kaarie Makinen	Finland
Featherweight	Allie Morrison	USA
Lightweight	Osvald Kapp	Estonia
Welterweight	Arve Haavisto	Finland
Middleweight	Ernst Kyburz	Switzerland
Light-Heavyweight	Thure Sjostedt	Sweden
Heavyweight	John C. Richtoff	Sweden

Graeco-Roman style
Bantamweight	Karl Leucht	Germany
Featherweight	Voldemar Vali	Estonia
Lightweight	Lajos Keresztes	Hungary
Middleweight	Vaino A. Kokkinen	Finland
Light-Heavyweight	Ibrahim Moustafa	Egypt
Heavyweight	Rudolph Svensson	Sweden

Yachting
6-metre class	Prince Olav	Norway
8-metre class	Mme V. Herict	France
12-foot dinghy	Sven Thorell	Sweden

---

the judging that won the headlines —some of it was so bad as to be unbelievable. It seems that mauling, butting, and boring were all one to the gentlemen who did the scoring.

German fencer Helen Mayer, who took the gold in the individual foil, the only women's event, won every match throughout the competition and received only nine hits in the process. German fencers also came third and fourth in this event. France, Italy, and Hungary each scored doubles in the six men's events.

Switzerland won three of the five gymnastic events. Women gymnasts had given exhibitions at previous Games, but at Amsterdam a women's team event was included for the first time. They had to wait another 24 years before more gymnastic events for women competitors were staged.

Among the oarsmen only the Americans gained more than a single victory. Paul Costello won his third gold medal in successive Olympics in the double sculls, this time with Charles McIlvaine as his partner. An American crew also won the eights, for the third time in succession, roared on mercilessly to victory by their vociferous cox, Don Blessing. Bobbie Pearce of Australia won the single sculls by a good four lengths.

Hockey, dropped from the 1924 Games, was reintroduced—much to India's satisfaction. They gained the first of six Olympic wins in succession, scoring 29 goals throughout the competition without conceding one. There were no shooting events, because of trouble over amateurism, and the tennis competitions were dropped (for ever) because of a similar controversy.

Perhaps the last word on the Amsterdam Olympic Games should rest with General Mac-Arthur, who described them with somewhat exaggerated if not pardonable pride as 'a model for all future Olympics'.

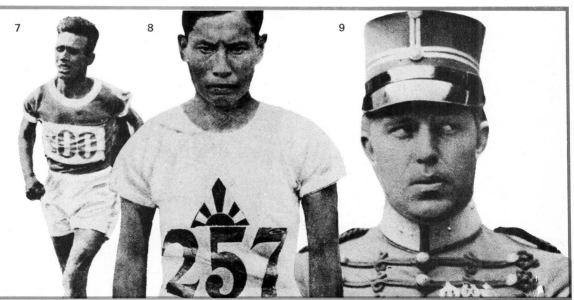

7 The dynamic Finn, Willie Ritola, relentlessly upheld his country's great tradition in the distance events, already established by Kolehmainen and Nurmi. At Amsterdam in the 10,000 metres he matched Nurmi stride for stride until the last lap, but was beaten at the tape by less than a second. A few days later he had his revenge by defeating his great rival in the 5,000 metres.
8 Grim-faced Mikio Ada produced a historic leap of nearly 50 ft in the triple jump to win Japan's first ever gold medal.
9 Sven Thofelt won the modern pentathlon for Sweden with a total of 47 points on the old reckoning.

Los Angeles Olympic Games (1932)

The ninth in the series of modern Olympic Games was held at Los Angeles in late July and early August 1932, the first Games to be held in the Americas since the St Louis celebrations of 1904. In many ways they were the first of the highly organized promotions that typified the Games afterwards. For the first time an 'Olympic village', housing the 1,300 male athletes, was especially constructed, while the 120 women competitors (in three sports—athletics, swimming, and fencing) were located in an hotel. Although 40 countries were represented in Los Angeles, the travelling distance and the time and expense involved resulted in very small entries from the European countries.

Athletics

Thirty-four nations sent some 400 men and women to Los Angeles to compete for 23 men's and 6 women's titles. The United States, of course, had a full team, but other countries could not afford to be so well represented. The women were competing in their second track and field Olympics, and their programme had been expanded by the inclusion of the 80 metres hurdles and javelin, but the 800 metres was dropped.

The United States won 11 men's titles, with Finland the next most successful team with 3. American women won five out of the six events, while their only failure was in the 100 metres, won by Stanislawa Walasiewicz—representing Poland, her native country, but a resident—known as Stella Walsh—in the United States since she was two years old. The track events were notable for the introduction of an experimental electric timing mechanism, while hand-operated stop watches and a movie camera were also used.

Eddie Tolan became the first coloured man to win a gold medal in the 100 or 200 metres. In fact he won both, beating his fellow-American Ralph Metcalfe by an inch in the 100 metres and equalling the world record of 10.3 sec. In the 200 metres he beat George Simpson (also of the United States) by two yards in 21.2 sec with Metcalfe third. The only European to reach either final was Arthur Jonath of Germany, who took the bronze in the 100 metres and was fourth in the 200. Tolan was not included in America's 4 by 100 metres relay team, and nor was Metcalfe. But the quartet showed the United States' remarkable depth of sprinting ability, winning by 10 yards in 40.0 sec, a world record.

The 400 metres final was also an all-American battle, between Bill

Official Report of the 1932 Olympics

1 The scene in the Los Angeles Coliseum as the Games of the Xth Olympiad were opened on July 30, 1932.
2 George Gulack won a gold medal for America on the rings. American gymnasts won 5 of the 11 gymnastic events contested in the Games. **3** Jean Shiley won the high jump after a jump-off with her American teammate Mildred Zaharias. Both girls were credited with a world record height of 5 ft. 5 in. **4** Finland's Lauri Lehtinen just holds off America's Ralph Hill in the 5,000 metres. Some people thought that the Finn had impeded the American, and demanded his disqualification, but the result was allowed to stand.

Official Report of the 1932 Olympics

Central Press

Official Report of the 1932 Olympics

5 A well judged race by Britain's Tom Hampson gave him the 800 metres title by 0.2 sec from Canada's Alex Wilson in a world record of 1 min 49.8 sec. **6** The American yacht *Angelita* had only one opponent, Canada's *Santa Maria*, in the 8-metre class.

Carr and Ben Eastman (the world 440 and 880 yards record holder). Carr won by 0.2 sec, setting a world record of 46.2 sec, with Eastman second, a second ahead of Canada's Alex Wilson. Eastman did not feature in his country's 4 by 400 metres relay team, but the Americans still won, beating Great Britain by 3 seconds in 3 min 8.2 sec—a world record.

Three days before the 400 metres final, Wilson had been even closer to a gold medal. Britain's Tom Hampson, who was fifth at the half-way stage, won his country's fourth consecutive 800 metres title after a tremendous battle with Wilson down the home straight. His time of 1 min 49.7 sec was officially rounded off to 1 min 49.8 sec—a world record and the first time a man had broken 1 min 50 sec.

The 5,000 metres produced a controversial finish between Finland's Lauri Lehtinen and the American champion Ralph Hill. In a desperate last lap Hill tried to pass his opponent, and there can be no doubt that Lehtinen, albeit unintentionally, impeded the American. Some of the judges and a section of the crowd thought that the Finn should have been disqualified, but the chief judge ruled otherwise and the announcer settled the crowd with the words 'Remember, please, these people are our guests'.

The '3,000 metres' steeplechase was an extraordinary race on account of a strange error on the part of the officials. Finland's Volmari Iso-Hollo had won his heat in an Olympic record time of 9 min 14.6 sec, but in the final he recorded 10 min 33.4 sec. It was later discovered that the official responsible for counting the laps had been taken ill and his substitute had failed to record one of the laps—in all a distance of 3,460 metres was run.

The finish of the marathon was one of the closest in history, with just 65 seconds covering the first four men. Argentina's Juan Zabala beat Britain's Sam Ferris by 19 seconds for the gold medal. Another close finish came in the 110 metres hurdles. The movie film of the race was instrumental in clarifying the placings. The race was clearly won by America's George Saling, with his team-mate Percy Beard in second place. The bronze medal was at first awarded to another American Jack Keller, but the film showed that he had been beaten by Britain's Don Finlay, and Keller went to the British team's quarters personally to give Finlay the medal.

For the first time, the United States failed to win the high jump, which crossed the border into Canada. Duncan McNaughton won the jump-off against Robert van Osdel and Cornelius Johnson of the United States and Simeon Toribio of Argentina. Two other jumping events—the

pole vault and long jump—went to American competitors, but Japan won the triple jump through Chuhei Nambu, whose 51 ft. 7 in. clearance was over a foot better than the silver-medal-winning effort of Sweden's Erik Svensson.

The outstanding female athlete of the Games was Mildred 'Babe' Didrikson, who won the 80 metres hurdles and the javelin, and was second in the high jump, in which she shared a new world record with the winner Jean Shiley.

Swimming

Japan, inspired by the victory of Yoshiyuki Tsuruta in the 200 metres breaststroke at the 1928 Games, set off for America with the firm belief that what one could do, they could all do. And how right they were. They won five of the six men's swimming titles, and even won their first women's Olympic swimming medal through Hideko Maehata who was second in the 200 metres breaststroke.

Yoshiyuki Tsuruta retained his breaststroke crown, with his team-mate Reizo Koike second. Kusuo Kitamura, at 14 years old the youngest man to win an Olympic swimming title, was first in the 1,500 metres freestyle and was followed home by Shozo Makino. And in the 100 metres freestyle, an American preserve since 1908, they took first and second places. They won all three medals in the 100 metres backstroke, and beat the United States by 12.1 sec to win the 4 by 200 metres relay in a world record time of 8 min 58.4 sec. Japan's tally of medals was 11 out of a possible 16, and they got all three of their permitted competitors through to the last six of every men's race.

American pride was salvaged in the diving where they took all 12 medals and in the women's swimming, in which the host country won four of the five events. Helene Madison won both the 100 and 400 metres freestyle (setting a world record in the latter) and took a third gold as a member of the winning American relay team. The only non-American women's winner was Australia's Clare Dennis, who set a world record in the 200 metres breaststroke. Her time of 3 min 6.3 sec was 0.1 sec faster than Miss Maehata. Britain's only medallist was Valerie Davies of Wales, third in the 100 metres backstroke.

Hungary, with 35 goals in their favour and only 2 scored against them, were conclusive winners of the water polo tournament for the first time. They beat the Japanese team 18-0.

Other sports

The gymnastics events saw the great Italian Romeo Neri in action. He was the most successful gymnast on show, winning three gold medals, in the combined exercises individual and team events and on the parallel bars. The United States team was much in evidence, with victories in the horizontal bar and the rings (both 'regular' gymnastic events) and in three more unusual competitions, rope climbing, tumbling, and Indian club swinging.

The rowing course at Long Beach could accommodate four crews abreast, but was made difficult by a tricky cross wind which made some of the times slower than usual. The United States were understandably the most successful team, with three victories—in the double sculls, coxed pairs, and eights. Great Britain's small team, which contested only four races and reached the final of each, won two golds, in the coxless pairs and the coxless fours. 'Jumbo' Edwards created something of a record by being a member of both winning crews. Australia's Henry Pearce retained the single sculls title he had won in Amsterdam in 1928, the first man to do so,

Shooting, omitted from the 1928 programme, returned with two events, the free pistol and small bore rifle. Both events were won by European marksmen, Renzo Morigi of Italy taking the pistol gold, and Bertil Ronnmark of Sweden the rifle.

The Swedish team was the most successful in the wrestling events, winning two freestyle and four Graeco-Roman golds. Ivar Johansson was their most outstanding competitor, winning the freestyle middleweight and the Graeco-Roman welterweight titles.

Although the relative isolation of California from the main population centres of the world had cut down the number of participants at the 1932 Olympics, the Games themselves were a success. It would be more than 20 years before the Olympics were again held outside Europe but the Los Angeles Games had shown that the Olympics could move from continent to continent.

LOS ANGELES OLYMPIC GAMES, 1932 Gold Medallists

Athletics—Men			
100 metres	Eddie Tolan	USA	10.3 sec
200 metres	Eddie Tolan	USA	21.2 sec
400 metres	Bill Carr	USA	46.2 sec
800 metres	Tommy Hampson	Great Britain	1 min 49.8 sec
1,500 metres	Luigi Beccali	Italy	3 min 51.2 sec
5,000 metres	Lauri Lehtinen	Finland	14 min 30.0 sec
10,000 metres	Janusz Kusocinski	Poland	30 min 11.4 sec
Marathon	Juan Zabala	Argentina	2 hr 31 min 36 sec
4 x 100 metres relay		USA	40.0 sec
4 x 400 metres relay		USA	3 min 8.2 sec
110 metres hurdles	George Saling	USA	14.6 sec
400 metres hurdles	Bob Tisdall	Eire	51.8 sec
Steeplechase*	Volmari Iso-Hollo	Finland	10 min 33.4 sec
50 kilometres walk	Thomas Green	Great Britain	4 hr 50 min 10 sec
High jump	Duncan McNaughton	Canada	6 ft 5½ in
Pole vault	William Miller	USA	14 ft 1¾ in
Long jump	Edward Gordon	USA	25 ft 0¾ in
Triple jump	Chuhei Nambu	Japan	51 ft 7 in
Shot	Leo Sexton	USA	52 ft 6 in
Discus	John Anderson	USA	162 ft 4½ in
Hammer	Patrick O'Callaghan	Eire	176 ft 11 in
Javelin	Matti Jarvinen	Finland	238 ft 6½ in
Decathlon	James Bausch	USA	8,462.23 pts (6,588 pts by 1962 tables)
Athletics—Women			
100 metres	Stanislawa Walasiewicz	Poland	11.9 sec
4 x 100 metres relay		USA	47.0 sec
80 metres hurdles	Mildred Didrikson	USA	11.7 sec
High jump	Jean Shiley	USA	5 ft 5 in
Discus	Lilian Copeland	USA	133 ft 1¾ in
Javelin	Mildred Didrikson	USA	143 ft 4 in
Boxing			
Flyweight	Istvan Enekes	Hungary	
Bantamweight	Horace Gwynne	Canada	
Featherweight	Carmelo Robledo	Argentina	
Lightweight	Lawrence Stevens	South Africa	
Welterweight	Edward Flynn	USA	
Middleweight	Carmen Barth	USA	
Light-heavyweight	David Carstens	South Africa	
Heavyweight	Alberto Lovell	Argentina	
Cycling			
1,000 metres sprint	Jacobus van Egmond	Netherlands	
1,000 metres time trial	Edgar Gray	Australia	1 min 13.0 sec
2,000 metres tandem	Maurice Perrin, Louis Chaillot	France	
4,000 metres team pursuit		Italy	4 min 52.9 sec
Road race	Attilio Pavesi	Italy	2 hr 28 min 5.6 sec
Equestrian			
Dressage—individual	Francois Lesage	France	
—team		France	
Show jumping —individual	Takeichi Nishi	Japan	
—team		No complete team finished	
Three day event—individual	Ferdinand de Mortanges	Netherlands	
—team		USA	
Fencing—Men			
Foil—individual	Gustavo Marzi	Italy	
—team		France	
Epee—individual	Giancarlo Medici	Italy	
—team		France	
Sabre—individual	Gyorgy Piller	Hungary	
—team		Hungary	
Fencing—Women			
Foil—individual	Ellen Preis	Austria	
Hockey		India	
Gymnastics			
Combined exercises—individual	Romeo Neri	Italy	
—team		Italy	
Floor exercises	Istvan Pelle	Hungary	
Horizontal bar	Dallas Bixler	USA	
Parallel bars	Romeo Neri	Italy	
Pommell horse	Istvan Pelle	Hungary	
Vault	Savino Guglielmetti	Italy	
Rings	George Gulack	USA	
Rope climbing	Raymond Bass	USA	
Tumbling	Rowland Wolfe	USA	
Indian club swinging	George Roth	USA	
Modern Pentathlon	Johan Oxenstierna	Sweden	
Rowing			
Single sculls	Henry Pearce	Australia	7 min 44.4 sec
Double sculls	William Garrett-Gilmore, Kenneth Myers	USA	7 min 17.4 sec
Coxless pairs	'Jumbo' Edwards, Lewis Clive	Great Britain	8 min 0.0 sec
Coxed pairs	Charles Kieffer, Joseph Schauers, Edward Jennings (cox)	USA	8 min 25.8 sec
Coxless fours		Great Britain	6 min 58.2 sec
Coxed fours		Germany	7 min 19.0 sec
Eights		USA	6 min 37.6 sec
Shooting			
Free pistol	Renzo Morigi	Italy	
Small bore rifle	Bertil Ronnmark	Sweden	
Swimming—Men			
100 metres freestyle	Yasuji Miyazaki	Japan	58.2 sec
400 metres freestyle	Clarence Crabbe	USA	4 min 48.4 sec
1,500 metres freestyle	Kusuo Kitamura	Japan	19 min 12.4 sec
200 metres breaststroke	Yoshiyuki Tsurata	Japan	2 min 45.4 sec
100 metres backstroke	Masaji Kiyokawa	Japan	1 min 8.6 sec
4 x 200 metres freestyle relay		Japan	8 min 58.4 sec
Springboard diving	Michael Galitzen	USA	
Highboard diving	Harold Smith	USA	
Swimming—Women			
100 metres freestyle	Helene Madison	USA	1 min 6.8 sec
400 metres freestyle	Helene Madison	USA	5 min 28.5 sec
200 metres breaststroke	Clare Dennis	Australia	3 min 6.3 sec
100 metres backstroke	Eleanor Holm	USA	1 min 19.4 sec
4 x 100 metres freestyle relay		USA	4 min 38.0 sec
Springboard diving	Georgia Coleman	USA	
Highboard diving	Dorothy Poynton	USA	
Water Polo		Hungary	
Weightlifting			
Featherweight	Raymond Suvigny	France	633¾ lb
Lightweight	Rene Duverger	France	716½ lb
Middleweight	Rudolf Ismayr	Germany	760½ lb
Light-heavyweight	Louis Hostin	France	804¾ lb
Heavyweight	Jaroslav Skobla	Czechoslovakia	837¾ lb
Wrestling			
Freestyle			
Bantamweight	Robert Pearce	USA	
Featherweight	Hermanni Pihlajamaki	Finland	
Lightweight	Charles Pacome	France	
Welterweight	Jack van Bebber	USA	
Middleweight	Ivar Johansson	Sweden	
Light-heavyweight	Peter Mehringer	USA	
Heavyweight	Johan Richtoff	Sweden	
Graeco-Roman			
Bantamweight	Jakob Brendel	Germany	
Featherweight	Giovanni Gozzi	Italy	
Lightweight	Erik Malmberg	Sweden	
Welterweight	Ivar Johansson	Sweden	
Middleweight	Vaino Kokkinen	Finland	
Light-heavyweight	Rudolf Svensson	Sweden	
Heavyweight	Carl Westergren	Sweden	
Yachting			
Monotype	Jacques Lebrun	France	
Star	Gilbert Gray, Andrew Libano	USA	
6-metre		Sweden	
8-metre		USA	

* An extra lap was run through 'official error', and the distance run in the final was 3,460 metres.

Eddie Tolan (left) winning the 100 metres from Ralph Metcalfe. Tolan followed this victory with another in the 200 metres.

Central Press

Ireland's Bob Tisdall (right) wins the 400 metres hurdles. Fourth (second from left) was the 1928 champion, Lord Burghley.

Central Press

Official Report of the 1936 Olympics

Fox Photos

Associated Press

Berlin Olympic Games (1936)

An 'infamous festival dominated by Jews' was the first published Nazi verdict on the Olympic Games when it was learned in 1931 that the games of the XIth Olympiad would be held in Berlin four years later. It was hardly an auspicious start to a pageant designed to foment international amity through sport. But at that time Hitler was not yet undisputed master of Germany. As the deadline for the Games approached, he awoke to their immense propaganda value, and spared no expense to make the occasion the best organized and the most efficiently equipped in the history of the Olympics.

Many nations were beginning to flex their muscles before plunging into the maelstrom of World War II, and a number of private scraps broke out in the months preceding the Berlin Olympics, any one of which might have persuaded the organizers to call the whole thing off. Russia was making threatening gestures at China and Japan. France, Greece, and Austria were riven with political dissension. Japan invaded Manchuria, and Italy helped herself to Ethiopia. Spain exploded into civil war, and over all hung the brooding shadow of the swastika.

In 1913 the Kaiser had dedicated a 60,000-seat stadium at Grunewald, a suburb of Berlin, in preparation for the 1916 Games, which had been awarded to Germany, but which never took place. When Hitler came to power in 1933 the Germans extended the site to produce a magnificent stadium holding 100,000 spectators, and a sumptuous Olympic village to house 4,000 competitors — and conveniently adaptable to military needs. State money was poured out to make the Berlin Games the best ever, for the glory of sport—and of the Third Reich.

1 Lit by Greek virgins from the light of the sun, the first Olympic flame to burn in the modern Olympics nears the brazier at Berlin. **2** Czechoslovakia's Alois Hudec, strongman of the rings and gold medallist at Berlin. **3** Bespectacled Godfrey Brown, baton in hand, wins the 4 x 400 metres for Britain. Frederick Wolff, Godfrey Rampling, and William Roberts had built up a 5-yard lead and Brown made no mistake.

Germany, as expected, won most gold medals at the Olympics in Berlin. They took 33 golds to America's 24, but most of them were in the more esoteric events. **1** There was a close finish in the eights, with the USA crew from Washington University winning by 0.2 sec from Italy (2nd) and Germany. German oarsmen won medals in all the Berlin rowing events. **2** Ken Carpenter of America broke the German monopoly of throwing events to beat the German world record holder Willie Schroeder with a throw of 50.48 metres, an Olympic record. **3** Britain won only two gold medals in track and field at Berlin. One of them, came from Harold Whitlock in the 50 km walk. **4** Winner of three gold medals, Karl Schwarzmann shows his technique on the parallel bars. Germany dominated the gymnastic events and won 6 out of the 8 golds at stake in this sport.

Nazi ideology inevitably produced problems in the realm of sport. In Britain, and more particularly the United States, there was widespread agitation to boycott the Games. Assurances were sought, and glibly given, that there would be no racial discrimination against the selection of non-Aryans to represent Germany, if they reached the required athletic standard.

But official anti-Jewish sentiment soon made itself evident. Dr Lewald, the head of the German organizing committee at that time, was of partly Jewish descent. The Nazis began by forcing him to resign from the national athletic committee; they then tried to remove him from the German and International Olympic committees. They did everything they could to take over the jurisdiction of the Games. Count Baillet Latour, president of the IOC, and his fellow members refused to kowtow to the Fuehrer's demands and stood courageously behind Dr Lewald. They insisted that the Games must be presented in the spirit of the Olympic ideal; that the preparations for the Games were to be carried out by the organizing committee, supervised by the IOC; and that the whole tournament must be entirely non-political in character. Finally they threatened that if these conditions were not met, they would cancel the 1936 Olympic Games. Hitler reluctantly acquiesced.

A gigantic bell, some 9 feet in diameter and weighing more than 14 tons, summoned the youth of the world to Berlin. It was hung in a special tower at the Olympic Stadium. Swastikas outnumbered Olympic flags in this great Nazi showpiece. The torch relay was instituted for the first time. On July 30 a torch was lit by the rays of the sun at Olympia, in Greece, and carried by nearly 3,000 athletes who each ran one kilometre, through Greece, Bulgaria, Yugoslavia, Hungary, Austria, Czechoslovakia, and Germany to reach the Olympic Stadium on August 1.

On the opening day 110,000 spectators squeezed into the huge stadium to watch the march-past. A military band perched on the top of the towers that flanked the Marathon Gate heralded the arrival of the Fuehrer. The Germans sang 'Deutschland Uber Alles' and the 'Horst Wessel' song, the flags of the competing nations fluttered to the mastheads, and the Olympic bell tolled its message.

The 50-nation march-past began. Hitler took the salute—which was revealing in its variety. The French team favoured the Olympic salute, similar to the Nazi salute, and were given a tremendous reception. The British immediately behind, gave a curt 'eyes right' and were greeted with stony silence. The political implications could not be disguised.

The German team, nearly 500 strong, brought up the rear of the procession, marching with military precision. Thousands of doves soared skywards to signal the arrival of a beautifully proportioned, flaxen-haired athlete holding the Olympic torch in his right hand. He came down a long flight of steps, ran halfway round the track looking for all the world like some athlete from the pages of Greek mythology, then plunged the torch into a brazier. The Olympic flame burst forth, to thunderous applause from the delighted multitude. Spiridon Louis, winner of the first marathon, in 1896, impressively attired in Greek national costume, presented Hitler with an olive branch; the Olympic oath was taken; a message from Baron de Coubertin was relayed over the loudspeakers; the crowd joined in the singing of the 'Hallelujah' chorus—and the opening ceremony was over.

There were 130 gold medals to be won (counting each of the team events as one medal) in the 19 sports.

Athletics

Track and field events consisted of 23 events for men (nowadays there are 24—there is a 20 km as well as a 50 km walk), and six for women. More than 700 men from 42 nations, and just over 100 women competitors from 20 nations, competed.

The outstanding athlete of the Berlin Games was the American Negro Jesse Owens. He gained three individual gold medals and was the first runner of the American quartet in the sprint relay, which they won by a good three yards in a new world record time. In both the 100 metres and the 200 metres he stormed through four rounds to head the field easily on each occasion. His times in the 100 metres were 10.3, 10.2, 10.4, and 10.3 sec. His 10.2 sec was disallowed as a world record because of a following wind of slightly more than two metres a second. In the 200 metres he produced times of 21.1, 21.1, 21.3, and 20.7 sec. He thus equalled the Olympic record for the 100 metres and beat the previous record for the 200 metres by half a second.

The long jump turned out to be one of the most exciting contests of all time. Owens, to the dismay of his fans, started with two foul jumps and faced elimination. It was then, according to Owens, that the German champion Luz Long (later killed on the Eastern Front) almost certainly saved him by pointing out that his run-up mark was wrong. With three final jumps to go, Owens led Long by just over an inch, but with his fifth leap the German equalled Owen's best effort of 25 ft 9¾ in. Methodically, almost casually, Owens sprinted down the track and cleared 26 ft 0½ in. The jump was immortalized in Leni Riefenstahl's historic film of the 1936 Games, which shows Owens jumping and Long watching. In the final jumps, Long fouled and Owens, with the pressure off, did 26 ft 5¼ in, more than a foot further than the previous Olympic record.

There was hardly an event during the eight full days of competition that did not excite the crowd. The stadium was always full, even for the heats. In the 400 metres, the duel between the two Americans, Archie Williams and Jimmy Luvalle, and Godfrey Brown and Bill Roberts from Britain was magnificent. Williams, running in lane 5, beat Brown in lane 6 by a very short yard, while Luvalle in lane 3 was inches ahead of Roberts in lane 4. Brown and Roberts gained their revenge in the relay team which pushed the Americans into second place in the 4 by 400 metres relay. The only other British gold medal was won by Harold Whitlock in the 50 km walk.

The 1,500 metres was a triumph for Jack Lovelock from New Zealand, who defeated the finest field of middle distance runners to date. Glenn Cunningham, the great American miler, was in the lead 400 metres from home, when suddenly a wispy figure in black streaked past him and stayed in front all the way to the tape. The fair-haired New Zealand medical student covered

1 Cyclists from 27 nations contested the 100 km race which was eventually won by Robert Charpentier of France. The French cyclists also took the team medals for the best overall result in the event. Germans were never famous for their cycling prowess, but the competitors from the host country won two of the six cycling titles at Berlin. **2** One of the most touching moments in Olympic history was when Spiridon Louis, who was the first Olympic marathon champion when he ran from Marathon to Athens in 1896, presented the German Chancellor with the age-old symbol of peace, an olive branch. The Berlin Games were full of incidents of this kind, most of them arranged by the German stage managers to make the Games the most successful ever. Germany's sportsmen were trained for the Games so that they would not be disgraced by the 'black auxiliaries' included in other countries' teams. The opening ceremony was marked by the release of thousands of doves; there was a special performance of a festival play, *Olympic Youth*, written by Dr Carl Diem, one of the Olympic committee; and a performance of Beethoven's Ninth Symphony, the choral movement of which was used as an anthem for all-German teams until the 1964 Games, when the combined German team was split into East/West.

Pictorial Press

Fox Photos

BERLIN OLYMPIC GAMES, 1936 Gold Medallists

Athletics—Men			
100 metres	Jesse C. Owens	USA	10.3 sec
200 metres	Jesse C. Owens	USA	20.7 sec
400 metres	Archie F. Williams	USA	46.5 sec
800 metres	John Woodruff	USA	1 min 52.9 sec
1,500 metres	John E. Lovelock	New Zealand	3 min 47.8 sec
5,000 metres	Gunnar Hoeckert	Finland	14 min 22.2 sec
10,000 metres	Ilmari Salminen	Finland	30 min 15.4 sec
3,000 metres Steeplechase	Volmari Iso-Hollo	Finland	9 min 03.8 sec
110 metres Hurdles	Forrest G. Towns	USA	14.2 sec
400 metres Hurdles	Glenn F. Hardin	USA	52.4 sec
50 kilometres Walk	Harold H. Whitlock	GB	4 hr 30 min 41.4 sec
Marathon	Kitei Son	Japan	2 hr 29 min 19.2 sec
4 x 100 metres Relay		USA	39.8 sec
4 x 400 metres Relay		GB	3 min 09.0 sec
High Jump	Cornelius C. Johnson	USA	6 ft 8 in
Pole Vault	Earle Meadows	USA	14 ft 3¼ in
Long Jump	Jesse C. Owens	USA	26 ft 5¼ in
Triple Jump	Naoto Tajima	Japan	52 ft 6 in
Shot	Hans Woellke	Germany	53 ft 1¾ in
Discus	Kenneth Carpenter	USA	165 ft 7½ in
Hammer	Karl Hein	Germany	185 ft 5 in
Javelin	Gerhard Stoeck	Germany	235 ft 8½ in
Decathlon	Glenn Morris	USA	
Athletics—Women			
100 metres	Helen H. Stephens	USA	11.5 sec
80 metres Hurdles	Trebisonda Valla	Italy	11.7 sec
4 x 100 metres Relay		USA	46.9 sec
High Jump	Ibolya Csak	Hungary	5 ft 3 in
Discus	Gisela Mauermeyer	Germany	156 ft 3¼ in
Javelin	Tilly Fleischer	Germany	148 ft 2¾ in
Basketball		USA	
Boxing			
Flyweight	Willi Kaiser	Germany	
Bantamweight	Ulderico Sergo	Italy	
Featherweight	Oscar Casanovas	Argentina	
Lightweight	Imre Harangi	Hungary	
Welterweight	Sten Suvio	Finland	
Middleweight	Jean Despeaux	France	
Light-Heavyweight	Roger Michelot	France	
Heavyweight	Herbert Runge	Germany	
Canoe Racing			
10,000 metres			
One seater collapsable	Gregor Hradetzky	Austria	50 min 01.2 sec
Two seater collapsable	Sven Johansson, Eric Blandstroem	Sweden	45 min 48.9 sec
One seater Kayak	Ernst Krebs	Germany	46 min 01.7 sec
Two seater Kayak	Paul Wevers, Ludwig Landen	Germany	41 min 45.0 sec
Two seater Canadian	Vaclav Mottl, Zdenek Skrdlant	Czechoslovakia	50 min 33.8 sec
1,000 metres			
One seater Kayak	Gregor Hradetzky	Austria	4 min 22.9 sec
Two seater Kayak	Adolph Kainz, Alfonz Dorfner	Austria	4 min 03.8 sec
One seater Canadian	Francis Amyot	Canada	5 min 32.1 sec
Two seater Canadian	R. Vladimir Syrovatka, Felix J. Brzak	Czechoslovakia	4 min 50.1 sec
Cycling			
1,000 metres Scratch	Toni Merkens	Germany	
1,000 metres Time Trial	Arie G. van Vliet	Netherlands	1 min 12.0 sec
2,000 metres Tandem	Ernst Ihbe, Carl Lorenz	Germany	
4,000 metres Team Pursuit		France	4 min 45.0 sec
Road Race—Individual	Robert Charpentier	France	2 hr 33 min 05.0 sec
—Team		France	7 hr 39 min 16.2 sec
Equestrian Sports			
Dressage—Individual	Heinrich Pollay	Germany	
—Team		Germany	
Three Day Event			
—Individual	Ludwig Stubbendorff	Germany	
—Team		Germany	
Jumping Prix de Nations			
—Individual	Kurt Hasse	Germany	
—Team		Germany	
Fencing			
Foil—Individual	Giulio Gaudini	Italy	
—Team		Italy	
Foil (Ladies)	Ilona Schacherer-Elek	Hungary	
Epee—Individual	Franco Riccardi	Italy	
—Team		Italy	
Sabre—Individual	Endre Kabos	Hungary	
—Team		Hungary	
Football		Italy	
Gymnastics			
Individual championship—Men	Karl A. M. Schwarzmann	Germany	
Team championship—			
Men		Germany	
Women		Germany	
Apparatus championship—men			
Horizontal Bar	Aleksanteri Saarvala	Finland	

Rings	Alois Hudec	Czechoslovakia	
Pommelled Horse	Konrad Frey	Germany	
Free Exercises	Georges Miez	Switzerland	
Parallel Bars	Konrad Frey	Germany	
Long Horse	Karl A. M. Schwarzmann	Germany	
Handball		Germany	
Hockey		India	
Modern Pentathlon			
Individual	Gotthardt Handrick	Germany	
Team		USA	
Polo		Argentina	
Rowing			
Single Sculls	Gustav Schaefer	Germany	8 min 21.5 sec
Double Sculls	Jack Beresford, Leslie F. Southwood	GB	7 min 20.8 sec
Coxless Pairs	Willi Eichhorn, Hugo Strauss	Germany	8 min 16.1 sec
Coxed Pairs	Gerhard Gustmann, Herbert Adamski, Dieter Arend (Cox)	Germany	8 min 36.9 sec
Coxless Fours		Germany	7 min 01.8 sec
Coxed Fours		Germany	7 min 16.2 sec
Eights		USA	6 min 25.4 sec
Shooting			
Automatic pistol or revolver (25 metres)	Cornelius M. van Oyen	Germany	
Target—pistol (50 metres)	Torsten Ullman	Sweden	
Miniature rifle (50 metres)	Willy Roegeberg	Norway	
Swimming and Diving —Men			
100 metres Freestyle	Ferenc Czik	Hungary	57.6 sec
400 metres Freestyle	Jack Medica	USA	4 min 44.5 sec
1,500 metres Freestyle	Noboru Terada	Japan	19 min 13.7 sec
200 metres Breaststroke	Tetsuo Hamuro	Japan	2 min 42.5 sec
100 metres Backstroke	Adolph Keifer	USA	1 min 5.9 sec
4 x 200 metres Freestyle Relay		Japan	8 min 51.5 sec
Springboard Diving	Richard Degener	USA	
High Diving	Marshall Wayne	USA	
Swimming and Diving —Women			
100 metres Freestyle	Hendrika Mastenbroek	Netherlands	1 min 5.9 sec
400 metres Freestyle	Hendrika Mastenbroek	Netherlands	5 min 26.4 sec
200 metres Breaststroke	Hideko Maehata	Japan	3 min 3.6 sec
100 metres Backstroke	Dina Senff	Netherlands	1 min 18.9 sec
4 x 100 metres Freestyle Relay		Netherlands	4 min 36.0 sec
Springboard Diving	Marjorie Gestring	USA	
High Diving	Dorothy Poynton Hill	USA	
Water Polo		Hungary	
Weight lifting			
Featherweight	Anthony Terlazzo	USA	688½ lb
Lightweight	Mohammed Ahmed Mesbah	Egypt	754¼ lb
Middleweight	Khadr el Touni	Egypt	854 lb
Light-Heavyweight	Louis Hostin	France	821 lb
Heavyweight	Josef Manger	Germany	903½ lb
Wrestling			
Catch as Catch Can			
Bantamweight	Odon Zombori	Hungary	
Featherweight	Kustaa Pihlajamaeki	Finland	
Lightweight	Karoly Karpati	Hungary	
Welterweight	Frank W. Lewis	USA	
Middleweight	Emile Poilve	France	
Light-Heavyweight	Knut Fridell	Sweden	
Heavyweight	Kristjan Palusalu	Estonia	
Greco-Roman Style			
Bantamweight	Marton Loerincz	Hungary	
Featherweight	Yasar Erkan	Turkey	
Lightweight	Lauri Koskela	Finland	
Welterweight	Rudolph Suedberg	Sweden	
Middleweight	Ivar Johansson	Sweden	
Light-Heavyweight	Axel Cadier	Sweden	
Heavyweight	Kristjan Palusalu	Estonia	
Yachting			
6-metre class		GB	
8-metre class		Italy	
International Star class		Germany	
Olympic Monotype	Daniel Kabchelland	Netherlands	

'Storm-troopers march with a steady, quiet tread . . .' sang the Germans, but their dreams of athletic supremacy were shattered by the 'Tan Streak from Ohio State'—Jesse Owens. Legend has it that Hitler, who met and congratulated the Aryan winners of the first three finals, deliberately snubbed Owens. If he snubbed anyone it was Cornelius Johnson and David Allbritton, American negroes who were first and second in the high jump, the fourth event. In fact Hitler had overstayed his intended visit and, by design or not, had left the stadium before the result was announced. The IOC

1 the last lap in an amazing 55.7 sec and won by five yards in a world record time of 3 min 47.8 sec. Cunningham also finished inside the old world record, and the next three runners broke the Olympic record.

Finland won the 5,000 metres, 10,000 metres, and steeplechase, but were rather surprisingly defeated in the javelin by the German Gerhard Stoeck. Another surprise German victory was in the shot, which went to Hansje Woellke, with Stoeck third. The world record holder Jack Torrance of the United States who in 1934 had put up a remarkable world record of 57 ft 1 in, was more than six feet below his best, and nearly three feet behind the winning put of 53 ft 1¾ in. The third German men's victory came in the hammer. Carpenter Karl Hein, in the presence of the Fuehrer, achieved a tremendous throw of 185 ft 5 in, beating the 24-year-old Olympic record by nearly six feet. But in the discus, world record holder Willie Schroeder of Germany was nearly 20 feet below his best, and Americans finished first and second.

The pole vault produced a duel that continued into the night. In the glare of the floodlights, the American Earl Meadows soared to a victorious 14 ft 3¼ in, within three inches of the world record. His two Japanese rivals were beaten by four inches. World and

Olympic records were shattered in the decathlon, that awe-inspiring 10-event contest decided over two days, with Americans in the three first places. In the marathon, the brash Argentine newsboy Juan Carlos Zabala, defending his title, collapsed exhausted, and Korean-born Kitei Son of Japan romped home by a clear two minutes.

The American women won the sprint relay by default—the German women dropped the baton when yards ahead. The American sprinter Helen Stephens beat Stella Walsh of Poland, the 1932 winner, by two yards in the 100 metres. Tribisonda Valla of Italy equalled the world record of 11.6 sec in the 80 metres hurdles, and Ibolya Csak of Hungary took the high jump. In that event Britain's Dorothy Odam, just 16 years old, cleared the same height as the winner, but lost the jump-off. When the next Games took place in London 12 years later, Dorothy, then Mrs Tyler and the mother of two children, again cleared the same height as the winner, but had to be content with second place because of the rule for deciding ties. This rule was changed after the 1936 Games. Had the new rule been in operation in 1936, Dorothy would have won the gold, while had the old rule been in existence in 1948 she would also have won the gold.

The United States won 12 of the 23 men's track and field events,

told Hitler it was not his job to congratulate anyone—but if he did he should not discriminate. Thereafter Hitler did not congratulate anyone—in public at least. 1 Owens wins the long jump with a leap of 26 ft 5¼ in, an Olympic record that stood until 1960. 2 In the heat of the 100 metres Owens equalled the Olympic record of 10.3 sec. 3 Germany's Anny Steuer (right) and Italy's Trebisonda Valla (far left) were second and first in a blanket finish of the hurdles.
4 German girls set a world record in the heat of the 400 metres relay but dropped the baton in the final.

thanks largely to their 'black auxiliaries', as they were described in the Nazi press. These 10 negroes, headed by Jesse Owens, won a total of six gold, three silver, and two bronze medals—a score superior to that of any other single nation, including the rest of the American team. They were the victors in every flat race from 100 to 800 metres.

Swimming and diving
In the 18,000-seat swimming pool, next to the athletics stadium, Japan ruled the ripples. The Japanese splashed their way to 10 out of a possible 17 medals in the men's events, and took another in the women's events. But the Netherlands dominated the women's races, winning the other four titles.

In the diving, the United States were supreme. They made a clean sweep of the medals in the men's and women's springboard and were first and second in both highboard events—Germany won the bronzes—for a total of 10 out of 12 medals. Thirteen-year-old Marjorie Gestring, who won the springboard title, became the youngest champion of the modern Olympic Games.

One of the surprises was the victory of Hungary's Ferenc Csik in the 100 metres freestyle race. With all eyes on the favoured Americans and Japanese in the centre lanes, Csik crept forward on the outside to gain a shock first place.

The men's breaststroke set a new style. For the first time in the Olympics, the over-water arm recovery, the 'high sail' (later to become the butterfly), was used by some swimmers for part of the race. Despite this display of power, particularly by Germany's Erwin Sietas, little Tetsuo

Pictorial Press

Mansell Collection

Central Press

Hamuro of Japan, using a neat, orthodox, underwater recovery throughout, was victorious.

Dina Senff from the Netherlands created a sensation in the 100 metres backstroke. She missed her touch at the turn and had to swim back to the wall again. Astonishingly, she still won. Another great Dutch girl, Ria Mastenbroek, took the 100 and 400 metres freestyle—the only woman yet to achieve this double—and won the silver in the backstroke. Hideko Maehata became Japan's first and only woman Olympic swimming champion in taking the 200 metres breaststroke, with Denmark's tiny 13-year-old Inge Sorensen, third.

Rowing
Rowing was a triumph for the Germans. They won five of the seven events, and a silver and a bronze medal in the other two. Their only defeats occurred in the double sculls, where Jack Beresford (competing in his fifth successive Olympics) and Leslie Southwood of Britain won a brilliant victory over the Germans who had defeated them in the heats; and in the eights, in which the first three crews finished within a second of each other, the United States defeating Italy by three-fifths of a second.

Other events
In the boxing events, although the continental judges appeared to favour attack unduly when awarding points, there was next to no criticism of the decisions. France and Germany each won two gold medals.

A new event was canoe racing—in which Austria won three golds, and Germany and Czechoslovakia two each.

France gained three of the six

gold medals for cycling, finishing first and second in the 100 km road race, which was held for the first time under massed-start conditions. All six equestrian events—three individual and three team—were won by Germany, and the seven gold medals for fencing were shared by Italy (four) and Hungary (three).

In securing their hockey title, India played five matches, scoring 39 goals and conceding only one —to Germany in the final.

Among the gymnasts, two magnificent German athletes, Karl Swharzmann and Konrad Frey, won three gold medals each; and such was the appeal of the weightlifters that more than 20,000 people crammed into the arena to watch their hero, Joseph Manger of Germany, win the heavyweight crown.

The Germans scooped a total of 35 gold, 23 silver, and 29 bronze medals in the summer Olympics of 1936. Equestrian events, gymnastics, and rowing—for which they had prepared massively—accounted for 16 of their golds. The United States, who came next overall, were consoled with their 12 golds in men's track and field events—one more than all the other nations put together. In those events, five world records had been broken and one equalled and 17 new Olympic records set.

On the final day the Olympic fire flickered out and the five-ringed flag was struck in the Berlin twilight. The best organized, and for that reason possibly least truly Olympian Games, had come to an end. It was to be 12 years in time, and a whole lifetime in experience, before the world would awake to the austerity Games in the battle-weary, bomb-scarred London of 1948.

1 Ernst Krebs from Munich won the 10,000 metres single kayak event from 15 other competitors. This is one of the events no longer included in the Games.
2 Germany's first ever track and field gold medal was won by Hans Wollke in the shot put. Like all other winners in the Games he received his medal and a potted oak tree.
3 One of the last of the flying Finns, Gunnar Hoeckert, won the 5,000 metres in an Olympic record time. His win was helped by the collision of his compatriots, Lauri Lehtinen and Ilmari Salminen, who lost valuable ground and could finish only second and fourth. Henry Jonsson of Sweden picked up the bronze.
4 The podgy, 150-lb Dutch girl Hendrika Mastenbroek (lane 5) won the 100 metres freestyle in an Olympic record time—65.9 sec. Her medal collection at the Games amounted to three golds (two individual and one team) and a silver in the backstroke.

Pictorial Press

Diving has been an Olympic sport since 1904, at St Louis, when a competition for men, with dives from both highboard and springboard, was held. A women's diving competition was held at Stockholm in 1912, but it was not until 1928 that the Olympic diving programme was limited to its present four-event formula—highboard and springboard for men and women.

London Olympic Games (1948)

After six years in which most of the world had been locked in World War II, the Olympic Games were revived after a 12-year gap. The war had caused the scheduled Games of 1940 and 1944 to be cancelled, but in October 1945 London applied to stage the Games of 1948. This privilege was granted in March 1946, and in a little over two years the Games were planned and carried out.

The economic situation in the post-war years did not make things easy for the organizing committee. They were fortunate in having in London—at Wembley—the buildings of the 1924 British Empire Exhibition, which were more suitable than the White City site of the 1908 Olympics. The Empire Stadium was the scene of the athletics, the soccer semi-finals and final, the hockey semi-finals and final, and the equestrian show jumping. The Empire Pool, close by, accommodated the swimming and boxing (a special bridge was built across the pool). The basketball was held at Harringay Arena, cycling at Herne Hill in South London, and the yachting at Tor Bay in Devon. It had originally been decided to hold the gymnastics in the stadium, but the inclement weather forced the gymnasts to go indoors, to the Empress Hall in the Earl's Court exhibition complex, where the weightlifting and wrestling events had already been held.

Fifty-nine countries sent 4,030 men and 438 women to compete in the Games. They were housed in special centres around London, as there was insufficient capital to provide an Olympic Village as at Los Angeles and Berlin. Notable absentees were, not surprisingly, the Germans and Japanese, while the USSR were not affiliated to the International Olympic Committee and thus could not compete.

Athletics

The original running track in the Empire Stadium had not been used for over 20 years, and had been covered with a greyhound track. Laying a special cinder track and other 'temporary works' cost the organizing committee nearly £80,000, while compensation paid to the proprietors of the stadium for loss of revenue from greyhound racing amounted to £90,000. There was intensive press, radio, and—for the first time—television coverage of the track events. Belgium, Czechoslovakia, and Jamaica won their first Olympic athletics gold medals.

The track and field events in which there were 600 men and nearly 150 women entrants, got off to an inauspicious start when the first event, the heats of the 400

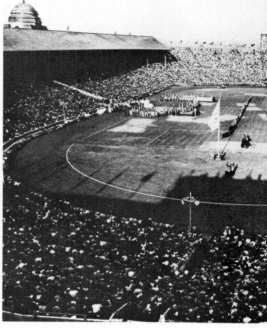

metres hurdles, was delayed for a good half-hour because the marks for spacing the hurdles had not been laid down. The one track final that day—the 10,000 metres—more than made up for any organizational chaos. Viljo Heino of Finland, the world record holder, was the favourite, although he was threatened by a new name, Emil Zatopek of Czechoslovakia who had recently come within a few seconds of the Finn's time. For the first eight laps Heino was in front, but after 10 laps Zatopek took the lead and never relinquished it. Heino tried to follow the Czech, but with 9 laps to go, to everyone's astonishment, he left the track. Thereafter Zatopek went farther and farther ahead, winning by over three-quarters of a minute, and becoming the first man to beat the half-hour in an Olympic Games. Three days later, Zatopek was involved in another race, the final of the 5,000 metres. He had qualified for that final the day after the 10,000 metres in a peculiar heat, in which he and Sweden's Erik Ahlden had raced

neck and neck for the tape—an unnecessary duel as the third man was over 80 yards behind. The track for the final was sodden by heavy rain. Zatopek set a fast pace, and by the half-distance only he, Ahlden, Gaston Reiff of Belgium, and the Dutchman Willem Slykhuis were in the hunt. In the tenth lap, Reiff 'jumped' the opposition and at the bell was 20 yards ahead of Slykhuis, with Zatopek another 50 yards behind. With 300 yards left Zatopek made one of those apparently mad rushes which were to be such a feature of his performances in years to come. First he caught and passed the Dutchman, and then he cut into Reiff's lead at an alarming rate. The Belgian seemed to be on his last legs, and a victory for Zatopek appeared certain, but half-a-dozen yards from the tape Reiff glanced over his shoulder, and hung on grimly to win by 0.2 sec. Zatopek seemed to have misjudged his race, but years later claimed he was very tired three laps from home, and then found a new lease of life at the bell.

The last running event was the marathon. At half-way, a former Belgian paratrooper, 21-year-old Etienne Gailly, was over half-a-minute clear of the field, and nearly two minutes ahead of the British favourite, Jack Holden, who later dropped out. With 12 kilometres to go, Gailly was still half-a-minute in front, but in the next 5,000 metres was passed by Choi of Korea and Delfo Cabrera of Argentina. Gailly, hardly able to drag one foot after the other, somehow regained the lead, while Choi dropped out. He entered the stadium a few yards ahead of Cabrera and Welshman Tommy Richards. In the final circuit of the track, Gailly was passed by Cabrera, the winner, and Richards, both still full of running. The marathon had once again produced a dramatic finish.

At the other end of the distance scale, the 100 metres produced an upset of form. The United States were represented in the final by Mel Patton, the world 100 yards record holder, Barney Ewell, who held the world 100 metres record,

1 Australia's John Winter won the high jump with a leap of 6 ft. 6 in. He was the last eastern cut-off jumper to win an Olympic gold medal.
2 Although Belgium's Etienne Gailly (left) was the first marathon runner to enter the stadium, he was overtaken in the last yards by Argentina's Delfo Cabrera (right) and Britain's Tom Richards.
3 Cycling at Herne Hill. Italy (white shirts) beating Britain in the tandem final.
4 America's mighty John Davis won the first of his two Olympic heavyweight titles with a total of 996½ lb.
5 The Empire Stadium laid out for the show jumping. The hockey and soccer finals were also held there.
6 The 17-year-old American Bob Mathias caused a shock in the decathlon. After being in the stadium for over 12 hours on the second day, he won by 165 points.

and Harrison Dillard, world record holder for the 120 yards hurdles who had failed to make the team in the hurdles and had scraped into third place in the American trials for the 100 metres. Dillard—the dark horse—won clearly from Ewell. And Ewell was to gain a second silver, in the 200 metres, which was won by Mel Patton, who had been pushed into fifth place in the 100.

Another world record holder, Jamaica's Herb McKenley, was relegated to second place, in the 400 metres. McKenley, the first man to beat 46 seconds for the distance, was beaten by his fellow-Jamaican Arthur Wint. Jamaica were, not surprisingly, favourites for the 4 by 400 metres relay, but their chances of winning were obliterated on the third leg when Arthur Wint collapsed with cramp. Wint also featured in the 800 metres final, in which he was beaten by three yards by America's Mal Whitfield.

The two hurdles events produced some outstanding performances. The 110 metres saw

William Porter lead home the American trio of medal winners in an Olympic record 13.9 sec. And in the 400 metres 29-year-old Roy Cochran—who had won the American championship in 1939—gained a six-yard victory over Duncan White of Ceylon, who thus became the first Ceylonese to win an Olympic athletics medal.

The United States won three of the eight field events—the pole vault, long jump (Willie Steele won by nearly a foot from Australia's Thomas Bruce), and the shot. Australia won her first high jump title through John Winter (with a modest 6 ft. 6 in. clearance), and Adolfo Consolini and Giuseppe Tosi took first and second places in the discus for Italy. The real surprise was a 17-year-old American, Bob Mathias. He gained a brilliant victory in the decathlon, winning by 165 points from France's Ignace Heinrich. The Americans also won the 4 by 100 metres relay. At first it was announced that they had been disqualified, and the gold medals were to be awarded to the British

quartet. The crowd did not relish a home victory being earned in this way, and they were very relieved when the initial decision was reversed and the medals were awarded to the Americans.

Fanny Blankers-Koen dominated the women's events, winning four gold medals in the nine-event programme. She won the 100 and 200 metres with some ease, was pushed all the way in the 80 metres hurdles by Britain's Maureen Gardner, and ran a fine anchor leg for the Netherlands in the 4 by 100 metres relay to pull up from fourth to first place. Mrs Blankers-Koen held the world records for the high and long jump, but did not compete in those events at London.

The high jump produced a great struggle between Britain's Dorothy Tyler, who as Dorothy Odam had been second at Berlin in 1936, and America's Alice Coachman. Both girls cleared 5 ft. 6⅛ in. and the gold medal went to the American because she had cleared the final height at her first attempt while Mrs Tyler needed a second jump.

Micheline Ostermeyer of France gained a shot-discus double, and Austria's Hermine Bauma gained her country's first Olympic athletics title, in the javelin. She had missed a bronze medal at Berlin in 1936 by a mere 6 inches.

Despite the bad weather—it was rainy and cold on several days—the track and field events were conducted in front of a very interested crowd, and there was no 'incident' that soured the happy atmosphere of this first Olympic Games for 12 years.

Swimming

The Empire Pool, built for the 1934 British Empire Games but closed to aquatic activities since World War II, was reopened for the Olympics and proved to be a magnificent arena.

The absence of Germany, and more particularly Japan, opened the way to American pre-eminence in the men's events. American swimmers won all the swimming events—five individual titles and the 4 by 200 metres relay (which produced the only swimming world record of the Games)—and took 5 of the other 10 medals open to them.

But Japan had the last laugh on their wartime enemies. On the days that Bill Smith won the 400 metres freestyle in 4 min 41.0 sec and Jim McLane the 1,500 metres in 19 min 18.5 sec, Hironashin Furuhashi was demonstrating just what those two medals were worth. In Tokyo, in the Japanese championships which were timed to coincide with the Olympic programme, he swam 400 metres in 4 min 33.0 sec, and 1,500 metres in 18 min 37.0 sec—world best times which were never ratified as world records as Japan had not then been readmitted to the International Swimming Federation.

The Americans did not have it all their own way in the five women's swimming events, winning two titles—the 400 metres freestyle (through Ann Curtis) and the 4 by 100 metres relay. Denmark challenged strongly for Olympic honours, with Greta Andersen taking the 100 metres freestyle, Karen Harup the 100 metres backstroke, and this pair helping their country to silver medals in the freestyle relay.

There were signs of an Australian revival in both men's and women's events. John Marshall took a bronze in the 400 metres and a silver in the 1,500 metres; Nancy Lyons was second in the 200 metres breaststroke (behind Nel van Vliet of the Netherlands), and Judy Joy Davies was third in the backstroke. Britain's only medal—a bronze—went to Cathie Gibson in the 400 metres. She closed right up on backstroke champion Karen Harup to miss the silver medal by 1.3 sec.

The Americans achieved a clean sweep of diving gold medals. Victoria Draves became the first woman to win both highboard and springboard titles at the same Games, and Sammy Lee and Bruce Harlan took the men's crowns. American divers, in fact, won 10 of the 12 medals, and only Mexico's Joaquin Capilla and the Danish girl Birte Christoffersen intervened, both with bronze medals in the highboard.

European champions in 1947, Italy won the water polo gold medals for the first time, in a tournament which was criticized—as all water polo tournaments tend to be—for the amount of fouling and inefficient refereeing.

Other Sports
When Sweden were announced as winners of the dressage team event, few people could have guessed that they would be stripped of their medals. It was subsequently discovered, however, that one of their team—Gehnall Persson, who finished 6th—was not an officer, and thus ineligible to compete. The gold medals were therefore belatedly awarded to France.

In the team sports, the United States retained their basketball title, and India beat Great Britain 4-0 to win their fourth successive hockey gold medals. Sweden, with their brilliant inside-forward trio of Gunnar Gren, Gunnar Nordahl, and Nils Liedholm, beat Yugoslavia 3-1 in a splendid soccer final.

Henley was the scene of the canoeing and rowing events. Gert Fredriksson won both individual kayak titles—over 1,000 and 10,000 metres—while his fellow Swedes took both K-2 events. British oarsmen won two of the seven rowing golds—the double sculls and the coxless pairs. John Wilson and Stanley Laurie, the 1938 Silver Goblets winners back from 10 years service in the Sudan, won the coxless pairs, and Herbert Bushnell and Richard Burnell won the double sculls. Mervyn Wood gave Australia her third single sculls title when he beat Uruguay's Eduardo Risso by a 14-second margin.

On the fencing *piste*, the most remarkable performance came from 41-year-old Ilona Elek of Hungary who retained the women's foil title she had won 12 years before, with Ellen Muller-Preiss, the 1932 champion, adding another bronze to the one she gained in 1936. Finnish gymnasts were supreme, winning four of the eight titles, including a unique triple tie for the pommel horse gold medal. The women's team event, the only women's gymnastic event on the programme, went to Czechoslovakia.

Of the 59 competing nations, 17 failed to place a competitor in the first six in any event. The United States were by far the most successful team, winning 35 gold medals, while Sweden were next with 13. The significance of the Games of the XIV Olympiad, however, was not to be gauged in terms of world records or gold medals, or even in national domination, but in the way that countries of the world had come together to compete in London in a friendly way. The scars of the war—many of the belligerents in which came face to face again at Wembley—were hardly healed, but the Olympics did do something towards restoring a shattered world to the sanity it so badly needed.

1 The Dutch goalkeeper gropes helplessly as the Italians score their second goal in a 4-2 victory. Italy won the gold medals in the water polo tournament, and the Netherlands the bronzes.
2 A happier moment for the Dutch—Fanny Blankers-Koen wins the 100 metres from Britain's Dorothy Manley (691)—one of the Flying Dutchwoman's four gold medals. **3** Richard Burnell and Herbert Bushnell winning the double sculls for Britain by 4 seconds from the Danish pair.

LONDON OLYMPIC GAMES, 1948 Gold Medallists

Athletics—Men			
100 metres	Harrison Dillard	USA	10.3 sec
200 metres	Mel Patton	USA	21.1 sec
400 metres	Arthur Wint	Jamaica	46.2 sec
800 metres	Mal Whitfield	USA	1 min 49.2 sec
1,500 metres	Henry Eriksson	Sweden	3 min 49.8 sec
5,000 metres	Gaston Rieff	Belgium	14 min 17.6 sec
10,000 metres	Emil Zatopek	Czechoslovakia	29 min 59.6 sec
Marathon	Delfo Cabrera	Argentina	2 hr 34 min 51.6 sec
4 x 100 metres relay		USA	40.6 sec
4 x 400 metres relay		USA	3 min 10.4 sec
110 metres hurdles	William Porter	USA	13.9 sec
400 metres hurdles	Roy Cochran	USA	51.1 sec
3,000 metres steeplechase	Tore Sjostrand	Sweden	9 min 4.6 sec
10 kilometres walk	John Mikaelsson	Sweden	45 min 13.2 sec
50 kilometres walk	John Ljunggren	Sweden	4 hr 41 min 52 sec
High jump	John Winter	Australia	6 ft 6 in
Pole vault	Guinn Smith	USA	14 ft 1¼ in
Long jump	Willie Steele	USA	25 ft 8 in
Triple jump	Arne Ahman	Sweden	50 ft 6¼ in
Shot	Wilbur Thompson	USA	56 ft 2 in
Discus	Adolfo Consolini	Italy	172 ft 2 in
Hammer	Imre Nemeth	Hungary	183 ft 11½ in
Javelin	Tapio Rautavaara	Finland	228 ft 11 in
Dacathlon	Bob Mathias	USA	7,139 pts (1934 tables)
Athletics—Women			
100 metres	Fanny Blankers-Koen	Netherlands	11.9 sec
200 metres	Fanny Blankers-Koen	Netherlands	24.4 sec
4 x 100 metres relay		Netherlands	47.5 sec
80 metres hurdles	Fanny Blankers-Koen	Netherlands	11.2 sec
High jump	Alice Coachman	USA	5 ft 6⅛ in
Long jump	Olga Gyarmati	Hungary	18 ft 8¼ in
Shot	Micheline Ostermeyer	France	45 ft 1½ in
Discus	Micheline Ostermeyer	France	137 ft 6 in
Javelin	Hermine Bauma	Austria	149 ft 6 in
Basketball		USA	
Boxing			
Flyweight	Pascual Perez	Argentina	
Bantamweight	Tibor Csik	Hungary	
Featherweight	Ernesto Formenti	Italy	
Lightweight	Gerald Dreyer	South Africa	
Welterweight	Julius Torma	Czechoslovakia	
Middleweight	Laszlo Papp	Hungary	
Light-heavyweight	George Hunter	South Africa	
Heavyweight	Rafael Iglesias	Argentina	
Canoeing			
1,000 metres—Men			
Kayak singles	Gert Fredriksson	Sweden	4 min 33.2 sec
Kayak pairs	Hans Berglund, Lennart Klingstrom	Sweden	4 min 7.3 sec
Canadian singles	Josef Holecek	Czechoslovakia	5 min 42 sec
Canadian pairs	Jan Brzak, Bohumil Kudrna	Czechoslovakia	5 min 7.1 sec
10,000 metres—Men			
Kayak singles	Gert Fredriksson	Sweden	50 min 47.7 sec
Kayak pairs	Gunnar Akerlund, Hans Wetterstrom	Sweden	46 min 9.4 sec
Canadian singles	F. Capek	Czechoslovakia	62 min 5.2 sec
Canadian pairs	Stephen Lysak, Stephen Macknowski	USA	55 min 55.4 sec
500 metres—Women			
Kayak singles	K. Hoff	Denmark	2 min 31.9 sec
Cycling			
1,000 metres sprint	Mario Ghella	Italy	
1,000 metres time trial	Jacques Dupont	France	1 min 13.5 sec
2,000 metres tandem	Renato Perona, Ferdinando Teruzzi	Italy	
4,000 metres team pursuit		France	4 min 57.8 sec
Road race—individual	Jose Beyaert	France	5 hr 18 min 12.6 sec
Road race—team		Belgium	15 hr 58 min 17.4 sec
Equestrian			
Dressage—individual	Hans Moser	Switzerland	
Dressage—team		France	
Show jumping—individual	Humberto Mariles	Mexico	6.25 pts
Show jumping—team		Mexico	34.25 pts
Three day event—individual	Bernard Chevalier	France	
Three day event—team		USA	
Fencing—Men			
Foil—individual	Jean Buhan	France	
Foil—team		France	
Epee—individual	Luigi Cantone	Italy	
Epee—team		France	
Sabre—individual	Aladar Gerevich	Hungary	
Sabre—team		Hungary	
Fencing—Women			
Foil—individual	Ilona Elek	Hungary	

Football		Sweden	
Gymnastics—Men			
Combined exercises—Individual	Veikko Huhtanen	Finland	
Combined exercises—team		Finland	
Floor exercises	Ferenc Pataki	Hungary	
Horizontal bar	Josef Stalder	Switzerland	
Parallel bars	Michael Reusch	Switzerland	
Pommel horse	Paavo Aaltonen	Finland	
	Veikko Huhtanen	Finland	
	Heikki Savolainen	Finland	
Vault	Paavo Aaltonen	Finland	
Rings	Karl Frei	Switzerland	
Gymnastics—Women			
Combined exercises—team		Czechoslovakia	
Hockey		India	
Modern Pentathlon	William Grut	Sweden	
Rowing			
Single sculls	Mervyn Wood	Australia	7 min 24.4 sec
Double sculls	Herbert Bushnell, Richard Burnell	Great Britain	6 min 51.3 sec
Coxless pairs	John Wilson, Stanley Laurie	Great Britain	7 min 21.1 sec
Coxed pairs	T. Henriksen, F. Pedersen, C. Andersen (cox)	Denmark	8 min 0.5 sec
Coxless fours		Italy	6 min 39.0 sec
Coxed fours		USA	6 min 50.3 sec
Eights		USA	5 min 56.7 sec
Shooting			
Free pistol	E. Vasquez	Peru	
Automatic pistol	Karoly Takacs	Hungary	
Free rifle	Emil Grunig	Switzerland	
Small-bore rifle	Arthur Cook	USA	
Swimming—Men			
100 metres freestyle	Walter Ris	USA	57.3 sec
400 metres freestyle	Bill Smith	USA	4 min 41.0 sec
1,500 metres freestyle	Jim McLane	USA	19 min 18.5 sec
200 metres breaststroke	Joe Verdeur	USA	2 min 39.3 sec
100 metres backstroke	Allan Stack	USA	1 min 6.4 sec
4 x 200 metres freestyle relay		USA	8 min 46.0 sec
Springboard diving	Bruce Harlan	USA	
Highboard diving	Sammy Lee	USA	
Swimming—Women			
100 metres freestyle	Greta Andersen	Denmark	1 min 6.3 sec
400 metres freestyle	Ann Curtis	USA	5 min 17.8 sec
200 metres breaststroke	Petronella van Vliet	Netherlands	2 min 57.2 sec
100 metres backstroke	Karen Harup	Denmark	1 min 14.4 sec
4 x 100 metres freestyle relay		USA	4 min 29.2 sec
Springboard diving	Victoria Draves	USA	
Highboard diving	Victoria Draves	USA	
Water Polo		Italy	
Weightlifting			
Bantamweight	Joseph de Pietro	USA	678 lb
Featherweight	Mahmoud Fayad	Egypt	733 lb
Lightweight	Ibrahim Shams	Egypt	793½ lb
Middleweight	Frank Spellman	USA	860 lb
Light-heavyweight	Stanley Stanczyk	USA	920½ lb
Heavyweight	John Davis	USA	996½ lb
Wrestling			
Freestyle			
Flyweight	Lennart Viitala	Finland	
Bantamweight	Nasuk Akkar	Turkey	
Featherweight	Gazanfer Bilge	Turkey	
Lightweight	Cedal Atik	Turkey	
Welterweight	Yasar Dogu	Turkey	
Middleweight	Glen Brand	USA	
Light-heavyweight	Henry Wittenberg	USA	
Heavyweight	Gyula Bobis	Hungary	
Graeco-Roman			
Flyweight	Pietro Lombardi	Italy	
Bantamweight	Kurt Petterson	Sweden	
Featherweight	Mohammed Oktav	Turkey	
Lightweight	Karl Freij	Sweden	
Welterweight	Gosta Andersson	Sweden	
Middleweight	Axel Gronberg	Sweden	
Light-heavyweight	Karl Nilsson	Sweden	
Heavyweight	Ahmed Kirecco	Turkey	
Yachting			
6-metres		USA	
Dragon		Norway	
Star	Hilary Smart, Paul Smart	USA	
Swallow	S. Morris, D. Bond	Great Britain	
Firefly	Paul Elvstrom	Denmark	

Helsinki Olympic Games (1952)

One of the closest secrets at any Olympic Games is the name of the runner who carries the flame on the last leg of its journey from Olympia to light the fire that burns for the duration of the Games. When the runner appeared in the Helsinki stadium in 1952 there was a mighty shout from the 70,500 crowd. He was a balding 55-year-old whose athletics feats had thrilled the world 30 years before—Paavo Nurmi. With his characteristic upright gait he completed nearly a lap and lit the flame. Then he handed the torch to Hannes Kolehmainen, the first of the Flying Finns, winner of the 5,000 and 10,000 metres at Stockholm in 1912—who was taken by a lift to the top of a 250-ft. tower to light another flame.

Heavy downpours of rain could not quench the Finns' enthusiasm, but one incident was out of place. Soon after the lighting of the flame, a woman dressed in white entered the stadium, ran gracefully round the track, and tried to address the crowd from the rostrum where the oath had been taken minutes before. Gripping the microphone, she started to speak, but was cut off and hustled out of the arena. She was, it transpired, a 23-year-old student from Stuttgart, and a fanatical peace enthusiast. Her entrance was perfectly timed, and most of the crowd, though puzzled, did not really resent the intrusion.

The Olympics were 12 years late arriving in Helsinki. Tokyo and Helsinki were the two applicants for the 1940 Games, which were awarded to Tokyo. In 1938, Japan, because of her military commitments in Asia, abandoned the project, and Helsinki offered to stage them. The outbreak of World War Two put paid to the idea, and it was not until 1952 that the Games were staged in their country.

As was generally expected, the Finns' organization was superb in every way. Sixty-nine nations sent more than 6,000 men and nearly 800 women to take part in 17 different sports. Men from 61 nations were housed in an Olympic Village (new blocks of flats afterwards let to the public) at Kapyla, about 1½ miles from the stadium. Other teams both male and female, including the USSR, Bulgaria, Hungary, and Poland, were quartered at Otaniemi, 5 miles from Helsinki, while the main women's village was a nurses training college half-a-mile from the stadium, accommodating more than 600 competitors. Over 1,800 journalists, broadcasters, and photographers were catered for.

The main stadium was full to capacity for the opening ceremony, and nearly so for many of the track and field events. The football matches attracted a total of about 370,000, and swimming 110,000.

Athletics

In 19 of the 24 men's events the Olympic record was beaten, and in two others it was equalled, while in the nine women's events, seven new Olympic records were set. Six world records, three men's and three women's, were established. Unhappily for the Finns, there were no gold medals for them, while the Russians, competing in

1 **Finland's athletics hero Paavo Nurmi lights the flame.**
2 **Wilf White, on Nizefela, clears an obstacle during the show jumping, thus helping to win Britain's only gold medal.**
3 **Nina Romashkova won the women's discus—one of the USSR's two gold medals in the track and field events.**
4 **Werner Lueg leads the 1,500 metres field into the home straight. Josy Barthel (406) sprinted past him to win a surprise gold for Luxembourg, while Bob McMillen (992) pipped the German on the tape for the silver medal. Roger Bannister (177) was 4th.**

U.P.I.

Official Report of the 1952 Olympics

Central Press

Keystone

their first Olympics since 1912, had to rely on their women to win their two golds for athletics.

The outstanding competitor of the entire Games was seen in action in the long-distance running events—all three of them. He was Emil Zatopek, a Czechoslovakian army officer who ran as if every step would be his last, apparently in agony. This remarkable man retained the 10,000 metres title he had won in London four years previously, and improved from second to first in the 5,000 metres—setting Olympic records in both.

The 5,000 metres was Zatopek's severest test. With one lap left there were four men left in contention—Zatopek, Britain's Chris Chataway, Herbert Schade of Germany, and Alain Mimoun of France. Along the back straight Chataway made a burst, but was closely followed by the Czech. Around the final turn Chataway tripped on the kerb and fell, while Schade was visibly fading. Only Mimoun held on to the flying Zatopek, but he finally had to concede first place, just as he had a game few days earlier in the 10,000 metres. On the same day as Zatopek's 5,000 metres triumph, his wife, Dana, won the javelin.

Three days after that gruelling 5,000 metres, Zatopek lined up for what was—officially—the first marathon of his career. Though tiring towards the end, he won by over $2\frac{1}{2}$ minutes from Reinaldo Gorno of Argentina. His time was yet another Olympic record, and he had completed a unique treble that few men even attempt.

Athletes from the United States won 14 of the 24 men's events, and their victories were evenly split between track and field. Lindy Remigino's win in the 100 metres was an extremely close affair. Many people thought that Herb McKenley of Jamaica, the world record holder for 440 yards who had entered the 100 for a kind of training spin, should have had the verdict, but the photo-finish camera showed that Remigino had won by inches. McKenley won another silver medal in the 400 metres, where his fast finish was not quite good enough to catch his team-mate George Rhoden although they were both credited with an Olympic record time of 45.9 sec. Arthur Wint—another Jamaican—made a game bid to retain his 1948 title, but he lapsed into fifth place. These three West Indians teamed up with Leslie Laing to win the 4 by 400 metres relay, beating the world record by over 4 seconds in 3 min 3.9 sec.

Mal Whitfield retained his 800 metres title in 1 min 49.2 sec, the same time as at Wembley four years previously, with Arthur Wint again occupying second place. But in the 1,500 metres there was an unexpected win for Josy Barthel of Luxembourg, who beat another 'outsider', Bob McMillen of the United States, by inches, with the world record holder, Werner Lueg of Germany, 0.2 sec behind, third.

Apart from Zatopek and Whitfield, two other champions retained their titles, the American Bob Mathias in the decathlon and John Mikaelsson of Sweden in the 10 kilometres track walk. Harrison Dillard, who won the 100 metres in London, won his favourite event, the 100 metres hurdles, from his fellow-American Jack Davis, both being timed at 13.5 sec.

While the USSR did not secure a single victory in the men's events,

5 André Noyelle of Belgium is the triumphant winner of the 190.4-km cycling road race. Noyelle also led home the winning team in the event.
6 The 1948 champion, Bob Mathias, in the second event of the decathlon—the long jump. Mathias retained his title with a world record score of 7,887 points—912 more than the runner-up, Milton Campbell.
7 Australia's Marjorie Jackson wins the 100 metres in 11.5 sec, a world record.
8 Valeria Gyenge—one of the all-conquering Hungarian women's swimming team—won the 400 metres freestyle in an Olympic record time of 5 min 12.1 sec, just 1.6 sec in front of her team rival Eva Novak, the runner-up in the 200 metres breaststroke.

Associated Press

5

U.P.I.

Central Press

Official Report of the 1952 Olympics

8

their women excelled, winning the shot and discus with new Olympic records. The United States, in contrast, had only one victory, and a lucky one at that. At the last changeover of the 4 by 100 metres relay the Australian team fumbled while in the lead, Marjorie Jackson and Winsome Cripps contriving to drop the baton. The team recovered, but the time lost in the adventure was too great and the Australian girls did not even win a medal. In the 80 metres hurdles, Shirley Strickland, the bronze medallist in London, beat a field including defending champion Fanny Blankers-Koen who struck a hurdle and failed to finish.

Swimming

The swimming events were dominated by the Hungarian women's team who won four out of the five events. They were given a special award for the greatest achievement of the swimming section of the Games for their world record winning time of 4 min 24.4 sec in the 4 by 100 metres relay.

Three members of this team also won individual medals. Katalin Szoke was first, and Judit Temes third, in the 100 metres freestyle. It was a remarkable final in which only 0.3 sec covered the first five swimmers, while the lead changed

HELSINKI OLYMPIC GAMES, 1952 Gold Medallists

Athletics—Men			
100 metres	Lindy Remigino	USA	10.4 sec
200 metres	Andy Stanfield	USA	20.7 sec
400 metres	George Rhoden	Jamaica	45.9 sec
800 metres	Malvin Whitfield	USA	1 min 49.2 sec
1,500 metres	Josef Barthel	Luxembourg	3 min 45.2 sec
5,000 metres	Emil Zatopek	Czechoslovakia	14 min 6.6 sec
10,000 metres	Emil Zatopek	Czechoslovakia	29 min 17.0 sec
Marathon	Emil Zatopek	Czechoslovakia	2 hr 23 min 3.2 sec
110 metres hurdles	Harrison Dillard	USA	13.7 sec
400 metres hurdles	Charles Moore	USA	50.8 sec
3,000 metres steeplechase	Horace Ashenfelter	USA	8 min 45.4 sec
10 kilometres walk	John Mikaelsson	Sweden	45 min 2.8 sec
50 kilometres walk	Giuseppe Dordoni	Italy	4 hr 28 min 7.8 sec
4 x 100 metres relay		USA	40.1 sec
4 x 400 metres relay		Jamaica	3 min 3.9 sec
High Jump	Walter Davis	USA	6 ft 8¼ in
Pole Vault	Robert Richards	USA	14 ft 11¼ in
Long Jump	Willie Steele	USA	25 ft 8 in
Triple Jump	Adhemar da Silva	Brazil	53 ft 2½ in
Shot	Wilbur Thompson	USA	56 ft 2 in
Discus	Sim Iness	USA	180 ft 6½ in
Hammer	Josef Csermak	Hungary	197 ft 11½ in
Javelin	Cyrus Young	USA	240 ft 0½ in
Decathlon	Robert Mathias	USA	8,887 pts
Athletics—Women			
100 metres	Marjorie Jackson	Australia	11.5 sec
200 metres	Marjorie Jackson	Australia	23.7 sec
80 metres hurdles	Shirley Strickland	Australia	10.9 sec
4 x 100 metres relay		USA	45.9 sec
High Jump	Esther Brand	South Africa	5 ft 5¾ in
Long Jump	Yvette Williams	New Zealand	20 ft 5¾ in
Shot	Galina Zybina	USSR	50 ft 1½ in
Discus	Nina Romashkova	USSR	168 ft 8½ in
Javelin	Dana Zatopkova	Czechoslovakia	165 ft 7 in
Basketball		USA	
Boxing			
Flyweight	Nathan Brooks	USA	
Bantamweight	Pentti Hamalainen	Finland	
Featherweight	Jan Zachara	Czechoslovakia	
Lightweight	Aureliano Bolognesi	Italy	
Light-welterweight	Charles Adkins	USA	
Welterweight	Zygmunt Chychla	Poland	
Light-middleweight	Laszlo Papp	Hungary	
Middleweight	Floyd Patterson	USA	
Light-heavyweight	Norvel Lee	USA	
Heavyweight	Edward Sanders	USA	
Canoeing			
1,000 metres—Men			
Kayak singles	Gert Fredriksson	Sweden	4 min 7.9 sec
Kayak pairs	Kurt Wires, Yrjo Hietanen	Finland	3 min 51.1 sec
Canadian singles	Josef Holecek	Czechoslovakia	4 min 53.6 sec
Canadian doubles	Bent Rasch, Finn Haunstoft	Czechoslovakia	4 min 38.3 sec
500 metres—Women			
Kayak singles	Sylvi Saimo	Finland	2 min 18.4 sec
Cycling			
1,000 metres sprint	Enzo Sacchi	Italy	
1,000 metres time trial	Russell Mockridge	Australia	1 min 11.1 sec
2,000 metres tandem	Russell Mockridge, Lionel Cox	Australia	
4,000 metres team pursuit		Italy	4 min 46.1 sec
Road race—individual	Andre Noyelle	Belgium	5 hr 6 min 3.4 sec
Road race—team		Belgium	15 hr 20 min 46.6 sec
Equestrian			
Dressage—individual	Henri St Cyr	Sweden	
—team		Sweden	
Show jumping			
—individual	Pierre d'Oriola	France	
—team		Great Britain	
Three day event			
—individual	Hans von Blixen-Finecke	Sweden	
—team		Sweden	
Fencing—Men			
Foil—individual	Christian d'Oriola	France	
—team		France	
Epee—individual	Edoardo Mangiarotti	Italy	
—team		Italy	
Sabre—individual	Pal Kovacs	Hungary	
—team		Hungary	
Fencing—Women			
Foil—individual	Irene Camber	Italy	
Football		Hungary	
Gymnastics—Men			
Combined exercises			
—individual	Viktor Chukarin	USSR	
—team		USSR	
Floor exercises	Karl Thoreson	Sweden	
Horizontal bar	Jack Gunthard	Switzerland	
Parallel bars	Hans Eugster	Switzerland	
Pommell Horse	Viktor Chukarin	USSR	
Vault	Viktor Chukarin	USSR	
Rings	Grant Shaginyan	USSR	
Gymnastics—Women			
Combined exercises			
—individual	Maria Gorokhovskaya	USSR	
—team		USSR	
Floor exercises	Agnes Keleti	Hungary	
Asymmetrical bars	Margit Korondi	Hungary	
Beam	Nina Bocharyova	USSR	
Vault	Yekaterina Kalinchuk	USSR	
Hockey		India	
Modern Pentathlon			
Individual	Lars Hall	Sweden	
Team		Hungary	
Rowing			
Single sculls	Yuri Tyukalov	USSR	8 min 12.8 sec
Double sculls	Tranquilo Copozzo, Eduardo Guerrero	Argentina	7 min 32.2 sec
Coxless pairs	Charles Logg, Thomas Price	USA	8 min 20.7 sec
Coxed pairs	Raymond Salles, Gaston Mercier, Bernard Malivoire (Cox)	France	8 min 28.6 sec
Coxless fours		Yugoslavia	7 min 16.0 sec
Coxed fours		Czechoslovakia	7 min 33.4 sec
Eights		USA	6 min 25.9 sec
Shooting			
Sport pistol	Huelet Benner	USA	
Rapid fire pistol	Karoly Takacs	Hungary	
Free rifle	Anatoliy Bogdanov	USSR	
Small-bore rifle, prone	Josif Sarbu	Romania	
Small-bore rifle, three positions	Erling Kongshaug	Norway	
Clay pigeon	Georges Genereux	Canada	
Swimming and Diving—Men			
100 metres freestyle	Clarke Scholes	USA	57.4 sec
400 metres freestyle	Jean Boiteux	France	4 min 30.7 sec
1,500 metres freestyle	Ford Konno	USA	18 min 30.0 sec
200 metres breaststroke	John Davies	Australia	2 min 34.4 sec
100 metres backstroke	Yoshi Oyakawa	USA	1 min 5.4 sec
4 x 200 metres freestyle relay		USA	8 min 31.1 sec
Springboard diving	David Browning	USA	
Highboard diving	Sammy Lee	USA	
Swimming and Diving—Women			
100 metres freestyle	Katalin Szoke	Hungary	1 min 6.8 sec
400 metres freestyle	Valeria Gyenge	Hungary	5 min 12.1 sec
200 metres breaststroke	Eva Szekely	Hungary	2 min 51.7 sec
100 metres backstroke	Joan Harrison	South Africa	1 min 14.3 sec
4 x 100 metres freestyle relay		Hungary	4 min 24.4 sec
Springboard diving	Pat McCormick	USA	
Highboard diving	Pat McCormick	USA	
Water Polo		Hungary	
Weightlifting			
Bantamweight	Ivan Udodov	USSR	694.5 lb
Featherweight	Rafael Chimiskyan	USSR	774 lb
Lightweight	Thomas Kono	USA	799 lb
Middleweight	Peter George	USA	882 lb
Light-heavyweight	Trofim Lomakin	USSR	920.5 lb
Middle-heavyweight	Norbert Schemansky	USA	903.75 lb
Heavyweight	John Davis	USA	1,014 lb
Wrestling			
Freestyle			
Flyweight	Hasan Gemici	Turkey	
Bantamweight	Schoohachi Ishii	Japan	
Featherweight	Bayram Sit	Turkey	
Lightweight	Olle Anderberg	Sweden	
Welterweight	William Smith	USA	
Middleweight	David Cimakuridze	USSR	
Light-heavyweight	Wiking Palm	Sweden	
Heavyweight	Arsen Mekokishvili	USSR	
Graeco-Roman			
Flyweight	Boris Gurevich	USSR	
Bantamweight	Imre Hodos	Hungary	
Featherweight	Yakov Punkin	USSR	
Lightweight	Khasame Safin	USSR	
Welterweight	Miklos Szilvasi	Hungary	
Middleweight	Axel Gronberg	Sweden	
Light-heavyweight	Kaelpo Grondhal	Finland	
Heavyweight	Johannes Kotkas	USSR	
Yachting			
Single-handed	Paul Elvstrom	Denmark	
Star	Agostino Straulino, Nicole Rode	Italy	
Dragon		Norway	
5.5 metres		USA	
6.0 metres		USA	

1

Official Report of the 1952 Olympics

1 New Zealand's Yvette Williams won the long jump by clearing 20 ft 5¾ in. **2** Jean Boiteux led from start to finish to win the 400 metres freestyle. His victory so excited his father that he jumped into the water to congratulate him. **3** Emil Zatopek leads Alain Mimoun of France and Herbert Schade of Germany into the home straight of the 5,000 metres. They finished in that order, and the fallen Chris Chataway came fifth. **4** Hungary's goalkeeper, Gyula Grosics, plucks a cross out of the air during the final against Yugoslavia. Hungary won 2-0, and in five matches scored 20 goals, conceding only 2. **5** The photo-finish of the men's 100 metres shows Lindy Remigino (third from top) nosing Herb McKenley (second from top) out of the gold medal spot, while Britain's McDonald Bailey (second from bottom) clinches the bronze medal. **6** A baton mix-up between Winsome Cripps (left) and Marjorie Jackson left the Australians floundering in the women's relay, but they still managed to finish fifth. **7** Viktor Chukarin—the winner of the combined exercises, pommel horse, and vault—in action on the parallel bars, in which he was placed second.

2

Keystone

hands three times in the last 10 metres. The versatile Eva Novak added two silvers—in the 400 metres freestyle and the 200 metres breaststroke—to her relay gold. Other Hungarians beat her in both races, Valeria Gyenge in the 400 metres, and Eva Szekely in the breaststroke. In 1952, breaststroke and butterfly had not been made separate strokes and Eva (whose husband Deszo Gyarmati won a water polo gold at these games) used the 'butterfly' recovery while Miss Novak kept to the classic orthodox underwater breaststroke arm action. Britain's Elenor Gordon, also an orthodox breaststroke swimmer, was third.

The men's events were not without their surprises and incidents. Clarke Scholes of the United States took the 100 metres freestyle after his team-mate Dick Cleveland, the world record holder, had failed to reach the final. Jean Boiteux became, in the 400 metres freestyle, France's first Olympic swimming champion. As soon as the race was over his father, fully clothed, jumped into the water to embrace his son.

There were protests galore in the water polo tournament. Russia got FINA secretary Max Ritter out of bed at six in the morning to protest over the draw—and a re-

draw was made. And Yugoslavia protested over the Belgian referee who handled their match against the Netherlands, which they lost. They had no grounds for complaint, yet were given a replay, which they won. The Yugoslavs went on to win the silver medals, while the Netherlands, one of the best teams at Helsinki, failed to get into the last four.

Equestrianism
Great Britain won her only gold medal of the Games in the Grand Prix show jumping team event. Sixteen teams, comprising 48 riders, lined up for the big equestrian test, which started at 8 a.m. Britain's hero was Fox-

hunter, the horse that had helped Britain to win the bronze medals in London at the previous Games. The crucial round was Foxhunter's final trial: Britain were five points clear of Chile, so Foxhunter and Harry Llewellyn could afford just one fence down. But they did not even need that. A clear round made sure of the golds.

There was a five-way jump-off for the individual medals. Pierre d'Oriola of France on Ali Baba went first and set such a hot pace that nobody could match him. He went round clear in 40 seconds. The nearest challenger to his supremacy was Oscar Christi of Chile on Bambi who collected four faults in a 44 second round.

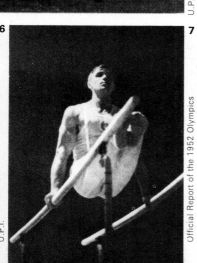

Germany's Fritz Thiedemann on Meteor went round in 38.5 seconds, but had two fences down for eight faults and finished third.

Other Sports
A total of 27 nations claimed gold medals at Helsinki, and the honours were fairly widely distributed. Australia's Russell Mockridge won two golds in cycling—the 1,000 metres time trial and the 2,000 metres tandem. He was not entered in his favourite event, the 1,000 metres sprint, and had not partnered Lionel Cox (the silver medallist in the sprint) on a tandem before the Games.

The United States won five of

the 10 boxing championships, including the newly introduced light-welterweight. Two future world heavyweight champions were on show. Floyd Patterson, aged 17, won the middleweight crown, and turned professional on returning to America. Some four years later he became the youngest ever world heavyweight champion. Ingemar Johansson—who beat Patterson to win the world heavyweight championship in 1959—found himself disqualified in the heavyweight final for not trying.

The outstanding woman fencer of the Games was the silver medallist Hungary's Ilona Elek, champion in 1936 and 1948. A 45-year-old, she fought her way through a fiercely contested competition to tie for first place in the final—only to lose in the fight-off to Irene Camber of Italy, a girl she had already beaten twice on the way. In the men's foil Christian d'Oriola, the 1948 silver medallist, won all his eight bouts in the final pool to clinch the title, and he was a member of the winning foil team.

The Hungarian soccer team won their first Olympic tournament, and in the team were such outstanding names as Ferenc Puskas, Josef Bozsik, Sandor Kocsis, Zoltan Czibor, and Nandor Hidegkuti. They beat Yugoslavia 2-0 in the final.

The USSR made a great impact on the gymnastics world, winning 22 medals in all, including eight golds. It was the first time that Russia had been prominent in this sport.

The masters of the hockey field, however, were still India, who gained their fifth successive title and conceded only two goals in the competition, and scored 13.

Six nations won rowing gold medals, the United States winning two—the coxless pairs and the eights. Russia's team were outstanding in this sport as well, claiming one gold and two silver medals. They excelled in weightlifting, too, winning three gold medals. The United States claimed four. Forty nations took part in the weightlifting, and seven world records were set up and five equalled, while Olympic bests were equalled 16 times and beaten 18 times. John Davis, the 1948 heavyweight champion, was the only man to repeat his success. Wrestling was also a sport contested by many nations—37—but this time the honours were more widespread. The USSR won four Greco-Roman and two free-style titles, but 14 countries won medals of some sort.

From the moment Nurmi set foot in the stadium with the torch, until the flame was allowed to die at the conclusion of the Games, the Finns did everything to ensure that their Olympics were a success. In a city of 400,000 people this was no small accomplishment, and the packed stadiums were a witness to the enthusiasm of the Finnish people for one of the most successful Olympic celebrations ever.

53

Melbourne Olympic Games (1956)

In 1956, for the first time, the Olympic Games were celebrated in the Southern Hemisphere. And for the first time, too, they were held as late in the year as November and December. Ten of the previous 12 Games had been held in July and August. Nevertheless, 67 nations sent some 2,800 men and 370 women to compete in the 16 sports. The suppression of the Hungarian uprising by the Russians and the British and French adventure in the Middle East had resulted in the withdrawal of Egypt, Iraq, Lebanon, the Netherlands, and Spain. But Ethiopia, Kenya, and Malaya were represented for the first time.

More than 88,000 people were present for the opening ceremony, which the Duke of Edinburgh performed. The final lap of the Olympic torch relay was run by the young Ron Clarke, Australia's junior mile record holder. World mile record holder John Landy took the Olympic Oath.

Athletics

The Melbourne Cricket Ground, with a newly laid track, provided a fine setting for the athletics events, as well as for the hockey and soccer finals and the opening and closing ceremonies.

The outstanding competitor in the track events was the Russian Vladimir Kuts, who won the 5,000 and 10,000 metres gold medals, the former in a Games record which stood for the next three Olympiads. His 10,000 metres victory on the first day of the athletics was Russia's first ever gold medal in Olympic track and field events. He had set a world record of 28 min 30.4 sec in Moscow some 10 weeks earlier, and in Melbourne set out to burn up the field with a fast early pace. By the 5,000 metres mark, Kuts had disposed of all his rivals except Britain's Gordon Pirie. Pirie was weakened by the Russian's constant variations of pace, and after 8,000 metres dropped

back, eventually to finish in eighth position. This left Kuts out on his own, and he won easily.

The second leg of Kuts' double came five days later, in the 5,000 metres final. Although he was trailed for much of the way by two Englishmen, Pirie and Derek Ibbotson, he was never in much danger, and 1,000 metres from home was in complete command. He won by 11 seconds from Pirie in 13 min 39.6 sec, thus beating the Olympic record by 27 seconds.

Bobby Morrow's 100-200 metres double was the first by a man in the Olympics since 1936. In each event he was followed home by other Americans. It was in the 100 metres that 'hustling' Hec Hogan won Australia's first men's sprint medal since 1900, a bronze. America's depth of sprinters made the result of the 4 by 100 metres relay a foregone conclusion, and Bobby Morrow thus gained his third gold of the Games in anchoring his country's winning squad in world record time. The United States also took the first three places in the 110 metres hurdles. Lee Calhoun won by a whisker from Jack Davis, who thus gained his second successive silver medal in this event.

Whereas only one European reached a sprint final, three got through to the 400 metres final. America's Lou Jones, the world record holder, was an early leader in the outside lane, but faded to fifth place, at least 15 yards behind the winner, his team-mate Charles Jenkins. Tying for third place—the only instance of such an occurrence on the track—were Russia's Ardalion Ignatyev and Finland's Voitto Hellsten, both timed at 47.0 sec.

For the fourth Olympics in succession, the United States provided the winner of the 800 metres. But Tom Courtney won only after a fierce battle down the finishing straight with Britain's Derek Johnson.

The 1,500 metres lived up to its reputation as one of the Games' most exciting races, and produced a surprise winner in Ireland's Ron Delany, whose searing burst over the last 300 metres was too good for the others, including the Australian John Landy who came third. The first nine finishers beat Josy Barthel's 1952 Olympic record.

The longest running event—the marathon—enabled Alain Mimoun of France to win, at last, an Olympic gold medal. Three times an Olympic runner-up behind Emil Zatopek, the determined French-Algerian won by over half a minute. Zatopek, a pale shadow of his former self, was 4½ minutes behind Mimoun in sixth place.

The 3,000 metres steeplechase provided the most controversial event of the Games. Britain's unfancied third string Chris Brasher surprised the field with a last-lap burst to win by nearly 20

1 America's Hal Connolly won the gold medal in the hammer with a throw of 207 ft. 3½ in. It was over 17 ft. below his three-week old world record of 224 ft. 10 in.
2 Britain's Gillian Sheen (left) takes on Renée Garilhe of France in the women's foil event. Miss Sheen won the gold medal—Britain's first Olympic fencing title—and Mlle Garilhe the bronze.
3 Vladimir Kuts breaks away from the British trio of Gordon Pirie (189—2nd), Derek Ibbotson (188—3rd) and Chris Chataway (11th) in the final of the 5,000 metres.

yards. But he had to survive a disqualification for obstruction and a long wait before the jury of appeal allowed him to call the gold medal his own. It was Britain's only athletics gold at Melbourne and their first individual track title since the 1932 Olympics.

Of the nine field events (including the decathlon), the United States won seven. Charles Dumas, the first man to clear 7 feet, beat Australia's Charles Porter by $\frac{3}{4}$ in., with an Olympic record of 6 ft. $11\frac{1}{2}$ in. In the pole vault Bob Richards successfully defended his title, but not without a couple of missed heart beats when he took three tries to get over 13 ft. $1\frac{1}{2}$ in. in the qualifying competition. In the final, however, he set an Olympic record of 14 ft. $11\frac{1}{2}$ in. to beat his compatriot Bob Gutowski by $1\frac{1}{4}$ in.

Conditions for record breaking in the long jump were non-existent, with a wind veering from not far short of 30 mph against to 20 mph in favour of the jumpers. Only 2 of the 13 finalists exceeded 25 feet —the winner Gregory Bell (25 ft. $8\frac{1}{4}$ in.) and his fellow-American, silver medallist John Bennett (25 ft. $2\frac{1}{4}$ in.). Further United States successes came through Parry O'Brien in the shot, the 20-year-old Al Oerter in the discus, Harold Connolly in the hammer, and Milton Campbell in the decathlon.

Brazilian triple jump specialist Adhemar Ferreira da Silva retained his title with an Olympic record combination jump of 53 ft. $7\frac{3}{4}$ in., though he was hard pressed by Iceland's Vilhjálmur Einarsson (53 ft. $4\frac{1}{4}$ in.). In the javelin, Egil Danielsen of Norway deprived Poland's Janusz Sidlo of both the Olympic title and his world record with a throw of 281 ft. $2\frac{1}{2}$ in.— more than 40 feet farther than his own next best throw in the competition.

The heroine of the women's events was the 18-year-old Betty Cuthbert who won the 100 and 200 metres, and anchored Australia to a world record and a close victory over Great Britain in the 4 by 100 metres relay. Shirley De la Hunty, competing in her third Olympic Games, retained her 80 metres hurdles title and was also a member of Australia's winning relay team. Of the other Australians, Marlene Mathews was third in both the 100 and the 200 metres, and Norma Thrower was third in the hurdles.

America's Mildred McDaniel was a clear winner of the high jump with a world record of 5 ft. $9\frac{1}{4}$ in., $3\frac{1}{2}$ inches better than Thelma Hopkins of Britain and Maria Pisaryeva of Russia, who were both awarded silver medals. In the long jump Elzbieta Krzesinka of Poland equalled her own world record of 20 ft. 10 in. to win by nearly a foot.

Czechoslovakia's Olga Fikotova won the discus gold medal with a throw of 176 ft. $1\frac{1}{2}$ in., but while at Melbourne she also gained a husband, the American hammer thrower Harold Connolly. The pair were married in 1957, only after much diplomatic dithering, and the Connollys continued to compete, though without repeating their Melbourne successes, in the next three Olympic Games.

Russia's contribution to the women's athletics events came through two throwers. The massive, 17-stone Tamara Tyshkyevich won the shot with her last throw to beat defending champion Galina Zybina by $2\frac{1}{4}$ inches. And in the javelin Inese Jaunzeme won by over 11 feet from Chile's Marlene Ahrens with Russia's world record holder Nadyezhda Konyayeva third.

Swimming

In the new 5,500-seat swimming pool in Olympic Park, the Games were an unqualified triumph for Australia, and equally disastrous for the United States, although the absence of the Dutch girls affected the outcome somewhat.

Australia's Jon Henricks, John Devitt, and Gary Chapman took first, second, and third places respectively in the 100 metres freestyle, and Murray Rose won both the 400 and 1,500 metres freestyle. In both of these events Japan's Tsuyoshi Yamanaka was second and America's George Breen (who set a world 1,500 metres record of 17 min 52.9 sec in his heat) third. Rose, Devitt, and Henricks were joined by Kevin O'Halloran in the 4 by 200 metres relay which they won in a world record of 8 min 23.6 sec, 7.9 sec in front of the Americans.

The Australian girls emulated their men in the 100 metres freestyle, with Dawn Fraser first, Lorraine Crapp second, and Faith Leech third. Sandra Morgan helped these three to win the 4 by 100 metres relay. America's only individual women's freestyle medal came through Sylvia Ruuska, third in the 400 metres. She was well beaten by Lorraine Crapp and Dawn Fraser, who thus claimed two gold and one silver medal each.

Britain claimed her first Olympic swimming champion in 32 years through Judy Grinham in the 100 metres backstroke, and had the added pleasure of Margaret

4 Norman Read of New Zealand (No. 10) leads the field at the start of the 50-km walk. He stayed in front to win the gold medal from Russia's Yevgeniy Maskinskov with over two minutes to spare. **5** Women's 100 metres final: Betty Cuthbert of Australia (466) was first, Christa Stubnick of Germany (right) second, and Australia's Marlene Mathews (470) third. **6** Chris Brasher takes the final water jump on his way to a surprise gold medal in the 3,000 metres steeplechase. Though at first disqualified, he was later reinstated.

Edwards and Julie Hoyle coming third and sixth, respectively. American wins came through Bill Yorzyk in the men's butterfly, and Shelley Mann in the women's butterfly.

America won three of the four diving titles, with Pat McCormick retaining the springboard and highboard crowns she had won at Helsinki in 1952—the first diver of either sex to achieve this feat. But the men's highboard went to Mexico's Joaquin Capilla—who had been third in 1948 and second in 1952—by 0.03 of a point.

Hungary, whose team had got out of Budapest only days after the rebellion in their country, retained the water polo title, but not without a real blood battle with the Soviet Union, who tried to match technical and tactical excellence with rough play. It required police assistance to calm infuriated spectators and players alike after Hungary's Ervin Zador had his eyebrow split. But Hungary beat the Russians 4-0 and won their final game 2-1, against runners-up Yugoslavia, to emerge undefeated champions.

Other Sports

If the United States had claimed the lion's share of honours in athletics and Australia in swimming, it was the turn of Russia to come good in the other sports. It was in shooting, wrestling, and gymnastics that the Russians showed their prowess to the full.

The gymnastics events were very closely contested, but Russia's well balanced men's team came away with six outright wins, and one shared. Viktor Chukarin won three gold medals—in the team, individual combined exercises, and parallel bars. He won the combined title from Japan's Takashi Ono by 0.05 of a point. The gold medals in the women's events were shared evenly between Russia and Hungary. Hungary's Agnes Keleti and Russia's Larissa Latynina were joint champions in the floor exercises, and won two individual and one team title each.

Two sons of famous fathers competed for the United States in the rowing events, John B. Kelly Jr and Bernard Costello Jr. John Kelly and Paul Costello had won

1 British flyweight Terry Spinks lays into René Libeer of France during their semi-final bout. Spinks won, and went on to beat Romania's Mircea Dobrescu in the final. **2** The American Yale crew (top) won the eights gold from Canada (bottom). **3** A thrilling 1,500 metres final saw Ron Delany of Eire come through with a well-timed burst to take the gold medal in front of Germany's Klaus Richtzenhain (134—2nd) and Australia's John Landy. **4** The 800 metres was equally exciting. America's Tom Courtney had to fight right to the end to hold off the challenge of Britain's Derek Johnson. Courtney's winning time— 1 min 47.7 sec—beat the Olympic record by $1\frac{1}{2}$ sec.

Sport & General

MELBOURNE OLYMPIC GAMES, 1956 Gold Medallists

Athletics—Men			
100 metres	Bobby Morrow	USA	10.5 sec
200 metres	Bobby Morrow	USA	20.6 sec
400 metres	Charles Jenkins	USA	46.7 sec
800 metres	Tom Courtney	USA	1 min 47.7 sec
1,500 metres	Ron Delany	Eire	3 min 41.2 sec
5,000 metres	Vladimir Kuts	USSR	13 min 39.6 sec
10,000 metres	Vladimir Kuts	USSR	28 min 45.6 sec
Marathon	Alain Mimoun	France	2 hr 25 min 0.0 sec
4 x 100 metres relay		USA	39.5 sec
4 x 400 metres relay		USA	3 min 4.8 sec
110 metres hurdles	Lee Calhoun	USA	13.5 sec
400 metres hurdles	Glenn Davis	USA	50.1 sec
3,000 metres steeplechase	Chris Brasher	Great Britain	8 min 41.2 sec
20 kilometres walk	Leonid Spirin	USSR	1 hr 31 min 27.4 sec
50 kilometres walk	Norman Read	New Zealand	4 hr 30 min 42.8 sec
High jump	Charles Dumas	USA	6 ft 11¼ in
Pole vault	Bob Richards	USA	14 ft 11½ in
Long jump	Gregory Bell	USA	25 ft 8¼ in
Triple jump	Adhemar da Silva	Brazil	53 ft 7½ in
Shot	Parry O'Brien	USA	60 ft 11 in
Discus	Al Oerter	USA	184 ft 10½ in
Hammer	Hal Connolly	USA	207 ft 3½ in
Javelin	Egil Danielsen	Norway	281 ft 2 in
Decathlon	Milton Campbell	USA	7,937 pts
Athletics—Women			
100 metres	Betty Cuthbert	Australia	11.5 sec
200 metres	Betty Cuthbert	Australia	23.4 sec
4 x 100 metres relay		Australia	44.5 sec
80 metres hurdles	Shirley De la Hunty	Australia	10.7 sec
High jump	Mildred McDaniel	USA	5 ft 9¼ in
Long jump	Elzbieta Krzesinka	Poland	20 ft 10 in
Shot	Tamara Tyshkyevich	USSR	54 ft 5 in
Discus	Olga Fikotova	Czechoslovakia	176 ft 1½ in
Javelin	Inese Jaunzeme	USSR	176 ft 8½ in
Basketball		USA	
Boxing			
Flyweight	Terry Spinks	Great Britain	
Bantamweight	Wolfgang Behrandt	Germany	
Featherweight	Vladimir Safranov	USSR	
Lightweight	Dick McTaggart	Great Britain	
Light-welterweight	Vladimir Enguibarian	USSR	
Welterweight	Necolae Linca	Romania	
Light-middleweight	Laszlo Papp	Hungary	
Middleweight	Genadiy Schatkov	USSR	
Light-heavyweight	James Boyd	USA	
Heavyweight	Peter Rademacher	USA	
Canoeing			
1,000 metres—Men			
Kayak singles	Gert Fredriksson	Sweden	4 min 12.8 sec
Kayak pairs	Michel Scheuer, Meinrad Miltenberger	Germany	3 min 49.6 sec
Canadian singles	Leon Rottman	Romania	5 min 5.3 sec
Canadian pairs	Alexe Dumitru, Simion Ismailciuc	Romania	4 min 47.4 sec
10,000 metres—Men			
Kayak singles	Gert Fredriksson	Sweden	47 min 43.4 sec
Kayak pairs	Janos Uranyi, Laszlo Fabian	Hungary	43 min 37.0 sec
Canadian singles	Leon Rottman	Romania	56 min 41.0 sec
Canadian pairs	Pavel Kharine, Gratsian Botev	USSR	54 min 2.4 sec
500 metres—Women			
Kayak singles	Elisaveta Dementieva	USSR	2 min 18.9 sec
Cycling			
1,000 metres sprint	Michel Rousseau	France	
1,000 metres time trial	Leandro Faggin	Italy	1 min 9.8 sec
2,000 metres tandem	Ian Browne, Anthony Marchant	Australia	
4,000 metres team pursuit		Italy	4 min 37.4 sec
Road race (116 miles, 1,144 yards)			
—individual	Ercole Baldini	Italy	5 hr 21 min 17 sec
—team		France	
Fencing—Men			
Foil—individual	Christian d'Oriola	France	
—team		Italy	
Epee—individual	Carlo Pavesi	Italy	
—team		Italy	
Sabre—individual	Rudolf Karpati	Hungary	
—team		Hungary	
Fencing—Women			
Foil—individual	Gillian Sheen	Great Britain	
Football		USSR	
Gymnastics—Men			
Combined exercises			
—individual	Viktor Chukarin	USSR	
—team		USSR	
Floor exercises	Valentin Muratov	USSR	
Horizontal bar	Takashi Ono	Japan	
Parallel bars	Viktor Chukarin	USSR	
Pommel horse	Boris Shakhlin	USSR	
Vault	Helmuth Bantz	Germany	
	Valentin Muratov	USSR	
Rings	Albert Azarian	USSR	

Gymnastics—Women			
Combined exercises team		USSR	
Team drill		Hungary	
Combined exercises individual	Larissa Latynina	USSR	
Floor exercises	Agnes Keleti	Hungary	
	Larissa Latynina	USSR	
Asymmetrical bars	Agnes Keleti	Hungary	
Beam	Agnes Keleti	Hungary	
Vault	Larissa Latynina	USSR	
Hockey		India	
Modern Pentathlon			
Individual	Lars Hall	Sweden	
Team		USSR	
Rowing			
Single sculls	Vyacheslav Ivanov	USSR	8 min 2.5 sec
Double sculls	Aleksandr Berkutov, Yuri Tyukalov	USSR	7 min 24.0 sec
Coxless pairs	James Fifer, Duvall Hecht	USA	7 min 55.4 sec
Coxed pairs	Arthur Ayrault, Conn Findlay, Kurt Seiffert (cox)	USA	8 min 26.1 sec
Coxless fours		Canada	7 min 8.8 sec
Coxed fours		Italy	7 min 19.4 sec
Eights		USA	6 min 35.2 sec
Shooting			
Free pistol	Pentti Linnosvuo	Finland	
Silhouette pistol	Stefan Petrescu	Romania	
Free rifle	Vasiliy Borissov	USSR	
Running deer	Vitalii Romanenko	USSR	
Small bore rifle			
—three positions	Anatoliy Bogdanov	USSR	
—prone	Gerald Quellette	Canada	
Clay pigeon	Galliano Rossini	Italy	
Swimming—Men			
100 metres freestyle	Jon Henricks	Australia	55.4 sec
400 metres freestyle	Murray Rose	Australia	4 min 27.3 sec
1,500 metres freestyle	Murray Rose	Australia	17 min 58.9 sec
200 metres breaststroke	Masaru Furukawa	Japan	2 min 34.7 sec
200 metres butterfly	Bill Yorzyk	USA	2 min 19.3 sec
100 metres backstroke	David Theile	Australia	1 min 2.2 sec
4 x 200 metres freestyle relay		Australia	8 min 23.6 sec
Springboard diving	Robert Clotworthy	USA	
Highboard diving	Joaquin Capilla	Mexico	
Swimming—Women			
100 metres freestyle	Dawn Fraser	Australia	1 min 2.0 sec
400 metres freestyle	Lorraine Crapp	Australia	4 min 54.6 sec
200 metres breaststroke	Ursula Happe	Germany	2 min 53.1 sec
100 metres butterfly	Shelley Mann	USA	1 min 11.0 sec
100 metres backstroke	Judy Grinham	Great Britain	1 min 12.9 sec
4 x 100 metres freestyle relay		Australia	4 min 17.1 sec
Springboard diving	Pat McCormick	USA	
Highboard diving	Pat McCormick	USA	
Water Polo		Hungary	
Weightlifting			
Bantamweight	Charles Vinci	USA	759 lb
Featherweight	Isaac Berger	USA	776½ lb
Lightweight	Igor Rybak	USSR	837½ lb
Middleweight	Fyeodor Bogdanovskiy	USSR	925¾ lb
Light-heavyweight	Tommy Kono	USA	986¼ lb
Mid-heavyweight	Arkhadiy Vorobiev	USSR	1,019¼ lb
Heavyweight	Paul Anderson	USA	1,102 lb
Wrestling			
Freestyle			
Flyweight	Mirian Tsalkalamanidze	USSR	
Bantamweight	Mustafa Dagistanli	Turkey	
Featherweight	Shozo Sasahara	Japan	
Lightweight	Emamali Habibi	Iran	
Welterweight	Mitsuo Ikeda	Japan	
Middleweight	Nikola Nikolov	Bulgaria	
Light-heavyweight	Gholam-Reza Takhti	Iran	
Heavyweight	Hamit Kaplan	Turkey	
Graeco-Roman			
Flyweight	Nikolay Solovyev	USSR	
Bantamweight	Konstantin Vyroupaev	USSR	
Featherweight	Rauno Makinen	Finland	
Lightweight	Kyosto Lehtonen	Finland	
Welterweight	Mithat Bayrak	Turkey	
Middleweight	Guivi Kartosia	USSR	
Light-heavyweight	Valentin Nikolaev	USSR	
Heavyweight	Anatoliy Parfenov	USSR	
Yachting			
Finn	Paul Elvstrom	Denmark	
Star	Herbert Williams, Lawrence Low	USA	
12 square metres	Peter Mander, John Cropp	New Zealand	
5.5 metres		Sweden	
Dragon		Sweden	

the double sculls together in 1920 and 1924, but their sons were less successful. Kelly Jr was third in the single sculls, and Costello Jr second in the double sculls.

Yale University achieved America's eighth successive victory in the eights—but first had to fight their way through the repechage, having been beaten into third place in their heat. They won the final by a small margin from Canada.

All thoughts of Budapest and the Gaza Strip were dispelled from the Olympic arena during the closing ceremony. On the suggestion of a Chinese-Australian

Official Report of the 1956 Olympics

17-stone Tamara Tyshkyevich won the women's shot with a throw of 54 ft. 5 in.

schoolboy, the competitors in the Games marched together in a single body for the first time— possibly an omen of better things to come in the world outside sport.

Equestrian Sports
Because of Australia's strict quarantine regulations, the equestrian events were held in July 1956 in Stockholm—the first instance of an individual sport being held in a different country from the main summer Games.

The Swedish dressage ace Henri St Cyr brought his tally of Olympic titles to four by retaining his individual title and gaining a gold medal as a member of the Swedish team, who won the dressage team title for the third successive time. Hans Winkler of Germany won two golds in the show jumping, one individual and one team. He collected 4 faults, with the Italian brothers Raimondo d'Inzeo (8 faults) and Piero d'Inzeo (11 faults) second and third.

Associated Press

Opposite page: **The winner of the silver medal in the decathlon at Melbourne was the American Rafer Johnson. At Rome four years later in 1960, he was to beat the Formosan Yang to take the gold medal.**
1 The long jump was one of Johnson's best events. Although he did not compete he was selected for the long jump for the United States in the 1956 Olympic Games.
2 An ungainly high jump landing during the AAU decathlon championships in 1960. Johnson cleared 5 ft 10 in to help him take yet another world record.
3 The final event of the decathlon at Rome was the 1500 metres. Yang had to beat Johnson by more than 11 seconds to win the gold medal, but Johnson held on to keep the margin down to 1.2 seconds and thus success.
4 Vyacheslav Ivanov, the world's leading sculler of the 1950s and 1960s, won the first of his three Olympic Golds at Melbourne.
5 Just 20 and little known outside the United States, Al Oerter won the first of a record consecutive discus golds at Melbourne with a first throw distance of 184 ft 11 in.

4

5

1956 OLYMPIC GAMES
Equestrian events held in Stockholm
Gold Medallists

Dressage		
individual Henri St Cyr	Sweden	
team	Sweden	
Show jumping		
individual Hans Winkler	Germany	
team	Germany	
Three-day event		
individual Petrus		
Kastenman	Sweden	
team	Great Britain	

Armin Hary, specialist of the
blitz start, appears confident on
the blocks before the start of
the 1960 Olympic 100 metres.

Rome Olympic Games
(1960)

A record number of 5,337 competitors—4,800 men and 537 women—gathered in Rome in late August and early September 1960 to contest 150 separate events in 18 different sports. The total number of competitors exceeded the previous record—4,925 at Helsinki in 1952—by over 400.

The Olympics were over 50 years late in arriving at 'the Eternal City.' The 1908 Games were originally scheduled for Rome. But some two years earlier the Italians had to stand down, and Britain stepped into the breach to organize what is generally recognised as the first of the great modern Games. But the 50-year wait did not affect the Italians' enthusiasm. Cash from football pool profits supported the Olympic movement financially, and in the city new sports stadiums had been built to accommodate the biggest sporting occasion to grace the Italian capital since the fall of the Roman Empire.

Athletics

In the men's track and field events, only four countries won more than one gold medal—the United States (nine), the USSR (five), New Zealand (two), and Poland (two). The Russians dominated the women's events, with 6 wins in 10 events; America won three titles, and Romania one.

For the first time since 1928 the men's sprint title eluded the Americans. The 100 metres went to the newly crowned world record holder, Armin Hary, who thus proved that his 10.0 sec world record in Zurich three months earlier was no fluke. He

1 Armin Hary blazes through the tape to win the 100 metres title from Dave Sime of the United States (far right).
2 New Zealand's Peter Snell pips Belgium's Roger Moens to win the 800 metres title.
3 A second gold for New Zealand came from Murray Halberg, 5,000 metres winner.
4 Herb Elliott (9) won the 1,500 metres in record time.

was Germany's first ever male track gold medallist, and he also won a second gold medal. In the 4 by 100 metres relay Germany finished second to the United States but the Americans were disqualified for a faulty take-over. The discomfiture of American sprinters was completed by the result of the 200 metres. Despite the competition from no fewer than three co-holders of the world record, Italy's Livio Berruti himself equalled the record in the semi-final and final to win the country's first athletics gold since 1936. The Roman crowd celebrated by lighting hundreds of paper torches as Berruti, who always

ran in dark glasses, acknowledged the cheers by removing them.

New Zealand's two gold medals came on a single afternoon, September 2. The first came in the 800 metres. The 21-year-old Peter Snell had come to the Games with a personal best time of 1 min 49.2 sec for 880 yards. But he improved to 1 min 46.3 sec to win the final by inches from the Belgian world record holder Roger Moens. An hour later came the 5,000 metres final, and New Zealand's hope in this race was 27-year-old Murray Halberg. He ran the race of a lifetime, breaking away boldly 1,000 metres from the finish with a 61.5 sec lap to open up a 30-yard lead before the rest of the field were aware of it. Though his last lap took 73.0 sec and he collapsed at the end of it, he still won by 1.2 sec from Hans Grodotzki of Germany who was 0.2 sec in front of the bronze medallist Kazimierz Zimny of Poland. Six days later Grodotzki won a second silver medal, in the 10,000 metres. In that race he was second to Russia's Pyotr Bolotnikov, who beat Vladimir Kuts's

1956 Olympic record by 13 seconds with 28 min 32.2 sec.

But the showpiece of the track events was the 1,500 metres. Australia's Herb Elliott, the world record holder, was the favourite, and he made winning in world record time look almost simple. He took the lead soon after passing the 800-metre mark, and surged majestically away from the others to finish in 3 min 35.6 sec. A distant second was the young Frenchman Michel Jazy in 3 min 38.4 sec: the first six to finish beat the previous Olympic record of 3 min 41.2 sec.

If Elliott's victory was sweeping, the finish of the 400 metres was desperately close. The final resolved into a battle between America's Otis Davis and Carl Kaufmann, representing Germany but born in New York. The early leader was South Africa's Malcolm Spence, but he faded to finish third, and in the home straight it was Davis who led by about 5 yards. Kaufmann produced a tremendous finish and it took a photograph to decide that Davis had just held him off. Both

shared a new world record of 44.9 sec.

Otis Davis teamed up with Glenn Davis, Jack Yerman, and Earl Young to win the 4 by 400 metres relay in a world record 3 min 0.7 sec, with Kaufmann anchoring the German team to the silver medals. Glenn Davis was the first champion ever to retain the 400 metres hurdles title, and the same thing happened in the 110 metres, which Lee Calhoun retained. Americans took all three medals in both hurdles events.

The steeplechase, on the other hand, was an all-European affair. The 1958 European 5,000 and 10,000 metres champion Zdzislaw Krzyszkowiak took the title in 8 min 34.2 sec—less than 3 seconds outside his world record—and two Russians, Nikolai Sokolov and Semyon Rzhishchin, the silver and bronze respectively.

Honours were evenly divided between the United States and Europe in the jumps, with Don

record throw of 194 ft. 2 in., nearly 4 feet better than Rink Babka's silver medal throw of 190 ft. 4¼ in. In the shot, the gold went to a late addition to the American team, Bill Nieder, and the silver to twice-winner Parry O'Brien.

The javelin and hammer went to the Soviet Union. Defending champion Hal Connolly could do no better than place eighth in the hammer although he had only three weeks earlier set a world record of 230 ft. 9 in. He threw only 208 ft. 7½ in., whereas the winner, Vasiliy Rudenkov, managed 220 ft. 1¾ in. and the runner-up Gyula Zsivotsky of Hungary, 215 ft. 10¼ in. In the javelin it was a case of third time lucky for Viktor Tsibulenko, fourth in 1952 and third in 1956, who won with 277 ft. 8¼ in. The 1956 champion, Egil Danielsen of Norway, failed to qualify for the final rounds.

The two-day battle for the decathlon honours was one of the closest in Olympic history. There

was never more than 144 points between America's Rafer Johnson and Formosa's Yang Chuan-kwang, and the result was in doubt until the final event, the 1,500 metres. Yang tried to run away from Johnson, but the American hung on to win the competition.

Two days after the last track and field event came the marathon, an event that heralded the arrival of African runners into the Olympic honours list. Two men, Abebe Bikila from Ethiopia and Rhadi Ben Abdesselm of Morocco broke away from the field, and Abebe went into a lead—narrow but decisive—only in the last kilometre. Abebe won, in a world best time of 2 hr 15 min 16.2 sec; Rhadi was second and Barry Magee of New Zealand was third.

The outstanding woman athlete of the Games was 20-year-old Wilma Rudolph from Tennessee, who became the third woman since World War II to win

1 Britain's Don Thompson steps out towards a gold medal in the 50 kilometres walk.
2 Abebe Bikila of Ethiopia won the marathon—barefoot— in the fastest time ever recorded for the distance.
3 Tennessee State's Wilma Rudolph wins the 200 metres. She collected two more gold medals, in the 100 metres and the 4 x 100 metres relay.
4 Russia's Irina Press just outpaced Britain's Carole Quinton to win the 80 metres hurdles. Britain's Mary Rand (left) came home fourth.
5 A statuesque encounter in the freestyle wrestling, a sport in which the United States, uncharacteristically, were extremely successful. But Turkey, with seven gold and two silver medals, were the dominant wrestling team.
6 Future world heavyweight champion Cassius Clay stands at the top of the Olympic light-heavyweight boxing tree.

Bragg winning the States' fourteenth successive pole vault title and Ralph Boston taking the long jump with a historic 26 ft. 7¾ in.— thus beating Jesse Owen's 24-year-old Olympic record set at Berlin by 2½ inches. The favourite for the high jump, world record holder John Thomas, was relegated to third place by two Russians, Robert Shavlakadze and Valeriy Brumel. Thomas was more than 3 inches below his world record, while Shavlakadze won the gold medal on the fewer misses rule after clearing 7 ft. 1 in. In the triple jump five men beat Ferreira da Silva's 1956 Olympic record, with world record holder Jozef Schmidt of Poland beating them all with 55 ft. 1¾ in. Da Silva, in his fourth Olympic Games, finished a sad 14th.

Russia and the United States divided the gold medals in the throwing events. But America won all three discus and shot medals. Al Oerter retained his discus title with an Olympic

Olympic golds in the 100 and 200 metres and the 4 by 100 metres relay. In the two individual events she was in a class of her own, winning each by at least three yards. In her semi-final of the 100 metres she equalled the world record of 11.3 sec, and in the final—with a following wind just over the maximum allowed—she returned 11.0 sec. In the 200 metres, after coming within 0.3 sec of her own world record (22.9 sec) in her heat, she won the final in 24.0 sec (against a strong head-wind) by 0.4 sec from Germany's Jutta Heine. And in the relay final, after sharing in a new world record in the heat, she took over some yards behind Miss Heine but still managed to finish in front.

After a gap of 32 years, the women's programme included an 800 metres again, and unlike the race at Amsterdam in 1928 this one produced no undue distress in any of the finalists. Ludmilla Shevtsova of the USSR had to equal her world record of 2 min

4.3 sec to hold off the challenge of Australia's Brenda Jones. Another win for Russia on the track came through Irina Press in the 80 metres hurdles. She was closely challenged by Britain's Carole Quinton who hurdled better than the Russian holder of the world pentathlon record, but Miss Press was the more powerful and won by 0.1 sec.

Four field events fell to athletes from Russia. The 'strong woman' of the Games was Tamara Press, elder sister of Irina: she took the gold medal in the shot with 56 ft. 10 in., an Olympic record, and the silver medal in the discus, over 8 feet behind the winner, Nina Ponomaryeva, another Russian. Mrs. Ponomaryeva thus regained the title she had won in 1952 and lost in 1956, when she was third. The 1956 discus winner—Olga Fikotova of Czechoslovakia, but by now Mrs. Hal Connolly of the United States—was seventh. The javelin title went to 20-year-old Elvira Ozolina, the world record

holder, and the long jump to Vyera Krepkina who beat the defending champion Elzbieta Krzesinska of Poland into second place by 4 inches. Mrs. Krepkina's winning jump, 20 ft. 10¾ in., was only one inch below the world record.

The only field event not won by a Russian was the high jump, and somewhat inevitably the winner was Iolanda Balas from Romania, whose winning 6 ft. 0¾ in. jump was more than 5 inches better than the joint silver medallist—Dorothy Shirley of Britain and Jaroslawa Jozwiakowska of Poland.

Swimming

The magnificent Stadio del Nuoto was the scene of an American comeback in Olympic swimming. Smarting from their trouncing at Melbourne, the Americans made amends by winning 9 of the 15 swimming events and both men's diving titles. Their gold medals tally could have been one more but

for the disputed decision in the 100 metres freestyle in which Australia's John Devitt was given the victory over Lance Larson of the United States.

Australians were first home in four men's events: Murray Rose became the first man to retain the Olympic 400 metres title, and David Theile also retained his 1956 title, in the 100 metres back-stroke. Devitt took the 100 metres, and John Konrads edged Murray Rose out of first place in the 1,500 metres. The only Australian woman to win was Dawn Fraser, who retained her 100 metres free-style title. But for Australia this was a poor return: bad weather spoilt the team's training, their plane was held up for 24 hours in the steamy heat of Bahrein on the way to Rome, and in Rome a number of the team—including Melbourne 100 metres winner Jon Henricks—went down with 'Roman tummy' (gastroenteritis).

The British team had their best Games since 1924. Anita Lons-

Associated Press

brough won the 200 metres breaststroke in world record time —the only title that did not go to Australia or America, Natalie Steward won a silver in the backstroke and a bronze in the 100 metres freestyle, and to their surprise the men's 4 by 200 metres squad set a European record in coming fourth.

In the diving, Ingrid Kramer of Germany became the first non-American to win both women's titles. Bronze medals for Britain came through Liz Ferris in the women's springboard and Brian Phelps in the men's highboard. And for the hosts, Italy, gold medals came from victory in the water polo.

Other Sports
Traditionally a strong cycling nation, Italy missed only one gold medal in the six-event programme. Italians won the first event, the newly instituted road team time trial by over two minutes from Germany, and proceeded to monopolize the honours until the very last race, the individual road race. Sante Gaiardoni won the 1,000 metres sprint and the 1,000 metres time trial, the first time this particular double had been accomplished in the Olympics. But a historic clean sweep eluded

Central Press

the host country: Viktor Kapitonov
of Russia beat Livio Trape of
Italy in a sprint finish to the road
race with the pursuing 'bunch'
some 20 seconds in arrears. It was
Russia's first Olympic cycling
gold. One unfortunate incident
soured this part of the Games:
Denmark's Knud Jensen died in
hospital after collapsing during the
team trial. Autopsy reports suggested that his death may have
been due to the effects of drugs,
but his collapse was later officially
ascribed to sunstroke.

Another traditional winner to
triumph—yet again—was the
United States basketball team who
won their fifth Olympic tournament. But some favourites who
failed were India, winners since
1928 of the hockey. A goal
scored after 13 minutes in the
final was sufficient for Pakistan to
defeat them.

The perennial Gert Fredriksson
added two more Olympic canoeing medals to his collection which
began with two golds in 1948. At
Rome he was third in the kayak
singles, less then 3 seconds
behind the winner, and first, with
Sven Sjodelius, in the kayak
doubles. Rome proved to be his
last Olympics, and his tally stood
at six Olympic golds, one silver,
and one bronze. But in another
water sport, rowing, a new name
began to become known—the
Ratzeburg Ruder Club. Coached
by Karl Adam, the German eight,
composed of Ratzeburg members,
broke the 40-year-old American
hold on this title: it was also
Germany's first win in the event.

The soccer title went again to
eastern Europe, and this time it
was the turn of Yugoslavia who
defeated Denmark 3-1 in the
final. This victory came despite
the dismissal of captain Milan
Galic after only 39 minutes when
Yugoslavia were leading 2-0.
Hungary won the bronze medals
by beating Italy 2-1 in their play-
off.

The outstanding part of the
equestrian events was the success
of Australia in the three-day
competition. Not only did the
Australian team of Laurie Morgan, Neale Lavis, and Bill Roycroft win the team event with only
128.18 penalty points (against
runners-up Switzerland's 386.02),
but Morgan took the individual
gold and Lavis the silver. And
they were Australia's first equestrian medallists in Olympic competition.

Far away in the Bay of Naples,
the heir to the Greek throne,
Prince Constantine, was at the
helm of the winning Dragon class
vessel. The Prince, a better sailor
than politician, had been sailing a
Dragon for less than 18 months.
One very experienced competitor
whose victory was less of a surprise
was Paul Elvstrom, who won his
fourth successive gold medal in
single-handed events and his third
successive gold in the Finn
category.

1 Russia's first Olympic gold
in cycling went to Viktor
Kapitonov (left) who held off
a strong challenge from
Italy's Livio Trape to win
the 109-mile road race.
2 Gert Fredriksson (left)
took his collection of Olympic
canoeing gold medals to six.
3 Laurie Morgan won the three-
day event title with a rare
'plus' score, and added a
second gold as a member of
Australia's winning team.
4 Prince Constantine of
Greece helmed his Dragon class
yacht to win an Olympic gold
medal. It was the only medal
of any colour won by Greece
at these Olympic Games.

Keystone

Italy's Raimondo d'Inzeo, gold medallist at Rome ahead of his brother, Piero. The brothers completed a family set of medals by collecting a bronze in the team event.

The great Herb Elliott (2), whose greatest race was undoubtedly the 1960 Olympic 1,500 metres final. Into the last 400 metres, Elliott had opened up a 10-yard lead, and at the finish was almost 3 seconds ahead, winning his gold medal in world-record time.

ROME OLYMPIC GAMES, 1960 Gold Medallists

Athletics—Men			
100 metres	Armin Hary	Germany	10.2 sec
200 metres	Livio Berruti	Italy	20.5 sec
400 metres	Otis Davis	USA	44.9 sec
800 metres	Peter Snell	New Zealand	1 min 46.3 sec
1,500 metres	Herb Elliott	Australia	3 min 35.6 sec
5,000 metres	Murray Halberg	New Zealand	13 min 43.4 sec
10,000 metres	Pyetor Bolotnikov	USSR	28 min 32.2 sec
Marathon	Abebe Bikila	Ethiopia	2 hr 15 min 16.2 sec
4 x 100 metres relay		Germany	39.5 sec
4 x 400 metres relay		USA	3 min 2.2 sec
110 metres hurdles	Lee Calhoun	USA	13.8 sec
400 metres hurdles	Glenn Davis	USA	49.3 sec
3,000 metres steeplechase	Zdzislaw Krzyszkowiak	Poland	8 min 34.2 sec
20 kilometres walk	Vladimir Golubnichiy	USSR	1 hr 34 min 7.2 sec
50 kilometres walk	Don Thompson	Great Britain	4 hr 25 min 30.0 sec
High jump	Robert Shavlakadze	USSR	7 ft 1 in
Pole vault	Don Bragg	USA	15 ft 5 in
Long jump	Ralph Boston	USA	26 ft $7\frac{3}{4}$ in
Triple jump	Jozef Schmidt	Poland	55 ft $1\frac{3}{4}$ in
Shot	Bill Nieder	USA	64 ft $6\frac{3}{4}$ in
Discus	Al Oerter	USA	194 ft 2 in
Hammer	Vasiliy Rudenkov	USSR	220 ft $1\frac{3}{4}$ in
Javelin	Viktor Tsibulenko	USSR	277 ft $8\frac{1}{4}$ in
Decathlon	Rafer Johnson	USA	8,392 points
Athletics—Women			
100 metres	Wilma Rudolph	USA	11.0 sec
200 metres	Wilma Rudolph	USA	24.0 sec
800 metres	Ludmilla Shevtsova	USSR	2 min 4.3 sec
4 x 100 metres relay		USA	44.5 sec
80 metres hurdles	Irina Press	USSR	10.8 sec
High Jump	Iolanda Balas	Romania	6 ft $0\frac{3}{4}$ in
Long jump	Vyera Krepkina	USSR	20 ft $10\frac{3}{4}$ in
Shot	Tamara Press	USSR	56 ft 10 in
Discus	Nina Ponomaryeva	USSR	180 ft $9\frac{1}{4}$ in
Javelin	Elvira Ozolina	USSR	183 ft 8 in
Basketball		USA	
Boxing			
Flyweight	Gyula Torok	Hungary	
Bantamweight	Oleg Grigoryev	USSR	
Featherweight	Francesco Musso	Italy	
Lightweight	Kazimierz Pazdzior	Poland	
Light-welterweight	Bohumil Nemecek	Czechoslovakia	
Welterweight	Giovanni Benvenuti	Italy	
Light-middleweight	Wilbert McClure	USA	
Middleweight	Edward Crook	USA	
Light-heavyweight	Cassius Clay	USA	
Heavyweight	Franco de Piccoli	Italy	
Canoeing—Men			
1,000 metres K-1	Erik Hansen	Denmark	3 min 53.00 sec
1,000 metres K-2	Gert Fredriksson Sven Sjodelius	Sweden	3 min 34.73 sec
4 x 500 metres K-1 relay		Germany	7 min 39.43 sec
1,000 metres C-1	Janos Parti	Hungary	4 min 33.03 sec
1,000 metres C-2	Leonid Geyshter Stephan Makarenko	USSR	4 min 17.04 sec
Canoeing Women			
500 metres K-1	Antonina Seredina	USSR	2 min 8.08 sec
500 metres K-2	Maria Shubina Antonina Seredina	USSR	1 min 54.76 sec
Cycling			
1,000 metres sprint	Sante Gaiardoni	Italy	
1,000 metres time trial	Sante Gaiardoni	Italy	1 min 7.27 sec
2,000 metres tandem	Sergio Bianchetto Giuseppe Beghetto	Italy	
4,000 metres team pursuit		Italy	4 min 38.41 sec
Road team time trial (100 km)		Italy	2 hr 14 min 33.53 sec
Road race (175.38 km)	Viktor Kapitonov	USSR	4 hr 20 min 37 sec
Equestrian			
Dressage—Individual	Sergey Filatov	USSR	
Show jumping			
—individual	Raimondo d'Inzeo	Italy	
—team		Germany	
Three day event			
—individual	Laurie Morgan	Australia	
—team		Australia	
Fencing—Men			
Foil—individual	Viktor Zhdanovich	USSR	
—team		USSR	
Epee—individual	Giuseppe Delfino	Italy	
—team		Italy	
Sabre—individual	Rudolph Karpati	Hungary	
—team		Hungary	
Fencing—Women			
Foil individual	Heidi Schmid	Germany	
—team		USSR	
Football		Yugoslavia	
Gymnastics—Men			
Combined exercises			
—individual	Boris Shakhlin	USSR	
—team		Japan	
Floor exercises	Nobuyuki Aihara	Japan	
Horizontal bar	Takashi Ono	Japan	
Parallel bars	Boris Shakhlin	USSR	
Pommell horse	Boris Shakhlin Eugen Ekman	USSR Finland	

Vault	Takashi Ono Boris Shakhlin	Japan USSR	
Rings	Albert Azaryan	USSR	
Gymnastics—Women			
Combined exercises			
—individual	Larissa Latynina	USSR	
—team		USSR	
Floor exercises	Larissa Latynina	USSR	
Asymmetrical bars	Polina Astakhova	USSR	
Beam	Eva Bosakova	Czechoslovakia	
Vault	Margarita Nikolayeva	USSR	
Hockey		Pakistan	
Modern Pentathlon			
Individual	Ferenc Nemeth	Hungary	
Team		Hungary	
Rowing			
Singe sculls	Vyacheslav Ivanov	USSR	7 min 13.96 sec
Double sculls	Vaclav Kozak Pavel Schmidt	Czechoslovakia	6 min 47.50 sec
Coxless pairs	Valentin Boreyko Oleg Golovanov	USSR	7 min 2.01 sec
Coxed pairs	Bernhard Knubel Heinz Renneburg Klaus Zerta (cox)	Germany	7 min 29.14 sec
Coxless fours		USA	6 min 26.26 sec
Coxed fours		Germany	6 min 39.12 sec
Eights		Germany	5 min 57.18 sec
Shooting			
Free pistol	Alexei Gustchin	USSR	
Rapid fire pistol	William McMillan	USA	
Free rifle	H. Hammerer	Austria	
Small bore rifle			
—three positions	Vicktor Shamburkin	USSR	
—prone	Peter Kohnke	Germany	
Clay pigeon	Ion Dumitrescu	Romania	
Swimming—Men			
100 metres freestyle	John Devitt	Australia	55.2 sec
400 metres freestyle	Murray Rose	Australia	4 min 18.3 sec
1,500 metres freestyle	John Konrads	Australia	17 min 19.6 sec
200 metres breaststroke	Bill Mulliken	USA	2 min 37.4 sec
200 metres butterfly	Mike Troy	USA	2 min 12.8 sec
100 metres backstroke	David Theile	Australia	1 min 1.9 sec
4 x 200 metres freestyle relay		USA	8 min 10.2 sec
4 x 100 metres medley relay		USA	4 min 5.4 sec
Springboard diving	Gary Tobian	USA	
Highboard diving	Bob Webster	USA	
Swimming—Women			
100 metres freestyle	Dawn Fraser	Australia	1 min 1.2 sec
400 metres freestyle	Chris von Saltza	USA	4 min 50.6 sec
200 metres breastroke	Anita Lonsbrough	Great Britain	2 min 49.5 sec
100 metres butterfly	Carolyn Schuler	USA	1 min 9.5 sec
100 metres backstroke	Lynn Burke	USA	1 min 9.3 sec
4 x 100 metres freestyle relay		USA	4 min 8.9 sec
4 x 100 metres medley relay		USA	4 min 41.1 sec
Springboard diving	Ingrid Kramer	Germany	
Highboard diving	Ingrid Kramer	Germany	
Water Polo		Italy	
Weightlifting			
Bantamweight	Charles Vinci	USA	760 lb
Featherweight	Evgeniy Minayev	USSR	821 lb
Lightweight	Viktor Bushuyev	USSR	876 lb
Middleweight	Aleksandr Kurynov	USSR	$964\frac{1}{4}$ lb
Light-heavyweight	Ireneusz Palinski	Poland	$975\frac{1}{4}$ lb
Mid-heavyweight	Arkhadiy Vorobyev	USSR	$1,014\frac{1}{4}$ lb
Heavyweight	Yuri Vlasov	USSR	$1,184\frac{1}{2}$ lb
Wrestling			
FREESTYLE			
Flyweight	A. Bilek	Turkey	
Bantamweight	Terrence McCann	USA	
Featherweight	Mustafa Dagistanli	Turkey	
Lightweight	Shelby Wilson	USA	
Welterweight	Douglas Blubaugh	USA	
Middleweight	Hassan Gungor	Turkey	
Light-heavyweight	Ismet Atli	Turkey	
Heavyweight	Wilfred Dietrich	Germany	
GRAECO-ROMAN			
Flyweight	Dumitru Pirvulescu	Romania	
Bantamweight	Oleg Karavayev	USSR	
Featherweight	Muzanir Sille	Turkey	
Lightweight	Avtandil Koridze	USSR	
Welterweight	Mithat Bayrak	Turkey	
Middleweight	Dimitar Dobrev	Bulgaria	
Light-heavyweight	Trofim Kis	Turkey	
Heavyweight	Ivan Bogdan	USSR	
Yachting			
Finn	Paul Elvstrom	Denmark	
Flying Dutchman	Peter Lunde, Bjorn Bergvall	Norway	
Star	Timir Pinegin, Fyedor Shutkov	USSR	
Dragon	Prince Constantine, Odysseus Eskidjoglou, Georges Zaimis	Greece	
5.5 metres	George O'Day, James Hunt, David Smith	USA	

Britain's golden girl at the Tokyo Olympics, Mary Rand. Her victory in the long jump, together with Lynn Davies's success in the men's event, brought Britain a memorable 'double'.

Tokyo Olympic Games

(1964)

In the afternoon of October 10, 1964, Yoshinoro Sakai performed an act of dual significance in the Olympic stadium in Tokyo. By running the last lap of the Olympic torch relay and lighting the flame, he formed an integral part of the opening ceremony of the Games of the XVIIIth Olympiad. But, more important perhaps, this young man, born under the shadow of the mushroom cloud of the atomic bomb dropped on Hiroshima in 1946, was a symbol of his country's acceptance of a new role in the world, and the world's acceptance of Japan.

An age had passed since 1940, when Japan was originally due to host the Games, the first of two Olympic celebrations which were cancelled as a result of the various wars taking place around the world. Japan, as a defeated nation, had not even been invited to the London Games of 1948, but Japanese sportsmen had competed at Helsinki in 1952. And despite inclement weather all concerned agreed that the 1964 Games were, as the latest Games always seem to be, the biggest and the best. They were not quite the biggest, as travelling distances had cut down on the number of competitors, but the stadiums, almost all built new for the Games, made them the costliest—more than £200,000,000.

The magnificent venues certainly inspired the competitors to reach new heights, and four of them claimed their third successive gold medals: Al Oerter in athletics, Dawn Fraser in swimming, Vyacheslav Ivanov in sculling, and Hans Winkler in the equestrian show jumping team event.

Athletics—Men

Twice a winner of the discus already, Al Oerter became the second man in Olympic athletics history to win an individual event for the third time (the first being John Flanagan in the hammer in 1900, 1904, and 1908). But this time he was not only opposed by stiff opposition, including the new world record holder Ludvik Danek of Czechoslovakia, but handicapped by the effects of a dislocated neck sustained earlier in the year and a strained cartilage of the trunk incurred just before the Games opened. Oerter, however, was not going to let mere

Left, **Symbolizing Japan's rebirth as a world power, Yoshinoro Sakai lights the flame of the Tokyo Olympics.**
Below, **American unknown Billy Mills streaks past world record holder Ron Clarke to win the 10,000 metres title.**

U.P.I.

injury stop him. He discarded his surgical collar and took cortizone to allay the pain in his body. But as Danek went into the lead in the first round of the final with 195 ft. 11½ in. and improved with his fourth throw to 198 ft. 6½ in., it looked all over for the champion. Yet with his fifth effort, Oerter sent the discus flying beyond the 200-ft. mark, to 200 ft. 1½ in., to earn him his third consecutive gold medal. Danek won the silver medal, and Oerter's team-mate, David Weill, the bronze.

The previous day, the first of the athletics events, the United States had had an unexpected triumph in the 10,000 metres. The favourite was Australia's Ron Clarke, holder of the world record for this distance and many others, and he led the field of 38 through the first few laps. By half-way he had dropped most of the others, but with a lap to go he was being pressed by Mohamed Gammoudi of Tunisia and Billy Mills of the

United States. As they moved over the track to pass lapped runners, it was first Clarke in the lead, and then Mills appeared on his shoulder. But Gammoudi suddenly burst between them, opening up a 10-yard gap with 250 yards to go, a lead that lasted until 50 yards from the tape. Clarke came up to challenge first, and then Mills stormed past to win his country's first Olympic title in the longer track events. Gammoudi held on for the silver, and Clarke had to be content with the bronze.

Clarke had even less reward in the 5,000 metres. He made much of the pace, but when it came to the last lap he could not match the fast finishing of the others and wound up ninth. The winner, after a 54.8 sec last 400 metres, was America's Bob Schul, with his team-mate, 30-year-old Bill Dellinger, third.

Matching Oerter's achievement was Peter Snell's complete domination of the 800 and 1,500 metres. A surprise winner of the 800 metres at Rome in 1960, he had since developed into one of the finest middle-distance talents ever, with world records for 800 metres, 880 yards, and one mile. In the 800 metres he came through the preliminary rounds untroubled, although in other heats George Kerr of Jamaica and Wilson Kiprugut of Kenya reduced the Olympic record to 1 min 46.1 sec. In the final Kiprugut led the eight finalists round the first lap, with Snell in seventh position. But moving with unmistakable power, the black-vested New Zealander simply ran round his opponents to take the lead with 200 metres to go and won unpressed in 1 min 45.1 sec—the second fastest time ever recorded for the distance. In the 1,500 metres he was opposed by his team-mate John Davies, whose pre-Games performances had been better than Snell's. But once again the big figure of Snell was dominant in the final, and he won by 1½ seconds from Josef Odlozil of Czechoslovakia in 3 min 38.1 sec. Davies, who had made much of the early pace, was third.

The traditional domination of the United States in the sprint events, somewhat eroded at the Rome Olympics, was reasserted in no uncertain way. Powerful Bob Hayes, who looked menacing enough in qualifying, simply destroyed his rivals in the final, which he won in a world-record-equalling 10.0 sec, after recording a wind-assisted 9.9 sec in the semi-final. Enrique Figuerola of Cuba took the silver, and erratic Harry Jerome of Canada the bronze. Hayes's amazing speed stood the United States in good stead in the 4 by 100 metres relay. Running the last leg in the final he received the baton in fifth position. Not only did he make up lost ground, but he exploded into action to win by three yards to make the team's final time 39.0 sec—a world record. Seven of the eight teams in the final broke the 1960 Olympic record.

In contrast to Hayes's almost animal power, grace and technique triumphed in the 200 metres in the person of Henry Carr. He glided round the bend to win the gold medal by 0.2 sec from his team-mate Paul Drayton in an Olympic record of 20.3 sec.

Britain's best hopes for a gold medal on the track appeared to be vested in team captain Robbie Brightwell in the 400 metres. But the opposition was too strong for him and he came home a disappointed man in fourth place, behind the American winner, 30-year-old Mike Larrabee (45.1 sec), Wendell Mottley of Trinidad and Tobago (45.2 sec), and the Pole Andrzej Badenski (45.6 sec). However Brightwell had his revenge on the place-medallists when it came to the 4 by 400 metres relay. Britain had a useful quartet entered—including Tim Graham, sixth in the 400 metres; John Cooper, silver medallist in the 400 metres hurdles; Adrian Metcalfe, Britain's joint-fastest ever man over 400 metres, and Brightwell. Larrabee, running second for America, put his team well in front and as Brightwell took over for the last leg he was third, behind Henry Carr of the United States and Mottley, Trinidad and Tobago's last man. Running with the same style that had taken him to the 200 metres gold, Henry Carr swept on to his second gold medal. Behind him Brightwell was running the race of a lifetime to oust Mottley from second place. The United States (3 min 0.7 sec), Britain (3 min 1.6 sec) and Trinidad and Tobago (3 min 1.7 sec) all beat the existing world record.

This race capped a most successful Games for Britain's men,

their best since 1908. In the marathon, behind Abebe Bikila, Basil Heatley won the silver medal. Abebe, only recently having had his appendix removed, was never in danger and won by over 4 minutes in a world best time of 2 hr 12 min 11.2 sec, and when he had finished treated the crowd to an impromptu display of limbering down exercises. Heatley, third as he entered the stadium, mortified the Japanese fans by overtaking their champion Kokichi Tsuburaya within sight of the tape. It was Britain's fourth silver medal in this Olympic event. In the 3,000 metres steeplechase Maurice Herriott picked up a well deserved silver behind the Belgian Gaston Roelants. And in the 50 kilometres walk, Paul Nihill pressed the great Italian Abdon Pamich almost all the way to claim his reward of a silver.

Britain's male heroes, however, were Ken Matthews and Lynn Davies. Matthews, who had col-

Central Press

Keystone

Europeans. In the high jump the world record holder Valeriy Brumel, second at the Rome Olympics, improved to take the gold medal with an Olympic record of 7 ft. 1¾ in., the same height as runner-up John Thomas of the United States. But Brumel was a safe winner on the fewer failures rule. In the pole vault the supremacy of the United States was sorely put to the test during a competition which lasted 13 hours and finished under floodlights. The lone American during the final stages of the contest was Fred Hansen. He had passed at 16 ft. 6¾ in., a height cleared first time by Germany's Wolfgang Reinhardt, so Hansen, a dental student from Texas, had to clear 16 ft. 8¾ in. to win. This he did at his third attempt, and in a tense atmosphere he watched Reinhardt fail. America's run of wins, unbroken since 1896, was safe, although Germans were placed second, third, and fourth.

The first eight places in the triple jump were filled by Europeans. The winner, almost inevitably, was the incomparable Pole Jozef Schmidt, the champion in Rome. He went into the lead in the second round with 54 ft. 7½ in., and with his final effort reached out to 55 ft. 3½ in. Russians were second and third, while Britain's Fred Alsop was fourth.

The throwing events were equally divided between the Old World and the New. American giants Dallas Long and Randy Matson were first and second in the shot, with veteran Parry O'Brien relegated to fourth place behind Vilmos Varju of Hungary. And Oerter took the discus gold. The hammer final was held in the rain, and was a complete triumph for the Eastern Europeans. The gold medallist was the 31-year-old Russian Romuald Klim, who threw over 2 feet farther than his perennial rival Gyula Zsivotsky of Hungary (228 ft. 10½ in. to 226 ft. 8 in.). Finland's Pauli Nevala revived memories of his country's greatness by winning the javelin. Once again, this event was hampered by rain, which accounted for his relatively modest winning distance of 271 ft. 2½ in.

Athletics—Women

American women won only two events in track and field—the sprints—and once again they had their long-striding negro girls to thank. In the 100 metres Wyomia Tyus beat her team-mate Edith McGuire by 0.2 sec to take the gold medal, with Poland's Ewa Klobukowska in third place. Miss McGuire took the 200 metres title in 23.0 sec, only 0.1 sec away from the world record. Miss Klobukowska (later to have world records but not her Olympic medals taken away from her after failing a 'sex test') and Irene Kirszenstein, the 200 metres silver medallist, were both members of Poland's winning 4 by 100 metres relay team who set a world record of 43.6 sec.

There was a new event on the women's programme, the 400 metres, which provided Australia's 'golden girl' of the 1956 Olympics, Betty Cuthbert, with an opportunity to win her fourth Olympic gold. Miss Cuthbert, starting very fast and taking a breather down the back straight, made no mistake in beating Britain's Ann Packer by 0.2 sec in 52.0 sec. Miss Packer had been a pre-Games favourite for this event, but she had a second chance in the 800 metres, in which she had not had much experience. But running a more relaxed race, the British girl used her speed well to come through in the final straight to take a surprise gold medal and set an even more surprising world record of 2 min 1.1 sec, which was not beaten until 1968.

Miss Packer's gold medal was, in fact, Britain's second ever women's athletics title. The first had come only six days previously—in the long jump. And the winner of this event, in another world record, was Mary Rand. As Mary Bignal in 1960, she had had the mortifying experience of failing to qualify for the final six, but she was now a far more mature athlete. In the qualifying round this time Mrs Rand cleared an Olympic record of 21 ft. 4½ in., and in the final she improved to the world record distance of 22 ft. 2¼ in. Mrs Rand collected a full set of Olympic medals at these games. She was runner-up to Russia's Irina Press in the pentathlon although she put up better performances than Miss Press in four of the five events. And her bronze came in the 4 by 100 metres relay.

Irina Press's sister, Tamara, was an impressive winner of the shot and discus gold medals, improving on her Rome performances in both events. But

1 Veteran Mike Larrabee (709) pips Wendell Mottley (613) for the 400 metres gold, as Britain's Robbie Brightwell (153) comes home fourth.
2 Master of the marathon Abebe Bikila was head and shoulders above his rivals, winning for the second time in a world's best performance.
3 Another champion who dominated his opponents was Belgium's Gaston Roelants in the 3,000 metres steeplechase.
4 A gripping struggle in the 50 kilometres walk resulted in a win for Italy's Abdon Pamich (left) over Britain's Paul Nihill. The margin of victory was a mere 18.8 sec in over 4 hours walking.
5 Familiar conditions of rain and wind hampered Welsh long jumper Lynn Davies less than the redoubtable Ter-Ovanesyan and Boston as he soared to win Britain's first field event gold medal since 1908.

lapsed while in the lead in the 20 kilometres walk at Rome four years before, made no mistakes this time in adding the Olympic gold medal to his European championship of 1962 by a margin of over 1½ minutes. But the man who captured the imagination of the British public was long-jumper Lynn Davies. Faced by men whose best performances were as much as a foot longer than his, he responded better than anyone else to the challenge of competing in rainy and windy conditions. With his penultimate effort in the final he made the best of a lull in the wind to reach 26 ft. 5¾ in. and claim Britain's first Olympic field event gold medal since 1908, with America's world record holder and 1960 Olympic champion Ralph Boston relegated to second place and Russia's European champion Igor Ter-Ovanesyan third.

The medals in the other jumping events also went mostly to

the javelin was a surprise win for Mihaela Penes of Romania. At 17 years and 2 months she became the youngest Olympic athletics champion ever. The high jump, in contrast, was a complete triumph for 27-year-old Iolanda Balas, another Romanian, whose winning height of 6 ft. 2¾ in. was almost 4 inches better than that of the runner-up, Michele Brown of Australia.

Swimming

The superb, brand new swimming pool brought out the best in the competitors. World records were set in all but 2 of the 10 men's races, and 4 of the 8 women's. But overshadowing even this aggregate of achievement were the feats of Dawn Fraser and Don Schollander.

Australia's Miss Fraser became the first woman in any Olympic sport to win three successive gold medals in the same event—in her case the 100 metres freestyle which she had previously won at Melbourne in 1956 and Rome in 1960. America's Don Schollander became the first swimmer to win four gold medals at the same Games, in the 100 and 400 metres freestyle and both freestyle relays. He took the 100 metres freestyle by 0.1 sec from Britain's Bobby McGregor, and in the longer event he swam both 200 metres at almost even pace and broke the world record with 4 min 12.2 sec, finishing 2.7 sec ahead of the East German Frank Wiegand, who swam for the combined German team.

The United States took 13 of the 18 swimming titles, but Australians won 3 of the 6 individual men's races. Bob Windle (1,500 metres freestyle), Ian O'Brien (200 metres breaststroke), and Kevin Berry (200 metres butterfly) saved Australia from a total rout, and Berry and O'Brien also set world records in winning.

The only European to win a gold medal was Galina Prosumenschikova from Moscow, who won Russia's first Olympic swimming gold, by leading the 200 metres breaststroke finalists home with a world record. And East Germany's Ingrid Engel-Kramer successfully defended her springboard diving title (Europe's only success in this field), but lost the highboard by 1.35 points to America's Lesley Bush.

In the water polo, Hungary won the gold medals for the third time in four games, but this time their victory came only as a result of their having a superior goal average to Yugoslavia. Completing a customary European sweep of the medals, the USSR were third.

Other Sports

Dominating the rowing on the Toda course, some 15 miles from Tokyo, was the Russian sculler Vyacheslav Ivanov. Champion in 1956 and 1960, he caused a sen-

1 Wyomia Tyus (217) leads the way in the 100 metres, but Ewa Klobukowska (166) had revenge in the relay, 2, in which she anchored Poland to victory with the USA second. 3 Mary Rand won a rare set of gold, silver, and bronze medals at the Tokyo Games. 4 Long-legged Iolanda Balas won the high jump by a 3¾-in. margin to win one of Romania's two athletics golds. 5 Triple gold medallist Dawn Fraser (left) and challenger Sharon Stouder pose after the 100 metres freestyle final.

sation in the heats by being beaten by America's Don Spero. But he fought back to win his repechage easily, and then in the final he finished nearly 4 seconds ahead of Germany's Achim Hill (as he had also done in 1960) to take his third straight gold medal. In the eights, the classic rowing event, Germany's crew, defending the title won by Ratzeburg at Rome, were beaten in a storming finish by America's Vesper Boat Club. Another man who won a third

gold medal was Hans Winkler, in Germany's grand prix show jumping team. In 1956 (when he also won the individual title) and 1960, Winkler had ridden Halla, but this time his gold medal was won on a new horse, Fidelitas. Even Winkler's achievement was overshadowed by that of the French veteran, Pierre d'Oriola. Olympic show jumping champion in 1952, he found a touch of genius to produce a clear round when it really mattered to take a second gold medal after a 12-year gap and also take his team into second place.

The Tokyo Olympics saw judo assume a place in the Olympic programme. It was suited to the Games not only because of the fact that Japan gave this sport to the world, but also because the sporting conventions of this combat make it ideal for the Olympic Games. And of course the Japanese were hoping that their champions would win them justly deserved gold medals. Although the home team won gold medals in the three restricted categories, they failed in their real objective—

to beat the giant Dutch world champion Anton Geesink. The Japanese hope, Kaminaga, had been drawn against Geesink in the preliminaries, and lost. But he fought his way through four more eliminations to enter the final. There, after 9 min 22 sec, the Japanese was pinned to the mat and Geesink took the gold medal to add to the world title he had won in 1961—again at Japan's expense.

But the Japanese enjoyed their share of success in, for them, other traditionally successful sports. In gymnastics, led by Yukio Endo, the Japanese won five out of the eight events—the team, combined exercises and parallel bars (Endo), rings (Takuji Hayata), and vault (Haruhiro Yamashita). Pushing the Japanese were the Russians, led by their veteran champion Boris Shakhlin who won the horizontal bar. The women's events were divided between the Russian girls and Czechoslovakia's Vera Caslavska. Vera won golds in the combined exercises, vault, and beam to be the Games outstanding individual

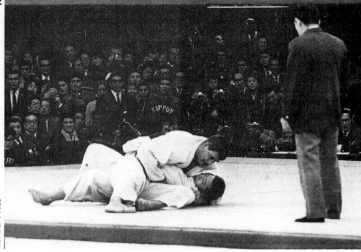

1 Pierre d'Oriola, champion in 1952, claimed his second individual show jumping gold medal and helped the French to win their first ever team medals—silvers—behind a German squad which included Hans Winkler, who was winning his third successive gold in the competition.

2 Giant Dutchman Anton Geesink mortified the Japanese by beating their judo champion Akio Kaminaga to win the unlimited category gold. 3 A new Olympic sport, volleyball, resulted in the USSR winning the men's competition and the highly trained Japanese the women's.

gymnast, but Russia won the team event for the fourth consecutive time.

In the wrestling events Japan's Osamu Watanbe won his 186th consecutive victory to take the freestyle featherweight title. Japan won four other gold medals, two freestyle and two Graeco-Roman, to emerge as the world's top wrestling nation.

For controversy, the boxing events took first prize. Two boxers were suspended (one for life) for assaulting, or trying to assault, referees who—they thought—did not come up to their own standards of judging. Another man sat in his corner for 51 minutes after being disqualified and would not be moved. In national terms, Poland and the USSR tied with three gold medals each. America's one gold medal winner was rather more significant: six years later Joe Frazier won the world's professional heavyweight title as well.

In the team sports the *status quo* prevailed. The United States once again went through the basketball tournament without losing a game, and Russia were second for the fourth consecutive Olympics, while Brazil were third, as they had been in Rome. In hockey, India regained the title they had lost in Rome, beating Pakistan 1-0 in the final. In Rome, Pakistan had won 1-0. Hungary, champions in 1952 won their second Olympic soccer title in grand style, with their ace forward Ferenc Bene scoring 12 goals to head the list of goalscorers. Hungary beat Czechoslovakia 2-1 in the final, and a combined Germany beat the United Arab Republic 3-1 in the play-off for third place.

Taking all sport into consideration, the USSR headed the medal table with 30 golds, 31 silver, and 35 bronze—a total of 96. The United States were relegated to second place with 90—no fewer than 37 of which had come in swimming. But as 41 countries won a medal of one sort or another, perhaps it was not such a 'two-horse race' after all.

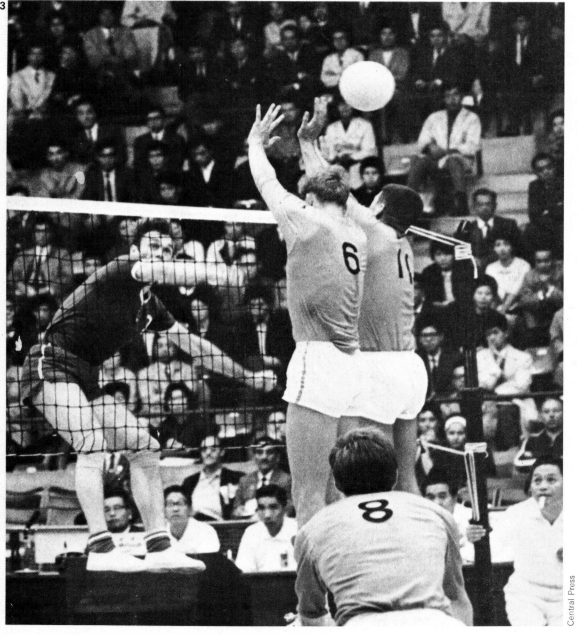

TOKYO OLYMPIC GAMES, 1964 Gold Medallists

Athletics—Men			
100 metres	Bob Hayes	USA	10.0 sec
200 metres	Henry Carr	USA	20.3 sec
400 metres	Mike Larrabee	USA	45.1 sec
800 metres	Peter Snell	New Zealand	1 min 45.1 sec
1,500 metres	Peter Snell	New Zealand	3 min 38.1 sec
5,000 metres	Bob Schul	USA	13 min 48.8 sec
10,000 metres	Billy Mills	USA	28 min 24.4 sec
Marathon	Abebe Bikila	Ethiopia	2 hr 12 min 11.2 sec
4 x 100 metres relay		USA	39.0 sec
4 x 400 metres relay		USA	3 min 0.7 sec
110 metres hurdles	Hayes Jones	USA	13.6 sec
400 metres hurdles	Warren Cawley	USA	49.6 sec
3,000 metres steeplechase	Gaston Roelants	Belgium	8 min 30.8 sec
20 kilometres walk	Ken Matthews	Great Britain	1 hr 29 min 34.0 sec
50 kilometres walk	Abdon Pamich	Italy	4 hr 11 min 12.4 sec
High jump	Valeriy Brumel	USSR	7 ft 1$\frac{3}{4}$ in
Pole vault	Fred Hansen	USA	16 ft 8$\frac{3}{4}$ in
Long jump	Lynn Davies	Great Britain	26 ft 5$\frac{3}{4}$ in
Triple jump	Jozef Schmidt	Poland	55 ft 3$\frac{1}{2}$ in
Shot	Dallas Long	USA	66 ft 8$\frac{1}{2}$ in
Discus	Al Oerter	USA	200 ft 1$\frac{1}{2}$ in
Hammer	Romuald Klim	USSR	228 ft 10$\frac{1}{2}$ in
Javelin	Pauli Nevala	Finland	271 ft 2$\frac{1}{2}$ in
Decathlon	Willi Holdorf	Germany	7,887 pts
Athletics—Women			
100 metres	Wyomia Tyus	USA	11.4 sec
200 metres	Edith McGuire	USA	23.0 sec
400 metres	Betty Cuthbert	Australia	52.0 sec
800 metres	Ann Packer	Great Britain	2 min 1.1 sec
4 x 100 metres relay		Poland	43.6 sec
80 metres hurdles	Karin Balzer	Germany	10.5 sec
High jump	Iolanda Balas	Romania	6 ft 2$\frac{3}{4}$ in
Long jump	Mary Rand	Great Britain	22 ft 2$\frac{1}{4}$ in
Shot	Tamara Press	USSR	59 ft 6 in
Discus	Tamara Press	USSR	187 ft 10$\frac{1}{2}$ in
Javelin	Mihaela Penes	Romania	198 ft 7$\frac{1}{2}$ in
Pentathlon	Irina Press	USSR	5,246 pts
Basketball		USA	
Boxing			
Flyweight	Fernando Otzori	Italy	
Bantamweight	Takao Sakurai	Japan	
Featherweight	Stanislav Stepashkin	USSR	
Lightweight	Jozef Grudzien	Poland	
Light-welterweight	Jerzy Kulej	Poland	
Welterweight	Marian Kasprzyk	Poland	
Light-middleweight	Boris Lagutin	USSR	
Middleweight	Valeriy Popenchenko	USSR	
Light-heavyweight	Cosimo Pinto	Italy	
Heavyweight	Joe Frazier	USA	
Canoeing			
1,000 metres—Men			
Kayak singles	Rolf Peterson	Sweden	3 min 57.13 sec
Kayak pairs	Sven Sjodelius, Gunnar Utterberg	Sweden	3 min 38.54 sec
Kayak fours		USSR	3 min 14.67 sec
Canadian singles	Jurgen Eschert	Germany	4 min 35.14 sec
Canadian pairs	Andrei Khimich, Stepan Oschepkov	USSR	4 min 4.65 sec
500 metres—Women			
Kayak singles	Ludmilla Khvedosink	USSR	2 min 12.87 sec
Kayak pairs	Roswitha Esser, Annemie Zimmermann	Germany	1 min 56.95 sec
Cycling			
1,000 metres sprint	Giovanni Pettenella	Italy	
1,000 metres time trial	Patrick Sercu	Belgium	1 min 9.59 sec
2,000 metres tandem	Sergio Bianchetto, Angelo Damanio	Italy	
4,000 metres pursuit	Jiri Daler	Czechoslovakia	5 min 4.75 sec
4,000 metres team pursuit		Germany	4 min 35.67 sec
Road team time trial (109.89 km)		Netherlands	2 hr 26 min 31.19 sec
Road race (194.83 km)	Mario Zanin	Italy	4 hr 39 min 51.63 sec
Equestrian			
Dressage—individual	Henri Chammartin	Switzerland	
—team		Germany	
Show jumping—individual	Pierre d'Oriola	France	
—team		Germany	
Three day event			
—individual	Mauro Checcoli	Italy	
—team		Italy	
Fencing—Men			
Foil —individual	Egon Franke	Poland	
—team		USSR	
Epee —individual	Grigory Kriss	USSR	
—team		Hungary	
Sabre —individual	Tibor Pezsa	Hungary	
—team		USSR	
Fencing—Women			
Foil —individual	Ildko Rejto	Hungary	
—team		Hungary	
Gymnastics—Men			
Combined exercises			
—individual	Yukio Endo	Japan	
—team		Japan	
Floor exercises	Franco Menicelli	Italy	
Horizontal bar	Boris Shakhlin	USSR	
Parallel bars	Yukio Endo	Japan	
Pommell horse	Miroslav Cerar	Yugoslavia	
Vault	Haruhiro Yamashita	Japan	
Rings	Takuji Hayata	Japan	
Gymnastics—Women			
Combined exercises			
—individual	Vera Caslavska	Czechoslovakia	
—team		USSR	
Floor exercises	Larissa Latynina	USSR	
Asymmetrical bars	Polina Astakhova	USSR	
Beam	Vera Caslavska	Czechoslovakia	
Vault	Vera Caslavska	Czechoslovakia	
Hockey		India	
Judo			
Lightweight	Takehide Nakatani	Japan	
Middleweight	Isao Okanao	Japan	
Heavyweight	Isao Inokuma	Japan	
Open division	Anton Geesink	Netherlands	
Modern Pentathlon			
Individual	Ferenc Toerek	Hungary	
Team		USSR	
Rowing			
Single sculls	Vyacheslav Ivanov	USSR	8 min 22.51 sec
Double sculls	Oleg Tyurin, Boris Dubrovsky	USSR	7 min 10.66 sec
Coxless pairs	George Hungerford, Roger Jackson	Canada	7 min 32.94 sec
Coxed pairs	Edward Ferry, Conn Findlay, Kent Mitchell (cox)	USA	8 min 21.33 sec
Coxless fours		Denmark	6 min 59.30 sec
Coxed fours		Germany	7 min 0.44 sec
Eights		USA	6 min 18.23 sec
Shooting			
Small bore rifle			
—three positions	Lones Wigger	USA	
—prone	Laszlo Hammerl		
Free pistol	Vaino Markkanen	Finland	
Free rifle	Gary Anderson	USA	
Rapid fire pistol	Pentti Linnosvuop	Finland	
Clay pigeon	Ennio Mattarelli	Italy	
Soccer		Hungary	
Swimming—Men			
100 metres freestyle	Don Schollander	USA	53.4 sec
400 metres freestyle	Don Schollander	USA	4 min 12.2 sec
1,500 metres freestyle	Bob Windle	Australia	17 min 1.7 sec
200 metres breaststroke	Ian O'Brien	Australia	2 min 27.8 sec
200 metres butterfly	Kevin Berry	Australia	2 min 6.6 sec
200 metres backstroke	Jed Graef	USA	2 min 10.3 sec
400 metres individual medley	Dick Roth	USA	4 min 45.4 sec
4 x 100 metres freestyle relay		USA	3 min 33.2 sec
4 x 200 metres freestyle relay		USA	7 min 52.1 sec
4 x 100 metres medley relay		USA	3 min 58.4 sec
Springboard diving	Ken Sitzberger	USA	
Highboard diving	Bob Webster	USA	
Swimming—Women			
100 metres freestyle	Dawn Fraser	Australia	59.5 sec
400 metres freestyle	Ginny Duenkel	USA	4 min 43.3 sec
200 metres breaststroke	Galina Prozumenschikova	USSR	2 min 46.4 sec
100 metres butterfly	Sharon Stouder	USA	1 min 4.7 sec
100 metres backstroke	Cathie Ferguson	USA	1 min 7.7 sec
400 metres individual medley	Donna de Varona	USA	5 min 18.7 sec
4 x 100 metres freestyle relay		USA	4 min 3.8 sec
4 x 100 metres medley relay		USA	4 min 33.9 sec
Springboard diving	Ingrid Engel-Kramer	Germany	
Highboard diving	Lesley Bush	USA	
Volleyball—Men		USSR	
Volleyball—Women		Japan	
Water Polo		Hungary	
Weightlifting			
Bantamweight	Alexey Vakhonin	USSR	787$\frac{3}{4}$ lb
Featherweight	Yoshinobu Miyake	Japan	876 lb
Lightweight	Waldemar Baszanowski	Poland	953$\frac{1}{4}$ lb
Middleweight	Hans Zdrazila	Czechoslovakia	980$\frac{3}{4}$ lb
Light-heavyweight	Rudolf Plyukeider	USSR	1,046 lb
Mid-heavyweight	Vladimir Golovanov	USSR	1,074$\frac{1}{2}$ lb
Heavyweight	Leonid Zhabotinsky	USSR	1,262 lb
Wrestling			
Freestyle			
Flyweight	Yoshikatsu Yoshida	Japan	
Bantamweight	Yojiro Uetake	Japan	
Featherweight	Osamu Watanabe	Japan	
Lightweight	Enio Dimor	Bulgaria	
Welterweight	Ismail Ogan	Turkey	
Middleweight	Prodan Gardjer	Bulgaria	
Light-heavyweight	Alexandr Medved	USSR	
Heavyweight	Alexandr Wanitsky	USSR	
Graeco-Roman			
Flyweight	Tsutomu Hanahara	Japan	
Bantamweight	Masamitsu Ichiguchi	Japan	
Featherweight	Imre Polyak	Hungary	
Lightweight	Kazim Ayvaz	Turkey	
Welterweight	Anatoly Koleslav	USSR	
Middleweight	Branislav Simic	Yugoslavia	
Light-heavyweight	Boyan Alexandrov	Bulgaria	
Heavyweight	Istvan Kozma	Hungary	
Yachting			
Finn	Willi Kuhweide	Germany	
Star	D. Knowles, C. Cook	Bahamas	
Flying Dutchman	Helman Pederson, E. Wells	New Zealand	
5.5 metres		Australia	
Dragon		Denmark	

One of the truly outstanding sports photos captures the power and determination that won America's Willie Davenport his gold medal in the 110 metres hurdles at Mexico City.

Mexico City Olympic Games (1968)

Politics, sex, commercialism . . . and sport—these four topics dominated the Games of the XIXth Olympiad held in Mexico City in October 1968, the most controversial Olympics ever.

The most argued-about decision was to hold the Games in Mexico City at all. The capital of Mexico is situated some 7,347 feet above sea level, a height at which the air is so rarefied that a man normally living at sea level may take more than a month to become used simply to living there. For an athlete, the time required to acclimatize for events lasting more than one and a half minutes is longer than a month.

The decision to award the Games to Mexico City was made at the 1963 meeting of the IOC in Baden-Baden. It excited no special comment at first and the IOC must have thought it a progressive step to hold the Games in one of the more developed Latin-American countries. But in 1964, Onni Niskanen, the Swedish coach to Abebe Bikila, brought the issue to a head when he stated quite bluntly: 'There will be those who will die.'

The altitude issue was quite straightforward. Lowland athletes in any endurance event would have to get used to competing in a rarified atmosphere. Some athletes, such as Mexicans, Kenyans, and Ethiopians, already lived in such conditions. For the rest of the

world there was the choice between competing at a grave disadvantage or breaking the IOC's rule that no competitor could train at high altitudes for more than four weeks in the three months preceding the Games. The French built a high-altitude sports centre at Font Romeu in the Pyrenees. The town of South Lake Tahoe built the United States team a training centre at a height of 6,000 feet in Nevada, where the team trained as part of the 'South Lake Tahoe United States Olympic Medical and Testing Program'.

In addition to the altitude controversy, there was another cloud on the Olympic scene—the world of power politics. In August 1968, the invasion of Czechoslo-

Enriqueta Basilio holds the Olympic torch aloft after igniting the flame—the first woman in the history of the Olympic Games to do so.

vakia by the armies of the Warsaw Pact countries to suppress the liberal Dubcek regime cast a dark shadow over the Games.

The IOC was itself very concerned with the increasing commercialization of the Olympic movement. In Mexico, the markings on running shoes was their chief cause for concern, mainly because some athletes were known to wear the distinctively marked shoes of two German companies only if they were paid to do so. But there was nothing the IAAF or the

IOC could do about it.

Even the internal conditions in Mexico did not augur well. Violent riots broke out before the Games opened, and were ruthlessly repressed. The state of public order made it uncertain that the Games would take place at all. But eventually, and in time for the Olympics to begin, Mexico City was quiet again.

The Games were formally opened on October 12, with troops arranged in force outside the new Olympic Stadium. Diaz Ordaz, the Mexican President, and IOC president Avery Brundage made the speeches, and for the first time, a woman—Enriqueta Basilio, who ran for Mexico in the 400 metres—lit the Olympic flame.

Athletics—Men

By tradition, the men's 10,000 metres was held as a final on the first day of the athletics events, and the fears of the world's lowland distance runners were confirmed in this event. The winner's time— 29 min 27.4 sec—was 1 min 48 sec slower than Ron Clarke's world record, and a slow time for even the most tactical of races. The early pace was easy, sensibly so at this altitude, but it would have been funereal at sea level. And so it continued for the first 8,400 metres. Then, with four laps to go, the pace suddenly hotted up. Seven men broke away—Kenya's Naftali Temu and Kipchoge Keino, Australia's Ron Clarke, Tunisia's Mohamed Gammoudi, the hero of the Mexico crowd Juan Martinez, Russia's Nikolai Sviridov, and Mamo Wolde of Ethiopia. Of these, only Ron Clarke was not born or domiciled at a high altitude but he had lived for some time at Font Romeu. Wolde, Temu, Keino, and Martinez actually live at altitude, and Gammoudi and Sviridov were known to have trained for months in the highlands.

Clarke himself was eventually dropped by the other six, and Keino dropped out, suffering from a stomach complaint. With only two laps left Temu and Wolde accelerated, dragging Gammoudi with them, Wolde leading this sudden rush because of his lack of a finishing sprint. But Temu held on and sprinted ahead in the straight to win by 0.6 sec from Wolde, with a well-beaten Gammoudi just holding off Martinez for third place. It was a gripping struggle between great runners, none of whom was prepared to let up for a moment, and yet it lost much of its meaning because of the effects of the altitude. Ron Clarke collapsed after finishing 6th and was given oxygen by the Australian team doctor. Jurgen Haase, the European champion, finished 15th. Even Russia's Leonid Mikityenko, the fifth fastest man in the world in 1968, was relegated to 17th position. Their times were, of course, much slower than their best performances at a lower altitude. The only lowlander who was at all prominent was Britain's Ron Hill, who had for a moment led the field to show that he was not in Mexico just for a ride, and he finished 7th.

It was the same story in the 5,000 metres and the steeplechase. The first four men in the 5,000 metres—Gammoudi, Keino, Temu, and Martinez—and the first two in the steeplechase— Amos Biwott and Benjamin Kogo (both of Kenya)—were altitude men. The 5,000 metres was won by Gammoudi from Keino in a desperate sprint finish. Gammoudi's last 400-metre lap took him only 54.8 sec, an indication of the overall slowness of the race. Eight of the first nine places were filled by men with experience of high altitudes, gained either at home or in special training camps.

In the 3,000 metres steeplechase, runners whose performances before the Games would have made them hot favourites for medals were unceremoniously eliminated in the heats, while less experienced — and slower — 'highlanders' qualified. The Tokyo silver medallist, Britain's Maurice Herriott, was put out with a heat time of 9 min 33.0 sec, over a minute slower than his best sea-level time. And the final was perhaps one of the most bizarre Olympic races ever. The Kenyan team included a peculiar runner named Amos Biwott. He had the most rudimentary style of hurdling, and would make every effort to avoid putting his feet in the water jump. He had little idea of tactics, and with a lap to go was 30 yards behind the leaders. As his team-mate Ben Kogo, America's George Young, Australia's Kerry O'Brien, the defending champion from Belgium, Gaston Roelants, and Russia's Viktor Kudinskiy battled for the major prizes—or so they thought—Biwott suddenly tore past them all to win by five yards in 8 min 51.0 sec.

The marked advantages of the highlanders were not so apparent in the other endurance events on the track and road. True, Mamo Wolde won the marathon, but he was followed by other men without vast altitude experience. Second to Wolde was Kenji Kimihara of Japan, 3rd New Zealand's Mike Ryan, 4th Ismail Akcay of Turkey, 5th Britain's Bill Adcocks, and 6th Merawi Gebru of Ethiopia. But what of the great Abebe Bikila, who had threatened to win his third Olympic marathon? He had been suffering from a leg injury and in fact retired after 17 of the 42 kilometres. In the walks, the 'highland' countries had never been a force to be reckoned with, and their only medal came through José Padraza of Mexico in the 20 kilometres. He entered the stadium third, close behind two Russians— Vladimir Golubnichiy and Nikolai Smaga. Experienced commentators were unanimous in their view that if ever a man ran in a walking race, Pedraza did on the last hectic lap of the Olympic stadium. First he cut down Smaga in the back straight, and then he went after Golubnichiy. But the experienced

Mexico's Juan Martinez leads the 10,000 metres field. Ron Clarke is second, with the eventual winner Naftali Temu of Kenya (No. 575) on his shoulder. 'High-altitude men' dominated the 5,000 and 10,000 metres events.

Rex Features

Britain's only athletics gold at Mexico City
came in the 400 metres hurdles, when David
Hemery, here working out over the high
hurdles, simply annihilated his opposition to
win in a world record 48.1 sec, 0.7 sec faster
than the previous record.

Kenya's Kipchoge Keino, gold medallist in the Mexico City 1,500 metres and the torch-bearer of black Africa's dramatic entry on to the sports fields of the world.

Russian held him off to claim his second Olympic title in this event. The 50 kilometres was won, as expected, by East Germany's Christoph Hohne—by over 10 minutes from Hungary's Antal Kiss.

In the 1,500 metres, the front-running tactics of Kenya's Kip Keino and the finishing burst of world record holder Jim Ryun were expected to produce the Games' greatest race. Ryun had been suffering from glandular fever early in the year, but he expected to be able to win with a time in the region of 3 min 38 sec. He did not reckon with the form of Keino, who ran one of his best races despite having already run in the 10,000 and 5,000 metres. Keino's team-mate Ben Jipcho set a fast early pace, passing 400 metres in 56.0 sec, and Keino then took over to pass 800 metres in 1 min 55.3 sec, a fast pace even at sea level. Keino continued to pour on the pressure and was well ahead at 1,200 metres. Ryun, then, at last, began to move, but despite his last 400 metres in 55.7 sec was never a danger to the brave Kenyan who eventually beat him by about 20 yards. Here was a case of the highland runner beating the sea level man entirely on merits. Keino's time—3 min 34.9 sec—was the second fastest ever.

A Kenyan also took second place in the 800 metres, which was the real meeting point between the highland and lowland runner. The winner here was Australia's Ralph Doubell, and he equalled the world record of 1 min 44.3 sec in beating Kenya's Wilson Kiprugut by 0.2 sec.

If the distance runners suffered from the altitude, whatever their origin, the sprinters came into their own in the thin air. And the United States, whose only middle- and long-distance honours had been bronzes in the 800 metres and 50-kilometre walk, swept up 9 of the 11 medals open to them in the 100, 200, and 400 metres, and the two relays. Jim Hines equalled the world record of 9.9 sec in the 100 metres, and Lee Evans chopped 0.3 sec off the world record in the 400 metres. American quartets set new world marks in both relays, and averaged just over 44 sec apiece in the 4 by 400 metres.

The talking point of the sprints was the victory of Tommie Smith in the 200 metres. He won easily in 19.8 sec—a world record—from Australia's Peter Norman and his fellow-American Negro John Carlos. It was a beautiful run, with no inhibitions, and once the long-legged Smith had got into his stride he was clearly the only man in the race. But the aftermath of the race was the victory ceremony, which is the most notorious incident of its kind in the history of the Games. Smith and Carlos walked to the rostrum clad in official United States tracksuits, embellished with

a badge of the Olympic Project for Human Rights. Smith wore a black leather glove on his right hand, Carlos one on his left. Both carried an easily identified running shoe. They received their medals with dignity from Lord Burghley, and turned to face the flags of their country as the national anthem was played. Then they raised their gloved hands in the 'black power' salute and bowed their heads. The crowd was taken aback, and some elements began booing and whistling. Smith explained his motive simply and succinctly: it was only through running that he could approach the prestige of any white American. 'If I win I am an American, not a black American. But if I did something bad then they would say a Negro.' Both Smith and Carlos were sent home.

The United States retained their grip on the high hurdles title, which American athletes had won in 13 of the 15 previous Games. Willie Davenport more than made up for his disappointing showing in the 1964 Games (when eliminated in his semi-final) by winning in an Olympic record of 13.3 sec. The 400 metres hurdles title was expected to go to the United States, where it had remained since 1936. But the Americans had played host to Britain's Dave Hemery at Boston University since 1964, and during his stay there he had matured from being a fair 110 metres hurdler to a good 400 metres man —just how good had to be put to the test. And although the Americans had been prominent in the preliminary rounds, British observers could see Hemery holding himself back. In the final, Hemery appeared to be in the lead from the first barrier onwards, and won by seven yards in a world and Olympic record of 48.1 sec, 0.7 sec faster than Geoff Vanderstock's world record set in the United States trials at Lake Tahoe. Second in 49.0 sec, was West Germany's Gerhard Hennige, and third—in the same time—Britain's John Sherwood.

In the tense, but less immediate, world of the field events some remarkable happenings were taking place, including perhaps the most amazing single performance in the history of athletics. In the long jump, Bob Beamon, with his first effort—and the first 'legal' jump of the final rounds—soared to a world record of 29 ft. 2½ in., 21 inches farther than the previous best. It killed the event as a competition, but provided a talking point for years to come. And if the triple jump record was not improved by such a vast margin, the fact that no fewer than five improvements were made in the world mark is a testimony to the keen competition and the helpful effects of the thin air. Giuseppe Gentile of Italy started the ball rolling with the first world mark—56 ft. 1¼ in.— in the qualifying rounds. And in

the final the next day, his first jump was another world record— 56 ft. 6 in. It was short-lived, however, as in the third round Viktor Saneyev of the USSR added a centimetre to Gentile's mark (56 ft. 6¼ in.). The title looked set to go to Brazil after the fifth round, in which Nelson Prudencio reached 56 ft. 8 in. Yet Saneyev reacted to the Brazilian's effort with a hop, step, and jump of 57 ft. 0¾ in. with his final jump to snatch the gold.

If no records fell in the pole vault, this did not stop the event being one of the most exciting ever held, with the United States desperately close to losing their record of having won every Olympic pole vault. The first three men, Bob Seagren (United States), Claus Schiprowski (West Germany) and Wolfgang Nordwig (East Germany), tied, each with a clearance of 17 ft. 8½ in. They were placed in that order on the 'count-back' rule. The competition lasted 7½ hours, and was continually interrupted by victory ceremonies, including that of the 200 metres.

For sheer individualism, the winner of the high jump, Dick Fosbury of the United States, took the prize. Using his personal back lay-out style, he would run flat out up to the bar, turn onto his back, and land on his shoulders on the inflated mattress in the pit. He delighted the capacity crowd with his display, and emerged a clear winner: he was the only man to jump 2.24 metres (7 ft. 4¼ in.).

The most acclaimed feat in the throwing events was the victory of Al Oerter in the discus.

Champion three times before—in 1956, 1960, and 1964—this remarkable man, whose best throw before the Games in 1968 was 205 ft. 10 in.—far inferior to his compatriot Jay Silvester's world record of 224 ft. 5 in.—unleashed his best ever throw of 212 ft. 6½ in. to win the title from men who before the Games had been his superiors.

Silvester was completely unnerved by Oerter's competitiveness, and finished fifth with 202 ft. 8 in., and nobody else could rival the veteran Long Islander.

Randy Matson duly added the Mexico City gold to his Tokyo silver in the shot. And in the hammer, Gyula Zsivotsky brought his career to a wonderful climax by adding a gold to the silvers he had won in Rome and Tokyo. After a ding-dong battle with his perennial rival Romuald Klim, Zsivotsky reached his winning distance of 240 ft. 8 in. in the fifth round to win by 3 inches.

Janis Lusis, Russia's world record holder, added the Olympic javelin gold to his two European championships with a winning effort of 295 ft. 7 in. In the decathlon, Bill Toomey of the United States beat West Germany's Hans Joachim Walde by 82 points with a total score of 8,193 pts. Toomey dominated the first day's events— his 400 metres of 45.6 sec earned him 1,021 pts—to lead at the halfway stage by 4,499 pts to 4,384 over East Germany's Joachim Kirst, and held on to his advantage to beat the fast-finishing Walde by a relatively scant margin.

MEXICO CITY OLYMPIC GAMES, 1968 Gold Medallists—Athletics			
Men			
100 metres	Jim Hines	USA	9.9 sec
200 metres	Tommie Smith	USA	19.8 sec
400 metres	Lee Evans	USA	43.8 sec
800 metres	Ralph Doubell	Australia	1 min 44.3 sec
1,500 metres	Kipchoge Keino	Kenya	3 min 34.9 sec
5,000 metres	Mohamed Gammoudi	Tunisia	14 min 5.0 sec
10,000 metres	Naftali Temu	Kenya	29 min 27.4 sec
Marathon	Mamo Wolde	Ethiopia	2 hr 20 min 26.4 sec
4 x 100 metres relay		USA	38.2 sec
4 x 400 metres relay		USA	2 min 56.1 sec
110 metres hurdles	Willie Davenport	USA	13.3 sec
400 metres hurdles	David Hemery	Great Britain	48.1 sec
3,000 metres steeplechase	Amos Biwott	Kenya	8 min 51.0 sec
20 kilometres walk	Viktor Golubnichiy	USSR	1 hr 33 min 58.4 sec
50 kilometres walk	Christoph Hohne	East Germany	4 hr 20 min 13.6 sec
High jump	Dick Fosbury	USA	7 ft 4¼ in
Pole vault	Bob Seagren	USA	17 ft 8½ in
Long jump	Bob Beamon	USA	29 ft 2½ in
Triple jump	Viktor Saneyev	USSR	57 ft 0¾ in
Shot	Randy Matson	USA	67 ft 4¾ in
Discus	Al Oerter	USA	212 ft 6½ in
Hammer	Gyula Zsivotsky	Hungary	240 ft 8 in
Javelin	Janis Lusis	USSR	295 ft 7 in
Decathlon	Bill Toomey	USA	8,193 pts
Women			
100 metres	Wyomia Tyus	USA	11.0 sec
200 metres	Irena Szewinska	Poland	22.5 sec
400 metres	Colette Besson	France	52.0 sec
800 metres	Madeline Manning	USA	2 min 0.9 sec
4 x 100 metres relay		USA	42.8 sec
80 metres hurdles	Maureen Caird	Australia	10.3 sec
High jump	Miroslava Rezkova	Czechoslovakia	5 ft 11¾ in
Long jump	Viorica Viscopoleanu	Romania	22 ft 4½ in
Shot	Margit Gummel	East Germany	64 ft 4 in
Discus	Lia Manoliu	Romania	191 ft 2½ in
Javelin	Angela Nemeth	Hungary	198 ft 0½ in
Pentathlon	Ingrid Becker	West Germany	5,098 pts

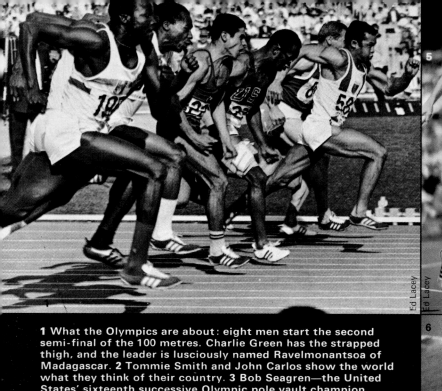

1 What the Olympics are about: eight men start the second semi-final of the 100 metres. Charlie Green has the strapped thigh, and the leader is lusciously named Ravelmonantsoa of Madagascar. 2 Tommie Smith and John Carlos show the world what they think of their country. 3 Bob Seagren—the United States' sixteenth successive Olympic pole vault champion. 4 David Hemery clears the penultimate hurdle well ahead of the field. 5 Poland (left), Britain (centre) and the Ivory Coast contest the minor placings in the first 4 x 100 metres relay semi-final. 6 His lungs burning from lack of air, an exhausted runner breathes in much needed oxygen after competing—a familiar sight in the athletics area at Mexico City. 7 Tommie Smith (in the black socks) strides to victory in the second heat of the 200 metres. 8 Individualism triumphs yet again—Dick Fosbury 'flops' in the high jump. 9 Even the lowliest finisher gave his all—Perera of Ceylon, after coming 51st in the marathon. 10 Heat 1 of the 400 metres hurdles: West Germany's Gerhard Hennige (16) leads Geoff Vanderstock of America (312), and Russia's deaf-mute Vyacheslav Skomorokhov (828). 11 Thirty-seven men started the 50-km walk, and 28 finished. Paul Nihill (centre) was one of those forced to drop out.

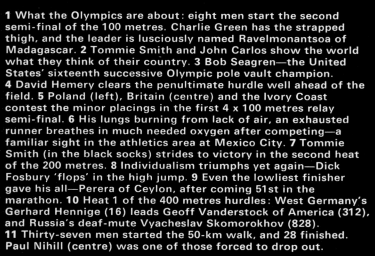

Athletics—Women

For the first time, sex tests for women were held at an Olympic Games. And although they had been used in the Asian and Commonwealth Games and in the 1966 European athletics championships, with embarrassing results for some, there was no such incident in Mexico City. This, at least, was a happy omen for world sport.

Three 1964 champions defended their titles—Wyomia Tyus in the 100 metres, Karin Balzer in the 80 metres hurdles, and Mihaela Penes in the javelin. Of these, only Miss Tyus was successful, and she thus became the first sprinter—man or woman—to retain the 100 metres crown. She won by 0.1 sec from her compatriot Barbara Ferrell in a world record of 11.0 sec. Third was Irena Kirszenstein-Szewinska, who had equalled the old world record of 11.1 sec in the second round.

Mrs Szewinska claimed the 200 metres gold medal with a world record run of 22.5 sec, 0.2 faster than her own existing record. She was a clear winner from two young Australian girls, Raelene Boyle and Jennifer Lamy. The American team won the 4 by 100 metres relay, and set two world records in that event during the Games. They won their heat in a record 43.4 sec, and saw it equalled by the Netherlands in the second heat. But in the final they improved to 42.8 sec, with a well-drilled Cuban quartet second in 43.3 sec.

There had been no hotter favourite before the Games than Britain's Lillian Board in the 400 metres. This burden—foisted on her largely by the British press—undoubtedly affected her running. She was warned by the judges for not having her feet in contact with the ground at the start, but led by a few yards as the field entered the home straight. She was visibly tiring, and was caught on the line by a little-known French girl, Colette Besson, who equalled the Olympic record of 52.0 sec. Miss Board, aged only 19, set a national record of 52.1 sec to take the silver medal.

In the 800 metres, the world record holder Vera Nikolic of Yugoslavia had impressed observers in training, but when she competed it was clear she was not in the peak of condition. She won her heat easily enough in 2 min 5.7 sec, but in her semi-final she ran off the track after 300 metres. The girl was certainly upset, and it was said she tried to commit suicide after the race. But what was more certain was that she had been called upon to carry too great a burden, mentally and physically. She was training even on the morning of her semi-final. The absence of this fine runner who had set her world record of 2 min 0.5 sec in the British championships earlier in the year rendered the final a little anti-climatic, but this could not detract from the fine running of Madeline

Above, **Wyomia Tyus is well ahead as she receives the baton from Mildrette Netter and takes the United States to victory in the women's relay, with Cuba (third from outside) second.**

Ed Lacey

1 Margitta Lange claimed the silver medal in the women's shot behind her team-mate Margit Gummel. 2 Madeline Manning wins the 800 metres from Ileana Silai of Romania (215—2nd) and the Netherland's Mia Gommers (148—3rd) in 2 min 0.9 sec.

Manning of the United States. After Romania's Ileana Silai had set the pace through the first lap (59.1 sec), Miss Manning broke away around the final bend to win in 2 min 0.9 sec—the third fastest time ever recorded.

The hurdles, too, provided an upset of form. Russia's new world record holder, Vera Korsakova, did not even reach the final, and the defending champion, Karin Balzer, was placed fifth. Maureen Caird, a 17-year-old from New South Wales, led from start to finish to defeat her more experienced team-mate Pam Kilborn. Miss Caird thus became the youngest Olympic athletics champion ever.

With recent memories of the Russian invasion of Czechoslovakia still fresh, there was no more popular winner than Milena Rezkova in the high jump. Miss Rezkova had to clear the final height—5 ft. 11¾ in.—to win, because her opponents, Russia's Antonina Okorokova had a sup-

erior record at lower heights. But the Czech girl, 18 years old and 5 ft. 6½ in. tall, went over to the delight of the crowd with her final try, leaving the two Russians to pick up the place medals.

Mexico City must have been the favourite venue of long jumpers. The world record was broken in the women's event as well, by Romania's Viorica Viscopoleanu. She cleared 22 ft. 4½ in. with her first jump in the final rounds to clinch the title. Britain gained a silver medal in this event through Sheila Sherwood, wife of the 400 metres hurdles bronze medallist.

The gold medals in the three throwing events went behind the Iron Curtain. The shot was a complete triumph for the East Germans Margit Gummel and Margitta Lange. Miss Gummel set two world records in Mexico City, 62 ft. 6¾ in. and 64 ft. 4 in., and won by a clear margin from her team-mate, whose best effort was 61 ft. 7½ in. Mihaela Penes,

the defending champion, lost her javelin title to Hungary's Angela Nemeth. Miss Penes started well with a throw of 196 ft. 7 in., but the Hungarian girl came through in the second round with 198 ft. 0½ in. to make sure of the gold. The win of Lia Manoliu in the discus was a triumph for perseverance. This 36-year-old engineer from Bucharest was competing in her fifth Olympic Games, and had been third twice, in 1960 and 1964. She was the only thrower to overcome the wet conditions, and although her winning throw of 191 ft. 2½ in. was over 10 feet less than the world record, it was more than her rivals, better throwers on paper, could manage.

West German Ingrid Becker's score of 5,098 points in the pentathlon could not match the Olympic and world record of 5,246 set by Irina Press in the Tokyo Olympics, but it was enough to beat Austria's Liese Prokop by 132 points. Miss Becker overtook her rival on the last event, the 200 metres, which she ran in 23.5 sec, worth 1,077 points, while the Austrian could achieve only 25.1 sec (923 points).

1 Debbie Meyer was hailed as Olympic champion three times in the swimming events—in the 200, 400, and 800 metres freestyle.
2 The start of the men's 100 metres freestyle. Winner Mike Wenden of Australia (in 52.2 sec—a world record) is in lane 4. Zac Zorn of America (lane 5) took an early lead, but made his effort too soon and finished 8th. Britain's Bobby McGregor, the only survivor from the Tokyo final, is in lane 6 and came 4th.
3 All action in the water polo, won by Yugoslavia.

MEXICO CITY OLYMPIC GAMES, 1968 Gold Medallists—Swimming

Men

100 metres freestyle	Mike Wenden	Australia	52.2 sec
200 metres freestyle	Mike Wenden	Australia	1 min 55.2 sec
400 metres freestyle	Mike Burton	USA	4 min 9.0 sec
1,500 metres freestyle	Mike Burton	USA	16 min 38.9 sec
100 metres breaststroke	Don McKenzie	USA	1 min 7.7 sec
200 metres breaststroke	Felipe Munoz	Mexico	2 min 28.7 sec
100 metres butterfly	Doug Russell	USA	55.9 sec
200 metres butterfly	Carl Robie	USA	2 min 8.7 sec
100 metres backstroke	Roland Matthes	East Germany	58.7 sec
200 metres backstroke	Roland Matthes	East Germany	2 min 9.6 sec
200 metres individual medley	Charles Hickcox	USA	2 min 12.0 sec
400 metres individual medley	Charles Hickcox	USA	4 min 48.4 sec
4 x 100 metres freestyle relay		USA	3 min 31.7 sec
4 x 200 metres freestyle relay		USA	7 min 52.3 sec
4 x 100 metres medley relay		USA	3 min 54.9 sec
Springboard diving	Bernie Wrightson	USA	
Highboard diving	Klaus Dibiasi	Italy	

Women

100 metres freestyle	Jan Henne	USA	1 min 0.0 sec
200 metres freestyle	Debbie Meyer	USA	2 min 10.5 sec
400 metres freestyle	Debbie Meyer	USA	4 min 31.8 sec
800 metres freestyle	Debbie Meyer	USA	9 min 24.0 sec
100 metres breaststroke	Djurdjica Bjedov	Yugoslavia	1 min 15.8 sec
200 metres breaststroke	Sharon Wichman	USA	2 min 44.4 sec
100 metres butterfly	Lyn McClements	Australia	1 min 5.5 sec
200 metres butterfly	Ada Kok	Netherlands	2 min 24.7 sec
100 metres backstroke	Kaye Hall	USA	1 min 6.2 sec
200 metres backstroke	Pokey Watson	USA	2 min 24.8 sec
200 metres individual medley	Claudia Kolb	USA	2 min 24.7 sec
400 metres individual medley	Claudia Kolb	USA	5 min 8.5 sec
4 x 100 metres freestyle relay		USA	4 min 2.5 sec
4 x 100 metres medley relay		USA	4 min 28.3 sec
Springboard diving	Sue Gossick	USA	
Highboard diving	Milena Duchkova	Czechoslovakia	
Water Polo		Yugoslavia	

Swimming

The pre-Olympic spotlight was not focused on the problems of altitude in relation to swimming. Yet it was in the pool that there were many collapses, in a sport for which post-racing distress is the exception and not the rule. The most dramatic incident concerned America's John Ferris, the bronze medallist in the 200 metres individual medley. He had to be supported during the medal presentation ceremony by the winner, his team-mate Charles Hickcox, and fell to the ground at the foot of the rostrum as soon as the presentations were over. Oxygen was needed to revive him, and he later fainted again during the medal winners' interview and had to have more oxygen.

It was not only the altitude

that affected the results. A stomach virus infection—'Montezuma's revenge'—also claimed many victims. They included America's Catie Ball, holder of all the world breaststroke records. She lost 10 lb in weight, was relegated to fifth place in the 100 metres breaststroke, and was too ill even to start in the heats of the 200 metres. But others — including Djurdijca Bjedov, the shock winner of the 100 metres breaststroke and Yugoslavia's first individual swimming medallist—were completely unaffected by the conditions.

The combination of these factors affected the general level of performance, and only three individual world records were broken during the 29-event swimming programme. Australia's Mike Wenden claimed one, in winning the 100 metres freestyle in 52.2 sec. Kaye Hall of the United States trimmed the women's 100 metres backstroke mark to 66.2 sec. And Roland Matthes swam the first leg—100 metres backstroke—in East Germany's medley relay squad in 58.0 sec.

Backstroker Matthes, who won both individual battles, was one of the outstanding competitors in

Mexico City, and his apparently effortless successes were among the highlights of the Games. Three other men won two individual titles—Mike Wenden the 100 and 200 metres freestyle, Mike Burton the 400 and 1,500 metres freestyle, and Charles Hickcox the 200 and 400 metres individual medley.

But the swimmer who won most gold medals was America's Debbie Meyer. Helped by the introduction of two new events in the programme, she became the first swimmer to win three individual titles—all for freestyle—at the same Games. She took 11½ seconds off the 1964 Olympic record in the 400 metres and also won the newly instituted 200 and 800 metres. Her team-mate Claudia Kolb won two titles, the

200 and 400 metres individual medley, to add two golds to the silver she had won in the Tokyo 200 metres breaststroke.

The United States, in fact, dominated the swimming section of the Games, winning 10 of a possible 15 men's titles, and 11 of a possible 14 women's. Don Schollander, the quadruple gold medallist at Tokyo in 1964, could not qualify for the American team to defend his 100 and 400 metres titles, but was in the 200 metres, and finished second behind Wenden. Britain's only medal in the pool came through Martyn Woodroffe, who shocked everyone by splitting America's Carl Robie and John Ferris to win the silver in the 200 metres butterfly.

Both the springboard diving titles went to America, but the highboard crowns went to countries who had never before claimed an individual title in the pool. Italy's Klaus Dibiasi won the men's, and Czechoslovakia's Milena Duchkova beat her Russian rival Natalia Lobanova by 4.45 marks in the women's, only two months after Russian troops had entered her home city of Prague.

The Russian invasion of Czecho-slovakia had meant that many Czechoslovak sportsmen and women had to curtail their preparation for the Games, none more than Vera Caslavska, the blonde gymnast who had gathered three gold medals at the 1964 Olympic Games. But once she arrived in Mexico the stresses of the invasion were behind her. Miss Caslavska turned on immaculate performances to win the combined exercises title by 1.40 points and two of the four individual events—the vault and the asymmetrical bars—outright, tie for first place in the floor exercises and gain silver medals in the beam and the team events. After the Games she married the Czech middle-distance runner Josef Odlozil, the 1,500 metres silver medallist in 1964.

There was no such outstanding performer in the men's events, but Miroslav Cerar, the Yugoslav pommel horse expert, staked a claim as one of the most consistent gymnasts ever. He maintained an unbeaten record in world and Olympic events on this apparatus which had lasted from 1962. In national terms, the Japanese challenge to the supremacy of the Russians was the outstanding feature. They won five of the eight titles at stake, tied for another, and won 12 of a possible 22 medals.

It was expected that the United States might, after taking all six previous titles, lose the basketball event at last. But despite losing many of their top college players to the professional ranks, the Americans proved to be unbeatable. The Russians, four times winners of the silver medals, went down narrowly to the Yugoslavs—63-62—and had to settle for the bronzes.

India, who had never failed to finish first or second in the hockey, were surprisingly beaten 2-1 by Australia in the semi-finals. Australia met Pakistan in the final, and despite at one stage holding the Asians to 1-1, they were eventually beaten 2-1. India beat West Germany 2-1 for the bronze medals, but must have been far from satisfied with their performance.

The Japanese women, who had been so outstanding in winning the volleyball golds in Tokyo, were this time without the services of their legendary coach Hirofumi Daimatsu, and they succumbed to the power of the Russian women, whose men also won their event. But Japan, not a traditional power in the sport, won the bronze medals in soccer, thanks largely to the efforts of their tall striker Kunigishe Kamamoto. They beat Mexico 2-0 in the third place match, both goals coming from Kamamoto. In the final Hungary beat Bulgaria 4-1. No fewer than four players were sent off in this game by the referee, three

Morley L. Pecker

Bulgarians and one Hungarian, and the Mexican fans showed their disapproval by showering the field with cushions. This tournament, the customary blooding ground of many Iron Curtain players for the harsher tests of the World Cup, was played in the venues of the 1970 World Cup tournament, and the success of the World Cup organization was in no small way due to the Olympic competition.

The Mexican organization was much in evidence at the Xochimilco rowing course, and only the altitude prevented it from being one of the best meetings in Olympic

history. Rowing events normally last about 6 minutes for the 2,000 metres course, and this period of exertion proved too much even for these tough, highly trained athletes. Martin Studach, the Swiss sculler, unbeaten in major events since 1965, collapsed in his heat and was carried away on a stretcher. The United States, for the first time, failed to win a single gold medal, and their tally amounted to just one silver and one bronze. East Germany won two of the seven events and also a silver medal. New Zealand's coxed four led from start to finish to win their event by nearly three

seconds from the East Germans, but despite a good effort in the eights final New Zealand had to be content with fourth place. The gold medals, almost as a matter of course, went to the West German team coached by the redoubtable Karl Adam. Russia, normally a force to be reckoned with in the world of rowing, won two medals, a gold and a bronze. The canoeing events were held over the same course and, as usual, were dominated by European paddlers of both sexes. No 'high-altitude' country won medals of any sort in rowing or canoeing.

It was the same story in the

1 The Olympic flame still burns, but was extinguished soon after the team show jumping—the final event of the Games. **2** Waldemar Baszanowski of Poland successfully defended his lightweight title with a total of 964¼ lb. **3** Rodney Pattisson and Iain Macdonald-Smith (K 163) were convincing winners of the Flying Dutchman gold medals. **4** The modernistic basketball arena dominated the hockey field: Australia (white) beat India 2-1 in the semi-final to reach their first-ever final.

cycling, in which all the medals were claimed by European riders. The most bemedalled cyclist was the Frenchman Pierre Trentin, who won golds in the 1,000 metres time trial and tandem sprint, and was third in the 1,000 metres sprint. But the talking point of the meeting was the disqualification of the West German quartet in the 4,000 metres team pursuit. In the final race, between Denmark and West Germany, the Germans seemed to have an easy victory, but one of their team appeared to receive assistance on the last lap, an illegal procedure in this form of racing. The Danes protested, and

the Germans were disqualified. Denmark were thus awarded the gold medals, and the silvers were withheld. West Germany, by virtue of reaching the final, did get the silver medals some weeks after the end of the Games.

Britain's heroes were few and far between in Mexico, but Rodney Pattisson and Iain Macdonald-Smith were out on their own in the Flying Dutchman yachting event held on the beautiful waters of Acapulco Bay. After being disqualified in the first race, they won five races in succession and were a careful second in the last to win the gold medal with 3.0 penalty points

to runner-up West Germany's 43.7. Paul Elvström, four times an Olympic winner, was fourth in the Star class.

In the equestrian events, the gold medals in the three-day event went to Britain. The bad weather and tough cross-country course suited the British riders, and 54-year-old Major Derek Allhusen, Sergeant Ben Jones, Richard Meade, and Jane Bullen (the first woman to feature in a winning Olympic three-day team) collected 175.93 penalty points to win by nearly 70 points from the United States. Britain's chances of team medals in the show jumping

disappeared when Marion Coakes, winner of the silver medal in the individual competition, crashed into one of the bigger fences with her tiny pony Stroller. Winners of this team prize were Canada, relative newcomers to this type of competition, thanks to a careful last round by Jim Elder.

The show jumping team event was the last competition of the Games, held in the Olympic stadium just before the closing ceremony. It brought to an end an Olympic Games filled with controversy but in which the Olympic ideals, if sorely tried, tested, and tempted, had at least survived.

MEXICO CITY OLYMPIC GAMES, 1968 Gold Medallists

Basketball		USA	
Boxing			
Light-flyweight	Francisco Rodriguez	Venezuela	
Flyweight	Ricardo Delgado	Mexico	
Bantamweight	Valeriy Sokolov	USSR	
Featherweight	Antonio Roldan	Mexico	
Lightweight	Ronnie Harris	USA	
Light-welterweight	Jerzy Kulej	Poland	
Welterweight	Manfred Wolke	East Germany	
Light-middleweight	Boris Lagutin	USSR	
Middleweight	Chris Finnegan	Great Britain	
Light-heavyweight	Dan Pozdniak	USSR	
Heavyweight	George Foreman	USA	
Canoeing			
1,000 metres—Men			
Kayak singles	Mihaly Hesz	Hungary	4 min 2.63 sec
Kayak pairs	Alexander Shaparenko, V. Morosov	USSR	3 min 37.54 sec
Kayak fours		Norway	3 min 14.38 sec
Canadian singles	Tibor Tatai	Hungary	4 min 36.14 sec
Canadian pairs	Ivan Patazichin, S. Covakiov	Romania	4 min 7.18 sec
500 metres—Women			
Kayak singles	Ludmilla Pinaeva	USSR	2 min 11.09 sec
Kayak pairs	A. Zimmermann, R. Esser	West Germany	1 min 56.44 sec
Cycling			
1,000 metres sprint	Daniel Morelon	France	
1,000 metres time trial	Pierre Trentin	France	
2,000 metres tandem	Daniel Morelon, Pierre Trentin	France	
4,000 metres team pursuit		Denmark	4 min 22.44 sec
Road team time trial (104 km)		Netherlands	2 hr 7 min 49.06 sec
Road race (196.2 km)	Pierfranco Vianelli	Italy	4 hr 41 min 25.24 sec
Equestrian			
Dressage —individual	Ivan Kizimov	USSR	
—team		West Germany	
Show jumping—individual	Bill Steinkraus	USA	
—team		Canada	
Three day event—individual	Jean Guyon	France	
—team		Great Britain	
Fencing—Men			
Foil —individual	Ion Drimba	Romania	
—team		France	
Epee —individual	Gyozo Kulcsar	Hungary	
—team		Hungary	
Sabre —individual	Jerzy Pawlowski	Poland	
—team		USSR	
Fencing—Women			
Foil —individual	Elena Novikova	USSR	
—team		USSR	
Football		Hungary	
Gymnastics—Men			
Combined exercises			
—individual	Sawao Kato	Japan	
—team		Japan	
Floor exercises	Sawao Kato	Japan	
Horizontal bar	Mikhail Voronin Akinari Nakayama.	USSR Japan	
Parallel bars	Akinari Nakayama	Japan	
Pommell horse	Miroslav Cerar	Yugoslavia	
Vault	Mikhail Voronin	USSR	
Rings	Akinari Nakayama	Jaapn	
Gymnastics—Women			
Combined exercises			
—individual	Vera Caslavska	Czechoslovakia	
—team		USSR	
Floor exercises	Larissa Petrik Vera Caslavska	USSR Czechoslovakia	
Asymmetrical bars	Vera Caslavska	Czechoslovakia	
Beam	Natalia Kuchinskaya	USSR	
Vault	Vera Caslavska	Czechoslovakia	
Hockey		Pakistan	
Modern Pentathlon			
Individual	Bjorn Ferm	Sweden	
Team		Hungary	
Rowing			
Single sculls	Henri Wienese	Netherlands	7 min 47.80 sec
Double sculls	Anatoly Sass, Alexander Timoshinin	USSR	6 min 51.82 sec
Coxless pairs	Jorg Lucke, Heinz Bothe	East Germany	7 min 26.56 sec
Coxed pairs	P. Baran, R. Sambo, B. Cipolla (cox)	Italy	8 min 4.81 sec
Coxed fours		New Zealand	6 min 45.62 sec
Coxless fours		East Germany	6 min 39.18 sec
Eights		West Germany	6 min 7.00 sec
Shooting			
Small bore rifle			
—three positions	Bernd Klingner	West Germany	
—prone	Jan Kurka	Czechoslovakia	
Free pistol	Gregory Kosyth	USSR	
Free rifle	Gary Anderson	USA	
Rapid fire pistol	Jozef Zapedzki	Poland	
Clay pigeon	Bob Braithwaite	Great Britain	
Skeet	Evgeny Petrov	USSR	
Volleyball—Men		USSR	
Volleyball—Women		USSR	
Weightlifting			
Bantamweight	Mohamed Nassiri	Iran	809¾ lb
Featherweight	Yoshinobu Miyake	Japan	865 lb
Lightweight	Waldemar Baszanowski	Poland	964¼ lb
Middleweight	Viktor Kurentsov	USSR	1,046¾ lb
Light-heavyweight	Boris Selitsky	USSR	1,068¾ lb
Mid-heavyweight	Kaarlo Kangasniemi	Finland	1,140½ lb
Heavyweight	Leonid Zhabotinsky	USSR	1,261¾ lb
Wrestling			
Freestyle			
Flyweight	Shigeo Nakata	Japan	
Bantamweight	Yojiro Uetake	Japan	
Featherweight	Masaaki Kaneko	Japan	
Lightweight	Abdollah Mohaved	Iran	
Welterweight	Mahmut Atalay	Turkey	
Middleweight	Boris Gurevitch	USSR	
Light-heavyweight	Ahmed Ayuk	Turkey	
Heavyweight	Alexandr Medved	USSR	
Graeco-Roman			
Flyweight	Petar Kirov	Bulgaria	
Bantamweight	Janos Varga	Hungary	
Featherweight	Roman Rurua	USSR	
Lightweight	Muneji Munemura	Japan	
Welterweight	Rudolf Vesper	East Germany	
Middleweight	Lothar Metz	East Germany	
Light-heavyweight	Boyan Radev	Bulgaria	
Heavyweight	Istvan Kozma	Hungary	
Yachting			
Finn	Valentin Mankin	USSR	
Star	Lowel North, Peter Barrett	USA	
Flying Dutchman	Rodney Pattisson, Iain Macdonald-Smith	Great Britain	
5.5 metres		Sweden	
Dragon		USA	

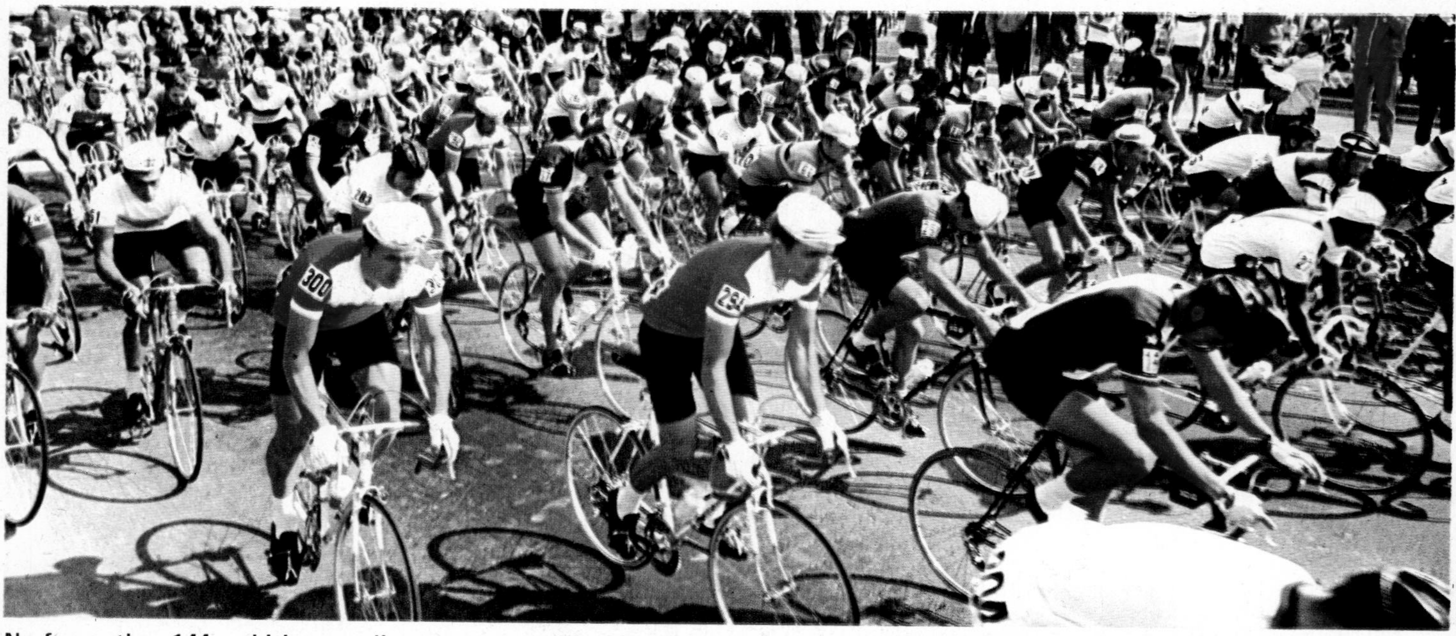

Rex Features

No fewer than 144 ambitious cyclists set out on the 122-mile road race, won by 22-year-old Pierfranco Vianelli of Italy.

Munich Olympic Games (1972)

On September 5 1972, the Olympic Games finally lost the battle to disassociate itself from the pernicious influence of world politics on sport. In the early hours of that fateful day, war came to the XXth Olympiad, and in those moments the considerable efforts of the West German organisers to present the largest, the most smoothly run, and the most costly Games were completely tarnished.

The Olympic Village became the platform for political propaganda of the most cold-blooded variety. A squad of Palestinian guerrillas invaded the Israeli team headquarters, claimed hostages in a violent struggle during which two members of the Israeli team received fatal injuries, and demanded the release of 200 Arab political prisoners. The intensive world-wide interest in the Games afforded them the very maximum publicity for their grievance.

All athletic activity immediately ceased and for several hours a complete cancellation appeared possible. The Olympic Games stood still and watched with the rest of the world as the West German Government and its security forces grappled with the problem. After a day of impasse their first positive move was directed at removing the conflict out of its sporting setting. Around 10.00 pm, three helicopters flew out of the Village, two containing the guerrillas with their hostages; the third had government officials aboard.

Their destination was the air-base at Fuerstenfeldbruck. Here the tragedy was compounded. Shortly after 11.30 pm, news bulletins around the world carried the story that, after an exchange of gunfire at the airfield, the hostages had all been safely recovered. It was a story without substance, and within four hours came the bitter retraction. True, there had been shots fired, but the tactics of local police had turned sour.

A troop of crack marksmen had been delegated to shoot down the Arabs the moment that they disembarked from the helicopters to transfer to the jet which they had demanded for a safe passage to Cairo. Four of the eight guerrillas moved forward to inspect the jet; as they returned to their comrades the police opened fire. Three were hit but the fourth reached the sanctuary of the helicopters. And then there was silence—for over an hour.

In that time the police prepared for an assault with armoured cars. It took too long. For, just after midnight, the hostages were murdered, some as a result of a hand-grenade tossed into one helicopter by a fleeing guerrilla, the rest shot. In all, 11 Israelis had been killed; five Arabs also died while three were taken into custody; another victim was a policeman slain by a terrorist bullet.

While the initial post-mortem centred on a security system that allowed any person wearing a track-suit, as the guerrillas had done, to enter the Olympic Village without a pass, and on the housing of the athletes, which had put the Israelis in a vulnerable station near the perimeter rather than in a more easily guarded and central post, the value of the Olympic Games and its uneasy tendency to arouse nationalism was also questioned.

Its cause was not helped on that Wednesday morning when a memorial service was held for the dead Israelis. Avery Brundage, at 84 in his last few days as chairman of the International Olympic Congress, appeared to lack any sensitivity when, in his address, he compared the killings to the problems over the inclusion of Rhodesia in the Games as 'commercial, political and now criminal pressure'. And there seemed a hurry which was almost indecent about the resumption of competition.

The Rhodesian question had ensured that politics was never far from the mind at the outset of these sumptuous Olympics which cost £300 million to stage. The IOC in 1971 had consented to the Rhodesian application for entry, on the grounds that they competed as a British colony, and duly a team of 30 athletes had arrived in Munich. But the African nations, surprised that Rhodesia had for sporting purposes rejected her independence, protested and threatened a boycott if Rhodesia took part. This was tantamount to 'blackmail', the word used by Avery Brundage after the event, but the IOC were forced to retract and the Rhodesian team were expelled.

Nor did the tragedy of the Israelis bring an end to nationalist overtones. The very day after the memorial service, two black Americans, Vince Matthews and Wayne Collett, stood relaxed, hands on hips and holding a conversation while the American national anthem was being played at their victory ceremony for the 400 metres final. It was every bit

Munich's day of mourning: the Israeli flag, along with the flags of all the competing nations, flies at half mast; a small group of Israelis, with a crepe covered flag, sit in silence during the memorial service to the 11 Israeli team members killed by Palestinian terrorists.

Colorsport

Associated Press

as much a demonstration for Black Power as the raised fists of Tommie Smith and Juan Carlos four years earlier, and the IOC duly banned the two athletes from any further Olympic competition, though they were allowed to retain their gold and silver medals.

Though the competition in all sports was of the usual elevated standards, the XXth Olympiad seemed even further removed from the original ideal. Even at the outset, amateurism was far removed when it was learned that the West German athlete, Heidi Schuller, who took the Olympic oath at the opening ceremony, had charged photographers for taking her picture in the preceding days. It provided an appropriate beginning for the fortnight.

Athletics—Men

Though world records were not achieved with the ease of the Mexican Games and its rarified air, the athletics stadium was the scene of intense and often spectacular competition. And on the track the extreme competition in the 10,000 metres and the 400 metres hurdles did stimulate the winners to exceed the previous world's best times.

Both races provided distinct disappointments for British hopes. In the 10,000 metres, 22-year-old David Bedford entered the final as the holder of the world record. But Bedford had endured an unhappy preparation for the Games. A week before Munich, he had been disastrously defeated in a two-mile race in Sweden; a stomach bug had been sapping his strength throughout that week; and when he arrived in Germany he was charged with infringing his amateur status through advertising—charges that were eventually dropped.

Yet he performed well enough in his heat, coming second to Emile Puttemans of Belgium by a fifth of a second, both running half a minute inside the previous Olympic record. They were the fastest qualifiers, but only the Belgian could recreate that form in the final. Bedford, without the security of a finishing sprint, had to set the pace from the front if he was to win; but he never freed himself from the pack.

By the end of the 14th lap his challenge was finished. The race was left for the sprinters and the fastest finish belonged to a 23-year-old policeman from Finland, Lasse Viren. Viren had good fortune when, in colliding with

the Tunisian, Mohamed Gammoudi, the Finn stumbled to the ground but recovered, while Gammoudi tumbled out of the race. Only Puttemans could match Viren, but not for long enough, and the Finn won easily in the world record time of 27 min 38.4 sec.

In the 400 metres hurdles, David Hemery was bidding to retain the Olympic title he had gained so worthily in Mexico. He might have done so but for the emergence of a remarkable and relatively unknown athlete. The Ugandan, John Akii-Bua, one of a family of 43 children, completely rewrote the standard for the event with a breathtaking win in 47.8 sec. Hemery lost second place to the American, Ralph Mann, almost at the tape, but took the bronze medal; there was little despondency from him when he said: 'I'm glad that my medal and world record have gone in this way. I'd have hated it to have gone in a slow time.'

Mann's silver medal was one consolation for the United States men's team which experienced a series of disasters, some of them of their own design. First, their two leading 100 metres men, Eddie Hart and Rey Robinson, failed to appear on the blocks for the second round of the heats, a complete misunderstanding of the schedule for the events. And Robert Taylor, who just arrived in time to qualify for the final, was completely outclassed by the powerful Russian, Valeri Borzov, who won the gold medal in 10.14 sec, only the second non-American victor in this event since 1932.

The Americans have shown even greater dominance in the pole vault—they had provided winners since 1896—but now Bob Seagren, gold medallist in Mexico, found his 'Catapult' style vaulting pole banned and lost his title to Wolfgang Nordwig of East Germany. The shot, too, escaped the Americans, George Woods being unable to match the winning effort of Komar of Poland, who achieved 69 ft 6 in. And then came the ignominious behaviour of Matthews and Collett, whose subsequent ban destroyed the USA 4 x 400 metres relay team.

The final disaster came in a 1,500 metres heat in which, by some strange quirk of the computer which controlled the composition of the heats, Mexico silver medallist Jim Ryun was drawn with the reigning champion Kip Keino. All might have been well, with Ryun comfortably placed to make his bid for qualification with 500 metres left, but as he moved out to step up his pace he collided with another runner and crashed on to the track. Though he bravely pursued the field his chance had disintegrated in that desperate moment.

Apart from Matthews' 400

The Soviet Union's Valeri Borzov (932) cruises to a comfortable win over Roberts of Trinidad and Jamaica's Hardware in his first-round heat of the 200 metres. In the two sprint finals, Borzov eclipsed his opposition to complete the first men's 100-200 double since 1956.

1 In middle-distance events, Finland returned to the fore, mainly through Lasse Viren, here winning the 5,000 metres to complete the seemingly impossible 5,000-10,000 metres double. **2** Wolfgang Nordwig, here dramatically falling away from the skylights of the Cosford indoor arena, ended America's reign in the pole vault. **3** The uninhibited John Akii-Bua took David Hemery's Olympic title and world record in the 400 metres hurdles: Hemery finished third behind America's Ralph Mann.

Colorsport

metres success, the United States men were limited to athletics golds from Rod Milburn in the 110 metres hurdles, Frank Shorter in the marathon, Randy Williams in the long jump (with a frantic effort in his first jump after straining a leg while warming-up), the 4 x 100 metres relay, and Dave Wottle in the 800 metres. And Wottle embarrassed himself considerably by forgetting to remove his trademark, a peaked cap, during the national anthem on the victors rostrum.

If the Americans struggled it was Finland who made the advance. The success of Viren in the 10,000 metres was compounded

within a few hours on Sunday, September 10. In the 5,000 metres David Bedford again took up the challenge with Viren, and again could not match him. On the final lap the Finn was left to duel with Gammoudi, the reigning champion, and it was the younger man who came home more than five yards clear. Behind Gammoudi, Ian Stewart outlasted the field to win a bronze medal for Great Britain. Viren's winning time, 13 min 26.4 sec, was an Olympic record.

A British runner, Brendan Foster, played an influential part in the 1,500 metres. He acted as pacemaker for the opening two

laps, until Keino, gold medallist in Mexico, eased his way to the front. With him went Finland's Pekka Vasala, and it was Vasala who kicked off the final bend to make the day belong entirely to Finland. Foster finished gallantly in fifth place.

Keino had been forced to withdraw from the 5,000 metres, his other main event, because of a clash in the timings of the heats with those of the 1,500 metres. But he had trained hard for the 3,000 metres steeplechase, a completely new event to him. And though he had run the race only four times before in his career, his sheer pace brought

him Olympic gold, though his style made the purists shudder. He won in an Olympic record time of 8 min 23.6 sec, beating his team-mate Ben Jipcho, with Kantanen giving the Finns further joy with a bronze medal.

Valeri Borzov duly completed the sprint double for Russia; his smooth, powerful stride beating three Americans and the Italian, Mennea, in a time of 20 sec dead. Sadly, the greatness of his dual triumph may always be open to question because he never had the opportunity to beat Hart and Robinson, the Americans who missed their heats. That criticism probably does disservice to an

athlete who seemed a class above all his rivals, particularly when many judges felt that Taylor, who took the silver in the 100 metres, was the most effective of the United States entrants.

For the USSR—the satisfaction of the only athlete who retained his title. Viktor Saneyev took his second successive gold medal in the triple jump, though his winning leap of 56 ft 11 in was 13 inches less than he achieved in Mexico. The Russians also took gold in the high jump, where no one could match the 7 ft 4¼ in leap with which Dick Fosbury flopped to fame in 1968, but Tarmak won the Olympic title

with a jump of just half an inch less. They also won the hammer competition, where Bondarchuk broke the Olympic record, and the decathlon, in which Avilov's 8454 pts was a world record.

Jay Silvester could not succeed to the crown handed down by the great Al Oerter, and he could only finish second in the discus to Danek of Czechoslovakia, while Klaus Wolfermann of West Germany raised the Olympic javelin standard with a winning throw of 296 ft 10 in. In the walking event there was a gold medal for Frenkel of East Germany in the 20 km, and for Kannenberg of West Germany in the 50 km.

The performance of the fancied Paul Nihill in the former event highlighted a problem in the approach of many of the British team to the competition.

Nihill, like many others, had trained at altitude to improve his performance when he came to compete at the lower level of Munich. But during the 20 km walk he complained that his legs had never felt as tired before; he felt that he had returned from altitude too late and that the benefits of this type of training had been slightly misunderstood by the doctors who had recommended the idea. It was perhaps a partial explanation of the poor showing

of the British team.

Nevertheless, the last male track event did provide some consolation, when the 4 x 400 metres relay team of Martin Reynolds, Alan Pascoe, David Hemery and David Jenkins came second behind Kenya. Hemery, running third, produced an inspired lap of 44.9 sec to hand over to Jenkins in fourth place. The West German leader tied up in sight of home, and Sang of Kenya took the lead while Jenkins showed all his promising power to overtake both German and French runners; the silver medal came in a new British record of 3 min 0.5 sec.

Athletics—Women

It was a new Olympic event for women, the 1,500 metres, which provided perhaps the most outstanding performance in a series of excellent contests. At the start of 1972, the world record for the event stood at 4 min 9.6 sec, but throughout the Games, Ludmilla Bragina of the USSR clinically made such a time seem increasingly archaic. In her first round heat, this 5 ft 7 in girl, who weighs a mere 110 lb, was a winner in 4 min 6.5 sec; in her semi-final she sliced that time down to 4 min 5.1 sec.

Then in the final she produced an even better performance. After two fast opening laps, the 29-year-old Russian took over chased by Sheila Carey from Coventry. The English girl held her own on lap three, but understandably faded over the last 250 yards, nevertheless finishing fifth in a new British record. But Bragina raced home, slaughtering her own previous best of a few days earlier with yet another world record of 4 min 1.4 sec, and really placing the four minute mile for women within reach.

For Great Britain, an athletics gold medal became reality when 33-year-old Mary Peters of Belfast won the pentathlon. Her triumph was based on a tremendous effort on the first day of this two-day event; it was then that she established a strong lead with her performances in three of the five events. By sprinting the 100 metres hurdles in 13.29 sec; by putting the shot 53 ft 1¼ in, and by high jumping a personal best of 5 ft 10½ in, she totalled 2969 points, the best ever first day score in the women's pentathlon. As she battled to get some sleep that night, she must have reflected on the proximity of the world record holder Pollak of East Germany, just 97 points behind, and the West German, Heidi Rosendahl, then in fifth place, but with her two strongest events, the long jump and the 200 metres, Mary's weakest, to follow.

The drama took its predictable course. Rosendahl, who had already won the gold medal in the women's long jump, even improved on that winning leap; her 22 ft 5 in was nearly two feet in front of Mary Peters' best jump. And to add further bite to the tension, the two girls were drawn in the same heat of the 200 metres. Again the West German girl responded to the occasion; her 22.9 sec was a career best, but the 11 stone Irish girl clung on to record 24.08, and to win the gold medal by

2 just 10 points!

Apart from that success for Great Britain, the women's events were shared between three nations, USSR and East and West Germany. In the short sprints, Renate Stecher of East Germany, a strongly built girl, emulated the achievement of Borzov in the men's events with a double in the 100 and 200 metres, her 22.40 sec in the latter equalling the world record; both silvers went to the Australian, Raelene Boyle. East Germany, an increasing force in the Games, also won the 400 metres with M. Zehrt, the 110 metres hurdles through A. Ehrhardt, the 4 x 400 metres relay, while Ruth Fuchs set a new Olympic record in winning the javelin.

The West German success belonged almost exclusively to Heidi Rosendahl, who came back in the most decisive fashion from the disappointment of an injury in Mexico which cost her the gold medal in the pentathlon. After her long jump win and her second place to Mary Peters, she played the vital part in a thrilling 4 x 100 metres relay. In front of a packed and intensely partisan crowd she took the last leg, and in a frenzy of excitement held off the great Renate Stecher and East Germany by .14 of a second; the winning time of 42.81 equalled the world and Olympic record.

But there was even more of the fairytale about the triumph of 16-year-old Ulrike Meyfarth in the high jump. Before the Games began, her best jump was just $\frac{3}{4}$ in over 6 ft, but she took the gold medal by equalling the world record of 6 ft $3\frac{1}{2}$ in, and above all she showed remarkable composure and maturity in withstanding the pressure of a competition which lasted four and a half hours. Britain's Barbara Inkpen finished a creditable fourth with a jump of 6 ft $0\frac{1}{2}$ in.

There was a victory, too, for the home team in the 800 metres, an Olympic record run from Hildergard Falck, while the Russian team, without a gold in the women's track and field in Mexico City, responded to the example set by Ludmila Bragina and were victorious in both discus and shot. Faina Melnik took the discus title by over five feet with another Olympic record, 218 ft 7 in, and the giant Nadizhda Chizhova set new world standards in the shot putt. She pushed her own world record up to 69 ft an advance of over a foot, and she won by the impressive margin of 3 ft 8 in.

For Great Britain there was Mary Peters to remember . . . and very little else.

1 Pentathlon gold medallist Mary Peters in a moment of intense concentration.
2 Heidi Rosendahl—darling of the German supporters.

Swimming

The 1972 Olympic swimming competition will be remembered entirely for the performance of one man whose phenomenal success is unlikely to ever be equalled. Mark Spitz, a 22-year-old Californian, won seven gold medals; he accomplished this feat over a period of just eight days, and in each event a world record was broken.

His haul comprised four golds for individual races and three for relays, and in most cases he won with great ease. He took the 100 metres and 200 metres free-style titles, and also the 100 and 200 metres butterfly, and was a key figure in the USA successes in all three relay events. In the individual races his narrowest success came in the 100 metres freestyle, when another American, Jerry Heidenreich, finished four tenths of a second behind him, but even that represented a comfortable margin for the supremely talented and confident Spitz.

Fifteen-year-old Shane Gould from Australia made a creditable effort to emulate Spitz in the women's competition. She had three golds—and world records—in the 200 and 400 metres free-style and in the 200 metres medley relay, winning the 400 metres freestyle in the most impressive

fashion by 3.4 seconds; in an event in which the United States had traditionally excelled, they were out of the medals when Novella Calligaris of Italy and Gudrun Wegner of East Germany followed Miss Gould home. The young Australian, however, could only manage a well-beaten second in the 800 metres and a bronze medal in the 100 metres freestyle.

Undoubtedly the saddest saga of the swimming tournament concerned the young American Rick Demont, who failed a dope test after he had won the 400 metres freestyle. He admitted to using the drug ephedrine as a prescribed aid to an asthmatic condition, but had been unaware that it could also be construed as a stimulant. After a lengthy debate, Brad Cooper of Australia, who had come second by one hundredth of a second to Demont, was finally awarded the gold medal, and as further punishment the 16-year-old from California was barred from competing in the final of the 1,500 metres freestyle.

That race turned out to be one of the most exciting of the Games, and the United States had some consolation for Demont's absence by winning the gold medal. Mike Burton, the gold medallist in Mexico City, became engaged in

1 If Mark Spitz's was the supreme performance, Shane Gould's was the one that drew the public to her. The 15-year-old Australian won three golds (200m freestyle, 400m freestyle, and 200m medley), a silver (800m freestyle) and a bronze (100m freestyle)—the most medals by a woman swimmer in a single Games. 2 Medley king at Munich was Sweden's Gunnar Larsson, who did most of his training in the United States. However, his gold medal victory in the 400 metres medley could not have been closer: the electronic timing separated him from America's Tim McKee by a mere 1/500th of a second. 3 'Golden Boy' was an apt description of Mark Spitz; for after his unparalleled performance in the Munich pool—seven gold medals, seven world records—he turned professional as the million-dollar offers poured in. 4 The distinguished style of East Germany's Roland Matthes. Arguably the best backstroke exponent the swimming world has known, he retained both his Mexico City Olympic titles in Munich.

3

4

MUNICH OLYMPIC GAMES, 1972 Gold Medallists—Swimming			
Men			
100 metres freestyle	Mark Spitz	USA	51.22 sec
200 metres freestyle	Mark Spitz	USA	1 min 52.78 sec
400 metres freestyle	Rick Demont	USA	4 min 00.26 sec
	disqualified for taking a banned drug – gold medal went to		
	Brad Cooper	Australia	4 min 00.27 sec
1500 metres freestyle	Mike Burton	USA	15 min 52.58 sec
100 metres breaststroke	Nabutaka Taguchi	Japan	1 min 04.94 sec
200 metres breaststroke	John Hencken	USA	2 min 21.55 sec
100 metres butterfly	Mark Spitz	USA	54.27 sec
200 metres butterfly	Mark Spitz	USA	2 min 00.70 sec
100 metres backstroke	Roland Matthes	East Germany	56.58 sec
200 metres backstroke	Roland Matthes	East Germany	2 min 02.82 sec
200 metres individual medley	Gunnar Larsson	Sweden	2 min 07.17 sec
400 metres individual medley	Gunnar Larsson	Sweden	4 min 31.98 sec
4 x 100 metres freestyle relay		USA	3 min 26.42 sec
4 x 200 metres freestyle relay		USA	7 min 35.78 sec
4 x 100 metres medley relay		USA	3 min 48.16 sec
Springboard diving	Vlademir Vasin	USSR	594.09 pts
Highboard diving	Klaus Dibiasi	Italy	504.12 pts
Women			
100 metres freestyle	Sandra Neilson	USA	58.59 sec
200 metres freestyle	Shane Gould	Australia	2 min 03.56 sec
400 metres freestyle	Shane Gould	Australia	4 min 19.04 sec
800 metres freestyle	Keena Rothammer	USA	8 min 53.68 sec
100 metres breaststroke	Catharine Carr	USA	1 min 13.58 sec
200 metres breaststroke	Beverley Whitfield	Australia	2 min 41.71 sec
100 metres butterfly	Mayumi Aoki	Japan	1 min 03.34 sec
200 metres butterfly	Karen Moe	USA	2 min 15.57 sec
100 metres backstroke	Melissa Belote	USA	1 min 5.78 sec
200 metres backstroke	Melissa Belote	USA	2 min 19.19 sec
200 metres individual medley	Shane Gould	Australia	2 min 23.07 sec
400 metres individual medley	Gail Neall	Australia	5 min 02.97 sec
4 x 100 metres freestyle relay		USA	3 min 55.19 sec
4 x 100 metres medley relay		USA	4 min 20.75 sec
Springboard diving	Micki King	USA	450.03 pts
Highboard diving	Ulrika Knape	Sweden	390.00 pts
Water Polo		USSR	

an enthralling duel with
Australia's Graham Windeatt.
First Burton led, then, at the
halfway mark, Windeatt took
such a lead that the contest
seemed to be over. But in the last
quarter mile, Burton reduced the
margin and stormed to the front
and finally won in the world
record time of 15 minutes 52.58
seconds. Such had been the competition between the two men that
Burton's winning time had been
pushed to an incredible 46.3 sec
greater than in his winning race
in 1968.

The British team again disappointed by winning, for the
third successive Olympics, only
one single medal. This time it was
a success for Scotland, with
David Wilkie from Edinburgh
coming second to John Hencken
of the United States in the 200
metres breaststroke. Wilkie, who
had prepared in America, also
broke the European and
Commonwealth records with his
time of 2 min 23.67 sec. Wilkie
also won a final place in the 100
metres breaststroke final, a race
won by Taguchi of Japan, but
his performance could scarcely
compensate for the failure of a
British squad which had had the
benefit of more pre-Games
training than those of former
years.

In the diving, Micki King of the
United States, who had seemed
certain of a medal in 1968 until
she broke a wrist in the competition, took the women's
springboard title, but again the
Americans, for so long the most
influential diving nation, faltered.
Ulrike Knape, of Sweden, second
to the King in the springboard,
took the highboard title with the
American girls fourth and fifth.
Klaus Dibiasi retained his men's
highboard diving title for Italy,
who also won a bronze and silver
through Cagnotto in the two
competitions. The springboard
title went to a Russian for the
first time in Olympic history, when
Vladimir Vasin edged the Italian
out of first place.

And the drama of the Olympic
pool extended into the water
polo competition. The successful
Hungary team, who have claimed
medals in every Olympics since
1928, met Russia in the last
match knowing that a win would
give them the gold medal again.
But in a thrilling game Russia
held out for a 3-3 draw and thereby took the title for themselves,
for the first time.

1 Akinori Nakayama, winner of
three gold medals in Mexico
City, collected two (on the
rings and team), plus a silver
and bronze at Munich.
2 The incomparable Olga, the
17-year-old Russian whose
charisma charmed the watching
world as her captivating
routines brought her three
golds and a silver.

Alan E. Burrows

Colorsport

Other Sports

In the 18 other sports outside the main athletic and swimming events, the most enchanting performance came from perhaps the smallest competitor. The delightful Russian gymnast, Olga Korbut, 17 years old, under five feet tall and weighing around six stone, possessed all the precocious appeal of a young child, and her genuine charisma charmed both spectators and judges—and she was in the Russian team as a late replacement only. Her phenomenal agility and the captivating manner in which she performed her routines brought her gold medals in the individual floor exercises and beam, and also a team gold in the combined exercises.

The boxing arena provided heroes of different stature, and three bronze medals for Britain. Ralph Evans, in the light-flyweight division, George Turpin, bantamweight, and Alan Minter, light-middleweight, were all losing semi-finallists in a very popular sport at the Games—all the seats in the hall were sold out for every night of the tournament. But though Britain achieved more than might have been expected, the surprise nation was Cuba who provided three gold medallists and the biggest puncher of the competition in Teofilo Stevenson. Among a series of spectacular wins during his progress to the heavyweight final there was included the destruction of a much-praised white American, Duane Bobeck, who many experts had predicted would break the coloured domination of professional heavyweight boxing. But there was no sensational final performance from the Cuban; his Romanian opponent rather wisely withdrew through injury.

Wrestling and weightlifting provided two strongmen, both Russians. Alex Medved won a third successive Olympic medal with his winning performance in the super-heavyweight freestyle class, while Alexeyev earned his title as the strongest man in the Games by recording a total of $1409\frac{1}{4}$ lb in the super-heavyweight lifting contest.

If Britain achieved their expected success in the equestrian events—Richard Meade took the gold medal in the individual three-day event, with Meade, Mary Gordon-Watson, Bridget Parker and Mark Phillips winning the team gold, and Anne Moore earning the silver in the individual show jumping—medals came from an unexpected source in the judo competition. David Starbrook won Britain's first ever Olympic medal in this sport when he took the second place in the middle-heavyweight division, and later Brian Jacks, middleweight, and Angelo Parisi, open, won bronze medals. Their success was part of the breaking of the traditional Japanese domination of this sport. In the six judo events, the Japanese claimed only three golds and one bronze medal.

A more expected success for Great Britain came at Kiel, where the yachting competition was held. Rodney Pattison, who won the Flying Dutchman gold medal in Mexico with Iain Macdonald-Smith, triumphed again with a new partner, Chris Davies. Pattison's total dedication in his preparation for the Olympics typified the overriding approach of the successful competitors in the Games. Britain had a silver medal to enjoy, too, as Alan Warren and David Hunt sailed in second to the Russian yacht in the Tempest Class. Another medal, a bronze, came in the cycling team pursuit race when the British team of Mick Bennett, Ian Hallam, Ronald Keeble and Willie Moore came in behind West Germany and East Germany, whilst John Kynoch also took a bronze medal in the moving target shooting event, improving 11 points on his previous personal best.

The ball sports provided moments of drama and controversy. Russia ended the American domination of the basketball, scoring the winning points in the very last second of the final, stunning the holders who had, at one time, been cruising to victory. Not even lengthy post-match protests from the United States' squad, who claimed that time had run out, could reverse what was, perhaps, the most sensational finish in the entire games. Hockey had its controversy when the whole of the Pakistan team were banned from further Olympic competition for their behaviour while losing their title to West Germany. Football brought success again to an Eastern European nation, this time Poland, whose footballers are as near full-time as professionals in the West. The volleyball golds went to Japan in the men's competition, and the Russian women's team; the latter defeated Japan in the final, which was perhaps only just, as a Munich observer had taken out a law suit against the coach of the Japanese squad for brutal training methods!

1 Russia's Vasili Alexeyev, super-heavyweight gold medallist with an Olympic record total of 1,410¾ lb.
2 For Britain there was double gold in the three-day event, with Richard Meade, on Major Derek Allhusen's Laurieston, taking the individual title and leading the team—Mary Gordon-Watson, Bridget Parker and Mark Phillips.
3 Dave Starbrook won a surprise bronze for Britain in the light-heavy judo.

Keystone

In the inevitable though un-official, medal table that intro-duces nationalistic feeling to a competition which is essentially between individuals, Russia were the most successful country with 50 golds and a total of 99 medals, five more than the United States. But East Germany, third in the table with 20 gold medals and 66 medals in all, made the most decisive steps forward since Mexico City, and had the two Germanys competed as one nation, they would have been the most successful, totalling 106 medals between them. Britain equalled their Mexico City total with 18 medals, but of the four gold, only that won by Mary Peters was a pure athletic success; the other three victories had either horse or yacht to aid the competitor.

But for all the improvement in competition, the 1972 Olympic Games will always leave a taste that is tainted. Commercialism, professionalism and nationalism had all been threats to an insti-tution which had at least been peaceable if not wholly resistable. Munich must now be remem-bered for its violence, and the death of 11 members of a team. That is a cross that the Olympic Games, in the lavish, expensive and enormous form expressed by the XXth Olympiad, will find very hard to bear.

1 Rodney Pattison, this time with Chris Davies crewing, retained his title in the Flying Dutchman class.
2 New Zealand, East Germany, Denmark, Romania, USSR, and West Germany battle out the coxless fours.

MUNICH OLYMPIC GAMES, 1972 Gold Medallists

Archery
Men	John Williams	USA	2,538 pts
Women	Doreen Wilber	USA	2,424 pts
Basketball		USSR	
Boxing			
Light-flyweight	Gyoergy Gedo	Hungary	
Flyweight	Gheorgi Kostadinov	Bulgaria	
Bantamweight	Orlando Martinez	Cuba	
Featherweight	Boris Kousnetsov	USSR	
Lightweight	Jan Sczcepanski	Poland	
Light-welterweight	Ray Seales	USA	
Welterweight	Emilio Correa	Cuba	
Light-middleweight	Dieter Kottysch	West Germany	
Middleweight	Viatchesian Lemenchev	USSR	
Light-heavyweight	Mate Parlov	Yugoslavia	
Heavyweight	Teofilo Stevenson	Cuba	
Canoeing—Slalom			
Men			
Kayak singles	Siegbert Horn	East Germany	4 min 28.56 sec
Canadian singles	Reinhard Eiben	East Germany	5 min 15.84 sec
Canadian pairs	Walter Hoffman	} East Germany	310.68 pts
	Rolf-Dieter Amend		
Women			
Kayak singles	Angelika Bahmann	East Germany	364.50 pts
Canoeing—Straight Races			
Men			
Kayak singles	Aleksandr Shaparenko	USSR	3 min 48.06 sec
Kayak pairs	Nikolai Gorbachev	} USSR	3 min 31.23 sec
	Viktor Kratassyuk		
Kayak fours		USSR	3 min 14.02 sec
Canadian singles	Ivan Patzaichin	Romania	4 min 08.94 sec
Canadian Pairs	Vladas Chessyunas	} USSR	3 min 52.60 sec
	Yuri Lobanov		
Women			
Kayak singles	Yulia Ryabchinskaya	USSR	2 min 03.17 sec
Kayak pairs	Ludmila Pinayeva	} USSR	1 min 53.50 sec
	Ekaterina Kuryshko		

Cycling
1000 metres time trial	Niels Fredborg	Denmark	1 min 06.44 sec
1000 metres sprint	Daniel Morelon	France	
Tandem sprint		USSR	
4000 metres individual pursuit	Knut Knudsen	Norway	4 min 45.74 sec
Team pursuit		West Germany	4 min 22.14 sec
100 kilometres team time trial		USSR	2 hr 11 min 17.8 sec
Individual road race	Henry Kuyper	Netherlands	4 hr 14 min 37.0 sec
Equestrian			
Three-day event—individual	Richard Meade	GB	
—team		GB	
Show jumping —individual	Graziano Mancinelli	Italy	
—team		West Germany	
Dressage —individual	Liselott Linsenhoff	West Germany	
—team		USSR	
Fencing			
Men			
Foil —individual	Witold Woyda	Poland	
—team		Poland	
Epee —individual	Csaba Fenyvesi	Hungary	
—team		Hungary	
Sabre —individual	Viktor Sidiak	USSR	
—team		Italy	
Women			
Foil —individual	Antonella Ragno Lonzi	Italy	
—team		USSR	
Football		Poland	
Gymnastics			
Men			
Combined exercises —individual	Sawao Kato	Japan	
—team		Japan	
Floor exercises	Nikolai Andrianov	USSR	
Horizontal bar	Mitsuo Tsukahara	Japan	
Parallel bars	Sawao Kato	Japan	
Pommell horse	Viktor Klimenko	USSR	
Long horse	Klaus Koeste	East Germany	
Rings	Akinori Nakayama	Japan	
Women			
Combined exercises —individual	Ludmilla Tourischeva	USSR	
—team		USSR	

Floor exercises	Olga Korbut	USSR
Asymmetrical bars	Karin Janz	East Germany
Beam	Olga Korbut	USSR
Long Horse	Karin Janz	East Germany
Handball		Yugoslavia
Hockey		West Germany
Judo		
Lightweight	Takeo Kawaguchi	Japan
Welterweight	Kazutoyo Nomura	Japan
Middleweight	Shinobu Sekine	Japan
Light-heavy	Shota Chochoshvili	USSR
Heavyweight	Willem Ruska	Netherlands
Open	Willem Ruska	Netherlands
Modern Pentathlon		
Individual	Andras Balczo	Hungary
Team		USSR
Rowing		
Single sculls	Yuri Malishev	USSR
Double sculls	Aleksandr Timoshinin	} USSR
	Gennadi Korshikov	
Coxless pairs	Siegfried Brietzke	} East Germany
	Wolfgang Mager	
Coxed pairs	Wolfgang Gunkel	} East Germany
	Joerg Lucke	
Coxed fours		West Germany
Coxless fours		East Germany
Eights		New Zealand
Shooting		
Small bore rifle		
—3 positions	John Writer	USA
—prone	Ho Jun Li	North Korea
Free pistol	Ragnar Skanaker	Sweden
Free rifle	Lones Wigger	USA
Rapid fire pistol	Josef Zapedzki	Poland
Clay pigeon	Angelo Scalzone	Italy
Skeet	Konrad Wirnhier	West Germany
Moving target	Lakov Zhelezniak	USSR
Volleyball		
Men		Japan
Women		USSR

Weightlifting			
Flyweight	Zygmunt Smalcerz	Poland	743¾ lb
Bantamweight	Imre Foeldi	Hungary	831¾ lb
Featherweight	Norair Nurikyan	Bulgaria	887 lb
Lightweight	Mukharbi Kirzhinov	USSR	1013¾ lb
Middleweight	Yordan Bikov	Bulgaria	1068¾ lb
Light-heavyweight	Leif Jensen	Norway	1118¾ lb
Middle-heavyweight	Andon Nikolov	Bulgaria	1157 lb
Heavyweight	Yan Talts	USSR	1278¼ lb
Super-heavyweight	Vasili Alexeyev	USSR	1409¼ lb
Wrestling			
Freestyle			
Light-flyweight	Roman Dmitriev	USSR	
Flyweight	Kiyomi Kato	Japan	
Bantamweight	Hideaki Yanagida	Japan	
Featherweight	Zagalav Abdulbekov	USSR	
Lightweight	Dan Gable	USA	
Welterweight	Wayne Wells	USA	
Middleweight	Levan Tedioshvili	USSR	
Light-heavyweight	Ben Peterson	USA	
Heavyweight	Ivan Yarygin	USSR	
Super-heavyweight	Alexandr Medved	USSR	
Graeco-Roman			
Light-flyweight	Gheorghe Berceanu	Romania	
Flyweight	Petar Kirov	Bulgaria	
Bantamweight	Rustem Kazakov	USSR	
Featherweight	Gheorghi Markov	Bulgaria	
Lightweight	Shamil Khisamutdinov	USSR	
Welterweight	Vitezspav Macha	Czechoslovakia	
Middleweight	Csaba Hegedus	Hungary	
Light-heavyweight	Valeri Rezantsev	USSR	
Heavyweight	Nicolae Martinescu	Romania	
Super-heavyweight	Anotoly Roshin	USSR	
Yachting			
Finn	Serge Maury	France	
Star	David Forbes	Australia	
Flying Dutchman	Rodney Pattison	} GB	
	Chris Davies		
Soling	Harry Melges	USA	
Tempest	Valentin Mankin	USSR	
Dragon	John Cuneo	Australia	

Montreal Olympic Games (1976)

There were no riots in Montreal beyond a one-day demonstration by under-employed taxi drivers and nobody was killed, and if that has become the mark of a successful Olympic Games, Montreal came out of their Games on the winning side. But never before has a Games cost its hosts so much, never before have so many nations used it for political ends and never have so many of the world's leading athletes been prevented from competing.

Some of the problems were of the IQC's own making, but in the end it could only be described as an unhappy Games, throttled by its own security, its own expense and its own vastness.

Monique Berlioux, the executive director of the IOC, described the security as a 'collar of iron', re-gretted the absence of freedom and 'a bit of anarchy', and though she was hated by the local citizenry for saying as much, it was obvious that the Games of the XXIst Olympiad in Montreal did nothing to further the Olympic movement.

Certainly they did little to en-hance Montreal. A long overdue sewage treatment plant had to be postponed, major parks acquisi-tions and a sub-way extension cancelled and even the municipal recreation services cut back to pay for the Games. Mayor Jean Drapeau had promised that the Games would not cost the taxpayers one cent but instead they cost somewhere around $1 billion.

Even after the Games, the bills continued to flood into the treasuries of Montreal and Quebec. The stadium alone, unfinished and under-used, was costing $50,000 a day to maintain, and Drapeau's promise of a 'modest and self-financing' Games, a promise which won the city the Games, was shown up as the pious hope of a vain and egotistical man.

But in the end, it will be neither the financing, nor the terrible wor-ries in the preceding months that the facilities would not be ready, that will be remembered as the legacy of Montreal. Far worse was the political domination of the Olympic movement there.

The last-minute Canadian deci-sion to bar the team of the Republic of China, thus breaking the Olympic charter it had sworn to maintain, and the boycott of the Games by African nations and their cohorts dealt a more serious blow to the Olympic ideal.

The African nations also left their action until the last moment. A letter signed by 16 of them demanded the expulsion of New Zealand on the grounds that the New Zealand rugby union team was touring South Africa. The IOC refused, thankfully standing by its principles, and 16 African countries, Iraq and Guyana withdrew, taking with them 441 athletes, affecting 14 sports and leaving only 88 nations to compete.

That said, there were things to admire in Montreal, the magnifi-cence of The Forum and the Velo-drome not least among them. Some day it will be remembered for the athletic deeds performed there but in the short term it may be seen only as the beginning of what Lord Killanin called rather pompously 'the retreat into barbarism'.

Athletics – Men

The Africans had gone home, rob-bing the distance events of some of the glamour but not, as it turned out, lowering the standards. Five world records fell, three of them on the track, and another ten Olympic records, and the conspicuous absence of the great Kenyan, Ugan-dan, Ethiopian and Tanzanian champions did not in any way reduce the achievements of those who did win. Indeed, in three events that the Africans might have hoped to win, the 800 metres, the 400 metres hurdles and the 3,000 metres steeplechase, the winners had to set new world records.

mark in 50sec, and though he lost the lead briefly, won in 1min 43.5sec. Could he complete the double with the 400 metres? Not since 1952 had a non-American won, but Juantorena was unstoppable. He had an adolescent starting style, which left him trailing badly in his semi-final, but in the final he won by two of his own huge strides in the fastest time ever run on a sea-level track.

That 400 metres world and Olympic record had stood since the high-altitude Olympics of Mexico, but the 400 metres hurdles world record fell for the third consecutive Games. Dave Hemery had clocked 48.12sec in 1968, the Ugandan John Akii-Bua 47.82sec in 1972 and this time Ed Moses, a 20-year-old who six months before had only raced the event once, took the title back to the United States with a record of 47.64sec. His winning margin of more than a second was the widest in Olympic history.

The steeplechase was even more remarkable, not only for the final time but for the way in which it was achieved. Two men had been expected to dominate the race, Anders Garderud, the world record holder from Sweden, and the European champion, Bronislaw Malinowski, from Poland. But a third, Frank Baumgartl, of East Germany, intervened and when Garderud struck out 300 metres from home, it was the German and not the Pole who went with him.

Finally, at the last hurdle, the German came level. But his stride faltered as he took the obstacle, his heel struck it and he crashed. Malinowski avoided him but Garderud was home in a world record of 8min 8sec, and the German had to be consoled with the bronze medal after climbing to his feet and finishing within half a second of the old world record.

Great though these performances were, they paled beside those of the

Memorable scenes from Montreal: the Olympic flame, recurring symbol of the Games; Lasse Viren, who won both the 5,000m and 10,000m for the second successive Games; and Nadia Kim, displaying the coolness and grace of a champion.

It is difficult to choose between the winners of these three but pride of place must go to Albertos Juantorena, a 6ft 3in Cuban with a huge loping stride and a high back-lift. He had only run four 800 metres races before the Games, and none before 1976, but he had decided after a summer's programme in Europe to add the event to his speciality, the 400 metres. The odds had to be against him. Nobody had achieved the double, and the 800 had always been won by an athlete from an English-speaking nation.

The 800 came first on the programme. Juantorena, who looked more like a sprinter than a half-miler, flashed through the halfway

What Montreal intended: a model of the Olympic Stadium and surrounding buildings produced four years before the XXI Olympiad. Delays and soaring costs, affecting the building of the main stadium, led to one of the worst crises ever to face the International Olympic Committee

Finn Lasse Viren. Defending an Olympic title has always been a thankless task but defending two has never proved possible. In distance events, only Vladimir Kuts, Emil Zatopek and Hannes Kolehmainen, had previously achieved this double at a single Games. Viren wanted to achieve it for a second time. 'I just want to stop my countrymen talking about Paavo Nurmi as THE Flying Finn,' he said.

Viren, a Finnish policeman, had set a new world record in the 10,000 metres in Munich, but in Montreal, the first half of the race was run at a funereal pace. After 10 laps only one runner had dropped off the main pack, and the halfway mark came up in 14min 8.94sec. Then the pace quickened.

Portugal's Carlos Lopes gradually forced others to drop away until, after 8,000 metres, only Viren was still in contention, with Britain's Brendan Foster a long way back in third place. But Lopes could not match Viren's finishing speed. With 450 metres to go, Viren struck, storming round the last lap in an incredible 61 seconds. Unbelievably, the second half of the race had been run in 13min 31.5sec, and the final time of 27min 40.4sec was only two seconds slower than his 1972 world record time.

The 5,000 metres was dominated just as surely by Viren. 'He mesmerized the race, like a rattlesnake,' said former Canadian star, Bruce Kidd. Not until Viren took charge after 4,000 metres did a race begin in earnest, and with every other runner waiting for his move, Viren held back until the bell before outsprinting them. His time was two seconds faster than his Munich time but not an Olympic record this time. Brendan Foster had set that in an earlier heat, only to finish fifth in the final.

The Americans, after their great disasters in Munich, had their moments but too few of them for their own comfort. They won only four titles, Moses' 400 metres hurdles, the long jump (Arnie Robinson), the discus (Mac Wilkins), and the decathlon. But the last at least was a triumph to savour. It was forecast that it would be the greatest decathlon ever, a classic contest between the reigning champion Nikolay Avilov, of the Soviet Union, and the world record holder, Bruce Jenner, of the United States.

Jenner did not disappoint us, but for Avilov the contest was over after the first event in which he had come out of his blocks so slowly that he was 70 points behind Jenner in an event he should have won. The rest was a formality for Jenner but he won like a champion. He had personal best scores in the first five events, and in the end he needed only to run the 1,500 metres in 4min 30sec to break the world record. He ran it in 4min 12.6sec to beat it by a margin of 164 points.

Britain managed only one medal — Foster's 10,000 metres bronze — but the biggest disappointment of

the Games for everybody was the 1,500 metres. With world record holder Filbert Bayi absent, world mile record holder John Walker led a pedestrian race, winning in a time nearly seven seconds or 50 yards slower than Bayi's record.

The men of the Soviet Union won only two titles – Viktor Saneev becoming only the third athlete ever to win an event for the third time when he won the triple jump and Yuriy Sedyh beating his own coach, Anatoliy Bondarchuk, in the hammer. But that was not much consolation for the Americans. They failed to regain the pole vault they had lost for the first time in 1972, lost the 110 metres hurdles for the first time since 1928 and for the first time for 40 years did not have a medallist in the shot.

Athletics – Women
Women did not run 1,500 metres at Olympic Games before 1972 but if any further proof was needed that

the longer events of athletics hold no dangers for the fairer sex it was offered by a Russian girl, Tatiana Kazankina, in Montreal when she won both the 800 and 1,500 metres.

Kazankina was sent to the Games as the Soviet Union's first string 1,500 metres runner. She had set a world record of 3min 56sec before the Games. On the last day for entries, she was added to the 800 metres, and proceeded to win it in one of the biggest break-throughs seen in any event at these Games.

Four girls broke the existing world record for the 800 metres – and one of them, Anita Weiss, did not win a medal even though she had set an Olympic record in the heats, and slashed three-tenths of a second off the world record in the final. She was still a second behind Kazankina, who had sprinted from fifth to first place in the last 80 metres, almost exactly the tactics she adopted later in the week to win the 1,500 metres.

But if the Russian's performances have lasting significance for women's running, the outstanding achievement of the women's track competitions was the 400 metres victory of Irene Szewinska, a 30-year-old Polish mother, who had won the 200 metres title in 1968, and medals in Tokyo and Munich. No other woman has ever won a medal at four consecutive Games, and she did it in the style always associated with her.

Although she was still one of the world's best sprinters, she had decided to concentrate exclusively on 400 metres, an event in which she had become the first woman to break 50 seconds. It was a wise decision; she overwhelmed the opposition with a new world record of 49.29sec and a margin of 10 metres over the runner-up, a girl 12 years her junior.

In Mrs Szewinska's absence from the sprints, they were dominated by Germans. Annagret Richter set the

Two undisputed champions of very different sports. *Right,* Cuba's Teofilo Stevenson wins his second heavyweight gold, and, *left,* Nadia Comaneci of Rumania, whose stunning perfection was unequalled.

first world record of the athletics competition in a semi-final of the 100 metres, and then ran slower to win the final for West Germany. She had to take second place to East Germany's Barbel Eckert in the 200 metres but Annagret still went home with a gold, two silvers and a world record.

The East Germans dominated just about everything else in women's track and field. Their women athletes finally overtook their swimmers when they won nine of the 14 gold medals and four of the 12 silvers available to them. It was a crushing victory for them, and left the West with only one gold medal – Richter's in the 100 metres.

Indeed, so overwhelming was East German superiority that when, in the 100 metres hurdles, their world record holder and reigning Olympic champion, Annelie Ehrhardt failed to make the final because of injury, their second string, Johanna Schaller still won the gold medal.

Perhaps more curious was the failure of another defending champion, Faina Melnik, in the discus. She had thrown five feet more than any other woman before the Games but she could not find her rhythm until the fifth round when she threw 225ft 1in to move into second place.

Unfortunately, Melnik had walked out of the circle before making her throw, and the fifth throw was disqualified, leaving her in fourth place and promoting an East German girl, Evelyn Schlaak, to second.

For Britain there was no consolation in any of the women's events. Only one girl, Andrea Lynch, made a track final, and she finished seventh, the highest position Britain's women managed at these Games.

Swimming

The swimming events at the 1976 Games were the exclusive preserve of two countries – the United States and East Germany. It was rather like an international match between the two, with guest swimmers from elsewhere.

There were always only two questions to be answered. Would the American men win all the Olympic titles? And would East Germany win all the women's? As it happened, the answer was no to both, but it was a near thing. The Americans won 34 of the 78 medals, and 13 of the 26 gold medals; the East German women won all but two of the 13 Olympic titles.

Only two of the other nations, the Soviet Union and Great Britain, won titles, and only six other countries won any medals. The American men were so powerful

that they won 12 of the 13 golds open to them, won 25 of the 33 individual medals, won all three medals in four of the events and were first and second in five more.

But even their achievements were no more than equal to those of East Germany's women. Before Montreal, no East German woman had won an Olympic title in the swimming pool, and in 1972 had won only four medals. Between the Games, they had blossomed, winning eight of the 12 titles at the 1973 and 1975 world championships. But even that did not prepare their opponents for their feats in Montreal.

Outstanding among their team was Kornelia Ender, a 13-year-old at Munich who had won one of East Germany's two silver medals there. She was now a powerful and tall girl, and virtually unbeatable. She won the 100 and 200 metres freestyle in world records, set another world record in winning

the 100 metres butterfly and anchored her country to a winning world record in the medley relay.

In only one event did she swim without winning a gold medal, and that was when the East German coaches made the strange tactical decision to have her swim the first leg in the freestyle relay. In that race, in spite of the early lead Ender established, the United States broke the East German monopoly on women's titles. But for her the climax of the Games was the announcement of her forthcoming marriage to another Olympic swimming champion, Roland Matthes.

The Ender of the men's competition was, undoubtedly, John Naber, whose 6ft 6in frame took him to two backstroke gold medals, two relay golds and a silver in the 200 metres freestyle when he swam only 35 minutes after another final.

It was a successful Games, too, for Britain. Fifth overall in the total medal table with one gold, one

silver and one bronze, they had the satisfaction of the incomparable achievement of David Wilkie, the first British man to win a swimming gold since 1908. Wilkie won a silver in the 100 metres breaststroke in a time which would have won gold in 1972, and then had easily the most decisive win of the entire swimming competitions in the 200 metres when he won in a new world record of 2min 15.11sec, more than two seconds ahead of the second man.

Other highlights were the breaking of the 50 second barrier in the 100 metres freestyle by American Jim Montgomery, a studious, bespectacled figure who won three golds at the Games but will be remembered for his time of 49.99sec; the 17-year-old Brian Goodell's world record in the 1,500 metres freestyle; and the fact that only four of the 26 world records and only one Olympic record survived. Appropriately the latter belonged to

eft, David Wilkie, who won Britain's first swimming gold or 68 years in a world-record ime.

Above, a model of Montreal's Olympic Village.

he greatest swimming Olympian of ll, Mark Spitz.

Diving had its heroes, too. Dibiasi created a record when he von the highboard title for the third uccessive Games, and the Italian id it by scoring the first maximum :n points at an Olympics to win by 3 points with a total of more than 00. Similarly impressive was the pringboard winner, Phil Boggs, a Jnited States Air Force captain, vho had been world champion in 973 and 1975. The women's spring-oard also went to the United tates, and Elena Vaytsekhovskaia, n 18-year-old, won the Soviet Jnion its first women's Olympic iving title in the highboard.

The Soviet Union were far less uccessful in water polo. The de-:nding champions were beaten out f qualifying for the final pool of ix, and even failed to win the osers' pool. The gold medal went nstead to Hungary, the runners-up Munich, who were led by Tamas iargo, a trainee veterinary surgeon

who scored 22 goals in eight games.

Other sports
No sport in Montreal won more hearts around the world, through its television coverage, than gymna-stics – this time because of one girl, Nadia Comaneci, a small, 5ft tall, 14-year-old Rumanian.

In 1972 it had been the Soviet Union's Olga Korbut who had begun the tidal wave of interest in the sport. With her tiny, almost child-like physique and her frighten-ing back somersaults, she won the adoration and enthusiasm of the world's children. Suddenly, every mother's child wanted a try on the bars and beams.

Comaneci was a different crea-ture, a girl with an orphan look but without Korbut's fallibility. She made her enormous impact on the Games quite simply because of her ultimate perfection. Never before had any gymnast achieved a perfect score of ten at an Olympics, but Nadia did it in her first day's competition. She was to achieve that perfect score seven times over before the Games ended, emerging from the Games with three gold medals: the beam, the asymmetric bars and the supreme title, the combined exercises.

The Russians were shaken by her superiority. Nelli Kim won them two individual golds but their great champion Ludmila Tourisheva had to be content with two silver and one bronze medal and Olga Korbut with a single silver. Their only consolation was the team prize remaining their property, as it had since the Soviet Union first entered the Olympic arena in 1952.

The men's gymnastics never ap-peals to audiences as much as the women's but there was plenty of drama still in the intense competi-tion between Japan and the Soviet Union, and in the brilliance of one Russian, Nikolai Andrianov, the 22-year-old European champion. Adrianov was not as adventurous as the women had been but he was consistently uniform. He never re-ceived less than a mark of 9.65 points for any apparatus, and fin-ished as the all-round champion with another three individual gold medals. Japan, however, won the team prize – by just 0.4 of a point.

Britain's most unexpected success came in the modern pentathlon, that five-point sport created origin-ally for the modern Olympics in 1912 as an event for military men. Britain had never so much as won a medal at it but in Montreal with

two civilians, Adrian Parker and Danny Nightingale, and an army sergeant, Jim Fox, they won the team gold medal in a tense and unforgettable finish. Britain were only fifth at the start of the fifth day, 537 points behind the leading nation, Czechoslovakia. But all three Britons were runners, and the final event was the 4,000 metres cross country.

Parker was the first runner out, and finished in 12min 9sec, a staggering time which earned him 1,378 points. He was placed first, Nightingale was fourth and Fox, at the age of 34 and in his fourth Games, ran himself to complete collapse. Between them they had not only pulled back the 537 points but won by 108.

There were few other British successes. European three day event champion Lucinda Prior-Palmer's horse Be Fair went lame, Princess Anne fell and was slightly concussed and Britain won nothing from that equestrian event. The show jumping was similarly unrewarding, al-though Debbie Johnsey on Moxy was involved in a jump off for the silver and bronze medals, finally finishing fourth.

In the judo, Japan won only three of the six gold medals, which was a disaster for them, but Britain's Keith Remfry won a silver in the open category and David Star-brook, silver medallist in 1972, won a bronze, this time in the light-heavyweights, an outstanding Games for a country not noted for its martial arts.

More predictably, there were medals for Britain in the yachting at Kingston. Rodney Pattisson, attempting to win his third con-secutive gold medal in the Flying Dutchman class, had the edge until the fifth race of the series but finally had to settle for the silver. More successful were Reg White and John Osborn, brothers-in-law from Essex, who won the Tornado cata-maran class – new to the Games – so convincingly that they did not bother to sail in the final race after winning the first four.

The Americans, who had slipped badly in the boxing rings of Munich, restored their supremacy by win-ning five titles while the Cubans proved the newest force by winning three. The United States climbed back on the winner's rostrum, too, in basketball, sweet revenge for their controversial beating by the Soviet Union in 1972.

For the hosts, the Canadians, the vast financial support for amateur sport over the previous four years, the importing of many top foreign coaches and the serious bid for medals was not rewarded as well as they had hoped. Canadian stan-dards had improved immeasurably, but the Olympics had come too soon.

They did not win a gold medal – Greg Joy's high jump silver medal was the best performance – but eight medals in swimming put them among the world's strongest in that sport.

Olympic Football

As regular as the Olympic tournament itself is the well-worn controversy about the 'shamateurism' of the East Europeans in Olympic football. Munich and 1972 were no different. This time it was the turn of Stanley Rous to right the wrongs. His answer was to ban all World Cup players from the Olympics, thereby seriously weakening the strength of the Eastern European countries and, hopefully, allowing the emerging soccer nations to compete on more equal terms.

Excellent as it seemed, Rous' proposal was greeted with predictable hostility by anyone who felt that it affected their interests for the worse. And so the 1972 Olympics went as almost everyone predicted they would, Eastern European countries dominating the qualifying groups and monopolizing the semi-finals. It was left to Poland, who had never before won a major honour, to provide the one real surprise of the tournament when they, and not Hungary, won the final to take the gold medal.

There was a trace of irony in Rous' proposal, for without the success of Olympic football in the 1920s, the World Cup would have taken a longer time to materialize. Football had been introduced to the Olympics at Paris in 1900, but only as an exhibition, when Upton Park (representing Britain) beat France 4-0. It was eventually adopted in London in 1908, though only six teams took part and two were from France. The British side (all English) beat Sweden 12-1, the Netherlands 4-0, and Denmark 2-0 (in front of 8,000 people at the White City) to take the gold medal.

The 1912 tournament at Stockholm produced 11 entrants, all from Europe, but the same finalists. In intense heat Britain defeated Hungary 7-0 and Finland 4-0 before overcoming by 4-2 an injury-hit Danish side, who had eliminated Norway and the Netherlands.

Britain's dominance ended ignominiously when the Olympics were resumed at Antwerp in 1920. The FA stormed out of the Games, claiming that they had been playing against professionals. Professionalism was indeed already seeping through in the form of lavish expenses and broken-time payments (for time lost from work), but a more likely explanation for Britain's chagrin was their 3-1 defeat at the hands of Norway, one of the few amateur sides present.

Czechoslovakia emerged as new stars, beating Yugoslavia 7-0, Norway 4-0, and France 4-1 to reach the final where they met Belgium—the home side. The Czechs, however, were to go home without reward. They disagreed strongly with many decisions, some justifiably, and when the referee awarded Belgium their second goal, and let it stand after furious protest, they left the pitch and were disqualified. After a complicated play-off system Spain, beaten by Belgium 3-1 in the second round, took the silver medal, while the Dutch had to be content with the bronze for the third successive time, despite having won the match for third place before the disqualification of Czechoslovakia.

Soon after the Antwerp Games several European nations legalized various forms of broken-time payments for amateurs. In 1923 FIFA refused to accept the British definition of the term, and both Britain and Denmark did not compete in 1924. The four British associations finally withdrew from FIFA after that body had insisted the Olympic committee legalize broken-time payments for their members during the Amsterdam tournament, and did not rejoin until 1946. Football was dropped from the 1932 Games at Los Angeles, and in 1936 there was a return to the strict definition of the amateur: Britain and Denmark reappeared, but Uruguay, Argentina, Belgium, and Switzerland refused to participate.

With the emergence of government-assisted athletes from the Eastern European bloc, the FA attitude softened after the Second World War and in 1948 the FA gave tentative approval to broken-time payments for representative matches.

At Paris in 1924 football had really made its mark. A quarter of a million people saw the 21 games, including 41,000 for the final, and soccer contributed over a third of the total Olympic revenue. The entry (22) was considerably broad-ended, and one of the two major surprises was Egypt's 3-0 win over Hungary, the favourites. The other was Sweden's elimination of the holders, Belgium, by 8-1. But attention fixed on the South American champions Uruguay, who defeated Yugoslavia 7-0, USA 3-0, France 5-1, and the Netherlands 2-1 to make the final, where after an even first half they put three goals past Switzerland.

The 1928 competition endorsed the New World's success with an all-South American final. Argentina scored 23 goals against USA, Belgium, and Egypt, while Uruguay, if less spectacular statistically, had little trouble with greater opposition in the Netherlands, Germany, and Italy. Uruguay overcame their neighbours and old rivals after a replay in a foretaste of the first World Cup final two years later.

When soccer returned to the Olympic agenda at Berlin in 1936, the competition was organized with Teutonic thoroughness and efficiency.

The 16 teams were seeded—8 strong ones playing 8 weaker ones in the first round—but there were plenty of surprises to upset the officials' calculations. Newcomers Japan upset the ratings by beating Sweden 3-2, before losing 8-0 to Vittorio Pozzo's Italy. Norway held out against the meticulously prepared Germans—who were sent away in disgrace—and Britain, who had beaten China 2-0 in the first round, went down 5-4 to Poland after trailing 5-1 at one stage. Italy and Austria, coached by Jimmy Hogan, beat Norway and Poland respectively to reach the final, where the Italians needed extra time and a lucky goal to win the gold medal.

The London Olympics of 1948 were won in grand style by Sweden, coached by George Raynor and full of players later to make their mark with European clubs. They beat Austria 3-0, Korea 12-0, Denmark 4-2 and, in the final, Yugoslavia, who had beaten Great Britain (managed by Matt Busby), 3-1 in the semi-final. Britain had earlier beaten the Netherlands and France, who in turn had struggled in beating India, who had nine players competing without boots.

If 1948 belonged to Sweden, 1952 and Helsinki was the story of Hungary. They eliminated Romania, Italy, Turkey, and Sweden (6-0) before meeting Yugoslavia, who had scored 26 goals in their five matches. The Hungarians—10 of whom were to be in the side that shattered England at Wembley the following year—brought that run to an abrupt end in the final and won 2-0, despite Puskas missing a penalty. The shock of the competition was provided by Luxembourg with a 5-3 win over Britain in the preliminary round.

The 1956 series in Melbourne was a dull affair. Many countries, including Hungary, stayed out because of the travelling expense, and the entry went down from the 25 of 1952 to 11—the lowest since 1912. England were invited after being eliminated in the qualifiers by Bulgaria—who promptly beat them 6-1 in the second round. The Russians, fielding their full international side, beat Yugoslavia, and the luckless Yugoslavs thus took their third successive silver medal.

Yugoslavia's turn was to come at Rome in 1960 when—with the help of five full caps—they beat Denmark in the final. It was unfortunate that their success was clouded by the situation in the semi-final, when they won through on the drawing of lots after fruitless extra time with Italy. For the first time the competition employed groups, with the top club from each qualifying for the semi-finals. There the series produced its one upset, with Denmark beating a star-studded Hungarian side 2-0.

Eastern Europe again provided

Above: **Great Britain, Olympic champions in 1908 and 1912, got close to the honours at the second London Olympics, in 1948. But in the semi-final, Britain (white) lost 1-3 to Yugoslavia and then went down 3-5 to Denmark in the third-place match. 1 Sweden (dark shirts), with their famed Grenoli trio, took the gold medals at London. 2 Hungary's Lajos Szucs scores against Japan in their 1968 semi-final in Mexico City. Japan, surprisingly, won the bronze medals. Less of a shock was the east European final between Hungary and Bulgaria. Unfortunately, the game developed into a brawl, with four players being sent off and the officials being bombarded with cushions (3). 4 The magnificent setting for the 1972 Olympic football final in Munich.**

OLYMPIC GOLD MEDAL SIDES

Britain (1908): Bailey; Corbett, Smith; Hunt, Chapman, Hawkes; Berry, Woodward, Stapley, Purnell, Hardman
Britain (1912): Brebner; Burn, Knight; Littlewort, Hanney, Dines; Berry, Woodward, Walden, Hoare, Sharpe
Belgium (1920): De Bie; Swartenbroecks, Verbeek; Masch, Hause, Fierens; van Hegge, Coppee, Bragard, Larnoe, Bastin
Uruguay (1924): Mazzali: Nasazzi, Arispe; Andrade, Vidal, Ghierra; A. Urdinaran, Scarone, Petrone, Cea, Romano
Uruguay (1928): Mazzali; Nasazzi, Arispe; Andrade, Fernandez, Gestido; S. Urdinaran, Scarone, Petrone, Cea, Castro
Italy (1936): Venturini, Foni, Rava; Baldo, Piccini, Locatelli; Frossi, Marchini, Bertoni, Biagi, Gabriotti
Sweden (1948): Lindberg; K. Nordahl, Nilsson; Rosengren, B. Nordahl, Andersson; Rosen, Gren, G. Nordahl, Carlsson, Liedholm
Hungary (1952): Grosics; Buzansky, Lantos; Bozsik, Lorant, Zakarias; Hidegkuti, Kocsics, Palotas, Puskas, Czibor
USSR (1956): Yachin; Kuznetsov, Ogonkinov; Maslenkin, Bachachkin, Netto; Tatouchkin; Issaev, Simonian, Salnikov, Ilyin
Yugoslavia (1960): Vidinic; Durkovic, Jusufi; Zanetic, Roganovic, Perusic; Ankovic, Matous, Galic, Knez, Kostic
Hungary (1964): Szentmihalyi; Novak, Iliasz; Szepesi, Orban, Nogradi; Farkas, Csernai, Bene, Komora, Katona
Hungary (1968): Fater; Novak, Drestyak; Pancsics, Menczel, Szucs; Fazekas, A. Dunai, Nagy, Nosko, Juhasz
Poland (1972): Kostka; Gut, Gorgon; Cmikiewicz, Anczok, Szoltysik; Masczyk, Kraska, Deyna, (s. Szynczak), Lubanski, Godocha

1 The Hungarians celebrate Varadi's goal in the usual manner, but it was the Poles, with two goals by Deyna, who took the football gold medals at Munich.
2 Quick thinking by Gunnar Nordahl brought Sweden a goal in the 1948 semi-final with Denmark. Realizing he could be off-side, he stepped into the net—and out of play—and Carlsson's goal stood.

Colorsport

1 the winner at Tokyo in 1964, with Hungary beating Czechoslovakia. East Germany took third place, but there was no other European opposition. The 14 sides were arranged in two groups of four and two of three, with the top eight forming the quarter-finalists. Hungary, having beaten Morocco and Yugoslavia (6-5) in their group, then eliminated Romania and the UAR to reach the final.

For 1968 in Mexico two genuinely amateur European countries, France and Spain, returned to the fray and both won their sections. The relatively un-advanced soccer nations of Asia, Africa, and Central America provided nine entrants, but it was two of the three state-sponsored teams—Hungary and Bulgaria, again using the Olympics as a practice for the subsequent World Cup—who provided the finalists. The final, however, was ruined by a mixture of violent play and over-zealous refereeing, and four players were sent off. Conduct was to improve, but abuse of the system was not, in 1972.

OLYMPIC SOCCER

Year	Venue	Teams	First		Second		Third		Fourth	
1908	London	†6	Great Britain	2	Denmark	0	Netherlands	2	Sweden	1
1912	Stockholm	11	Great Britain	4	Denmark	2	Netherlands	9	Finland	0
1920	Antwerp	14	‡Belgium		‡Spain		‡Netherlands		‡France	
1924	Paris	22	Uruguay	3	Switzerland	0	Sweden	1:3	Netherlands	1:1
1928	Amsterdam	17	Uruguay	1:2	Argentina	1:1	Italy	11	Egypt	3
1936	Berlin	16	*Italy	2	Austria	1	*Norway	3	Poland	2
1948	London	18	Sweden	3	Yugoslavia	1	Denmark	5	Great Britain	3
1952	Helsinki	25	Hungary	2	Yugoslavia	0	Sweden	3	Germany	0
1956	Melbourne	11	USSR	1	Yugoslavia	0	Bulgaria	3	India	1
1960	Rome	16	Yugoslavia	3	Denmark	1	Hungary	2	Italy	1
1964	Tokyo	14	Hungary	2	Czechoslovakia	1	East Germany	3	UAR	1
1968	Mexico City	16	Hungary	4	Bulgaria	1	Japan	2	Mexico	0
1972	Munich	16	Poland	2	Hungary	1	*§East Germany	2	§USSR	2
1976	Montreal	16	East Germany	3	Poland	1	USSR	2	Brazil	0

* after extra time † including two French sides. ‡ Czechoslovakia, losing 2-0 to Belgium in the final, walked off the field and were disqualified. Spain, Sweden, Italy, and Norway played off for the right to meet the Netherlands (beaten by Belgium in the semi-final) for second place, and Spain then beat the Netherlands 3-1. France had earlier lost to the Netherlands in the play-off between the losing semi-finalists. § East Germany and USSR shared third place.

The Winter Olympic Games

Tony Nash and Robin Dixon
overcame tremendous
handicaps to become Britain's
first ever bobsleigh Olympic
champions, at Igls in 1964.

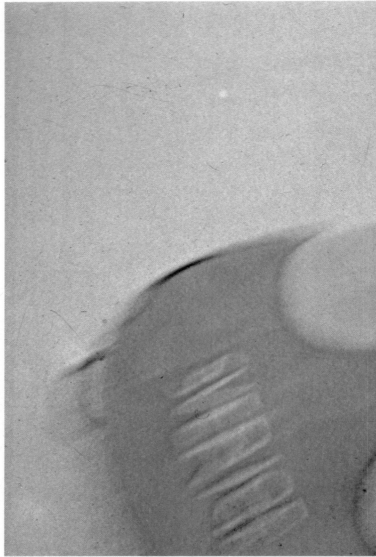

The speed skater striving for the extra yard of pace; the ski jumper defying gravity to the utmost; the bobsleigh crew hurtling down a funnel of ice; the figure skater entrancing with breathtaking spins and jumps; the skier twisting and weaving downhill through the slalom poles . . . all contribute to making the Winter Olympics an absorbing spectacle of speed and grace, courage and self-expression.

Above: **Jean-Claude Killy, sex symbol of the slopes and the second Alpine skier, after Austria's Toni Sailer, to win three gold medals in one Winter Olympics. Soon after achieving this, at Grenoble, Killy turned professional.**

Left: **The Special Jump, which has been a largely Scandinavian preserve since its Olympic inception in 1924. It was first practised in Norway as early as 1866.**

Although ice figure skating competitions were included in the original list of proposed Olympic events drawn up at the first Olympic conference, at Paris on June 23, 1894, which led to the revival of the Olympic Games, skating had to wait until 1908 and the first London Olympics to make its debut in the Games.

But from this belated beginning arose the Winter Olympic Games, officially the 'Olympic Winter Games', held quadriennially since 1924 as a separate celebration. The early listing of skating was due to its being one of the earliest sports to be organized internationally, and its delayed appearance in the Games was due only to the difficulty of finding a suitable rink in the host cities. London was the first able to provide it.

The second Olympic contest in figure skating, together with the first Olympic ice hockey tournament, took place at the Antwerp

Games of 1920. And although such events could have continued to form part of the summer Games, the growing popularity of Nordic skiing prompted the logical setting up of a separate winter programme. Thus the first Winter Olympic Games were held at Chamonix in 1924. There, Nordic ski racers and jumpers, four-man bobsledders, and speed skaters joined the figure skaters and ice hockey players in a self-contained schedule.

For the second Winter Olympics, at St Moritz in 1928, skeleton tobogganing was included on the Cresta Run. (This competition was revived in 1948 at the same venue, but was not held at any other Winter Olympics.) In other fields, too, the programme expanded. For the third meeting, at Lake Placid, New York, two-man bobsledding was added. Alpine skiing was included at the 1936 Games at Garmisch-Partenkirchen, and the popularity of the Winter Games was such that they were revived immediately after World War II, at St Moritz in 1948.

The 1952 events were the first to be staged near a capital city, Oslo, and this factor considerably boosted the attendance figures. By this time the Games were an integral feature of the winter sports calendar, and the three gold medals won by Toni Sailer at Cortina in 1956 made his name as well known throughout the world as those of the heroes of the summer Olympics.

For the Squaw Valley Games of 1960, the second to be held in the United States, the programme was strengthened by the inclusion of women's speed skating and the men's biathlon—a combination cross-country skiing and shooting event—though bobsleigh was temporarily excluded. And though the number of entrants may have been reduced because of the distance of Squaw Valley from Europe, when the 1964 Games were staged in Innsbruck they attracted over 1,000 competitors from a record 36 countries. These Games also saw the introduction of luge tobogganing. Further records were broken at Grenoble in 1968, when 1,293 competitors from 37 nations attended.

The Winter Olympic Games are the one occasion every four years when all the major snow and ice sports are being staged in one

Above: **The opening ceremony of the 1968 Winter Olympics at Grenoble, the 10th to be held since 1924, when 293 men and women met at Chamonix. At Grenoble there were 1,293 competitors. 1 Bobsleigh was an Olympic sport from the very start, but 2 alpine skiing, perhaps the most publicized of winter sports, did not join the list until 1936. 3 Ice hockey, for a long time the domain of the Canadians, and 4 figure skating preceded the Winter Olympics by appearing in earlier Olympic Games.**

area. Even so, because of the disparate nature of many of the sports involved, which require differing facilities, the competitions tend to be rather dispersed. This, however, is true of any major event, and is a reflection of the difficulty of staging the winter Games. Consequently, the cost to the host city is enormous, and it may be indicative that Denver, in Colorado, USA, withdrew as the venue for the 1976 Winter Olympics; and it was decided to hold them at Innsbruck, where winter sport facilities were available without the burden of unnecessary expense.

WINTER OLYMPIC GAMES

Year	Venue	Date	Competitors		
			Men	Women	Total
1924	Chamonix	25 Jan—4 Feb	280	13	293
1928	St Moritz	11-19 Feb	484	27	491
1932	Lake Placid	4-13 Feb	277	30	307
1936	Garmisch	6-16 Feb	680	76	756
1948	St Moritz	30 Jan—8 Feb	636	77	713
1952	Oslo	14-25 Feb	624	108	732
1956	Cortina	26 Jan—5 Feb	778	146	924
1960	Squaw Valley	18-28 Feb	521	144	665
1964	Innsbruck	29 Jan—9 Feb	914	197	1,111
1968	Grenoble	6-18 Feb	1,065	228	1,293
1972	Sapporo	3-13 Feb	911	217	1,128
1976	Innsbruck	4-15 Feb	1092	276	1,368

Figure skating events were also held in 1908 and 1920 as part of the main Olympic celebrations.

Chamonix Winter Olympic Games (1924)

Nobody knew it then, but a competitor who finished last at the Chamonix Winter Olympics was later to become the most famous of all Winter Olympics entrants. These first Winter Olympics marked the international debut of a tiny, 11-year-old Norwegian schoolgirl —Sonja Henie—who was later to reign as queen of the ice with three Olympic and 10 world championship crowns.

But in these early days of Winter Olympics, the big talking point was whether they would take place at all. Despite Chamonix's favourable climatic record, there was at first no snow; and when it did snow on the French Alpine resort, 36,000 cubic metres of it had to be cleared from the ice rink. With only a week to go, rain transformed the speed-skating rink into a lake. Fortunately, frosts returned, and conditions were ideal when Monsieur Gaston Vidal, French Undersecretary of State, declared the Games open.

Although figure skating had already formed part of the 1908 London Olympic Games, and was again contested, along with ice hockey, at Antwerp in 1920, the Chamonix Games were the first occasion on which other snow and ice sports gained Olympic status. And so Nordic skiers, bobsledders, and speed skaters joined figure skaters and ice hockey players at Chamonix for the first self-contained, separate Winter Olympics.

One hundred and two skiers, 82 ice hockey players, 39 bobsledders, 31 speed skaters, and 29 figure skaters representing 16 nations contested the 14 titles. The only women competitors were the 13 figure skaters, 5 of whom took part in the pairs as well as the solo event. Norway and Finland finished the most successful countries, winning 4 gold medals each, followed by Austria with 2, and the United States, Switzerland, Canada, and Sweden with 1 each.

The outstanding individuals were the Norwegian skier Thorleif Haug and the Finnish skater Clas Thunberg, both winning three gold

Competitors gather in the French Alpine resort of Chamonix for the opening of the first Winter Olympics.

medals each. In addition, Thunberg collected a silver and a bronze, and Haug also won a bronze. In a sense, one of Thunberg's gold medals was complimentary because it was awarded to the best overall performer in the four speed-skating events, the only time a combination award has been made for Olympic speed skating.

Haug led a strong team of Norwegian skiers who, in the 1920s, were acknowledged world masters both of cross-country and jumping events. His superiority was most marked in the gruelling 50 kilometres cross-country, in which only 21 of the 33 contestants finished a course made hazardous by several frozen downhill slopes. Haug's three team-mates followed him to take the next places and little more than five minutes separated the four. The fifth-placed competitor, however, was more than 21 minutes slower than Haug.

The story was much the same in the 18 kilometres, except that a Finn took the bronze. And by winning the Nordic combination, a challenging test of overall cross-country and jumping skill, Haug illustrated his versatility and collected his third gold.

The Norwegian skiers completed the grand slam when Jacob Thams won the specialized jump event. It was held on a hill erected with possible leaps of 60 metres in mind, but the jury shortened the in-run and so lessened the distance potential. Thams took the title with two leaps of 49 metres in the adjudged best style. The longest clearance, 50 metres, was made by an American Anders Haugen, who eventually finished fourth.

Successful though the Norwegians were in skiing, their eclipse in all the speed-skating events was a major surprise, for this was another sport in which the nation had distinguished traditions. Thunberg convincingly won the two middle distances, 1,500 metres and 5,000 metres, finished second in the 10,000 to his fellow Finn Julius Skutnabb, and tied for third place

1 Sonja Henie made her debut at Chamonix, placing last in a field of eight: an inauspicious start to a remarkable career.
2 The jumping was won by Jacob Tham, and the other three Nordic events by his compatriot, Thorleif Haug (3).

American runner-up, was followed by Britain's Ethel Muckelt, with an endearingly diminutive Sonja Henie last in the field of eight. In the pairs, Alfred Berger and Helene Engelmann struck another blow for the Viennese school by outpointing the Finns, Walter and Ludovika Jakobsson.

Bobsledding at Chamonix was confined to one event, for crews of four or five riders. The bob run at the time was considered pretty hazardous and technically below the top international standards, and there were some nasty incidents. Although the Swiss won the gold medal, they had mixed fortunes. Their number one sled had to withdraw after a serious crash, and it was left to their second crew, driven by Eduard Scherrer, to clock the fastest times in each of the first three runs to take the title.

The ice hockey was, as it has been since, the big spectator draw, and Europeans were dazzled by the consistently high standard of the Canadian and American teams, which they were unable to match. Goals galore in uneven games seldom failed to mesmerize onlookers, who admired and respected a brand of play they had not been accustomed to.

The transatlantic teams overwhelmed the best Europe could offer, Canada running up scores of 30-0 against Czechoslovakia and 22-0 against Sweden. Their least one-sided game was their 6-1 victory over the United States, America's only defeat. Great Britain, though losing 2-19, were the only side to score more than once against the champions, and by beating Sweden 4-3 they earned the bronze medal.

It is an Olympic tradition that the host country may present in the programme two additional sports as demonstration events. At Chamonix, the chosen demonstration events were curling and a military patrol race. Three nations contested the curling—the more widely practised rules of Scottish origin were used—which was won by a British team led by T. S. Aikman, with Sweden runners-up.

The military patrol race, combining skiing and rifle marksmanship over a difficult 30 kilometres course, was a forerunner of the modern biathlon. The earlier sport had a more military appearance than its successor, and was especially popular in Switzerland whose team narrowly defeated Finland.

The Chamonix Games had made a great start for separate Winter Olympics. Other events have been added since then, and at Grenoble in 1968, more than double the nations represented at Chamonix sent over five times the number of competitors to contest more than twice the events.

1 Herma Plank-Szabo, five times world champion, was a convincing winner of the women's figure skating.
2 A goalmouth incident in the ice hockey final between the United States (dark shirts) and Canada, who won 6-1.

CHAMONIX WINTER OLYMPIC GAMES, 1924 Gold Medallists			
Nordic Skiing			
18 kilometres	Thorleif Haug	Norway	1 hr 14 min 31.0 sec
50 kilometres	Thorleif Haug	Norway	3 hr 44 min 32.0 sec
Jumping	Jacob Thams	Norway	
Combination	Thorleif Haug	Norway	
Figure Skating			
Men	Gillis Grafstrom	Sweden	
Women	Herma Plank-Szabo	Austria	
Pairs	Alfred Berger, Helene Engelmann	Austria	
Speed Skating			
500 metres	Charles Jewtraw	USA	44.0 sec
1,500	Clas Thunberg	Finland	2 min 20.8 sec
5,000 metres	Clas Thunberg	Finland	8 min 39.0 sec
10,000 metres	Julius Skutnabb	Finland	18 min 4.8 sec
Combined	Clas Thunberg	Finland	
Bobsleigh		Switzerland	
Ice Hockey		Canada	

in the 500 metres sprint, won by the American Charles Jewtraw.

All the ice events were held in a stadium that was admirable by the standards of the time. A complex arena, capable of holding more than 10,000 spectators, it included a 400 metres speed-skating perimeter around two ice hockey rinks, with the end semicircles used by figure skaters.

The individual figure-skating golds each went to the respected greats in the sport's history. Sweden's Gillis Grafström gained a narrow verdict over his Austrian rival Willy Böckl, being placed first by only four of the seven judges. And Herma Plank-Szabó, one of the early exponents of the Viennese school of technique and world champion for five consecutive years from 1922, took the women's title by a unanimous vote. Beatrix Loughran, the

St Moritz Winter Olympic Games (1928)

A sharp increase in the number of entries for the second Winter Olympics, at the Swiss glamour resort of St Moritz in 1928, reflected the substantial rise in popularity of snow and ice sports during the four years since the first Winter Games at Chamonix, France. The 491 competitors— 464 men and 27 women—numbered almost 200 more than in 1924, and represented 25 participating nations, an increase of 9.

Despite the high altitude of 6,066 feet, an unseasonably mild westerly *fohn* wind caused a dramatic thaw which affected many performances and caused the 10,000 metres speed skating to be cancelled. In fact a deluge of rain, almost unheard of in this area during February, caused one completely blank day in the middle of the meeting. Fortunately, a rapid freeze followed in time to save the programme. One new event on the programme was skeleton tobogganing on the challenging Cresta Run.

In unusually heavy conditions, Per Erik Hedlund's victory for Sweden in the 50 kilometres cross-country ski marathon took 68

minutes longer than Thorleif Haug's in 1924. This underlined the difficulty of comparing the times in cross-country ski races at different dates or venues, with weather conditions variable enough to make the going more than an hour slower. Swedes took all the medals in this event but it was Norway's turn for a grand

Above: An ice-hockey match in the picturesque setting of St Moritz during the 1928 Winter Olympics. Canada won the second of four successive gold medals in this event.
Below: Per Erik Hedlund led a clean sweep for Sweden in the 50 kilometres cross-country Nordic skiing event.

slam in the 18 kilometres. On a contrasting course, crackling with frost, Johan Grottumsbraaten finished a full two minutes ahead of two compatriots. In convincing style, Grottumsbraaten also won the Nordic combination (18 kilometres cross-country and ski jumping) in which Norwegians once more monopolized the medals.

Although hampered by a short in-run for the take-off, Alf Andersen clinched another gold for Norway in the jumping, after Jacob Tullin-Thams, the defending champion, crashed when landing what would have been a winning leap. Sigmund Ruud took the silver for Norway but third place went surprisingly to a Czech, Rudolf Burkert, the only Central European to win a medal in this event before World War II.

The Finnish speed skater Clas Thunberg, although nearly 35 years old, proved still a master by winning two gold medals for the two shorter distances, the 500 and 1,500 metres. But in the 500 metres sprint, Norwegian Bernt Evensen also took a gold with an equal time, the first winter Olympic occasion when two golds were awarded for an individual event. A triple dead heat for third place meant the award of three bronze medals.

The 5,000 metres revealed the early world-beating class of yet another Norwegian, Ivar Ballangrud, who was almost 9 seconds in

front of Julius Skutnabb of Finland, the runner-up. The cancellation of the 10,000 metres was a bitter disappointment to the United States because, at the time of curtailment, the American racer Irving Jaffee had been leading the Norwegian favourite Evensen.

The figure skating saw the last of Gillis Grafstrom's three men's victories for Sweden and the first of Sonja Henie's three women's wins for Norway—a master at his peak and a prodigy on her way up. The elegant Grafstrom, 30, skated a freestyle programme clearly better than his previous performances, appreciably superior to that of the young fourth-placed Austrian Karl Schafer, who was to be Grafstrom's successor four years later. But the runner-up was another Austrian, Willy Bockl, who closely challenged Grafstrom all the way.

Miss Henie, already the world champion but not quite 16, enjoyed a more comfortable passage and introduced a refreshingly more athletic element into women's freestyle. In the pairs event, the French partnership of Pierre Brunet and Andree Joly set a high standard in well timed lifts.

Despite their home course advantage, the Swiss were disappointing in the five-man bobsleigh event, contested by 23 teams from 14 countries. The thawing course allowed only two runs instead of the usual four. The American sleds took the first two places, with William Fiske ably piloting the winner. Jennison Heaton, who drove the second bob, won the first Olympic skeleton toboggan event on the separate Cresta Run, with his brother John in second place, ahead of Britain's Earl of Northesk.

The ice hockey tournament emphasized that a wide gulf still existed between the Canadians and the 10 other competing nations. The United States did not enter and, because of their obvious superiority, the Canadians were granted exemption until the semi-finals, a stage also reached by Sweden, Switzerland,

1 Alpine forests form a scenic backdrop to the ski jumping.
2 The great Nordic skier Johan Grottumsbraaten won the 18-km cross-country and the Nordic combined competitions for Norway.
3 Norway also came home first in the Military Ski Patrol: this demonstration event was the forerunner of the skiing-shooting biathlon which was included in the 1960 Olympics.

and Great Britain.

Scoring double figures without conceding a goal against each of the other three (an aggregate of 38–0), Canada displayed complete mastery, while the Swedes proved best of the rest by defeating third placed Switzerland 4–0 and Great Britain 3–1. The Swiss beat the British 4–0 to take the bronze medals.

A military patrol ski event was demonstrated at these Games, and this was a basic forerunner of the shooting/cross-country-skiing biathlon, which gained full Olympic status in 1960. But perhaps the most significant development at St Moritz really took place at the conference table, for it was there that Arnold Lunn seized an opportunity to persuade the then Nordic-biased International Ski Federation to agree in principle on the future Olympic inclusion of Alpine skiing, even though the motion took another eight years to reach reality. As someone observed at the time, Lunn's achievement was comparable to a Norwegian's getting the rules of cricket changed.

ST MORITZ WINTER OLYMPIC GAMES, 1928 Gold Medallists			
Nordic Skiing			
18 kilometres	Johan Grottumsbraaten	Norway	1 hr 37 min 1.0 sec
50 kilometres	Per Hedlund	Sweden	4 hr 52 min 3.0 sec
Combination	Johan Grottumsbraaten	Norway	17.8 pts
Jumping	Alf Andersen	Norway	19.2 pts
Figure Skating			
Men	Gillis Grafstrom	Sweden	2,698.2 pts
Women	Sonja Henie	Norway	1,455.8 pts
Pairs	Pierre Brunet, Andree Joly	France	100.5 pts
Speed Skating			
500 metres	Clas Thunberg	Finland	43.4 sec
	Bernt Evensen	Norway	43.4 sec
1,500 metres	Clas Thunberg	Finland	2 min 21.1 sec
5,000 metres	Ivar Ballangrud	Norway	8 min 50.5 sec
Bobsleigh			
5 man		USA	3 min 20.5 sec
Skeleton Tobogganing			
	Jennison Heaten	USA	3 min 1.8 sec
Ice Hockey		Canada	

Lake Placid Winter Olympic Games (1932)

In 1932, both summer and winter Olympic Games were held in the United States, the Winter Olympics at Lake Placid in northern New York State, and the summer Games at Los Angeles, 3,000 miles away in California. Only once previously, in 1904, had an Olympic celebration been held outside Europe, and the long travelling distances and enormous expenses involved kept the number of participants at Lake Placid down to a total of 262 competitors from 17 nations, compared with the 1928 total of 494 entrants from 25 nations.

Scandinavians dominated the four Nordic skiing events, held at an altitude of 1,860 ft. There were, in fact, Norwegian clean sweeps in both the jumping and the combination contests. Norway's Hans Beck jumped 5 metres farther than his team-mate Birger Ruud with his first attempt in the ski jump. But in the second round Beck played for safety—as he thought—and Ruud, possibly the best ski-jumper of all time, out-jumped him by 5½ metres to snatch the gold medal. Ruud was to add a second gold and a silver

19-year-old Norwegian ski jumper Birger Ruud soars through the American air to a narrow Olympic victory at Lake Placid in 1932.

in the two subsequent Winter Games in 1936 and 1948. In the Nordic combination event the versatile Johan Grottumsbraaten, another of Norway's giants, crowned a glorious career by winning the gold for the second time running, having been second at Chamonix in 1924 behind fellow-Norwegian Thorleif Haug.

The 50 kilometres cross-country marathon provided a close and exciting duel between two Finns, Veli Saarinen and Väinö Liikkanen. After nearly 4½ hours of gruelling skiing, Saarinen finished just 20 seconds clear of his compatriot, with the third-placed man, Norway's Arne Rustadstuen, 3 minutes behind them. But the 18-kilometres event was a clear win for Sweden's Sven Utterström, who came in a clear two minutes ahead of fellow-Swede Axel Wikström.

In 1932 Sonja Henie was at the zenith of her career, and it came as no surprise when she won her second Olympic figure skating gold medal with a unanimous judges' verdict over Fritzi Burger of Austria. But even the popular Norwegian's magnificent display was overshadowed by the interest taken in the men's event. The

question was, could the remarkable Swedish skater Gillis Grafström, who had won gold medals in this event at Antwerp in 1920 (when figure skating was included in the Summer Games), at Chamonix in 1924, and at St Moritz in 1928, win for a fourth successive time at the remarkable age of 38? The rising star of men's figure skating was the Austrian Karl Schäfer, a youngster of 22, and he won a thrilling tussle by a 5–2 decision and went on to retain the title in 1936. In fairness to Grafström it must be recorded that he was suffering from a knee injury, and this probably cost him the chance of becoming the first man to win four successive Olympic titles. He still finished an easy second, 66.2 points ahead of the bronze medallist, Montgomery Wilson of Canada.

The pairs title was retained by the French couple, Pierre and Andrée Brunet, who had married since their 1928 victory. Their nearest challengers, Sherwin Badger and Beatrix Loughran from the United States, came close enough to take better marks from two of the seven judges.

American skaters won all four of the men's speed skating events, John Shea winning the 500 and 1,500 metres, and Irving Jaffee the 5,000 and 10,000 metres. Their successes were gained with more than the usual home advantages. For the only time in an Olympic Games or world championship event, the customary international rules of skating in pairs were suspended, and the races were run according to the American rules of 'pack' starts with heats and finals. This meant a complete revolution in tactics for the European competitors, who were more used to the international format, the strategy of spurting and the use of 'elbowing' techniques being completely new to them. The redoubtable Finn Clas Thunberg (co-champion in 1928) declined to take part in these controversial circumstances, and the only two Europeans able to gain medals were the Norwegians Ivar Ballangrud (second in the 10,000 metres) and Bernt Evensen (second in the 500 metres). John Shea equalled the Olympic record for the 500 metres with 43.4 sec, but his victory in the 1,500 metres and both of Irving Jaffee's wins in the longer distances were the slowest Olympic successes ever recorded. The Americans were conclusively outpaced during the annual world championships held later that year on the same track under normal two-at-a-time rules. Ivar Ballangrud won all four events.

Only four nations—the United States, Canada, Germany, and Poland—contested the ice hockey and each played the other teams twice. The United States, with a much improved side, came close to toppling the Canadians (champions in 1920, 1924, and 1928). The

two Canada v USA matches decided the issue: in the first Canada won 2–1 in extra time, and drew the other 2–2 after three additional periods.

The bobsleigh course, at Mount Van Hoevenberg, was long and dangerous. It measured 1½ miles instead of the generally accepted 1 mile, and was a challenging snaking ice chute demanding special care at the now famous Shady Corner and Zigzag turns. A crash in training put one German sled and crew out of action, and it was replaced by an American bob and a new crew hastily recruited from German residents in the United States. American bobs won both the events, and the status of bobsledding was enhanced by the introduction of 2-man bobs, only a 4-man event being contested at the two previous Winter Games. William Fiske steered cleverly to win his second 4-man bob title in successive Games, while one of the crew, Clifford Gray, had also shared in the 1928 triumph. Fiske and Gray thus became the first men to win two Olympic bobsleigh gold medals. The American No. 2 crew, led by Henry Homburger, were 2.2 sec slower, but they won the silvers, and in the 2-man event the American brothers Hubert and Curtis Stevens had just 1.44 sec in hand over the runners-up Switzerland's Reto Capadrutt and Oscar Geier.

Supporting the official Olympic programme at Lake Placid were demonstration events, contested by Americans and Canadians alone, in curling, dogsleigh races, and women's speed skating. Of these, the women's speed skating found a place on the Olympic schedule in 1960.

1 Sven Utterström of Sweden easily won the 18-kilometre cross-country skiing race. 2 Ice hockey has drawn large crowds in post-war years, but in 1932 few spectators were on hand to watch Canada crush Germany 4-1 in the Olympic series at Lake Placid. The Canadian team won the gold medal. 3 Two Lake Placid brothers, Hubert and Curtis Stevens, won the first 2-man Olympic bob sled event over 1½ slippery miles. Americans also won the 4-man race. 4 Irving Jaffee, winner of the 5,000 and 10,000 speed-skating races. 5 Jack Shea won the 500 and 1,500 metres to give the United States a clean sweep. 6 Norway's Johan Grottumsbraaten recorded the second Olympic triumph in the Nordic combination event.

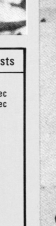

LAKE PLACID WINTER OLYMPIC GAMES, 1932 Gold Medallists

Nordic Skiing—Men

18 kilometres	Sven Utterstrom	Sweden	1 hr 23 min 7.0 sec
50 kilometres	Veli Saarinen	Finland	4 hr 28 min 0.0 sec
Combination event	Johan Grottumsbraaten	Norway	446.0 pts
Jumping	Birger Ruud	Norway	228.1 pts
Figure Skating			
Men	Karl Schafer	Austria	2,602.0 pts
Women	Sonja Henie	Norway	2,302.5 pts
Pairs	Pierre Brunet, Andree Brunet	France	76.7 pts
Speed Skating—Men			
500 metres	John Shea	USA	43.4 sec
1,500 metres	John Shea	USA	2 min 57.5 sec
5,000 metres	Irving Jaffee	USA	9 min 40.8 sec
10,000 metres	Irving Jaffee	USA	19 min 13.6 sec
Bobsleigh			
2-man	Hubert Stevens, Curtis Stevens	USA	8 min 14.74 sec
4-man		USA	7 min 53.68 sec
Ice Hockey		Canada	

Garmisch Winter Olympic Games (1936)

Fourteen thousand incredulous spectators packed the elaborate new Olympic Ice Stadium at Garmisch as Carl Erhardt led Britain's ice hockey team in a historic victory over Canada, the acknowledged masters of the game who had won every previous Olympic contest. Yet Britain beat them 2–1 and by holding the United States to a goal-less draw in the final game, they not only won the gold medal but showed that the North American teams were not invincible.

Fewer reserves were carried then than there are today, and just 12 players—Sandy Archer, James Borland, Ed Brenchley, Jimmy Chappell, John Coward, Gordon Dailley, John Davey, Carl Erhardt, Jimmy Foster, John Kilpatrick, Archie Stinchcombe, and Bob Wyman—accomplished this once seemingly impossible task to provide the surprise result of the fourth Winter Olympics.

Staged in and around the picturesque Bavarian resort of Garmisch-Partenkirchen, these Games attracted a then record entry of 755 competitors from 28 nations. Australia, Bulgaria, Greece, Liechtenstein, Spain, and Turkey all participated for the first time.

Separate winter Olympic meetings were, by this time, an undoubted success, and, with the host country intent on prestige, money was available to organize a meeting on a scale hitherto unparalleled. And the easily accessible location, midway between Munich and Innsbruck, enabled half a million spectators to attend the 17 events.

For the first time, Baron Pierre de Coubertin, founder of the modern Olympic series, excused himself from attending the opening ceremony. It was Hitler's turn to inaugurate the Games, and though no serious political incident occurred, the swastika's appearance ominously heralded the eclipse of the Winter Olympics for 12 years.

Alpine skiing was included for the first time and, when a crowd of 70,000 turned up to see the men's slalom, the sport's pioneer Arnold Lunn, who was referee, must have been proud to see his brainchild so enthusiastically acclaimed. Men's and women's downhill slalom contests were held, but medals were awarded only to the best overall performers, Franz Pfnür and Christel Cranz, both Germans. Fraulein Cranz's victory gave her the distinction of being the first women's skiing gold medallist. But because women were not yet represented in nordic

1 The ice hockey gold medal at Garmisch was won by Great Britain who created the sensation of the Games when they beat previous champions Canada by two goals to one.
2 Christel Cranz fell in the downhill race but overcame a loss of 19 seconds to win the ladies' Alpine combination.
3 The bobsleigh gold medals were won by the United States (two-man) and Switzerland (four-man), so ending hopes of a home success on the new, steeply banked Riessersee course. 4 The jumping event saw Norway's Birger Ruud keep the title he won in 1932.

skiing or speed skating, the extremely versatile Norwegian girl Schou Nilsen was deprived of even greater fame. Only 16, she dominated the downhill and took the bronze medal in the alpine combination — a sensational achievement for one of the prominent tennis players of the day who also held no fewer than five world speed skating records.

Not surprisingly, Scandinavians monopolized the nordic skiing honours. Swedes won both the individual cross-country races—the gruelling 50 kilometres test of endurance going to Elis Wiklund and the relatively short 18 kilometres to Erik Larsson. A Finnish quartet took the first Olympic relay title to be contested but they beat the Norwegians by only 6 seconds, a small margin after four legs of 10 kilometres each.

Oddbjörn Hagen retained the nordic combination for Norway. And thanks to his stylish compatriot, Birger Ruud, who with leaps of 75 and 77.5 metres, withstood a spirited challenge from the Swede Sven Eriksson in the special ski jumping, Norway remained undefeated in the event after four Olympics. For this event 150,000 awe-struck onlookers clustered around the 'horse-shoe' below the impressive Olympic jump tower.

But it was another Norwegian, speed skater Ivar Ballangrud, who was the real star of the Garmisch Games. In his third Olympics and less than a month from his 32nd birthday, Ballangrud won three gold medals, in the 500, 5,000 and 10,000 metres, and also took the silver in the 1,500 metres, finishing just one second slower than his fellow countryman Charles Mathiesen.

Inevitably the figure skating will be remembered most for Sonja Henie's third Olympic victory. But whereas she had clearly dominated the event previously, the gap between her and her rivals had now decreased. Though eight years Sonja's junior, Bri-

tain's Cecilia Colledge, who was to become world champion the following season, proved a dangerous challenger. No longer did the Norwegian star enjoy a unanimous verdict—one judge placed the two girls equal—and she was perhaps wise to turn professional soon afterwards.

Karl Schäfer, a star pupil of the Vienna Skating School's most glorious era, comfortably retained the men's crown he had captured in 1932. His nearest challenger, Ernst Baier, was compensated with a hard-earned victory for Germany in the pairs contest, partnered by his future wife, Maxi Herber. The pairs was something of a cliff-hanger, with a young Viennese brother and sister, Erik and Ilse Pausin, stealing the spectators' hearts with a skilful interpretation of a lilting Strauss waltz. But the Germans' more experienced technique split the judges voting 7–2 in their favour.

In the bobsleigh, a home success had been expected on the new, steeply banked Riessersee course, but it was not to be. In the two-man event, Ivan Brown, with Alan Washbond as brakeman, piloted the United States boblet to victory, just half a second clear of the Swiss sled driven by Fritz Feierabend. The Swiss made no mistake, however, in the four-man event. Their second and first crews—led by Pierre Musy and Reto Capadrutt respectively—took the gold and silver medals in that order, with Fred McEvoy guiding the British sled home for the bronze.

As had now become a customary feature of the Winter Olympics, there were two demonstration events—a ski military patrol race, forerunner of the present-day biathlon, and German-style curling. No medals are awarded for these supporting contests, but the skiing and shooting, over a 25-km course, produced an unexpected victory for Italy, led by Captain Silvestri, and the curling honours went to Austria.

GARMISCH WINTER OLYMPIC GAMES, 1936 Gold Medallists			
Nordic Skiing			
18 kilometres	Erik Larsson	Sweden	1 hr 14 min 38.0 sec
50 kilometres	Elis Wiklund	Sweden	3 hr 30 min 11.0 sec
4 × 10 km relay		Finland	2 hr 41 min 33.0 sec
Jumping	Birger Ruud	Norway	
Combination	Oddbjorn Hagen	Norway	
Alpine Skiing—Men			
Combination	Franz Pfnur	Germany	
Alpine Skiing—Women			
Combination	Christel Cranz	Germany	
Figure Skating			
Men	Karl Schafer	Austria	
Women	Sonja Henie	Norway	
Pairs	Ernst Baier / Maxi Herber	Germany	
Speed Skating			
500 metres	Ivar Ballangrud	Norway	43.4 sec
1,500 metres	Charles Mathiesen	Norway	2 min 19.2 sec
5,000 metres	Ivar Ballangrud	Norway	8 min 19.6 sec
10,000 metres	Ivar Ballangrud	Norway	17 min 24.3 sec
Bobsleigh			
2-man	Ivan Brown / Alan Washbond	USA	5 min 29.29 sec
4-man		Switzerland	5 min 19.85 sec
Ice Hockey		Great Britain	

Alpine skiing consists of three different disciplines—downhill
slalom, and giant slalom. Downhill courses usually have a vertical
descent of between 2,500 metres and 3,000 feet and vary between
1½ to 3 miles according to the terrain. Slalom courses are
considerably shorter and comprise a series of 'gates' through
which the skier must pass. The giant slalom blends characteristics
of the downhill and slalom in one event.

St Moritz Winter Olympic Games (1948)

After 20 years and a world war, the Winter Olympic Games returned to St Moritz in 1948. Lack of training facilities and the paltry allowance of only five Swiss francs a day for the members of some teams made participation in these Games a truly remarkable achievement. The Germans and Japanese were excluded from this bold revival. The Americans appeared monetarily unfettered, staying at the best hotels in a resort famous for luxurious living. In striking contrast, their wartime British allies suffered the humility of appearing the poor relations through having to economize drastically with regard to accommodation and everything that had to be paid for in foreign currency.

For a nation that had contributed so much towards Europe's liberation, the situation was ludicrous enough to inspire a *Daily Express* Giles cartoon which showed the British team encamped under canvas in the snow beside a five-star hotel and one of the competitors calling to a dignified waiter: 'Garcon, would you mind fetching us a can of water for our cocoa?'

This humorous exaggeration bore a strong element of truth. Several European nations were severely handicapped financially, but their admirable determination to overcome this difficulty did much to put the Olympic movement unsteadily back on its feet. The International Olympic Committee somehow rode a multiplicity of administrative problems which reached a climax when separate icy hockey teams claimed to represent the same nation.

Even this early, the pseudo-amateur controversy was rearing its head. Critics on the spot had harsh words to say about the supplanting of true sporting traditions by purely commercial interests, and some eminent observers made no attempt to disguise their opinions that certain competitors were as good as committing perjury by signing the Olympic oath.

Petty squabbles—and they were mostly petty—were numerous enough to inspire one reporter to comment: 'In an assembly of feuding factions whose dogmatic attitude sometimes reduced the Games to a farcical level, it was a pity that some organisations did not settle their domestic differences at home beforehand instead of airing their grievances in public while the Olympics were on.'

The fifth Winter Olympic meeting was originally scheduled for 1940 at Sapporo, Japan, but World War II intervened and

Sapporo has had to wait until 1972. The selection of St Moritz for a second time was the result of the resort's suitability in almost every respect, especially its facilities, and Switzerland's central location and political stability. The atmosphere throughout the programme appeared to be that of a brave front being put on by Europeans still suffering in many respects from the aftermath of war, but the important thing was that the Olympic flame could be rekindled despite countless frustrations.

In the circumstances, the entry of 28 nations was encouraging, equal to that of 1936, though the total number of competitors, 636

men and 77 women, fell 40 short of the Garmisch figures—understandably, in view of various travel and financial problems which also greatly reduced the numbers of spectators. But for the first time there were Chilean, Danish, Icelandic, Korean, and Lebanese competitors.

The development of Alpine skiing since 1936 justified the extension of medals for these competitions to include separate awards for downhill, slalom, and combined. Significantly, 25 nations were represented in the downhill—10 more than in any Nordic ski event. Ideal weather was temporarily interrupted by a thawing *fohn* wind, less severe

1 France's Henri Oreiller was the most successful Alpine skier at St Moritz, with wins in the downhill and combined events, and a slalom bronze.
2 Switzerland's Edi Reinalter wins a slalom event.
3 Gretchen Frazer of the United States won her country's only Alpine skiing medals at St Moritz—a slalom gold and a combined silver.

than 20 years previously, but sufficient to affect the 10,000 metres speed skating and some of the ice hockey matches. Fortunately, this time no event had to be cancelled.

The Swedes proved supreme in

the cross-country skiing, taking all three medals in the 18 kilometres, the first two places in the 50 kilometres, and leading the Finnish runners-up by 9 seconds in the 18 kilometres.

Martin Lundstrom, victor in the 18 kilometres, got his second gold medal in the relay, but the Swedish strength in depth was underlined by the ability to win the latter without the services of Nils Karlsson, an impressive 50 kilometres champion despite being more troubled than most by an altitude to which he was unaccustomed.

The all-round ability of two Finns earned gold and silver in the Nordic combination for Heikki Hasu and Martti Huhtala. Switzerland's Niklaus Stump, fourth, achieved the highest place in this event yet by a central European, with the best Norwegian sixth.

The Norwegians reasserted their traditional supremacy in the jumping, taking all the medals for an event in which they had yet to concede first place. The winner, Petter Hugsted, owed his victory more to near-perfect posture than to sheer distance. His longest jump was 3 metres shorter than the 138 metres covered by the fourth placed Matti Pietikainen from Finland, whose style cannot have pleased the judges. At 36 years of age, Birger Ruud gained a noteworthy bronze medal—16 years after his first gold for the same event.

In the men's Alpine skiing, a downhill triumph with more than four seconds in hand and third place in the slalom gave Frenchman Henri Oreiller the academic combined title to total two gold medals and a bronze. Edi Reinalter won the slalom for Switzerland with an aggregate for the two runs just half a second faster than another Frenchman, James Couttet.

The women's honours were shared by three nations. Hedy Schlunegger took the downhill for Switzerland. Gretchen Frazer, at 29, was a surprise American slalom winner—the first skiing medal to be won by the United States. Austrian Trude Beiser, second in the downhill, was unplaced in the slalom but her overall performance was just good enough to pip Miss Frazer for the combined title.

The figure skating saw the American continent take the top honours through the United States' Dick Button and Canada's Barbara Ann Scott who gave Europe a first glimpse of the new American school of theatrical athleticism in jumps. Displaying a new degree of physical strength and suppleness, Button was the forerunner of a revolutionary trend that was to characterize future men's free-skating. The more orthodox Swiss, Hans Gerschwiler, held second place only by virtue of his figures, having been outpointed in free-style by another American, John

Lettengarver. Miss Scott serenely withstood hard pressure from Britain's Jeannette Altwegg in the figures and from Austrian's Eva Pawlik in the free-skating. The Belgians Pierre Baugniet and Micheline Lannoy, a gracefully authentic partnership, clinched the pairs title after a resolute Hungarian bid from Ede Kiraly and Adrea Kekessy.

Norwegians won three of the four speed skating events. Finn Helgesen snatched the 500 metres by a tenth of a second from his compatriot Thomas Byberg and two Americans, Ken Bartholomew and Robert Fitzgerald, whose equal times earned the first Winter Olympic triple tie for silver medals. Sverre Farstad won the 1,500 metres and Reidar Liaklev the 5,000. But a Swede, Ake Seyffarth, was the most noteworthy speed skater on view. A decisive winner of the 10,000 metres with nearly 10 seconds to spare, he was also runner-up in the 1,500; he was a powerful racer who had passed his peak form, after establishing world records over two distances during the war years.

An intimate knowledge of their home course enabled the Swiss to secure gold and silver medals in the two-man bobsleigh event. The Americans took first and third places in their four-man sleds, separated by a Belgian crew in second spot.

Skeleton tobogganing made its second Olympic appearance on

the Cresta Run. The event provided Italy's first gold medal in winter sports, thanks to the rare skill of Nino Bibbia, the cleverest exponent the course had known, no doubt due largely to his being a St Moritz resident. Another man who was familiar with the course, American John Heaton, gained a notable silver medal—repeating his achievement of 20 years previously, when runner-up to his brother Jennison.

The Canadians recaptured the ice hockey title, avenging their unexpected defeat by the British in 1936, but only by a goal-average verdict over the Czechs. Each won seven of their eight matches, their direct encounter ending in a rare goalless stalemate. The Czech line-up included a player who gained greater fame as a tennis star—Jaroslav Drobny.

There was confusion and embarrassment concerning the American ice hockey entry. Two United States teams arrived at St Moritz and the one eventually allowed to compete finished fourth, only to be disqualified by the IOC because it was not affiliated to the American Olympic Association.

Two supporting demonstration events were a military patrol ski race, won by the host nation in a field of eight teams, and an enterprising winter pentathlon, comprising cross-country skiing, pistol shooting, a downhill race, fencing, and horse-riding. In this widely varied combination the Swedes proved best.

This second St Moritz Winter Olympic presentation determinedly overcame unenviable difficulties and emphasized the compactness and easy access of all the sites, in very favourable comparison to some of the subsequent venues. The palpable will to revive the Games was the most heartening element of all.

1 The two-man bobsleigh contest proved to be a triumph for the Swiss hosts: their No. 2 bob won first place, and the No. 1 bob was second, with the United States pair third, 5 seconds behind.
2 Nino Bibbia negotiates Church Leap on his way to a gold medal in the skeleton tobogganing on the Cresta Run—an event held twice and only when the Olympic Games have been at St Moritz.
3 Not many spectators watch this speed skating event. Norway, Finland, Sweden, and the United States won all the medals in this sport, with Norway's skaters winning three titles.
4 The Olympic flame burns in the ice stadium. The mere fact that these Games were held at all was a sign of hope for a world only just at peace and beset with political worries.

ST MORITZ WINTER OLYMPIC GAMES, 1948 Gold Medallists

Nordic Skiing

18 kilometres	Martin Lundstrom	Sweden	1 hr 13 min 50.0 sec
50 kilometres	Nils Karlsson	Sweden	3 hr 47 min 48.0 sec
4 x 10 km relay		Sweden	2 hr 32 min 8.0 sec
Combination	Heikki Hasu	Finland	448.8 pts
Jumping	Petter Hugsted	Norway	228.1 pts

Alpine Skiing—Men

Downhill	Henri Oreiller	France	2 min 55.0 sec
Slalom	Edi Reinalter	Switzerland	2 min 10.3 sec
Combined	Henri Oreiller	France	3.2 pts

Alpine Skiing—Women

Downhill	Hedy Schlunegger	Switzerland	2 min 28.3 sec
Slalom	Gretchen Frazer	USA	1 min 57.2 sec
Combined	Trude Beiser	Austria	6.5 pts

Figure Skating

Men	Dick Button	USA	1,720.6 pts
Women	Barbara Ann Scott	Canada	1,467.7 pts
Pairs	Pierre Baugniet, Micheline Lannoy	Belgium	123.5 pts

Speed Skating

500 metres	Finn Helgesen	Norway	43.1 sec
1,500 metres	Sverre Farstad	Norway	2 min 17.6 sec
5,000 metres	Reidar Liaklev	Norway	8 min 29.4 sec
10,000 metres	Ake Seyffarth	Sweden	17 min 26.3 sec

Bobsleigh

2 man	Felix Endrich, Fritz Waller	Switzerland	5 min 29.2 sec
4 man		USA	5 min 20.1 sec

Skeleton Tobogganing

	Nino Bibbia	Italy	5 min 23.2 sec

Ice Hockey

	Canada	

Above: A well-nigh perfect performance in the compulsory figures gave Britain's Jeanette Altwegg a valuable start in the figure skating at Oslo, for though she was bettered by Tenley Albright in the free skating, she held her overall lead to add a gold medal to the bronze she had won four years earlier in London. *Below:* Another 1948 medallist was America's Dick Button. His medal, however, was a gold, and he won another at Oslo, where his skating spearheaded a new athleticism in jumping on skates. His *tour de force* was the triple jump—three mid-air revolutions before landing, and at Oslo he unleashed the first real triple loop.

Oslo Winter Olympic Games (1952)

The first Winter Olympics to be held in a capital city, the Oslo Games of 1952 drew a record entry of 30 nations. Germany and Japan made their first post-World War II appearances in the Olympic arena, and New Zealand and Portugal made their Winter Games debuts. Even so, the total number of competitors—624 men and 108 women—fell slightly short of the record 1936 figures.

The siting of the events was relatively compact for a Winter Games. The cross-country and ski jumping were held at Holmenkollen, only a few miles from the city centre, and the slalom events took place on the nearby Rodkleiva slope. All the ice sports were located within the Oslo area, and only the downhill and giant slalom contests were any distance from the city—at Norefjell, some 75 miles to the north-west.

It was the first time that the Games had gone to the country that pioneered sport on skis, and appropriately the Olympic flame was lit not in Greece, as is the custom, but in Morgedal, the village in the Norwegian province of Telemark where Sondre Nordheim, the 'father of skiing', had been born in 1825. The torch was carried by 94 skiers along the 137 miles to Oslo, where Eigil Nansen, grandson of the famous explorer Fridtjof Nansen, ran the final lap in the Bislet Stadium. In the opening ceremony, a minute's silence was observed to mark the death of Britain's King George VI.

Attendances were very high. Over half a million people paid to see the events: 130,000 witnessed the four speed skating competitions, and a similar number watched the ski jumping finale.

Hallgeir Brenden took the 18 kilometres cross-country ski sprint title to Norway for the first time since Johnn Grottumsbraaten's success at St Moritz in 1928. Another home triumph came in the Nordic combination event, consisting of 18 kilometres cross-country and ski jumping. Simon Slattvik's 1 hr 5 min 40 sec and three jumps of 67.5, 67, and 66.5 metres gave him 451.6 points, 4 more than the runner-up, Heikki Hasu of Finland. Hasu was a member of Finland's winning

4 by 10 kilometres relay team who beat Norway by nearly 3 minutes. Further success for Finland came in the 50 kilometres cross-country, won by Veikko Hakulinen with team-mate Eero Kolehmainen second. Finland's women cross-country skiers won all three medals in their 10-kilometre event, the first held in an Olympic Games. The winner was the robust and well-schooled Lydia Wideman.

The Scandinavian monopoly in the Nordic events was not as surprising as the significant success of Stein Eriksen in the giant slalom, and his silver, and Gutterm Berge's bronze, in the slalom. The other Alpine events went to true Alpine skiers. Othmar Schneider of Austria won the slalom, and was runner-up to Zeno Colo of Italy in the downhill.

1 Norway's Stein Eriksen was a surprise winner of the giant slalom—an alpine event. 2 Another Norwegian to shine before his home audience was triple gold medallist speed skater Hjalmar Andersen.

Twenty-seven of the 30 competing nations were represented in the men's downhill and slalom—more than in any other events.

America's Andrea Mead-Lawrence was a double winner in the women's Alpine skiing. She took the gold medals in the slalom and giant slalom, but a crash put paid to her chances in the downhill, which was won by Austria's Trude Jochum-Beiser.

The outstanding individual of the Games was the Norwegian speed skater Hjalmar Andersen, who won three events—the 1,500,

5,000, and 10,000 metres, setting Olympic records in the two longer distances. Only a week previously he had set a world record for 10,000 metres that was not beaten until 1960. Ken Henry won the 500 metres, America's third gold medal in this event in six Winter Games, with his team-mate Donald McDermott second. Norway's Arne Johansen and Canada's Gordon Audley dead-heated for the bronze medals.

The figure skating audience saw America's Dick Button retain his title. As a result of arduous practice he made the first ever triple loop jump in winning comfortably for a second time. In the women's figures Jeanette Altwegg made well-nigh perfect compulsory figures to add the Olympic gold to her bronze of 1948 and the world championship she had won

the previous year. Even so, she was surpassed in free skating by the American Tenley Albright who won the silver medal and Jacqueline du Bief of France who was third. The pairs gold medals went to the German husband and wife team, Paul and Ria Falk, whose precision timing in lifts and skilful 'shadow' jumps and spins were quite unusual.

Germany also excelled in the bobsleigh events. Cashing in on what was then a legitimate weight advantage, German crews won both 2-man and 4-man events. Andreas Ostler (driver) and Lorenz Nieberl (brakeman) were in both winning crews, and in each case they won by more than two seconds. The advantage the Germans gained by having heavy crews prompted the International Bobsleigh Federation to amend

the rules, setting maximum combined weights of sleds and riders to create fairer conditions.

Canada won the ice hockey for the sixth time in seven Games. In eight matches they conceded only one point—in a tie with the United States, who were runners-up. In a play-off for third place Sweden beat Czechoslovakia after the Czechs had established a 3-0 lead. By way of a contrast, bandy —a form of hockey on ice, with rules similar to soccer's—was the official demonstration sport, and in this Sweden won a three-way contest against Norway and Finland.

The final event, and the climax of the Games, was the ski jumping at Holmenkollen. A vast crowd in festive mood assembled to watch, and they were not disappointed when local hero Arnfinn Bergmann retained the title for Norway.

OSLO WINTER OLYMPIC GAMES, 1952 Gold Medallists

Nordic Skiing—Men			
18 Kilometres	Hallgeir Brenden	Norway	1 hr 1 min 34.0 sec
50 kilometres	Veikko Hakulinen	Finland	3 hr 33 min 33.0 sec
4 x 10 km relay		Finland	2 hr 20 min 16.0 sec
Combination	Simon Slattvik	Norway	451.6 pts
Jumping	Arnfinn Bergmann	Norway	226.0 pts
Nordic Skiiing—Women			
10 kilometres	Lydia Wideman	Finland	41 min 40.0 sec
Alpine Skiing—Men			
Downhill	Zeno Colo	Italy	2 min 30.8 sec
Slalom	Othmar Schneider	Austria	2 min 0.0 sec
Giant slalom	Stein Eriksen	Norway	2 min 25.0 sec
Alpine Skiing—Women			
Downhill	Trude Jochum-Beiser	Austria	1 min 47.1 sec
Slalom	Andrea Mead-Lawrence	USA	2 min 10 6 sec
Giant slalom	Andrea Mead-Lawrence	USA	2 min 6.8 sec
Figure Skating			
Men	Dick Button	USA	1,730.3 pts
Women	Jeannette Altwegg	Great Britain	1,455.8 pts
Pairs	Paul Falk & Ria Falk	Germany	102.6 pts
Speed Skating			
500 metres	Ken Henry	USA	43.2 sec
1,500 metres	Hjalmar Andersen	Norway	2 min 20.4 sec
5,000 metres	Hjalmar Andersen	Norway	8 min 10.6 sec
10,000 metres	Hjalmar Andersen	Norway	16 min 45.8 sec
Bobsleigh			
2-man	Andreas Ostler, Lorenz Nieberl	Germany	5 min 22.54 sec
4-man		Germany	5 min 7.84 sec
Ice Hockey		Canada	

1 Dick Button of the United States, who retained his Olympic figure skating title at Oslo with comparative ease.
2 Norway's Arnfinn Bergmann collected 226 points to take first place in the ski-jumping. Altogether the host country won seven gold medals—almost a third of the total. **3** Like all the other teams in the two-man bobsleigh, Guillard and Chatelus of France found that German combination of Andreas Ostler and Lorenz Nieberl too powerful.

Cortina Winter Olympic Games (1956)

Millions of people watched on television, and 13,000 gaily expectant onlookers packed the newly built stands of the £750,000 Olympic Ice Stadium for the opening of the seventh Winter Olympics, at the picturesque Italian resort of Cortina d'Ampezzo. And after the speech by President Giovanni Gronchi, Italian ice racer Guido Caroli skated the final lap with the Olympic Flame, which had been brought 500 miles in relay from Rome's ruined Temple of Jupiter. Then, diminutive Italian skier Juliana Minuzzo took the Olympic oath on behalf of the others.

The Cortina Olympics were one of the most colourful and lavish ever. Profits from Italy's nationalized football pools had largely subsidized the elaborately erected sites, and it mattered little that the 231 million lire netted from the 157,000 admission tickets repaid only a proportion of the £2½ million promotional costs.

In addition, as these were the first Winter Olympics to be internationally televised, world-wide publicity brought substantial long-term commercial benefits to both Italy in general and Cortina in particular, as well as to winter sports. Such obvious assets ensured no shortage of applicants to stage subsequent Olympics.

At least one outstanding performer emerges from most Olympic meetings and Cortina was no exception. The big name on this occasion was the Austrian Alpine skier, Toni Sailer, a 20-year-old plumber from Kitzbühel.

Sailer was hailed as the most brilliant and daring Alpine skier yet seen, not just because he won all of his events, but because of his impressive, hip-swinging style and the decisive time margins that quite outclassed the opposition.

His giant slalom time was 6.2 seconds better than that of the runner-up, fellow Austrian Anderl Molterer. And in the slalom, 4 clear seconds separated him from the American-based Chiharu Igaya, the first Japanese to win an Olympic Winter Games medal. Finally, the icy, windswept downhill gave Sailer a 3.5 seconds lead over the second-placed Swiss, Raymond Fellay, and brought him his third gold medal.

But the Swiss had more glory in the women's events. Dairymaid Madeleine Berthod was the most successful, winning the downhill and coming fifth in the slalom. Her compatriot, Renée Collard, triumphed in the slalom, but Ossi Reichert, a German hotelier's daughter, took the giant slalom.

Competing for the first time in the Winter Olympics, the Russians took the lion's share of medals and earned respect as an obviously increasing force. Their well-balanced Nordic ski team earned a convincing team relay win, but the individual cross-country stars were the seemingly indefatigable Swede Sixten Jernberg and the never-flagging Finn Heikko Hakulinen. Jernberg's medal tally—a gold, two silver, and a bronze—was one more than even Sailer's. In all six previous Winter Olympics Norway had won each jumping gold, but their dominance was at last cracked at Cortina, by a Finn, Antti Hyvärinen, who won with a new aerodynamic drop style.

An unprecedented spate of speed-skating records on the outdoor circuit at Lake Misurina was due to rapidly improving techniques at high altitude. In the four events, three skaters set new world records, while 73 competitors were inside the previous best Olympic times for their distances.

Soviet racers gained four gold medals for winning three events, because compatriots Jurij Mikailov and Eugenij Grischin tied in the 1,500 metres, both clocking a new world-record time. Grischin, the outstanding ice sprinter of his day, also established a new world time to win the 500 metres. For the

Right, **Ossi Reichert shows the form that won her a gold medal in the giant slalom.**
Below, **Toni Sailer, skiing star of the Cortina Olympics.**

first time since 1932, Norway failed to get a speed-skating gold.

The technical and spectacular highlight of the figure skating was the freestyle of the dominant American men's trio, Hayes Jenkins, Ronnie Robertson, and David Jenkins, Hayes' younger brother, who finished in that order. Hayes Jenkins won by virtue of a slender lead gained in the figures, and though his free-skating was excellent, its contents were not quite as difficult as those displayed by Robertson.

Robertson was a sensational, at times almost acrobatic, free-skater, and he gave everything he had on this occasion. He touched a hand down when landing in a triple loop jump, then completed a triple salchow to perfection, and concluded with a fast cross-toe spin, altogether a thrilling programme for the mesmerized audience.

In the women's contest, Tenley Albright, runner-up in the previous Winter Olympics to Britain's Jeannette Altwegg, presented a wonderfully delicate programme, dramatically timed to *Tales of Hoffman* in a seemingly effortless, graceful style, ending splendidly with a rapid cross-foot spin.

But if a miracle were needed by Carol Heiss to overtake her brilliant compatriot, this she nearly achieved. Very speedy and impressive, she not only scored almost as many marks as Tenley, but was actually placed first in the freestyle by 5 of the 11 judges.

In the pairs event, the elegant Viennese partnership of Kurt Oppelt and Sissy Schwartz gained a controversial verdict over Canada's Norris Bowden and Frances Dafoe, both couples synchronizing superbly.

The ice hockey, as usual, drew the greatest number of spectators. At their first attempt, the Russians emerged victorious and unbeaten in their five final pool matches against the previously fancied United States, who were second, and Canada, Sweden, Czechoslovakia, and Germany.

Scoring 25 goals and conceding only 5, the Russian players never looked unduly ruffled. Their clever stick-handling and superior skating, in both defence and attack, decided the issue in the two games that mattered most, and they defeated the United States 4-0, and Canada, who finished third, 2-0.

Forty-six-year-old Franz Kapus became the oldest gold medallist in any Winter Olympics when he cannily piloted the Swiss sled to victory in the four-man bobsleigh event, 1.26 seconds ahead of the Italian ace Eugenio Monti. Monti was pipped again in the two-man boblet, but this time by his fellow Italian Dalla Costa—a popular home success and a triumph for the new Podar-designed sleds, which were subsequently adopted by nearly every nation.

CORTINA WINTER OLYMPIC GAMES, 1956 Gold Medallists

Nordic Skiing—Men

15 kilometres	Hallgeir Brendan	Norway		49 min	39.0 sec
30 kilometres	Veikko Hakulinen	Finland	1 hr	44 min	6.0 sec
50 kilometres	Sixten Jernberg	Sweden	2 hr	50 min	27.0 sec
4 x 10 km relay		USSR	2 hr	15 min	30.0 sec
Jumping	Antti Hyvärinen	Finland			
Combination	Sverre Stenersen	Norway			

Nordic Skiing—Women

10 kilometres	Ljubov Kozyreva	USSR		38 min	11.0 sec
3 x 5 km relay		Finland	1 hr	9 min	1.0 sec

Alpine Skiing—Men

Downhill	Toni Sailer	Austria
Slalom	Toni Sailer	Austria
Giant Slalom	Toni Sailer	Austria

Alpine Skiing—Women

Downhill	Madeleine Berthod	Switzerland
Slalom	Renee Colliard	Switzerland
Giant Slalom	Ossi Reichert	Germany

Figure Skating

Men	Hayes Jenkins	USA
Women	Tenley Albright	USA
Pairs	Kurt Oppelt	Austria
	Elisabeth Schwarz	

Speed Skating

500 metres	Eugenyi Grischin	USSR			40.2 sec
1,500 metres	Eugenyi Grischin	USSR		2 min	8.6 sec
	Jurij Mikailov	USSR			
5,000 metres	Boris Schilkov	USSR		7 min	48.7 sec
10,000 metres	Sigvard Ericsson	Sweden		16 min	35.9 sec

Bobsleigh

2-man	Lamberto Dalla Costa	Italy
	Giacomo Conti	
4-man		Switzerland
Ice Hockey		USSR

1 Hayes Jenkins, gold medallist in the men's figure skating.
2 Soviet speed skating star Boris Schilkov won the 5,000 metres in Olympic record time.
3 The Italian boblet, piloted by Lamberto Dalla Costa.
4 Toni Sailer swings into action in the giant slalom.

Squaw Valley Winter Olympic Games

(1960)

'The gamble that came off' is a phrase aptly describing the choice of venue for the eighth Winter Olympics. In face of keen competition from three well-established European resorts, Squaw Valley, an empty, scarcely known Californian site where everything had to be built from scratch, won the International Olympic Committee vote. On the eastern side of the Sierra Nevada, 200 miles from San Francisco, and at an altitude of 6,230 feet, this location seemed like a risky throw of the dice. But Alexander Cushing, who owned the land, insisted with oratorical conviction that the compactness would be a key feature—and so it proved.

As pageantry committee chairman, filmdom's Walt Disney supervised all the ceremonial arrangements, and he did not miss a trick. But the miracle of these Games was the weather. After weeks of rain had threatened to wash away the courses, snow and wind threatened to ruin the elaborately planned opening by Vice-President Nixon. Then, with only 15 minutes to go, as if by magic, the clouds cleared and the sun shone, and only the humorist attributed this dramatic effect to Disney.

Throughout the entire 11-day meeting, warm Californian sunshine on incongruous-looking snow and ice dominated the proceedings. The great asset of Squaw Valley, and a boon to the spectators, was that, except for the cross-country ski courses 17 miles away on the McKinney Creek, everything was within short walking distance. Sometimes it was possible to watch speed skating, figure skating, ice hockey, downhill skiing, and ski jumping simultaneously from the same spot—something that could not be done anywhere else in the world.

The entry for these Games, the second to be held outside Europe, totalled 521 men and 144 women from 30 countries, which was not quite as good as Cortina because many nations pruned their numbers to reduce travel costs. But an increase of 13 countries since the Lake Placid Games in 1932 reflected the widening of winter sports interest through three decades.

There was some dissension because no bobsleigh or tobogganing runs were built, but this was the only real shortcoming, and it was somewhat atoned for by the friendly spirit so prevalent among competitors and spectators. Andrea Mead-Lawrence, an alpine skier from the United States, carried the torch, lit at Morgedal, Norway, as in 1952, on its last ski-borne relay, and the American ice racer Ken Henry skated a final lap with it before igniting the sacred flame.

Five inside the world record, 8 inside the Olympic record, and 12 inside their national records—all in one event: that, in the history-making 10,000 metres, was the speed skating highlight. Norwegian Knut Johannesen fairly whistled through to chop 46 seconds off the 1952 record established by the great Hjalmar Andersen, and even Britain's Terence Monaghan, who came fifth, was a full second faster than Andersen's previous world best.

Eugenii Grischin equalled his own world record time of 40.2 sec in winning the 500 metres for the USSR, emphasizing that, at 28, he still had no peers as a sprinter. He also tied with the Norwegian Roald Aas to share the 1,500 metres gold medal award. In the Czech Karol Divin. Jenkins's compatriot and future sister-in-law, Carol Heiss, won the women's event by a comfortable margin, and the Canadian combination Robert Paul and Barbara Wagner were equally convincing in the pairs.

The United States really clinched the ice hockey issue with a 2-1 upset of form-favoured Canada. It was their first win over Canada in any major international competition since 1956, and only their third since 1920. Both the Canadians and the Americans defeated the Russians, the Soviet side suffering a clear setback after their 1956 triumph.

The general atmosphere of goodwill during these Games was exemplified by a Russian suggestion to the American ice hockey team to take oxygen during second intervals. At this altitude, the tip paid handsome dividends. Never before had United States ice hockey players shadowed by less publicized team colleagues.

Canadian Anne Heggtveit, victor of the women's slalom, did well enough in the other races to register the best all-round performance, but Yvonne Ruegg, a downhill specialist, confounded the experts by winning the giant slalom for Switzerland. Heidi Biebl took the downhill for Germany and Americans came second in all three events. Penny Pitou got silvers for the downhill and giant slalom—pipped in the latter by a mere tenth of a second—and Betsy Snite was runner-up in the slalom.

Nobody ever did discover why the mountain used for the men's slalom and women's downhill was called KT-22, but there was no lack of suggestions—ranging from that of the 22 kick-turns it took the first skier to get down it to that of a historic fight with red-skins that resulted in these words being carved on a tree: 'Killed by

5,000 metres, Russian Viktor Kosichkin was nearly 10 sec faster than Johannesen.

Women's speed skating was included for the first time, and another Russian, Lidia Skoblikova, had the distinction of being the only contestant in the Games to win two outright individual golds, for the 1,500 metres and the 3,000 metres, setting a new world record in the former. The 500 metres was won by Helga Haase of Germany, and the 1,000 by Klara Guseva of the USSR.

In the men's figure skating at the architectural prize-winning Blyth Arena, American David Jenkins included in his free-skating high triple and double jumps of a standard no European could match, to overhaul a lead in the compulsory figures by the won Olympic gold medals, but they made a dour, persevering side, based on a sound defence well marshalled by Jack Mc-Carten, the best goalkeeper in the contest.

No outstanding alpine skier hogged the honours as Toni Sailer had done in 1956. Roger Staub won the giant slalom for Switzerland's first Alpine men's victory since 1948, Ernst Hinterseer took the slalom for Austria, and Jean Vuarnet of France came first in the downhill. Another Frenchman Guy Perillat was the most consistent performer, gaining a bronze in the downhill and finishing sixth in each of the other two events. The Austrians clearly slipped in the downhill. Sailer's heir-apparent, Karl Schranz, failed to fulfil expectations and was over-

One of Squaw Valley's assets as venue of the 1960 Winter Olympics was that almost all the events were within close walking distance. An added advantage was the California sun that shone throughout.

tomahawk, 22'. They say the tree is still there, but perhaps the etchings were obliterated by snow . . . .

The cross-country skiing showed the two Olympic veterans Sixten Jernberg and Veikko Hakulinen to be still well up among the best. Sweden's Jernberg scored a gold and silver in the two shorter distances and came fifth in the marathon 50 km, won by the Finn Kalevi Hamalainen. Hakulinen gained the 50 km silver, got a bronze in the 15

km sprint, won by Norway's Haakon Brusveen, and was hero of Finland's remarkable victory in the relay. In a dramatic duel on the last 10 km leg, Hakulinen made up a 22 seconds leeway to pass Brusveen and win by just the length of a ski.

Although the men's cross-country events continued very much as the prerogative of Scandinavia, there was a major surprise when a German postman, Georg Thoma, emerged as winner of the Nordic combination, a stern test of all-round skill in cross-country and ski jumping. It was the first time a non-Scandinavian had won the event. And Germany was to defy the critics still more. Few expected Helmut Recknagel to win the spectacular 80 metres jumping, but he did it by a comfortable margin, impressing with his extra-rapid take-off and an outmoded orthodox arms-forward style. The sunshine on this calm day showed enormous shadows ahead of each silent jumper, further enhancing the theatrical effect that fascinated the awe-inspired crowds thronging the foot of the impressive jump hill.

The newly introduced biathlon, combining cross-country ski running and rifle marksmanship, was won by Klas Lestander, of Sweden, whose 20 shots without a miss made up for a lagging pace along the track.

Four Russians, headed by Marija Gusakova, filled the first four places in the women's 10 km race. Consequently the Soviet team's defeat by the Swedes in the relay was sensational, but this was mainly because a Russian racer fell and broke a ski during the first leg, so costing irretrievable time.

The gay informality of the closing ceremony reflected the true international friendship that the competitions and the off-stage Olympic village community had fostered. In contrast to the team-by-team parade on opening day, all the competitors at the end inter-mingled in such obvious harmony that one could not help but recall the famous words of Baron Pierre de Coubertin, pioneer of the modern Olympics: 'May the Olympic flame shed its light on all generations and prove a blessing to mankind on its journey ever upward to a nobler and braver world.'

Opposite, **Knut Johannesen led a spree of record-breaking in the 10,000 metres speed skating. He lowered the old mark by 46 seconds, and four others also bettered it. In second place was the Russian 5,000 metres gold medallist Viktor Kosichkin (1, on left). 2 Lidia Skoblikova became the first double gold medallist of the 1960 Games when she added the 3,000 metres title to the 1,500 metres, in which she set a new world record. 3 The Canadian pair Barbara Wagner and Robert Paul were convincing winners in the pairs figure skating. 4 Roger Staub's victory in the giant slalom came on the strangely named KT-22 mountain. 5 His fellow-Swiss Yvonne Ruegg won the women's equivalent.**

SQUAW VALLEY WINTER OLYMPIC GAMES, 1960
Gold Medallists

Nordic Skiing—Men			
15 kilometres	Haakon Brusveen	Norway	51 min 55.5 sec
30 kilometres	Sixten Jernberg	Sweden	1 hr 51 min 3.9 sec
50 kilometres	Kalevi Hamalainen	Finland	2 hr 59 min 6.3 sec
4 x 10 km relay		Finland	2 hr 18 min 45.6 sec
Combination	Georg Thoma	Germany	457.9 pts
80 metres jumping	Helmut Recknagel	Germany	227.2 pts
Biathlon	Klas Lestander	Sweden	1 hr 33 min 21.6 sec
Nordic Skiing—Women			
10 kilometres	Marija Gusakova	USSR	39 min 46.6 sec
3 x 5 km relay		Sweden	1 hr 4 min 21.4 sec
Alpine Skiing—Men			
Downhill	Jean Vuarnet	France	2 min 6.0 sec
Slalom	Ernst Hinterseer	Austria	2 min 8.9 sec
Giant Slalom	Roger Staub	Switzerland	1 min 48.3 sec
Alpine Skiing—Women			
Downhill	Heidi Biebl	Germany	1 min 37.6 sec
Slalom	Anne Heggtveit	Canada	1 min 49.6 sec
Giant Slalom	Yvonne Ruegg	Switzerland	1 min 39.9 sec
Figure Skating			
Men	David Jenkins	USA	1,440.2 pts
Women	Carol Heiss	USA	1,490.1 pts
Pairs	Robert Paul & Barbara Wagner	Canada	80.4 pts
Speed Skating—Men			
500 metres	Eugenii Grischin	USSR	40.2 sec
1,500 metres	Roald Aas	Norway	2 min 10.4 sec
	Eugenii Grischin	USSR	
5,000 metres	Viktor Kosichkin	USSR	7 min 51.3 sec
10,000 metres	Knut Johannesen	Norway	15 min 46.6 sec
Speed Skating—Women			
500 metres	Helga Haase	Germany	45.9 sec
1,000 metres	Klara Guseva	USSR	1 min 34.1 sec
1,500 metres	Lidia Skoblikova	USSR	2 min 25.2 sec
3,000 metres	Lidia Skoblikova	USSR	5 min 14.3 sec
Ice Hockey		USA	

The anxiety of the long wait until the finish of the competition is etched on the face of Switzerland's teenage heroine, Marie-Therese Nadig, as she watches the opposition trying to beat her time in the giant slalom at Sapporo, where she won two gold medals.

2 1 Britain's Tony Nash and Robin Dixon propel their two-man bobsleigh down the Igls run to claim a surprise gold medal for their 'lowland' country—Britain's first Winter Games gold since 1952.
2 The flags of 36 competing nations dip at the colourful opening ceremony held in the natural amphitheatre which formed the base of the ski jump at Bergisel.

Innsbruck Winter Olympic Games

(1964)

The ancient Tyrolean city of Innsbruck experienced its mildest February for 58 years in 1964, just when snow was needed for the tenth winter Olympic Games. The Austrian organizers staged the Games with an efficiency belying their financial limitations, and with some astute re-timetabling and considerable help from the army they promoted a most successful Olympic celebration.

Nearly a million spectators attended the Games, and they witnessed some thrilling events during the 12-day programme. The Russian speed skater Lidia Skoblikova won all four individual gold medals—the first woman to do so. In Alpine skiing, the French sisters Christine and Marielle Goitschel won a gold and a silver medal apiece. The biggest surprise came in the bobsleigh, when Tony Nash and Robin Dixon of Britain—a country with no courses for the sport —won Britain's first Olympic gold medal in the winter Games since 1952.

For the first time in the history of the winter Games, the opening ceremony was not held in an ice rink, but in the natural amphitheatre that formed the base of the scenic Bergisel ski jump, thus enabling more than 60,000 people to watch. There was a sad moment as the crowd stood silent in memory of Australian skier Ross Milne and Britain's tobogganist Kay Skrzypecki, who had both been killed in training before the Games.

The ceremony over, 1,186 competitors—the highest number ever at a Winter Olympics—from 36 countries set about winning the 34 gold medals at stake. The USSR, with 11 gold, 8 silver, and 6 bronze, claimed the lion's share, while the host nation, Austria, were the next best with 4 gold, 5 silver, and 3 bronze. The United States—the largest team present—did surprisingly badly, and Switzerland, a country whose name is synonymous with winter sports, did not obtain any awards at all.

The outstanding individual of the Games was Lidia Skoblikova, who was the 1960 champion over 1,500 and 3,000 metres. She won her four gold medals in four days and set three Olympic records—a feat that caused the 24-year-old blonde Soviet speedster to be acclaimed as the greatest woman ice racer ever seen. A surprising bronze medallist in the 3,000 metres speed skating was Pil Hwa Han of North Korea, who won her country's first ever medal in the Winter Olympics.

Two Olympic records were shattered in the men's speed skating. Richard McDermott, a Michigan barber, shaved a tenth of a second off the previous 500 metres record, finishing half-a-second ahead of three men who tied for the silver medal, including the former record-holder Eugeniv Grischin of the USSR. In the 5,000 metres the veteran Norwegian Knut Johannesen clipped 10.3 sec off the world mark.

With six out of nine judges giving her 5.9 marks out of a possible 6 for technical merit, the Dutch figure skater Sjoukje Dijkstra captured her country's first Olympic gold medal since 1948. It was the climax of a distinguished career for the 22-year-old Amsterdam girl, who turned pro-

fessional later in the year. Man- **1**
fred Schnelldorfer took the men's
title for the combined German
team after seeing his French rival
Alain Calmat fall twice. The
classic skating of the veteran
Russian pair, Oleg Protopopov
and Ludmilla Belousova, won a
tight struggle with the German
world and European champions,
Hans Bäumler and Marika Kilius.
Protopopov's powerful lifts and
his wife's control were decisive
factors in the battle between the
two best partnerships seen for
years.

Five of the six Alpine skiing
events were held at Axamer
Lizum, about 10 miles south-west
of Innsbruck, and the men's
downhill on the Patscherkofel
mountain near Igls. Austrian and
French skiers won all six gold
medals at stake, gaining three
each.

The French sisters Marielle and
Christine Goitschel scored a
unique Olympic double: Christine
beat her sister in the slalom by
nearly a second over the two runs,
and in the giant slalom it was
Marielle's turn to win, with her
sister sharing second place with
the American Jean Saubert who
had been third in the slalom. The
Austrian women had a grand
slam in the downhill event in
which 20-year-old Christl Haas
won the gold, Edith Zimmermann the silver, and Traudl
Hecher the bronze.

In the three men's events, the
German Ludwig Leitner, who
was eighth in the giant slalom and
fifth in the slalom and the downhill, was the best all-rounder. But
in terms of medals the most
successful skier was the Austrian
Josef Stiegler, champion in the
slalom and bronze medallist in
the giant slalom. His team-mate
Karl Schranz, who had surprisingly lapsed at the 1960
Games, recaptured some of his
old form to take the giant slalom
silver. But he had to concede
first place by 0.38 seconds to
François Bonlieu of France.

At Seefeld, a few miles up the
Inn valley, the Nordic skiing fans
were able to see the indefatigable
Swedish veteran Sixten Jernberg
win his third and fourth Olympic
gold medals. The 50-km cross-
country champion in 1956 and
the 30-km champion in 1960, this
grand old man of *langlauf* was
greeted with sentimental cheers as
he came home to win the 50-km,
and as he won his fourth gold
in the final Nordic skiing event,
the 4 by 10 kilometres team event.
The 35-year-old Swede thus
brought his medal tally in three
Olympic Games to four gold,
three silver, and two bronze.

Had it not been for Jernberg's
feat, the star of the Nordic events
would have been Claudia Boyarskikh of the USSR who won golds
in all three women's events. Yet
another Russian success came in
the men's biathlon, which had
been introduced experimentally

for the 1960 Squaw Valley Games.
Vladimir Melanin beat his compatriot Aleksandr Privalov by
over three minutes in this skiing-
shooting combination event.

The Commonwealth successes
of Britain and Canada in the two
bobsleigh events were something
of a surprise, completely upsetting the form book, which
favoured the Italians. The wins
were, as the driver of the Canadian four-man bobsleigh, Vic
Emery, was at pains to point out,
'a triumph for countries without
a single course of their own'.
Tony Nash and Robin Dixon,
the British No. 1 two-man crew,
had spent much time and money
training together and really earned
their gold medals. It was only
Britain's third gold medal won
at a Winter Olympic Games.
They had perfected their run on
the Igls course to the utmost
degree, and won by just 12-
hundredths of a second from the
Italian No. 2 crew, Sergio Zardini
and Romano Bonagura, with the
Italian No. 2 bob piloted by the
redoubtable Eugenio Monti in
third place.

Germans took all of the men's
single toboggan medals. The
event, held at Igls, was won by
23-year-old Thomas Köhler, with
Klaus Bonsack in second place.
Köhler's aggregate time over the

four runs was less than 0.3 sec
faster than Bonsack's. In the
two-seater, the host nation, Austria, won both gold and silver
medals, but the Germans were
again victors in the women's
single-seater, in which Ortrun
Enderlein defeated the world
champion Ilse Geisler.

The Innsbruck Games were
the first at which luge tobogganing
had been included, and for many
onlookers it was a new experience
to see the luge tobogganists
adopt a sitting position, steering
by skilfully transferring their
weight and delicately controlling
the sharp-edged runners, in contrast to the forward-prone position of the Cresta-style of the
other tobogganists. Possibly because of the novelty of the event,
some riders looked decidedly un-
safe on their sleds, although the
experienced German and Austrian experts seldom gave cause
for anxiety.

The USSR, with seven wins
and 14 points for seven games,
appeared to win the ice hockey
with plenty to spare from the
Canadian team who won five of
their seven games. In fact, the
title was decided by Russia's
final game, against Canada. Had
Canada won, they would have
finished equal on points with the
USSR, and would have won the

gold medals because Olympic
rules stated that, in the event of a
tie between countries, the result
of a match between the two would
have decided the issue. As it
happened, Russia beat Canada
3-2, and Canada were relegated
to fourth position in the final
table, Sweden taking the silvers
and Czechoslovakia the bronzes.
But there was no question that
the best team—the only team to
win all seven of its matches, and
the team with the best goal
average—won. The Russians were
superbly fit—a factor that gave
them superiority in the closing
stages of their matches, were much
better skaters than their opponents, while their forwards
were adept at keeping possession
of the puck until a clear scoring
chance appeared.

A colourful finale to the Games
was provided by the thrilling
spectacle of 52 ski jumpers
soaring silently over the Bergisel
hill, the scene of the opening
ceremony. After the Finn Veikko
Kankkonen had beaten him and
won the gold medal in the newly
introduced 'little' 70-metre jump
at Seefeld, the Norwegian Toralf
Engan proved supreme in the
traditional 90-metre event with
Kankkonen second. In both ski-
jumps Engan's team-mate Tor-
geir Brandtzaeg was third.

Associated Press

INNSBRUCK WINTER OLYMPIC GAMES, 1964 Gold Medallists

Nordic Skiing—Men

15 kilometres	Eero Mantyranta	Finland	50 min 54.1 sec
30 kilometres	Eero Mantyranta	Finland	1 hr 30 min 50.7 sec
50 kilometres	Sixten Jernberg	Sweden	2 hr 43 min 52.6 sec
4 x 10 km relay		Sweden	2 hr 18 min 34.6 sec
Combination	Termod Knutsen	Norway	469.28 pts
70 metres jumping	Veikko Kankkonen	Finland	229.9 pts
90 metres jumping	Toralf Engan	Norway	230.7 pts
Biathlon	Vladimir Melanin	USSR	1 hr 20 min 26.8 sec

Nordic Skiing—Women

5 kilometres	Claudia Boyarskikh	USSR	17 min 50.5 sec
10 kilometres	Claudia Boyarskikh	USSR	40 min 24.3 sec
3 x 5 km relay		USSR	59 min 20.2 sec

Alpine Skiing—Men

Downhill	Egon Zimmermann	Austria	2 min 18.16 sec
Slalom	Josef Stiegler	Austria	2 min 11.13 sec
Giant Slalom	Francois Bonlieu	France	1 min 46.71 sec

Alpine Skiing—Women

Downhill	Christl Haas	Austria	1 min 55.39 sec
Slalom	Christine Goitschel	France	1 min 29.86 sec
Giant Slalom	Marielle Goitschel	France	1 min 52.24 sec

Figure Skating

Men	Manfred Schelldorfer	Germany	1,916.9 pts
Women	Sjoukje Dijkstra	Netherlands	2,018.5 pts
Pairs	Oleg Protopopov & Ludmilla Belousova	USSR	104.4 pts

Speed Skating—Men

500 metres	Richard McDermott	USA	40.1 sec
1,500 metres	Ants Antson	USSR	2 min 10.3 sec
5,000 metres	Knut Johannesen	Norway	7 min 38.4 sec
10,000 metres	Jonny Nilsson	Sweden	15 min 50.1 sec

Speed Skating—Women

500 metres	Lidia Skoblikova	USSR	45.0 sec
1,000 metres	Lidia Skoblikova	USSR	1 min 33.2 sec
1,500 metres	Lidia Skoblikova	USSR	2 min 22.6 sec
3,000 metres	Lidia Skoblikova	USSR	5 min 14.9 sec

Bobsleigh

2-man	Tony Nash & Robin Dixon	Great Britain	4 min 21.90 sec
4-man		Canada	4 min 14.46 sec

Luge Tobogganing—Men

Single	Thomas Köhler	Germany	3 min 26.77 sec
2-man	Josef Feistmantl & Manfred Stengl	Austria	1 min 41.62 sec

Luge Tobogganing—Women

Single	Ortrun Enderlein	Germany	3 min 24.67 sec
Ice Hockey		USSR	

1 Hardly any snow is visible as this ski jumper soars over Innsbruck. **2** Lidia Skoblikova won all four women's speed skating golds. **3** Marielle Goitschel matched her sister's tally of one gold and one silver in Alpine skiing. **4** Thomas Köhler won the first Olympic luge tobogganing gold medal. **5** Awnings prevented the remaining ice from melting on the bobsleigh course.

U.P.I.

Central Press

Grenoble Winter Olympic Games (1968)

Sixty-thousand people packed the amphitheatre that had been constructed especially for the opening ceremony of the Tenth Winter Olympic Games. After France's President de Gaulle had declared the Games open, the temporary construction was dismantled—a typical example of the efforts of the French to provide a spectacular presentation for the first Olympic competitions held in that country since 1924.

The traditional Olympic pageantry was brought up to date when showers of artificial roses—the rose being the symbol of Grenoble—were dropped from helicopters; the five Olympic rings were woven in smoke in the sky; and Olympic flags fluttered through the air hanging from parachutes. Stereophonic music accompanied the 1,560 competitors from 37 nations as they marched past. Alain Calmat, the former world figure skating champion, brought in the torch that had been carried from Olympia, and Leo Lacroix, the French Alpine skier, took the oath of amateurism. It was a memorable ceremony, the start of 13 days of intense competition that were marred only slightly by the unseasonably mild weather that necessitated some rearrangement of the timetables of the bobsleigh, luge, and Alpine skiing events.

The Grenoble Games were dominated by Jean-Claude Killy, a French hotelier whose consistency brought him all three gold medals in Alpine skiing. His victories were among the most controversial in the history of the Olympics, for he had been accused of professionalism; but the charges were of a type that could never be proved or disproved satisfactorily. Then, after the slalom, Karl Schranz, the evergreen Austrian whose skiing career had extended to its eleventh season, asked for an inquiry after being disqualified for allegedly missing a gate during a second descent which gave him a faster aggregate time than Killy. Doubts were raised and feelings ran high, but the jury stood by their decision and disqualified Schranz, leaving Killy the champion.

These were not the only skiing controversies. The sport's very future was threatened by the demands of the International Olympic Committee's president, Avery Brundage, that trade marks and names on skis should be removed. Brundage's unenforced demand escalated an already inflamed situation concerning problems of professional involvement that remained unresolved for years afterwards.

But none of this marred the real Killy glory. Poor visibility impaired the view of the challenging Chamrousse courses, but the runs were good, technically difficult, and a fair test for the world's best skiers. On the awesome-looking downhill course Killy exceeded 60 mph to win by 0.08 sec, and he won the slalom equally narrowly—by 0.09 sec. His giant slalom victory was the most clear-cut: Killy had more than 2 seconds in hand over the Swiss runner-up Willy Favre. But even with Killy's supremacy and the silver medal in the downhill of his compatriot Guy Perillat, France lacked some of the dominance that had been so obvious two years previously in the world championships at Portillo in Chile. Switzerland, led by Favre, Jean Daetwyler, and Duman Giovanoli, and the Austrians—notably Schranz and Heinrich Messner— were a constant danger.

Canada's Nancy Greene was the most successful woman Alpine racer despite a suspect ankle that had hindered her in previous events that season. The winner of the first World Alpine Ski Cup the previous year, she regained peak form to take the giant slalom gold and the slalom silver.

Ahead of Miss Greene in the slalom was Marielle Goitschel, perhaps the greatest woman skier of all time, who was in 1968 nearing the end of a great career. Reaching her best form of the Games in the slalom she started each run with amazing speed, and steered her way carefully to the finish. Her style—with its distinctive body-lean and perfect turning technique—allied to her superb anticipation and tall, powerful build brought her her third Olympic medal in two Games.

In contrast to Mlle Goitschel, her diminutive team-mate Annie Famose was second in the giant slalom and third in the slalom. Isabelle Mir, runner-up in the downhill, was yet another French medallist. But it was the Austrian girls who shone in the downhill, with Olga Pall taking the gold and the veteran Christl Haas third. Spear-heading a British revival was Gina Hathorn, who missed a bronze in the slalom by just three-hundredths of a second.

The outstanding woman of the Grenoble Games was the Swedish cross-country skier Toini Gustafsson. She left the opposition standing in the 5 km event, which she won with over 3 seconds in hand, and took the 10 km by over a minute. To her two gold medals she added a silver in the 3 by 5 km relay, anchoring the Swedish trio who were second to Norway.

The Scandinavians were unexpectedly outpaced in the men's 30 km by an Italian, Franco Nones, but the other cross-country races went to Norwegians. Ole Ellefsaeter was only 16.7 seconds ahead of Russia's Viatches Vedenin after a savage duel in the

1 A crowd of over 50,000 was at St Nizier to watch Vladimir Beloussov win the 90 metres ski-jumping from Czechoslovakia's Jiri Raska, who won the 70 metres event.
2 The medallists in the men's figure skating. Left to right, Tim Wood (silver), Emmerich Danzer (gold), and Patrick Pera (bronze). 3 The man who dominated the Grenoble Winter Olympics—Jean-Claude Killy. He won all three alpine skiing events, the downhill, slalom, and giant slalom, to emulate Toni Sailer's grand-slam in 1956. 4 Overcoming an ankle injury suffered during her preparations for the Games, Canada's Nancy Greene won the giant slalom by an amazing 2.5 seconds and was second in the slalom behind, 5 Marielle Goitschel, whose victory was the culmination of her fine career. In 1964, she had won the gold medal in the giant slalom. Third in the slalom and second in the giant slalom was another French skier Annie Famose. 6 Austria's Olga Pall won the women's downhill convincingly from Isabelle Mir of France and the Austrian Christl Haas, the defending Olympic champion.
7 An Austrian competitor in the 70 metres jumping, which was held at Autrans. Only the ice hockey and skating events were held in Grenoble itself.

50 km, and Harald Groenningen was less than 2 seconds faster than Finland's experienced Eero Maentyranta in the 15 km. The two Norwegians were joined by Odd Martinsen and Paal Tyldum in the winning 4 by 10 km relay team. The individual biathlon was also won by a Norwegian, Magnar Solberg, but his team were second to the Russians in the relay.

Franz Keller underlined a rising of West German strength in Nordic skiing when he won the 15 km and ski-jumping combination gold medal. Scandinavian pride was hurt further in the special jumps. On the 70 metres hill at Autrans, Jiri Raska leapt to a surprise victory for Czechoslovakia, followed by two Austrians, Reinhold Bachler and Balder Reiml. Björn Wirkola, the great Norwegian world champion of 1966, finished fourth.

A crowd of 58,000 people watched the spectacular climax of the ski-jumping from the 90 metres tower at St Nizier, where once more the Norwegians were put to shame. With the two best jumps of the contest, Russia's Vladimir Beloussov beat Jiri Raska, who proved his earlier win from the 70 metres tower was no flash in the pan. In fact, the successes in Nordic skiing were more widely

distributed than ever before, with Austria, Czechoslovakia, and Italy gaining their first Olympic medals in this branch of the sport.

The bobsleigh events were held at Alpe d'Huez, and provided a fitting climax to the long career of the Italian driver Eugenio Monti, the sport's outstanding exponent who had previously won no less than nine world titles but never an Olympic victory. This time, aged 40, he made no mistakes and in a memorable farewell performance clinched both two-man and four-man titles. The two-man was a real cliff-hanger: the West German boblet piloted by Horst Floth equalled Monti's aggregate time for the four runs and both he and Monti thought that two sets of gold medals would be awarded. But the regulations clearly stated that the fastest single run would decide such a tie, and although it was disappointing for Floth, popular sentiment rejoiced over Monti's triumphant finale. The weather interfered with the four-man bobsleigh. Although the floodlit course had three artificially frozen bends, the sun melted so much of the rest of the course that very early morning starts became inevitable, and the result was decided over two runs instead of the normal four.

The luge tobogganing at Villard-de-Lans was similarly inconvenienced. The woman's winner, Erica Lechner of Italy, prevented the Austrians and the two German teams from gaining a monopoly of the medals. That traditionally strong nation in this event, Poland, was completely overshadowed. Manfred Schmid of Austria narrowly pipped the East German Thomas Köhler to win the men's singles, but Köhler, partnered by Klaus Bonsack, reversed the order in the two-seaters. The clear, blue Olympic skies were momentarily clouded by the disqualification of the East German women's team by the Polish judge for heating the runners of their toboggan. The East Germans roundly condemned this 'capitalist, revanchist conspiracy', but to no avail.

The speed skating arena was enlivened to a cup-tie atmosphere by bands of Dutch and Norwegian supporters armed with rosettes, banners, motor horns, and bells. Predictions that the outdoor skating oval would not provide such a fast surface as similar rinks at higher altitudes were confounded as Anton Maier of Norway set a world record in the 5,000 metres and as no fewer than 52 improvements were made on the Olympic records. An important contribu-

tory factor to fast times may have been the ideally moist ice which had been chemically softened and demineralized to match ice formed naturally at mountain rinks. Maier, the 5,000 metres champion, was beaten by 1.2 seconds in the 10,000 metres by Sweden's Johnny Hoeglin. In the 1,500 metres Kees Verkerk defeated his fellow-Dutchman Ard Schenk, and Erhard Keller of West Germany took the 500 metres sprint.

The Netherlands' high reputation in women's ice racing was upheld by Johanna Schut and Carolina Geijssen, who won the 3,000 and 1,000 metres respectively. But their much-fancied compatriot Stien Kaiser managed only to win two bronze medals in the 1,500 and 3,000 metres after apparently reaching top form too early. Russian women speed skaters, previously renowned, had only one medallist: Ludmilla Titova won the 500 metres and was second in the 1,000 metres. An unprecedented event occurred in the 500 metres when the three United States competitors—Jenny Fish, Dianne Holum, and Mary Meyers—tied for second place and were all awarded silver medals.

The indoor Olympic Ice Stadium, a spacious and pillarless masterpiece of modern architec-

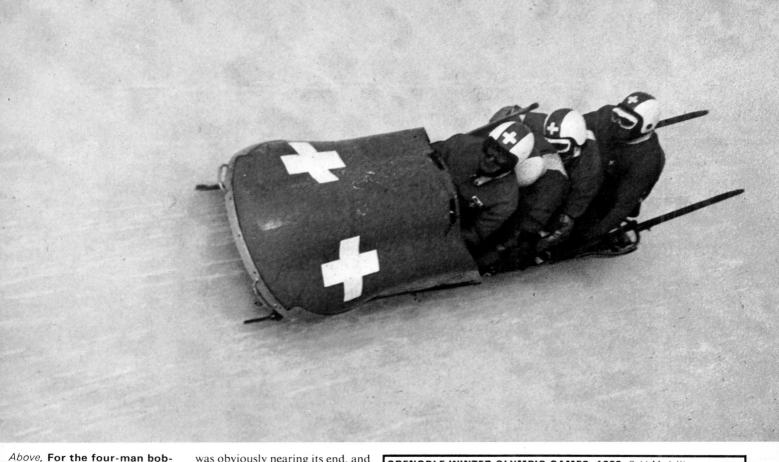

Above, **For the four-man bob-sleigh events, only two runs instead of the customary four decided the event as the sun melted so much of the course.** *Left,* **The ice hockey gold was won by the Russians (red).**

ture, was designed to seat 11,500 people, but this figure was exceeded at all three free skating events and for all the crucial ice hockey games.

A general trend of upsets of form extended to the men's figure skating when Emmerich Danzer, the world champion, dropped to fourth place, and his fellow-Austrian Wolfgang Schwarz, long accustomed to being Danzer's 'shadow', took the gold medal with a dominant display of free-skating highlighted by well-timed triple salchow, double axel, and double flip jumps.

A feature of the women's free-skating was the contrasting techniques of the classical, frail-looking winner, Peggy Fleming of the United States, and the robust runner-up, East German Gabriele Seyfert. The outcome was never in doubt because of Miss Fleming's substantial lead in the figures, but her slender frame belied a remarkable stamina which sustained a widely varied repertoire of gracefully fast spins, and smooth landings from her double jumps.

The retention of the pairs title by the Soviet husband and wife partnership Oleg Protopopov and Ludmilla Belousova was a commendable achievement in view of their ages: 35 and 32 respectively. Their long and successful career

was obviously nearing its end, and loud applause greeted their skilfully timed split lutz lift and characteristic one-handed death spiral.

The Russian stick-handlers began the eight-team ice hockey contest in unbeatable fashion, outclassing Finland 8-0 and East Germany 9-0. But they did not appear such clear favourites when they just beat Sweden 3-2. Then, in the outstanding match of the series, Czechoslovakia beat them 5-4 in a tense end-to-end affair which kept the excited spectators on the edges of their seats. Had the Czechs not drawn 2-2 with Sweden in the penultimate match of the tournament they would have been level with the Russians on points, in which case the result of the USSR-Czechoslovakia match would have decided the final order and not goal average. So the Russians did not win as easily as had been anticipated: they had 12 points from seven games, followed by Czechoslovakia with 11, and Canada with 10. Anatolii Firsov was the Soviet Union's star, being top scorer with 12 goals in the competition.

In common with the Innsbruck Games four years previously, the diverse nature of the terrain and the distances of up to 20 miles between venues caused considerable discomfort and frustration. But a most rewarding feature of the Games was that the Grenoble authorities had the foresight to build the Olympic facilities so they could be readily converted for the use of the people of the town after the Games had finished.

GRENOBLE WINTER OLYMPIC GAMES, 1968 Gold Medallists			
Nordic Skiing—Men			
15 kilometres	Harald Groenningen	Norway	47 min 54.2 sec
30 kilometres	Franco Nones	Italy	1 hr 35 min 39.2 sec
50 kilometres	Ole Ellefsaeter	Norway	2 hr 28 min 45.8 sec
4 x 10 km relay		Norway	2 hr 8 min 33.5 sec
Combination	Franz Keller	West Germany	449.04 pts
70 metres jumping	Jiri Raska	Czechoslovakia	216.5 pts
90 metres jumping	Vladimir Beloussov	USSR	231.3 pts
Biathlon	Magnar Solberg	Norway	1 hr 13 min 45.9 sec
Biathlon relay		USSR	2 hr 13 min 2.4 sec
Nordic Skiing—Women			
5 kilometres	Toini Gustafsson	Sweden	16 min 45.2 sec
10 kilometres	Toini Gustafsson	Sweden	36 min 46.5 sec
3 x 5 km relay		Norway	57 min 30.0 sec
Alpine Skiing—Men			
Downhill	Jean-Claude Killy	France	1 min 59.85 sec
Slalom	Jean-Claude Killy	France	1 min 39.73 sec
Giant slalom	Jean-Claude Killy	France	3 min 29.28 sec
Alpine Skiing—Women			
Downhill	Olga Pall	Austria	1 min 40.87 sec
Slalom	Marielle Goitschel	France	1 min 25.86 sec
Giant slalom	Nancy Greene	Canada	1 min 51.97 sec
Figure Skating			
Men	Wolfgang Schwarz	Austria	1,904.1 pts
Women	Peggy Fleming	USA	1,970.5 pts
Pairs	Oleg Protopopov & Ludmila Belousova	USSR	315.2 pts.
Speed Skating—Men			
500 metres	Erhard Keller	West Germany	40.3 sec
1,500 metres	Kees Verkerk	Netherlands	2 min 3.4 sec
5,000 metres	Anton Maier	Norway	7 min 22.4 sec
10,000 metres	Johnny Hoeglin	Sweden	15 min 23.6 sec
Speed Skating—Women			
500 metres	Ludmila Titova	USSR	46.1 sec
1,000 metres	Carolina Geijssen	Netherlands	1 min 32.6 sec
1,500 metres	Kaija Mustonen	Finland	2 min 22.4 sec
3,000 metres	Johanna Schut	Netherlands	4 min 56.2 sec
Bobsleigh			
2-man	Eugenio Monti & Luciano De Paolis	Italy	4 min 41.54 sec
4-man		Italy	2 min 17.39 sec
Luge Tobogganing—Men			
Single	Manfred Schmid	Austria	2 min 52.48 sec
2-man	Klaus Bonsack & Thomas Kohler	East Germany	1 min 35.85 sec
Luge Tobogganing—Women			
Single	Erica Lechner	Italy	2 min 28.66 sec
Ice Hockey		USSR	

Sapporo Winter Olympic Games
(1972)

Grenoble in 1968 had seen the problems of professionalism and commercialism brought out into the open as the competitors gathered for the opening ceremony. Then the centre of the controversy was the flamboyant French skier Jean-Claude Killy, against whom charges could never be proved and who went on to a 'grand slam' of skiing gold medals.

Four years later, at Sapporo, status again set off controversy and for a time threatened the first Winter Olympics held in Asia. At the centre this time was the veteran Austrian, Karl Schranz, one-time heir apparent to the great Toni Sailer and usurped by Killy. Now he was to return home hailed as the hero—not because of any medal haul, but because he wore the mantle of the martyr.

In a week of bitterness, wrangling, probes into commercialism and professionalism, Schranz's suspension for allegedly profiting from advertising was the spark that set off the boycott threats, and endangered the Games that were costing the Japanese £17 million to stage. Perhaps it was just wild talk engendered by the high winds that blustered around Sapporo; perhaps it was because of the long distances travelled by competitors; perhaps it was courtesy to the host nation. Whatever the reason, there was no boycott and the controversy, seemingly customary as an *hors d'oeuvre* to modern major sports encounters, subsided to make way for the pageantry of the opening ceremony.

An entry of 1,128 competitors (911 men, 217 women), from 35 countries, had gathered by February 3 for the 11th Winter Olympics when Emperor Hirohito of Japan declared them open, and some 18,000 balloons took to the air, replacing the customary pigeons who, in turn, were mere substitutes for the doves of peace. A nice touch to the ceremony was the choice of the injured French skier, Ingrid Lafforgue,

1 Karl Schranz, the veteran Austrian star whose suspension just before the Olympics sparked the boycott threats at the Sapporo Games.
2 Britain's Galina Hathorn in the women's downhill, in which she finished 25th.
Opposite page: The Asians try their hand at Nordic skiing—the 15 km cross-country.

1 America's 16-year-old Anne Henning, the youngest gold medallist at Sapporo and the first competitor to set a Winter Olympic record twice in the same event—the women's 500m speed skating. 2 Marie-Therese Nadig—17-year-old schoolgirl double gold medallist, in the downhill and giant slalom. 3 Exhilaration and grace from the 70-metre tower.

to carry in the Olympic flag. Such moments of sympathy and the emotion of the ceremony itself helped to push less sporting matters into the background.

In the absence of a Killy, the star of the Sapporo Games emerged not in the alpine skiing but in the speed skating. Ard Schenk, a strongly built, blond Dutchman with a long, sweeping stride, took three of the four speed skating golds and in two events, 1,500 metres and 10,000 metres, set Olympic records to stamp his personality on both the Games and the sport. His compatriot Kees Verkerk, 1,500 metres gold medallist at Grenoble,

was runner-up in the 10,000 metres; while Roar Gronvald, with silvers in the 1,500 and 5,000, and Sten Stenson, with bronzes in the 5,000 and 10,000, kept Norway well to the fore.

There was another Olympic record in the 500 metres, to the reigning champion, Erhard Keller of West Germany, and all four women's speed skating events brought new records. Amazingly the sprint record went twice; to 16-year-old American Anne Henning, who was allowed a second attempt after being baulked in her first record-breaking run. The Russians Vera Krasnova and Ludmila Titova

had to be content with the minor medals. Miss Henning added a bronze to her 500 metres gold in the 1,000 metres, which was won by Monika Pflug by just a hundredth of a second from Atje Keulen-Deelstra of the Netherlands. The latter showed her tremendous all-round ability with bronze medals in the 1,500 metres and the 3,000 metres, and was sixth in the sprint. Further proof of Dutch superiority came with the gold of Stien Baas-Kaiser in the 3,000 metres and her silver in the 1,500 metres behind America's Dianne Holum, who in turn followed Mrs Baas-Kaiser in the longer distance.

The alpine skiing, so often the centre-piece of the Winter Olympics, produced only one dual winner—and an amazing one at that. Marie-Therese Nadig, a 17-year-old Swiss schoolgirl, had not won a major race throughout the season, but she chose Sapporo to oust Austria's Anne-Marie Proell, the favourite, in both the downhill and the giant slalom. Heavy snow slowed the track in Miss Nadig's favour, but nonetheless hers was a most impressive performance. America's Susan Corrock took the bronze in the downhill and Austria's Wiltrud Drexel placed third in the giant slalom. The slalom went to

America—and Barbara Cochran —for their first alpine gold medal since 1952, and then only just: there was a mere two-hundredth of a second between the winner and France's Daniele Debernard. The French also took the bronze through Florence Steurer, which compensated in a small way for the disappointments of the season. In addition to Ingrid Lafforgue, the strong French team had lost Patrick Russel, Jacqueline Rouvier, and Francoise Macchi through injuries—Francoise Macchi's, coming during training at Sapporo, being the cruellest of all.

Nor was there any joy for the French in the men's alpine. There, the surprise was Francisco Fernandez-Ochoa, whose victory over Italy's Theoni brothers in the slalom—it was his first win in a major international—made him Spain's first Winter Olympic gold medallist. Gustavo Thoeni, the holder of the World Ski Cup, took the silver ahead of his brother Rolando, but showed true form in his second run in the giant slalom. For the first time, the Olympic event was decided on a two-runs aggregate, and after finishing third on his first run, Thoeni produced the fastest run next time round. With Norway's Erik Haaker,

fastest first time down, falling, it was left to the Swiss Edmund Bruggmann and Werner Mattle to take the minor medals. The Swiss finished 1-2 in the downhill with Bernhard Russi and Roland Colombin in that order, while Heini Messner, another of Austria's veterans, helped salvage some of his country's honour by finishing third despite a heavy attack of 'flu.

In the other ski sport, Nordic skiing, the inroads made into the Scandinavian dominance at Grenoble continued. This was not especially so across country, where the Norwegians and Swedes shared a virtual monopoly

with the Russians, but it was most definite in the jumping. A home hat-trick in the 70 metres jump was given an enthusiastic welcome as Yukio Kasaya, Akitsugo Konno, and Seiji Aochi took the medals in that order. The 1968 gold medallist, Jiri Raska of Czechoslovakia, could finish only fifth. But if home advantage could be given as a reason for the Japanese triumph, there could be no such excuse for the magnificent and brave jumping of Poland's Wojciech Fortuna from the 90-metre tower. His first leap of 367 feet left the others with too much to do, and Switzerland's Walter

Steiner outjumped Rainer Schmidt of East Germany for the silver medal.

There was gold, however, for the East Germans in the combined ski-jumping and 15 km cross-country. A Japanese, Hideki Nakano, led after the jumping section from Finland's Miettinen, but while the Finn sustained his challenge across country, the Japanese somewhat ironically came in last. East Germany's Ulrich Wehling came through to win the gold with Miettinen separating him from his compatriot Karl Luck in the medal order.

But for Sweden's Sven-Ake Lundback in the 15 kilometres, the men's cross-country would have been all Norway and Russia. Fedor Simaschov and Ivar Formo respectively gave Russia the silver and Norway the bronze behind Lundback, while in the 30 kilometres Vyacheslav Vedenine came through in a final powerful burst to relegate the Norwegians Paal Tyldum and Johs Harviken to minor placings. Surprisingly, considering Russia's 10-second success over Norway in a thrilling 4 x 10 kilometres relay, Vedenine's gold was only the second by a non-Scandinavian in the men's cross-country. Tyldum gained his revenge in the 50 kilometres, but Vedenine split Magne Myrmo and Reider Hjermstad to prevent Norway taking all three medals.

In the women's cross-country, the Russians, so supreme since Olympic ski-racing was introduced in 1952, dominated both events in the person of Galina Koulakova, 5 kilometres bronze medallist at Grenoble. In the 5 kilometres she led from the start, the other medals going to Finland's Marjatta Kajosmaa, 34-year-old mother of 11-year-old twins, and the Czech Helene Sikolova. Over the longer distance Miss Koulakova was followed home by fellow-countrywoman

Alvetina Olynina, with Mrs Kajosmaa third. For Miss Koulakova there was a further taste for gold in the relay, the silver going to Finland and the bronze to Norway.

The biathlon gold medals went to the same recipients as in 1968: the individual to Magnar Solberg of Norway; the relay to Russia. Silver and bronze medallists, respectively, were Hansjoerg Knauthe of East Germany and Sweden's Lars Ardwidson in the individual; Finland and East Germany in the relay.

When the final tally of medals was reckoned, the 14 to East Germany was an appropriate reminder of its growing power in all international competition. However, of those 14, eight came in the luge tobogganing—a remarkable monopoly of three races. Wolfgang Scheidel attacked the 14-curve run from the first and held his position throughout, while Harald Ehrig and Wolfram Fielder shut out the opposition. Incredibly, the remaining member of the East German squad, Klaus Bonsack, took fourth place. The two-man luge ended in a dead-heat, and to some extent, therefore, the Italians Paul Hildgartner and Walter Plaikner broke the East Germany monopoly. They shared the same two-run aggregate as Horst Hornlein and Reinhard Bredow, while Bonsack and Fiedler followed their individual showings with the bronze. In the women's, the three East German entrants Anna Muller, Ute Ruhrold, and Margit Schumann finished in that order.

In the bobsleigh it was the other Germany who held the stage, taking gold and silver in the two-man and bronze in the four. Wolfgang Zimmerer steered both the gold and bronze medal winning sleds, while his opposite number in the leading Swiss sled, Jean Wicki, accomplished the same feat but in reverse order.

1 Home-crowd support for a Japanese entrant in the women's 10 km cross-country. Both the women's cross-country events were won by the Russian, Galina Koulacova, who won a third gold with the relay team. **2** Jean Wicki drives his four-man bob to victory and the security of the finishing line. **3** The two-man bob saw West Germany come out on top through Wolfgang Zimmerer and Peter Utzschneider.

The figure skating was memorable for the superb figures traced by Austria's Trixi Schuba. If she lacked the uninhibited freestyling of Canada's Karen Magnussen (silver) and America's Janet Lynn (bronze), the tall Austrian took full advantage of her superiority in the compulsory section. There was some controversial scoring, as there often is, but few knew how to react to the maximum six awarded to Janet Lynn for artistic impression after her fall.

There was a notable fall in the men's event, too. Ondrej Nepela, while attempting a triple toe loop jump, fell for the first time in four years, but this did not prevent the Czech, whose performance included an excellent triple salchow, from winning the gold medal. France's Patrick Pera failed to hold his position in the freestyle and had to be content with the bronze medal behind Sergei Tchetveroukhin of Russia.

The pairs, for so long the preserve of Oleg Protopopov and Ludmilla Belousova, saw two Russian pairs battle for their Olympic crown and ended with victory for Moscovites Alexei Ulanov and Irena Rodnina over the Leningrad pair, Andrei Suraikin and Ludmila Smirnova. East Germany's Uwe Kagelmann

and Manuela Gross added a bronze to their country's medal tally.

For the first time since the inaugural Winter Olympics, Canada did not compete in the ice hockey—the problem again being the question of status. As expected, the Russians won the gold medal, and only Sweden, with a 3-3 draw, stopped them winning every game. That draw, however, could have opened the way for the Czechs, had they not gone down 5-1 to the young United States team. Consequently the Czechs had to beat Russia in the final match, which they were unable to do. America's upsetting of the form book gave them the silver medal over the Czechs, as both finished the group with 6 points. In Group B, West Germany topped the table ahead of Norway and Japan.

Success in the ice hockey gave the Russians their eighth gold medal, and they ended the Games with 16 medals (five silver, three bronze), two ahead of East Germany (4-3-7). Once again, however, the dividing problems had remained unsolved, and the suspension of Schranz did little except rob the Games of a leading personality. With the threat of possible walk-outs and boycotts at forthcoming winter Olympics, plus the prohibitive cost of staging the events, it was not surprising that so few venues were coming forward to host the Games and it remained with the administrators to put the Olympic house in order long before the competitors arrived for the 1976 Winter Olympics at Innsbruck.

1 Italy (left), Switzerland and West Germany at the four-man bob medal ceremony.
2 Practising Soviet-American relations in the ice hockey.
3 Alexei Ulanov and Irena Rodnina. **4** Trixi Schuba.

SAPPORO WINTER OLYMPIC GAMES, 1972 Gold Medallists			
Nordic Skiing—Men			
15 kilometres	Sven Lundback	Sweden	45 min 28.24 sec
30 kilometres	Vyacheslav Vedenine	USSR	1 hr 36 min 31.15 sec
50 kilometres	Paal Tyldum	Norway	2 hr 43 min 14.75 sec
4 x 10 km relay		USSR	2 hr 04 min 47.94 sec
Combination	Ulrich Wehling	East Germany	413.34 pts
70 metres jumping	Yukio Kasaya	Japan	244.2 pts
90 metres jumping	Wojciech Fortuna	Poland	219.9 pts
Biathlon	Magnar Solberg	Norway	1 hr 15 min 55.50 sec
Biathlon relay		USSR	1 hr 51 min 44.92 sec
Nordic Skiing—Women			
5 kilometres	Galina Koulacova	USSR	17 min 00.50 sec
10 kilometres	Galina Koulacova	USSR	34 min 17.82 sec
3 x 5 km relay		USSR	48 min 46.15 sec
Alpine Skiing—Men			
Downhill	Bernhard Russi	Switzerland	1 min 51.43 sec
Slalom	Francisco Fernandez-Ochoa	Spain	1 min 49.27 sec
Giant slalom	Gustavo Thoeni	Italy	3 min 09.62 sec
Alpine Skiing—Women			
Downhill	Marie-Therese Nadig	Switzerland	1 min 36.68 sec
Slalom	Barbara Cochran	USA	1 min 31.24 sec
Giant slalom	Marie-Therese Nadig	Switzerland	1 min 29.90 sec
Figure Skating			
Men	Ondrej Nepela	Czechoslovakia	2,739.1 pts
Women	Trixi Schuba	Austria	2,751.5 pts
Pairs	Alexei Ulanov and Irena Rodnina	USSR	420.4 pts
Speed Skating—Men			
500 metres	Erhard Keller	West Germany	39.44 sec
1,500 metres	Ard Schenk	Netherlands	2 min 02.96 sec
5,000 metres	Ard Shenk	Netherlands	7 min 23.61 sec
10,000 metres	Ard Shenk	Netherlands	15 min 01.35 sec
Speed Skating—Women			
500 metres	Anne Henning	USA	43.33 sec
1,000 metres	Monika Pflug	West Germany	1 min 31.40 sec
1,500 metres	Dianne Holum	USA	2 min 20.85 sec
3,000 metres	Stien Baas-Kaiser	Netherlands	4 min 52.14 sec
Bobsleigh			
2-man	Wolfgang Zimmerer and Peter Utzschneider	West Germany	4 min 57.07 sec
4-man		Switzerland I	4 min 43.06 sec
Luge Tobogganing—Men			
Individual	Wolfgang Scheidel	East Germany	3 min 27.58 sec
2-man	Horst Hornlein and Reinhard Bredow	East Germany	
	Paul Hildgartner and Walter Plaikner	Italy	1 min 28.35 sec
Luge Tobogganing—Women			
Individual	Anna Muller	East Germany	2 min 59.18 sec
Ice Hockey		USSR	

Innsbruck Winter Olympic Games (1976)

After the problems of professionalism and commercialism at the previous two Olympic Games, the XIIth Winter Olympics was a blast of fresh air to the Olympic movement. Two competitors failed dope tests but both were the unwitting victims of drugs given to combat a flu epidemic in the Olympic Village, and that was typical of a Games with the right spirit.

Innsbruck was in many ways a test case for future Olympiads. The small and ancient Tyrolean city had staged efficient and friendly Games in 1964, and it was a novel step to entrust the staging of another Games to the same city so soon after its first. But Innsbruck rose to the occasion, not only proving that the small city can afford a Games but that it can be afforded by using existing facilities and making the best possible use of them by using them for a second Games.

Not that the Austrians tried to

keep commercialism totally out of their Games. Their national ski industry depended too greatly on a local success. But even that was offered them when Franz Klammer, after a slow first half, literally flew downhill to win the downhill title by just half a second.

Winter Olympics are growing all the time. At Innsbruck in 1964, a record of 1,186 competed; in 1976 there were 1,368 competitors from 37 countries, 12 of whom won gold medals – including, for the first time since the other Innsbruck Games 12 years earlier, Britain.

Just as they had in 1964, the Austrians opened their Games in the natural amphitheatre of the Bergisel ski jump where the country's president, Dr Rudolf Kirchschalager, conducted the formal ceremony in the presence of 60,000 spectators. Leading the British team was an appropriate choice, ice skater John Curry.

Curry had finished 11th in the men's figure skating at the previous Olympics. But in 1973 he had gone to the United States to train under the Italian coach Carlo Fassi, coach to former Olympic champion Peggy Fleming and then coaching Dorothy Hammill. It was an inspired move. From being on the fringe of world class, Curry's balletic style soon began to set a trend, and in 1975 he was second in the European Championships and third in the World Championships.

In Innsbruck there was no other skater in the same class. The Russians, Sergei Volkov and Vladimir Kovalev, and the Canadian

Toller Cranston performed well but Curry was brilliant, a perfectly choreographed programme of jumps, lutzs, axels and spins winning him many 5.9 markings and a convincing victory. It was the first time a British man had won the Olympic title, and Curry, a 26-year-old from Birmingham, went on to win the European and World titles, too.

For Britain, naturally, it made a Games which traditionally passes them by in mid-soccer season. The real star of the Games, however, was a German, Rosi Mittermaier, an attractive girl who became the first woman to gain two golds and a silver in Alpine skiing.

Incredibly, the grand slam of all three Olympic Alpine skiing titles has been achieved twice, by Austria's Toni Sailer and Jean Claude Killy, of France. Mittermaier failed to emulate them by a margin of just 0.12 sec.

She won the downhill, even though she was skiing in the event for the first time. The slalom was made slightly easier for her when the Swiss, Lise-Marie Morerud, fell, and she won that too. But the triple crown was taken from her by Kathy Kreiner, the first Canadian gold medallist for eight years, who beat her by 0.12 sec in the giant slalom.

Inevitably, the Games were dominated by the Eastern European bloc. The Soviet Union and East Germany won 46 of the 111 medals between them, leaving the others to be shared by 14 other countries, with little Lichtenstein, who won

two bronze medals, winning its first Olympic medals in either summer or winter Games, and France, which spends a fortune on its skiers, collecting just one bronze medal as their reward.

The Soviet Union lost one medal in the 5,000 metres cross country skiing when Galina Koulakova was dope tested after taking third place, and found to have traces of a prohibited drug in her blood. The drug came from a nasal spray she had been taking for a cold but because the IOC's medical commission had not been informed in advance that it had been prescribed for her, she lost her medal. The Soviet Union did not lose; the upgraded fourth place competitor was also one of theirs.

The same harsh judgement was passed on the Czechoslovakian ice hockey team. Their captain, Frantisek Pospisil, was found to have taken an antibiotic prescribed by the team doctor, and the IOC deducted two points from the Czechs' total and banned the player. The International Ice Hockey Federation protested bitterly but in the end it made no difference. The Czechs still reached the final comfortably and five minutes from the end led 3–2, only to lose 4–3 to two late Soviet goals.

Innsbruck did more than just offer its 1964 facilities. It added where necessary, as at the speed skating stadium in Innsbruck itself which became one of the world's biggest electrically refrigerated surfaces. It was there that, in the four women's events, no fewer than 36

Above, **Toller Cranston, one of Canada's three medallists at the Innsbruck Games.**
Left, **Dorothy Hamill on her way to winning the women's figure skating event.**

Left, **East German Danneberg took the silver in the 70m ski jump, whilst Zimmerer's West German four-man bob team had to be content with a bronze medal.**

Olympic records were broken and where Tatiana Averina, of the Soviet Union, won two gold and two bronze medals.

There was also the incredible, new combined bobsledding and tobogganing course at Igls, the largest artificially frozen track in the world with more than 50 miles of cooling pipes. The East Germans, who have a similar track at home, were totally dominant there, using men such as former world class athletes Meinhard Nehmer and Bernhard Germeshausen to power the bobs. Those two won the two-man event by more than half a second.

The East Germans also won on the 70 metres ski jump, taking the first two places to keep out local hero Karl Schnabl – but his moment of glory followed in the 90 metre jump, the most spectacular event of the Winter Games. His consistency won it, but the longest jump of the competition was performed by Tony Innauer, a 17-year-old Austrian, who took the silver medal in this final event of the Games to make his country's day.

Even without Curry's victory for Britain, the figure skating again captured most of the attention of the world outside the few Alpine countries. It was a particularly exciting Games for skaters, since most medals remained wide open to be won until the end.

Dorothy Hamill made a clean sweep for coach Fassi when she emulated Curry's success by winning the women's title, just ahead of an American-bred, Dutch-born and qualified skater, Dianne de Leeuw, who had beaten Dorothy at the 1975 World Championships. But the Russians again won the pairs, with the partnership of Alek Zaitsev and Irina Rodnina, the latter for the second successive Games but with a different partner. And the Russians won, too, in the only new Olympic event in Innsbruck, the ice dancing. Alex Gorshkov and Ludmila Pakhomova won the honour of being the first Olympic champions in that event.

For Innsbruck itself, the Games were an enormous success. They managed to contain all the different sports within a 15-mile radius, had none of 1964's problems with lack of snow and actually ended with a working profit. And that did not count one of the estimated one million spectators and tourists who flocked into the Tyrol during the Games period.

Because it was staging its second Games, Innsbruck was allowed to burn two flames throughout the Games. A third resort will take a second turn to host them in 1980, Lake Placid, and it is now obvious that the IOC has seen the wisdom of rotating the Games between those cities which have existing facilities. It surely must be a lesson that it will soon learn can also be applied to the summer Games.

Moscow Olympic Games (1980)

'The Soviet Union has given the IOC its guarantee that the Games will be held in accordance with the Olympic Charter. We guarantee that, and the Soviet government does not give guarantees for nothing and without thought.'

Sergëi Pavlov, chairman of the USSR Committee for Physical Education and Sport.

When Montreal won the right to host the 1976 Olympic Games, its mayor, Jean Drapeau, guaranteed they would not cost the city's taxpayers a cent. 'There is no more chance of the Games losing money than of a man having a baby,' he boasted. Drapeau's dream eventually cost the taxpayers of Montreal and Quebec province around $1 billion.

Guarantees made when cities are putting themselves forward to host the Games six years ahead are meaningless. How could Mexico have guaranteed in 1962 that there would be no riots at the time of their Games six years later? How could Munich guarantee there would be no massacre of Israeli competitors?

But Moscow has made that one guarantee on which the future of the whole Olympic movement must depend. Money is not a problem for the Soviet Union. Indeed, the careful selection of Western companies to help them could give the organizing committee at least a working profit.

'Our Games will not be any cheaper than those in Munich. This we are not very much worried about. Cost is of no interest to us,' says Pavlov.

Certainly, security at a Games will never have been easier to ensure than at the first Games ever to have been held in Eastern Europe. Only those foreigners who have bought tickets and hotel accommodation in advance will even be granted entry visas.

But for the IOC at least, that guarantee made by Pavlov is paramount. Riots and black power in Mexico, killings in Munich and boycotts in Montreal are as much as the Olympic movement can stand. Trouble in Moscow would be disastrous.

The Olympic rules, as amended in 1974, state categorically that 'no discrimination in them is allowed against any country or person on grounds of race, religion or politics.' It further states that the IOC 'shall secure the widest possible audience' for the Games.

The Soviet Union is the first country in which a Games have been held which demands that every single person entering the country must have a visa issued by the Soviet government. This even applies to the accredited competitors, officials and media representatives,

all normally permitted to enter an Olympic host country merely on production of their Olympic credentials.

The dangers are obvious. The Soviet government, and not the IOC, is retaining the right to refuse entry. It has already stated that it will not give press accreditation to the representatives of two American radio stations which beam programmes into Eastern Europe. Four years ago, when Moscow staged the World Student Games, some

Israelis were refused visas.

What about them this time, and what about the Chinese should they be welcomed back into the Olympic fold? What about countries which have cut off diplomatic ties with the Soviet Union? Will Chilean competitors, whose football team was refused entry to play a World Cup preliminary in 1974 and whose Olympic federation is the fifth oldest, be welcome?

All this is speculation. Pavlov has promised publicly that journalists

and other visitors will have the right to travel all over the Soviet Union.

What those visitors will see once there will almost certainly be the most superb facilities ever offered a modern Games. No city in the world probably knows more about sport. There are more Olympic champions (238) among Moscow's inhabitants than any city in the world. According to the Organizing Committee, spending just half a day in each of Moscow's sports installations would take you ten years.

Scenes from Moscow's preparations for hosting the 1980 Games: a dress rehearsal for the opening ceremony in the vast Lenin Stadium and, *(top)*, the specially-commissioned cycling stadium.

Even so, more have had to be built to accommodate the Games. A modern rowing canal, complete with a return channel, has been built. Next to it, an indoor cycling track with a perimeter of 333.3 metres and with a seating capacity for 6,000 has been erected. An archery stadium with movable grandstands and a circuit road for cycling have been built at Krylatskoye, the first time Olympic cyclists will have a special course and not just a section of public highway.

For the first time, too, all the equestrian events will be held in the same place, a southern suburb of Moscow where the complex comprises a hurdle-race stadium, a steeplechase course and a show ring overlooked by a 20,000-seater red-brick and wood grandstand.

For the first time, too, swimming and diving will be given their own separate buildings, and a 500 metre corridor will connect the aquatic centre with an indoor arena seating 45,000, the largest of Moscow's new Olympic projects, which can be divided into two by a sound-proof, eight-storey high, metal curtain. In one half, 18,000 will watch the boxing, while in the other 16,000 will be watching basketball matches.

But the main Olympic arena is not new. The Central Lenin Stadium at Luzhniki is already the country's biggest sports complex, occupying an area of 450 acres and with 140 various sports installations. The main arena, where the athletics and football will be held, will seat 103,000, while the smaller arena there will hold the gymnastics, judo and wrestling events.

There are also existing facilities being modernized, like the famous Dynamo stadium for soccer and hockey, the Young Pioneers' Stadium for hockey and the Sokolniki Park hall for handball.

Accommodation for the anticipated 300,000 visitors, however, has had to be extensively built. A hotel in Ismailovo will consist of five 30-storey buildings to accommodate 10,000 (and will include its own cinema and concert hall). Two other smaller hotels are being built, and the radio and television journalists

will have a new hotel to themselves.

The Olympic Village itself is also new, built on 270 acres and consisting of 18 16-storey buildings with single and double rooms arranged as apartments. Each group of six buildings will have its own courtyard with summer houses and flower beds, and the Village will have a shopping centre, concert hall, cinemas, and a cafe.

Most important for the athletes is its proximity to extensive training areas and the main stadia.

Of course, when Munich and Montreal paid out vast sums for capital projects, the bill was passed on to the heads of the Olympic Organizing Committees as part of their debt. Moscow does not see it in that light. "All the construction is incorporated in the Master Plan of the city's development until the end of the century, says the Organizing Committee. 'The Olympic Games has just caused some of the dates to be brought forward.'

Only the Village was not a part of any master plan, and the new Northern Ray, a city highway connecting the city centre with its northern suburbs, was brought forward by ten years. But when the Games are finished the city of Moscow will not be presenting bills for these, nor for the new air terminal which will handle up to 2,100 passengers an hour.

The Organizing Committee argues that all would have been built anyway, at least in some shape or form, and though the Village was not planned, arrangements have now been made to house 14,000 Muscovites in it after the Games.

Indeed, the Games will benefit Moscow hugely. Around $50 million of television equipment is being left behind after the Games by NBC, the television company which won the lucrative North American rights to screen the Games. Several artificial pitches have been given by a company which wanted the right to claim their pitches were used for the 1980 Games. Vast sums in hard Western currency will be earned from the 300,000 spectators expected.

Certainly it will be the culmination of a long struggle by the Soviet Union to bring the Olympic Games to Eastern Europe and, particularly, to Moscow. They tried to do it for 1976 but faced with awarding it for a second time to capitalistic Los Angeles or for the first time to communist Moscow, the IOC came up with one of its traditional compromises. It awarded it to Montreal.

So six years later in Vienna, at the 1974 Olympic Congress, Moscow tried again. This time the only opposition was Los Angeles, and even they were reputed to have let their name be put forward only to save the IOC from the embarrassment of having no choice. Even so, unofficial voting returns – the actual figures are never released – gave Moscow only 39 of the 61 votes cast. But it was enough.

Curiously, the IOC chose the same Congress to allow Olympic

A reminder of the venue for the 1980 Games – one of the fabulous displays at the opening ceremony in Moscow.

Gymnastics is an increasingly popular sport in the West, but the Eastern bloc countries can usually expect to dominate with stars such as, *left,* Rumania's Nadia Comaneci. *Above,* Britain's Sebastian Coe is one of the favourites for the middle distance events in Moscow.

competitors unlimited training and broken-time payments for doing it, thus giving Western athletes the legal means to begin doing what the Eastern bloc has been doing for 20 years. It could make a substantial difference in 1980.

Already, Britain, one of the most poverty-stricken of the world's sporting powers, has used the new rule to give vast sums to its best athletes—through an organization called the Sports Aid Foundation, funded partly by the Sports Council but largely by commercial concerns.

No athlete, it claims, with any chance of competing in the Olympics will have been in need of money.

The French have done the same by a different method, selecting about 30 outstanding prospects for Olympic medals and supporting them directly from the Sports Ministry of the French government.

The United States, following a presidential commission, set aside about $30 million to support its Olympic Committee, and for the first time amateur athletes have been encouraged to use their fame to endorse commercial products in advertising campaigns, with the fees going to their sports federations.

But the Soviet Union will still be better prepared than any other country. Its swimmers showed a few signs in Montreal that they were becoming a force to be reckoned with, and in Berlin at the 1978 World Championships, they

were ranked second only to the United States. In athletics, gymnastics, shooting and indeed every sport with the exception of field hockey, it will start among the favourites.

Even in yachting, that most capitalistic pastime, the Soviet Union had boats placed in the first six in all but one class at the last Games. The Olympic organizers are even building a special harbour at Tallinn, capital of Estonia, where the yachting events will be held – not for the competitors but for guests arriving aboard their own yachts and motorboats.

Sport in the Soviet Union is simply a part of the culture. Government statistics show that 55 million participate, one in five of the population. The facilities for them to enjoy are extensive. As part of its planning requirement, any new housing development in Moscow must have its own stadium for soccer and athletics, a swimming pool, a gymnasium and sports fields.

There are now more than 80,000 professional sports coaches in the Soviet Union, with six million volunteer assistants, most graduates of the external departments of higher education establishments. The coaches must have graduated from one of the 23 state institutes of physical culture.

For those children who show promise there are nearly 6,000 junior sports schools, one in ten of them specializing in a particular sport. The children will go there to be coached six to eight hours each week, and later as much as three hours a day.

After school, there are the voluntary sports societies where, for a fee of just 30 kopecks – the price of a Soviet chocolate bar – and on production of a medical certificate of good health anybody may use the sports facilities for a year. For that price you can even join flying, yachting and riding clubs, all paid for from an annual budget from central government.

Yet anybody believing that the Soviet teams are mass-produced on one production line should know that the Soviet team at the Montreal Games came from 85 different cities and towns.

What will be unusual about the Moscow Games will be the prices charged—visitors from abroad having to pay about ten times as much as the locals.

Hard currency is what the Games are about for the Soviet Union. It will bring them prestige, show their country in a good light and boost the morale of their own people. Most of all, however, it will bring foreign exchange. Take the television contracts. The National Broadcasting Corporation of America is paying $100 million for 150 hours of coverage. That is $11,200 per minute, but tiny compared with the $150,000 a minute they are demanding from advertisers and sponsors.

The Soviet Union received the first $20 million instalment in 1977, a further $30 million in 1978 and finally $50 million in equipment which will be left in Moscow after the Games. Even the other nations, like Britain and West Germany, who plan comprehensive coverage, are only being allowed to bring in the special equipment they need on condition they pay a fee in foreign currency or leave the equipment behind on departure.

The Organizing Committee is also taking advantage of a massive commemorative coins campaign throughout the world, not a new idea since the Governor of Messina in 480 B.C. is said to have done it after winning a chariot race at an Olympics. But never has such a scheme been so successful. The Canadians made around $300 million from their coins in 1976 but the Soviet coins are selling more quickly because they have made them more expensive but in smaller, more exclusive editions.

Then there are the commercial supporters of the Games from the West, companies like Coca-Cola, Olivetti, Swiss Timing, Adidas and BAT-Taraflex. At least two of those are reported to have paid a seven-figure sum for various rights. Adidas

and its associates are clothing 35,000 Soviet officials and Olympic workers right down to the level of the chauffeurs.

Nor has Moscow missed a trick in exploiting its symbol and mascot, the former a stylized representation of the Kremlin and the latter a bear cub called Misha. Already the bear has starred in an American cartoon film. Soon bags, clothing, umbrellas and every other conceivable piece of merchandize will be carrying that famous bear.

Olympic Games are like travelling circuses, all the same old sideshows and traders coming together every four years to exploit Coubertin's ideal. This time, though, there is the unusual complication of the totalitarian state whose citizens even need visas to travel from one state to another within the Soviet Union. 'It will not be a problem,' says David Dryer, head of the British consortium of travel agencies. 'We've been organizing tours there for five years and I can't remember the last visa application which was refused.'

Indeed, he points out, Intourist, a Soviet travel agency, is offering

30 tours within the Soviet Union during the Games. One tour will even take in Siberia, and another reach the Asiatic half of the vast country. Each country has been allocated places and tickets based on the number of tickets they bought for the Games in Montreal and Munich. Britain has about 100,000 tickets, enough to cater for 15,000 since everybody must have a ticket for every day of their stay in Moscow.

The Organizing Committee is expecting 12,000 athletes and officials, 900 judges from international federations and at least 7,000 representatives from the world's media. They will also be entertaining Lord Killanin in his last Games as the IOC president.

Killanin has been a president of a different kind to his predecessor, Avery Brundage. He is not the autocrat but the diplomat. He does not demand or tell; he talks and negotiates. He has become the Kissinger of the Olympic movement. But his successes in the end are few enough. The Games are not smaller. Indeed, in Moscow, women's hockey will be contested

for the first time, just as women's basketball made its debut in 1976. They are not cheaper, nor any freer from politics. They have not yet resolved the membership of the two Chinas, although they have come closer to doing it. They have suffered their first mass boycott and their first refusal by a host government to allow free access to a Games, something the Canadians succeeded in achieving where Hitler in 1936 had failed.

They have suffered all this and survived. What they cannot survive is any further erosion of the Olympic ideal. As Killanin said before Montreal: 'We all have our own beliefs; we all have our friends and enemies; but the aim of the Olympic Movement is to subjugate these in the fellowship enshrined in the intertwining Olympic rings . . . if this is not accomplished then the Olympic Movement and all sport, whether amateur or professional, is doomed.'

The largest sporting complex in Europe, Moscow's Lenin Central Stadium, seen here from across the River Moscva.

Olympic Medallists

G = Gold S = Silver B = Bronze

Archery
MENS DOUBLE F.I.T.A. ROUND
1896–1968 Event not held
1972 G,John C. Williams (USA) 2,528 pts S,Gunnar Jarvil (Sweden) 2,481 B,Kyoesti Laasonen (Finland) 2,467
1976 G,D. Pace (USA) 2,571 pts S,H. Michinaga (Japan) 2,502 B, C. C. Ferrari (Italy) 2,495

WOMENS DOUBLE F.I.T.A. ROUND
1896–1968 Event not held
1972 G,Doreen Wilbur (USA) 2,424 pts S,Irena Szydlwska (Poland) 2,407 B,Emma Gapchenko (USSR) 2,403
1976 G,L. Ryon (USA) 2,499 pts S,V. Kovpan (USSR) 2,460 B, Z. Rustamova (USSR) 2,407

Basketball (Men)
1896–1932 Event not held
1936 G,USA (Francis Johnson, Carl Knowles, Joe Fortenberry, William Wheatly, Jack Ragland. Ralph Bishop, Carl Shy, Duane Swanson, Samuel Balter, Gibbons, Lubin, Mollner, Piper, Schmidt) S,Canada B,Mexico
1948 G,USA (Clifford Barker, Donald Barksdale, Ralph Beard, Louis Beck, Vincent Borzla, Gordon Carpenter, Alexander Groza, Wallace Jones, Robert Kurland, Raymond Lumpp, R. C. Pitts, Jesse Renick, R. Jackie Robinson, Kenneth Rollins) S,France B,Brazil
1952 G,USA (Charles Hoag, William Houghland, J. Keller, Dean Kelley, Robert Kenney. W. Lienhard, Clyde Lovellette, Marcus Frieberger, Wayne Glasgow, Frank McCabe, Daniel Pippin, Howard Williams, Ronald Bontemps, Robert Kurland) S,USSR B,Uruguay
1956 G,USA (Carl Cain, William Houghland, K. C. Jones, William Russell, James Walsh, William Evans, Burdette Haldorson, Ronald Tomsic, Richard Boushka, Gilbert Ford, Robert Jeangerard, Charles Darling) S,USSR B,Uruguay
1960 G,USA (Jerry West, Walter Bellamy, Robert Boozer, Terry Dischinger, Burdette Haldorson, Darrall Imhoff, Allen Kelley, Lester Lane, Jerry Lucas, Adrian Smith, Jay Arnette, Oscar Robertson) S,USSR B,Brazil
1964 G,USA (Jim Barnes, William Bradley, Lawrence Brown, Joe Caldwell, Mel Counts, Richard Davies, Walter Hazzard, Lucius Jackson, John McCaffrey, Jeffrey Mullins, Jerry Shipp, George Wilson) S,USSR B,Brazil
1968 G,USA (M. Barret, J. Clawson, D. Dee, C. Fowler, S. Haywood, W. Hosket, J. King, G. Saulters, C. Scott, M. Silliman, K. Spain, J. White) S,Yugoslavia B,USSR
1972 G,USSR (A. Pooivoda, M. Paulauskas, Z. Sakandelidze, A. Sharmukhamedov, A. Boloshev, Y. Edeshko, S. Belov, M. Korkia, Y. Dvorni, G. Volnov,

A. Belov. S. Kovalenko, V. Kondrashin) S,USA B,Cuba
1976 G,USA (P. Ford, S. Sheppard, A. Dantley, W. Davis, W. Buckner, E. Grunfeld, K. Carr, S. May, M. Armstrong, T. La Garde, P. Hubbard, M. Kupchak) S,Yugoslavia B,USSR

Basketball (Women)
1896–1972 Event not held
1976 G,USSR (A. Rupshene, T. Zakharova, O. Barisheva, T. Ovetchkina, N. Shuvaeva, I. Semenova, N. Zakharova, N. Feryabuikova, O. Sukharova, T. Daunene, N. Klimova) S,USA B,Bulgaria

Boxing
LIGHT FLYWEIGHT
1896–1964 Event not held
1968 G,Francisco Rodriguez (Venezuela) S,Yung-Ju Jee (South Korea) B,Harlan Marbley (USA), Hubert Skrzypczak (Poland)
1972 G,Gyoergy Gedo (Hungary) S,U. Gil Kim (Korea) B,Ralph Evans (Great Britain), Enrique Rodriguez (Spain)
1976 G,J. Hernadez (Cuba) S,B. U. Li (Korea) B,B. Pooltarat (Thailand), O. Maldonado (Puerto Rico)

FLYWEIGHT
1896–1900 Event not held
1904 G,George Finnegan (USA) S,Miles Burke (USA)
1908–1912 Event not held
1920 G,Frank De Genaro (USA) S,Anders Petersen (Denmark) B,W. Cuthbertson (Great Britain)
1924 G,Fidel La Barba (USA) S,James McKenzie (Great Britain) B,Raymond Fee (USA)
1928 G,Antal Kocsis (Hungary) S,Armand Apell (France) B,Carlo Cavagnoli (Italy)
1932 G,Istvan Enekes (Hungary), S,Francisco Cabanas (Mexico) B, Louis Salica (USA)
1936 G,Willi Kaiser (Germany) S,Gavino Matta (Italy) B,Louis Laurie (USA)
1948 G,Paschal Perez (Argentina) S,Spartaco Bandinelli (Italy) B,Soo Ann Han (Korea)
1952 G,Nathan Brooks (USA) S,Edgar Basel (Germany) B,Anatoliy Bulakov (USSR), Willie Toweel (South Africa)
1956 G,Terry Spinks (Great Britain) S,Mircea Dobrescu (Rumania) B,John Caldwell (Eire), Rene Libeer (France)
1960 G,Gyula Torok (Hungary) S,Sergey Sivko (USSR) B,Kiyoshi Tanabe (Japan), Abdelmoneim Elgvindi (UAR)
1964 G,Fernando Atzori (Italy) S,Artur Olek (Poland) B,Robert Carmody (USA), Stanislav Sorokin (USSR)
1968 G,Ricardo Delgado (Mexico) S,Artur Olek (Poland) B,Servilio de Oliveira (Brazil), Leo Rwabogo (Uganda)
1972 G,Gheorghi Kostadinov (Bulgaria) S,Leo Rwabogo (Uganda) B,Leszek Blazynski (Poland). Douglas Rodriguez (Cuba)
1976 G,L. Randolph (USA) S,R. Duvalong (Cuba) B,D. Torosayan (USSR), L. Blazynski (Poland)

BANTAMWEIGHT
1896–1900 Event not held
1904 G,O. L. Kirk (USA)

S,George Finnegan (USA)
1908 G,A. Thomas (Great Britain) S,J. Condon (Great Britain) B,W. Webb (Great Britain)
1912 Event not held
1920 G,Clarence Walker (South Africa) S,C. Graham (Canada) B,James McKenzie (Great Britain)
1924 G,William Smith (South Africa) S,Salvatore Tripoli (USA) B,Jean Ces (France)
1928 G,Vittorio Tamagnini (Italy) S,John Daley (USA) B,Harry Isaacs (South Africa)
1932 G,Horace Gwynne (Canada) S,Hans Ziglarski (Germany) B,Jose Villaneuva (Philippines)
1936 G,Ulderico Sergo (Italy) S,Jack Wilson (USA) B,Fidel Ortiz (Mexico)
1948 G,Tibor Csik (Hungary)· S,Giovanni Zuddas (Italy) B,Juan Venegas (Puerto Rico)
1952 G,Pentti Hamalainen (Finland) S,John McNally (Eire) B,Gennadiy Garbuzov (USSR), Joon Kang (South Korea)
1956 G,Wolfgang Behrendt (Germany) S,Soon Chun Song (Korea) B,Frederick Gilroy (Eire), Claudio Barrientos (Chile)
1960 G,Olyeg Grigoryev (USSR) S,Primo Zamparini (Italy) B,Brunoh Bendig (Poland), Oliver Taylor (Australia)
1964 G,Takao Sakurai (Japan) S,Shin Cho Chung (South Korea) B,Juan Fabila (Mexico), Washington Rodriguez (Uruguay)
1968 G,Valery Sokolov (USSR) S,Eridadi Mukwanga (Uganda) B,E. Morioka (Japan) Soon-Kill Chang (South Korea)
1972 G,Orlando Martinez (Cuba) S,George Turpin (Great Britain) B,John M. Nderu (Kenya), Ferry E. Moniaga (Indonesia)
1976 G,Y. G. Gu (Korea) S,C. Mooney (USA) B,P. Cowdell (Great Britain), C. Hwang (Korea)

FEATHERWEIGHT
1896–1900 Event not held
1904 G,O. L. Kirk (USA) S,Frank Haller (USA)
1908 G,R. K. Gunn (Great Britain) S,C. Morris (Great Britain) B,H. Roddin (Great Britain)
1912 Event not held
1920 G,Paul Fritsch (France) S,Gauchet (France) B,Edoardo Garzena (Italy)
1924 G,John Fields (USA) S,Joseph Salas (USA) B,Pedro Quartucci (Argentina)
1928 G,L. van Klaveren (Netherlands) S,Victor Peralta (Argentina) B,Harold Devine (USA)
1932 G,Carmelo Robledo (Argentina) S,Josef Schleinkofer (Germany) B,Carl Carlsson (Sweden)
1936 G,Oscar Casanova (Argentina) S,Charles Catterall (South Africa) B,Joseph Miner (Germany)
1948 G,Ernesto Formenti (Italy) S,Denis Shepherd (South Africa) B,Aleksey Antkiewicz (Poland)
1952 G,Jan Zachara (Czechoslovakia) S,Sergio Caprari (Italy) B,Joseph Ventaja (France), Leonard Leisching (South Africa)
1956 G,Vladimir Safronov

(USSR) S, Tommy Nicholls (Great Britain) B,Henryk Niedzwiedzki (Poland), Pentti Hamalainen (Finland)
1960 G,Francesco Musso (Italy) S,Jerzy Adamski (Poland) B,William Meyers (South Africa) Jorma Limmonen (Finland)
1964 G,Stanislav Stepashkin (USSR) S,Antony Villanueva (Philippines) B,Charles Brown (USA), Heinz Schultz (Germany)
1968 G,Antonio Roldan (Mexico) S,Albert Robinson (USA) B,Philip Waruinge (Kenya), Ivan Michailov (Bulgaria)
1972 G,Boris Kousnetsov (USSR) S,Andras Botos (Hungary) B,Kazuo Kobayashi (Japan), Gabriel Pometcu (Rumania)
1976 G,A. Herrera (Cuba) S,R. Nowakowski (East Germany) B,J. Paredes (Mexico), L. Kosedowski (Poland)

LIGHTWEIGHT
1896–1900 Event not held
1904 G,H. J. Spangler (USA) S,James Eagan (USA) B,R. Van Horn (USA)
1908 G,F. Grace (Great Britain) S,F. Spiller (Great Britain) B,H. Johnson (Great Britain)
1912 Event not held
1920 G,Samuel Mosberg (USA) S,Gotfred Johanssen (Denmark) B,Newton (Canada)
1924 G,Hans Nielsen (Denmark) S,Alfredo Copello (Argentina) B,Frederick Boylstein (USA)
1928 G,Carlo Orlando (Italy) S,Stephen Halaiko (USA) B,Gunnar Berggren (Sweden)
1932 G,Lawrence Stevens (South Africa) S,Thure Alhquist (Sweden) B,Nathan Bor (USA)
1936 G,Imre Harangi (Hungary) S,Nikolai Stepulov (Estonia) B,Erik Agren (Sweden)
1948 G,Gerald Dreyer (South Africa) S,Joseph Vissers (Belgium) B,Svend Wad (Denmark)
1952 G,Aureliano Bolognesi (Italy) S,Aleksey Antkiewicz (Poland) B,Gheorghe Fiat (Rumania), Erkki Pakkanen (Finland)
1956 G,Dick McTaggart (Great Britain) S,Harry Kurschat (Germany) B,Anthony Byrne (Eire), Anatoliy Laguetko (USSR)
1960 G,Kazimierz Pazdzior (Poland) S,Sandro Lopapoli (Italy) B,Dick McTaggart (Great Britain), Alberto Lavdiono (Argentina)
1964 G,Jozef Grudzien (Poland) S,Vellikton Barannikov (USSR) B,Ronnie Harris (USA) James McCourt (Ireland)
1968 G,Ronnie Harris (USA) S,Jozef Grudzien (Poland) B,Calistrast Cutov (Rumania), Zvonimir Vujin (Yugoslavia)
1972 G,Jan Szczepanski (Poland) S,László Orban (Hungary) B,Samuel Mbugue (Kenya), Alfonso Perez (Columbia)
1976 G,H. Davis (USA) S,S. Cutov (Rumania) B,A. Rusevski (Yugoslavia), V. Solomin (USSR)

LIGHT-WELTERWEIGHT
1896–1948 Event not held
1952 G,Charles Adkins (USA) S,Viktor Mednov (USSR)

B,Erkki Malenius (Finland),
Bruno Visintin (Italy)
1956 G,Vladimir Jengibarian
(USSR) S,Franco Nenci (Italy)
B,Henry Loubscher (South
Africa), Constantin Dumitrescu
(Rumania)
1960 G,Bohumil Nemecek
(Czechoslovakia) S,Clement
Quartey (Ghana) B,Quincy
Daniels (USA), Marian
Kasprzyk (Poland)
1964 G,Jerzy Kulej (Poland)
S,Evgeniy Frolov (USSR)
B,Eddie Blay (Ghana), Habib
Galhia (Tunisia)
1968 G,Jerzy Kulej (Poland)
S,Enrique Regueiferos (Cuba)
B,Arto Nilsson (Finland), James
Wallington (USA)
1972 G,Ray Seales (USA)
S,Anghel Anghelov (Bulgaria)
B,Zvonimir Vujin (Yugoslavia),
Issaka Daborg (Nigeria)
1976 G,R. Leonard (USA)
S,A. Adalma (Cuba) B, V. Kolev
(Bulgaria), K. Szczerba (Poland)

WELTERWEIGHT
1896-1900 Event not held
1904 G,Albert Young (USA)
S,H. Spanger (USA) B,Joseph
Lydon (USA)
1908-1912 Event not held
1920 G,T. Schneider (Canada)
S,A. Ireland (Great Britain)
B,Frederick Colberg (USA)
1924 G,Jean Delarge (Belgium)
S,Hector Mendez (Argentina)
B,Douglas Lewis (Canada)
1928 G,Edward Morgan (New
Zealand) S,Paul Landini
(Argentina) B,Raymond Smillie
(Canada)
1932 G,Edward Flynn (USA)
S,Erich Campe (Germany)
B,Bruno Ahlberg (Finland)
1936 G,Sten Suvio (Finland)
S,Michael Murach (Germany)
B,Gerhard Petersen (Denmark)
1948 G,Julius Torma
(Czechoslovakia) S,Horace
Herring (USA) B,Alessandro
Ottavio (Italy)
1952 G,Zyugmunt Chychla
(Poland) S,Sergey Shcherbakov
(USSR) B,Victor Jorgensen
(Denmark), Gunther Herdmann
(Germany)
1956 G,Nicolae Linca
(Rumania) S,Fredrick Tiedt
(Eire) B,Kevin Hogarth
(Australia), Nicholas Gargano
(Great Britain)
1960 G,Giovanni Benvenuti
(Italy) S,Yuriy Radnoyak
(USSR) B,Leszek Drogosz
(Poland), James Lloyd (Great
Britain)
1964 G,Marian Kasprzyk
(Poland) S,Richards Tamulis
(USSR) B,Pertti Purhonen
(Finland), Silvano Bertini (Italy)
1968 G,Manfred Wolke (East
Germany) S,Joseph Bessala
(Cameroon) B,Vladimir
Masalimov (USSR), Mario
Guilloti (Argentina)
1972 G,Emilio Correa (Cuba)
S,Janos Kajdi (Hungary)
B,Dick T. Murunga (Kenya),
Jesse Valdez (USA)
1976 G,J. Bachfeld (East
Germany) S,P. J. Gamarro
(Venezuela) B,R. Skricek (West
Germany), V. Zilberman
(Rumania)

LIGHT-MIDDLEWEIGHT
1896-1948 Event not held
1952 G,Laszlo Papp (Hungary)
S,Theunis Van Schalkwyk
(South Africa) B,Boris Tishin
(USSR), Eladio Herrera (Argentina)

1956 G,Laszlo Papp (Hungary)
S,Jose Torres (USA) B,John
McCormack (Great Britain),
Zbigniew Pietrzykowski
(Poland)
1960 G,Wilbert McClure (USA)
S,Carmelo Bossi (Italy)
B,Boris Lagutin (USSR),
William Fisher (Great Britain)
1964 G,Boris Lagutin (USSR)
S,Josef Gonzales (France)
B,Nojim Maiyegun (Nigeria),
Jozef Grzesiak (Poland)
1968 G,Boris Lagutin (USSR)
S,Rolando Garbey (Cuba)
B,John Baldwin (USA),
Gunther Meyer (West Germany)
1972 G,Dieter Kottysch (West
Germany) S,Wieslaw Rudkowski
(Poland) B,Alan Minter (Great
Britain), Peter Tiepold (East
Germany)
1976 G,J. Rybicki (Poland)
S,T. Kacar (Yugoslavia)
B,V. Savchenko (USSR),
R. Garbey (Cuba)

MIDDLEWEIGHT
1896-1900 Event not held
1904 G,Charles Mayer (USA)
S,Benjamin Spradley (USA)
1908 G,John Douglas (Great
Britain) S,Reginald Baker
(Australasia) B,W. Philo (Great
Britain)
1912 Event not held
1920 G,Harry Mallin (Great
Britain) S,Prudhomme (Canada)
B,Herzowitch (Canada)
1924 G,Harry Mallin (Great
Britain) S,John Elliott (Great
Britain) B,Joseph Beecken
(Belgium)
1928 G,Piero Toscani (Italy)
S,Jan Hermanek (Czecho-
slovakia) B,Lenard Steyaert
(Belgium)
1932 G,Carmen Barth (USA)
S,Amado Azar (Argentina)
B,Ernest Pierce (South Africa)
1936 G,Jean Despeaux (France)
S,Henry Tiller (Norway)
B,Raul Villareal (Argentina)
1948 G,Laszlo Papp (Hungary)
S,John Wright (Great Britain)
B,Ivano Fontana (Italy)
1952 G,Floyd Patterson (USA)
S,Vasile Tita (Rumania)
B,Boris Nikolov (Bulgaria),
Karl Sjolin (Sweden)
1956 G,Genadiy Schatkov
(USSR) S,Ramon Tapia (Chile)
B,Gilbert Chapron (France),
Victor Zalazar (Argentina)
1960 G,Edward Crook (USA)
S,Tadeusz Walasek (Poland)
B,Ion Monea (Rumania),
Evgeniy Feofanov (USSR)
1964 G,Valeriy Popenchenko
(USSR) S,Emil Schultz
(Germany) B,Franco Valla
(Italy), Tadeusz Walasek
(Poland)
1968 G,Chris Finnegan (Great
Britain) S,Aleksey Kiselyov
(USSR) B,Agustin Zaragoza
(Mexico), Alfred Jones (USA)
1972 G,Viatcheslav Lemechev
(USSR) S,Reima Virtanen
(Finland) B,Prince Amartey
(Ghana), Marvin Johnson
(USA)
1976 G,M. Spinks (USA)
S,R. Riskiev (USSR)
B,A. Nastac (Rumania),
L. Martinez (Cuba)

LIGHT-HEAVYWEIGHT
1896-1912 Event not held
1920 G,Edward Eagan (USA)
S,Sverre Sorsdal (Norway)
B,H. Frank (Great Britain)
1924 G,Harry Mitchell (Great
Britain) S,Thyge Petersen

(Denmark) B,Sverre Sorsdal
(Norway)
1928 G,Victorio Avendano
(Argentina) S,Ernst Pistulla
(Germany) B,Karel Miljon
(Netherlands)
1932 G,David Carstens (South
Africa) S,Gino Rossi (Italy)
B,Peter Jorgensen (Denmark)
1936 G,Roger Michelot
(France) S,Richard Voigt
(Germany) B,Francisco
Risiglione (Argentina)
1948 G,George Hunter (South
Africa) S,Donald Scott (Great
Britain) B,M. Cia (Argentina)
1952 G,Norvel Lee (USA)
S,Antonio Pacenza (Argentina)
B,Anatoliy Perov (USSR),
Harry Siljander (Finland)
1956 G,James Boyd (USA)
S,Gheorghe Negrea (Rumania)
B,Carlos Lucas (Chile),
Romualdas Morauskas (USSR)
1960 G,Cassius Clay (USA)
S,Zbigniew Pietrzykowski
(Poland) B,Anthony Madigan
(Australia), Giulio Saraudi
(Italy)
1964 G,Cosimo Pinto (Italy)
S,Aleksey Kiselyov (USSR)
B,Alexander Nicolov (Bulgaria),
Zbigniew Pietrzykowski
(Poland)
1968 G,Dan Pozniak (USSR)
S,Dan Pozniak (USSR) S,Ion
Monea (Rumania) B,Guerogui
Stankov (Bulgaria), Stanislaw
Dragan (Poland)
1972 G,Mate Parlov (Yugoslavia)
S,Gilberto Carrillo (Cuba)
B,Isaac Ikhouria (Nigeria),
Janusz Gartat (Poland)
1976 G,L. Spinks (USA)
S,S. Soria (Cuba) B,C. Dafinoiu
(Rumania), J. Gortat (Poland)

HEAVYWEIGHT
1896-1900 Event not held
1904 G,Samuel Berger (USA)
S,Charles Mayer (USA)
1908 G,A. L. Oldman (Great
Britain) S,S. Evans (Great
Britain) B,F. Parks (Great
Britain)
1912 Event not held
1920 G,R. Rawson (Great
Britain) S,Soren Petersen
(Denmark) B,Elvere (France)
1924 G,Otto von Porat
(Norway) S,Soren Petersen
(Denmark) B,Alfredo Porzio
(Argentina)
1928 G,Arturo Rodriguez Jurado
(Argentina) S,Nils Ramm
(Sweden) B,Michael
Michaelson (Denmark)
1932 G,Alberto Lovell
(Argentina) S,Luigi Rovati
(Italy) B,Frederick Feary (USA)
1936 G,Herbert Runge
(Germany) S,Guillermo Lovell
(Argentina) B,Erling Nilsen
(Norway)
1948 G,Rafael Iglesias
(Argentina) S,Gunnar Nilsson
(Sweden) B,John Arthur
(South Africa)
1952 G,Edward Sanders (USA)
S,Withheld B,Andries Nieman
(South Africa), Ilkka Koski (Finland)
1956 G,Peter Rademacher
(USA) S,Lev Mukhin (USSR)
B,Daniel Bekker (South Africa)
Giacomo Bozzano (Italy)
1960 G,Franco de Piccoli
(Italy) S,Daniel Bekker (South
Africa) B,Josef Nemec
(Czechoslovakia), Gunter
Siegmund (Germany)
1964 G,Joe Frazier (USA)
S,Hans Huber (Germany)
B,Guiseppe Ros (Italy), Vadim

Yemelyanov (USSR)
1968 G,George Foreman
(USA) S,Iones Chepulis
(USSR) B,Giorgio Bambini
(Italy), Joaquin Rocha (Mexico)
1972 G,Teofilio Stevenson
(Cuba) S,Ion Alexe (Rumania)
B,Peter Hussing (West Germany)
Hasse Thomsen (Sweden)
1976 G,T. Stevenson (Cuba)
S,M. Simon (Rumania) B,J. Tate
(USA), C. Hill (Bermuda)

Canoeing (Men)
KAYAK SINGLES
500 METRES
1896-1972 Event not held
1976 G,V. Diba (Rumania)
S,Z. Sztanity (Hungary)
B,R. Helm (East Germany)
1976 G,V. Diba (Rumania)
1m 46.41s S,Z. Sztanity
(Hungary) 1m 46.95s B,R. Helm
(East Germany) 1m 48.30s

KAYAK PAIRS
500 METRES
1896-1972 Event not held
1976 G,East Germany (Mattern,
Olbricht) 1m 35.87s S,USSR
1m 36.81s B,Rumania 1m 37.43s

KAYAK SINGLES
1000 METRES
1896-1932 Event not held
1936 G,Gregor Hradetzky
(Austria) 4m 22.9s S,Helmut
Cammerer (Germany) 4m 25.6s
B,Jacob Kraaier (Netherlands)
4m 35.1s
1948 G,Gert Frederiksson
(Sweden) 4m 33.2s
S,J. Andersen (Denmark)
4m 39.9s B,Henri Eberhardt
(France) 4m 41.4s
1952 G,Gert Frederiksson
(Sweden) 4m 07.9s S,Thorvald
Stromberg (Finland) 4m 09.7s
B,Louis Gantois (France)
4m 20.1s
1956 G,Gert Frederiksson
(Sweden) 4m 12.8s S,Igor
Pisaryev (USSR) 4m 15.3s
B,Lajos Kiss (Hungary) 4m 16.2s
1960 G,Erik Hansen (Denmark)
3m 53.0s S,Imbre Szoellosi
(Hungary) 3m 54.0s B,Gert
Frederiksson (Sweden) 3m 55.8s
1964 G,Rolf Peterson (Sweden)
3m 57.13s S,Mihaly Hesz
(Hungary) 3m 57.28s B,Aurel
Vernescu (Rumania) 4m 00.7s
1968 G,Mihaly Hesz (Hungary)
4m 02.63s S,Aleksandr
Shaparenko (USSR) 4m 03.58s
B,Erik Hansen (Denmark) 4m 04.39s
1972 G,Aleksandr Shaparenko
(USSR) 3m 48.06s S,Rolf
Peterson (Sweden) 3m 48.35s
B,Geza Csapo (Hungary)
3m 49.38s
1976 G,R. Helm (East Germany)
3m 48.20s S,G. Csapo (Hungary)
3m 48.84s B,V. Diba (Rumania)
3m 49.65s

KAYAK PAIRS
1000 METRES
1896-1932 Event not held
1936 G,Austria (Adolf Kainz,
Alfonz Dorfner) 4m 03.8s
S,Germany 4m 09.9s
B,Netherlands 4m 12.2s
1948 G,Sweden (Hans
Berglund, Lenart Klingstrom)
4m 07.3s S,Denmark 4m 07.5s
B,Finland 4m 08.7s
1952 G,Finland (Kurt Wires,
Yrjo Hietanen) 3m 51.1s
S,Sweden 3m 51.1s
B,Austria 3m 51.4s
1956 G,Germany (Michel
Scheuer, Meinrad Miltenberger)
3m 49.6s S,USSR 3m 51.4s
B,Austria 3m 55.8s

1960 G,Sweden (Gert Fredriksson, Sven Sjodelius) 3m 34.7s S,Hungary 3m 34.9s B,Poland 3m 37.3s
1964 G,Sweden (Sven Sjoedelius, Gunnar Utterberg) 3m 38.54s S,Netherlands 3m 39.30s B,Germany 3m 40.69s
1968 G,USSR (A. Shaparenko, V. Morozov) 3m 37.54s S,Hungary 3m 38.44s B,Austria 3m 40.71s
1972 G,USSR (N. Gorbachev, V. Kratassyuk) 3m 31.23s S,Hungary 3m 32.00s B,Poland 3m 33.83s
1976 G,USSR (S. Nagorny, V. Ramonovskiy) 3m 29.01s S,East Germany 3m 29.33s B,Hungary 3m 30.36s

KAYAK FOURS 1000 METRES
1896–1960 Event not held
1964 G,USSR (N. Chuzhikov, A. Grishin, V. Ionov, V. Morozov) 3m 14.67s S,Germany 3m 15.39s B,Rumania 3m 15.51s
1968 G,Norway (S. Amundsen, E. Soby, T. Berger, J. Johansen) 3m 14.38s S,Rumania 3m 14.81s B,Hungary 3m 15.10s
1972 G,USSR (Y. Filatov, Y. Stezenko, V. Morozov, V. Didenko) 3m 14.02s S,Rumania 3m 15.07s B,Norway 3m 15.27s
1976 G,USSR (S. Chuhray, A. Degtiarev, Y. Filatov, V. Morozov) 3m 08.69s S,Spain 3m 08.95s B,East Germany 3m 10.76s

CANADIAN SINGLES 500 METRES
1896–1972 Event not held
1976 G,A. Rogov (USSR) 1m 59.23s S,J. Wood (Canada) 1m 59.58s B,M. Ljubek (Yugoslavia) 1m 59.60s

CANADIAN PAIRS 500 METRES
1896–1972 Event not held
1976 G,USSR (Petrenko, Vinogradov) 1m 45.81s S,Poland 1m 47.77s B,Hungary 1m 48.35s

CANADIAN SINGLES 1000 METRES
1896–1932 Event not held
1936 G,Francis Amyot (Canada) 5m 32.1s S,Bohuslav Karlik (Czechoslovakia) 5m 36.9s B,Erich Koschik (Germany) 5m 39.0s
1948 G,Josef Holecek (Czechoslovakia) 5m 42.0s S,D. Bennett (Canada) 5m 53.3s B,Robert Boutigny (France) 5m 55.9s
1952 G,Josef Holecek (Czechoslovakia) 4m 56.3s S,Janos Parti (Hungary) 5m 03.6s B,Olavi Ojanpera (Finland) 5m 08.5s
1956 G,Leon Rottman (Rumania) 5m 05.03.3s S,Istvan Hernek (Hungary) 5m 06.2s B,Gennadiy Bukharin (USSR) 5m 12.7s
1960 G,Janos Parti (Hungary) 4m 33.0s S,Aleksandr Silayev (USSR) 4m 34.4s B,Leon Rottman (Rumania) 4m 35.8s
1964 G,J. Eschert (Germany) 4m 35.14s S,A. Igorov (Rumania) 4m 37.89s B,E. Penyayev (USSR) 4m 38.31s
1968 G,Tibor Tatai (Hungary) 4m 36.14s S,Detlef Lewe (West Germany) 4m 38.31s B,Vitaly Galkov (USSR) 4m 40.42s
1972 G,Ivan Patzaichin (Rumania) 4m 08.94s S,Tamas Wichmann (Hungary) 4m 12.42s B,Detlef Lewe (West Germany) 4m 13.63s
1976 G,M. Ljubek (Yugoslavia) 4m 09.51s S,V. Urchenko (USSR) 4m 12.57s B,T. Wichmann (Hungary) 4m 14.11s

CANADIAN PAIRS 1000 METRES
1896–1932 Event not held
1936 G,Czechoslovakia (Vladimir Syrovatka, Felix Brzak) 4m 50.1s S,Austria 4m 53.8s B,Canada 4m 56.7s
1948 G,Czechoslovakia (Jan Brzak, Bohumil Kudrna) 5m 07.1s S,USA 5m 08.2s B,France 5m 15.2s
1952 G,Denmark (Bent Rasch, Finn Haunstoft) 4m 38.3s S,Czechoslovakia 4m 42.9s B,Germany 4m 48.3s
1956 G,Rumania (Alexe Dumitru, Simion Ismailciuo) 4m 47.4s S,USST 4m 48.6s B,Hungary 4m 54.3s
1960 G,USSR (Leonid Geyshter, Sergey Makharenko) 4m 17.0s S,Italy 4m 20.7s B,Hungary 4m 20.8s
1964 G,USSR (Andrey Khimich, Stepan Oschepkov) 4m 04.65s S,France 4m 06.52s B,Denmark 4m 07.48s
1968 G,Rumania (Patzaichin, Covaliov) 4m 07.18s S,Hungary 4m 08.77s B,USSR 4m 11.30s
1972 G,USSR (V. Chessyunas, Y. Lobanov) 3m 52.60s S,Rumania 3m 52.63s B,Bulgaria 3m 58.10s
1976 G,USSR (V. Petrenko, A. Vinogradov) 3m 52.76s S,Rumania 3m 54.28s B,Hungary 3m 55.66s

Canoeing (Women)
KAYAK SINGLES
1896–1936 Event not held
1948 G,K. Hoff (Denmark) 2m 31.9s S,Alide Van de Anker-Doedans (Netherlands) 2m 32.8s B,Fritzi Schwingl (Austria) 2m 32.9s
1952 G,Sylvi Saimo (Finland) 2m 18.4s S,Gertrude Liebhart (Austria) 2m 18.8s B, Nina Savina (USSR) 2m 21.6s
1956 G,Elisaveta Dementyeva (USSR) 2m 18.9s S,Therese Zenz (Germany) 2m 19.6s B,Tove Soby (Denmark) 2m 22.3s
1960 G,Antonina Seredina (USSR) 2m 08.0s S,Therese Zenz (Germany) 2m 08.2s B,Daniela Walkowiak (Poland) 2m 10.4s
1964 G,Ludmila Khvedosinka (USSR) 2m 12.87s S,Hilde Lauer (Rumania) 2m 15.35s B,Marcia Jones (USA) 2m 15.68s
1968 G,Lyudmila Pinaeva (USSR) 2m 11.09s S,Renate Breuer (West Germany) 2m 12.71s B,Viorica Dumitru (Rumania) 2m 13.22s
1972 G,Yulia Ryabchinskaya (USSR) 2m 03.17s S,Mieke Jaapies (Holland) 2m 04.03s B,Anna Pfeffer (Hungary) 2m 05.50s
1976 G,C. Zirzow (East Germany) 2m 01.05s S,T. Korshunova (USSR) 2m 03.07s B,K. Rajnai (Hungary) 2m 05.01s

KAYAK PAIRS
1896–1956 Event not held
1960 G,USSR (Maria Shubina, Antonina Seredina) 1m 54.7s S,Germany 1m 56.6s B,Hungary 1m 58.2s
1964 G,Germany (Roswitha Esser, Annemie Zimmerman) 1m 56.95s S,USA 1m 59.16s B,Rumania 2m 00.25s
1968 G,West Germany (Zimmerman, Esser) 1m 56.44s S,Hungary 1m 58.60s B,USSR 1m 58.61s
1972 G,USSR (Pinayeva, Kuryshko) 1m 53.50s S, East Germany 1m 54.30s B, Rumania 1m 55.01s
1976 G,USSR (N. Gopova, G. Kreft) 1m 51.15s S,Hungary (A. Pfeffer, K. Rajnai) 1m 51.69s B,East Germany (B. Koster, C. Kirzow) 1m 51.81s

Cycling
1000 METRES SPRINT
1896 Event not held
1900 G,G. Taillandier (France) 2m 16.0s S,Vasserot (France) B,Lanz (France)
1904–1912 Event not held
1920 G,Mauritius Peeters (Netherlands) 1m 38.3s S,H. T. Johnson (Great Britain) B,Harry Ryan (Great Britain)
1924 G,Lucien Michard (France) S,Jacob Meyer (Netherlands) B,Jean Cugnot (France)
1928 G,R. Beaufrand (France) S,A. Mazairac (Netherlands) B,Willy Falck-Hahsen (Denmark)
1932 G,Jacobus van Egmond (Netherlands) S,Louis Chaillot (France) B,Bruno Pellizzari (Italy)
1936 G,Toni Merkens (Germany) S,Arie van Vliet (Netherlands) B,Louis Chaillot (France)
1948 G,Mario Ghella (Italy) S,Reginald Harris (Great Britain) B,Axel Schandorff (Denmark)
1952 G,Enzo Sacchi (Italy) S,Lionel Cox (Australia) B,Werner Potzernheim (Germany)
1956 G,Michel Rousseau (France) S,Guglielmo Pesenti (Italy) B,Richard Ploog (Australia)
1960 G,Sante Gaiardoni (Italy) S,Leon Sterckx (Belgium) B,Valentino Gasparella (Italy)
1964 G,Giovanni Pettenella (Italy) S,Sergio Bianchetto (Italy) B,Daniel Morelon (France)
1968 G,Daniel Morelon (France) S,Giordano Turrini (Italy) B,Pierre Trentin (France)
1972 G,Daniel Morelon (France) S,John M. Nickolson (Australia) B,Omari Phakadze (USSR)
1976 G,A. Tkac (Czecho-slovakia) S,D. Morelon (France) B,H-J. Geschke (East Germany)

1000 METRES TIME TRIAL
1896–1924 Event not held
1928 G,Willy Falck-Hansen (Denmark) 1m 14.4s S,Bosch van Drakestein (Netherlands) 1m 15.2s B,Edgar Gray (Australia) 1m 15 6s
1932 G,Edgar Gray (Australia) 1m 13.0s S,Jacobus van Egmond (Netherlands) 1m 13.3s B,Charles Rampelberg (France) 1m 13.4s
1936 G,Arie van Vliet (Netherlands) 1m 12.0s S,Pierre Georget (France) 1m 12.8s B,Rudolf Karsch (Germany) 1m 13.2s
1948 G,Jacques Dupont (France) 1m 13.5s S,Pierre Nihant (Belgium) 1m 14.5s B,Thomas Godwin (Great Britain) 1m 15.0s
1952 G,Russell Mockridge (Australia) 1m 11.1s S,Marino Morettini (Italy) 1m 12.7s B,Raymond Robinson (South Africa) 1m 13.0s
1956 G,Leandro Faggin (Italy) 1m 09.8s S,Ladislav Foucek (Czechoslovakia) 1m 11.4s B,Alfred Swift (South Africa) 1m 11.6s
1960 G,Sante Gaiardoni (Italy) 1m 07.27s S,Dieter Gieseler (Germany) 1m 08.75s B,Rostislav Vargashkin (USSR) 1m 08.86s
1964 G,Patrick Sercu (Belgium) 1m 09.59s S,Giovanni Pettenella (Italy) 1m 10.09s B,Pierre Trentin (France) 1m 10.42s
1968 G,Pierre Trentin (France) 1m 03.91s S,Niels-Christian Fredborg (Denmark) 1m 04.61s B,Janusz Kierzkowski (Poland) 1m 04.63s
1972 G,Niels-Christian Fredborg (Denmark) 1m 06.44s S,Daniel Clark (Australia) 1m 06.87s B,Juergen Schuetze (East Germany) 1m 07.02s
1976 G,K-J. Grunke (East Germany) 1m 05.927s S,M. Vaarten (Belgium) 1m 07.516s B,N. Fredborg (Denmark) 1m 07.617s

4000 METRES INDIVIDUAL PURSUIT
1896–1960 Event not held
1964 G,Jiri Daler (Czecho-slovakia) 5m 04.75s S,Giorgio Ursi (Italy) 5m 05.96s B,Preben Isaksson (Denmark) 5m 01.90s
1968 G,Daniel Rebillard (France) 4m 41.71s S, Mogens Jensen (Denmark) 4m 42.43s B,Xavier Kurmann (Switzerland) 4m 39.42s
1972 G,Knut Knudsen (Norway) 4m 45.74s S,Xaver Kurmann (Switzerland) 4m 51.96s B,Hans Lutz (West Germany) 4m 50.80s
1976 G,G. Braun (West Germany) 4m 47.61s S,H. Ponsteen (Holland) 4m 49.72s B,T. Huschke (East Germany) 4m 52.71s

4000 METRES TEAM PURSUIT
1896–1912 Event not held
1920 G,Italy (Franco Giorgetti, Ruggero Ferrario, Arnaldo Carli, Primo Magnani) 5m 20.0s S,Great Britain B,South Africa
1924 G,Italy (Alfredo Dinale, Francesco Zucchetti, Angelo de Martino, Alerado Menegazzi) 5m 12.0s S,Poland B,Belgium
1928 G,Italy (Luigi Tasselli, Giacomo Gaioni, Cesare Facciani, Mario Lusiani) 5m 06.25s S,Netherlands B,Great Britain
1932 G,Italy (Marco Cimatti, Paolo Pedretti, Alberto Ghilardi, Nino Borsari) 4m 52.9s S,France 4m 55.7s B,Great Britain 4m 56.0s

1936 G,France (Robert Charpentier, Jean Goujon, Guy Lapebie, Roger Le Nizerhy) 4m 45.0s S,Italy 4m 51.0s B,Great Britain 4m 52.6s
1948 G,France (Pierre Adam, Serge Blusson, Charles Coste, Ferdinand Decanali) 4m 57.8s S,Italy 5m 36.7s B,Great Britain 5m 55.8s
1952 G,Italy (Marino Morettini, Guido Messina, Mino de Rossi, Loris Campana) 4m 46.1s S,South Africa 4m 53.6s B,Great Britain 4m 51.5s
1956 G,Italy (Leandro Faggin, Valentino Gasparella, Franco Gandini, Tonino Domenicali) 4m 37.4s S,France 4m 39.4s B,Great Britain 4m 42.2s
1960 G,Italy (Luigi Arienti, Franco Testa, Mario Vallotto, Marino Vigna) 4m 30.90s S,Germany 4m 35.78s B,USSR 4m 34.05s
1964 G,Germany (Lothar Claesges, Karl-Heinz Henrichs, Karl Link, Ernest Streng) 4m 35.67s S,Italy 4m 35.74s B,Netherlands 4m 38.99s
1968 G,Denmark (G. Asmussen, P. Lyngemark, R. Olsen, M. Frey) S,West Germany B,Italy
1972 G,West Germany (J. Colombo, G. Haritz, U. Hempel, G. Schumacker) S,East Germany B,Great Britain
1976 G,West Germany (G. Braun, H. Lutz, G. Schumacher, P. Vonhof) 4m 21.06s S,USSR B,Great Britain

ROAD-RACE
1896 G,A. Konstantinidis (Greece) 3h 22m 31.0s S,A. Goedrich (Germany) 3h 42m 18.0s B,F. Battel (Great Britain)
1900–1908 Event not held
1912 G,Ruldolph Lewis (South Africa) 10h 42m 39.0s S,Frederick Grubb (Great Britain) 10h 51m 24.2s B,Carl Schutte (USA) 10h 52m 38.8s
Teams—
G,Sweden (Eric Friborg, Ragnar Malm, Axel Persson, Algot Lonn) 44h 35m 33.6s S,Great Britain 44h 44m 39.2s B,USA 44h 47m 55.5s
1920 G,Harry Stenquist (Sweden) 4h 40m 01.8s S,Henry Kaltenbrun (South Africa) 4h 41m 26.6s B,F. Canteloube (France) 4h 42m 54.4s
Teams—
G,France (F. Canteloube, G. Detreille, Souchard, Gobillot) 19h 16m 43.2s S,Sweden 19h 23m 10.0s B,Belgium 19h 28m 44.4s
1924 G,Armand Blanchonnet (France) 6h 20m 48.0s S,Henry Hoevenaers (Belgium) 6h 30m 27.0s B,Rene Hamel (France) 6h 30m 51.6s
Teams—
G,France (Armand Blanchonnet, Rene Hamel, Georges Wambst) 19h 30m 14.0s S,Belgium 19h 46m 55.4s B,Sweden 19h 59m 41.6s
1928 G,Henry Hansen (Denmark) 4h 47m 18.0s S,Frank Southall (Great Britain) 4h 54m 44.0s B,Gosta Carlsson (Sweden)

4h 59m 55.0s
Teams—
G,Denmark (Henry Hansen, Leo Nielsen, Orla Jorgensen) 15h 09m 14.0s S,Great Britain 15h 14m 44.0s B,Sweden 15h 27m 22.0s
1932 G,Attilio Pavesi (Italy) 2h 28m 05.6s S,Guglielmo Segato (Italy) 2h 29m 21.4s B,Bernhard Britz (Sweden) 2h 29m 45.2s
Teams—
G,Italy (Attilio Pavesi, Guglielmo Segato, Giuseppe Olmo) 7h 27m 15.2s S,Denmark 7h 38m 50.2s B,Sweden 7h 39m 12.6s
1936 G,Robert Charpentier (France) 2h 33m 05.0s S,Guy Lapebie (France) 2h 33m 05.2s B,Ernst Nievergelt (Switzerland) 2h 33m 05.8s
Teams—
G,France (Robert Charpentier, Guy Lapebie, Robert Dorgebray) 7h 39m 16.2s S,Switzerland 7h 39m 20.4s B,Belgium 7h 39m 21.0s
1948 G,Jose Beyaert (France) 5h 18m 12.6s S,Geerit Voorting (Netherlands) 5h 18m 16.2s B,Louis Wouters (Belgium) 5h 18m 16.2s
Teams—
G,Belgium (Louis Wouters, Leon Delathouwer, Eugene van Roosbroeck) 15h 58m 17.4s S,Great Britain 16h 03m 31.6s B,France 16h 08m 19.4s
1952 G,Andre Noyelle (Belgium) 5h 06m 03.4s S,Robert Grondelaers (Belgium) 5h 06m 51.2s B,Edi Ziegler (Germany) 5h 07m 47.5s
Teams—
G,Belgium (Andre Noyelle, Robert Grondelaers, Lucien Victor) 15h 20m 46.6s S,Italy 15h 33m 27.3s B,France 15h 38m 58.1s
1956 G,Ercole Baldini (Italy) 5h 21m 17.0s S,Arnaud Geyre (France) 5h 23m 16.0s B,Alan Jackson (Great Britain) 5h 23m 17.0s
G,France (Arnaud Geyre, Maurice Moucheraud, Michel Vermeulin) 22 pts. S,Great Britain 23 B,Germany 27
1960 G,Viktor Kapitanov (USSR) 4h 20m 37.0s S,Livio Trape (Italy) 4h 20m 37.0s B,Willy van den Berghen (Belgium) 4h 20m 57.0s
1964 G,Mario Zanin (Italy) 4h 39m 51.63s S,Kjell Rodian (Denmark) 4h 39m 51.65s B,Walter Godefroot (Belgium) 4h 39m 51.74s
1968 G,Pierfranco Vianelli (Italy) 4h 41m 25.24s S,Leif Mortensen (Denmark) 4h 42m 49.71s B,Gosta Pettersson (Sweden) 4h 43m 15.24s
1972 G,Hennie Kuiper (Holland) 4h 14m 37.0s S,Kevin C. Sefton (Australia) 4h 15m 04.0s B,Jaime Huelamo (Spain) 4h 15m 04.0s
1976 G,B. Johansson (Sweden) 4h 46m 52.0s S,G. Martinelli (Italy) 4h 47m 23.0s B,M. Noeicki (Poland) 4h 47m 23.0s

ROAD-TEAM TIME-TRIAL
1896–1956 Event not held
1960 G,Italy (Antonio Bailetti, Ottavio Cogliati, Giacomo Fornoni, Livio Trape) 2h 14m 33.53s S,Germany 2h 16m 56.31s B,USSR 2h 18m 41.67s
1964 G,Netherlands (Gerben Karstens, Evert Dolman, Johannes Pieterse, Hubertus Zort) 2h 26m 31.19s S,Italy 2h 26m 55.39s B,Sweden 2h 27m 11.72s
1968 G,Netherlands (M. Pijnen, F. Den Hertog, J. Krekela, G. Zoetemelk) 2h 07m 49.06s S,Sweden 2h 09m 26.60s B,Italy 2h 10m 18.74s
1972 G,USSR (B. Chouhov, V. Iardy, G. Komnatov, V. Likhachev) 2h 11m 17.8s S,Poland 2h 11m 47.5s B,Netherlands 2h 12m 27.1s
1976 G,USSR (A. Chukanov, V. Chaplygin, V. Kaminsky, A. Pikkuus) 2h 8m 53.0s S,Poland 2h 9m 13.0s B,Denmark 2h 12m 20.0s

Equestrian Sports
GRAND PRIX (JUMPING)
1896–1908 Event not held
1912 G,J. Cariou (France) 186 pts. S,von Krocher (Germany) 186 pts. B, Emanuel Blommaert de Soye (Belgium) 185 pts
Teams—
G,Sweden (Casimir Lewenhaupt, Hans von Rosen, Gustaf Kilman) 545 pts. S,France 538 B,Germany 530
1920 G,Tommaso Lequio (Italy) no faults S,Alessandro Valerio (Italy) 3 B,Gustaf Lewenhaupt (Sweden) 4
Teams—
G,Sweden (Hans von Rosen, Claes Konig, Daniel Norling) 14 faults S,Belgium 16.25 B,Italy 18.75
1924 G,Alphons Gemuseus (Switzerland) 6 pts. S, Tommaso Lequio (Italy) 8.75 B,Adam Krolikiewicz (Poland) 10
Teams—
G,Sweden (Ake Thelning, Axel Stahle, Age Lundstrom) 42.5 pts. S,Switzerland 50 B,Portugal
1928 G,F. Ventura (Czechoslovakia) no faults S,M. L. M. Bertran (France) 2 B,Chasimir Kuhn (Switzerland) 4
Teams—
G,Spain (Marquis de los Trujillos, J. Morenes Navarro, J. Garcia Fernandez) 4 faults S,Poland 8 B,Sweden 10
1932 G,Takeichi Nishi (Japan 8 pts. S,Harry Chamberlin (USA) 12 B,Clarence von Rosen (Sweden) 16
1936 G,Kurt Hasse (Germany) 4 pts. S,Henri Rang (Rumania) 4 B,Jozsef Platthy (Hungary) 8
Teams—
G,Germany (Kurt Hasse, Marten von Barnekow, Heinz Brandt) 44 pts. S,Netherlands 51.5 B,Portugal 56
1948 G,Humberto Mariles (Mexico) 6.25 pts. S,Ruben Uriza (Mexico) 8 B,Jeann d'Orgeix (France) 8
Teams—
G,Mexico (Humberto Mariles, Ruben Uriza, R. Valdes)

34.25 pts. S,Spain 56 B,Great Britain 67
1952 G,Pierre Jonqueres d'Oriola (France) no faults S,Oscar Cristi (Chile) 4 B,Fritz Thiedemann (Germany) 8
Teams—
G,Great Britain (Douglas Stewart, Wilfred White, Henry Llewellyn) 40.75 faults S,Chile 45.75 B,USA 52.25
1956 G,Hans Winkler (Germany) 4 faults S, Raimondo d'Inzeo (Italy) 8 B,Piero d'Inzeo (Italy) 11
Teams—
G,Germany (Hans Winkler, Fritz Thiedemann, August Lutge-Westhues) 40 S,Italy 66 B,Great Britain 69
1960 G,Raimondo d'Inzeo (Italy) 12 faults S,Piero d'Inzeo (Italy) 16 B,David Broome (Great Britain) 23
Teams—
G,Germany (Alwin Schockemohle, Fritz Thiedemann, Hans Winkler) 46.50 S,USA 66 B,Italy 80.50
1964 G,Pierre Jonquieres d'Oriola (France) 9 faults S,Herman Schridde (Germany) 13.75 faults B,Peter Robeson (Great Britain) 16 faults
Teams—
G,Germany (Herman Schridde, Kurt Jarasinki, Hans Winkler) 68.50 S,France 77.75 B,Italy 88.50
1968 G,Bill Steinkraus (USA) 4 faults S,Marion Coakes (Great Britain) 8 B,David Broome (Great Britain) 12
Teams—
G,Canada (Tom Gayford, Jim Day, Jim Elder) 102.75 faults S,France 110.50 B,West Germany 117.25
1972 G,Graziano Mancinelli (Italy) 8 faults S,Ann Moore (Great Britain) 8 B,Neal Shapiro (USA) 8
Teams—
West Germany (Fritz Ligges, Gerhard Wiltfang, Hartwig Steenken, Hans Gunter Winkler) 32 faults S,USA 32.25 B,Italy 48
1976 G,A. Schockemoehle (West Germany) no faults S, M. Vaillancourt (Canada) 12 B,F. Mathy (Belgium) 12
Teams—
G,France (H. Parot, M. Rozier, M. Roche, M. Roguet) 40 faults S,West Germany 44 B,Belgium 63

GRAND PRIX (DRESSAGE)
1896 Event not held
1900 G,C. Haegeman (Belgium) S,van der Poele (Belgium) B,de Champsavin (France)
1904–08 Event not held
1912 G,Carl Bonde (Sweden) 15 pts. S,Gustav Boltenstern (Sweden) 21 B,Hans von Blixen-Finecke (Sweden) 32
1920 G,Janne Lundblad (Sweden) 27.937 pts. S,Bertil Sandstrom (Sweden) 26,312 B,Hans von Rosen (Sweden) 25,125
1924 G,Ernst Linder (Sweden) 276.4 pts. S,Bertil Sandstrom (Sweden) 275.8 B,Francois Lesage (France) 268.5
1928 G,Carl von Langen (Germany) 237,42 pts. S,Charles Marion (France)

231.00 B,Ragnar Olsson (Sweden) 229.78
Teams—
G,Germany (Carl von Langen, Linkenbach, von Lotzbeck) 669.72 pts. S,Sweden 650.86 B,Netherlands 642.96
1932 G,Francois Lesage (France) 1,031.25 pts. S,Charles Marion (France) 916.25 B,Hiram Tuttle (USA) 901.50
Teams—
G,France (Francois Lesage, Charles Marion, Andre Jousseaume) 2,818.75 pts. S,Sweden 2,678.00 B,USA 2,576.75
1936 G,Heinrich Pollay (Germany) 1,760.0 pts. S,Friedrich Gerhard (Germany) 1,745.5 B,Alois Podhajsky (Austria) 1,721.5
Teams—
G,Germany (Heinrich Pollay, Friedrich Gerhard, Hermann Bronikowski) 5,074 pts. S,France 4,846 B,Sweden 4,660.5
1948 G,Hans Moser (Switzerland) 492.5 pts. S,Andre Jousseaume (France) 480.0 B,Gustav Boltenstern (Sweden) 477.5
Teams—
G,France (Andre Jousseaume, Jean Paillard, Maurice Buret) 1,269 pts. S,USA 1,256 B,Portugal 1,182
1952 G,Henri St. Cyr (Sweden) 561.0 pts. S,Lis Hartel (Denmark) 541.5 B,Andre Jousseaume (France) 541.0
Teams—
G,Sweden (Gustav Boltenstern, Henri St. Cyr, Gehnall Persson) 1,597.5 pts. S,Switzerland 1,579.0 B,Germany 1,501.0
1956 G,Henri St. Cyr (Sweden) 860 pts. S,Lis Hartel (Denmark) 850 B,Liselott Linsenhoff (Germany) 832
Teams—
G,Sweden (Henri St. Cyr Gehnall Persson, Gustav Boltenstern) 2,475 pts. S,Germany 2,346 B,Switzerland 2,346
1960 G,Sergey Filatov (USSR) 2,144 pts. S,Gustav Fischer (Switzerland) 2,087 B,Josef Neckermann (Germany) 2,082
1964 G,Henri Chammartin (Switzerland) 1,504 pts. S,Harry Boldt (Germany) 1,503 B,Sergey Filatov (USSR) 1,486
Teams—
G,Germany (Harry Boldt, Josef Neckermann, Reiner Klimke) 2,558 pts. S, Switzerland 2,526 B,USSR 2,311
1968 G,Ivan Kizimov (USSR) 1,572 pts. S,Josef Neckermann (West Germany) 1,546 B,Reinert Klimke (West Germany) 1,537
Teams—
G,West Germany (Josef Neckermann, Liselott Linsenhoff, Reinert Klimke) 2,699 pts. S,USSR 2,657 B,Switzerland 2,547
1972 G,Liselott Linsenhoff (West Germany) 1,229 pts. S,Elena Petuchkova (USSR) 1,185 B,Josef Neckermann (West Germany) 1,177
Teams—
G,USSR (Elena Petuchkova,

Ivan Kizimov, Ivan Kalita) 5,095 pts. S,West Germany 5,083 B,Sweden 4,849
1976 G,C. Stueckelberger (Switzerland) 1,486 pts. S,H. Boldt (West Germany) 1,435 B,R. Klimke (West Germany) 1,395
Teams—
G,West Germany (H. Boldt, R. Klimke, G. Grillo) 5,155 pts. S,Switzerland 4,684 B,USA 4,647

THREE-DAY EVENT
1896–1908 Event not held
1912 G,Axel Norlander (Sweden) 46,59 pts. S,von Rochow (Germany) 46,42 B,J. Cariou (France) 46,32
Teams—
G,Sweden (Nils Adlercreutz, Axel Nordlander, E. Casparsson) 139.06 pts. S,Germany 138.48 B,USA 137.33
1920 G,Helmer Morner (Sweden) 1,775 pts. S,Age Lundstrom (Sweden) 1,738 B,Ettore Caffaratti (Italy) 1,733.75
Teams—
G,Sweden (Helmer Morner, Age Lundstrom, Georg von Braun) 5,057.5 pts. S, Italy 4,735 B,Belgium 4,660
1924 G,Adolph van Zijp (Netherlands) 1,976 pts. S,Frode Kirkebjerg (Denmark) 1,873.5 B,Sloan Doak (USA) 1,845.5
Teams—
G,Netherlands (Adolph van Zijp, Ferdinand de Mortanges, G. P. de Kruyff) 5,294.5 pts. S,Sweden 4,743.5 B,Italy 4,512
1928 G,Ferdinand de Mortanges (Netherlands) 1,969.82 pts. S,G. P. de Kruyff (Netherlands) 1,967.26 B,Bruno Neumann (Germany) 1,934.42
Teams—
G,Netherlands (Ferdinand de Mortanges, G. P. de Kruyff, Adolph van Zijp) 5,865.68 pts. S,Norway 5,395.68 B,Poland 5,067.92
1932 G,Ferdinand de Mortanges (Netherlands) 1,813.83 pts. S,Earl Thomson (USA) 1,811 B,Clarence von Rosen (Sweden) 1,809.42
Teams—
G,USA (Earl Thomson, Harry Chamberlin, Edwin Argo) 5,038.08 pts. S,Netherlands 4,689.08
1936 G,Ludwig Stubbendorff (Germany) 37.7 faults B,Earl Thomson (USA) 99.9 B,Hans Lunding (Denmark) 102.2
Teams—
G,Germany (Ludwig Stubbendorff, Rudolf Lippert Konrad von Wangenheim) 676.75 pts. S,Poland 991.70 B,Great Britain 1,195.50
1948 G,Bernard Chevalier (France) plus 4 pts. S,Frank Henry (USA) minus 21 B,J. R. Selfelt (Sweden) minus 25
Teams—
G,USA (Frank Henry, Charles Anderson, Earl Thomson) 161.50 faults S,Sweden 165.00 B,Mexico 305.25
1952 G,Hans von Blixen-Finecke (Sweden) 28.33 faults S,Guy Lefrant (France) 54.50

B,Wilhelm Bussing (Germany) 55.50
Teams—
G,Sweden (Hans von Blixen-Finecke, Nils Stahre, Karl Frolen) 221.94 S,Germany 235.49 B,USA 587.16
1956 G,Petrus Kastenman (Sweden) 66.53 faults S,August Lutge-Westhues (Germany) 84.87 B,Francis Weldon (Great Britain) 85.48
Teams—
G,Great Britain (Albert Hill, Francis Weldon, A. Lawrence Rook) 355.48 S,Germany 475.91 B,Canada 572.72
1960 G,Lawrence Morgan (Australia) plus 7.15 pts. S,Neale Lavis (Australia) minus 16.50 B,Anton Buhler (Switzerland) minus 51.21
Teams—
G,Australia (Lawrence Morgan, Neale Lavis, William Roycroft) 128.18 pts. S,Switzerland 386.02 B,France 515.71
1964 G,Mauro Checcoli (Italy) 64.40 pts. S,Carlos Moratono (Argentina) 56.40 B,Fritz Ligges (Germany) 49.20
Teams—
G,Italy (Mauro Checcoli, Paolo Angioni, Giuseppe Ravano) 85.80 pts. S,USA 65.86 B,Germany 56.73
1968 G,Jean Guyon (France) 38.86 faults S,Derek Allhusen (Great Britain) 41.61 B,Michael Page (USA) 52.31
Teams—
G,Great Britain (Derek Allhusen, Richard Meade, Ben Jones) 175.93 faults S,USA 245.87 B,Australia 331.26
1971 G,Richard H. Meade (Great Britain) 57.73 pts. S,Alessa Argenton (Italy) 43.33 B,Jan Jonsson (Sweden) 39.67
Teams—
Great Britain (Mary D. Gordon-Watson, Bridget Parker, Richard H. Meade, Mark A. Phillips) 95.53 pts. S,USA 10.81 B,West Germany minus 18.00
1976 G,E. Coffin (USA) 114.99 pts. S,J. Plumb (USA) 125.85 B,K. Schultz (West Germany) 129.45
Teams—
G,USA 441 pts. S,West Germany 584.60 B,Australia 599.54

Fencing (Men)
FOIL (INDIVIDUAL)
1896 G,E. Gravelotte (France) 4 wins S,Henri Callott (France 3 B,Perikles Pierrakos (Greece) 2
1900 G,C. Coste (France) 6 wins S,Henry Masson (France) 5 B,Jacques Boulanger (France) 4
1904 G,Ramon Fonst (Cuba) S,Albertson Post (Cuba) B,Charles Tatham (Cuba)
1908 Event not held
1912 G,Nedo Nadi (Italy) 7 wins S,Pietro Speciale (Italy) 5 B,Richard Verderber (Austria) 4
1920 G,Nedo Nadi (Italy) 10 wins S,Philippe Cattiau (France) 9 B,Roger Ducret (France) 9
1924 G,Roger Ducret (France) 6 wins S,Philippe Cattiau (France) 5 B,Maurice van Damme (Belgium) 4
1928 G,Lucien Gaudin (France) 9 wins S,Erwin Casmir (Germany) 9 B,Giulio Gaudini (Italy) 9

1932 G,Gustavo Marzi (Italy) 9 wins S,Joseph Levis (USA) 6 B,Guilo Gaudini (Italy) 5
1936 G,Guilo Gaudini (Italy) 7 wins S,Edouard Gardere (France) 6 B,Giorgio Bocchino (Italy) 4
1948 G,Jean Buhan (France) 7 wins S,Christian d'Oriola (France) 5 B,Lajos Maszlay (Hungary) 4
1952 G,Christian d'Oriola (France) 8 wins S,Edoardo Mangiarotti (Italy) 6 B,Manlio di Rosa (Italy) 5
1956 G,Christian d'Oriola (France) 6 wins S,Giancarlo Bergamini (Italy) 5 B,Antonio Spallino (Italy) 5
1960 G,Viktor Zhdanovich (USSR) 7 wins S,Yuriy Sisikin (USSR) 4 B,Albert Axelrod (USA) 3
1964 G,Egon Franke (Poland) 3 wins S,Jean Magnan (France) 2 B,Daniel Revenu (France) 1
1968 G,Ion Drimba (Rumania) 4 wins S,Jeno Kamuti (Hungary) 3 B,Daniel Revenu (France) 3
1972 G,Witold Woyda (Poland) 5 wins S,Jeno Kamuti (Hungary) 4 B,Christian Noel (France) 2
1976 G,F. Dal Zotto (Italy) 4 wins S,A. Romankov (USSR) 4 B,B. Talvard (France)
FOIL (TEAM)
1896–1912 Event not held
1920 G,Italy (Nedo Nadi, Aldo Nadi, Abelardo Olivier, Pietro Speciale. Rodolfo Terlizzi, Tomasso Costantino, Baldo Baldi, Oreste Puliti) S,France B,USA
1924 G,France (Lucien Gaudin, Roger Ducret, Philippe Cattiau, Henri Jobier, Jacques Coutrot, Guy de Luget, Andre Labattut, Joseph Peroteaux) S,Belgium B,Hungary
1928 G,Italy (Ugo Pignotti, Oreste Puliti, Giulio Gaudini, Giorgio Pessina. Giorgio Chiaviacci, Gioacchino Guaragna) S,France B, Argentina
1932 G,France (Edouard Gardere, Rene Lemoine, Rene Bougnol, Philippe Cattiau, Rene Bondoux, Jean Piot) S,Italy B,USA
1936 G,Italy (Gustavo Marzi, Gioacchino Guaragna, Manlio di Rosa, Ciro Verratti, Giulio Gaudini, Giorgio Bocchino) S,France B,Germany
1948 G,France (Andre Bonin, Christian d'Oriola, Jean Buhan, Rene Bougnol, Jacques Lataste, Adrien Rommel) S,Italy B,Belgium
1952 G,France (Jean Buhan, Christian d'Oriola, Adrien Rommel, Claude Netter, Jacques Noel, Jacques Lataste) S,Italy B,Hungary
1956 G,Italy (Edoardo Mangiarotti, Giancarlo Bergamini, Antonio Spallino, Vittorio Lucarelli, Manlio di Rosa, Luigi Carpaneda) S,France B,Hungary
1960 G,USSR (Viktor Zhdanovitch, Mark Midler, Yuny Sisikin, Gherman Sveshnikov, Yuriy Rudv) S,Italy B,Germany
1964 G,USSR (Gherman Sveshinikov, Yuriy Sisikin, Viktor Zhdanovitch, Mark Midler) S,Poland B,France
1968 G,France (Daniel

Revenu, G. Berolatti, Christian Noel, Jean Magnan, J. Dimont) S,USSR B,Poland
1972 G,Poland (W. Woyda, L. Koziejowski, J. Kaczmarek, M. Dabrowski, A. Godel) S,USSR B,France
1976 G,West Germany (M. Behr, T. Bach, H. Hein, K. Reichert) S,Italy B,France

EPEE (INDIVIDUAL)
1896 Event not held
1900 G,Ramon Fonst (Cuba) S,Louis Peree (France) B,Leon See (France)
1904 G,Ramon Fonst (Cuba) S,Charles Tatham (Cuba) B,Albertson Post (Cuba)
1908 G,Gaston Alibert (France) 5 wins S,Alexandre Lippmann (France) 4 B,Eugene Olivier (France) 4
1912 G,Paul Anspach (Belgium) 6 wins S,Ivan Osuer (Denmark) 5 B,Philippe de Beaulieu (Belgium) 4
1920 G,Armand Massard (France) S,Alexandre Lippmann (France) B,Ernest Gevers (Belgium)
1924 G,Charles Delporte (Belgium) S,Roger Ducret (France) B,Nils Hellsten (Sweden)
1928 G,Lucien Gaudin (France) 8 wins S,Georges Buchard (France) 7 B,George Calnan (USA) 6
1932 G,Giancarlo Medici (Italy) 9 wins S,Georges Buchard (France) 7 B,Carlo Agosti (Italy) 7
1936 G,Franco Riccardi (Italy) 13 pts. S,Saverio Ragno (Italy) 12 B,Giancarlo Medici (Italy) 12
1948 G,Luigi Cantone (Italy) 7 wins S,Oswald Zappelli (Switzerland) 5 B,Edoardo Mangiarotti (Italy) 5
1952 G,Edoardo Mangiarotti (Italy) 7 wins S,Dario Mangiarotti (Italy) 6 B,Oswald Zappelli (Switzerland) 6
1956 G,Carlo Pavesi (Italy) 5 wins S,Giuseppe Delfino (Italy) 5 B,Edoardo Mangiarotti (Italy) 5
1960 G,Giuseppe Delfino (Italy) 5 wins S,Allan Jay (Great Britain) 5 B,Bruno Khabarov (USSR) 4
1964 G,Grigory Kriss (USSR) S,William Hoskyns (Great Britain) B,Guram Kostava (USSR)
1968 G,Gyozo Kulcsar (Hungary) 4(14) S,Grigory Kriss (USSR) 4(19) B,Gianluigi Saccaro (Italy) 4(19)
1972 G,Csaba Fenyvesi (Hungary) 4 wins S,Jacques la Degaillerie (France) 3 B,Györö Kulcsár (Hungary) 3
1976 G,A. Pusch (West Germany) 3 wins S,J. Hehn (West Germany) 3 B,G. Kulcsar (Hungary) 3

EPEE (TEAM)
1896–1904 Event not held
1908 G,France (Gaston Alibert, Bernard Gravier, Alexandre Lippmann, Eugene Olivier, Jean Stern, Henry Berger, Charles Collignon) S,Great Britain B,Belgium
1912 G,Belgium (Paul Anspach, Henry Anspach, Fernand de Montigny, Jacques Ochs, Gaston Salmon, Francois Rom, Victor Willems, Robert Hennet) S,Great

Britain B,Netherlands
1920 G,Italy (Nedo Nadi, Aldo Nadi, Abelardo Olivier, Giovanni Canova, Dino Urbani, Giovanni Bozza, Andrea Marrazzi, Antonio Allocchio, Paolo di Revel) S,Belgium B,France
1924 G,France (Lucien Gaudin, Roger Ducret, Alexandre Lippmann, Gustave Buchard, Andre Labattut, Georges Teinturier, Lionel Liottel) S,Belgium B,Italy
1928 G,Italy (Carlo Agostoni, Marcello Bertinetti, Giancarlo Medici, Renzo Minoli, Guilio Basletta, Franco Riccardi) S,France B,Portugal
1932 G,France (Bernard Schmetz, Philippe Cattiau, Georges Buchard, Jean Piot, Fernand Jourdant, Georges Tainturier) S,Italy B,USA
1936 G,Italy (Giancarlo Medici, Edoardo Mangiarotti, Saverio Ragno, Alfredo Pezzano, Giancarlo Brusati, Franco Riccardi) S,Sweden B,France
1948 G,France (Henri Guerin, Henri Lepage, M. Desprets, Michel Pecheux, Maurice Huet, Edouard Artigas) S,Italy B,Sweden
1952 G,Italy (Edoardo Mangiarotti, Dario Mangiarotti, Carlo Pavesi, Giuseppe Delfino, Franco Bertinetti, Roberto Battaglia) S,Sweden B,Switzerland
1956 G,Italy (Giuseppe Delfino, Franco Bertinetti, Alberto Pellegrino, Giorgio Anglesio, Carlo Pavesi, Edoardo Mangiarotti) S,Hungary B,France
1960 G,Italy (Alberto Pellegrino, Carlo Pavesi, Giuseppe Delfino, Edoardo Mangiarotti, Gian Luigi Saccaro, Fiorenzo Marini) S,Great Britain B,USSR
1964 G,Hungary (Gyozo Kulscar, Zoltan Nemere, Tamas Gabor, Istvan Kausz) S,Italy B,France
1968 G,Hungary (C. Fenyvesi, Z. Nemere, P. Schmitt, G. Kulcsar, P. Nagy) S,USSR B,Poland
1972 G,Hungary (S. Erdoes, G. Kulcsár, C. Fenyvesi, P. Schmitt, I. Osztrics) S,Switzerland B,USSR
1976 G,Sweden (C. von Essen, H. Jacobson, L. Hagstrom, R. Eding) S,West Germany B,Switzerland

SABRE (INDIVIDUAL)
1896 G,Jean Georgiadis (Greece) 4 wins S,Telemachos Karakalos (Greece) 3 B,Holger Nielsen (Denmark) 2
1900 G,G. de la Falaise (France) S,Leon Thiebaut (France) B,Siegfried Flesch (Austria)
1904 G,Manuel Diaz (Cuba) S,William Grebe (USA) B,Albertson Post (Cuba)
1908 G,Jeno Fuchs (Hungary) 6 wins S,Bela Zulavsky (Hungary) 6 B,Vilem Goppold (Bohemia) 4
1912 G,Jeno Fuchs (Hungary) 6 wins S,Bela Bekessy (Hungary) 5 B,Ervin Meszaros (Hungary) 5
1920 G,Nedo Nadi (Italy) S,Aldo Nadi (Italy) B,A. E. W. de Jong (Netherlands)

1924 G,Sandor Posta (Hungary) 5 wins S,Roger Ducret (France) 5 B,Janos Garai (Hungary) 5
1928 G,Odon Tersztyanszky (Hungary) 9 wins S,Attila Petschauer (Hungary) 9 B,Bino Bini (Italy) 8
1932 G,Gyorgy Piller (Hungary) 8 wins S,Guilio Gaudini (Italy) 7 B,Endre Kabos (Hungary) 5
1936 G,Endre Kabos (Hungary) 7 wins S,Gustavo Marzi (Italy) 6 B,Aladar Gerevich (Hungary) 6
1948 G,Aladar Gerevich (Hungary) 7 wins S,Vincenzo Pinton (Italy) 5 B,Pal Kovacs (Hungary) 5
1952 G,Pal Kovacs (Hungary) 8 wins S,Aladar Gerevich (Hungary) 7 B,Tibor Berczelly (Hungary) 5
1956 G,Rudolf Karpati (Hungary) 6 wins S,Jerzy Pawlowski (Poland) 5 B,Lav Kuznyetsov (USSR) 4
1960 G,Rudolf Karpati (Hungary) 5 wins S,Zoltan Horvath (Hungary) 4 B,Wladimiro Calarese (Italy) 4
1964 G,Tibor Pezsa (Hungary) 2 wins S,Claude Arabo (France) 2 B,Umar Mavilkhanov (USSR) 1
1968 G,Jerzy Pawlowski (Poland) 4(18) S,Mark Rakita (USSR) 4(16) B,Tibor Pesza (Hungary) 3(16)
1972 G,Viktor Sidiak (USSR) 4 wins S,Peter Maroth (Hungary) 3 B,Vladimir Nazlimov (USSR) 3
1976 G,V. Krovopouskov (USSR) 5 wins S,V. Nazlymov (USSR) 4 B,V. Sidiak (USSR) 3

SABRE (TEAM)
1896–1904 Event not held
1908 G,Hungary (Jeno Fuchs, Oszkar Gerde, Peter Toth, Lajos Werkner, Dezso Foldes) S,Italy B,Bohemia
1912 G,Hungary (Laszlo Berti, Jeno Fuchs, Ervin Meszaros, Zoltan Schenker, Dezso Foldes, Oszkar Gerdes, Peter Toth, Lajos Werkner) S,Austria B,Netherlands
1920 G,Italy (Nedo Nadi, Aldo Nadi, Oreste Puliti, Federico Cesarano, Baldo Baldi, Francesco Gargano, Giorgio Santelli) S,France B,Netherlands
1924 G,Italy (Oreste Puliti, Giulio Sarrocchi, Marcello Bertinetti, Oreste Moricca, Renato Anselmi, Guido Balzarini, Bino Bini, Vincenzo Cuccia) S,Hungary B,Netherlands
1928 G,Hungary (Janos Garai, Gyula Glykais, Sandor Gombos, Jozsef Rady, Odon Tersztyanszky, Attila Petschauer) S,Italy B,Poland
1932 G,Hungary (Endre Kabos, Aladar Gerevich, Gyorgy Piller, Gyula Glykais, Attila Petschauer, Erno Nagy) S,Italy B,Poland
1936 G,Hungary (Tibor Berczelly, Aladar Gerevich, Endre Kabos, Laszlo Rajcsanyi, Imre Rajczy, Pal Kovacs) S,Italy B,Germany
1948 G,Hungary (Aladar Gerevich, Rudolf Karpati, Pal Kovacs, Tibor Berczelly, Laszlo Rajcsanyi, Bertalan Papp) S,Italy B,USA

1952 G,Hungary (Rudolf Karpati, Pal Kovacs, Tibor Berczelly, Laszlo Rajcsanyi, Bertalan Papp) S,Italy B,France
1956 G,Hungary (Attila Keresztes, Aladar Gerevich, Rudolf Karpati, Jeno Hamori, Pal Kovas) S,Poland B,USSR
1960 G,Hungary (Zoltan Horvath, Rudolf Karpati, Tamas Mendelenyi, Pal Kovacs, Gabor Delneki, Aladar Gerevich) S,Poland B,Italy
1964 G,USSR (Nagzar Asatiani, Yakov Rylsky, Mark Rakita, Umar Mavlikhanov) S,Italy B,Poland
1968 G,USSR (V. Nazimov, Z. Sidiak, E. Vinokurov, M. Rakita, U. Mavilkhanov) S,Italy B,Hungary
1972 G,Italy (M. Maffei, M. A. Montano, R. Rigoli, M. T. Montano, C. Salvadori) S,USSR B,Hungary
1976 G,USSR (V. Krovopouskov, E. Vinokurov, V. Sidiak, V. Nazlyov) S,Italy B,Rumania

Fencing (Women)
FOIL (INDIVIDUAL)
1896–1920 Event not held
1924 G,Ellen Osiier (Denmark) 5 wins S,Gladys Davis (Great Britain) 4 B,Grete Heckscher (Denmark)
1928 G,Helene Mayer (Germany) 7 wins S,Muriel Freeman (Great Britain) 6 B,Olga Oelkers (Germany) 4
1932 G,Ellen Preis (Austria) 9 wins S,Heather Guiness (Great Britain) 8 B,Ena Bogen (Hungary) 7
1936 G,Ilona Elek (Hungary) 7 wins S,Helene Mayer (Germany) 5 B,Ellen Preis (Austria) 5
1948 G,Ilona Elek (Hungary) 6 wins S,Karen Lachmann (Denmark) 5 B,Ellen Preis (Austria) 5
1952 G,Irene Camber (Italy) 5 wins S,Ilona Elek (Hungary) 5 B,Karen Lachmann (Denmark) 4
1956 G,Gillian Sheen (Great Britain) 6 wins S,Olga Orban (Rumania) 6 B,Renee Garilhe (France) 5
1960 G,Heidi Schmid (Germany) 6 wins S,Valentina Rastvorova (USSR) 5 B,Maria Vicol (Rumania) 4
1964 G,Ildiko Rejto (Hungary) S,Helga Mees (Germany) B,Antonella Ragno (Italy)
1968 G,Elena Novikova (USSR) 4 wins S,Pilar Roldan (Mexico) 3 B,Ildiko Rejto (Hungary) 3
1972 G,Antonella Ragno-Lonzi (Italy) 4 wins S,Ildiko Bobis (Hungary) 3 B,Galina Gorokhova (USSR) 3
1976 G,I. Schwarczenberger (Hungary) 4 wins S,A. Romankov (USSR) 4 B,B. Talvard (France) 3

FOIL (TEAM)
1896–1956 Event not held
1960 G,USSR (Valentina Rastvorova, Talyana Petrenko, Valentina Prudskova, Lyudmila Shishova, Galina Ghorokova, Aleksandara Zabelina) S,Hungary B,Italy
1964 G,USSR (Ildiko Retjo, Katalin Juhasz, Lidia Domolky, Judit Agoston) S,USSR B, Germany

1968 G,USSR (Elena Novikova, Galina Gorokhova, Samusenko, Zabelina) S,Hungary B,Rumania
1972 G,USSR (E. Belova, A. Zabelina, G. Gorokhova, T. Samusenko, S. Chirkova') S,Hungary B,Rumania
1976 G,USSR (E. Belova, O. Kniazeva, V. Sidorova, N. Guiliazova) S,France B,Hungary

Field Hockey
1896–1904 Event not held
1908 G,England (H. J. Wood, L. C. Baillon, H. Scott-Freeman, A. H. Noble, E. W. Page, J. Y. Robinson, E. H. Green, R. G. Pridmore, Stanley Shoveller, G. Logan, P. M. Rees) S,Ireland B,Scotland, Wales
1912 Event not held
1920 G,Great Britain (Harry Haslam, John Bennett, Charles Atkin, H. D. R. Cooke, Eric Crockford, Cyril Wilkinson, William Smith, George McGrath, John McBryan, Stanley Shoveller, R. W. Crummack, A. F. Leighton, C. H. Campbell, C. S. W. Marcon) S,Denmark B,Belgium
1924 Event not held
1928 G,India (Richard Allan, M. E. Rocque, L. C. Hammond, R. A. Norris, B. E. Pinniger, S. M. Yusuf, M. A. Goodsir-Cullen, M. A. Gately, G. E. Marthins, Dhyan Chand, F. S. Seaman) S,Netherlands B,Germany
1932 G,India (Mohammed Jaffar, Bais Roopsingh, Dhyan Chand, Gurmit Singh, R. J. Carr, S. J. S. Bokhari, B. E. Pinniger, M. A. K. Minhas, L. C. Hammond, Carlyle Tapsell, A. C. Hind) S,Japan B,USA
1936 G,India (Richard Allan, Carlyle Tapsell, Mohammed Hussain, Baboo Nimal, M. A. Goodsir-Cullen, Joseph Galibardy, Shabban Singh, Jatidar Dara, Dhyan Chand, Bais Roopsingh, Mohammed Jaffar) S,Germany B,Netherlands
1948 G,India (L. H. K. Pinto, T. Singh, Randhir Gentle, Keshav Datt, Amir Kumar, Maxie Vaz, Kishan Lal, Kunwar Singh, G. Singh, P. A. Jansen, L. Fernandes) S,Great Britain B,Netherlands
1952 G,India (Runganadhan Francis, Dharan Singh, Rhandir Gentle, Leslie Claudius, Keshav Datt, Govind Perumal, Raghbir Lal, Kunwar Singh, Balbir Dosanjh, Udham Singh, Muniswamy Rajagopal) S,Netherlands B,Great Britain
1956 G,India (Shankar Laxman, Bakshish Singh, Randhir Gentle, Leslie Claudius, Amir Kumar, Govind Perumal, S. Charles, Gurdev Singh, Balbir Singh, Udham Singh, Raghir Bhola, Runganadhan Francis, Balkishan Singh, Amit Singh, Hari Pal, Hardyal Singh, Raghbir Lal) S,Pakistan B,Germany
1960 G,Pakistan (Abdul Rashid, Bashir Ahmed, Manzur Atif, Ghulam Rasul, Anwar Ahmed, Ali Habib, Noor Alam, Abdul Hamid, Abdul Waheed, Nasser Ahmed, Moti Ullah,

Khurshid Aslam, Mushtag Ahmed) S,India B,Spain
1964 G,India (Shankar Laxman, Prithipal Singh, Dhara Singh, Lal Mohinder, Charanjit Singh, Gurbux Singh, Joginder Singh, John Peter, Harbinder Singh, Haripal Kashik, Darshan Singh, Jagjit Singh, Bandu Patil, Udham Singh, Ali Sayeed) S,Pakistan B,Australia
1968 G,Pakistan (Zakar Hussain, Tanvir Dar, Tariq Aziz, Saeed Anwar, Riaz Ahmed, Gulrez Akhtar, Khalid Mahmood, Mohammad Ashfaq, Mohammad Rashid, Asad Malik, Jehangir Butt) S,Australia B,India
1972 G,West Germany (P. Kraus, M. Peter, D. Freise, M. Krause, E. Thelen, H. Droese, C. Keller, U. Klaes, W. Baumgart, U. Vos, P. Trump) S,Pakistan B,India
1976 G,New Zealand (P. Ackerley, T. Borren, A. Chesney, J. Christensen, G. Dayman, T. Ineson, B. Maister, S. Maister, T. Manning, A. Parkin, R. Patel) S,Australia B,Pakistan

Gymnastics (Men)
COMBINED EXERCISES (INDIVIDUAL)
1896 Event not held
1900 G,S. Sandras (France) S,J. Bass (France) B,G. Demanet (France)
1904 G,Adolf Spinnler (Germany) 43.49 pts. S,Wilhelm Weber (Germany) 41.60 B,Hugo Peitsch (Germany) 41.56
1908 G,Alberto Braglia (Italy) 317 pts. S,S. W. Tysal (Great Britain) 312 B,Louis Segura (France) 297
1912 G,Alberto Braglia (Italy) 135 pts. S,Louis Segura (France) 132.5 B,Adolfo Tunesi (Italy) 113.5
1920 G,Giorgio Zampori (Italy) 88.35 pts. S,Marcel Torres (France) 87.62 B,Jean Gounot (France) 87.45
1924 G,Leon Stukelj (Yugoslavia) 110.34 pts. S,Robert Prazak (Czechoslovakia) 110.323 B,Bedrich Supcik (Czechoslovakia) 106.903
1928 G,Georges Miez (Switzerland) 247.625 pts. S,Hermann Hanggi (Switzerland) 246.625 B,Leon Stukelj (Yugoslavia) 244.875
1932 G,Romeo Neri (Italy) 140.625 pts. S,Istvan Pelle (Hungary) 134.925 B,Heikki Savolainen (Finland) 134.575
1936 G,Karl Schwarzmann (Germany) 113.100 pts. S,Eugen Mack (Switzerland) 112.234 B,Konrad Frey (Germany) 111.532
1948 G,Veikko Huhtanen (Finland) 229.7 pts. S,Walter Lehmann (Switzerland) 229.0 B,Paavo Aaltonen (Finland) 228.8
1952 G,Viktor Chukarin (USSR) 115.70 pts. S,Grant Shaginyan (USSR) 114.95 B,Josef Stalder (Switzerland) 114.75
1956 G,Viktor Chukarin (USSR) 114.25 pts. S,Takashi Ono (Japan) 114.20 B,Yuriy Titov (USSR) 113.80
1960 G,Boris Shakhlin (USSR) 115.95 pts. S,Takashi Ono (Japan) 115.90 B,Yuriy

Titov (USSR) 115.60
1964 G,Yukio Endo (Japan) 115.95 pts. S,Shuji Tsurumi (Japan) 115.40 B,Boris Shakhlin (USSR) Victor Libitsky (USSR) 115.40
1968 G,Sawao Kato (Japan) 115.90 pts. S,Michail Voronin (USSR) 115.85 B,Akinori Nakayama (Japan) 115.65
1972 G,Sawao Kato (Japan) 114.650 pts. S,Eizo Kenmotsu (Japan) 114.575 B,Akinori Nakayama (Japan) 114.325
1976 G,N. Andrianov (USSR) 116.650 pts. S,S. Kato (Japan) 115.650 B,M. Tsukahara (Japan) 115.575

COMBINED EXERCISES (TEAM)
1896–1920 Event not held
1924 G,Italy (Fernando Mandrini, Mario Lertora, Vittorio Lucchetti, Franco Martino, Luigi Cambiaso, Giuseppe Paris, Giorgio Zampori, Luigi Maiocco) 839.058 pts. S,France 820.528 B,Switzerland 816.66
1928 G,Switzerland (Georges Miez, Hermann Hanggi, Eugen Mack, M. Wezel, Ed Steinemann, August Guttinger, Hans Grieder, Otto Pfister) 1,718.625 pts. S,Czechoslovakia 1,711.5 B,Yugoslavia 1,648.5
1932 G,Italy (Romeo Neri, Mario Lertora, Savino Guglielmetti, Oreste Capuzzo, Franco Tognini) 541.850 pts. S,USA 522.275 B,Finland 509.995
1936 G,Germany (Franz Beckert, Konrad Frey, Karl Schwarzmann, Willi Stadel, Walter Steffens, Matthias Volz) 657.430 pts. S,Switzerland 654.802 B,Finland 638.468
1948 G,Finland (Veikko Huhtanen, Paavo Aaltonen, Heikki Savolainen, Olavi Rove, Einari Terasvirta, Aleksanteri Saarvala, Kalevi Laitinen, Sulo Salmi) 1,358.3 pts. S,Switzerland 1,356.7 B,Hungary 1,330.35
1952 G,USSR (Viktor Chukarin, Grant Shaginyan, Valentin Muratov, Yevgeniy Korolkov, Vladimir Belyakov, Yosif Berdiyev, Mihayl Perelman, Dimitriy Leonkin) 574.4 pts. S,Switzerland 567.5 B,Finland 564.2
1956 G,USSR (Viktor Chukarin, Valentin Muratov, Boris Shakhlin, Albert Azaryan, Yuriy Titov, Pavel Stolbov) 568.25 pts. S,Japan 566.40 B,Finland 555.95
1960 G,Japan (Takashi Ono, Shuji Tsurumi, Yukio Endo, Masao Takemoto, Nobuyuki Aihara, Takashi Mitsukuri) 575.20 pts. S,USSR 572.70 B,Italy 559.05
1964 G,Japan (Yukio Endo, Shuji Tsurumi, Haruhiro Yamashita, Takashi Mitsukuri, Takuji Hayata, Takashi Ono) 577.95 pts. S,USSR 575.45 B,Germany 565.10
1968 G,Japan 575.90 pts. S,USSR 571.10 B,East Germany 557.15
1972 G,Japan 571.25 pts. S,USSR 564.05 B,East Germany 559.70
1976 G,Japan 576.85 pts. S,USSR 576.45 B,East Germany 564.65

FLOOR EXERCISES
1896–1928 Event not held
1932 G,Istvan Pelle (Hungary) 28.8 pts. S,Georges Miez (Switzerland) 28.4 B,Mario Lertora (Italy) 27.7
1936 G,Georges Miez (Switzerland) 18.666 pts. S,Josef Walter (Switzerland) 18.5 B,Konrad Frey (Germany) 18.466, Eugene Mack (Switzerland) 18.466
1948 G,Ferenc Pataki (Hungary) 38.7 pts. S,Janos Mogyorosi (Hungary) 38.4 B,Zdenek Ruzicka (Czechoslovakia) 38.1
1952 G,Karl Thoresson (Sweden) 19.25 pts. S,Tado Uesako (Japan) 19.15, Jerzy Jokiel (Poland) 19.15
1956 G,Valentin Muratov (USSR) 19.20 pts. S,Nobuyuki Aihara (Japan) 19.10 William Thoresson (Sweden) 19.10 Viktor Chukarin (USSR) 19.10
1960 G,Nobuyuki Aihara (Japan) 19.45 pts. S,Yuriy Titov (USSR) 19.32 B,Franco Menichelli (Italy) 19.27
1964 G,Franco Menicelli (Italy) 19.45 pts. S,Victor Lisitsky (USSR) 19.35 B,Yukio Endo (Japan) 19.35
1968 G,Sawao Kato (Japan) 19.475 pts. S,Akinori Nakayama (Japan) 19.400 B,Takeshi Kato (Japan) 19.275
1972 G,Nikolai Andrianov (USSR) 19.175 pts. S,Akinori Nakayama (Japan) 19.125 B,Shigeru Kasamatsu (Japan) 19.025
1976 G,N. Andrianov (USSR) 19.450 pts. S,V. Marchenko (USSR) 19.425 B,P. Kormann (USA) 19.300

HORIZONTAL BAR
1896 G,Hermann Weingartner (Germany) S,Alfred Flatow (Germany) B, Petmesas (Greece)
1900 Event not held
1904 G,Anton Heida (USA) 40 pts. S,E. A. Hennig (USA) 40 B,George Eyser (USA) 39
1908–20 Event not held
1924 G,Leon Stukelj (Yugoslavia) 19.73 pts. S,Jean Gutweniger (Switzerland) 19.236 B,A. Higelin (France) 19.163
1928 G,Georges Miez (Switzerland) 19.17 pts. S,Romeo Neri (Italy) 19.00 B,Eugen Mack (Switzerland) 18.92
1932 G,Dallas Bixler (USA) 18.33 pts. S,Heikki Savolainen (Finland) 18.07 B,Einari Terasvirta (Finland) 18.07
1936 G,Aleksanteri Saarvala (Finland) 19.433 pts. S,Konrad Frey (Germany) 19.267 B,Karl Schwarzmann (Germany) 19.233
1948 G,Josef Stalder (Switzerland) 39.7 pts. S,Walter Lehmann (Switzerland) 39.4 B,Veikko Huhtanen (Finland) 39.2
1952 G,Jack Gunthard (Switzerland) 19.55 pts. S,Josef Stalder (Switzerland) 19.50 Karl Schwarzmann (Germany) 19.50
1956 G,Takashi Ono (Japan) 19.60 pts. S,Yuriy Titov (USSR) 19.40 B,Masao Takemoto (Japan) 19.30
1960 G,Takashi Ono (Japan)

19.60 pts. S, Masao Takemoto (Japan) 19.52 B, Boris Shakhlin (USSR) 19.47
1964 G, Boris Shakhlin (USSR) 19.625 pts. S, Yuriy Titov (USSR) 19.55 B, Miroslav Ceraf (Yugoslavia) 19.50
1968 G, Michail Voronin (USSR) 19.550 pts. Akinori Nakayama (Japan) 19.550 B, Eizo Kenmotsu (Japan) 19.375
1972 G, Mitsuo Tsukahara (Japan) 19.725 pts. S, Sawao Kato (Japan) 19.525 B, Shigeru Kasamatsu (Japan) 19.450
1976 G, M. Tsukahara (Japan) 19.675 pts. S, E. Kemmotsu (Japan) 19.500 B, E. Gienger (West Germany) 19.475

PARALLEL BARS
1896 G, Alfred Flatow (Germany) S, Hermann Weingartner (Germany) B, Louis Zutter (Switzerland)
1900 Event not held
1904 G, George Eyser (USA) 44 pts. S, Anton Heida (USA) 43 B, John Duha (USA) 40
1908—20 Event not held
1924 G, August Guttinger (Switzerland) 21.63 pts. S, Robert Prazak (Czechoslovakia) 21.61 B, Giorgio Zampori (Italy) 21.45
1928 G, Ladislav Vacha (Czechoslovakia) 18.83 pts. S, Josip Primozic (Yugoslavia) 18.50 B, Hermann Hanggi (Switzerland) 18.08
1932 G, Romeo Neri (Italy) 18.97 pts. S, Istvan Pelle (Hungary) 18.60 B, Heikki Savolainen (Finland) 18.27
1936 G, Konrad Frey (Germany) 19.067 pts. S, Michael Reusch (Switzerland) 19.034 B, Karl Schwarzmann (Germany) 18.967
1948 G, Michael Reusch (Switzerland) 39.5 pts. S, Veikko Huhtanen (Finland) 39.3 B, Christian Kipfer (Switzerland) 39.1, Josef Stalder (Switzerland) 39.1
1952 G, Hans Eugster (Switzerland) 19.65 pts. S, Viktor Chukarin (USSR) 19.60 B, Josef Stalder (Switzerland) 19.50
1956 G, Viktor Chukarin (USSR) 19.20 pts. S, Masami Kubota (Japan) 19.15 B, Takashi Ono (Japan) 19.10 Masao Takemoto (Japan) 19.10
1960 G, Boris Shakhlin (USSR) 19.40 pts. S, Gilvanni Carminucci (Italy) 19.37 B, Takashi Ono (Japan) 19.35
1964 G, Yukio Endo (Japan) 19.675 pts. S, Shuji Tsurumi (Japan) 19.45 B, Franco Menichelli (Italy) 19.35
1968 G, Akinori Nakayama (Japan) 19.475 pts. S, Michail Voronin (USSR) 19.425 B, Vladimir Klimenko (USSR) 19.225
1972 G, Sawao Kato (Japan) 19.475 pts. S, Shigeru Kasamatsu (Japan) 19.375 B, Eizo Kenmotsu (Japan) 19.250
1976 G, S. Kato (Japan) 19.675 pts. S, N. Andrianov (USSR) 19.500 B, M. Tsukahara (Japan) 19.475

POMMELLED HORSE
1896 G, Louis Zutter (Switzerland) S, Hermann Weingartner (Germany) B, Gyula Kokas (Hungary)

1900 Event not held
1904 G, Anton Heida (USA) 42 pts. S, George Eyser (USA) 33 B, W. A. Merz (USA) 29
1908—20 Event not held
1924 G, Josef Wilhelm (Switzerland) 21.23 pts. S, Jean Gutweniger (Switzerland) 21.13 B, Antoine Rebetez (Switzerland) 20.73
1928 G, Hermann Hanggi 19.75 pts. S, Georges Miez (Switzerland) 19.25 B, Heikki Savolainen (Finland) 18.83
1932 G, Istvan Pelle (Hungary) 19.07 pts. S, Omero Bonoli (Italy) 18.87 B, Frank Haubold (USA) 18.57
1936 G, Konrad Frey (Germany) 19.333 pts. S, Eugen Mack (Switzerland) 19.167 B, Albert Bachman (Switzerland) 19.067
1948 G, Paavo Aaltonen, Veikko Huhtanen, Heikki Savolainen (Finland) each 38.7 pts.
1952 G, Viktor Chukarin (USSR) 19.50 pts S, Yevgeniy Korolkov (USSR) 19.40 B, Grant Shaginyan (USSR) 19.40
1956 G, Boris Shakhlin (USSR) 19.25 pts. S, Takashi Ono (Japan) 19.20 B, Viktor Chukarin (USSR) 19.10 Shuji Tsurumi (Japan) 19.15
1960 G, Eugen Ekman (Finland) 19.37 pts. Boris Shakhlin (USSR) 19.37 B, Shuji Tsurumi (Japan) 19.15
1964 G, Miroslav Cerar (Yugoslavia) 19.525 pts. S, Shuji Tsurumi (Japan) 19.325 B, Yury Tsapenko (USSR) 19.20
1968 G, Miroslav Cerar (Yugoslavia) 19.325 pts. S, Olli Laiho (Finland) 19.225 B, Michail Voronin (USSR) 19.200
1972 G, Viktor Klimenko (USSR) 19.125 pts. S, Sawao Kato (Japan) 19.000 B, Eizo Kenmotsu (Japan) 18.950
1976 G, Z. Magyar (Hungary) 19.700 pts. S, E. Kenmotsu (Japan) 19.575 B, N. Andrianov (USSR) 19.525

LONG HORSE VAULT
1896 G, Karl Schumann (Germany) S, Louis Zutter (Switzerland)
1900 Event not held
1904 G, Anton Heida (USA) 36 pts. S, George Eyser (USA) 36 B, W. A. Merz (USA) 31
1908—20 Event not held
1924 G, Frank Kriz (USA) 9.98 pts. S, Jan Koutny (Czechoslovakia) 9.97 B, Bohumil Morkovsky (Czechoslovakia) 9.93
1928 G, Eugen Mack (Switzerland) 9.58 pts. S, E. Loffler (Czechoslovakia) 9.50 B, Stane Drganc (Yugoslavia) 9.46
1932 G, Savino Gughelmetti (Italy) 18.03 pts. S, Alfred Jochim (Germany) 17.77 B, Edward Carmichael (USA) 17.53
1936 G, Karl Schwarzmann (Germany) 19.20 pts. S, Eugen Mack (Switzerland) 18.967 B, Matthias Volz (Germany) 18.467
1948 G, Paavo Aaltonen (Finland) 39.1 pts. S, Olavi Rove (Finland) 39.0 B, Janos Mogyorosi (Hungary) 38.5 Ferenc Pataki (Hungary) 38.5

1952 G, Viktor Chukarin (USSR) 19.20 pts. S, Masao Takemoto (Japan) 19.15 B, Tadao Uesako (Japan) 19.05 Takashi Ono (Japan) 19.05
1956 G, Helmuth Bantz (Germany) 18.85 pts. Valentin Muratov (USSR) 18.85 B, Yuriy Titov (USSR) 18.75
1960 G, Takashi Ono (Japan) 19.35 pts. S, Boris Shakhlin (USSR) 19.35 B, Vladimir Portnoi (USSR) 19.22
1964 G, Haruhiro Yamashita (Japan) 19.660 pts. S, Victor Lisitsky (USSR) 19.325 B, Hannu Rantakari (Finland) 19.30
1968 G, Michail Voronin (USSR) 19.000 pts. S, Yukio Endo (Japan) 18.950 B, Sergei Diomidov (USSR) 18.925
1972 G, Klaus Koste (East Germany) 18.850 pts. S, Viktor Klimenko (USSR) 18.825 B, Nikolai Andrianov (USSR) 18.800
1976 G, N. Andrianov (USSR) 19.450 pts. S, M. Tsukahara (Japan) 19.375 B, H. Kajiyama (Japan) 19.275

RINGS
1896 G, Jean Mitropoulos (Greece) S, Hermann Weingartner (Germany) B, Persakis (Greece)
1900 Event not held
1904 G, Hermann Glass (USA) 45pts. S, W. A. Merz (USA) 35 B, E. Voight (USA) 32
1908—20 Event not held
1924 G Francesco Martino (Italy) 21.553 pts. S, Robert Prazak (Czechoslovakia) 21.483 B, Ladislav Vacha (Czechoslovakia) 21.43
1928 G, Leon Stukelj (Yugoslavia) 19.25 pts. S, Ladislav Vacha (Czechoslovakia) 19.17 B, E. Loffler (Czechoslovakia) 18.83
1932 G, George Gulack (USA) 18.97 pts. S, William Denton 18.60 B, Giovanni Lattuada (Italy) 18.50
1936 G, Alois Hudec (Czechoslovakia) 19.433 pts. S, Leon Stukelj (Yugoslavia) 18.87 B, Matthias Volz (Germany) 18.67
1948 G, Karl Frei (Switzerland) 39.6 pts. S, Michael Reusch (Switzerland) 39.1 B, Zdenek Ruzicka (Czechoslovakia) 38.5
1952 G, Grant Shaginyan (USSR) 19.75 pts. S, Viktor Chukarin (USSR) 19.55 B, Hans Eugster (Switzerland) 19.40 Dimitriy Leonkin (USSR) 19.40
1956 G, Albert Azarvan (USSR) 19.35 pts. S, Valentin Muratov (USSR) 19.15 B, Masao Takemoto (Japan) 19.10 Masami Kubota (Japan) 19.10
1960 G, Albert Azaryan (USSR) 19.72 pts. S, Boris Shakhlin (USSR) 19.50 B, Velik Kapsazov (Bulgaria) 19.42 Takashi Ono (Japan) 19.42
1964 G, Takuji Hayata (Japan) 19.475 pts. S, Franco Menichelli (Italy) 19.425 B, Boris Shakhlin (USSR) 19.40
1968 G, Akinori Nakayama (Japan) 19.450 pts. S, Michail Voronin (USSR) 19.325 B, Sawao Kato (Japan) 19.225
1972 G, Akinori Nakayama

(Japan) 19.350 pts. S, Mikhail Voronin (USSR) 19.275 B, Mitsuo Tsukahara (Japan) 19.225
1976 G, N. Andrianov (USSR) 19.650 pts. S, A. Ditiatin (USSR) 19.550 B, D. Grecu (Rumania) 19.500

Gymnastics (Women)
COMBINED EXERCISES (INDIVIDUAL)
1896—1948 Event not held
1952 G, Maria Gorokhovskaya (USSR) 76.78 pts. S, Nina Bocharyova (USSR) 75.94 B, Margit Korondi (Hungary) 75.82
1956 G, Larisa Latynina (USSR) 74.93 pts. S, Agnes Keleti (Hungary) 74.63 B, Sofia Muratova (USSR) 74.46
1960 G, Larisa Latynina (USSR) 77.03 pts. S, Sofia Muratova (USSR) 76.69 B, Polina Astakhova (USSR) 76.16
1964 G, Vera Caslavska (Czechoslovakia) 77.564 pts. S, Larisa Latynina (USSR) 76.998 B, Polina Astakhova (USSR) 76.965
1968 G, Vera Caslavska (Czechoslovakia) 78.25 pts. S, Zinaida Voronina (USSR) 76.85 B, Natalia Kuchinskaya (USSR) 76.75
1972 G, Lyudmila Tourischeva (USSR) 77.025 pts. S, Karin Janz (East Germany) 76.875 B, Tamara Lazakovitch (USSR) 76.850
1976 G, N. Comaneci (Rumania) 79.275 pts. S, N. Kim (USSR) 78.675 B, L. Tourischeva (USSR) 78.625

COMBINED EXERCISES (TEAM)
1896—1924 Event not held
1928 G, Netherlands (van Radwijk, van der Berg, Polak, Nordheim, van der Bos, van der Bos, van Rumst, van der Vegt, Burgerhof, Simons, de Levie, Stelma, Agsteribbe) 316.75 pts. S, Italy 289.00 B, Great Britain 258.25
1932 Event not held
1936 G, Germany (Anita Barwirth, Erna Burger, Isolde Frolian, Paula Pohlsen, Kathe Sohnemann, Trudi Meyer, Friedl Iby, Julie Schmitt) 506.50 pts S, Czechoslovakia 503.50 B, Hungary 499
1948 G, Czechoslovakia (Z. Honsova, M. Misakova, V. Ruzickova, Bozena Srncova, M. Mullerova, Zdenka Vermirovska, O. Silhanova, M. Kovarova) 445.45 pts. S, Hungary 440.55 B, USA 422.63
1952 G, USSR (Maria Gorokhovskaya, Nina Bocharyova, Galina Minaycheva, Galina Urbanovich, Pelageya Danilova, Galina Shamray, Medeya Dshugeli, Yekaterina Kalinchuk) 527.03 pts. S, Hungary 520.96 B, Czechoslovakia 503.32
1956 G, USSR (Larisa Latynina, Sofia Muratova, Tamara Manina, Lyudmila Egorova, Polina Astakhova, Lydia Kalinina) 444.80 pts. S, Hungary 443.50 B, Rumania 439.20
1960 G, USSR (Larisa Latynina, Sofia Muratova,

Polina Astakhova, Marganita Nikolayeva, Lydia Ivanova, Tamara Lyukhina) 382.32 pts. S,Czechoslovakia 373.32 B,Rumania 438.20
1964 G,USSR (Larisa Latynina, Elena Volchetskaya, Polina Astakhova, Tamara Zamotailova, Tamara Manina, Ludmila Gromova) 380.890 pts. S,Czechoslovakia 379.989 B,Japan 377.889
1968 G,USSR (Zinaida Voronina, Natalia Kuchinskaya, Arissa Petrik, Olga Karaseva) 382.85 pts. S,Czechoslovakia 382.20 B,East Germany 379.10
1972 G,USSR (L. Tourischeva, O. Korbut, T. Lazakovitch, L. Burda, E. Saadi, A. Koshel) 380.50 pts. S,East Germany 376.55 B,Hungary 368.25
1976 G,USSR 390.35 pts. S,Rumania 387.15 B,East Germany 385.10

BEAM
1896–1948 Event not held
1952 G,Nina Bocharyova (USSR) 19.22 pts. S,Maria Gorokhovskaya (USSR) 19.13 B,Margit Korondi (Hungary) 19.02
1956 G,Agnes Keleti (Hungary) 18.80 pts. S,Eva Bosakova (Czechoslovakia) 18.63 Tamara Manina 18.63
1960 G,Eva Bosakova (Czechoslovakia) 19.28 pts. S,Larisa Latynina (USSR) 19.233 B,Sofia Muratova (USSR) 19.232
1964 G,Vera Caslavska (Czechoslovakia) 19.449 pts. S,Tamara Manina (USSR) 19.399 B,Larisa Latynina (USSR) 19.382
1968 G,Natalia Kuchinskaya (USSR) 19.650 pts. S,Vera Caslavska (Czechoslovakia) 19.575 B,Arissa Petrik (USSR) 19.250
1972 G,Olga Korbut (USSR) 19.575 pts. S,Tamara Lazakovitch (USSR) 19.375 B,Karin Janz (East Germany) 18.975
1976 G,N. Comaneci (Rumania) 19.950 pts. S,O. Korbut (USSR) 19.725 B,T. Ungureanu (Rumania) 19.700

ASYMMETRICAL BARS
1896–1948 Event not held
1952 G,Margit Korondi (Hungary) 19.40 pts. S,Maria Gorokhovskaya (USSR) 19.26 B,Agnes Keleti (Hungary) 19.16
1956 G,Agnes Keleti (Hungary) 18.96 pts. S,Larisa Latynina (USSR) 18.83, B,Sofia Muratova (USSR) 18.80
1960 G,Polina Astakhova (USSR) 19.61 pts. S,Larisa Latynina (USSR) 19.41 B,Tamara Lyukhina (USSR) 19.39
1964 G,Polina Astakhova (USSR) 19.332 pts. S,Katalin Makray (Hungary) 19.216 B,Larisa Latynina (USSR) 19.199
1968 G,Vera Caslavska (Czechoslovakia) 19.650 pts. S,Karin Janz (West Germany) 19.500 B,Zinaida Voronina (USSR) 19.425
1972 G,Karin Janz (East Germany) 19.675 pts. S,Olga Korbut (USSR), Erika Zuchold (East Germany) 19.450
1976 G,N. Comaneci (Rumania)

20.00 pts. S,T. Ungureanu (Rumania) 19.80 B,M. Egervari (Hungary) 19.775

HORSE VAULT
1896–1948 Event not held
1952 G,Yekaterina Kalinchuk (USSR) 19.20 pts. S,Maria Gorokhovskaya (USSR) 19.19 B,Galina Minaycheva (USSR) 19.16
1956 G,Larisa Latynina (USSR) 18.83 pts. S,Tamara Manina (USSR) 18.80 B,Ann-Sofi Colling (Sweden) 18.73 Olga Tass (Hungary) 18.73
1960 G,Margarita Nikolayeva (USSR) 19.31 pts. S,Sofia Muratova (USSR) 19.04 B,Larisa Latynina (USSR) 19.01
1964 G,Vera Caslavska (Czechoslovakia) 19.483 pts. S,Larisa Latynina (USSR) 19.283 B,Birgit Radochla (Germany) 19.283
1968 G,Vera Caslavska (Czechoslovakia) 19.775 pts. S,Erika Zuchold (West Germany) 19.625 B,Zinaida Voronina (USSR) 19.500
1972 G,Karin Janz (East Germany) 19.525 pts. S,Erika Zuchold (East Germany) 19.275 B,Lyudmila Tourischeva (USSR) 19.250
1976 G,N. Kim (USSR) 19.800 pts. S,L. Tourischeva (USSR) 19.650 B,C. Dombeck (East Germany) 19.650

FLOOR EXERCISES
1896–1948 Event not held
1952 G,Agnes Keleti (Hungary) 19.36 pts. S,Maria Gorokhovskaya (USSR) 19.20 B,Margit Korondi (Hungary) 19.00
1956 G,Larisa Latynina (USSR) 18.73 pts. Agnes Keleti (Hungary) 18.73 B,Elena Leusteanu (Rumania) 18.70
1960 G,Larisa Latynina (USSR) 19.58 pts. S,Polina Astakhova (USSR) 19.53 B,Tamara Lyukhina (USSR) 19.44
1964 G,Larisa Latynina (USSR) 19.599 pts. S,Polina Astakhova (USSR) 19.50 B,Ducza Janosi (Hungary) 19.30
1968 G,Vera Caslavska (Czechoslovakia) 19.675 pts. Arissa Petrik (USSR) 19.675 B,Natalia Kuchinskaya (USSR) 19.650
1972 G,Olga Korbut (USSR) 19.575 pts. S,Lyudmila Tourischeva (USSR) 19.550 B,Tamara Lazakovitch (USSR) 19.450
1976 G,N. Kim (USSR) 19.850 pts. S,L. Tourischeva (USSR) 19.825 B,N. Comaneci (Rumania) 19.750

Handball (Men)
1896–1968 Event not held
1972 G,Yugoslavia (Z. Zivkovic, A. Arslanagic, M. Pribanic, P. Fajfric, M. Karalic, S. Miskovic, H. Horvat, B. Pokrajac, Z. Miljak, M. Lazarevic, N. Popovic) S,Czechoslovakia B,Rumania
1976 G,USSR (M. Istchenko, A. Fejukin, V. Maximov, S. Kushnirjuk, V. Kravsov, J. Klimov, A. Anpilogov, E. Tchernyshov, V. Gassiy, A. Tomin, J. Kidjaev, A. Rezanov) S,Rumania B,Poland

Handball (Women)
1896–1972 Event not held
1976 G,USSR (N. Sherstjuk, R. Shabanova, L. Berezhnaja, Z. Turchina, T. Makarets, M. Litoshenko, L. Bobrus, T. Glustchenko, L. Shubina, G. Zakharova, A. Chesaitite, N. Lobova, L. Pantchuk, L. Karlova) S,East Germany B,Hungary

Judo
Introduced in 1964
LIGHTWEIGHT
1964 G,T.Nakatani (Japan) S,E. Haenni (Switzerland) B,O. Stepanov (USSR), A. Bogulubov (USSR)
1968 Event not held
1972 G,T. Kawaguchi (Japan) S,B. Buidaa (Mongolia) B,Y. Ik Kim (Korea), J-J Mournier (France)
1976 G,H. Rodriguez (Cuba) S,E. Chang (Korea) B,F. Mariani (Italy), J. Tuncsik (Hungary)
WELTERWEIGHT
1964 Event not held
1968 Event not held
1972 G,T. Nomura (Japan) S,A. Zajkowski (Poland) B,D. Hoetger (East Germany) A. Novikov (USSR)
1976 G,V. Nevzorov (USSR) S,K. Kuramoto (Japan) B,P. Vial (France), M. Talaj'(Poland)
MIDDLEWEIGHT
1964 G,I. Okano (Japan) S,W. Hofmann (West Germany) B,J. Bregman (USA), E. Tae Kim (Korea)
1968 Event not held
1972 G,S. Sekine (Japan) S,Seung-Lip Oh (Korea) B,B. Jacks (Great Britain) J-P Coche (France)
1976 G,I. Sonoda (Japan) S,V. Dvoinikov (USSR) B,S. Obadov (Yugoslavia), Y. Park (Korea)
LIGHT HEAVYWEIGHT
1964 Event not held
1968 Event not held
1972 G,S. Chochoshvili (USSR) S,D. C. Starbrook (Great Britain) B,C. Ishii (Brazil), P. Barth (West Germany)
1976 G,K. Ninomiya (Japan) S,R. Harshiladze (USSR) B,D. C. Starbrook (Great Britain), J. Roethlisberger (Switzerland)
HEAVYWEIGHT
1964 G,I. Inokuma (Japan) S,A. H. Rogers (Canada) B,P. Chikviladze (USSR) A. Kiknadze (USSR)
1968 Event not held
1972 G,W. Ruska (Holland) S,K. Glahn (West Germany) B,G. Onashvili (USSR), M. Nishimura (Japan)
1976 G,S. Novikov (USSR) S,G. Neureuther (West Germany) B,S. Endo (Japan), A. Coage (USA)
OPEN CATEGORY, NO WEIGHT LIMIT
1964 G,A. Geesink (Holland) S,A. Kaminaga (Japan) B,T. Boronovskis (Australia), K. Glahn (Germany)
1968 Event not held
1972 G,W. Ruska (Holland) S,V. Kusnezov (USSR) B,J-C Brondani (France), A. Parisi (Great Britain)
1976 G,H. Uemura (Japan) S,K. Remfry (Great Britain) B,S. Chochishvili (USSR), J. Cho (Korea)

Modern Pentathlon
1896–1908 Event not held
1912 G,Gustaf Lilliehook (Sweden) 27 pts. S,Gosta Asbrink (Sweden) 28 B,George de Laval (Sweden) 30
1920 G,Gustaf Dyrssen (Sweden) 18 pts. S,Erik de Laval (Sweden) 23 B,G. Runo (Sweden) 27
1924 G,Bo Lindman (Sweden) 18 pts. S,Gustaf Dyrssen (Sweden) 39 B,Bertil Uggla (Sweden) 45
1928 G,Sven Thofelt (Sweden) 47 pts. S,Bo Lindman (Sweden) 50 B,Helmuth Kahl (Germany) 52
1932 G,Johan Oxenstierna (Sweden) 32 pts. S,Bo Lindman (Sweden) 35.5 B,Richard Mayo (USA) 38.5
1936 G,Gotthardt Handrick (Germany) 31.5 pts. S,Charles Leonard (USA) 39.5 B,Silvano Abba (Italy) 45.5
1948 G,William Grut (Sweden) 16 pts. S,George Moore (USA) 47 B,Gosta Gardin (Sweden) 49
1952 G,Lars Hall (Sweden) 32 pts. S,Gabor Benedek (Hungary) 32 B,Istvan Szondi (Hungary) 41
Teams—
G,Hungary (Gabor Benedek, Istvan Szondi, Aladar Kovacsi) 166 pts. S,Sweden 182 B,Finland 213
1956 G,Lars Hall (Sweden) 4,833 pts. S,Olavi Mannonen (Finland) 4,774.5 B,Vaino Korhonen (Finland) 4,750
Teams—
USSR (Igor Novikov, Aleksandr Tarasov, Ivan Deryugin) 13,609.5 pts. S,USA 13,482 B,Finland 13,185.5
1960 G,Ferenc Nemeth (Hungary) 5,024 pts. S,Imre Nagy (Hungary) 4,988 B,Robert Beck (USA) 4,981
Teams—
G,Hungary (Ferenc Nemeth, Imre Nagy, Andras Balczo) 14,863 pts. S,USSR 14,309 B,USA 14,192
1964 G,Ferenc Toerek (Hungary) 5,116 pts. S,Igor Novikov (USSR) 5,067 B,Albert Mokeyev (USSR) 5,039
Teams—
G,USSR (Igor Novikov, Albert Mokeyev, Victor Mineyev) 14,961 pts. S,USA 14,189 B,Hungary 14,173
1968 G,Bjorn Ferm (Sweden) 4,964 pts. S,Andras Balczo (Hungary) 4,953 B,Pavel Lednev (USSR) 4,795
Teams—
G,Hungary (Andras Balczo, Istvan Mona) 14,325 pts. S,USSR 14,248 B,France 13,289
1972 G,Andras Balczo (Hungary) 5,412 pts. S,Boris Onischenko (USSR) 5,335 B,Pavel Lednev (USSR) 5,328
Teams—
G,USSR (Boris Onischenko, Pavel Lednev, Vladimir Shmelev) 15,968 pts. S,Hungary 15,348 B,Finland 14,812
1976 G,J. Pyciak-Peciak (Poland) 5,520 pts. S,P. Lednev (USSR) 5,485 B,J. Bartu (Czechoslovakia) 5,466
Teams—
G,Great Britain (A. Parker, R. Nightingale, J. Fox) 15,559 pts. S,Czechoslovakia 15,451 B,Hungary 15,395

Rowing (Men)

SINGLE SCULLS
1896 Event not held
1900 G,H. Barrelet (France) 7m 35.6s S,Gaudin (France) 7m 41.6s B,George St. Ashe (Great Britain) 8m 15.6s
1904 G,Frank Greer (USA) 10m 08.5s S,James Juvenal (USA) B,Constance Titus (USA)
1908 G,Harry Blackstaffe (Great Britain) 9m 26.0s S,Alexander McCullough (Great Britain)
1912 G,William Kinnear (Great Britain) 7m 47.6s S,Polydore Veirman (Belgium) 7m 56.0s
1920 G,John Kelly (USA) 7m 35.0s S,Jack Beresford (Great Britain) 7m 36.0s B,Clarence Hadfield d'Arcy (New Zealand) 7m 48.0s
1924 G,Jack Beresford (Great Britain) 7m 49.2s S,William Garrett-Gilmore (USA) 7m 54.0s B,Josef Schneider (Switzerland) 8m 01.0s
1928 G,Henry Pearce (Australia) 7m 11.0s S,Kenneth Myers (USA) 7m 20.8s B,T. David Collet (Great Britain) 7m 19.8s
1932 G,Henry Pearce (Australia) 7m 44.4s S,William Miller (USA) 7m 45.2s B,Guillermo Douglas (Uruguay) 8m 13.6s
1936 G,Gustav Schafer (Germany) 8m 21.5s S,Josef Hasenohrl (Austria) 8m 25.8s B,Daniel Barrow (USA) 8m 28.0s
1948 G,Mervyn Wood (Australia) 7m 24.4s S,Eduardo Risso (Uruguay) 7m 38.2s B,Romolo Catasta (Italy) 7m 51.4s
1952 G,Yuri Tyukalov (USSR) 8m 12.8s S,Mervyn Wood (Australia) 8m 14.5s B,Teodor Kocerka (Poland) 8m 19.4s
1956 G,Vyacheslav Ivanov (USSR) 8m 02.5s S,Stuart Mackenzie (Australia) 8m 07.7s B,John B. Kelly (USA) 8m 11.8s
1960 Vyacheslav Ivanov (USSR) 7m 13.96s S,Achim Hill (Germany) 7m 20.21s B,Teodor Kocerka (Poland) 7m 21.26s
1964 G,Vyacheslav Ivanov (USSR) 8m 22.51s S,Achim Hill (Germany) 8m 26.34s B,Gottfried Kottman (Switzerland) 8m 29.68s
1968 G,Henri Wienese (Netherlands) 7m 47.80s S,Jochen Meissner (West Germany) 7m 52.00s B,Alberto Demiddi (Argentina) 7m 57.19s
1972 G,Yuri Malishev (USSR) 7m 10.12s S,Alberto Demiddi (Argentina) 7m 11.53s B,Wolfgang Gueldenpfennig (East Germany) 7m 14.45s
1976 G,P. Karppinen (Finland) 7m 29.03s S,P-M. Kolbe (West Germany) 7m 31.67s B,J. Dreifke (East Germany) 7m 38.03s

DOUBLE SCULLS
1896–1900 Event not held
1904 G,USA (Atlanta BC, New York) 10m 03.2s S,USA (Ravenswood BC, Long Island) B,USA (Independent RC, New Orleans)
1908–1912 Event not held
1920 G,USA (John Kelly, Paul Costello) 7m 09.0s S,Italy

7m 19.0s B,France 7m 21.0s
1924 G,USA (John Kelly, Paul Costello) 7m 45.0s S,France 7m 54.8s B,Switzerland
1928 G,USA (Charles McIlvaine, Paul Costello) 6m 41.4s S,Canada 6m 51.0s B,Austria 6m 48.8s
1932 G,USA (William Garrett-Gilmore, Kenneth Myers) 7m 17.4s S,Germany 7m 22.8s B,Canada 7m 27.6s
1936 G,Great Britain (Leslie Southwood, Jack Beresford) 7m 20.8s S,Germany 7m 26.2s B,Poland 7m 36.2s
1948 G,Great Britain (B. Herbert Bushnell, Richard Burnell) 6m 51.3s S,Denmark 6m 55.3s B,Uruguay 7m 12.4s
1952 G,Argentina (Tranquilo Copozzo, Eduardo Guerrero) 7m 32.2s S,USSR 7m 38.3s B,Uruguay 7m 43.7s
1956 G,USSR (Aleksandr Berkutov, Yuriy Tyukalov) 7m 24.0s S,USA 7m 32.2s B,Australia 7m 37.4s
1960 G,Czechoslovakia (Vaclav Kozak, Pavel Schmidt) 6m 47.50s S,USSR 6m 50.48s B,Switzerland 6m 50.59s
1964 G,USSR (Oleg Tyurin, Boris Dubrovsky) 7m 10.66s S,USA 7m 13.16s B,Czechoslovakia 7m 14.23s
1968 G,USSR (Anatoly Sass, Alexander Timoshinin) 6m 51.82s S,Netherlands 6m 52.80s B,USA 6m 54.21s
1972 G,USSR (Aleksandr Timoshinin, Gennadi Korshikov) 7m 01.77s S,Norway 7m 02.58s B,East Germany 7m 05.55s
1976 G,Norway (F. Hensen, A. Hensen) 7m 13.20s S,Great Britain (C. Baillieu, M. Hart) 7m 15.26s B,East Germany (U. Schmied, J. Bertow) 7m 17.45s

COXLESS FOURS SCULLS
1896–1972 Event not held
1976 G,East Germany (W. Guildenpfennig, R. Reiche, K. Bussert, M. Wolfgramm) 6m 18.65s S,USSR 6m 19.89s B,Czechoslovakia 6m 21.77s

COXLESS PAIRS
1896 Event not held
1900 G,Belgium I (van Crombuge, de Sonville) S,Belgium II B,France
1904 G,USA (Seawanhaka C) 10m 57.0s S,USA (Atlanta BC) B,USA (Western RC)
1908 G,Great Britain (Leander I. J. Fenning, Gordon Thomson) 9m 41.0s S,Great Britain (Leander II) 2¼ lengths B,Canada
1912 Event not held
1920 G,Italy (Ercole Olgeni, Giovanni Scatturin) 7m 56.0s S,France 7m 57.0s B,Switzerland
1924 G,Netherlands (W. Rosingh, A. Beynen) 8m 19.4s S,France 8m 21.6s
1928 G,Germany (Bruno Muller, Kurt Moeschter) 7m 06.4s S,Great Britain 7m 08.8s B,USA 7m 20.4s
1932 G,Great Britain (Arthur Edwards, Lewis Clive) 8m 00.0s S,New Zealand 8m 02.4s B,Poland 8m 08.2s
1936 G,Germany (Hugo Strauss, Willi Eichhorn) 8m 16.1s S,Denmark 8m 19.2s B,Argentina 8m 23.0s
1948 G,Great Britain (John Wilson, W. Stanley Laurie)

7m 21.1s S,Switzerland 7m 23.9s B,Italy 7m 31.5s
1952 G,USA (Charles Logg, Thomas Price) 8m 20.7s S,Belgium 8m 23.5s B,Switzerland 8m 32.7s
1956 G,USA (James Fifer, Duvall Hecht) 7m 55.4s S,USSR 8m 03.9s B,Austria 8m 11.8s
1960 G,USSR (Valentin Boreyko, Olyeg Golovanov) 7m 02.01s S,Austria 7m 03.69s B,Finland 7m 03.80s
1964 G,Canada (George Hungerford, Roger Jackson) 7m 32.94s S,Netherlands 7m 33.40s B,Germany 7m 38.63s
1968 G,East Germany (Jorg Lucke, Heinz Bothe) 7m 26.56s S,USA 7m 26.71s B,Denmark 7m 31.84s
1972 G,East Germany (Siegfried Brietzke, Wolfgang Mager) 6m 53.16s S,Switzerland 6m 57.06s B,Netherlands 6m 58.70s
1976 G,East Germany (J. Lanvoigt, B. Landvoigt) 7m 23.31s S,USA (C. Cofey, M. Staines) 7m 26.73s B,West Germany (P. Vanroye, T. Strauss) 7m 30.03s

COXED PAIRS
1986 Event not held
1900 G,Netherlands (Minerva, Amsterdam) 7m 34.2s S,France I 7m 34.4s B,France II 7m 57.2s
1904–1920 Event not held
1924 G,Switzerland (Eduard Candeveau, Alfred Felber, Emil Lachapelle (cox)) 8m 39.0s S,Italy 8m 39.1s B,USA
1928 G,Switzerland (Hans Schochlin, Karl Schochlin, H. Bourquin (cox)) 7m 42.6s S,France 7m 48.4s B,Belgium 7m 59.4s
1932 G,USA (Charles Kieffer, Joseph Schauers, Edward Jennings (cox)) 8m 25.8s S,Poland 8m 31.2s B,France 8m 41.2s
1936 G,Germany (Herbert Adamski, Gerhard Gustmann, Dieter Arend (cox)) 8m 36.9s S,Italy 8m 49.7s B,France 8m 54.0s
1948 G,Denmark (T. Henriksen, F. Pedersen, C. Anderson (cox)) 8m 00.5s S,Italy 8m 12.2s B,Hungary 8m 25.2s
1952 G,France (Raymond Salles, Gaston Mercier, Bernard Malivoire (cox)) 8m 28.6s S,Germany 8m 32.1s B,Denmark 8m 34.9s
1956 G,USA (Arthur Ayrault, F. Conn Findlay, Kurt Seiffert (cox)) 8m 26.1s S,Germany 8m 29.2s B,USSR 8m 31.0s
1960 G,Germany (Bernhard Knubel, Heinz Rennenberg, Klaus Zerta (cox)) 7m 29.14s S,USSR 7m 30.17s B,USA 7m 34.58s
1964 G,USA (Edward Ferry, Conn Findlay, Kent Mitchell (cox)) 8m 21.33s S,France 8m 23.15s B,Netherlands 8m 23.42s
1968 G,Italy (P Baran, R. Sambo, B. Cipolla) 8m 04.81s S,Netherlands 8m 06.80s B,Denmark 8m 08.07s
1972 G,East Germany (W. Gunkel, J. Lucke, K-D Neubert) 7m 17.25s S,Czechoslovakia 7m 19.57s B,Rumania 7m 21.36s

1976 G,East Germany (H. Jahrling, F. Ulrich, G. Spohr) 7m 58.99s S,USSR 8m 01.82s B,Czechoslovakia 8m 03.28s

COXLESS FOURS
1896 Event not held
1900 G,France I (Roubaix) 7m 11.0s S,France II 7m 18.0s B,Germany 7m 18.2s
1904 G,USA (Century BC. St Louis) 9m 53.8s S,USA (Western RC) B,USA (Independent RC, New Orleans)
1908 G,Great Britain (Magdalen BC. Oxford, Robert Cudmore, James Gillan, Duncan McKinnon, John Somers-Smith) 8m 34.0s S,Great Britain (Leander) 1¼ lengths
1912–1920 Event not held
1924 G,Great Britain (Trinity BC. Cambridge, Charles Eley, James McNabb, Robert Morrison, Robert Sanders) 7m 08.6s S,Canada 7m 18.0s B,Switzerland
1928 G,Great Britain (Trinity BC. Cambridge, Edward Bevan, Richard Beesly, M. Warriner, J. Lander) 6m 36.0s S,USA 6m 37.0s B,Italy 6m 37.0s
1932 G,Great Britain (George Rowland, Jack Beresford, Hugh Edwards, John Badcock) 6m 58.2s S,Germany 7m 03.0s B,Italy 7m 04.0s
1936 G,Germany (Wilhelm Menne, Martin Karl, Anton Romm, Rudolf Eckstein) 7m 01.8s S,Great Britain 7m 06.5s B,Switzerland 7m 10.6s
1948 G,Italy (Franco Faggi, Giovanni Invernizzi, Elio Morille, Giuseppe Moioli) 6m 39.0s S,Denmark 6m 43.5s B,USA 6m 47.7s
1952 G,Yugoslavia (Duje Bonacic, Velimir Valenta, Mate Trojanovic, Petar Sergvic) 7m 16.0s S,France 7m 18.9s B,Finland 7m 23.3s
1956 G,Canada (Archibald McKinnon, Lorne Loomer, I. Walter d'Hondt, Donald Arnold) 7m 08.8s S,USA 7m 18.4s B,France 7m 20.9s
1960 G,USA (Arthur Ayrault, Theodore Nash, John Sayre, Richard Wailes) 6m 26.26s S,Italy 6m 28.78s B,USSR 6m 29.62s
1964 G,Denmark (John Orsted Hansen, Bjorn Haslov, Erik Petersen, Kurt Helmudt) 6m 59.30s S,Great Britain 7m 00.47s B,USA 7m 01.37s
1968 G,East Germany (F. Forberger, D. Grahn, F. Ruhle, D. Schubert) 6m 39.18s S,Hungary 6m 41.64s B,Italy 6m 44.01s
1972 G,East Germany (F. Forberger, F. Ruhle, D. Grahn, D. Schubert) 6m 24.27s S,New Zealand 6m 25.64s B,West Germany 6m 28.41s
1976 G,East Germany (S. Brietzke, A. Decker, St. Semmler, W. Mager) 6m 37.42s S,Norway 6m 41.22s B,USSR 6m 42.52s

COXED FOURS
1896 Event not held
1900 G,Germany (Germania, Hamburg, Oskar Gossler, Katzenstein, Tietgens, G. Gossler, C. Gossler (cox)) 5m 59.0s S,Netherlands 6m 33.0s B,Germany 6m 35.0s

1904–1908 Event not held
1912 G,Germany (Ludwigshafen, Albert Arnheiter, Otto Fickeisen, Rudolf Fickeisen, Herman Wilker, Karl Leister (cox)) 6m 59.4s S,Great Britain
1920 G,Switzerland (Hans Walter, Max Rudolf, Willy Broderlin, Paul Rudolf) 6m 54.0s S,USA 6m 58.0s B,Norway 7m 01.0s
1924 G,Switzerland (Hans Walter, Alfred Probst, Emile Albrecht, Eugen Sigg, Walter Loosli (cox)) 7m 18.4s S,France 7m 21.6s B,USA
1928 G,Italy (Valerio Perentin, Giliante d'Este, Nicolo Vittori, Giovanni Delise, Renato Petronio (cox)) 6m 47.8s S,Switzerland 7m 03.4s B,Poland 7m 12.8s
1932 G,Germany (Joachim Spemberg, Walter Meyer, Horst Hoeck, Hans Eller, Karl Neumann (cox)) 7m 19.0s S,Italy 7m 19.2s B,Poland 7m 26.8s
1936 G,Germany (Paul Sollner, Ernst Gaber, Walter Voole, Hans Maier, Fritz Bauer (cox)) 7m 16.4s S,Switzerland 7m 24.3s B,France 7m 33.3s
1948 G,USA (Gordon Giovanelli, Robert Will, Robert Martin, Warren Westlund, Allen Morgan (cox)) 6m 50.3s S,Switzerland 6m 53.3s B,Denmark 6m 58.6s
1952 G,Czechoslovakia (Karel Mejta, Jiri Havlis, Jan Jindra, Stanislav Lusk, Miroslav Koranda (cox)) 7m 33.4s S,Switzerland 7m 36.5s B,USA 7m 37.0s
1956 G,Italy (Alberto Winkler, Romano Sgheiz, Angelo Vanzin, Franco Trincavelli, Ivo Stefanoni (cox)) 7m 19.4s S,Sweden 7m 22.4s B,Finland 7m 30.9s
1960 G,Germany (Gerd Cintl, Horst Effertz, Jurgen Litz, Klaus Riekemann, Michael Obst (cox)) 6m 39.12s S,France 6m 41.62s B,Italy 6m 43.72 s
1964 G,Germany (Peter Neusal, Bernhard Britting, Joachim Werner, Egbert Hirschfelder, Jurgen Oelke (cox)) 7m 00.44s S,Italy 7m 02.84s B,Netherlands 7m 06.46s
1968 G,New Zealand (R. Joyce, D. Storey, W. Cole, R. Collinge, S. Dickie) 6m 45.62s S,East Germany 6m 48.20s B,Switzerland 6m 49.04s
1972 G,West Germany (P. Berger, H-J Faerber, G. Auer, A. Bierl, U. Benter) 6m 31.85s S,East Germany 6m 33.30s B,Czechoslovakia 6m 35.64s
1976 G,USSR (V. Eshinov, N. Ivanov, M. Kuznetsov, A. Klepikov, A. Lukianov) 6m 40.22s S,East Germany 6m 42.70s B,West Germany 6m 46.96s

EIGHTS
1896 Event not held
1900 G,USA (Vesper BC, Philadelphia) 6m 09.8s S,Belgium (Club Nautique de Ghent) 6m 13.8s B,Netherlands (Minerva, Amsterdam) 6m 23.0s
1904 G,USA (Vesper BC, Philadelphia) 7m 50.0s S,Canada (Argonaut, Toronto)
1908 G,Great Britain (Leander, Albert Gladstone, Frederick Kelly, Banner Johnstone, Guy

Nickalls, Charles Burnell, Ronald Sanderson, Raymond Etherington-Smith, Henry Bucknall, Gilchrist Maclagen (cox)) 7m 52.0s S,Belgium (Club Nautique de Ghent) 2 lengths B,Great Britain (Cambridge University BC)
1912 G,Great Britain (Leander Club, Sidney Swann, Leslie Wormald, Ewart Horsfall, James Gillan, Arthur Garton, Alister Kirby, Philip Fleming, E. Burgess, Henry Wells (cox)) 6m 15.0s S,Great Britain (New College, Oxford) 6m 19.0s B,Germany
1920 G,USA (Navy) (Virgil Jacomini, Edwin Graves, William Jordan, Edward Moore, Allen Sanborn, Donald Johnston, Vincent Gallacher, Clyde King, Sherman Clark (cox)) 6m 02.6s S,Great Britain (Leander Club) 6m 05.8s B,Norway 6m 36.0s
1924 G,USA (Yale BC, Carpentier, Kingsbury, Frederick, Lindley, Miller, Rockefeller, Sheffield, Spock, Stoddard (cox)) 6m 33.4s S,Canada 6m 49.0s B,Italy
1928 G,USA (University of California, M. Stalder, J. Brinck, F. Frederick, Walter Thompson, W. Dally, J. Workman, Hubert Caldwell, P. Donlon, Donald Blessing (cox)) 6m 03.2s S,Great Britain 6m 03.6s B,Canada 6m 03.8s
1932 G,USA (University of California, Winslow Hall, Harold Tower, Charles Chandler, Burton Jastram, David Dunlap, Duncan Gregg, James Blair, Edwin Salisbury, Norris Graham (cox)) 6m 37.6s S,Italy 6m 37.8s B,Canada 6m 40.4s
1936 G,USA (Washington University, Donald Hume, Joseph Rantz, George Hunt, James McMillin, John White, Gordon Adam, Charles Day, Herbert Morris, Robert Moch (cox)) 6m 25.8s S,Italy 6m 26.0s B,Germany 6m 26.4s
1948 G,USA (University of California, John Stack, Justus Smith, David Brown, Lloyd Butler, George Ahlgreen, James Hardy, David Turner, Jean Turner, Ralph Purchase (cox)) 5m 56.7s S,Great Britain 6m 06.9s B,Norway 6m 10.3s
1952 G,USA (Navy, Frank Shakespeare, William Fields, James Dunbar, Richard Murphy, Robert Detweiler, Henry Proctor, Wayne Frye, Edward Stevens, Charles Manring (cox)) 6m 25.9s S,USSR 6m 31.2s B,Australia 6m 33.1s
1956 G,USA (Yale University, Thomas Charlton, David Wight, John Cooke, Donald Beer, Caldwell Esselstyn, Charles Grimes, Richard Wailes, Robert Morey, William Becklean (cox)) 6m 35.2s S,Canada 6m 37.1s B,Australia 6m 39.2s
1960 G,Germany (Klaus Bittner, Karl-Heinz Hopp, Hans Lenk, Manfred Rulffs, Frank Schepke, Kraft Schepke, Walter Schroder, Karl von Groddeck, Willi Padge (cox)) 5m 57.18s S,Canada 6m 01.52s B,Czechoslovakia 6m 04.84s

1964 G,USA (Joseph Amlong, Thomas Amlong, Harold Budd, Emory Clark, Stanley Cwiklinski, Hugh Foley, William Knecht, William Stowe, Robert Zimonyi (cox)) 6m 18.23s S,Germany 6m 23.29s B,Czechoslovakia 6m 25.11s ·
1968 G,West Germany (Meyer, Schreyer, Henning, Ulbricht, Hottenrott, Hirschfelder, Siebert, Bose, Thiersch) 6m 07.00s S,Australia 6m 07.98s B,USSR 6m 09.11s
1972 G,New Zealand (Hurt, Veldman, Joyce, Hunter, Wilson, Earl, Coker, Robertson, Dickie) 6m 08.94s S,USA 6m 11.61s B,East Germany 6m 11.67s
1976 G,East Germany (B. Baumgart, G. Dohn, W. Klatt, J. Luck, D. Wendisch, R. Kostulski, U. Karnatz, K. Prudohl, K. Danielowski) 5m 58.29s S,Great Britain 6m 00.82s B,New Zealand 6m 03.51s

Rowing (Women)
SINGLE SCULLS
1896–1972 Event not held
1976 G,C. Sheiblich (East Germany) 4m 05.56s S,J. Lind (USA) 4m 06.21s B,E. Antonova (USSR) 4m 10.24s
DOUBLE SCULLS
1896–1972 Event not held
1976 G,Bulgaria (S. Otzetova, Z. Yordanova) 3m 44.36s S,East Germany 3m 47.86s B,USSR 3m 49.93s
COXED FOURS SCULLS
1896–1972 Event not held
1976 G,East Germany (A. Borchmann, J. Lau, V. Poley, R. Zobelt, L. Weigelt) 3m 29.99s S,USSR 3m 32.76s B,Bulgaria 3m 34.13s
COXLESS PAIRS
1896–1972 Event not held
1976 G,Bulgaria (S. Kelbetcheva, S. Grouitcheva) 4m 01.22s S,East Germany 4m 01.64s B,West Germany 4m 02.35s
COXED FOURS
1896–1972 Event not held
1976 G,East Germany (K. Metze, B. Schwede, G. Lohs, A. Kurth, S. Hess) 3m 45.08s S,Bulgaria 3m 48.24s B,USSR 3m 49.38s
EIGHTS
1896–1972 Event not held
1976 G,East Germany (V. Goretzki, C. Knetsch, I. Richter, B. Ahrenholz, M. Kallies, H. Ebert, H. Lehmann, I. Muller, M. Wilke) 3m 32.48s S,USSR 3m 36.17s B,USA 3m 38.68s

Shooting
SPORT PISTOL (RANGE 50 METRES)
1936 G,Thorsten Ullman (Sweden) 559 pts. S,Erich Krempel (Germany) 544 B,Charles des Jammonieres (France) 540
1948 G,Cam Vasquez (Peru) 545 pts. S,Rudolf Schnyder (Switzerland) 539 B,Thorsten Ullmann (Sweden) 539
1952 G,Huelet Benner (USA) 553 pts. S,Angel Leon (Spain) 550 B,Ambrus Balogh (Hungary) 549
1956 G,Pentti Linnosvuo (Finland) 556 pts. S,Makhmoud Oumarov (USSR) 556 B,Offutt Pinion

(USA) 551
1960 G,Aleksey Gustchin (USSR) 560 pts. S,Makhmoud Oumarov (USSR) 552 B,Yoshihisa Yoshikawa (Japan) 552
1964 G,Vaino Markkanen (Finland) 560 pts. S,Franklin Green (USA) 557 B,Yoshihisa Yoshikawa (Japan) 554
1968 G,Gregory Kosykh (USSR) 562 pts. S, Heinz Mertel (West Germany) 562 B,Harald Vollmar (East Germany) 560
1972 G,Ragnar Skanakar (Sweden) 567 pts. S,Dan Iuga (Rumania) 562 B,Rudolf Dollinger (Austria) 560
1976 G,U. Potteck (East Germany) 573 pts. S,H. Vollmar (East Germany) 567 B,R. Dollinger (Austria) 562

RAPID FIRE PISTOL (RANGE 25 METRES)
1948 G,Karoly Takacs (Hungary) 580 pts. S,Enrique Diaz Saenz Valiente (Argentina) 571 B,S. Lundquist (Sweden) 569
1952 G,Karoly Takacs (Hungary) 579 pts. S,Szilard Kun (Hungary) 578 B,Gheorghe Lichiardopol (Rumania) 578
1956 G,Stefan Petrescu (Rumania) 587 pts. S,Evgeniy Tcherkassov (USSR) 585 B,Gheorghe Lichiardopol (Rumania) 581
1960 G,William McMillan (USA) 587 pts. S,Pentti Linnosvuo (Finland) 587 B,A. Zabelin (USSR) 587
1964 G,Pentti Linnosvuop (Finland) 592 S,Ion Tripsa (Rumania) 591 B,Lubomi Nacovsky (Czechoslovakia) 590
1968 G,Jozef Zapedzki (Poland) 593 pts. S,Marcel Rosca (Rumania) 591 B,Renart Sulleimanov (USSR) 591
1972 G,Jozef Zapedzki (Poland) 595 pts. S,Ladislav Faita (Czechoslovakia) 594 B,Victor Torshin (USSR) 593
1976 G,N. Klaar (East Germany) 597 pts. S,J. Wiefel (East Germany) 596 B,R. Ferraris (Italy) 595

SMALL-BORE RIFLE— PRONE
1896 Event not held
1900 G,A. Carnell (Great Britain)
1904 Event not held
1908 G,A. Carnell (Great Britain) 387 pts. S,H. Humby (Great Britain) 386 B,G. Barnes (Great Britain) 385
1912 G,Frederick Hird (USA) 194 pts. S,W. Milne (Great Britain) 193 B,H. Burt (Great Britain) 192
1920 G,Lawrence Nuesslein (USA) 391 pts. S,Arthur Rothrock (USA) 386 B,Dennis Fenton (USA) 385
1924 G,Charles Coquelin de Lisle (France) 398 pts. S,M. Dinwiddie (USA) 396 B,Josias Hartmann (Switzerland) 394
1928 Event not held
1932 G,Bartil Ronmark (Sweden) 294 pts. S,Gustavo Huest (Mexico) 294 B,Zoltan Hradetsky-Soos (Hungary) 293
1936 G,Willy Rogeberg (Norway) 300 pts. S,Ralph Berzsenyi (Hungary) 296

Wladyslav Karas (Poland) 296
1948 G,Arthur Cook (USA)
599 pts. S,Walter Tomsen
(USA) 599 B,Jonas Jonsson
(Sweden) 597
1952 G,Josif Sarbu (Rumania)
400 pts. S,Boris Andreyev
(USSR) 400 B,Arthur Jackson
(USA) 399
1956 G,Gerald Quellette
(Canada) 600 pts. S,Vasiliy
Borisov (USSR) 599
B,Gilmour Boa (Canada) 598
1960 G,Peter Kohnke
(Germany) 590 pts. S,James
Hill (USA) 589 B,P. Forcella
(Venezuela) 587
1964 G,Laszlo Hammerl
(Hungary) 597 pts. S,Lones
Wigger (USA) 597 B,Tommy
Pool (USA) 596
1968 G,Jan Kurka
(Czechoslovakia) 598 pts.
S,Laszlo Hammer (Hungary)
598 B,Ian Ballinger (New
Zealand) 597
1972 G,Ho Jun Li (Korea)
599 pts. S,Victor Auer (USA)
598 B,Nicolae Rotaru
(Rumania) 598
1976 G,K. Smieszek (West
Germany) 599 pts. S,U. Lind
(West Germany) 597 B,G.
Lushchikov (USSR) 595

SMALL-BORE RIFLE—THREE POSITIONS
1896–1948 Event not held
1952 G,Erling Kongshaug
(Norway) 1,164 pts. S,Vilho
Ylonen (Finland) 1,164
B,Boris Andreyev (USSR)
1,163
1956 G,Anatoliy Bogdanov
(USSR) 1,172 pts. S,Otto
Horinek (Czechoslovakia)
1,172 B,Nils Sundverg
(Sweden) 1,167
1960 G,Viktor Shamburkin
(USSR) 1,149 pts. S,Marat
Nyesov (USSR) 1,145
B,Klaus Zaehriger (Germany)
1,139
1964 G,Lones Wigger (USA)
1,164 pts. S,Velitchko Hustov
(Bulgaria) 1,152 B,Laszlo
Hammerl (Hungary) 1,151
1968 G,Bernd Klingner (West
Germany) 1,157 pts. S,John
Writer (USA) 1,156 B,Vitaly
Parkhimovich (USSR) 1,154
1972 G,John Writer (USA)
1,166 pts. S,Lanny Bassham
(USA) 1,157 B,Werner Lippoldt
(East Germany) 1,153
1976 G,L. Bassham (USA)
1,162 pts. S,M. Murdock (USA)
1,162 B,W. Seibold (West
Germany) 1,160

OLYMPIC TRAP
1896 Event not held
1900 G,W. Ewing (Canada)
1904 Event not held
1908 G,W. Ewing (Canada)
72 pts. S,G. Beattie (Canada)
60 B,Alexander Maunder
(Great Britain) 57, Anastassios
Metaxas (Greece) 57
1912 G,James Graham (USA)
96 pts. S,Alfred Goeldel
(Germany) 94 B,Harry Blau
(Russia) 91

OLYMPIC SKEET
1920 G,Mark Arie (USA) 95
pts. S,Frank Troeh (USA)
93 B,Frank Wright (USA) 87
1924 G,Gyula Halasy
(Hungary) 98 pts. S,Konrad
Hubert (Finland) 98 B,Frank
Hughes (USA) 97
1928–1948 Event not held
1952 G,Georges Genereux
(Canada) 192 pts. S,Knut

Holmqvist (Sweden) 191
B,Hans Liljedahl (Sweden) 190
1956 G,Galliano Rossini
(Italy) 195 pts. S,Adam
Smelczynski (Poland) 190
B,Alessandro Ciceri (Italy) 188
1960 G,Ion Dumitrescu
(Rumania) 192 pts. S,Galliano
Rossini (Italy) 191 B,S. Kalinin
(USSR) 190
1964 G,Ennio Mattarelli (Italy)
198 pts. S,Pavel Senichev
(USSR) 194 B,William Morris
(USA) 194
1968 G,Robert Braithwaite
(Great Britain) 198 pts. S,Tom
Garrigus (USA) 196 B,Kurt
Czekalla (East Germany) 196
1972 G,Angelo Scalzone (Italy)
199 pts. S,Michel Carrega
(France) 198 B, Silvano
Basagni (Italy) 195
1976 G,D. Haldeman (USA)
190 pts. S,A. Silva Marques
(Portugal) 189 B,U. Baldi
(Italy) 189

RUNNING GAME TARGET
1896–1964 Event not held
1968 G,Evgeny Petrov (USSR)
198(25) pts. S,Romano
Garagnani (Italy) 198(24–25)
B,Konrad Wirnhier (West
Germany) 198 (24–23)
1972 G,Konrad Wirnhier (West
Germany) 195 pts. S,Evgeny
Petrov (USSR) 195 B,Mickael
Buchheim (East Germany) 195
1976 G,J. Panacek
(Czechoslovakia) 198 pts.
S,E. Swinkels (Holland) 198
B,W. Gawlikowski (Poland) 196
1896 Event not held
1900 G,Louis Debray (France)
20 S,P. Nivet (France) 20,
de Lambert (France) 19.
1904–1968 Event not held
1972 G,L. Zhelezniak (USSR)
569 S,H. Bellingrodt (Columbia)
565 B,J. Kynoch (Great Britain) 562
1976 G,A. Gazov (USSR) 579
S,A. Kedyarov (USSR) 576
B,J. Grezkiewicz (Poland) 571

Soccer
1896–1904 Event not held
1908 G,Great Britain (Harold
Bailey, W. S. Corbett, Herbert
Smith, Kenneth Hunt,
Frederick Chapman, Robert
Hawkes, Arthur Berry, Vivian
Woodward, Hubert Stapley,
Claude Purnell, Harold
Hardman) S,Denmark
B,Netherlands
1912 G,Great Britain (Ronald
Brebner, Thomas Burn, Arthur
Knight, Douglas McWhirter,
Horace Littlewort, James Dines,
Arthur Berry, Vivian Woodward,
Harold Walden, Gordon
Hoare, Ivan Sharpe, Hanney,
Stamper, Wright) S,Denmark
B,Netherlands
1920 G,Belgium (Jan de Bie,
Armand Swartenbroecks, Oscar
Verbeek, Joseph Masch,
Emile Hause, Andre Fierens,
Louis van Hegge, Robert
Coppee, Mathieu Bragard,
Henri Larnoe, Desire Bastin,
Nisot, Hebdin, Bally)
S,Spain. B,Netherlands
1924 G,Uruguay (Mazzali,
Jose Nasazzi, Arispe, Jose
Andrade, Vidal Ghierra,
A. Urdinaran, Hector Scarone.
Pedro Petrone, Cea, Romano,
Tomasina, Naya, Zibechi.
S. Urdinaran) S,Switzerland
B,Sweden
1928 G,Uruguay (Mazzali,

Jose Nasazzi, Arispe, Jose
Andrade, Lorenzo Fernandez,
Alvaro Gestido, S. Urdinaran,
Castro, Pedro Petrone, Pedro
Cea, Hector Scarone, Campolo,
Aremon, Borjas, Piriz, Canavesi,
Figueroa) S,Argentina B,Italy
1932 Event not held
1936 G,Italy (Bruno Venturini
Alfredo Foni, Pietro Rava,
Giuseppe Baldo, Achille Piccini,
Ugo Locatelli, Annibale Frossi,
Libero Marchini, Sergio
Bertoni, Carlo Biagi, Francesco
Gabriotti, Luigi Scarabello,
Giulio Cappelli, Alfonso Negro)
S,Austria B,Norway
1948 G,Sweden (Torsten
Lindberg, Knut Nordahl, Erik
Nilsson, Birger Rosengren,
Bertil Nordahl, Sune Andersson,
Kjell Rosen, Gunnar Gren,
Gunnar Nordahl, Henry
Carlsson, Nils Liedholm,
Borje Leander, Garvis Carlsson,
Rune Emanuelsson, Stellan
Nilsson, Stig Nystrom, Karl
Svensson) S,Yugoslavia
B,Denmark
1952 G,Hungary (Gyula
Grosics, Jeno Buzanszky, Gyula
Lorant, Mihaly Lantos,
Jozsef Bozsik, Nandor
Hidegkuit, Sandor Kocsis,
Peter Palotas, Ferenc Puskas,
Zoltan Csibor, Sandor Geller,
Janos Brozsei, Jeno Dalnoki,
Imre Kovacs, Ferenc Szojka
Laszlo Budai, Lajos Csordas)
S,Yugoslavia B,Sweden
1956 G,USSR (Lev Yashin,
Boris Kuznyetsov, Mikhail
Ogognikov, Aleksey
Paramanov, Anatoliy
Bashashkin, Igor Netto, Boris
Tatushin, Anatoliy Isayev,
Edouard Streltsov, Sergey
Salnikov, Anatoliy Ilin,
Anatoliy Maslenkin, Nikita
Simonian, Nikolay Tyshenko,
Vladimir Rykkin, Josif Betsa)
S,Yugoslavia B,Bulgaria
1960 G,Yugoslavia (Blagoje
Vidinic, Vladimir Djurkovic,
Fahrudin Yusufi, Ante Zanetic,
Novak Ragonovic, Zeljko
Perusic, Andreja Ankovic,
Zeljko Maius, Milan Galic,
Tomislav Knez, Borivoje Kostic,
Velimir Sambelac, Alexsandar
Kozlina, Dusan Maravic,
Silvester Takac, Milutin
Soskic) S,Denmark B,Hungary
1964 G,Hungary (Antal
Szentmihalyi, Dezso Novak,
Kalman Ihasz, Arpad Orban,
Ferenc Nogradi, Janos Farkas,
Tibor Csernai, Ferenc Bene,
Imre Komora, Gustav Szepesi,
Sandor Katona, Jozsef Gelei,
Karoly Palotai, Zoltan Varga)
S,Czechoslovakia B,Germany
1968 G,Hungary (Karoly Fater,
Dezso Novak, Lajos Drestyak,
Miklos Pancsics, Ivan Menczel,
Lajos Szucs, Laszlo Fazekas,
Antal Dunai, Laszlo Nagy,
Erno Nosko, Istvan Juhasz)
S,Bulgaria B,Japan
1972 G,Poland (Hubert Kostka,
Zbigniew Gut, Jerzy Gorgon,
Zygmunt Anczok, Leslaw
Cmikiewicz, Jerzy Kraska,
Kazimierz Deyna, Zygfryd
Szoltysik, Wlodzimierz Lubanski,
Robert Gadocha, Ryszard
Szymczak, Antoni Szymanowski
Marian Ostafinski, Kazimierz
Kmiecik, Zygmunt Maszczyk,
Joachim Marx, Grzegorz Lato)
S,Hungary B,East Germany.
USSR

1976 G,East Germany (Croy,
Dorner, Weise, Kurbjuweit,
Lauck, Hafner, Riediger
(Bransch), Hoffmann, Kische,
Lowe (Grobner), Schade)
S,Poland. B,USSR

Swimming and Diving (Men)
100 METRES BREASTSTROKE
1896–1964 Event not held
1968 G,Donald McKenzie
(USA) 1m 07.7s S,Valdamir
Kosinsky (USSR) 1m 08.0s
B,Nicolay Pankin (USSR)
1m 08.0s
1972 G,Nobutaka Taguchi
(Japan) 1m 04.94s S,Tom
Bruce (USA) 1m 05.43s
B,John Hencken (USA)1m 05.61s
1976 G,J. Hencken (USA)
1m 03.11s S,D. Wilkie (Great
Britain) 1m 03.43s B,A.
Iuozaytis (UUSR) 1m 04.23s
100 METRES BACKSTROKE
1896–1904 Event not held
1908 G,A. Bieberstein
(Germany) 1m 24.6s S,L. Dam
(Denmark) B,Haresnape
(Great Britain)
1912 G,H. Hebner (USA)
1m 21.2s S,O. Fahr (Germany)
B,P. Kellner (Germany)
1920 G,W. Kealoha (USA)
1m 15.2s S,R. K. Kergeris
(USA) B,G. Blitz (Belgium)
1924 G,W. Kealoha (USA)
1m 13.2s S,P. Wyatt (USA)
B,C. Bartha (Hungary)
1928 G,G. Kojac (USA)
1m 8.2s S,W. Laufer (USA)
B,P. Wyatt (USA)
1932 G,M. Kiyokawa (Japan)
1m 8.6s S,T. Irie (Japan)
B,K. Kawatsu (Japan)
1936 G,A. Kiefer (USA)
1m 5.9s S,A. van de Weghe
(USA) B,M. Kiyokawa (Japan)
1948 G,A. Stack (USA)
1m 6.4s S,R. Cowell (USA)
B,C. Vallery (France)
1952 G,Y. Oyakawa (USA)
1m 5.7s S,G. Bozon (France)
B,J. Taylor (USA)
1956 G,D. Theile (Australia)
1m 2.2s S,J. Monckton
(Australia) B,F. McKinney
(USA)
1960 G,D. Thiele (Australia)
1m 1.9s S,F. McKinney (USA)
B,R. Bennett (USA)
1964 Event not held
1968 G,Roland Matthes
(East Germany) 58.7s
S,Charles Hickcox (USA)
1m 00.2s B,Ronnie Mills (USA)
1m 00.5s
1972 G,Roland Matthes (East
Germany) 56.58 pts S,Mike
Stamm (USA) 57.70 B,John
Murphy (USA) 58.35
1976 G,J. Naber (USA) 55.49s
S,P. Rocca (USA) 56.34s
B,R. Matthes (East Germany)
57.22s
100 METRES FREESTYLE
1896 G,Alfred Hajos (Hungary)
1m 22.2s S,Gardrez Williams
(USA) 1m 23.0s B,Otto
Herschmann (Austria)
1900 Event not held
1904 G,Zoltan Halmay
(Hungary) 1m 02.8s S,Charles
Daniels (USA) B,Scott
Leary (USA) (100 yds)
1908 G,Charles Daniels (USA)
1m 05.6s S,Zoltan Halmay
(Hungary) 1m 06.2s B,Harald
Julin (Sweden) 1m 08.8s
1912 G,Duke Kahanamoku

(USA) 1m 03.4s S,Cecil Healy (Australia) 1m 04.6s B,Kenneth Huszagh (USA) 1m 05.6s
1920 G,Duke Kahanamoku (USA) 1m 00.4s S,Pua Kealoha (USA) 1m 02.2s B,William Harris (USA) 1m 03.2s
1924 G,Johnny Weismuller (USA) 59.0s S,Duke Kahanamoku (USA) 1m 01.4s B,Samuel Kahanamoku (USA) 1m 01.8s.
1928 G,Johnny Weismuller (USA) 58.6s S,Istvan Barany (Hungary) 59.8s B,Katsuo Takaishi (Japan) 1m 00.0s
1932 G,Yasuji Miyazaki (Japan) 58.2s S,Tatsugo Kawaishi (Japan) 58.6s B,Albert Schwartz (USA) 58.8s
1936 G,Ferenc Csik (Hungary) 57.6s S,Masanori Yusa (Japan) 57.9s B,Shigeo Arai (Japan) 58.0s
1948 G,Walter Ris (USA) 57.3s S,Alan Ford (USA) 57.8s B,Geza Kadas (Hungary) 58.1s
1952 G,C. Clarke Scholes (USA) 57.4s S,Hiroshi Suzuki (Japan) 57.4s B,Goran Larsson (Sweden) 58.2s
1956 G,Jon Henricks (Australia) 55.4s S,John Devitt (Australia) 55.8s B,Gary Chapman (Australia) 56.7s
1960 G,John Devitt (Australia) 55.2s S,Lance Larson (USA) 55.2s B,Manoel dos Santos (Brazil) 55.4s
1964 G,Donald Schollander (USA) 53.4s S,Robert McGregor (Great Britain) 53.5s B,Hans Klein (Germany) 54.0s
1968 G,Michael Wenderi (Australia) 52.2s S,Kenneth Walsh (USA) 52.8s B,Mark Spitz (USA) 53.0s
1972 G,Mark A. Spitz (USA) 51.22 pts S,Jerry Heidenreich (USA) 51.65 B,Vladimir Bure (USSR) 51.77
1976 G,J. Montgomery (USA) 49.99s S,J. Babashoff (USA) 50.81s B,P. Nocke (West Germany) 51.31s

200 METRES FREESTYLE
1896 Event not held
1900 G,Frederick Lane (Australia) 2m 25.29s S,Zoltan Halmay (Hungary) 2m 31.0s B,Karl Ruberl (Austria) 2m 32.0s
1904 G,Charles Daniels (USA) 2m 44.2s S,Francis Gailey (USA) 2m 46.0s B,Emil Rausch (Germany) 2m 56.0s
1908-1964 Event not held
1968 G,Michael Wenden (Australia) 1m 55.2s S,Don Schollander (USA) 1m 55.8s B,John Nelson (USA) 1m 58.1s
1972 G,Mark A. Spitz (USA) 1m 52.78s S,Steven Genter (USA) 1m 53.73s B,Werner Lampe (West Germany) 1m 53.99s
1976 G,B. Furniss (USA) 1m 50.29s S,J. Naber (USA) 1m 50.50s B,J. Montgomery 1m 50.58s

400 METRES FREESTYLE
1896-1900 Event not held
1904 G,Charles Daniels (USA) 6m 16.2s S,Francis Gailey (USA) 6m 22.0s B,Otto Wahle (Austria) 6m 39.0s (440 yds)

1908 G,Henry Taylor (Great Britain) 5m 36.8s S,Frank Beaurepaire (Australasia) 5m 44.2s B,Otto Scheff (Austria) 5m 46.0s
1912 G,George Hodgson (Canada) 5m 24.4s S,John Hatfield (Great Britain) 5m 25.8s B,Harold Hardwick (Australia) 5m 31.2s
1920 G,Norman Ross (USA) 5m 26.8s S,Ludy Langer (USA) 5m 29.2s B,George Vernot (Canada) 5m 29.8s
1924 G,Johnny Weismuller (USA) 5m 04.2s S,Arne Borg (Sweden) 5m 05.6s B,Andrew Charlton (Australia) 5m 06.6s
1928 G,Alberto Zorilla (Argentina) 5m 01.6s S,Andrew Charlton (Australia) 5m 03.6s B,Arne Borg (Sweden) 5m 04.6s
1932 G,Clarence Crabbe (USA) 4m 48.8s S,Jean Taris (France) 4m 48.5s B,Tsutoma Oyokota (Japan) 4m 52.3s
1936 G,Jack Medica (USA) 4m 44.5s S,Shumpei Uto (Japan) 4m 45.6s B,Shozo Makino (Japan) 4m 48.1s
1948 G,William Smith (USA) 4m 41.0s S,James McLane (USA) 4m 43.4s B,John Marshall (Australia) 4m 47.7s
1952 G,Jean Boiteux (France) 4m 30.7s S,Ford Konno (USA) 4m 31.3s B,Per-Olof Ostrand (Sweden) 4m 35.2s
1956 G,Murray Rose (Australia) 4m 27.3s S,Tsuyoshi Yamanaka (Japan) 4m 30.4s B,George Breen (USA) 4m 32.5s
1960 G,Murray Rose (Australia) 4m 18.3s S,Tsuyoshi Yamanaka (Japan) 4m 21.4s B,Jon Konrads (Australia) 4m 21.8s
1964 G,Donald Schollander (USA) 4m 12.2s S,Frank Wiegand (Germany) 4m 14.9s B,Allan Wood (Australia) 4m 15.1s
1968 G,Michael Burton (USA) 4m 09.0s S,Ralph Hutton (Canada) 4m 11.7s B,Alain Mosconi (France) 4m 13.3s
1972 G,Bradford P. Cooper (Australia) 4m 00.27s S,Steven Genter (USA) 4m 01.94 B,Tom McBreen (USA) 4m 02.64s
1976 G,B. Goodell (USA) 3m 51.93s S,T. Shaw (USA) 3m 52.54s B,V. Raskatov (USSR) 3m 55.76s

1500 METRES FREESTYLE
1896-1900 Event not held
1904 Emil Rausch (Germany) 27m 18.2s S,Geza Kiss (Hungary) -28m 28.2s B,Francis Gailey (USA) 28m 54.0s (1 mile)
1908 G,Henry Taylor (Great Britain) 22m 48.4s S,Thomas Battersby (Great Britain) 22m 51.2s B,Frank Beaurepaire (Australia) 22m 56.2s
1912 G,George Hodgson (Canada) 22m 00.0s S,John Hatfield (Great Britain) 22m 39.0s B,Harold Hardwick (Australia) 23m 15.4s
1920 G,Norman Ross (USA) 22m 23.2s S,George Vernot (Canada) 22m 36.4s B,Frank Beaurepaire (Australia) 23m 04.0s
1924 G,Andrew Charlton (Australia) 20m 06.6s S,Arne Borg (Sweden) 20m 41.4s

B,Frank Beaurepaire (Australia) 20m 48.4s
1928 G,Arne Borg (Sweden) 19m 51.8s S,Andrew Charlton (Australia) 20m 02.6s B,Clarence Crabbe (USA) 20m 28.8s
1932 G,Kusuo Kitamure (Japan) 19m 12.4s S,Shozo Makino (Japan) 19m 14.1s B,James Christy (USA) 19m 39.5s
1936 G,Norboru Terada (Japan) 19m 13.7s S,Jack Medica (USA) 19m 34.0s B,Shumpei Uto (Japan) 19m 34.5s
1948 G,James McLane (USA) 19m 18.5s S,John Marshall (Australia) 19m 31.3s B,Gyorgy Mitro (Hungary) 19m 43.2s
1952 G,Ford Konno (USA) 18m 30.3s S,Shiro Hashizume (Japan) 18m 41.4s B,Tetsuo Okamoto (Brazil) 18m 51.3s
1956 G,Murray Rose (Australia) 17m 58.9s S,Tsuyoshi Yamanaka (Japan) 18m 00.3s B,George Breen (USA) 18m 08.2s
1960 G,Jon Konrads (Australia) 17m 19.6s S,Murray Rose (Australia) 17m 21.7s B,George Breen (USA) 17m 30.6s
1964 G,Robert Windle (Australia) 17m 01.7s S,John Nelson (USA) 17m 03.0s B,Allan Wood (Australia) 17m 07.7s
1968 G,Michael Burton (USA) 16m 38.9s S,John Kinsella (USA) 16m 57.3s B,Gregory Brough (Australia) 17m 04.7s
1972 G,Michael J. Burton (USA) 15m 52.58s S,Graham Windeatt (Australia) 15m 58.48s B,Douglas Northway (USA) 16m 09.25s
1976 G,B. Goodell (USA) 15m 02.40s S,B. Hackett (USA) 15m 03.91s B,S. Holland (Australia) 15m 04.66s

200 METRES BREASTSTROKE
1896-1903 Event not held
1908 G,Frederick Holman (Great Britain) 3m 09.2s S,W. W. Robinson (Great Britain) 3m 12.8s B,Pontus Hansson (Sweden) 3m 11.6s
1912 G,Walter Bathe (Germany) 3m 01.8s S,Wilhelm Lutzow (Germany) 3m 05.0s B,Paul Malisch (Germany) 3m 08.0s
1920 G,Hakan Malmroth (Sweden) 3m 04.4s S, Thor Henning (Sweden) 3m 09.2s B,Arvo Aaltonen (Finland) 3m 12.2s
1924 G,Robert Skelton (USA) 2m 56.6s S,Joseph de Combe (Belgium) 2m 59.2s B,William Kirschbaum (USA) 3m 01.0s
1928 G,Yoshiyuki Tsuruta (Japan) 2m 48.8s S,Eirch Rademacher (Germany) 2m 50.6s B,Teofilo Yldefonso (Philippines) 2m 56.4s
1932 G,Yoshiyuki Tsuruta (Japan) 2m 45.4s S,Reizo Koike (Japan) 2m 46.4s B,Teofilo Yldefonso (Philippines) 2m 47.1s
1936 G,Tetsuo Hamuro (Japan) 2m 42.5s S,Erwin Sietas (Germany) 2m 42.9s B,Reizo Koike (Japan) 2m 44.2s
1948 G,Joseph Verdeur (USA) 2m 39.3s S,Keith

Carter (USA) 2m 40.2s B,Robert Sohl (USA) 2m 43.9s
1952 G,John Davies (Australia) 2m 34.4s S,Bowen Stassforth (USA) 2m 34.7s B,Herbert Klein (Germany) 2m 35.9s
1956 G,Masura Furukawa (Japan) 2m 34.7s S,Masahiro Yoshimura (Japan) 2m 36.7s B,Kharis Yunishev (USSR) 2m 36.8s
1960 G,William Mulliken (USA) 2m 37.4s S,Yoshihiko Ohsaki (Japan) 2m 38.0s B,Wieger Mensonides (Netherlands) 2m 39.7s
1964 G,Ian O'Brien (Australia) 2m 27.8s S,Georgy Prokopenko (USSR) 2m 28.2s B,Chester Jastremski (USA) 2m 29.6s
1968 G,Felipe Munoz (Mexico) 2m 28.7s S,Vladimir Kosinsky (USSR) 2m 29.2s B,Brian Job (USA) 2m 29.9s
1972 G,John Hencken (USA) 2m 2m 21.55s S,David A. Wilkie (Great Britain) 2m 23.67s B,Nobutaka Taguchi (Japan) 2m 23.88s
1976 G,D. Wilkie (Great Britain) 2m 15.11s S,J. Hencken (USA) 2m 17.26s B,R. Colella (USA) 2m 19.20s

100 METRES BUTTERFLY
1896-1964 Event not held
1968 G,Douglas Rusell (USA) 55.9s S,Mark Spitz (USA) 56.4s B,Ross Wales (USA) 57.2s
1972 G,Mark A. Spitz (USA) 54.27s S,Bruce Robertson (Canada) 55.56s B,Jerry Heidenreich (USA) 55.74s
1976 G,M. Vogel (USA) 54.35s S,J. Bottom (USA) 54.50s B,G. Hall (USA) 54.65s

200 METRES BUTTERFLY
1896-1952 Event not held
1956 G,William Yorzyk (USA) 2m 19.3s S,Takashi Ishimoto (Japan) 2m 23.8s B,Gyorgy Tumpek (Hungary) 2m 23.9s
1960 G,Michael Troy (USA) 2m 12.8s S,Neville Hayes (Australia) 2m 14.6s B,J. David Gillanders (USA) 2m 15.3s
1964 G,Kevin Berry (Australia) 2m 06.6s S,Carl Robie (USA) 2m 07.5s B,Fred Schmidt (USA) 2m 09.3s
1968 G,Carl Robie (USA) 2m 08.7s S,Martin Woodroffe (Great Britain) 2m 09.0s B,John Ferris (USA) 2m 09.3s
1972 G,Mark A. Spitz (USA) 2m 00.70s S,Gary Hall (USA) 2m 02.86s B,Robin Backhaus (USA) 2m 03.23s
1976 G,M. Bruner (USA) 1m 59.23s S,S. Gregg (USA) 1m 59.54s B,B. Forrester (USA) 1m 59.96s

200 METRES BACKSTROKE
1896 Event not held
1900 G,Ernst Hoppenberg (Germany) 2m 47.0s S,Karl Ruberl (Austria) 2m 56.0s B,F. Dooxt (Netherlands) 3m 01.0s
1904-1960 Event not held
1964 G,Jed Graef (USA) 2m 10.3s S,Gary Dilley (USA) 2m 10.5s B,Robert Bennett (USA) 2m 13.1s
1968 G,Roland Matthes (East Germany) 2m 09.6s S,Mitchell Ivey (USA) 2m 10.6s B,Jack

Horsley (USA) 2m 10.9s
1972 G,Roland Matthes (East Germany) 2m 02.82s S,Mike Stamm (USA) 2m 04.09s B,Mitchell Ivey (USA) 2m 04.33s
1976 G,J. Naber (USA) 1m 59.19s S,P. Rocca (USA) 2m 00.55s B,D. Harrigan (USA) 2m 01.35s

4×100 METRES INDIVIDUAL MEDLEY
1896–1960 Event not held
1964 G,Richard Roth (USA) 4m 45.5s S,Roy Saari (USA) 4m 47.1s B,Gerhard Hetz (Germany) 4m 51.0s
1968 G,Charles Hickcox (USA) 4m 48.4s S,Gary Hall (USA) 4m 48.7s B,Michael Holthaus (West Germany) 4m 51.4s
1972 G,Gunnar Larsson (Sweden) 4m 31.98s S,Tim McKee (USA) 4m 31.98s B,Andras Hargitay (Hungary) 4m 32.70s
1976 G,R. Strachan (USA) 4m 23.68s S,T. McKee (USA) 4m 24.62s B,A. Smirnov (USSR) 4m 26.90s

4×200 METRES FREESTYLE RELAY
1896–1904 Event not held
1908 G,Great Britain (John Derbyshire, Paul Radmilovic, Willie Foster, Henry Taylor) 10m 55.6s S,Hungary 10m 59.0s B,USA 11m 02.8s
1912 G,Australasia (Cecil Healy, Malcolm Champion, Leslie Boardman, Harold Hardwick) 10m 11.6s S,USA 10m 20.2s B,Great Britain 10m 28.2s
1920 G,USA (Perry McGillivray, Pua Kealoha, Norman Ross, Duke Kahanamoku) 10m 04.4s S,Australia 10m 25.4s B,Great Britain 10m 37.2s
1924 G,USA (Wallace O'Connor, Harry Glancy, Ralph Breyer, Johnny Weissmuller) 9m 53.4s S,Australia 10m 02.2s B,Sweden 10m 06.8s
1928 G,USA (Austin Clapp, Walter Laufer, George Kojac, Johnny Weissmuller) 9m 36.2s S,Japan 9m 41.4s B,Canada 9m 47.8s
1932 G,Japan (Yasuji Miyazaki, Takashi Yokoyama, Masanori Yusa, Hisakichi Toyoda) 8m 58.4s S,USA 9m 10.5s B,Hungary 9m 31.4s
1936 G,Japan (Masanori Yusa, Shigeo Shigeo Sugiura, Masaharu Taguchi, Shigeo Arai) 8m 51.5s S,USA 9m 03.0s B,Hungary 9m 12.3s
1948 G,USA (Walter Ris, Wallace Wolf, James McLane, William Smith) 8m 46.0s S,Hungary 8m 48.4s B,France 9m 08.0s
1952 G,USA (Wayne Moore, William Woolsey, Ford Konno, James McLane) 8m 31.1s S,Japan 8m 33.5s B,France 8m 45.9s
1956 G,Australia (Kevin O'Halloran, John Devitt, Murray Rose, Jon Henricks) 8m 23.6s S,USA 8m 31.5s
1960 G,USA (George Harrison, Richard Blick, Michael Troy, F. Jeffrey Farrell) 8m 10.2s S,Japan 8m 13.2s B,Australia 8m 13.8s
1964 G,USA (Stephen Clark, Roy Saari, Gary Ilman, Don Schollander) 7m 51.2s S,Germany 7m59.3s B,Japan 8m 03.8s

1968 G,USA (John Nelson, S. Rerych, Mark Spitz, Don Schollander) 7m 52.3s S,Australia 7m 53.7s B,USSR 8m 01.6s
1972 G,USA (John Kinsella, Frederick Tyler, Steven Genter, Mark A. Spitz) 7m 35.78s S,West Germany 7m 41.69s B,USSR 7m 45.76s
1976 G,USA (M. Brauner, B. Furniss, J. Naber, J. Montgomery) 7m 23.22s S,USSR 7m 27.97s B,Great Britain 7m 32.11s

4×100 METRES MEDLEY RELAY
1896–1956 Event not held
1960 G,USA (Frank McKinney, Paul Hait, Lance Larson, F. Jeffrey Farrell) 4m 05.4s S,Australia 4m 12.0s B,Japan 4m 12.2s
1964 G,USA (Harold Mann, William Craig, Fred Schmidt, Stephen Clark) 3m 58.4s S,Germany 4m 01.6s B,Australia 4m 02.3s
1968 G,USA (Charles Hickcox, Donald McKenzie, Douglas Russell, Kenneth Walsh) 3m 54.9s S,East Germany 3m 57.5s B,USSR 4m 00.7s
1972 G,USA (Mike Stamm, Tom Bruce, Mark A. Spitz, Jerry Heidenreich) 3m 48.16s S,East Germany 3m 52.12s B,Canada 3m 52.26s
1976 G,USA (J. Naber, J. Hencken, M. Vogel, J. Montgomery) 3m 42.22s S,Canada 3m 45.94s B,West Germany 3m 47.29s

PLATFORM DIVING
1896–1904 Event not held
1908 G,Hjalmar Johansson (Sweden) 83.75 pts. S,K. Malmstrom (Sweden) 78.73 B,A. Spangberg (Sweden) 74
1912 G,Erik Alderz (Sweden) 73.94 pts. S,Albert Zurner (Germany) 72.60 B,Gustaf Blomgren (Sweden) 69.56
1920 G,Clarence Pinkston (USA) 100.67 pts. S,Erik Adlerz (Sweden) 99.08 B,Harry Prieste (USA) 93.73
1924 G,Albert White (USA) 97.46 pts. S,D. Fall (USA) 97.30 B,Clarence Pinkston (USA) 94.60
1928 G,Peter Desjardins (USA) 98.74 pts. S,Farid Simaika (Egypt) 98.58 B,Michael Galitzen (USA) 92.34
1932 G,Harold Smith (USA) 124.80 pts. S,Michael Galitzen (USA) 124.28 B,Frank Kurtz (USA) 121.98
1936 G,Marshall Wayne (USA) 113.58 pts. S,Elbert Root (USA) 110.60 B,Hermann Stork (Germany) 110.31
1948 G,Samuel Lee (USA) 130.05 pts. S,Bruce Harlan (USA) 122.30 B,Joaquin Capilla (Mexico) 113.52
1952 G,Samuel Lee (USA) 156.28 pts. S,Joaquin Capilla (Mexico) 145.21 B,Gunther Haase (Germany) 141.31
1956 G,Joaquin Capilla (Mexico) 152.44 pts. S,Gary Tobian (USA) 152.41 B,Richard Connor (USA) 149.79
1960 G,Robert Webster (USA) 165.56 pts. S,Gary Tobian (USA) 165.25 B,Brian Phelps (Great Britain)

1964 G,Robert Webster (USA) 148.58 pts. S,Klaus Dibiasi (Italy) 147.54 B,Tom Gompi (USA) 146.57
1968 G,Klaus Dibiasi (Italy) 164.18 pts. S,Alvaro Gaxiola (Mexico) 154.49 B,Ed Young (USA) 153.93
1972 G,Klaus Dibiasi (Italy) 504.12 pts. S,Richard Rydze (USA) 480.75 B,Franco Cagnotto (Italy) 475.83
1976 G,K. Dibiasi (Italy) 600.51 pts. S,G. Louganis (USA) 576.99 B,V. Aleynik (USSR) 548.61

SPRINGBOARD DIVING
1896–1904 Event not held
1908 G,Albert Zurner (Germany) 85.5 pts. S,Kurt Behrens (Germany) 85.3 B, George Gaidzik (USA) 80.8 Gottlob Walz (Germany) 80.8
1912 G,Paul Gunther (Germany) 79.23 pts. S,Hans Luber (Germany) 76.78 B,Kurt Behrens (Germany) 73.73
1920 G,Louis Kuehn (USA) 675 pts. S,Clarence Pinkston (USA) 655.3 B,Louis Balbach (USA) 649.5
1924 G,Albert White (USA) 696.4 pts. S,Peter Desjardins (USA) 693.2 B,Clarence Pinkston (USA) 653
1928 G,Peter Desjardins (USA) 185.04 pts. S,Michael Galitzen (USA) 174.06 B,Farid Simaika (Egypt) 172.46
1932 G,Michael Galitzen (USA) 161.38 pts. S,Harold Smith (USA) 158.54 B, Richard Degener (USA) 151.82
1936 G,Richard Degener (USA) 163.57 pts. S,Marshall Wayne (USA) 159.56 B,Al Greene (USA) 146.29
1948 G,Bruce Harlan (USA) 163.64 pts. S,Miller Anderson (USA) 157.29 B,Samuel Lee (USA) 145.52
1952 G,David Browning (USA) 205.29 pts. S,Miller Anderson (USA) 199.84 B,Robert Clotworthy (USA) 184.92
1956 G,Robert Clotworthy (USA) 159.56 pts. S,Donald Harper (USA) 156.23 B,Joaquin Capilla (Mexico) 150.69
1960 G,Gary Tobian (USA) 170.00 pts. S,Samuel Hall (USA) 167.08 B,Juan Botella (Mexico) 162.30
1964 G,Ken Sitzberger (USA) 159.90pts. S,Frank Gorman (USA) 157.63 pts. B,Larry Andreasen (USA) 143.77
1968 G,Bernard Wrightson (USA) 170.15 pts. S,Klaus Dibiasi (Italy) 159.74 B,James Henry (USA) 158.09
1972 G,Vladimir Vasin (USSR) 594.09 pts. S,Franco Cagnotto (Italy) 591.63 B,Craig Lincoln (USA) 577.29
1976 G,P. Boggs (USA) 619.05 pts. S,F. Cagnatto (Italy) 570.48 B,A. Kosenkov (USSR) 567.24

Swimming and Diving (Women)
100 METRES FREESTYLE
1896–1908 Event not held
1912 G,Fanny Durack (Australasia) 1m 22.2s S,Wilhelmina Wylie (Australasia) 1m 25.4s B,Jennie Fletcher (Great Britain) 1m 27.0s
1920 G,Ethelda Bleibtrey

(USA) 1m 13.6s S,Irene Guest (USA) 1m 17.0s B,Frances Schroth (USA) 1m 17.2s
1924 G,Ethel Lackie (USA) 1m 12.4s S,Mariechen Wehselau (USA) 1m 12.8s B,Gertrude Ederle (USA) 1m 14.2s
1928 G,Albina Osipowich (USA) 1m 11.0s S,Eleonora Garatti (USA) 1m 11.4s B,Margaret Cooper (Great Britain) 1m 13.6s
1932 G,Helene Madison (USA) 1m 06.8s S,Willemijnte den Ouden (Netherlands) 1m 07.8s B,Eleonora Saville (USA) 1m 08.2s
1936 G,Hendrika Mastenbroek (Netherlands) 1m 05.9s S,Jeanette Campbell (Argentina) 1m 06.4s B,Gisela Arendt (Germany) 1m 06.6s
1948 G,Greta Andersen (Denmark) 1m 06.3s S,Ann Curtis (USA) 1m 06.5s B,Marie-Louise Vaessen (Netherlands) 1m 07.6s
1952 G,Katalin Szoke (Hungary) 1m 06.8s S,Johanna Termeulen (Netherlands) 1m 07.0s B,Judit Temes (Hungary) 1m 07.1s
1956 G,Dawn Fraser (Australia) 1m 02.0s S,Lorraine Crapp (Australia) 1m 02.3s B,Faith Leech (Australia) 1m 05.1s
1960 G,Dawn Fraser (Australia) 1m 01.2s S,Christine von Saltza (USA) 1m 02.8s B,Natalie Steward (Great Britain) 1m 03.1s
1964 G,Dawn Fraser (Australia) 59.5s S,Sharon Stouder (USA) 59.9s B,Kathleen Ellis (USA) 1m 00.8s
1968 G,Jan Henne (USA) 1m 00.0s S,Sue Pedersen (USA) 1m 00.3s B,Linda Gustavson (USA) 1m 00.3s
1972 G,Sandra Neilson (USA) 58.59s S,Shirley Babashoff (USA) 59.02s B,Shane E. Gould (Australia) 59.06s
1976 G,K. Ender (East Germany) 55.65s S,P. Priemer (East Germany) 56.49s B,E. Brigitha (Holland) 56.65s

220 METRES FREESTYLE
1896– 1964 Event not held
1968 G,Debbie Meyer (USA) 2m 10.5s S,Jan Henne (USA) 2m 11.0s B,Jane Barkman (USA) 2m 11.2s
1972 G,Shane E. Gould (Australia) 2m 03.56s S,Shirley Babashoff (USA) 2m 04.33s B,Keena Rothammer (USA) 2m 04.92s
1976 G,K. Ender (East Germany) 1m 59.26s S,S. Babashoff (USA) 2m 01.22s B,E. Brigitha (Holland) 2m 01.40s

400 METRES FREESTYLE
1896–1920 Event not held
1924 G,Martha Norelius (USA) 6m 02.2s S,Helen Wainwright (USA) 6m 03.8s B,Gertrude Ederle (USA) 6m 04.8s
1928 G,Martha Norelius (USA) 5m 42.8s S,Marie Braun (Netherlands) 5m 57.8s B,Josephine McKim (USA) 6m 00.2s
1932 G,Helene Madison (USA) 5m 28.5s S,Lenore Kight (USA) 5m 28.6s B,Jennie Maakal (South Africa) 5m 47.3s
1936 G,Hendrika Mastenbroek

(Netherlands) 5m 26.4s
S,Ranghild Hveger (Denmark)
5m 27.5s B,Lenore Wingard
(USA) 5m 29.0s
1948 G,Ann Curtis (USA)
5m 17.8s S,Karen Harup
(Denmark) 5m 21.2s B,Cathie
Gibson (Great Britain)
5m 22.5s
1952 G,Valeria Gyenge
(Hungary) 5m 12.1s S,Eva
Novak (Hungary) 5m 13.7s
B,Evelyn Kawamoto (USA)
5m 14.6s
1956 G,Lorraine Crapp
(Australia) 4m 54.6s S,Dawn
Fraser (Australia) 5m 02.5s
B,Sylvia Ruuska (USA)
5m 07.1s
1960 G,Christine von Saltza
(USA) 4m 50.6s S,Jane
Cederqvist (Sweden) 4m 53.9s
B,Tineke Lagerberg
(Netherlands) 4m 56.9s
1964 G,Virginia Duenkel
(USA) 4m 43.3s S,Marilyn
Ramenofsky (USA) 4m 44.6s
B,Terri Stickles (USA) 4m 47.2s
1968 G,Debbie Meyer (USA)
4m 31.8s S,Linda Gustavson
(USA) 4m 35.5s B,Karen
Moras (Australia) 4m 37.0s
1972 G,Shane E. Gould
(Australia) 4m 19.04s S,Novella
Calligaris (Italy) 4m 22.44s
B,Gudrun Weger (East Germany)
4m 23.11s
1976 G,P. Thumer (East
Germany) 4m 09.89s S,S.
Babashoff (USA) 4m 10.46s
B,S. Smith (Canada) 4m 14.60s

800 METRES FREESTYLE
1896–1964 Event not held
1968 G,Debbie Meyer (USA)
9m 24.0s S,Pam Kruse (USA)
9m 35.7s B,Maria Teresa
Ramirez (Mexico) 9m 38.5s
1972 G,Keena Rothhammer
(USA) 8m 53.68s S,Shane E.
Gould (Australia) 8m 56.39s
B,Novella Calligaris (Italy)
8m 57.46s
1976 G,P. Thumer (East
Germany) 8m 37.14s S,S.
Babashoff (USA) 8m 37.59s
B,W. Weinberg (USA) 8m 42.60s

200 METRES BUTTERFLY
1896–1964 Event not held
1968 G,Ada Kok (Netherlands)
2m 24.7s S,Helga Lindner
(East Germany) 2m 24.8s
B,Ellie Daniel (USA) 2m 25.9s
1972 G,Karen Moe (USA)
2m 15.57s S,Lynn Colella (USA)
2m 16.34s B,Ellie Daniel (USA)
2m 16.74s
1976 G,A. Pollack (East
Germany) 2m 11.41s
S,U. Tauber (East Germany)
2m 12.70s B,R. Gabriel (East
Germany) 2m 12.86s

200 METRES BACKSTROKE
1896–1964 Event not held
1968 G,Pokey Watson (USA)
2m 24.8s S,Elaine Tanner
(Canada) 2m 27.4s B,Kaye Hall
(USA) 2m 28.9s
1972 G,Melissa Belote (USA)
2m 19.19s S,Susie Atwood
(USA) 2m 20.38s B,Donna
Marie Gurr (Canada) 2m 23.22s
1976 G,U. Richter (East
Germany) 2m 13.43s S,B. Treiber
(East Germany) 2m 14.97s
B,N. Garapick (Canada)
2m 15.60s

100 METRES BREASTSTROKE
1896–1964 Event not held
1968 G,Djurdijca Bjedov

(Yugoslavia) 1m 15.8s
S,Galina Prozumenshikova
(USSR) 1m 15.9s B,Sharon
Wichman (USA) 1m 16.1s
1972 G,Catherine Carr (USA)
1m 13.58s S,Galina Stepanova
(USSR) 1m 14.99s B,Beverley
J. Whitfield (Australia)
1m 15.73s
1976 G,H. Anke (East Germany)
1m 11.16s S,L. Rusanova
(USSR) 1m 13.04s B,M.
Koshevaia (USSR) 1m 13.30s

200 METRES BREASTSTROKE
1896–1920 Event not held
1924 G,Lucy Morton (Great
Britain) 3m 33.2s S,Agnes
Geraghty (USA) 3m 34.0s
B,Gladys Carson (Great
Britain) 3m 35.4s
1928 G,Hilde Schrader
(Germany) 3m 12.6s S,Marie
Baron (Netherlands) 3m 15.2s
B,Lotte Muhe-Hildensheim
(Germany) 3m 17.6s
1932 G,Clare Dennis
(Australia) 3m 06.3s S,Hideko
Maehata (Japan) 3m 06.4s
B,Else Jacobson (Denmark)
3m 07.1s
1936 G,Hideko Maehata
(Japan) 3m 03.6s S,Martha
Genenger (Germany) 3m 04.2s
B,Inge Sorenson (Denmark)
3m 07.8s
1948 G,Petronella van Vliet
(Netherlands) 2m 57.2s
S,Beatrice Lyons (Australia)
2m 57.7s B,Eva Novak
(Hungary) 3m 00.2s
1952 G,Eva Szekely (Hungary)
2m 51.7s S,Eva Novak
(Hungary) 2m 54.4s B,Helen
Gordon (Great Britain)
2m 57.6s
1956 G,Ursula Happe
(Germany) 2m 53.1s S,Eva
Szekely (Hungary) 2m 54.8s
B,Eva-Maria ten Elsen
(Germany) 2m 55.1s
1960 G,Anita Lonsbrough
(Great Britain) 2m 49.5s
S,Wiltrud Urselmann
(Germany) 2m 50.0s
B,Barbara Gobel (Germany)
2m 53.6s
1964 G,Galina
Prozumenschikova (USSR)
2m 46.4s S,Claudia Kolb
(USA) 2m 47.6 B,Svetlana
Babanina (USSR) 2m 48.6s
1968 G,Sharon Wichman
(USA) 2m 44.4s S,Djurdjica
Bjedov (Yugoslavia) 2m 46.4s
B,Galina Prozumenshchikova
(USSR) 2m 47.0s
1972 G,Beverley J. Whitfield
(Australia) 2m 41.71s S,Dana
Schoenfield (USA) 2m 42.05s
B,Galina Stepanova (USSR)
2m 42.36s
1976 G,M. Koshevaia (USSR)
2m 33.35s S,M. Lurchenia
(USSR) 2m 36.08s B,L.
Rusanova (USSR) 2m 36.22s

100 METRES BUTTERFLY
1896–1952 Event not held
1956 G,Shelley Mann (USA)
1m 11.0s S,Nancy Jane
Ramey (USA) 1m 11.9s
B,Mary Jane Sears (USA)
1m 14.4s
1960 G,Carolyn Schuler (USA)
1m 09.5s S,Marian Heemskerk
(Netherlands) 1m 10.4s
B,Janice Andrew (Australia)
1m 12.2s
1964 G,Sharon Stouder (USA)
1m 04.7s S,Ada Kok
(Netherlands) 1m 05.6s

B,Kathleen Ellis (USA)
1m 06.0s
1968 G,Lynn McClements
(Australia) 1m 05.5s S,Ellie
Daniel (USA) 1m 05.8s
B,S. Shields (USA) 1m 06.2s
1972 G,Mayumi Aoki (Japan)
1m 03.34s S,Roswitha Beier
(East Germany) 1m 03.61s
B,Andrea Gyarmati (Hungary)
1m 03.73s
1976 G,K. Ender (East Germany)
1m 00.13s S,A. Pollack (East
Germany) 1m 00.98s
B,W. Boglioli (USA) 1m 01.17s

100 METRES BACKSTROKE
1896–1920 Event not held
1924 G,Sybil Bauer (USA)
1m 23.2s S,Phyllis Harding
(Great Britain) 1m 27.4s
B,Aileen Riggin (USA)
1m 28.2s
1928 G,Marie Braun
(Netherlands) 1m 22.0s
S,Elizabeth King (Great
Britain) 1m 22.2s B,Margaret
Cooper (Great Britain)
1m 22.8s
1932 G,Eleanor Holm (USA)
1m 19.4s S,Philomena Mealing
(Australia) 1m 21.3s
B,Elizabeth Davies (Great
Britain) 1m 22.5s
1936 G,Dina Senff
(Netherlands) 1m 18.9s
S,Hendrika Mastenbroek
(Netherlands) 1m 19.2s
B,Alice Bridges (USA)
1m 19.4s
1948 G,Karen Harup
(Denmark) 1m 14.4s
S,Suzanne Zimmermann (USA)
1m 16.0s B,Judy Joy Davies
(Australia) 1m 16.7s
1952 G,Joan Harrison (South
Africa) 1m 14.3s S,Geertje
Wielema (Netherlands)
1m 14.5s B,Jean Stewart
(New Zealand) 1m 15.8s
1956 G,Judy Grinham (Great
Britain) 1m 12.9s S,Carin
Cone (USA) 1m 12.9s
B,Margaret Edwards (Great
Britain) 1m 13.1s
1960 G,Lynn Burke (USA)
1m 09.3s S,Natalie Steward
(Great Britain) 1m 10.8s
B,Satoko Tanaka (Japan)
1m 11.4s
1964 G,Cathy Ferguson (USA)
1m 07.7s S,Christine Caron
(France) 1m 07.9s B,Virginia
Duenkel (USA) 1m 08.0s
1968 G,Kaye Hall (USA)
1m 06.2s S,Elaine Tanner
B,J. Swagerty (USA)
1m 08.1s
1972 G,Melissa Belote (USA)
1m 05.78s S,Andrea Gyarmati
(Hungary) 1m 06.26s B,Susie
Atwood (USA) 1m 06.34s
1976 G,U. Richter (East
Germany) 1m 01.83s S,B.
Treiber (East Germany)
1m 03.41s
B,N. Garapick (Canada)
1m 03.71s

4×100 METRES INDIVIDUAL MEDLEY
1896–1960 Event not held
1964 G,Donna de Varona
(USA) 5m 18.7s S,Sharon
Finneran (USA) 5m 24.1s
B,Martha Randall (USA)
2m 24.2s
1968 G,Claudia Kolb (USA)
5m 08.5s S,L. Vidali (USA)
5m 22.2s B,S. Steinbach
(East Germany) 5m 25.3s
1972 G,Gail Neall (Australia)
5m 02.97s S,Leslie Cliff

(Canada) 5m 03.57s
B,Novella Calligaris (Italy)
5m 03.99s
1976 G,U. Tauber (East
Germany) 4m 42.77s S,C.
Gibson (Canada) 4m 48.10s
B,B. Smith (Canada) 4m 50.48s

4×100 METRES FREESTYLE RELAY
1896–1908 Event not held
1912 G,Great Britain
(Bella Moore, Irene Steer,
Annie Speirs, Jennie Fletcher)
5m 52.8s S,Germany 6m 04.6s
B,Austria 6m 17.0s
1920 G,USA (Ethelda
Bleibtrey, Frances Schroth,
Irene Guest, Margaret
Woodbridge) 5m 11.6s
S,Great Britain 5m 40.8s
B,Sweden 5m 43.6s
1924 G,USA (Gertrude Ederle,
Mariechen Wehselau, Ethel
Lackie, Euphrasia Donelly)
4m 58.8s S,Great Britain
5m 17.0s B,Sweden 5m 35.8s
1928 G,USA (Adelaide
Lambert, Albina Osipowich,
Eleonora Garatti, Martha
Norelius) 4m 47.6s S,Great
Britain 5m 02.8s B,South
Africa 5m 13.4s
1932 G,USA (Josephine
McKim, Elenora Saville,
Helen Johns, Helene Madison)
4m 38.0s S,Netherlands
4m 46.5s B,Great Britain
4m 52.4s
1936 G,Netherlands
(Johanna Selbach, Catherina
Wagner, Willemijnte den
Ouden, Hendrika Mastenbroek)
4m 30.s S,Germany 4m 36.8s
B,USA 4m 40.2s
1948 G,USA (Marie Corridon,
Thelma Kalama, Brenda Helser,
Ann Curtis) 4m 20.2s
S,Denmark 4m 29.6s
B,Netherlands 4m 31.6s
1952 G,Hungary (Ilona Novak,
Judit Temes, Eva Novak, Katalin
Szoke) 4m 24.4s
S,Netherlands 4m 29.0s
B,USA 4m 30.1s
1956 G,Australia (Dawn
Fraser, Faith Leech, Sandra
Morgan, Lorraine Crapp)
4m 17.1s S,USA 4m 19.2s
B,South Africa 4m 25.7s
1960 G,USA (Joan Spillane,
Shirley Stobs, Carolyn Wood,
Christine von Saltza) 4m 08.9s
S,Australia 4m 11.3s
B,Germany 4m 19.7s
1964 G,USA (Sharon Stouder,
Donna de Varona, Lilian
Watson, Kathleen Ellis)
4m 33.9s S,Netherlands
4m 37.0s B,USSR 4m 39.2s
1968 G,USA (J. Barkman,
L. Gustavson, S. Pedersen,
J. Henne) 4m 02.5s S,East
Germany 4m 05.7s B,Canada
4m 07.2s
1972 G,USA (Sandra Neilson,
Jennifer Kemp, Jane Barkmann,
Shirley Babashoff) 3m 55.19s
S,East Germany 3m 55.55s
B,West Germany 3m 57.93s
1976 G,USA (K. Peyton,
W. Boglioli, J. Sterkel,
S. Babashoff) 3m 44.82s
S,East Germany 3m 45.50s
B,Canada 3m 48.81s

4×100 METRES MEDLEY RELAY
1896–1956 Event not held
1960 G,USA (Lynn Burke,
Patty Kempner, Carolyn
Schuler, Christine von Saltza)
4m 41.1s S,Australia 4m 45.9s
B,Germany 4m 47.6s

1964 G,USA (Cathy Ferguson, Cynthia Goyette Sharon Stouder, Kathleen Ellis) 4m 03.8s **S**,Australia 4m 06.9s **B**,Netherlands 4m 12.0s
1968 G,USA (Kaye Hall, Catie Ball, Ellie Daniel, Sue Pedersen) 4m 28.3s **S**,Australia 4m 30.0s **B**,West Germany 4m 36.4s
1972 G,USA (Melissa Belote, Catherine Carr, Deena Deardurff, Sandra Neilsen) 4m 20.75s **S**,East Germany 4m 24.91s **B**,West Germany 4m 26.46s
1976 G,East Germany (U. Richter, A. Hanelor, A. Pollack, K. Ender) 4m 07.95s **S**,USA 4m 14.55s **B**,Canada 4m 15.22s

PLATFORM DIVING
1896–1908 Event not held
1912 G,Greta Johansson (Sweden) 39.9 pts. **S**,Lisa Regnell (Sweden) 36 **B**,Isabelle White (Great Britain) 34
1920 G,Stefani Fryland-Clausen (Denmark) 34.6 pts. **S**,E. Armstrong (Great Britain) 33.3 **B**,Eva Ollivier (Sweden) 32.6
1924 G,Caroline Smith (USA) 10.5, 166 pts. **S**,Elisabeth Becker (USA) 11, 167 **B**,Hjordis Topel (Sweden) 15.5, 164
1928 G,Betty Pinkston (USA) 31.6 pts **S**,Georgia Coleman (USA) 30.6 **B**,Lala-Sjoquist (Sweden) 29.2
1932 G,Dorothy Poynton (USA) 40.26 pts **S**,Georgia Coleman (USA) 35.56 **B**,Marion Roper (USA) 35.22
1936 G,Dorothy Hill (USA) 33.93 pts. **S**,Velma Dunn (USA) 33.63 **B**,Kathe Kohler (Germany) 33.43
1948 G,Victoria Draves (USA) 68.87 pts. **S**,Patricia Elsener (USA) 66.28 **B**,Birte Christoffersen (Denmark) 66.04
1952 G,Patricia McCormick (USA) 79.37 pts. **S**,Paula Jean Myers (USA) 71.63 **B**,Juno Irwin (USA) 70.49
1956 G,Patricia McCormack (USA) 84.85 pts. **S**,Juno Irwin (USA) 81.64 **B**,Paula Jean Myers (USA) 81.58
1960 G,Ingrid Kramer (Germany) 91.28 pts. **S**,Paula Jean Pope (USA) 88.94 **B**,Ninel Krutova (USSR) 86.99
1964 G,Lesley Bush (USA) 99.80 pts. **S**,Ingrid Engel (Germany) 98.45 **B**,Galina Alekseyeva (USSR) 97.60
1968 G,Milena Duchkova (Czechoslovakia) 109.59 pts. **S**,Natalya Lobanova (USSR) 105.14 **B**,Ann Petersen (USA) 101.11
1972 G,Ulrika Knape (Sweden) 390.00 pts. **S**,Milena Duchková (Czechoslovakia) 370.92 **B**,Marina Janicke (East Germany) 360.54
1976 G,E. Vaytsekhovskaia (USSR) 406.59 pts. **S**,U. Knape (Sweden) 402.60 **B**,D. Wilson (USA) 401.07

SPRINGBOARD DIVING
1896–1912 Event not held
1920 G,Aileen Riggin (USA) 539.9 pts. **S**,Helen Wainwright (USA) 534.8 **B**,Thelma Payne (USA) 534.1
1924 G,Elisabeth Becker (USA) 474.5 pts. **S**,Aileen Riggin (USA) 460.4 **B**, Caroline Fletcher (USA) 434.4
1928 G,Helen Meany (USA) 78.62 pts. **S**,Dorothy Poynton (USA) 75.62 **B**,Georgia Coleman (USA) 73.38
1932 G,Georgia Coleman (USA) 87.52 pts. **S**,Katherine Rawls (USA) 82.56 **B**,Jane Fauntz (USA) 81.12
1936 G,Marjorie Gestring (USA) 89.27 pts. **S**,Katherine Rawls (USA) 88.35 **B**, Dorothy Hill (USA) 82.36
1948 G,Victoria Draves (USA) 108.74 pts. **S**,Zoe Ann Olsen (USA) 108.23 **B**,Patricia Elsener (USA) 101.30
1952 G,Patricia McCormick (USA) 147.30 pts. **S**,Madelaine Moreau (France) 139.34 **B**,Zoe Ann Jensen (USA) 127.57
1956 G,Patricia McCormick (USA) 142.36 pts. **S**,Jeanne Stunyo (USA) 125.89 **B**,Irene Macdonald (Canada) 121.40
1960 G,Ingrid Kramer (Germany) 155.81 pts. **S**,Paula Jean Pope (USA) 141.24 **B**,Elizabeth Ferris (Great Britain) 139.09
1964 G,Ingrid Engel (Germany) 145.00 pts. **S**,Jeanne Collier (USA) 138.36 **B**,Patsy Willard (USA) 138.18
1968 G,Sue Gossick (USA) 150.77 pts. **S**,Tamara Pogozheva (USSR) 145.30 **B**,Keala O'Sullivan (USA) 145.73
1972 G,Micki J. King (USA) 450.03 pts. **S**,Ulrika Knape (Sweden) 434.19 **B**,Marina Janicke (East Germany) 430.92
1976 G,J. Chandler (USA) 506.19 pts. **S**,C. Kohler (East Germany) 469.41 **B**,C. McIngvale (USA) 466.83

Track and Field Athletics (Men)
100 METRES
1896 G,Thomas Burke (USA) 12.0s **S**,Fritz Hofmann (Germany) **B**,Alajos Szokolyi (Hungary)
1900 G,Frank Jarvis (USA) 11.0s **S**,J. Walter Tewksbury (USA) **B**,Stan Rowley (Australia)
1904 G,Archie Hahn (USA) 11.0s **S**,Nathan Cartmell (USA) **B**,William Hogensen (USA)
1908 G,Reginald Walker (South Africa) 10.8s **S**,James Rector (USA) **B**,Robert Kerr (Canada)
1912 G,Ralph Craig (USA) 10.8s **S**,Alvah Meyer (USA) 10.9s **B**,Donald Lippincott (USA) 10.9s
1920 G,Carles Paddock (USA) 10.8s **S**,Morris Kirksey (USA) **B**,Harry Edward (Great Britain)
1924 G,Harold Abrahams (Great Britain) 10.6s **S**,Jackson Scholz (USA) **B**,Arthur Porritt (New Zealand)
1928 G,Percy Williams (Canada) 10.8s **S**,Jack London (Great Britain) **B**,Georg Lammers (Germany)
1932 G,Eddie Tolan (USA) 10.3s **S**,Ralph Metcalfe (USA) 10.3s **B**,Arthur Jonath (Germany) 10.4s
1936 G,Jesse Owens (USA) 10.3s **S**,Ralph Metcalfe (USA) 10.4s **B**,Martinus Osendarp (Netherlands) 10.5s

200 METRES
1896 Event not held
1900 G,J. Walter Tewksbury (USA) 22.2s **S**,Norman Pritchard (India) **B**,Stan Rowley (Australia)
1904 G,Archie Hahn (USA) 21.6s **S**,Nathan Cartmell (USA) **B**,William Hogenson (USA)
1908 G,Robert Kerr (Canada) 22.6s **S**,Robert Cloughen (USA) **B**,Nathan Cartmell (USA)
1912 G,Ralph Craig (USA) 21.7s **S**,Donald Lippincott (USA) 21.8s **B**,William Appelgarth (Great Britain) 22.0s
1920 G,Allen Woodring (USA) 22.0s **S**,Charles Paddock (USA) **B**,Harry Edward (Great Britain)
1924 G,Jackson Scholz (USA) 21.6s **S**,Charles Paddock (USA) **B**,Eric Liddell (Great Britain)
1928 G,Percy Williams (Canada) 21.8s **S**,Walter Rangeley (Great Britain) **B**,Helmut Kornig (Germany)
1932 G,Eddie Tolan (USA) 21.2s **S**,George Simpson (USA) 21.4s **B**,Ralph Metcalfe (USA) 21.5s
1936 G,Jesse Owens (USA) 20.7s **S**,Mack Robinson (USA) 21.1s **B**,Martinus Osendarp (Netherlands) 21.3s
1948 G,Melvin Patton (USA) 21.1s **S**,H. Norwood Ewell (USA) 21.1s **B**,Lloyd La Beach (Panama) 21.2s
1952 G,Andy Stanfield (USA) 20.7s **S**,W. Thane Baker (USA) 20.8s **B**,James Gathers (USA) 20.8s
1956 G,Bobby Morrow (USA) 20.6s **S**,Andy Stanfield (USA) 20.7s **B**,W. Thane Baker (USA) 20.9s
1960 G,Livio Berutti (Italy) 20.5s **S**,Les Carney (USA) 20.6s **B**,Abdoulaye Seye (France) 20.7s
1964 G,Henry Carr (USA) 20.3s **S**,Paul Drayton (USA) 20.5s **B**,Edwin Roberts (Trinidad) 20.6s
1968 G,Tommie Smith (USA) 19.8s **S**,Peter Norman (Australia) 20.0s **B**,John Carlos (USA) 20.0s
1972 G,Valeriy Borzov (USSR) 20.00s **S**,Larry J. Black (USA) 20.19s **B**,Pietro Mennea (Italy) 20.30s
1976 G,D. Quarrie (Jamaica) 20.23s **S**, M. Hampton (USA) 20.29s **B**, D. Evans (USA) 20.43s

400 METRES
1896 G,Thomas Burke (USA) 54.2s **S**,Herbert Jameson (USA) 55.2s **B**,Fritz Hofmann (Germany)
1900 G,Maxwell Long (USA) 49.4s **S**,William. Holland (USA) **B**,Ernst Schultz (Denmark)
1904 G,Harry Hillman (USA) 49.2s **S**,Frank Waller (USA) **B**,H. C. Groman (USA)
1908 G,Wyndham Halswell (Great Britain) 50.0s 'walk over' no other competitors
1912 G,Charles Reidpath (USA) 48.2s **S**,Hanns Braun (Germany) 48.3s **B**,Edward Lindberg (USA) 48.4s
1920 G,Bevil Rudd (South Africa) 49.6s **S**,Guy Butler (Great Britain) **B**,Nils Engdahl (Sweden)
1924 G,Eric Liddell (Great Britain) 47.6s **S**,Horatio Fitch (USA) 48.4s **B**,Guy Butler (Great Britain) 48.6s
1928 G,Raymond Barbuti (USA) 47.8s **S**,James Ball (Canada) 48.0s **B**,Joachim Buchner (Germany) 48.2s
1932 William Carr (USA) 46.2s **S**,Benjamin Eastman (USA) 46.4s **B**,Alex Wilson (Canada) 47.4s
1936 G,Archie Williams (USA) 46.5s **S**,A. Godfrey Brown (Great Britain) 46.7s **B**,James LuValle (USA) 46.8s
1948 G,Arthur Wint (Jamaica) 46.2s **S**,Herbert McKenley (Jamaica) 46.4s **B**,Malvin Whitfield (USA) 46.6s
1952 G,George Rhoden (Jamaica) 45.9s **S**,Herbert McKenley (Jamaica) 45.9s **B**,Ollie Matson (USA) 46.8s
1956 G,Charles Jenkins (USA) 46.7s **S**,Karl-Friedrich Haas (Germany) 46.8s **B**,Voitto Hellsten (Finland) 47.0s Ardalion Ignatyev (USSR) 47.0s
1960 G,Otis Davis (USA) 44.9s **S**,Carl Kaufmann (Germany) 44.9s **B**,Malcolm Spence (South Africa) 45.5s
1964 G,Michael Larrabee (USA) 45.1s **S**,Wendell Mottley (Trinidad) 45.2s **B**,Andrzej Badenski (Poland) 45.6s
1968 G,Lee Evans (USA) 43.8s **S**,Larry James (USA) 43.9s **B**,Ron Freeman (USA) 44.4s
1972 G,Vincent E. Matthews (USA) 44.66s **S**,Wayne C. Collett (USA) 44.80s **B**,Julius Sang (Kenya) 44.92
1976 G,A. Juantorena (Cuba) 44.26s **S**,F. Newhouse (USA) 44.40s **B**,H. Frazier (USA) 44.95s

800 METRES
1896 G,Edwin Flack (Australia) 2m 11.0s **S**,Nandor Dani (Hungary) 2m 11.8s **B**,Demetrius Golemis (Greece)
1900 G,Alfred Tysoe (Great Britain) 2m 01.2s **S**,John Cregan (USA) **B**,David Hall (USA)

1904 G,James Lghtbody (USA) 1m 56.0s S,Howard Valentine (USA) B,Emil Breitkreutz (USA)
1908 G,Melvin Sheppard (USA) 1m 52.8s S,Emilio Lunghi (Italy) 1m 54.2s B,Hanns Braun (Germany) 1m 55.4s
1912 G,James Meredith (USA) 1m 51.9s S,Melvin Sheppard (USA) 1m 52.0s B,Ira Davenport (USA) 1m 52.0s
1920 G,Albert Hill (Great Britain) 1m 53.4s S,Earl Eby (USA) B,Bevil Rudd (South Africa)
1924 G,Douglas Lowe (Great Britain) 1m 52.4s S,Paul Martin (Switzerland) 1m 52.6s B,Schuyler Enck (USA) 1m 53.0s
1928 G,Douglas Lowe (Great Britain) 1m 51.8s S,Erik Byhlen (Sweden) 1m 52.8s B,Hermann Engelhardt (Germany) 1m 53.2s
1932 G,Thomas Hampson (Great Britain) 1m 49.7s S,Alex Wilson (Canada) 1m 49.9s B,Philip Edwards (Canada) 1m 51.5s
1936 G,John Woodruff (USA) 1m 52.9s S,Mario Lanzi (Italy) 1m 53.3s B,Philip Edwards (Canada) 1m 53.6s
1948 G,Malvin Whitfield (USA) 1m 49.2s S,Arthur Wint (Jamaica) 1m 49.5s B,Marcel Hansenne (France) 1m 49.8s
1952 G,Malvin Whitfield (USA) 1m 49.2s S,Arthur Wint (Jamaica) 1m 49.4s B,Heinz Ulzheimer (Germany) 1m 49.7s
1956 G,Thomas Courtney (USA) 1m 47.7s S,Derek Johnson (Great Britain) 1m 47.8s B,Audun Boysen (Norway) 1m 48.1s
1960 G,Peter Snell (New Zealand) 1m 46.3s S,Roger Moens (Belgium) 1m 46.5s B,George Kerr (Jamaica) 1m 47.1s
1964 G,Peter Snell (New Zealand) 1m 45.1s S,William Crothers (Canada) 1m 45.6s B,Wilson Kiprugut (Kenya) 1m 45.9s
1968 G,Ralph Doubell (Australia) 1m 44.3s S,Wilson Kiprugut (Kenya) 1m 44.5s B,Tom Farrell (USA) 1m 45.4s
1972 G,David J. Wottle (USA) 1m 45.9s S,Evgeni Arzhanov (USSR) 1m 45.9s B,Michael Boit (Kenya) 1m 46.0s
1976 G,J. Juantorena (Cuba) 1m 43.50s S,I. Van Damme (Belgium) 1m 43.86s B.R. Wohlhuter (USA) 1m 44.12s

1500 METRES
1896 G,Edwin Flack (Australia) 4m 33.2s S,Arthur Blake (USA) B,Albin Lermusiaux (France)
1900 G,Charles Bennett (Great Britain) 4m 06.2s S,Henri Deloge (France) B,John Bray (USA)
1904 G,James Lightbody (USA) 4m 05.4s S,Frank Verner (USA) B,L. Hearn (USA)
1908 G,Melvin Sheppard (USA) 4m 03.4s S,Harold Wilson (Great Britain) 4m 03.6s B,Norman Hallows (Great Britain) 4m 0.40s
1912 G,Arnold Jackson (Great Britain) 3m 56.8s S,Abel Kiviat (USA) 3m 56.9s B,Norman Taber (USA) 3m 56.9s
1920 G,Albert Hill (Great Britain) 4m 01.8s S,Philip Baker (Great Britain) 4m 02.4s B,Lawrence Shields (USA)
1924 G,Paavo Nurmi (Finland) 3m 53.6s S,Willy Scherrer (Switzerland) 3m 55.0s B,Henry Stallard (Great Britain) 3m 55.6s
1928 G,Harri Larva (Finland) 3m 53.2s S,Jules Ladoumegue (France) 3m 53.8s B,Eino Purje (Finland) 3m 56.4s
1932 G,Luigi Beccali (Italy) 3m 51.2s S,John Cornes (Great Britain) 3m 52.6s B,Philip Edwards (Canada) 3m 52.8s
1936 G,John Lovelock (New Zealand) 3m 47.8s S,Glenn Cunningham (USA) 3m 48.4s B,Luigi Beccali (Italy) 3m 49.2s
1948 G,Henry Eriksson (Sweden) 3m 49.8s S,Lennart Strand (Sweden) 3m 50.4s B,Willem Slykhuis (Netherlands) 3m 50.4s
1952 G,Jose Barthel (Luxembourg) 3m 45.1s S,Robert McMillen (USA) 3m 45.2s B,Werner Lueg (Germany) 3m 45.4s
1956 G,Ron Delaney (Eire) 3m 41.2s S,Klaus Richtzenhain (Germany) 3m 42.0s B,John Landy (Australia) 3m 42.0s
1960 G,Herbert Elliott (Australia) 3m 35.6s S,Michel Jazy (France) 3m 38.4s B,Itsvan Rozsavolgyi (Hungary) 3m 39.2s
1964 G,Peter Snell (New Zealand) 3m 38.1s S,Josef Odlozil (Czechoslovakia) 3m 39.6s B,John Davies (New Zealand) 3m 39.6s
1968 G,Kipchoge Keino (Kenya) 3m 34.9s S,Jim Ryun (USA) 3m 37.8s B,Bodo Tummler (West Germany) 3m 39.0s
1972 G,Pekka Vasala (Finland) 3m 36.3s S,H. Kipchoge Keino (Kenya) 3m 36.8s B,Rodney Dixon (New Zealand) 3m 37.5s
1976 G,J. Walker (New Zealand) 3m 39.17s S,I. Van Damme (Belgium) 3m 39.27s B,P-H. Wellmann (West Germany) 3m 39.33s

5000 METRES
1896–1908 Event not held
1912 G,Hannes Kolehmainen (Finland) 14m 36.6s S,Jean Bouin (France) 14m 36.7s B,George Hutson (Great Britain) 15m 07.6s
1920 G,Joseph Guillemot (France) 14m 55.6s S,Paavo Nurmi (Finland) 15m 00.0s B,Eric Backman (Sweden) 15m 13.0s
1924 G,Paavo Nurmi (Finland) 14m 31.2s S,Ville Ritola (Finland) 14m 31.4s B,Edvin Wide (Sweden) 15m 01.8s
1928 G,Ville Ritola (Finland) 14m 38.0s S,Paavo Nurmi (Finland) 14m 40.0s B,Edvin Wide (Sweden) 14m 41.2s
1932 G,Lauri Lehtinen (Finland) 14m 30.0s S,Ralph Hill (USA) 14m 30.0s B,Lauri Virtanen (Finland) 14m 44.0s
1936 G,Gunnar Hockert (Finland) 14m 22.2s S,Lauri Lehtinen (Finland) 14m 25 8s

B,Henry Jonsson (Sweden) 14m 29.0s
1948 G,Gaston Rieff (Belgium) 14m 17.6s S,Emil Zatopek (Czechoslovakia) 14m 17.8s Willem Slykhuis (Netherlands) 14m 26.8s
1952 G,Emil Zatopek (Czechoslovakia) 14m 06.6s S,Alain Mimoun (France) 14m 07.4s B,Herbert Schade (Germany) 14m 08.6s
1956 G,Vladimir Kuts (USSR) 13m 39.6s S,D. A. Gordon Pirie (Great Britain) 13m 50.6s B,G. Derek Ibbotson (Great Britain) 13m 54.4s
1960 G,Murray Halberg (New Zealand) 13m 43.4s S,Hans Grodotzki (Germany) 13m 44.6s B,Kazimierz Zimmy (Poland) 13m 44.8s
1964 G,Robert Schul (USA) 13m 48.8s S,Harold Norpoth (Germany) 13m 49.6s B,William Dellinger (USA) 13m 49.8s
1968 G,Mohamed Gammoudi (Tunisia) 14m 05.0s S,Kipchoge Keino (Kenya) 14m 05.2s B,Naftali Temu (Kenya) 14m 06.4s
1972 G,Lasse Viren (Finland) 13m 26.4s S,Mohamed Gammoudi (Tunisia) 13m 27.4s B,Ian Stewart (Great Britain) 13m 27.6s
1976 G,L. Viren (Finland) 13m 24.76s S,D. Quax (New Zealand) 13m 25.16s B,K-P. Hildenbrand (West Germany) 13m 25.38s

10,000 METRES
1896–1904 Event not held
1908 G,Emil Voight (Great Britain) 25m 11.2s S,Edward Owen (Great Britain) 25m 24.0s B,John Svanberg (Sweden) 25m 37.2s
1912 G,Hannes Kolemainen (Finland) 31m 20.8s S,Lewis Tewanima (USA) 32m 06.6s B,Albin Stenroos (Finland) 32m 21.8s
1920 G,Paavo Nurmi (Finland) 31m 45.8s S,Joseph Guillemot (France) 31m 47.2s B,James Wilson (Great Britain) 31m 50.8s
1924 G,Ville Ritola (Finland) 30m 23.2s S,Edvin Wide (Sweden) 30m 55.2s B,Eero Berg (Finland) 31m 43.0s
1928 G,Paavò Nurmi (Finland) 30m 18.8s S,Ville Ritola (Finland) 30m 19.4s B,Edvin Wide (Sweden) 31m 00.8s
1932 G,Janusz Kusocinski (Poland) 30m 11.4s S,Volmari Iso-Hollo (Finland) 30m 12.6s B,Lauri Virtanen (Finland) 30m 35.0s
1936 G,Ilmari Salminen (Finland) 30m 15.4s S,Arvo Askola (Finland) 30m 15.6s B,Volmari Iso-Hollo (Finland) 30m 20.2s
1948 G,Emil Zapotek (Czechoslovakia) 29m 59.6s S,Alain Mimoun (France) 30m 47.4s B,Bertil Albertsson (Sweden) 30m 53.6s
1952 G,Emil Zatopek (Czechoslovakia) 29m 17.0s S,Alain Mimoun (France) 29m 32.8s B,Aleksandr Anufriayev (USSR) 29m 48.2s
1956 G,Vladimir Kuts (USSR) 28m 45.6s S,Jozsef Kovacs (Hungary) 28m 52.4s B,Allan Lawrence (Australia) 28m 53.6s
1960 G,Pyotr Bolotnikov

(USSR) 28m 32.2s S,Hans Grodotzki (Germany) 28m 37.0s B,W. David Power (Australia) 28m 38.2s
1964 G,William Mills (USA) 28m 24.4s S,Mohamed Gammoudi (Tunisia) 28m 24.8s B,Ronald Clarke (Australia) 28m 25.8s
1968 G,Naftali Temu (Kenya) 29m 27.4s S,Mamo Wolde (Ethiopia) 29m 28.0s B, Mohamed Gammoudi (Tunisia) 29m 34.2s
1972 G,Lasse Viren (Finland) 27m 38.4s S,Emiel Puttemans (Belgium) 27m 39.6s B,Meruts Yifter (Ethiopia) 27m 41.0s
1976 G,L. Viren (Finland) 27m 40.38s S,C. Sousa Lopes (Portugal) 27m 45.17s B,B. Foster (Great Britain) 27m 54.92s

MARATHON
1896 G,Spyridon Louis (Greece) 2h 58m 50.0s S,Charilaos Vasilakos (Greece) 3h 06m 03.0s B,Gyula Kellner (Hungary) 3h 09m 35.0s
1900 G,Michel Theato (France) 2h 59m 45.0s S,Emile Champion (France) 3h 04m 17.0s B,Ernst Fast (Sweden) 3h 37m 14.0s
1904 G,Thomas Hicks (USA) 3h 28m 53.0s S,Albert Corey (USA) 3h 34m 52.0s B,Arthur Newton (USA) 3h 47m 33.0s
1908 G,John Hayes (USA) 2h 55m 18.4s S,Charles Hefferon (USA) 2h 56m 06.0s B,Joseph Forshaw (USA) 2h 57m 10.4s
1912 G,Kenneth McArthur (South Africa) 2h 36m 54.8s S,Christopher Gitsham (South Africa) 2h 37m 52.0s B,Gaston Strobino (USA) 2h 38m 42.4s
1920 G,Hannes Kolehmainen (Finland) 2h 32m 35.8s S,Juri Lossman (Estonia) 2h 32m 48.6s B,Valerio Arri (Italy) 2h 36m 32.8s
1924 G,Albin Stenroos (Finland) 2h 41m 22.6s S,Romeo Bertini (Italy) 2h 47m 19.6s B,Clarence De Mar (USA) 2h 48m 14.0s
1928 G,El Ouafi (France) 2h 32m 57.0s S,Miguel Plaza (Chile) 2h 33m 23.0s B,Martti Marttelin (Finland) 2h 35m 02.0s
1932 G,Juan C. Zabala (Argentina) 2h 31m 36.0s S,Sam Ferris (Great Britain) 2h 31m 55.0s B,Armas Toivonen (Finland) 2h 32m 12.0s
1936 G,Kitei Son (Japan) 2h 29m 19.2s S,Ernest Harper (Great Britain) 2h 31m 23.2s B,Shoryu Nan (Japan) 2h 31m 42.0s
1948 G,Delfo Carbrera (Argentina) 2h 34m 51.6s S,Thomas Richards (Great Britain) 2h 35m 07.6s B,Etienne Gailly (Belguim) 2h 35m 33.6s
1952 G,Emil Zatopek (Czechoslovakia) 2h 23m 03.2s S,Reinaldo Gorno (Argentina) 2h 25m 35.0s B,Gustat Jansson (Sweden) 2h 26m 07.0s
1956 G,Allan Mimoun (France) 2h 25m 00.0s S,Franjo Mihalic (Yugoslavia) 2h 26m 32.0s B,Veikko Karvonen (Finland)

2h 27m 47.0s
1960 G,Abebe Bikila
(Ethiopia) 2h 15m 16.2s
S,Rhadi Ben Abdesselem
(Morocco) 2h 15m 41.6s
B,Barry Magee (New Zealand)
2h 17m 18.2s
1964 G,Abebe Bikila (Ethiopia)
2h 12m 11.2s S,Basil Heatley
(Great Britain) 2h 16m 19.2s
B,Kokichi Tsuburaya (Japan)
2h 16m 22.8s
1968 G,Mamo Wolde (Ethiopia)
2h 20m 26.4s S,Kenji
Kimihara (Japan) 2h 23m 31.0s
B,Mike Ryan (New Zealand)
2h 23m 45.0s
1972 G,Frank Shorter (USA)
2h 12m 19.8s S,Karel Lismont
(Belgium) 2h 14m 31.8s
B,Mamo Wolde (Ethiopia)
2h 15m 08.4s
1976 G,W. Cierpinski (East
Germany) 2h 09m 55.0s
S, F. Shorter (USA) 2h 10m
45.8s B,K. Lismont (Belgium)
2h 11m 12.6s

110 METRES HURDLES
1900 G,Alvin Kraenzlain (USA)
15.4s S,John McLean (USA)
B,Fred Moloney (USA)
1904 G,Fred Schule (USA)
16.0s S,Thaddeus Shideler
(USA) B,L. Ashburner (USA)
1908 G,Forrest Smithson
(USA) 15.0s S,John Garrels
(USA) B,Arthur Shaw (USA)
1912 G,Fred Kelly (USA) 15.1s
S,James Wendell (USA) 15.2s
B,Martin Hawkins (USA) 15.3s
1920 G,Earl Thomson (Canada)
14.8s S,Harold Barron (USA)
B,Fred Murray (USA)
1924 G,Daniel Kinsey (USA)
15.0s S,Sydney Atkinson
(South Africa) B,Sten
Petterson (Sweden)
1928 G,Sydney Atkinson
(South Africa) 14.8s S,Stephen
Anderson (USA) 14.8s B,John
Collier (USA) 15.0s
1932 G,George Saling (USA)
14.6s S,Percy Beard (USA)
14.7s B,Donald Finlay (Great
Britain) 14.8s
1936 G,Forrest Towns (USA)
14.2s S,Donald Finlay (Great
Britain) 14.4s B,Fred Pollard
(USA) 14.4s
1948 G,William Porter (USA)
13.9s S,Clyde Scott (USA)
14.1s B,Craig Dixon (USA)
14.1s
1952 G,W. Harrison Dillard
(USA) 13.7s S,Jack Davis
(USA) 13.7s B,Art Barnard
(USA) 14.1s
1956 G,Lee Calhoun (USA)
13.5s S,Jack Davis (USA)
13.5s B,Joel Shankle (USA)
14.1s
1960 G,Lee Calhoun (USA)
13.8s S,Willie May (USA)
13.8s B,Hayes Jones (USA)
14.0s
1964 G,Hayes Jones (USA)
13.6s S,Blaine Lindgren
(USA) 13.7s B,Anatol
Mikhailov (USSR) 13.7s
1968 G,Willie Davenport
(USA) 13.3s S,Erv Hall (USA)
13.4s B,Eddy Ottoz (Italy) 13.4s
1972 G,Rodney Milburn
(USA) 13.24s S,Guy Drut
(France) 13.34s B,Thomas
L. Hill (USA) 13.48s
1976 G,G. Drut (France)
13.30s S,A. Casanas (Cuba)
13.33s B,W. Davenport (USA)
13.38s
400 METRES HURDLES
1896 Event not held

1900 G,J. Walter Tewksbury
(USA) 57.6s S,Henri Tauzin
(France) B,George Orton (USA)
1904 G,Harry Hillman (USA)
53.0s S,Frank Waller (USA)
B,George Poage (USA)
1908 G,Charles Bacon (USA)
55.05s S,Harry Hillman (USA)
B,Leonard Tremeer (USA)
1912 Event not held
1920 G,Frank Loomis (USA)
54.0s S,John Norton (USA)
B,August Desch (USA)
1924 G,F. Morgan Taylor
(USA) 52.6s S,Erik Vilen
(Finland) 53.8s B,Ivan Riley
(USA) 54.2s
1928 G,Lord Burghley (Great
Britain) 53.4s S,Frank Cuhel
(USA) 53.6s B,F. Morgan
Taylor (USA) 53.6s
1932 G,Robert Tisdall (Eire)
51.8s S,Glenn Hardin (USA)
52.0s B,F. Morgan Taylor
(USA) 52.2s
1936 G,Glenn Hardin (USA)
52.4s S,John Loaring (Canada)
52.7s B,Miguel White
(Philippines) 52.8s
1948 G,Roy Cochran (USA)
51.1s S,Duncan White (Ceylon)
51.8s B,Rune Larsson
(Sweden) 52.2s
1952 G,Charles Moore (USA)
50.8s S,Yuriy Lituyev (USSR)
51.3s B,John Holland (New
Zealand) 52.2s
1956 G,Glenn Davis (USA)
50.1s S,S. Eddie Southern
(USA) 50.8s B,Joshua
Culbreath (USA) 51.6s
1960 G,Glenn Davis (USA)
49.3s S,Cliff Cushman (USA)
49.6s B,Richard Howard
(USA) 49.7s
1964 G,Warren Cawley (USA)
49.6s S,John Cooper (Great
Britain) 50.1s Salvador
Morale (Italy) 50.1s
1968 G,David Hemery (Great
Britain) 48.1s S,Gerhard
Hennige (West Germany)
49.0s B,John Sherwood
(Great Britain) 49.0s
1972 G,John Akii-bua (Uganda)
47.82s S,Ralph V. Mann
(USA) 48.51s B,David P.
Hemery (Great Britain) 48.52s
1976 G,E. Moses (USA)
47.64s S,M. Shine (USA)
48.69s B,E. Gavrilenko (USSR)
49.45s

3000 METRES
STEEPLECHASE
1896–1912 Event not held
1920 G,Percy Hodge (Great
Britain) 10m 00.4s S,Patrick
Flynn (USA) B,Ernesto
Ambrosini (Italy)
1924 G,Ville Ritola (Finland)
9m 33.6s S,Elias Katz (Finland)
9m 44.0s B,Paul Bontemps
(France) 9m 45.2s
1928 G,Toivo Loukola (Finland)
9m 21.8s S,Paavo Nurmi
(Finland) 9m 31.2s B,Ove
Andersen (Finland) 9m 35.6s
1932 G,Volmari Iso-Hollo
(Finland) 10m 33.4s S,Thomas
Evenson (Great Britain)
10m 46.0s B,Joseph
McCluskey (USA) 10m 46.2s
Run over 3400 metres in error
1936 G,Volmari Iso-Hollo
(Finland) 9m 03.8s S,Kaarlo
Tuominen (Finland) 9m 06.8s
B,Alfred Dompert (Germany)
9m 07.2s
1948 G,Tore Sjostrand
(Sweden) 9m 04.6s S,Erik
Elmsater (Sweden) 9m 08.2s
B,Gote Hagstrom (Sweden)

9m 11.8s
1952 G,Horace Ashenfelter
(USA) 8m 45.4s S,Vladimir
Kazantsev (USSR) 8m 51.6s
B,John Disley (Great Britain)
8m 51.8s
1956 G,Christopher Brasher
(Great Britain) 8m 41.2s
S,Sandor Rozsnyoi (Hungary)
8m 43.6s B,Ernst Larsen
(Norway) 8m 44.0s
1960 G,Zdzislaw Kryszkowiak
(Poland) 8m 34.2s S,Nikolay
Sokolov (USSR) 8m 36.4s
B,Semyon Rzhishchin (USSR)
8m 42.2s
1964 G,Gaston Roelants
(Belgium) 8m 30.8s
S,Maurice Herriott (Great
Britain) 8m 32.4s B,Ivan
Belyayev (USSR) 8m 33.8s
1968 G,Amos Biwott (Kenya)
8m 51.0s S,Benjamin Kogo
(Kenya) 8m 51.6s B,George
Young (USA) 8m 51.8s
1972 G,H. Kipchoge Keino
(Kenya) 8m 23.6s S,Benjamin
W. Jipcho (Kenya) 8m 24.6s
B,Tapio Kantanen (Finland)
8m 24.8s
1976 G,A. Garderud (Sweden)
8m 08.02s S,B. Malinowski
(Poland) 8m 09.11s B,F.
Baumgartl (East Germany)
8m 10.36s
4×100 METRES RELAY
1896–1908 Event not held
1912 Great Britain (David
Jacobs, Harold Macintosh,
Victor d'Arcy, William
Applegarth) 42.2s S,Sweden
42.6s
1920 G,USA (Charles Paddock,
Jackson Scholz, Loren
Murchison, Morris Kirksey)
42.2s S,France 42.6s
B,Sweden
1924 G,USA (Frank Hussey,
Louis Clark, Loren Murchison,
J. Alfred Leconey) 41.0s
S,Great Britain 41.2s
B,Netherlands 41.8s
1928 G,USA (Frank Wykoff,
James Quinn, Charles Borah,
Henry Russell) 41.0s
S,Germany 41.2s B,Great
Britain 41.8s
1932 G,USA (Robert Kiesel,
Emmett Toppino, Hector Dyer,
Frank Wykoff) 40.0s
S,Germany 40.9s B,Italy 41.2s
1936 G,USA (Jesse Owens,
Ralph Metcalfe, Foy Draper,
Frank Wykoff) 39.8 S,Italy
41.1s B,Germany 41.2s
1948 G,USA (H. Norwood
Ewell, Lorenzo Wright, W.
Harrison Dillard, Melvin Patton)
40.6s S,Great Britain 41.3s
B,Italy 41.5s
1952 G,USA (F. Dean Smith,
W. Harrison Dillard, Lindy
Remigino, Andy Stanfield)
40.1s S,USSR 40.3s
B,Hungary 40.5s
1956 G,USA (Ira Murchison,
Leamon King, W. Thane Baker,
Bobby Joe Morrow) 39.5s
S,USSR 39.8s B,Germany 40.3s
1960 G,Germany (Bernd
Cullman, Armin Hary, Wlater
Mahlendorf, Martin Lauer)
39.5s S,USSR 40.1s B,Great
Britain 40.2s
1964 G,USA (Paul Drayton,
Garry Ashworth, Richard
Stebbins, Robert Hayes) 39.0s
S,Poland 39.3s B,France 39.3s
1968 G,USA (Charlie Greene,
Mel Pender, Ronnie Ray Smith,
Jim Hines) 38.2s S,Cuba 38.3s
B,France 38.4s

1972 G,USA (Larry J. Black,
Robert Taylor, Gerland Tinker,
Eddie J. Hart) 38.19s S,USSR
38.50s B,West Germany
38.79s
1976 G,USA (H. Glance,
J. Jones, M. Hampton,
S. Riddick) 38.33s S,East
Germany 38.66s B,USSR
38.78s
4×400 METRES RELAY
1896–1908 Event not held
1912 G,USA (Melvin Sheppard,
Frank Lindberg, James
Meredith, Charles Reidpath)
3m 16.6s S,France 3m 20.7s
B,Great Britain 3m 23.2s
1920 G,Great Britain (Cecil
Griffiths, Robert Lindsay,
John Ainsworth-Davis, Guy
Butler) 3m 22.2s S,South
Africa B,France
1924 G,USA (C. S. Cochran,
William Stevenson, James
McDonald, Allan Hellfrich)
3m 16.0s S,Sweden 3m 17.0s
B,Great Britain 3m 17.4s
1928 G,USA (George Baird,
Emerson Spencer, Frederick
Alderman, Raymond Barbuti)
3m 14.2s S,Germany 3m 14.8s
B,Canada 3m 15.4s
1932 G,USA (Ivan Fuqua,
Edgar Ablowich, Karl Warner,
William Carr) 3m 08.2s
S,Great Britain 3m 11.2s
B,Canada 3m 12.8s
1936 G,Great Britain (Frederick
Wolff, Godfrey Rampling,
William Roberts, A. Godfrey
Brown) 3m 09.0s S,USA
3m 11.0s B,Germany 3m 11.8s
1948 G,USA (Arthur Harnden,
Clifford Bourland, Roy
Cochran, Malvin Whitfield)
3m 10.4s S,France 3m 14.8s
B,Sweden 3m 16.3s
1952 G,Jamaica (Arthur Wint,
Leslie Laing, Herbert McKenley,
George Rhoden) 3m 03.9s
S,USA 3m 04.0s B,Germany
3m 06.6s
1956 G,USA (Lou Jones,
Jesse Mashburn, Charles
Jenkins, Thomas Courtney)
3m 04.8s S,Australia 3m 06.2s
B,Great Britain 3m 07.2s
1960 G,USA (Jack Yerman,
Earl Young, Glenn Davis, Otis
Davis) 3m 02.2s S,Germany
3m 02.7s B,British West Indies
3m 04.0s
1964 G,USA (Ollan Cassell,
Michael Larrabee, Ulis
Williams, Henry Carr)
3m 00.7s S,Great Britain
3m 01.6s B,Trinidad
1968 G,USA (Vince Matthews,
Ron Freeman, Larry James,
Lee Evans) 2m 56.1s S,Kenya
2m 59.6s B,West Germany
3m 00.5s
1972 G,Kenya (Charles Asati,
Hezekia Nyamau, Robert Ouko,
Julius Sang) 2m 59.8s
S,Great Britain 3m 00.5s
B,France 3m 00.7s
1976 G,USA (H. Frazier,
B. Brown, F. Newhouse,
M. Parks) 2m 58.65s S,
Poland 3m 01.43s B,West
Germany 3m 01.98s
20,000 METRES WALK
1896–1952 Event not held
1956 G,Leonard Spirin (USSR)
1h 31m 27.4s S,Antonas
Mikenas (USSR) 1h 32m 03.0s
B,Bruno Junk (USSR)
1h 32m 12.0s
1960 G,V. Golubnichy (USSR)
1h 34m 07.2s S,Noel Freeman
(Australia) 1h 34m 16.4s

B,Stan Vickers (Great Britain) 1h 34m 56.4s
1964 G,Kenneth Matthews (Great Britain) 1h 29m 34.0s **S**,Dieter Lindner (Germany) 1h 31m 13.2s **B**,V. Golubnichy (USSR) 1h 31m 59.4s
1968 G,V. Golubnichy (USSR) 1h 33m 58.4s **S**,Jose Pedraza (Mexico) 1h 34m 00s **B**,Nikolai Smaga (USSR) 1h 34m 03.4s
1972 G,Peter Frenkel (East Germany) 1h 26m 42.4s **S**,Vladimir Golubnickiy (USSR) 1h 26m 55.2s **B**,Hans Reimann (East Germany) 1h 27m 16.6s
1976 G,D. Bautista (Mexico) 1h 24m 40.6s **S**,H. Reimann (East Germany) 1h 25m 13.8s **B**,P. Frenkel (East Germany) 1h 25m 29.4s

HIGH JUMP

1896 G,Ellery Clark (USA) 5' 11¼" **S**,James Connolly (USA) 5' 7¾" **B**,Robert Garrett (USA) 5' 7⅜"
1900 G,Irving Baxter (USA) 6' 2¾" **S**,Con Leahy (Great Britain) 5' 10⅜" **B**,Lajor Gonczy (Hungary) 5' 8⅞"
1904 G,Samuel Jones (USA) 5' 11" **S**,G. P. Serviss (USA) 5' 10" **B**,Paul Weinstein (Germany) 5' 10"
1908 G,Harry Porter (USA) 6' 3" **S**,Con Leahy (Great Britain) Istvan Somodi (Hungary) and Geo Andre (France) 6' 2"
1912 G,Alma Richards (USA) 6' 4" **S**,Hans Liesche (Germany) 6' 3¼" **B**,George Horine (USA) 6' 2⅞"
1920 G,Richmond Landon (USA) 6' 4⅜" **S**,Harold Muller (USA) 6' 2¾" **B**,Bo Ekelund (Sweden) 6' 2¾"
1924 G,Harold Obsorn (USA) 6' 6" **S**,Leroy Brown (USA) 6' 4¾" **B**,Pierre Lewden (France) 6' 3⅝"
1928 G,Robert King (USA) 6' 4⅜" **S**,Ben Hedges (USA) 6' 3¼" **B**,Claude Menard (France) 6' 3¼"
1932 G,Duncan McNaughton (Canada) 6' 5½" **S**,Robert Van Osdel (USA) 6' 5½" **B**,Simeon Toribio (Philippines) 6' 5½"
1936 G,Cornelius Johnson (USA) 6' 7⅞" **S**,David Allbritton (USA) 6' 6¾" **B**,Delos Thurber (USA) 6' 6¾"
1948 G,John Winter (Australia) 6' 6" **S**,Bjorn Paulsen (Norway) 6' 4¾" **B**,George Stanich (USA) 6' 4¾"
1952 G,Walter Davis (USA) 6' 8⅜" **S**,Kenneth Wiesner (USA) 6' 7⅛" **B**,Jose Tellesda Conceicao (Brazil) 6' 6"
1956 G,Charles Dumas (USA) 6' 11½" **S**,Charles Porter (Australia) 6' 10⅝" **B**,Igor Kashkarov (USA) 6' 9⅞"
1960 G,Robert Shavlakadze (USSR) 7' 1⅛" **S**,Valeriy Brumel (USSR) 7' 1⅛" **B**,John Thomas (USA) 7' 0¼"
1964 G,Valeriy Brumel (USSR) 7' 1¾" **S**,John Thomas (USA) 7' 1¾" **B**,John Rambo (USA) 7' 1"
1968 G,Richard Fosbury (USA) 7' 4¼" **S**,Ed Caruthers (USA) 7' 3½" **B**,Valentin Gavrilov (USSR) 7' 2⅝"
1972 G,Yuri Tarmak (USSR) 2.23m **S**,Stefan Junge (East Germany) 2.21m **B**,Dwight E. Stones (USA) 2.21m
1976 G,J. Wszola (Poland) 2.25m **S**,G. Joy (Canada) 2.23m **B**,D. Stones (USA) 2.21m

LONG JUMP

1896 G,Ellery Clark (USA) 20' 10" **S**,Robert Garrett (USA) 20' 3¼" **B**,James Connolly (USA) 20' 0½"
1900 G,Alvin Kraenzlein (USA) 23' 6⅞" **S**,Myer Prinstein (USA) 23' 6½" **B**,Con Leahy (Great Britain) 22' 9½"
1904 G,Myer Prinstein (USA) 24' 1" **S**,Daniel Frank (USA) 22' 7¼" **B**,R. Stangland (USA) 22' 7"
1908 G,Frank Irons (USA) 24' 6½" **S**,Daniel Kelly (USA) 23' 3¼" **B**,Calvin Bricker (Canada) 23' 3"
1912 G,Albert Gutterson (USA) 24' 11¼" **S**,Calvin Bricker (Canada) 23' 7¾" **B**,Georg Aberg (Sweden) 23' 6¾"
1920 G,William Pettersson (Sweden) 23' 5½" **S**,Carl Johnson (USA) 23' 3¼" **B**,Eric Abrahamsson (Sweden) 23' 2¾"
1924 G,William De Hart Hubbard (USA) 24' 5" **S**,Edward Gourdin (USA) 23' 10½" **B**,Sverre Hansen (Norway) 23' 9¾"
1928 G,Edward Hamm (USA) 25' 4¾" **S**,Silvio Cator (Haiti) 24' 10½" **B**,Alfred Bates (USA) 24' 3¼"
1932 G,Edward Gordon (USA) 25' 0¾" **S**,C. Lambert Redd (USA) 24' 11¼" **B**,Chuhei Nambu (Japan) 24' 5¼"
1936 G,Jesse Owens (USA) 26' 5¼" **S**,Luz Long (Germany) 25' 9¾" **B**,Naoto Tajima (Japan) 25' 4¾"
1948 G,Willie Steele (USA) 25' 8" **S**,Thomas Bruce (Australia) 24' 9¼" **B**,Herbert Douglas (USA) 24' 9"
1952 G,Jerome Biffle (USA) 24' 10" **S**,Meredith Gourdine (USA) 24' 8½" **B**,Odon Foldessy (Hungary) 23' 11½"
1956 G,Gregory Bell (USA) 25' 8¼" **S**,John Bennett (USA) 25' 2¼" **B**,Jorma Valkama (Finland) 24' 6½"
1960 G,Ralph Boston (USA) 26' 7½" **S**,Irvin Roberson (USA) 26' 7¼" **B**,Igor Ter-Ovanesyan (USSR) 26' 4¼"
1964 G,Lynn Davies (Great Britain) 26' 5¾" **S**,Ralph Boston (USA) 26' 4" **B**,Igor Ter-Ovanesyan (USSR) 26' 2½"
1968 G,Robert Beamon (USA) 29' 2½" **S**,Klaus Beer (East Germany) 26' 10½" **B**,Ralph Boston (USA) 26' 9¼"
1972 G,Randy L. Williams (USA) 8.24m **S**,Hans Baumgartner (West Germany) 8.18m **B**,Arnie Robinson (USA) 8.03m
1976 G,A. Robinson (USA) 8.35m **S**,R. Williams (USA) 8.11m **B**,F. Wartenberg (East Germany) 8.02m

TRIPLE JUMP

1896 G,James Connolly (USA) 44' 11¾" **S**,Alexandre Tuffere (France) 41' 8" **B**,Joannis Persakis (Greece) 41' 1"
1900 G,Myer Prinstein (USA) 47' 5¾" **S**,James Connolly (USA) 45' 10" **B**,L. P. Sheldon (USA) 44' 9"
1904 G,Myer Prinstein (USA) 47' 1" **S**,Fred Englehardt (USA) 45' 7¼" **B**,R. Stangland (USA) 43' 10¼"
1908 G,Timothy Ahearne (Great Britain) 48' 11¼" **S**,Garfield MacDonald (Canada) 48' 5¼" **B**,Edvard Larsen (Norway) 47' 2¾"
1912 G,Gustaf Lindblom (Sweden) 48' 5" **S**,Georg Aberg (Sweden) 47' 7¼" **B**,Erik Almlof (Sweden) 46' 5¾"
1920 G,Vilho Tuulos (Finland) 47' 7" **S**,Folke Jansson (Sweden) 47' 6" **B**,Erik Almolf (Sweden) 46' 10"
1924 G,Anthony Winter (Australia) 50' 11¼" **S**,Luis Brunetto (Argentina) 50' 7¼" **B**,Vilho Tuulos (Finland) 50' 5"
1928 G,Mikio Oda (Japan) 49' 10¾" **S**,Levi Casey (USA) 49' 9¼" **B**,Vilho Tuulos (Finland) 49' 7"
1932 G,Chuhei Nambu (Japan) 51' 7" **S**,Erik Svensson (Sweden) 50' 3¼" **B**,Kenkichi Oshima (Japan) 49' 7¼"
1936 G,Naoto Tajima (Japan) 52' 6" **S**,Masao Harada (Japan) 51' 4½" **B**,Jack Metcalfe (Australia) 50' 10¼"
1948 G,Arne Ahman (Sweden) 50' 6¼" **S**,George Avery (Australia) 50' 5" **B**,Rhui Sarialp (Turkey) 49' 3½"
1952 G,Adhemar Ferreira da Silva (Brazil) 53' 2½" **S**,Leonid Shcherbakov (USSR) 52' 5¼" **B**,Arnoldo Devonish (Venzuela) 50' 11"
1956 G,Adhemar Ferreira da Silva (Brazil) 53' 7¾" **S**,Vilhjalmur Einarsson (Iceland) 53' 4¼" **B**,Vitold Kreyer (USSR) 52' 6¾"
1960 G,Josef Schmidt (Poland) 55' 1¾" **S**,Vladimir Goryayev (USSR) 54' 6½" **B**,Vitold Kreyer (USSR) 53' 10¾"
1964 G,Josef Schmidt (Poland) 55' 3½" **S**,Olyeg Fyedoseyev (USSR) 54' 4¾" **B**,Victor Kravchenko (USSR) 54' 4¼"
1968 G,Viktor Saneyev (USSR) 57' 0¾" **S**,Nascimento Prudencio (Brazil) 56' 8" **B**,Giuseppe Gentile (Italy) 56' 6"
1972 G,Viktor Saneyev (USSR) 17.35m **S**,Joerg Drehmel (East Germany) 17.31m **B**,Nelson Prudencio (Brazil) 17.05m
1976 G,V. Saneyev (USSR) 17.29 **S**,J. Butts (USA) 17.18m **B**,J. C. De Oliviera (Brazil) 16.90m

POLE VAULT

1896 G,William Hoyt (USA) 10' 10" **S**,Albert Tyler (USA) 10' 8" **B**,Joannis Theodoropoulos (Greece) 9' 4¼"
1900 G,Irving Baxter (USA) 10' 10" **S**,M. B. Colkett (USA) 10' 8" **B**,Carl-Albert Andersen (Norway) 10' 6"
1904 G,Charles Dvorak (USA) 11' 6" **S**,Leroy Samse (USA) 11' 3" **B**,L. Wilkins (USA) 11' 3"
1908 G,Alfred Gilbert and Edward Cook (USA) 12' 2" **B**,Ernest Archibald (Canada) 11' 9" C. S. Jacobs (USA) 11' 9" B. Soderstrom (Sweden) 11' 9"
1912 G,Henry Babcock (USA) 12' 11½" **S**,Frank Nelson and Marc Wright (USA) 12' 7½"
1920 G,Frank Foss (USA) 13' 5" **S**,Henry Petersen (Denmark) 12' 1¾" **B**,Edwin Meyers (USA) 11' 9¾"
1924 G,Lee Barnes (USA) 12' 11½" **S**,Glenn Graham (USA) 12' 11½" **B**,James Brooker (USA) 12' 9½"
1928 G,Sabin Carr (USA) 13' 9¼" **S**,William Droegemuller (USA) 13' 5½" **B**,Charles McGinnis (USA) 12' 11½"
1932 G,William Miller (USA) 14' 1⅞" **S**,Shuhei Nishida (Japan) 14' 1¼" **B**,George Jefferson (USA) 13' 9½"
1936 G,Earle Meadows (USA) 14' 3¼" **S**,Shuhei Nishida (Japan) 13' 11¼" **B**,Sueo Oe (Japan) 13' 11¼"
1948 G,O. Guinn Smith (USA) 14' 1¼" **S**,Erkki Kataja (Finland) 13' 9½" **B**,Robert Richards (USA) 13' 9½"
1952 G,Robert Richards (USA) 14' 11¼" **S**,Donald Laz (USA) 14' 9¼" **B**,Ragnar Lundberg (Sweden) 14' 5¼"
1956 G,Robert Richards (USA) 14' 11½" **S**,Robert Gutowski (USA) 14' 10¼" **B**,Georgios Roubanis (Greece) 14' 9¼"
1960 G,Donald Bragg (USA) 15' 5" **S**,Ron Morris (USA) 15' 1¼" **B**,Eeles Landstrom (Finland) 14' 11¼"
1964 G,Fred Hansen (USA) 16' 8¾" **S**,Wolfgang Reinhardt (Germany) 16' 6¾" **B**,Klaus Lehnertz (Germany) 16' 5"
1968 G,Robert Seagren (USA) 17' 8½" **S**,Claus Schiprowski (West Germany) 17' 8½" **B**,Wolfgang Nordwig (East Germany) 17' 8½"
1972 G,Wolfgang Nordwig (East Germany) 5.50m **S**,Robert L. Seagren (USA) 5.40m **B**, Jan E. Johnson (USA) 5.35m
1976 G,T. Slusarski (Poland) 5.50m **S**,A. Kalliomaki (Finland) 5.50m **B**,D. Roberts (USA) 5.50m

SHOT PUT

1896 G,Robert Garrett (USA) 36' 9¾" **S**,Militiades Gouscos (Greece) 36' 9" **B**,Georgios Papasideris (Greece) 34' 0"
1900 G,Richard Sheldon (USA) 46' 3" **S**,Josiah McCracken (USA) 42' 2" **B**,Robert Garrett (USA) 40' 7"
1904 G,Ralph Rose (USA) 48' 7" **S**,Wesley Coe (USA) 47' 3" **B**,L. B. Feuerbach (USA) 43' 10½"
1908 G,Ralph Rose (USA) 46' 7½" **S**,Dennis Horgan (Great Britain) 44' 8¼" **B**,John Garrels (USA) 43' 3"
1912 G,Patrick McDonald (USA) 50' 4" **S**,Ralph Rose (USA) 50' 0½" **B**,Lawrence Whitney (USA) 45' 8½"
1920 G,Ville Porhola (Finland) 48' 7" **S**,Elmer Niklander (Finland) 46' 5¼" **B**,Harry Liversedge (USA) 46' 5"
1924 G,L. Clarence Houser (USA) 49' 2¼" **S**,Glenn Hartranft (USA) 49' 2" **B**,Ralph Hills (USA) 48' 0½"
1928 G,John Kuck (USA) 52' 0¾" **S**,Herman Brix (USA) 51' 8" **B**,Emil Hirschfield (Germany) 51' 7"
1932 G,Leo Sexton (USA) 52' 6⅛" **S**,Harlow Rothert (USA) 51' 5⅝" **B**,Frantisek Douda (Czechoslovakia) 51' 2½"

1936 G,Hans Wollke (Germany) 53' 1¾" S,Sulo Barlund (Finland) 52' 10¾" B,Gerhard Stock (Germany) 51' 4½"
1948 G,Wilbur Thompson (USA) 56' 2" S,James Delaney (USA) 54' 8¾" B,James Fuchs (USA) 53' 10½"
1952 G,W. Parry O'Brien (USA) 58' 1½" S,Darrow Hooper (USA) 57' 0¾" B,James Fuchs (USA) 55' 11¾"
1956 G,W. Parry O'Brien (USA) 60' 11¼" S,William Nieder (USA) 59' 7¾" B,Jiri Skobla (Czechoslovakia) 57' 11"
1960 G,William Nieder (USA) 65' 6¾" S,w. Parry O'Brien (USA) 62' 8¼" B,Dallas Long (USA) 62' 4¼"
1964 G,Dallas Long (USA) 66' 8½" S,Randall Matson (USA) 66' 3¼" B,Vilmos Varju (Hungary) 63' 7½"
1968 G,Randall Matson (USA) 67' 4¾" S,George Woods (USA) 66' 0¼" B,Eduard Gushchin (USSR) 65' 11"
1972 G,Wladyslaw Komar (Poland) 21.18m S,George R. Woods (USA) 21.17m B,Hartmut Briesenick (East Germany) 21.14m
1976 G,U. Beyer (East Germany) 21.05m S,E. Mironov (USSR) 21.03m B,A. Barisnikov (USSR) 21.00m

DISCUS THROW

1896 G,Robert Garrett (USA) 95' 7¾" S,Panagiotis Paraskevopoulos (Greece) 95' 0" B,Sotirios Versis (Greece) 91' 1¾"
1900 G,Rudolf Bauer (Hungary) 118' 3" S,Frantisek Janda (Bohemia) 115' 7¾" B,Richard Sheldon (USA) 113' 2¼"
1904 G,Martin Sheridan (USA) 128' 10½" S,Ralph Rose (USA) 128' 10½" B,Nicolas Georgantos (Greece) 123' 7½"
1908 G,Martin Sheridan (USA) 134' 2" S,M. H. Griffin (USA) 133' 6½" B,Marquis Horr (USA) 129' 5¼"
1912 G,Armas Taipale (Finland) 148' 4" S,Richard Byrd (USA) 138' 10" B,James Duncan (USA) 138' 8½"
1920 G,Elmer Niklander (Finland) 146' 7½" S,Armas Taipale (Finland) 144' 11½" B,Augustus Pope (USA) 138' 2½"
1924 G,L. Clarence Houser (USA) 151' 5" S,Vilho Niittymaa (Finland) 147' 5½" B,Thomas Lieb (USA) 147' 1"
1928 G,L. Clarence Houser (USA) 155' 3" S,Antero Kivi (Finland) 154' 11½" B,James Corson (USA) 154' 6½"
1932 G,John Anderson (USA) 162' 4½" S,Henri Laborde (France) 159' 0½" B,Paul Winter (France) 157' 0"
1936 G,Kenneth Carpenter (USA) 165' 7½" S,Gordon Dunn (USA) 161' 11" B, Giorgio Oberweger (Italy) 161' 6"
1948 G,Adolfo Consolini (Italy) 172' 2" S,Giuseppe Tosi (Italy) 169' 10½" B,Fortune Gordien (USA) 166' 7"
1952 G,Sim Iness (USA) 180' 6½" S,Adolfo Consolini (Italy) 176' 5" B,James Dillon (USA) 174' 9½"
1956 G,Alfred Oerter (USA) 184' 11" S,Fortune Gordien (USA) 179' 0" B,Desmond Koch (USA) 178' 5½"
1960 G,Alfred Oerter (USA) 194' 1¾" S,Rink Babka (USA) 190' 4¼" B,Richard Cochran (USA) 187' 6¼"
1964 G,Alfred Oerter (USA) 200' 1½" S,Ludvik Danek (Czechoslovakia) 198' 6½" B,David Weill (USA) 195' 2"
1968 G,Alfred Oerter (USA) 212' 6½" S,Lothar Milde (East Germany) 206' 11½" B,Ludvik Danek (Czechoslovakia) 206' 5"
1972 G,Ludvik Danek (Czechoslovakia) 64.40m S,L. Jay Silvester (USA) 63.50m B,Rickard Bruch (Sweden) 63.40m
1976 G,M. Wilkins (USA) 67.50m S,W. Schmidt (East Germany) 66.22m B,J. Powell (USA) 65.70m

HAMMER THROW

1896 Event not hled
1900 G,John Flanagan (USA) 163' 2" S,Truxton Hare (USA) 161' 2" B,Josiah McCracken (USA) 139' 3½"
1904 G,John Flanagan (USA) 168' 1" S,John DeWitt (USA) 164' 11" B,Ralph Rose (USA) 150' 0½"
1908 G,John Flanagan (USA) 170' 4¼" S,Matthew McGrath (USA) 167' 11" B,Con Walsh (USA) 159' 1½"
1912 G,Matthew McGrath (USA) 179' 7" S,Duncan Gillis (Canada) 158' 9" B,Clarence Childs (USA) 158' 0½"
1920 G,Patrick Ryan (USA) 173' 5½" S,Carl Johan Lind (Sweden) 160' 2¼" B,Basil Bennett (USA) 158' 3½"
1924 G,Fred Tootell (USA) 174' 10" S,Matthew McGrath (USA) 166' 9½" B,Malcolm Nokes (Great Britain) 160' 4"
1928 G,Patrick O'Callaghan (Eire) 168' 7" S,Ossian Skiold (Sweden) 168' 3" B,Edmund Black (USA) 160' 10"
1932 G,Patrick O'Callaghan (Eire) 176' 11" S,Ville Porhola (Finland) 171' 6" B,Peter Zaremba (USA) 165' 1½"
1936 G,Karl Hein (Germany) 185' 4" S,Erwin Blask (Germany) 180' 7" B,Fred Warngard (Sweden) 179' 10½"
1948 G,Imre Nemeth (Hungary) 183' 11½" S,Ivan Gubijan (Yugoslavia) 178' 0½" Robert Bennett (USA) 176' 3½"
1952 G,Joszef Csermak (Hungary) 197' 11½" S,Karl Storch (Germany) 193' 1" B,Imre Nemeth (Hungary) 189' 5"
1956 G,Harold Connolly (USA) 207' 3½" S,Mikhail Krivonosov (USSR) 206' 9½" B,Anatoliy Samotsvetov (USSR) 205' 3"
1960 G,Vasiliy Rudenkov (USSR) 220' 1¾" S,Gyula Zsivotzky (Hungary) 215' 10" B,Tadeusz Rut (Poland) 215' 4½"
1964 G,Romuald Klim (USSR) 228' 10½" S,Gyula Zsivotsky (Hungary) 226' 8" B,Uwe Beyer (Germany) 223' 4½"
1968 G,Gyula Zsivotsky (Hungary) 240' 8" S,Romuald Klim (USSR) 240' 5" B,Lazar Lovasz (Hungary) 228' 11"
1972 G,Anatoli Bondarchuk (USSR) 75.50m S,Jochen Sachse (East Germany) 74.96m B,Vasili Khmelevski (USSR) 74.04m
1976 G,Y. Sedyh (USSR) 77.52m S,A. Spiridonov (USSR) 76.08m B,A. Bondarchuk (USSR) 75.48m

JAVELIN THROW

1896–1904 Event not held
1908 G,Erik Lemming (Sweden) 179' 10½" S,Arne Halse (Norway) 165' 11" B,Otto Nilsson (Sweden) 154' 6¼"
1912 G,Erik Lemming (Sweden) 198' 11½" S,Juho Saaristo (Finland) 192' 5½" B,Mor Koczan (Hungary) 182' 1"
1920 G,Jonni Myyra (Finland) 215' 9½" S,Urko Peltonen (Finland) 208' 8" B,Pekka Johansson (Finland) 207' 0"
1924 G,Jonni Myyra (Finland) 206' 6½" S,Gunnar Lindstrom (Sweden) 199' 10½" B,Eugene Oberst (USA) 191' 5"
1928 G,Erik Lundkvist (Sweden) 218' 6" S,Bela Szepes (Hungary) 214' 1" B,Olav Sunde (Norway) 209' 10½"
1932 G,Matti Jaervinen (Finland) 238' 6½" S,Martti Sippala (Finland) 229' 0" B,Eino Penttila (Finland) 225' 4½"
1936 G,Gerhard Stock (Germany) 235' 8½" S,Yrjo Nikkanen (Finland) 232' 2" B,Kalervo Toivonen (Finland) 232' 0"
1948 G,Tapio Rautavaara (Finland) 228' 1" S,Steve Seymour (USA) 221' 8" B,Joszef Varszegi (Hungary) 219' 11"
1952 G,Cyrus Young (USA) 242' 0½" S,William Miller (USA) 237' 8½" B,Toivo Hyytiainen (Finland) 235' 10½"
1956 G,Egil Danielsen (Norway) 281' 2½" S,Janusz Sidlo (Poland) 262' 4½" B,Viktor Tsibulenko (USSR) 260' 10"
1960 G,Viktor Tsibulenko (USSR) 277' 8¼" S,Walter Kruger (Germany) 260' 4½" B,Gergely Kulcsar (Hungary) 257' 9¼"
1964 G,Pauli Nevala (Finland) 271' 2" S,Gergely Kulcsar (Hungary) 270' 0½" B,Janis Lusis (USSR) 264' 2"
1968 G,Janis Lusis (USSR) 295' 7" S,Jorma Kinnunen (Finland) 290' 7½" B,Gergely Kulcsar (Hungary) 285' 7½"
1972 G,Klaus Wolfermann (West Germany) 90.48m S,Janis Lusis (USSR) 90.46m B,William Schmidt (USA) 84.42m
1976 G,M. Nemeth (Hungary) 94.58m S,H. Siltonen (Finland) 87.92m B,G. Megelea (Rumania) 87.16m

DECATHLON

1896–1908 Event not held
1912 G,Hugo Wieslander (Sweden) 5.377 pts. S,Charles Lomberg (Sweden) 5.089 B,Gosta Holmer (Sweden) 5.161
1920 G,Helge Lovland (Norway) 5.190 pts. S,Brutus Hamilton (USA) 5.073 B,Bertil Ohlson (Sweden) 4.974
1924 G,Harold Osborn (USA) 6.163 pts. S,Emerson Norton (USA) 5.738 B,Aleksander Kolmpere (Estonia) 5.531
1928 G,Paavo Yrjola (Finland) 6.246 pts. S,Akilles Jaervinen (Finland) 6.379 B,Kenneth Doherty (USA) 6.039
1932 G,James Bausch (USA) 6.588 pts. S,Akilles Jaervinen (Finland) 6.707 B,Wolrad Eberle (Germany) 6.361
1936 G,Glenn Morris (USA) 7.310 pts. S,Robert Clark (USA) 7.002 B,Jack Parker (USA) 6.588
1948 G,Robert Mathias (USA) 6.386 pts. S,Ignace Heinrich (France) 6.264 B,Floyd Simmons (USA) 6,264
1952 G,Robert Mathias (USA) 8.887 pts. S,Milton Campbell (USA) 6.975 B,Floyd Simmons (USA) 6.788
1956 G,Milton Campbell (USA) 7.937 pts. S,Rafer Johnson (USA) 7.587 B,Vasiliy Kuznetsov (USSR) 7.465
1960 G,Rafer Johnson (USA) 8.392 pts. S,Yang Chuan-Kwang (Taiwan) 8.334 B,Vasiliy Kuznetsov (USSR) 7.809
1964 G,Willi Holdorf (Germany) 7.887 pts. S,Rein Aun (USSR) 7.842 B,Hans-Joachim Walde (Germany) 7.809
1968 G,William Toomey (USA) 8.193 pts. S,Hans-Joachim Wlade (West Germany) 8.111 B,Kurt Bendlin (West Germany) 8.064
1972 G,Nakolai Avilov (USSR) 8.454 pts. S,Leonid Litvinenko (USSR) 8.035 B,Ryszard Katus (Poland) 7.984
1976 G,B. Jenner (USA) 8.618 pts. S,G. Kratschmer (West Germany) 8.411 B,N. Avilov (USSR) 8.369

Track and Field Athletics (Women)

100 METRES

1928 G,Elizabeth Robinson (USA) 12.2s S,Fanny Rosenfeld (Canada) 12.2s B,Ethel Smith (Canada) 12.2s
1932 G,Stanislawa Walasiewicz (Poland) 11.9s S,Hilda Strike (Canada) 11.9s B,Wilhelmina von Bremen (USA) 12.0s
1936 G,Helen Stephens (USA) 11.5s S,Stanislawa Walasiewicz (Poland) 11.7s B,Kathe Krauss (Germany) 11.9s
1948 G,Francina Blankers-Koen (Netherlands) 11.9s S,Dorothy Manley (Great Britain) 12.2s B,Shirley Strickland (Australia) 12.2s
1952 G,Marjorie Jackson (Australia) 11.5s S,Daphne Hasenjager (South Africa) 11.8s B,Shirley Strickland (Australia) 11.9s
1956 G,Betty Cuthbert (Australia) 11.5s S,Christa

Stubnick (Germany) 11.7s
B,Marlene Mathews (Australia) 11.7s
1960 G,Wilma Rudolph (USA) 11.0s **S**,Dorothy Hyman (Great Britain) 11.3s
B,Giuseppina Leone (Italy) 11.3s
1964 G,Wyomia Tyus (USA) 11.4s **S**,Edith Maguire (USA) 11.6s **B**,Ewa Kobukowska (Poland) 11.6s
1968 G,Wyomia Tyus (USA) 11.0s **S**,Barbara Ferrell (USA) 11.1s **B**,Irena Kirszenstein (Poland) 11.1s
1972 G,Renate Stecher (East Germany) 11.07s **S**,Raelene A. Bayle (Australia) 11.23s
B,Silvia Chivas (Cuba) 11.24s
1976 G,A. Richter (West Germany) 11.08s **S**,R. Stecher (East Germany) 11.13s
B,I. Helten (West Germany) 11.17s

200 METRES

1928–36 Event not held
1948 G,Francina Blankers-Koen (Netherlands) 24.4s
S,Audrey Williamson (Great Britain) 25.1s **B**,Audrey Patterson (USA) 25.2s
1952 G,Marjorie Jackson (Australia) 23.7s **S**,Bertha Brouwer (Netherlands) 24.2s
B,Nadyezhda Khnykina (USSR) 24.2s
1956 G,Betty Cuthbert (Australia) 23.4s **S**,Christa Stubnick (Germany) 23.7s
B,Marlene Mathews (Australia) 23.8s
1960 G,Wilma Rudolph (USA) 24.0s **S**,Jutta Heine (Germany) 24.4s **B**,Dorothy Hyman (Great Britain) 24.7s
1964 G,Edith Maguire (USA) 23.0s **S**,Irena Kirszenstein (Poland) 23.1s
B,Marilyn Black (Australia) 23.1s
1968 G,Irena Kirszenstein (Poland) 22.5s **S**,Raelene Boyle (Australia) 22.7s
B,Jennifer Lamy (Australia) 22.8s
1972 G,Renate Stecher (East Germany) 22.40s **S**,Raelene A. Boyle (Australia) 22.45s
B,Irena Szewinska (Poland) 22.74s
1976 G,B. Eckert (East Germany) 22.37s **S**,A. Richter (West Germany) 22.39s
B,R. Stecher (East Germany) 22.47s

400 METRES

1928–60 Event not held
1964 G,Betty Cuthbert (Australia) 52.0s **S**,Ann Packer (Great Britain) 52.2s
B,Judith Amoore (Australia) 53.4s
1968 G,Colette Besson (France) 52.0s **S**,Lillian Board (Great Britain) 52.1s
B,Natalia Pechenkina (USSR) 52.2s
1972 G,Monika Zehrt (East Germany) 51.08s **S**,Rita Wilden (West Germany) 51.21s **B**,Kathy Hammond (USA) 51.64s
1976 G,I. Szewinska (Poland) 49.29s **S**,C. Brehmer (East Germany) 50.51s **B**,E. Streidt (East Germany) 50.55s

800 METRES

1928 G,Lina Radke (Germany) 2m 16.8s **S**,Kinuye Hitomi (Japan) 2m 17.6s **B**,Inga Gentzel (Sweden) 2m 17.6s
1932–56 Event not held
1960 G,Ludmila Shevtsova (USSR) 2m 04.3s **S**,Brenda Jones (Australia) 2m 04.4s
B,Ursula Donath (Germany) 2m 05.6s
1964 G,Ann Packer (Great Britain) 2m 01.1s **S**,Maryvonne Dupureur (France) 2m 01.9s
B,Marise Chamberlain (New Zealand) 2m 02.8s
1968 G,Madeleine Manning (USA) 2m 00.9s **S**,Irena Silai (Romania) 2m 02.5s
B,Maria Gommers (Netherlands) 2m 02.6s
1972 G,Hildegard Falck (West Germany) 1m 58.6s
S,Niole Sabaite (USSR) 1m 58.7s **B**,Gunhild Hoffmeister (East Germany) 1m 59.2s
1976 G,T. Kazankina (USSR) 1m 54.94s **S**,N. Chtereva (Bulgaria) 1m 55.42s
B,E. Zinn (East Germany) 1m 55.60s

1500 METRES

1928–1968 Event not held
1972 G,Lyudmila Bragina (USSR) 4m 01.4s **S**,Gunhild Hoffmeister (East Germany) 4m 02.8s **B**,Paola Cacchi-Pigni (Italy) 4m 02.9s
1976 G,T. Kazankina (USSR) 4m 05.48s **S**,G. Hoffmeister (East Germany) 4m 06.02s
B,U. Klapezynski (East Germany) 4m 06.09s

100 METRES HURDLES

1928–1968 Event not held
1972 G,A. Ehrhardt (East Germany) 12.59s **S**,V. Butanu (Rumania) 12.84s **B**,K. Balzer (East Germany) 12.90s
1976 G,J. Schaller (East Germany) 12.77s **S**,T. Anisimova (USSR) 12.78s
B,N. Lebedeva (USSR) 12.80s

4×100 METRES RELAY

1928 G,Canada (Myrtle Cook, Ethel Smith, Fanny Rosenfeld, F. Bell) 48.4s **S**,USA 48.8s
B,Germany 49.0s
1932 G,USA (Mary Carew, Evelyn Furtsch, Annette Rogers, Wilhelmina von Bremen) 47.0s **S**,Canada 47.0s **B**,Great Britain 47.6s
1936 G,USA (Harriett Bland, Annette Rogers, Elizabeth Robinson, Helen Stephens) 46.9s **S**,Great Britain 47.6s
B,Canada 47.8s
1948 G,Netherlands (Xenia de Jongh, Nettie Timmers, Gerda Koudijs, Francina Blankers-Koen) 47.5s **S**,Australia 47.6s
B,Canada 48.0s
1952 G,USA (Mae Faggs, Barbara Jones, Janet Moreau, Catherine Hardy) 45.9s
S,Germany 45.9s **B**,Great Britain 46.2s
1956 G,Australia (Shirley Strickland, Norma Crocker, Fleur Mellor, Betty Cuthbert) 44.5s **S**,Great Britain 44.7s
B,USA 44.9s
1960 G,USA (Martha Hudson, Lucinda Williams, Barbara Jones, Wilma Rudolph) 44.5s **S**,Germany 44.8s **B**,Poland 45.0s
1964 G,Poland (Teresa Ciepla, Irena Kirzsenstein, Halina Gorecka, Ewa Klobukowska) 43.6s **S**,USA 43.9s **B**,Great Britain 44.0s
1968 G,USA (Barbara Ferrell, H. Bailes, M. Netter, Wyomia Tyus) 42.8s **S**,Cuba 43.3s
B,USSR 43.4s
1972 G,West Germany (Christine Krause, Ingrid Mickler, Annegret Richter, Heidemarie Rosendahl) 42.81s
S,East Germany 42.95s
B,Cuba 43.36s
1976 G,East Germany (M. Oelsner, R. Stecher, C. Bodendorf, B. Eckert) 42.55s **S**,West Germany 42.59s **B**,USSR 43.09s

4×400 METRES RELAY

1928–1968 Event not held
1972 G,East Germany (D. Kasling, R. Kuhne, H. Seidler, M. Zehrt) 3m 23.00s
S,USA 3m 25.20s **B**,Germany 3m 26.50s
1976 G,East Germany (D. Maletzki, B. Rohde, E. Streidt, C. Brehmer) 3m 19.23s **S**,USA 3m 22.81s
B,USSR 3m 24.24s

HIGH JUMP

1928 G,Ethel Catherwood (Canada) 5′ $2\frac{5}{8}$″ **S**,Carolina Gisolf (Netherlands) and Mildred Wiley (USA) 5′ $1\frac{1}{2}$″
1932 G,Jean Shiley (USA) 5′ 5″ **S**,Mildred Didrikson (USA) 5′ 5″ **B**,Eva Dawes (Canada) 5′ 3″
1936 G,Ibolya Csak (Hungary) 5′ 3″ **S**,Dorothy Odam (Great Britain) 5′ 3″
B,Elfriede Kaun (Germany) 5′ 3″
1948 G,Alice Coachman (USA) 5′ $6\frac{1}{8}$″ **S**,Dorothy Tyler (Great Britain) 5′ $6\frac{1}{8}$″
B,Micheline Ostermeyer (France) 5′ $3\frac{3}{8}$″
1952 G,Esther Brand (South Africa) 5′ $5\frac{3}{4}$″ **S**,Sheila Lerwill (Great Britain) 5′ 5″
B,Alexandra Chudina (USSR) 5′ $4\frac{1}{8}$″
1956 G,Mildred McDaniel (USA) 5′ $9\frac{1}{4}$″ **S**,Thelma Hopkins (Great Britain) and Maria Pisaryeva (USSR) 5′ $5\frac{3}{4}$″
1960 G,Iolanda Balas (Romania) 6′ $0\frac{7}{8}$″
S,Jaroslawa Jozwiakowska (Poland) and Dorothy Shirley (Great Britain) 5′ $7\frac{1}{4}$″
1964 G,Iolanda Balas (Romania) 6′ $2\frac{3}{4}$″ **S**,Michele Brown (Australia) 5′ 11″
B,Taisia Chenchik (USSR) 5′ 10″
1968 G,Miloslava Rezkova (Czechoslovakia) 5′ $11\frac{3}{4}$″
S,Antonina Okorokova (USSR) 5′ $10\frac{3}{4}$″ **B**,Valentina Kozyr (USSR) 5′ $10\frac{3}{4}$″
1972 G,Ulrike Meyfarth (West Germany) 1.92m
S,Yordanka Blagoyeva (Bulgaria) 1.88m **B**,Ilona Gusenbauer (Austria) 1.88m
1976 G,R. Ackermann (East Germany) 1.93m **S**,S. Simeoni (Italy) 1.91m **B**,Y. Blagoeva (Bulgaria) 1.91m

LONG JUMP

1928–36 Event not held
1948 G,Olga Gyarmati (Hungary) 18′ $8\frac{1}{4}$″
S,Simonetto de Portela (Argentina) 18′ $4\frac{1}{2}$″ **B**,Anne Leyman (Sweden) 18′ $3\frac{3}{8}$″
1952 G,Yvette Williams (New Zealand) 20′ $5\frac{5}{8}$″ **S**,Alexandra Chudina (USSR) 20′ $1\frac{3}{4}$″
B,Shirley Cawley (Great Britain) 19′ 5″
1956 G,Elzbieta Krzesinska (Poland) 20′ 10″ **S**,Willye White (USA) 19′ $11\frac{3}{4}$″
B,Nadyezhda Dvalishvili (USSR) 19′ 11″
1960 G,Vyera Krepkina (USSR) 20′ $10\frac{3}{4}$″ **S**,Elzbieta Krzesinska (Poland) 20′ $6\frac{3}{4}$″
B,Hildrun Claus (Germany) 20′ $4\frac{1}{2}$″
1964 G,Mary Rand (Great Britain) 22′ $2\frac{1}{4}$″ **S**,Irena Kirszenstein (Poland) 21′ $7\frac{3}{4}$″
B,Tatyana Schelkanova (USSR) 21′ $0\frac{3}{4}$″
1968 G,Viorica Viscopoleanu (Romania) 22′ $4\frac{1}{2}$″ **S**,Sheila Sherwood (Great Britain) 21′ 11″ **B**,Tatyana Talycheva (USSR) 21′ $10\frac{1}{4}$″
1972 G,Heidemarie Rosendahl (West Germany) 6.78m
S,Diana Yorgove (Bulgaria) 6.77m **B**,Eva Suranova (Czechoslovakia) 6.67m
1976 G,A. Voigt (East Germany) 6.72m **S**,K. McMillan (USA) 6.66m **B**,L. Alfeeva (USSR) 6.60m

JAVELIN THROW

1928 Event not held
1932 G,Mildred Didrikson (USA) 143′ 4″ **S**,Ellen Braumüller (Germany) 142′ $8\frac{5}{8}$″
B,Tilly Fleischer (Germany) 141′ $6\frac{7}{8}$″
1936 G,Tilly Fleischer (Germany 148′ $2\frac{3}{4}$″ **S**,Luise Kruger (Germany) 142′ $0\frac{3}{8}$″
B,Marja Kwasniewska (Poland) 137′ $1\frac{1}{4}$″
1948 G,Hermine Bauma (Austria) 149′ 6″ **S**,Kaisa Parviäinen (Finland) 143′ $8\frac{1}{8}$″
B,Lily Carlstedt (Denmark) 140′ $5\frac{1}{8}$″
1952 G,Dana Zatopkova (Czechoslovakia) 165′ 7″
S,Alexandra Chudina (USSR) 164′ $0\frac{7}{8}$″ **B**,Yelena Gorchakova (USSR) 163′ $3\frac{1}{8}$″
1956 G,Inese Jaunzeme (USSR) 176′ $8\frac{1}{2}$″ **S**,Marlene Ahrens (Chile) 165′ $3\frac{1}{2}$″
B,Nadyezhda Konyayeva (USSR) 164′ $11\frac{1}{2}$″
1960 G,Elvira Ozolina (USSR) 183′ 8″ **S**,Dana Zatopkova (Czechoslovakia) 176′ $5\frac{1}{4}$″
B,Birute Kalediene (USSR) 175′ $4\frac{1}{2}$″
1964 G,Michaela Penes (Romania) 198′ $7\frac{1}{2}$″ **S**,Marta Rudasne (Hungary) 191′ 2″
B,Yelena Gorchakova (USSR) 187′ $2\frac{1}{2}$″
1968 G,Angela Nemeth (Hungary) 198′ $0\frac{1}{2}$″ **S**,Michaela Penes (Romania) 196′ 7″
B,Eva Janko (Austria) 190′ 5″
1972 G,Ruth Fuchs (East Germany) 63.88m **S**,Jacqueline Todten (East Germany) 62.54m **B**,Kathy Schmidt (USA) 59.94m
1976 G, R. Fuchs (East Germany) 65.94m **S**,M. Becker (West Germany) 64.70m **B**,K. Schmidt (USA) 63.96m

SHOT PUT

1928–36 Event not held
1948 G,Micheline Ostermeyer (France) 45′ $1\frac{1}{2}$″ **S**,Amelia Piccinini (Italy) 42′ $11\frac{1}{4}$″
B,Ina Schäffer (Austria) 42′ $10\frac{7}{8}$″
1952 G,Galina Zybina (USSR) 50′ $1\frac{1}{2}$″ **S**,Marianne Werner (Germany) 47′ $9\frac{5}{8}$″ **B**,Klavdia Tochenova (USSR) 47′ $6\frac{7}{8}$″
1956 G,Tamara Tyshkyevich (USSR) 54′ 5″ **S**,Galina

Zybina (USSR) 54' 2¾" **B**,Marianne Werner (Germany) 51' 2½"
1960 G,Tamara Press (USSR) 56' 10" **S**,Johanna Lüttge (Germany) 54' 6" **B**,Earlene Brown (USA) 53' 10½"
1964 G,Tamara Press (USSR) 59' 6" **S**,Renate Garisch (Germany) 57' 9¼" **B**,Galina Zybina (USSR) 57' 3"
1968 G,Margitta Gummel (East Germany) 64' 4" **S**,Marita Lange (East Germany) 61' 7½" **B**,Nina Chizhova (USSR) 59' 7¾"
1972 G,Nadyezhda Chizhova (USSR) 21.03m **S**,Margitta Gummel (East Germany) 20.22m **B**,Ivanka Khristova (Bulgaria) 19.35m
1976 G,I. Christova (Bulgaria) 21.16m **S**,N. Chijova (USSR) 20.96m **B**,H. Fibingerova (Czechoslovakia) 20.67m

DISCUS THROW

1928 G,Helena Konopacka (Poland) 129' 11¾" **S**,Lilian Copeland (USA) 121' 7⅞" **B**,Ruth Svedberg (Sweden) 117' 10¼"
1932 G,Lilian Copeland (USA) 133' 1¾" **S**,Ruth Osburn (USA) 131' 7½" **B**,Jadwiga Wajsowna (Poland) 127' 1¼"
1936 G,Gisela Mauermayer (Germany) 156' 3¼" **S**,Jadwiga Wajsowna (Poland) 151' 7¾" **B**,Paula Mollenhauer (Germany) 130' 6⅞"
1948 G,Micheline Ostermeyer (France) 137' 6⅛" **S**,Edera Gentile (Italy) 135' 0⅞" **B**,J. Mazeas (France) 132' 7⅜"
1952 G,Nina Romashkova (USSR) 168' 8½" **S**,Yelizaveta Bagryantseva (USSR) 154' 5⅝" **B**,Nina Dumbadze (USSR) 151' 10½"
1956 G,Olga Fikotova (Czechoslovakia) 176' 1½" **S**,Irina Beglyakova (USSR) 172' 4½" **B**,Nina Ponomaryeva (USSR) 170' 8"
1960 G,Nina Ponomaryeva (USSR) 180' 9¼" **S**,Tamara Press (USSR) 172' 6½" **B**,Lia Manoliu (Romania) 171' 9½"
1964 G,Tamara Press (USSR) 187' 10½" **S**,Ingrid Lotz (Germany) 187' 8½" **B**,Lia Manoliu (Romania) 186' 11"
1968 G,Lia Manoliu (Romania) 191' 2½" **S**,Liesel Westermann (West Germany) 189' 6" **B** Jolan Kleiber (Hungary) 180' 1½"
1972 G,Faina Melnik (USSR) 66.62m **S**,Argentina Menis (Rumania) 65.06m **B**,Vassilka Stoyeva (Bulgaria) 64.34m
1976 G,E. Schlaak (East Germany) 69.00m **S**,M. Vergova (Bulgaria) 67.30m **B**,G. Hinzmann (East Germany) 66.84m

PENTATHLON

1928–60 Event not held
1964 G,Irena Press (USSR) 5,246 pts. **S**,Mary Rand (Great Britain) 5,035 **B**,Galina Bystrova (USSR) 4,956
1968 G,Ingrid Becker (West Germany). 5,098 pts. **S**,Liese Prokop (Austria) 4,966 **B**,Anna Toth Kovacs (Hungary) 4,959
1972 G,Mary E. Peters (Great Britain) 4,801 pts. **S**,Heidemarie Rosendahl (West Germany) 4,791 **B**,Burglinde Pollak (East Germany) 4,768
1976 G,S. Siegl (East Germany) 4,745 pts. **S**,C. Laser (East Germany) 4,745 **B**,B. Pollak (East Germany) 4,740

Volleyball

MEN

1896–1960 Event not held
1964 G,USSR (Yury Chesnokov, Yury Vengerovsky, Eduard Sibiriakov, Dmitry Voskobornikov, Vazha Kacharava, Stanislaw Ljugailo, Vitaly Kovalenko, Yury Poyarkov, Ivan Bugaenkov, Nikolay Burobin, Valery Kalachikhin, Georgy Mondzolevsky) 17 pts. **S**,Czechoslovakia 17 **B**,Japan 16
1968 G,USSR (E. Sibiriakov, V. Kravchenko, V. Belyayev, E. Lapinsky, O. Antropov, V. Matushevas, V. Mikhalchuk, Y. Polarkov, B. Tereshuk, V. Ivanov, I. Bugayenkov, G. Modzolevsky) 17pts **S**,Japan 16 **B**,Czechoslovakia 16
1972 G,Japan (K. Nekoda, K. Kimura, Y. Fukao, J. Morita, T. Tokota, S. Oko, K. Shimaoka, Y. Nakamura, M. Minami, T. Sato, Y. Noguchi, T. Nishimoto) **S**,East Germany **B**,USSR
1976 G,Poland (W. Stefanski, B. Bebel, L. Lasko, T. Wojtowicz, E. Skorek, W. Gawlowski, M. Rybaczewski, Z. Lubiejewski, R. Bosek, W. Sadalski, Z. Zarzycki, M. Karbarz, H. Wagner, J. Welcz) **S**,USSR **B**,Cuba

WOMEN

1928–60 Event not held
1964 G,Japan (Masai Kasai, Emiko Miyamoto, Kinuko Tanida, Yuriko Handa, Yoshiko Matsumara, Sada Isobe, Masaku Kondo, Ayano Shibuki, Katsumi Matsumari, Yoko Shinozaki, Yuko Fujimoto) 10pts. **S**,USSR 9 **B**,Poland 8
1968 G,USSR (L. Buldakova, L. Mikhailovskaya, T. Veinberg, V. Lantratova, V. Gulashka, T. Sarycheva, T. Ponyayeva, N. Smoleyeva, I. Ryksal, G. Leontyeva, R. Salikhova, V. Vinogradova) 14 pts. **S**,Japan 13 **B**,Poland 12
1972 G,USSR (I. Ryskal, V. Douiounova, T. Tretiakova, N. Smoleeva, R. Salikhova, L. Buldakova, T. Gonobobeleva, L. Turina, G. Leontieva, T. Sarycheva, L. Borozna, N. Koudreva) **S**,Japan **B**,Korea
1976 G,Japan (T. Lida, M. Okamoto, E. Maeda, N. Matsuda, T. Shirai, K. Kato, Y. Arakida, K. Kanesaka, M. Yoshida, S. Takayanagi, H. Yano, J. Yokoyamma, S. Yamada, S. Maruyama) **S**,USSR **B**,Korea

Water Polo

1896 Event not held
1900 G,Great Britain **S**,Belgium **B**,France
1904 G,USA **S**,USA **B**,USA
1908 G,Great Britain (Charles Smith, G. Nevinson, George Cornet, T. Thould, George Wilkinson, Paul Radmilovic, C. G. E. Forsyth) **S**,Belgium **B**,Sweden
1912 G,Great Britain (Charles Smith, George Cornet, Charles Bugbee, Arthur Hill, George Wilkinson, Paul Radmilovic, Isaac Bentham) **S**,Sweden **B**,Belgium
1920 G,Great Britain (Charles Smith, Paul Radmilovic, Charles Bugbee, N. M. Purcell, C. Jones, W. Peacock, W. H. Dean) **S**,Belgium **B**,Sweden
1924 G,France (Paul Dujardin, Henri Padou, Rigal Deborgie, Delberghe, Desmettre, Mayraud) **S**,Belgium **B**,USA
1928 G,Germany (Erich Rademacher, Fritz Gunst, Otto Cordes, Emil Benecke, Joachim Rademacher, Karl Bähre, Max Amann) **S**,Hungary **B**,France
1932 G,Hungary (György Bródy, Sándor Ivády, Márton Hommonay, Olivér Halassy, József Vértesi, János Németh, Alajos Keserü, Béla Komjádi, István Barta, Miklós Sárkány) 8 pts. **S**,Germany 5 **B**,USA 5
1936 G,Hungary (György Bródy, Kálmán Hazai, Márton Hommonay, Olivér Halassy, Jenö Brandi, János Németh, György Kutasi, Mihály Bozsi, István Molnár, Sandor Tarics) 5 pts. **S**,Germany 5 **B**,Belgium 2
1948 G,Italy (Pasquale Buonocore, Emilio Bulgarelli, Cesare Rubini, Geminio Ognio, Ermenegildo Arena, Aldo Ghira, Tullio Pandolfini, Mario Majoni, Gianfranco Pandolfini) 6 pts. **S**,Hungary 3 **B**,Netherlands 2
1952 G,Hungary (László Jenei, György Vizvári, Dezsö Gyarmati, Kálmán Markovits, Antal Bolvári, István Szivós, György Kárpáti, Róbert Antal, Dezsö Fábián, Károly Szittya, Dezsö Lemhényi, István Hasznos, Miklós Martin) 5 pts. **S**,Yugoslavia 5 **B**,Italy 2
1956 G,Hungary (Otto Boras, Dezso Gyamati, Kálmán Markovits, István Hevesi, György Kárpáti, Mihály Mayer, Antal Bolvári, László Jenei, Tivadar Kanisza, István Szivós, Ervin Zador) 10 pts. **S**,Yugoslavia 7 **B**,USSR 6
1960 G,Italy (Danio Bardi, Giuseppe d'Altrui, Franco Lavoratori, Gianni Lonzi, Rosario Parmeggiani, Eraldo Pizzo, Dante Rossi, Amedeo Ambron, Salvatore Gionta, Luigi Mannelli, Brunello Spinelli) 5 pts. **S**,USSR 3 **B**,Hungary 2
1964 G,Hungary (Miklos Ambius, Lazslo Felkai, Janos Konrad, Zoltan Domotov, Tivador Kanizsa, Peter Rusoran, Gyorgy Karpati, Dezso Gyarmati, Denes Pocsik, Mihaly Mayer, Andras Bodnar, Otto Boros) 5 pts. **S**,Yugoslavia 5 **B**,USSR 2
1968 G,Yugoslavia (K. Stipanic, I. Trumbic, O. Bonacic, U. Marovic, R. Lopanty, Z. Jankovic, M. Poljak, D. Dabovic, D. Perisic, M. Sandic, Z. Hebel) 8 pts. **S**,USSR 8 **B**,Hungary 6
1972 G,USSR (V. Gulyaev, A. Akimov, A. Dreval, A. Dolgushin, V. Shmudski, A. Kabanov, A. Barkalov, A. Shidlovski, N. Melnikov, L. Ossipov, V. Sobchenko) **S**,Hungary **B**,USA
1976 G,Hungary (E. Molnar, Dr I. Szivos, T. Farago, Dr L. Sarosi, G. Horkai, G. Csapo, A. Sudar, G. Kenez, G. Gerendas, Dr F. Konrad, T. Cservenyak, D. Gyarmati) 9 pts. **S**,Italy 6 **B**,Holland 6

Weight-Lifting

Note: up until 1976 the competition result depended on the combined aggregate weight of three two-handed overhead lifts; the Press, the Snatch and the Jerk. In 1976 they were decided on the Snatch and the Jerk only.

FLYWEIGHT

1928–1968 Event not held
1972 G,Z. Smalcerz (Poland) 337.5 kg **S**,L. Szuecs (Hungary) 330 kg **B**,.S. Holczreiter (Hungary) 327.5 kg
1976 G,A. Voronin (USSR) 534.25 kg **S**,G. Koszegi (Hungary) 523.25 kg **B**,M. Nassiri (Iran) 517.75 kg

BANTAMWEIGHT

1896–1936 Event not held
1948 G,Joseph de Pietro (USA) 678 lb **S**,Julian Creus (Great Britain) 665¾ **B**,Robert Tom (USA) 650¼
1952 G,Ivan Udodov (USSR) 694½ lb **S**,Mahmoud Namdjou (Iran) 678 **B**,Ali Mirzai (Iran) 661¼
1956 G,Charles Vinci (USA) 754½ lb **S**,Vladimir Stogov (USSR) 743½ **B**,Mahmoud Namdjou (Iran) 732½
1960 G,Charles Vinci (USA) 759 lb **S**,Yoshinobu Miyake (Japan) 742½ **B**,Elm Khan (Iran) 726
1964 G,Alexey Vakhonin (USSR) 787¾ lb **S**,Imre Foldi (Hungary) 782¼ **B**,Shiro Ichinoseki (Japan) 765¾
1968 G,Mohamed Nassiri (Iran) 809¾ lb **S**,Imre Foldi (Hungary) 809¾ **B**,Henryk Trebicki (Poland) 787¾
1972 G,Imre Földi (Hungary) 377.5 kg **S**,Mohammad Nassiri (Iran) 370 kg **B**, Gennadi Chetin (USSR) 367.5 kg
1976 G,N. Nurikyan (Bulgaria) 262.5 kg **S**,G. Cziura (Poland) 252.5 kg **B**,K. Ando (Japan) 250 kg

FEATHERWEIGHT

1896–1912 Event not held
1920 G,F. de Haes (Belgium) 485 lb **S**,Alfred Schmidt (Estonia) 468½ **B**,E. Ritter (Switzerland) 463
1924 G,Pierino Gabetti (Italy) 887¼ lb **S**,Andreas Stadler (Austria) 848¾ **B**,A. Reinmann (Switzerland) 843¼
1928 G,Franz Andrysek (Austria) 633¾ lb **S**,Pierino Gabetti (Italy) 662¾ **B**,Hans Wölpert (Germany) 622¾
1932 G,Raymond Suvigny (France) 633¾ lb **S**,Hans Wölpert (Germany) 622¾ **B**,Anthony Terlazzo (USA) 617¼
1936 G,Anthony Terlazzo (USA) 689 lb **S**,Saleh Moh Soliman (Egypt) 672½ **B**,Ibrahim Shams (Egypt) 661¼

1948 G,Mahmoud Fayad (Egypt) 733 lb **S**,Rodney Wilkes (Trinidad) 700 **B**,Jaffar Salmassi (Iran) 689
1952 G,Rafael Chimishkyan (USSR) 774 lb **S**,Nikolay Saksonov (USSR) 733 **B**,Rodney Wilkes (Trinidad) 711
1956 G,Isaac Berger (USA) 776½ lb **S**,Evgeniy Minayev (USSR) 754¾ **B**,Marian Zielinski (Poland) 738
1960 G,Evgeniy Minayev (UUSR) 819½ lb **S**,Isaac Berger (USA) 797½ **B**,Sebastiano Mannironi (Italy) 775½
1964 G,Yoshinobu Miyake (Japan) 876 lb **S**,Isaac Berger (USA) 842 **B**,Mieczyslaw Nowak (Poland) 832
1968 G,Yoshinobu Miyake (Japan) 865 lb **S**,Dito Zhanidze (USSR) 854 **B**,Yoshiyuki Miyake (Japan) 848½
1972 G,Norair Nourikian (Bulgaria) 402.5 kg **S**,Dito Shanidze (USSR) 400 kg **B**,Janos Benedek (Hungary) 390 kg
1976 G,N. Kolesnikov (USSR) 285 kg **S**,G. Todorov (Bulgaria) 280 kg **B**,K. Hirai (Japan) 275 kg

LIGHTWEIGHT

1896–1912 Event not held
1920 G,Alfred Neyland (Estonia) 567¾ lb **S**,R. Williquet (Belgium) 529 **B**,J. Rooms (Belgium) 507
1924 G,Edmond Décottignies (France) 970 lb **S**,Anton Zwerzina (Austria) 942½ **B**,Bohumil Durdys (Czechoslovakia) 937
1928 G,Kurt Helbig (Germany) and Hans Haas (Austria) 711 lb **B**,F. Arnout (France) 667
1932 G,René Duverger (France) 716½ lb **S**,Hans Haas (Austria) 678 **B**,Gastone Pierini (Italy) 667
1936 G,Mohammed Mesbah (Egypt) and Robert Fein (Austria) 755 lb **B**,Karl Jansen (Germany) 722
1948 G,Ibrahim Shams (Egypt) 793½ lb **S**,Appia Hammouda (Egypt) 793½ **B**,James Halliday (Great Britain) 749½
1952 G,Thomas Kono (USA) 799 lb **S**,Yevgeniy Lopatin (USSR) 771½ **B**,Verdi Barberis (Australia) 771½
1956 G,Igor Rybak (USSR) 837½ lb **S**,Ravil Khabutdinov (USSR) 821 **B**,Chang Hee Kim (Korea) 815¼
1960 G,Viktor Bushuyev (USSR) 876 lb **S**,Tan Howe Liang (Korea) 837½ **B**,Abdul Wahid Aziz (Iraq) 837½
1964 G,Waldemar Baszanowski (Poland) 953¼ lb **S**,Vladimir Kaplunov (USSR) 953¼ **B**,Marian Zielihski (Poland) 925½
1968 G,Waldemar Baszanowski (Poland) 964¼ lb **S**,Parviz Jalayer (Iran) 931¼ **B**,Marian Zielinski (Poland) 925½
1972 G,Mujharbi Kirzhinov (USSR) 460 kg **S**,Mladen Koutchev (Bulgaria) 450 kg **B**,Zbigniew Kaczmarek (Poland) 437.5 kg
1976 G,K. Kaczmarek (Poland) 307.5 kg **S**,P. Korol (USSR) 305 kg **B**,D. Senet (France) 300 kg

MIDDLEWEIGHT

1896–1912 Event not held
1920 G,B. Gance (France) 540 lb **S**,Ubaldo Bianchi (Italy) 523½ **B**,Albert Pettersson (Sweden) 523½
1924 G,Carlo Galimberti (Italy) 1,085¾ lb **S**,Alfred Neyland (Estonia) 1,003 **B**,J. Kikkas (Estonia) 992
1928 G,Francois Roger (France) 738½ lb **S**,Carlo Galimberti (Italy) 733 **B**,A. Scheffer (Netherlands) 722
1932 G,Rudolf Ismayr (Germany) 760 ½ lb **S**,Carlo Galimberti (Italy) 749½ **B**,Karl Hipfinger (Austria) 744
1936 G,Khadr El Thouni (Egypt) 854¾ lb **S**,Rudolf Ismayr (Germany) 777 **B**,Adolf Wagner (Germany) 777
1948 G,Frank Spellman (USA) 860 lb **S**,Peter George (USA) 843¼ **B**,Sung Kim (Korea) 837¾
1952 G,Peter George (USA) 882 lb **S**,Gerald Gratton (Canada) 860 **B**,Sung Kim (South Korea) 843¼
1956 G,Fyeodor Bagdanovskiy (USSR) 925½ lb **S**,Peter George (USA) 909 **B**,Ermanno Pignatti (Italy) 843
1960 G,Aleksandr Kurynov (USSR) 964¼ lb **S**,Thomas Kono (USA) 942 **B**,Györzö Veres (Hungary) 895
1964 G,Hans Zdrazila (Czechoslovakia) 980¾ lb **S**,Victor Kurentsov (USSR) 969¾ **B**,Masashi Ohuchi (Japan) 964
1968 G,Victor Kurentsov (USSR) 1,046¾ lb **S**,Masashi Ohuchi (Japan) 1,002¾ **B**,Karoly Bakos (Hungary) 969¾
1972 G,Yordan Kikov (Bulgaria) 485 kg **S**,Mohamed Trabulsi (Lebanon) 472.5 kg **B**,Anselmo Silvino (Italy) 470 kg
1976 G,Y. Mitkov (Bulgaria) 335 kg **S**,V. Militosyan (USSR) 330 kg **B**,P. Wenzel (East Germany) 327.5 kg

LIGHT-HEAVYWEIGHT

1896–1912 Event not held
1920 G,E. Cadine (France) 639 lb **S**,Fritz Hünenberger (Switzerland) 606 **B**,Erik Pettersson (Sweden) 600½
1924 G,Charles Rigoulot (France) 1,107¾ lb **S**,Fritz Hünenberger (Switzerland) 1,080¼ **B**,Leopold Friedrich (Austria) 1,080¼
1928 G,Said Nosseir (Egypt) 782½ lb **S**,Louis Hostin (France) 777 **B**,J. Verheyen (Netherlands) 744
1932 G,Louis Hostin (France) 804¾ lb **S**,Svend Olsen (Denmark) 793½ **B**,Henry Duey (USA) 727½
1936 G,Louis Hostin (France) 820 lb **S**,Eugen Deutsch (Germany) 804¾ **B**,Ibrahim Wasif (Egypt) 793½
1948 G,Stanley Stanczyk (USA) 920½ lb **S**,Harold Sakata (USA) 837¾ **B**,Gösta Magnusson (Sweden) 826¾
1952 G,Trofim Lomakin (USSR) 920½ lb **S**,Stanley Stanczyk (USA) 915 **B**,Arkhadiy Vorobyev (USSR) 898¼
1956 G,Thomas Kono (USA) 986¼ lb **S**,Vasiliy Stepanov (USSR) 942 **B**,James George (USA) 920¼
1960 G,Ireneusz Palinski (Poland) 975¼ lb **S**,James George (USA) 947¾ **B**,Jan Bochenek (Poland) 925¾
1964 G,Rudolf Plyukbelder (USSR) 1,046¾ lb **S**,Geza Toth (Hungary) 1,030¼ **B**,Gyozo Veres (Hungary) 1,030
1968 G,Boris Selitsky (USSR) 1,068¾ lb **S**,Vladimir Belyaev (USSR) 1,068¾ **B**,Norbert Ozimek (Poland) 1,041¼
1972 G,Leif Jenssen (Norway) 507.5 kg **S**,Norbert Ozimek (Poland) 497.5 kg **B**,Gyorgy Horvath (Hungary) 495 kg
1976 G,V. Shary (USSR) 365 kg **S**,B. Blagoev (Bulgaria) 362.5 kg **B**,T. Stoichev (Bulgaria) 360 kg

MIDDLE-HEAVYWEIGHT

1896–1948 Event not held
1952 G,Norbert Schemansky (USA) 981 lb **S**,Grigoriy Novak (USSR) 903¾ **B**,Lennox Kilgour (Trinidad) 887¼
1956 G,Arkhadiy Vorobyev (USSR) 1,019¼ lb **S**,David Sheppard (USA) 975¼ **B**,Jean Debuf (France) 936¾
1960 G,Arkhadiy Vorobyev (USSR) 1,041¼ lb **S**,Trofim Lomakin (USSR) 1,008 **B**,Louis Martin (Great Britain) 980½
1964 G,Vladimir Golovanov (USSR) 1,074 lb **S**,Louis Martin (Great Britain) 1,046½ **B**,Ireneusz Palinski (Poland) 1,030
1968 G,Kaarlo Kangasniemi (Finland) 1,140½ lb **S**,Yan Talts (USSR) 1,118¼ **B**,Marek Golab (Poland) 1,091
1972 G,Andon Nikolav (Bulgaria) 525 kg **S**,Atanass Chopov (Bulgaria) 517.5 kg **B**,Hans Bettembourg (Sweden) 512.5 kg
1976 G,D. Rigert (USSR) 382.5 kg **S**,L. James (USA) 362.5 kg **B**,A. Shopov (Bulgaria) 360

HEAVYWEIGHT

1896–1912 Event not held
1920 G,Filippo Bottino (Italy) 595 lb **S**,Joseph Alzin (Luxemburg) 562 **B**,L. Bernot (France) 551
1924 G,Giuseppe Tonani (Italy) 1,140¾ lb **S**,Franz Aigner (Austria) 1,135¼ **B**,H. Tammer (Estonia) 1,096¾
1928 G,Josef Strassberger (Germany) 810 lb **S**,Arnold Luhaär (Estonia) 793½ **B**,Jaroslav Skobla (Czechoslovakia) 788
1932 G,Jaroslav Skobla (Czechoslovakia) 837¾ lb **S**,Vaclav Psenicka (Czechoslovakia) 832¼ **B**,Josef Strassberger (Germany) 832¼
1936 G,Josef Manger (Austria) 903¾ lb **S**,Vaclav Psenicka (Czechoslovakia) 887¼ **B**,Arnold Luhaär (Estonia) 882
1948 G,John Davis (USA) 996½ lb **S**,Norbert Schemansky (USA) 937 **B**,A. Charite (Netherlands) 909¼
1952 G,John Davis (USA) 1,014lb **S**,James Bradford (USA) 964½ **B**,Humberto Selvetti (Argentina) 953½
1956 G,Paul Anderson (USA) 1,102 lb **S**,Humberto Selvetti (Argentina) 1,102 **B**,Alberto Pigaiani (Italy) 997¼
1960 G,Yuriy Vlasov (USSR) 1,184½ lb **S**,James Bradford (USA) 1,129½ **B**,Norbert Schemansky (USA) 1,102
1964 G,Leonid Zhabotinsky (USSR) 1,262 lb **S**,Yuriy Vlasov (USSR) 1,256 **B**,Norbert Schemansky (USA) 1,184¾
1968 G,Leonid Zhabotinsky (USSR) 1,261¾ lb **S**,Serge Reding (Belgium) 1,223 **B**,Joseph Dube (USA) 1,223
1972 G,Jan Talts (USSR) 580 kg **S**,Alexandre Kraitchev (Bulgaria) 562.5 kg **B**,Stefan Fruetzner (East Germany) 555 kg
1976 G,V. Khristov (Bulgaria) 400 kg **S**,Y. Zaitsev (USSR) 385 kg **B**,K. Semerdijiev (Bulgaria) 385 kg

SUPER-HEAVYWEIGHT

1896–1968 Event not held
1972 G,V. Alexeev (USSR) 640 kg **S**,R. Mang (West Germany) 610 kg **B**,G. Bonk (East Germany) 572.5 kg
1976 G,V. Alexeev (USSR) 440 kg **S**,G. Bonk (East Germany) 405 kg **B**,H. Losch (East Germany) 387.5 kg

Wrestling

FREE-STYLE LIGHT-FLYWEIGHT

1896–1900 Event not held
1904 G,George Mennest (USA) **S**,Gustav Baners (USA) **B**,William Nelson (USA)
1906–1968 Event not held
1972 G,R. Dmitriev (USSR) **S**,O. Nikolov (Bulgaria) **B**,E. Javadpour (Iran)
1976 G,K. Issaev (Bulgaria) **S**,R. Dmitriev (USSR) **B**,A. Kudo (Japan)

FREE-STYLE —FLYWEIGHT

1896–1900 Event not held
1904 G,Robert Curry (USA) **S**,John Heim (USA) **B**,Gustav Thiefenthaler (USA)
1908–36 Event not held
1948 G,Lennart Viitala (Finland) **S**,Halit Balamir (Turkey) **B**,Thure Johansson (Sweden)
1952 G,Hasan Gemici (Turkey) **S**,Yushu Kitano (Japan) **B**,Mahmoud Mollaghassemi (Iran)
1956 G,Mirian Tsalkalamanidze (USSR) **S**,Mohamad Khojastehpour (Iran) **B**,Huseyin Akbas (Turkey)
1960 G,A. Bilek (Turkey) **S**,Masayuki Matsubara (Japan) **B**,S. Safepour (Iran)
1964 G,Yoshikatsu Yoshida (Japan) **S**,Chang-sun Chang (Korea) **B**,Said Alikbar Haydari (Iran)
1968 G,Shigeo Nakata (Japan) **S**,Dick Sanders (USA) **B**,Surenjav Sukhbaatar (Mongolia)
1972 G,Kiyomi Kato (Japan) **S**,Arsen Alakhverdiev (USSR) **B**,Kyong Kim Gwong (Korea)
1976 G,Y. Takada (Japan) **S**,A. Ivanov (USSR) **B**,H-S. Jeon (Korea)

FREE-STYLE —BANTAMWEIGHT

1896–1900 Event not held
1904 G,I. Niflot (USA) **S**,August Wester (USA)

B,Z. Strebler '(USA)
1908 G,George Mehnert (USA) S,W. Press (Great Britain) B,A. Cote (Canada)
1912–20 Event not held
1924 G,Kustaa Pihlajamäki (Finland) S,Kalle Makinen (Finland) B,Bryant Hines (USA)
1928 G,Kalle Makinen (Finland) S,Edmond Spapen (Belgium) B,James Trifonou (Canada)
1932 G,Robert Pearce (USA) S,Odön Zombori (Hungary) B,Aatos Jaskari (Finland)
1936 G,Odön Zombori (Hungary) S,Ross Flood (USA) B,Johannes Herbert (Germany)
1948 G,Nasuk Akkar (Turkey) S,Gerald Leeman (USA) B,Charles Kouyos (France)
1952 G,Shohachi Ishii (Japan) S,Rashid Mamedbekov (USSR) B,K. Jadav (India)
1956 G,Mustafa Dagistanli (Turkey) S,Mohamad Yaghoubi (Iran) B,Mihkail Chakhov (USSR)
1960 G,Terrence McCann (USA) S,Madjet Zalev (Bulgaria) B,Tadeusz Trojanowski (Poland)
1964 G,Yojiro Uetake (Japan) S,Huseyin Akbas (Turkey) B,Aidyn Ali Ogly (USSR) and A. Ibragimov (USSR)
1968 G,Yojiro Uetake (Japan) S,Donald Behm (USA) B,Gorgori Abutaleb (Iran)
1972 G,Hideaki Yanagide (Japan) S,Richard Sanders (USA) B,László Klinga (Hungary)
1976 G,V. Umin (USSR) S,H-D. Bruchert (East Germany) B,M. Arai (Japan)

FREE-STYLE —FEATHERWEIGHT
1896–1900 Event not held
1904 G,B. Bradshaw (USA) S,T. McLeer (USA) B,C. Clapper (USA)
1908 G,George Dole (USA) S,J. Slim (Great Britain) B,W. McKie (Great Britain)
1912 Event not held
1920 G,Charles Ackerley (USA) S,Samuel Gerson (USA) B,P. Bernard (Great Britain)
1924 G,Robin Reed (USA) S,Chester Newton (USA) B,Katsutoshi Naitoh (Japan)
1928 G,Allie Morrison (USA) S,Kustaa Pihlajamäki (Finland) B,Hans Minder (Switzerland)
1932 G,Hermanni Pihlajamäki (Finland) S,Edgar Nemir (USA) B,Einar Karlsson (Sweden)
1936 G,Kustaa Pihlajamäki (Finland) S,Francis Millard (USA) B,Gösta Jönsson (Sweden)
1948 G,Gazanfer Bilge (Turkey) S,Ivar Sjölin (Sweden) B,Adolf Müller (Switzerland)
1952 G,Bayram Sit (Turkey) S,Nasser Guivethchi (Iran) B,Josiah Henson (USA)
1956 G,Shozo Sasahara (Japan) S,Joseph Mewis (Belgium) B,Erkki Penttilä (Finland)
1960 G,Mustafa Dagistanli (Turkey) S,Stojan Ivanov (Bulgaria) B,Vladimir Rubashvili (USSR)
1964 G,Osamu Watanabe (Japan) S,Stantcho Ivanov (Bulgaria) B,Nodar Khokhash-vili (USSR)

1968 G,Masaaki Kaneko (Japan) S,Todorov Enio (Bulgaria) B,Seyed Abassy (Iran)
1972 G,Zagalav Abdulbekov (USSR) S,Vehbi Akdag (Turkey) B,Ivan Krastev (Bulgaria)
1976 G,J-M. Yang (Korea) S,Z. Oidov (Mongolia) B,G. Davis (USA)

FREE-STYLE —LIGHTWEIGHT
1896–1900 Event not held
1904 G,O. Roehm (USA) S, R. Tesing (USA) B,G. Zukel (USA)
1908 G,G. de Relwyskow (Great Britain) S, W. Wood (Great Britain) B,A. Gingell (Great Britain)
1912 Event not held
1920 G,Kalle Antilla (Finland) S,Gottfrid Svensson (Sweden) B,P. Wright (Great Britain)
1924 G,Russel Vis (USA) S,Volmar Wickström (Finland) B,Arve Haavisto (Finland)
1928 G,Osvald Käpp (Estonia) S,Charles Pacome (France) B,Eino Leino (Finland)
1932 G,Charles Pacome (France) S,Károly Kárpáti (Hungary) B,Gustaf Klarén (Sweden)
1936 G,Károly Kárpáti (Hungary) S,Wolfgang Ehrl (Finland) B,Hermanni Pihlajamäki (Finland)
1948 G,Celal Atik (Turkey) S,Gösta Fräandfors (Sweden) B,Hermann Baumann (Switzerland)
1952 G,Olle Anderberg (Sweden) S,Thomas Evans (USA) B,Djahanbakte Torfighe (Iran)
1956 G,Emamali Habibi (Iran) S,Shigeru Kasahara (Japan) B,Alimbeg Bestayev (USSR)
1960 G,Shelby Wilson (USA) S,Viktor Sinyavskiy (USSR) B,Enio Dimor (Bulgaria)
1964 G,Enio Dimor (Bulgaria) S,Klaus Rost (Germany) B,Iwao Horiuchi (Japan)
1968 G,Abdollah Movahed (Iran) S,Valychev Enio (Bulgaria) B,Sereeter Danzandarjaa (Mongolia)
1972 G,Dan Gable (USA) S,Kikou Wada (Japan) B,Ruslan Ashuraliev (USSR)
1976 G,P. Pinigin (USSR) S,L. Keaser (USA) B,Y. Sugarwara (Japan)

FREE-STYLE —WELTERWEIGHT
1896–1900 Event not held
1904 G,Charles Erickson (USA) S,William Beckmann (USA) B,J. Winholtz (USA)
1908–20 Event not held
1924 G,Hermann Gehri (Switzerland) S,Eino Leino (Finland) B,Adolf Müller (Switzerland)
1928 G,Arve Haavisto (Finland) S,Lloyd Appleton (USA) B,Morris Letchford (Canada)
1932 G,Jack van Bebber (USA) S,Daniel MacDonald (Canada) B,Eino Leino (Finland)
1936 G,Frank Lewis (USA) S,Ture Andersson (Sweden) B,Joseph Schleimer (Canada)
1948 G,Yasar Dogu (Turkey) S,Richard Garrard (Australia) B,Leland Mervill (USA)
1952 G,William Smith (USA)

S,Per Berlin (Sweden) B,Abdullah Modjtavabi (Iran)
1956 G,Mitsuo Ikeda (Japan) S,Ibrahim Zengin (Turkey) B,Vakhtang Balavadze (USSR)
1960 G,Douglas Blubaugh (USA) S,Ismail Ogan (Turkey) B,Muhammad Bashir (Pakistan)
1964 G,Ismail Ogan (Turkey) S,Guliko Sagaradze (USSR) B,Mohamad-Ali Sanatkaran (Iran)
1968 G,Mahmut Atalay (Turkey) S,Daniel Robin (France) B,Dagvas Purev (Mongolia)
1972 G,Wayne Wells (USA) S,Jan Karlsson (Sweden) B,Adolf Seger (West Germany)
1976 G,J. Date (Japan) S,M. Barzegar (Iran) B,S. Dziedzic (USA)

FREE-STYLE —MIDDLEWEIGHT
1896–1904 Event not held
1908 G,Stanley Bacon (Great Britain) S,G. de Relwyskow (Great Britain) B,F. Beck (Great Britain)
1912 Event not held
1920 G,Eino Leino (Finland) S,Väino Penttala (Finland) B,Charles Johnson (USA)
1924 G,Fritz Haggmann (Switzerland) S,Pierre Olivier (Belgium) B,Vilho Pekkala (Finland)
1928 G,Ernst Kyburz (Switzerland) S,D. Stockton (Canada) B,S. Rabin (Great Britain)
1932 G,Ivar Johansson (Sweden) S,Kyösti Luukko (Finland) B,Jozsef Tunyogi (Hungary)
1936 G,Emile Poilvé (France) S,Richard Voliva (USA) B,Ahmet Kirecci (Turkey)
1948 G,Glen Brand (USA) S,Adil Candemir (Turkey) B,Erik Linden (Sweden)
1952 G,David Cimakuridze (USSR) S,Gholamreza Takhti (Iran) B,György Gurics (Hungary)
1956 G,Nikola Nikolov (Bulgaria) S,Daniel Hodge (USA) B,Georgiy Skhirtladze (USSR)
1960 G,Hassan Gungor (Turkey) S,Georgiy Skhirtladze (USSR) B,Hans Antonsson (Sweden)
1964 G,Prodan Gardjev (Bulgaria) S,Hassan Gungor (Turkey) B,Daniel Brand (USA)
1968 G,Boris Gurevitch (USSR) S,Munkbhat Jigid (Mongolia) B,Prodane Gardjev (Bulgaria)
1972 G,Levan Tediashvili (USSR) S,John Peterson (USA) B,Vasile Jorga (Rumania)
1976 G,J. Peterson (USA) S,V. Novojilov (USSR) B,A. Seger (West Germany)

FREE-STYLE —LIGHT-HEAVYWEIGHT
1896–1912 Event not held
1920 G,Anders Larsson (Sweden) S,Charles Courant (Switzerland) B,Walter Maurer (USA)
1924 G,John Spellman (USA) S,Rudolf Svensson (Sweden) B,Charles Courant (Switzerland)
1928 G,Thure Sjöstedt (Sweden) S,Anton Bögli

(Switzerland) B,Henri Lefebre (France)
1932 G,Peter Mehringer (USA) S,Thure Sjöstedt (Sweden) B,Eddie Scarf (Australia)
1936 G,Knut Fridell (Sweden) S,August Néo (Estonia) B,Erich Siebert (Germany)
1948 G,Henry Wittenberg (USA) S,Fritz Stöckli (Switzerland) B,Bengt Fahlkvist (Sweden)
1952 G,Wiking Palm (Sweden) S,Henry Wittenberg (USA) B,Adil Atan (Turkey)
1956 G,Gholamreza Takhti (Iran) S,Boris Koulayev (USSR) B,Peter Blair (USA)
1960 G,Ismet Atli (Turkey) S,Gholamreza Takhti (Iran) B,Anatoliy Albul (USSR)
1964 G,Alexander Medved (USSR) S,Ahmed Ayuk (Turkey) B,Said Sherifov (Bulgaria)
1968 G,Ahmed Ayuk (Turkey) S,Shota Lomidze (USSR) B,Jozsef Csatari (Hungary)
1972 G,Ben Peterson (USA) S,Gennadi Strakhov (USSR) B,Karoly Bajko (Hungary)
1976 G,L. Tediashvili (USSR) S,B. Peterson (USA) B,S. Morcov (Rumania)

FREE-STYLE —HEAVYWEIGHT
1896 G,Karl Schumann (Germany) S,Georges Tsitas (Greece) B,Stephanos Christopulos (Greece)
1904 G,B. Hansen (USA) S,Frank Kungler (USA) B,F. Warmbold (USA)
1908 G,G. O'Kelly (Great Britain) S,Jacob Gundersen (Norway) B,Edward Barrett (Great Britain)
1912 Event not held
1920 G,Robert Rothe (Switzerland) S,Nathan Pendleton (USA) B,Ernst Nilsson (Sweden) and Frederick Meyer (USA)
1924 G,Harry Steele (USA) S,Henry Wernli (Switzerland) B,A. McDonald (Great Britain)
1928 G,Johan Richthoff (Sweden) S,Aukusti Sihvola (Finland) B,E. Dame (France)
1932 G,Johan Richthoff (Sweden) S,John Riley (USA) B,Nikolaus Hirschl (Austria)
1936 G,Kristjan Palusalu (Estonia) S,Josef Klapuch (Czechoslovakia) B,Hjalmar Nyström (Finland)
1948 G,Gyula Bóbis (Hungary) S,Bertil Antonsson (Sweden) B,Joseph Armstrong (Australia)
1952 G,Arsen Mekokishvili (USSR) S,Hans Antonsson (Sweden) B,Kenneth Richmond (Great Britain)
1956 G,Hamit Kaplan (Turkey) S,Hussein Alicher (Bulgaria) B,Taisto Kangasniemi (Finland)
1960 G,Wilfried Dietrich (Germany) S,Hamit Kaplan (Turkey) B,Sergey Sarasov (USSR)
1964 G,Alexander Ivanitsky (USSR) S,Liutvi Djiber (Bulgaria) B,Hamit Kaplan (Turkey)
1968 G,Alexandr Medved (USSR) S,Osman Douraliev (Bulgaria) B,Wilfried Dietrich (West Germany)
1972 G,Ivan Yarygin (USSR)

S,Khorloo Baianmunkh (Mongolia) B,Joszef Csatáti (Hungary)
1976 G,I. Yarygin (USSR) S,R. Hellickson (USA) B,D. Kostov (Bulgaria)

FREE-STYLE —SUPER HEAVYWEIGHT
1896–1968 Event not held
1972 G,A. Medved (USSR) S,O. Duraliev (Bulgaria) B,C. Taylor (USA)
1976 G,S. Andiev (USSR) S,J. Balla (Hungary) B,L. Simon (Rumania)

GRECO-ROMAN LIGHT-FLYWEIGHT
1896–1968 Event not held
1972 G,G. Berceanu (Rumania) S,R. Ahabadi (Iran) B,S. Anghelov (Bulgaria)
1976 G,A. Shumakov (USSR) S,G. Berceanu (Rumania) B,S. Anghelov (Bulgaria)

GRECO-ROMAN —FLYWEIGHT
1896–1936 Event not held
1948 G,Pietro Lombardi (Italy) S,Kenan Olcay (Turkey) B,Reino Kangasmäki (Finland)
1952 G,Boris Gurevich (USSR) S,Ignazio Fabra (Italy) B,Leo Honkala (Finland)
1956 G,Nikolay Solovyev (USSR) S,Ignazio Fabra (Italy) B,Dürsan Egribas (Turkey)
1960 G,Dumitru Pirvulescu (Romania) S,O. Sayed (UAR) B,Mohamad Paziraye (Iran)
1964 G,Tsutomu Hanahara (Japan) S,Angel Kerezov (Bulgaria) B,Dumitru Pirvulesco (Romania)
1968 G,Petar Kirov (Bulgaria) S,Vladimir Bakulin (USSR) B,Miroslav Zeman (Czechoslovakia)
1972 G,Petar Kirov (Bulgaria) S,Koichiro Hirayama (Japan) B,Giuseppe Bognanni (Italy)
1976 G,V. Konstantinov (USSR) S,N. Ginga (Rumania) B,K. Hirayama (Japan)

GRECO-ROMAN —BANTAMWEIGHT
1896–1920 Event not held
1924 G,Edvard Pütsep (Estonia) S,Anselm Ahlfors (Finland) B,Väinö Ikonen (Finland)
1928 G,Kurt Leucht (Germany) S,Josef Maudr (Czechoslavakia) B,Giovanni Gozzi (Italy)
1932 G,Jakob Brendel (Germany) S,Marcello Nizzola (Italy) B,Louis Francois (France)
1936 G,Marton Lorinc (Hungary) S,Egon Svensson (Sweden) B,Jakob Brendel (Germany)
1948 G,Kurt Pettersson (Sweden) S,Mahmoud Hassan Aly (Egypt) B,Hamit Kaya (Turkey)
1952 G,Imre Hódos (Hungary) S,Zakaria Khihab (Lebanon) B,Artem Teryan (USSR)
1956 G,Konstantin Vyrupayev (USSR) S,Edvin Vesterby (Sweden) B,Francisc Horvat (Romania)
1960 G,Olyeg Karavayev (USSR) S,Ion Cernea (Romania) B,Dimitar Stoikov (Bulgaria)
1964 G,Masamitsu Ichiguchi (Japan) S,Vladlen Trostiansky (USSR) B,Ion Cernea (Romania)

1968 G,Janos Varga (Hungary) S,Ion Baciu (Romania) B,Ivan Kochergin (USSR)
1972 G,Rustem Kazakov (USSR) S,Hans-Jürgen Veil (West Germany) B,Risto Bjorlin (Finland)
1976 G,P. Ukkola (Finland) S,I. Frgic (Yugoslavia) B,F. Mustafin (USSR)

GRECO-ROMAN —FEATHERWEIGHT
1896–1908 Event not held
1912 G,Kalle Koskelo (Finland) S,Georg Gerstacker (Germany) B,Otto Lasanen (Finland)
1920 G,Oskari Friman (Finland) S,Heikki Kähkönen (Finland) B,Fridtjof Svensson (Sweden)
1924 G,Kalle Antilla (Finland) S,Aleksanteri Toivola (Finland) B,Erik Malmberg (Sweden)
1928 G,Voldemar Väli (Estonia) S,Erik Malmberg (Sweden) B,Giacomo Quaglia (Italy)
1932 G,Giovanni Gozzi (Italy) S,Wolfgang Ehrl (Germany) B,Lauri Koskela (Finland)
1936 G,Yasar Erkan (Turkey) S,Aarne Reini (Finland) B,Einar Karlsson (Sweden)
1948 G,Mohammed Oktav (Turkey) S,Olle Anderberg (Sweden) B,Ferenc Tóth (Hungary)
1952 G,Yakov Punkin (USSR) S,Imre Polyák (Hungary) B,Abdel Rashed (Egypt)
1956 G,Rauno Mäkinen (Finland) S,Imre Polyák (Hungary) B,Roman Dzneladze (USSR)
1960 G,Müzanir Sille (Turkey) S,Imre Polyák (Hungary) B,Konstantin Vyrupayev (USSR)
1964 G,Imre Polyák (Hungary) S,Roman Rurua (USSR) B,Branko Martinovic (Yugoslavia)
1968 G,Roman Rurua (USSR) S,Hideo Fujimoto (Japan) B,Simion Popescu (Romania)
1972 G,Gheorghi Markov (Bulgaria) S,Heinz-Helmut Wehling (East Germany) B,Kozimierz Lipien (Poland)
1976 G,K. Lipien (Poland) S,N. Davidian (USSR) B,L. Reczi (Hungary)

GRECO-ROMAN —LIGHTWEIGHT
1896–1904 Event not held
1908 G,Enrico Porro (Italy) S,Nikolay Orlov (Russia) B,Arvo Linden-Linko (Finland)
1912 G,Eemil Wäre (Finland) S,Gustaf Malmström (Sweden) B,Edvin Matiasson (Sweden)
1920 G,Eemil Wäre (Finland) S,Taavi Tamminen (Finland) B,Fritjof Andersen (Norway)
1924 G,Oskari Friman (Finland) S,Lajos Keresztes (Hungary) B,Kalle-Westerlund (Finland)
1928 G,Lajos Keresztes (Hungary) S,Edvard Sperling (Germany) B,Edvard Westerlund (Finland)
1932 G,Erik Malmberg (Sweden) S,Abraham Kurland (Denmark) B,Edvard Sperling (Germany)
1936 G,Lauri Koskela (Finland) S,Josef Herda (Czechoslovakia) B,Voldemar Väli (Estonia)
1948 G,Karl Freij (Sweden) S,Aage Eriksen (Norway) B,Károly Ferencz (Hungary)

1952 G,Khasame Safin (USSR) S,Karl Freij (Sweden) B,Mikulas Athanasov (Czechoslovakia)
1956 G,Kyösti Lehtonen (Finland) S,Riza Dogan (Turkey) B,Gyula Tóth (Hungary)
1960 G,Avtandil Koridze (USSR) S,Bozidar Martinovic (Yugoslavia) B,Roland Freij (Sweden)
1964 G,Kazim Ayvaz (Turkey) S,Valerin Bularca (Romania) B,David Gvantseladze (USSR)
1968 G,Muneji Munemura (Japan) S,Stevan Horvat (Yugoslavia) B,Petros Galaktopoulos (Greece)
1972 G,Shamil Khisamutdinov (USSR) S,Stoyan Apostolov (Bulgaria) B,Gian Matteo Ranzi (Italy)
1976 G,S. Nalbandyan (USSR) S,S. Rusu (Rumania) B,H-H. Wehling (East|Germany

GRECO-ROMAN —WELTERWEIGHT
1896–1928 Event not held
1932 G,Ivar Johansson (Sweden) S,Väinö Kajander-Kajukorpi (Finland) B,Ercole Gallegatti (Italy)
1936 G,Rudolf Svedberg (Sweden) S,Fritz Schäfer (Germany) B,Eino Virtanen (Finland)
1948 G,Gösta Andersson (Sweden) S,Miklós Szilvási (Hungary) B,Carl Hansen (Denmark)
1952 G,Miklós Szilvási (Hungary) S,Gösta Andersson (Sweden) B,Khalil Taha (Lebanon)
1956 G,Mithat Bayrak (Turkey) S,Vladimir Maneyev (USSR) B,Per Berlin (Sweden)
1960 G,Mithat Bayrak (Turkey) S,Günther Maritschnigg (Germany) B,René Schiermeyer (France)
1964 G,Anatoly Kolesloav (USSR) S,Cyril Todorov (Bulgaria) B,Bertil Nyström (Sweden)
1968 G,Rudolf Vesper (East Germany) S,Daniel Robin (France) B,Karoly Bajko (Hungary)
1972 G,Vitezslav Mache (Czechoslovakia) S,Petros Galaktopoulos (Greece) B,Jan Karlsson (Sweden)
1976 G,A. Bykov (USSR) S,V. Macha (Czechoslovakia) B,K. Helbing (West Germany)

GRECO-ROMAN —MIDDLEWEIGHT
1896–1904 Event not held
1908 G,Fritjof Martensson (Sweden) S,Mauritz Andersson (Sweden) B,Anders Andersen (Denmark)
1912 G,Claes Johansson (Sweden) S,Max Klein (Russia) B,Alfred Asikainen (Finland)
1920 G,Carl Westergren (Sweden) S,Artur Lindfors (Finland) B,Massa Perttila (Finland)
1924 G,Edvard Westerlund (Finland) S,Artur Lindfors (Finland) B,Roman Steinberg (Estonia)
1928 G,Väinö Kokkinen (Finland) S,László Papp (Hungary) B,Albert Kusnetz (Sweden)
1932 G,Väinö Kokkinen (Finland) S,Johann Földeák

(Germany) B,Axel Cadier (Sweden)
1936 G,Ivar Johansson (Sweden) S,Ludwig Schweikert (Germany) B,József Palotás (Hungary)
1948 G,Axel Grönberg (Sweden) S,Mohamed Tayfur (Turkey) B,Ercole Gallegatti (Italy)
1952 G,Axel Grönberg (Sweden) S,Kalervo Rauhala (Finland) B,Nikolay Belov (USSR)
1956 G,Guivi Kartozia (USSR) S,Dimitar Dobrev (Bulgaria) B,Karl-Axel Jansson (Sweden)
1960 G,Dimitar Dobrev (Bulgaria) S,Lothar Metz (Germany) B,Ion Taranu (Romania)
1964 G,Branislav Simic (Yugoslavia) S,Jiri Kormanik (Czechoslovakia) B,Lothar Metz (Germany)
1968 G,Lothar Metz (East Germany) S,Valentin Olenik (USSR) B,Branislav Simic (Yugoslavia)
1972 G,Csaba Hegedus (Hungary) S,Anatoli Nazarenko (USSR) B,Milan Nenadic (Yugoslavia)
1976 G,M. Petkovic (Yugoslavia) S,V. Cheboksarov (USSR) B,I. Kolev (Bulgaria)

GRECO-ROMAN —LIGHT HEAVYWEIGHT
1896–1904 Event not held
1908 G,Verner Weckman (Finland) S,Yrjö Saarela (Finland) S,Karl Jensen (Denmark)
1912 G,Anders Ahlgren (Sweden) and Ivar Bohling (Finland) B,Béla Vargya (Hungary)
1920 G,Claes Johansson (Sweden) S,Edil Rosenquist (Finland) B,Johnsen Eriksen (Denmark)
1924 G,Carl Westergren (Sweden) S,Rudolf Svensson (Sweden) B,Onni Pellinen (Finland)
1928 G,Ibrahim Moustafa (Egypt) S,Adolf Rieger (Germany) B,Onni Pellinen (Finland)
1932 G,Rudolf Svensson (Sweden) S,Onni Pellinen (Finland) B,Mario Gruppioni (Italy)
1936 G,Axel Cadier (Sweden) S,Edwins Bietags (Lithuania) B,August Néo (Estonia)
1948 G,Karl Nilsson (Sweden) S,Kaelpo Gröndahl (Finland) B,Ibrahim Orabi (Egypt)
1952 G,Kaelpo Gröndahl (Finland) S,Shalva Shikhladze (USSR) B,Karl Nilsson (Sweden)
1956 G,Valentin Nikolayev (USSR) S,Petko Sirakov (Bulgaria) B,Karl Nilsson (Sweden)
1960 G,Trofim Kis (Turkey) S,Kraliu Bimbalov (Bulgaria) B,Guivi Kartozia (USSR)
1964 G,Boyan Alexandrov (Bulgaria) S,Pev Svensson (Sweden) B,Heinz Kiehl (Germany)
1968 G,Radev Boyan (Bulgaria) S,Nikolai Yakovenko (USSR) B,Martinescu Nicolae (Romania)
1972 G,Valeri Rezantsev (USSR) S,Josip Corak (Yugoslavia) B,Czeslaw Kwiecenski (Poland)
1976 G,V. Rezantsev (USSR) S,S. Ivanov (Bulgaria) B,C. Kwiecinski (Poland)

GRECO-ROMAN —HEAVYWEIGHT

1896–1904 Event not held
1908 G,Richard Weisz (Hungary) S,O. Petrov (Russia) B,Sören Jensen (Denmark)
1912 G,Yrjö Saarela (Finland) S,Johan Olin (Finland) B,Sören Jensen (Denmark)
1920 G,Adolf Lindfors (Finland) S,Paul Hansen (Denmark) B,Martti Nieminen (Finland)
1924 G,Henry Deglane (France) S,Edil Rosenquist (Finland) B,Raymund Badó (Hungary)
1928 G,Rudolf Svensson (Sweden) S,Hjalmar Nyström (Finland) B,Georg Gehring (Germany)
1932 G,Carl Westergren (Sweden) S,Josef Urban (Czechoslovakia) B,Nikolaus Hirschl (Austria)
1936 G,Kristjan Palusalu (Estonia) S,John Nyman (Sweden) B,Kurt Hornfischer (Germany)
1948 G,Ahmed Kirecci (Turkey) S,Tor Nilsson (Sweden) B,Guido Fantoni (Italy)
1952 G,Johannes Kotkas (USSR) S,Josef Ruzicka (Czechoslovakia) B,Tauro Kovanen (Finland)
1956 G,Anatoliy Parfenyov (USSR) S,Wilfried Dietrich (Germany) B,Adelmo Bulgarelli (Italy)
1960 G,Ivan Bogdan (USSR) S,Wilfried Dietrich (Germany) B,Karoly Kubat (Czechoslovakia)
1964 G,Istvan Kozma (Hungary) S,Anatoly Roskin (USSR) B,Wilfried Dietrich (Germany)
1968 G,Istvan Kozma (Hungary) S,Anatoly Roskin (USSR) B,Petr Kment (Czecgoslovakia)
1972 G,Nicolae Martinescu (Rumania) S,Nikolai Yakovenko (USSR) B, Ferenc Kiss (Hungary)
1976 G,N. Bolboshin (USSR) S,K. Goranov (Bulgaria) B,A. Skrzylewski (Poland)

GRECO-ROMAN —SUPER HEAVYWEIGHT

1896–1968 Event not held
1972 G,A. Roshin (USSR) S,A. Tomov (Bulgaria) B,V. Dolipschi (Rumania)
1976 G,A. Kolchinski (USSR) S,A. Tomov (Bulgaria) B,R. Codreanu (Rumania)

Yachting
INTERNATIONAL SOLING CLASS
1896–1968 Event not held
1972 G,USA (H. Melges Jr., W. Bentson, W. Allen) S,Sweden B,Canada
1976 G,Denmark (P. Jenson, V. Bandolowski, E. Hansen) 46.70 pts. S,USA 47.40 B,East Germany 47.40

INTERNATIONAL TEMPEST CLASS
1896–1968 Event not held
1972 G,USSR (V. Mankin, V. Dyrdyra) S,Great Britain|B,USA
1976 G,Sweden (J. Albrechtson, I. Hansson) 14.00 pts S,USSR 30.40|B,USA 32.70

INTERNATIONAL 470 CLASS
1896–1972 Event not held
1976 G,West Germany (F. Huebner, H. Bode)

42.00 pts S,Spain 49.70 B,Australia 57.00

INTERNATIONAL TORNADO CLASS
1896–1972 Event not held
1976 G,Great Britain (R. White, J. Osborn) 18.00 pts S,USA 36.00 B. West Germany 37.70

FLYING DUTCHMAN
1896–1956 Event not held
1960 G,Norway (Peter Lunde, Bjorn Bergvall) 6,774 pts S,Denmark 5,991 B,Germany 5,882
1964 G,New Zealand (Helman Pederson, E. Wells) 6,255 pts S,Great Britain 5,556 B,USA 5,158
1968 G,Great Britain (Rodney Pattisson, Iain Macdonald Smith) 3.0 pts S,West Germany 43.7 B,Brazil 48.4
1972 G,Great Britain (Rodney Pattisson, Christopher Davies) S,France B,West Germany
1976 G,West Germany (J. Diesch, E. Diesch) 34.7 pts. S,Great Britain 51.7 B,Brazil 52.1

FINN
1896–1952 Event not held
1956 G,Paul Elvström (Denmark) 7,509 pts S,Andre Nelis (Belgium) 6,254 B,John Marvin (USA) 5,953
1960 G,Paul Elvström (Denmark) 8,171 pts. S, Aleksandr Tyukelov (USSR) 6,250 B,Andre Nelis (Belgium) 5,934
1964 G,Willi Kuhweide (Germany) 7,638 pts. S,Peter Barrett (USA) 6,373 B,Henning Wind (Denmark) 6,190
1968 G,Valentin Mankin (USSR) 11.7 pts. S,Hubert Raudaschl (Austria) 53.4 B,Fabio Albarelli (Italy) 55.1
1972 G,Serge Maury (France) Ilias Hatzipavlis (Greece) B,Victor Potapov (USSR)
1976 G,J. Shumann (East Germany) 35.4 pts. S,A. Balashov (USSR) 39.7 B,J. Bertrand (Australia) 46.4

Nordic Ski-ing (Men)
15 KM CROSS-COUNTRY
1908–20 Event not held
1924 G,Thorleif Haug (Norway) 1h 14m 31.0s S,Johan Gröttumsbraaten (Norway) 1h 15m 51.0s B,Tipani Niku (Finland) 1h 26m 26.0s
1928 G,Johan Gröttumsbraaten (Norway) 1h 37m 01.0s S,Ole Hegge (Norway) 1h 39m 01.0s B,Reidar Odegaard (Norway) 1h 40m 11.0s
1932 G,Sven Utterström (Sweden) 1h 23m 07.0s S,Axel Wikström (Sweden) 1h 25m 07.0s B,Veli Saarinen (Finland) 1h 25m 24.0s
1936 G,Erik-August Larsson (Sweden) 1h 14m 38.0s S,Oddbjörn Hagen (Norway) 1h 15m 33.0s B,Pekki Niemi (Finland) 1h 16m 59.0s
1948 G,Martin Lundström (Sweden) 1h 13m 50.0s S,Nils Ostensson (Sweden) 1h 14m 22.0s B,Gunnar Eriksson (Sweden) 1h 16m 06.0s

1952 G,Hallgeir Brenden (Norway) 1h 1m 34.0s S,Tapio Mäkelä (Finland) 1h 2m 09.0s B,Paavo Lonkila (Finland) 1h 2m 20.0s
1956 G,Hallgeir Brenden (Norway) 49m 39s S,Sixten Jernberg (Sweden) 50m 14.0s B,Pavel Koltschin (USSR) 50m 17.0s
1960 G,Haakon Brusveen (Norway) 51m 55.5s S,Sixten Jernberg (Sweden) 51m 58.6s B,Veikko Hakulinen (Finland) 52m 03.0s
1964 G,Eero Mantyranta (Finland) 50m 54.1s S,Harald Gröenningen (Norway) 51m 34.8s B,Sixten Jernberg (Sweden) 51m 42.2s
1968 G,Harald Gröenningen (Norway) 47m 54.2s S,Eero Maentyranta (Finland) 47m 56.1s B,Gunnar Larsson (Sweden) 48m 33.7s
1972 G,Sven-Ake Lundback (Sweden) 45m 28.24s S, Fedor Simaschov (USSR) 46m 00.84s B,Ivar Formo (Norway) 46m 02.86s
1976 G,N. Bajukov (USSR) 43m 58.47s S,E. Beliaev (USSR) 44m 01.10s B,A. Koivisto (Finland) 44m 19.25s

30 KM CROSS-COUNTRY
1908–52 Event not held
1956 G,Veikko Hakulinen (Finland) 1h 44m 06.0s S,Sixten Jernberg (Sweden) 1h 44m 30.0s B,Pavel Koltschin (USSR) 1h 45m 45.0s
1960 G,Sixten Jernberg (Sweden) 1h 51m 03.9s S,Rolf Rämgard (Sweden) 1h 51m 16.9s B,Nikolay Anikin (USSR) 1h 52m 28.2s
1964 G,Eero Mantyranta (Finland) 1h 30m 50.7s S,Harald Gröenningen (Norway) 1h 32m 02.3s B,I. Voronchikin (USSR) 1h 32m 15.8s
1968 G,Franco Nones (Italy) 1h 35m 39.2s S,Odd Martinsen (Norway) 1h 36m 28.9s B,Eero Maentyranta (Finland) 1h 36m 55.3s
1972 G,Viaceseslav Vedenine (USSR) 1h 36m 31.2s S,Paal Tyldum (Norway) 1h 37m 25.3s B,Johs Harviken (Norway) 1h 37m 32.4s
1976 G,S. Saveliev (USSR) 1h 30m 29.38s S,W. Koch (USA) 1h 30m 57.84s B,I. Garanin (Finland) 1h 31m 09.29s

50 KM CROSS-COUNTRY
1908–20 Event not held
1924 G,Thorleif Haug (Norway) 3h 44m 32.0s S,Thoralf Strömstad (Norway) 3h 46m 23.0s B,Johan Gröttumsbraaten (Norway) 3h 47m 46.0s
1928 G,Per Erik Hedlund (Sweden) 4h 52m 03.3s S,Gustaf Jonsson (Sweden) 5h 05m 30.0s B,Volger Andersson (Sweden) 5h 05m 46.0s
1932 G,Veli Saarinen (Finland) 4h 28m 00.0s S,Väinö Liik-kanen (Finland) 4h 28m 20.0s B,Arne Rustadstuen (Norway) 4h 31m 20.0s
1936 G,Elis Wiklund (Sweden) 3h 30m 11.0s S,Axel Wikström (Sweden) 3h 33m 20.0s B,Nils-Joel

Englund (Sweden) 3h 34m 10.0s
1948 G,Nils Karlsson (Sweden) 3h 47m 48.0s S,Harald Eriksson (Sweden) 3h 52m 20.0s B,Benjamin Vanninen (Finland)|3h 57m 28.0s
1952 G,Veikko Hakulinen (Finland) 3h 33m 33.0s S,Eero Kolehmainen (Finland) 3h 38m 11.0s B,Magnar Estenstad (Norway) 3h 38m 28.0s
1956 G,Sixten Jerberg (Sweden) 2h 50m 27.0s S,Veikko Hakulinen (Finland) 2h 51m 45.0s B,Fyedor Terentyev (USSR) 2h 53m 32.0s
1960 G,Kalevi Hämäläinen (Finland) 2h 59m 06.3s S,Veikko Hakulinen (Finland) 2h 59m 26.7s B,Rolf Rämgard (Sweden) 3h 02m 46.7s
1964 G,Sixten Jernberg (Sweden) 2h 43m 52.6s S,A. Roennlund (Sweden) 2h 44m 58.2s B,A. Tiainen (Finland) 2h 45m 30.4s
1968 G,Ole Ellefsaeter (Norway) 2h 28m 45.8s S,Viatches Vedenine (USSR) 2h 29m 02.5s B,Josef Haas (Switzerland) 2h 29m 14.8s
1972 G,Paal Tyldrum (Norway) 2h 43m 14.75s S,Magne Myrmo (Norway) 2h 43m 29.45s B,Viaceslav Vedenine (USSR) 2h 44m 00.19s
1976 G,I. Formo (Norway) 2h 37m 30.05s S,G-D. Klause (East Germany) 2h 38m 13.21s B,B. Sodergren (Sweden) 2h 39m 39.21s

RELAY RACE 4×10 KM
1908–32 Event not held
1936 G,Finland (Nurmela, Karppnen, Lähde, Jalkanen) 2h 41m 33.0s S,Norway 2h 41m 39.0s B,Sweden 2h 43m 03.0s
1948 G,Sweden (Ostensson, Tapp, Eriksson, Lundström) 2h 32m 08.0s S,Finland 2h 41m 06.0s B,Norway 2h 44m 33.0s
1952 G,Finland (Hasu, Lonkila, Korhonen, Mäkelä) 2h 20m 16.0s S,Norway 2h 23m 13.0s B,Sweden 2h 24m 13.0s
1956 G,USSR (Terentyev, Koltschin, Anikin, Kusin) 2h 15m 30.0s S,Finland 2h 21m 31.0s B,Sweden 2h 17m 42.0s
1960 G,Finland (Alatalo, Mäntyrana, Huhtala, Hakulinen) 2h 18m 45.6s S,Norway 2h 18m 46.4s B,USSR 2h 21m 21.6s
1964 G,Sweden (Asph, Jernberg, Stefansson, Roennlund) 2h 18m 34.6s S,Finland 2h 18m 42.4s B,USSR 2h 18m 46.9s
1968 G,Norway (Martinsen, Tyldum, Groenningen, Ellefsaeter) 2h 8m 33.5s S,Sweden 2h 10m 13.2s B,Finland 2h 10m 56.5s
1972 G,USSR (Voronkov, Skobov, Simaschov, Vedenine) 2h 04m 47.94s S,Norway 2h 04m 57.06s B,Switzerland 2h 07m 00.06s
1976 G,Finland (M. Pitkaenen, J. Mieto, P. Teurajaervi, A. Koivisto) 2h 07m 59.72s S,Norway 2h 09m 58.36s B,USSR 2h 10m 51.46s

Nordic Ski-ing (Women)

5 KM CROSS-COUNTRY
1908–60 Event not held
1964 G,Klaudia Boyerskikh (USSR) 17m 50.5s S,M. Lehtonen (Finland) 17m 52.9s B,A. Kolchina (USSR) 18m 08.4s
1968 G,Toini Gustafsson (Sweden) 16m 45.2s S,Galina Koulakova (USSR) 16m 48.4s B,Alevtina Koltchina (USSR) 16m 51.6s
1972 G,Galina Kulakova (USSR) 17m 00.50s S, Marjatta Kajosmaa (Finland) 17m 05.50s B,Helena Sikolova (Czechoslovakia) 17m 07.32s
1976 G,H. Takalo (Finland) 15m 48.69s S,R. Smetanina (USSR) 15m 49.73s B,G. Kulakova (USSR) 16m 07.36s

10 KM CROSS-COUNTRY
1908–48 Event not held
1952 G,Lydia Widemen (Finland) 41m 40.0s S,Mirja Hietamies (Finland) 42m 39.0s B,Siiri Rantanen (Finland) 42m 50.0s
1956 G,Lyubov Kosyryeva (USSR) 38m 11.0s S,Radya Yeroschina (USSR) 38m 16.0s B,Sonja Edström (Sweden) 38m 23.0s
1960 G,Maria Gusakova (USSR) 39m 46.6s S,Lyubov Baranova-Kosyryeva (USSR) 40m 04.2s B,Radya Yeroschina (USSR) 40m 06.0s
1964 G,Klaudia Boyarskikh (USSR) 40m 24.3s S,E. Mekshilo (USSR) 40m 26.6s B,Maria Gusakova (USSR) 40m 46.6s
1968 G,Toini Gustafsson (Sweden) 36m 46.5s S,Berit Moerdre (Sweden) 37m 54.6s B,Inger Aufles (Norway) 37m 59.9s
1972 G,Galina Kulakova (USSR) 34m 17.8s S,Alevtina Olunina (USSR) 34m 54.1s B,Marjatta Kajosmaa (Finland) 34m 56.5s
1976 G,R. Smetanina (USSR) 30m 13.41s S,H. Takalo (Finland) 30m 14.28s B,G. Kulakova (USSR) 30m 38.61s

3×5 KM RELAY
1908–52 Event not held
1956 G,Finland (Polkunen, Hietamies, Rantanen) 1h 9m 01.0s S,USSR 1h 9m 28.0s B,Sweden 1h 9m 48.0s
1960 G,Sweden (Johansson, Strandberg, Ruthström-Edström) 1h 4m 21.4s S,USSR 1h 5m 2.6s B,Finland 1h 6m 27.5s
1964 G,USSR (Koltschina, Mekshilo, Boyarskikh) 59m 20.2s S,Sweden 1h 1m 27.0s B,Finland 1h 2m 45.1s
1968 G,Norway (Aufles, Damon, Moerdre) 57m 30.0s S,Sweden 57m 51.0s B,USSR 58m 13.6s
1972 G,USSR (Moukhateva, Olunina, Kulakova) 48m 46.15s S,Finland 49m 19.37s B,Norway 49m 51.49s
1976 G,USSR (Baldicheva, Amosova, Smetanina, Kulakova) 1h 07m 49.75s .S,Finland 1h 08m 36.57s B,East Germany 1h 09m 57.95s
*Race increased to four stages in 1976

Ski Jumping
SMALL HILL (70 metres)
1908–1960 Held on one hill only
1964 G,Veikko Kankkonen (Finland) 229.90 pts. S,Toralf Engan (Norway) 226.30 B,T. Brandtzaeg (Norway)¦222.90
1968 G,Jiri Raska (Czechoslovakia) 216.5 pts. S,Reinhold Bachler (Austria) 214.2 B,Baldur Preiml (Austria) 212.6
1972 G,Yakio Kasaya (Japan) 244.2 pts. S,Akitsugo Konno (Japan) 234.8 B,Seiji Aochi (Japan) 229.5
1976 G, H-G. Aschenbach (East Germany) 252.0 pts. S,J. Danneberg (East Germany) 246.2 B,K. Schnabl (Austria) 242.0

BIG HILL (90 metres)
1908–1960 Event not held
1964 G,Toralf Engan (Norway) 230.70 pts. S,Veikko Kankkonen (Finland) 228.90 B,Targeir Brandtzaeg (Norway) 227.20
1968 G,Vladimir Beloussov (USSR) 231.3 pts. S,Jiri Raska (Czechoslovakia) 229.4 B,Lars Grini (Norway) 214.3
1972 G,Wojciech Fortuna (Poland) 219.9 pts. S,Walter Steiner (Switzerland) 219.8 B, Rainer Schmidt (East Germany) 219.3
1976 G,K. Schnabl (Austria) 234.8 pts. S,A. Innauer (Austria) 232.9 B,H. Glass (East Germany) 221.7

NORDIC COMBINED (15 KM and jumping)
1908–20 Event not held
1924 G,Thorleif Haug (Norway) S,Thoralf Strömstad (Norway) B,Johan Gröttumsbraaten (Norway)
1928 G,Johan Gröttumsbraaten (Norway) S,Hans Vinjarengen (Norway) B,John Snersrud (Norway)
1932 G,Johan Gröttumsbraaten (Norway) 446.0 pts. S,Ole Stenen (Norway) 436.05 B,Hans Vinjarengen (Norway) 434.60
1936 G,Oddbjorn Hagen (Norway) 430.30 pts. S,Olaf Hoffsbakken (Norway) 419.80 B,Sverre Brodahl (Norway) 408.10
1948 G,Heikki Hasu (Finland) 448.80 pts. S,Martti Huhtala (Finland) 433.65 B,Sfen Israelsson (Sweden) 433.40
1952 G,Simon Slattvik (Norway) 451.952 pts. S,Heikki Hasu (Finland) 447.5 B,Sverre Stenersen (Norway) 436.335
1956 G,Sverre Stenersen (Norway) 455.0 pts. S,Bengt Eriksson (Sweden) 473.4 B,Franciszek Gron-Gasienica (Poland) 436.8
1960 G,Georg Thoma (Germany) 457.952 pts. S,Tormod Knutsen (Norway) 453.0 B,Nikolay Gusakow (USSR) 452.0
1964 G,Tormod Knutsen (Norway) 469.28 pts. S,N. Kiselev (USSR) 453.04 B,Georg Thoma (Germany) 452.88
1968 G,Franz Keller (West Germany) 240.1 pts. S,Hiroshi Itagaki (Japan) 237.4 B, Erwin Fiedor (Poland) 234.3
1972 G,Ulrich Wehling (East Germany) 413.34 pts. S,Rauno Mittinen (Finland)

405.55 B,Karl-Heinz Luck (East Germany) 398.80
1976 G,U. Wehling (East Germany) 423.39 pts. S,U. Hettich (West Germany) 418.90 B,K. Winkler (East Germany) 417.47

Biathlon
1908–56 Event not held
1960 G,Klas Lestander (Sweden) 1h 33m 21.6s S,Antti Tyrvainen (Finland) 1h 33m 57.7s B,Aleksandr Privalov (USSR) 1h 34m 54.2s
1964 G,Vladimir Melyanin (USSR) 1h 20m 26.8s S,Aleksandr Privalov (USSR) 1h 23m 42.5s B,O. Jordet (Norway) 1h 24m 38.8s
1968 G,Magnar Solberg (Norway) 1h 13m 45.9s S,Alexandr Tikhonov (USSR) 1h 14m 40.4s B,Vladimir Goundartsev (USSR) 1h 18m 27.4s
1972 G,Magnar Solberg (Norway) 1h 15m 55.5s S,Hans-Jürg Knauthe (East Germany) 1h 16m 07.6s B,Lars Arvidson (Sweden) 1h 16m 27.03s
1976 G,N. Kruglov (USSR) 1h 14m 12.26s S,H. Ikola (Finland) 1h 15m 54.10s B,A. Elizarov (USSR) 1h 16m 05.57s

BIATHLON RELAY
1908–1964 Event not held
1968 G,USSR (Alexandr Tikhonov, Nikolar Pousanov, Viktor Mamatov, Vladimir Goundartsev) 2h 13m 2.4s S,Norway 2h 14m 50.2s B,Sweden 2h 17m 26.3s
1972 G,USSR (Rinnat Safine, Ivan Biakov, Victor Mamatov, Alexandr Tikhonov) 1h 51m 44.92s S,Finland 1h 54m 37.22s B,East Germany 1h 54m 57.65s
1976 G,USSR (A. Elizarov, I. Bjakov, N. Kruglov, A. Tikhonov) 1h 57m 55.64s S,Finland 2h 01m 45.58s B,East Germany 2h 04m 08.61s

Alpine Ski-ing (Men)
GIANT SLALOM
1908–48 Event not held
1952 G,Stein Erikson (Norway) 2m 25.0s S,Christian Pravda (Austria) 2m 26.9s B,Toni Spiss (Austria) 2m 28.8s
1956 G,Anton Sailer (Austria) 3m 00.1s S,Andreas Molterer (Austria) 3m 0.63s B,Walter Schuster (Austria) 3m 07.2s
1960 G,Roger Staub (Switzerland) 1m 48.3s S,Josef Stiegler (Austria) 1m 48.7s B,Ernst Hinterseer (Austria) 1m 49.1s
1964 G,Francois Bonlieu (France) 1m 46.71s S,Karl Schranz (Austria) 1m 47.09s B,Josef Stiegler (Austria) 1m 48.05s
1968 G,Jean-Claude Killy (France) 3m 29.28s S,Willy Favre (Switzerland) 3m 31.50s B,Heinrich Messner (Austria) 3m 31.83s
1972 G,Gustavo Thoeni (Italy) 3m 09.62s S,Edmund Bruggmann (Switzerland) 3m 10.75s B,Werner Mattle (Switzerland) 3m 10.99s
1976 G,H. Hemmi (Switzerland) 3m 26.97s S,E. Good (Switzerland) 3m 27.17s

SLALOM
1908–36 Event not held
1948 G,Edi Reinalter (Switzerland) 2m 10.3s S,James Couttet (France) 2m 10.8s B,Henri Oreiller (France) 2m 12.8s
1952 G,Othmar Schneider (Austria) 2m 00.0s S,Stein Eriksen (Norway) 2m 01.2s B,Guttorm Berge (Norway) 2m 01.7s
1956 G,Anton Sailer (Austria) 3m 14.7s S,Chiharu Igaya (Japan) 3m 18.7s B,Stig Sollander (Sweden) 3m 20.2s
1960 G,Ernst Hinterseer (Austria) 2m 08.9s S,Matthias Lietner (Austria) 2m 10.3s B,Charles Bozon (France) 2m 10.4s
1964 G,Josef Stiegler (Austria) 2m 21.13s S,William Kidd (USA) 2m 21.27s B,James Heuga (USA) 2m 21.52s
1968 G,Jean-Claude Killy (France) 1m 39.73s S,Herbert Huber (Austria) 1m 39.82s B,Alfred Matt (Austria) 1m 40.09s
1972 G,Francisco Fernandez Ochoa (Spain) 1m 49.27s S,Gustavo Thoeni (Italy) 1m 50.28s B,Rolando Thoeni (Italy) 1m 50.30s
1976 G,P. Gros (Italy) 2m 03.29s S,G. Thoeni (Italy) 2m 03.73s B,W. Frommelt (Liechtenstein) 2m 04.28s

DOWNHILL
1908–36 Event not held
1948 G,Henri Oreiller (France) 2m 55.0s S,Franz Gabl (Austria) 2m 59.1s B,Karl Molitor (Switzerland) 3m 00.3s and Rolf Olinger (Switzerland) 3m 00.3s
1942 G,Zeno Colò (Italy) 2m 30.8s S,Othmar Schneider (Austria) 2m 32.0s B,Christian Pravda (Austria) 2m 32.4s
1956 G,Anton Sailer (Austria) 2m 52.2s S,Raymond Fellay (Switzerland) 2m 55.7s B,Andreas Molterer (Austria) 2m 56.2s
1960 G,Jean Vuarnet (France) 2m 06.0s S,Hans-Peter Lanig (Germany) 2m 06.5s B,Guy Perillat (France) 2m 06.9s
1964 G,Egon Zimmermann (Austria) 2m 18.16s S,L. Lacroix (France) 2m 18.90s B,W. Bartels (Germany) 2m 19.48s
1968 G,Jean-Claude Killy (France) 1m 59.85s S,Guy Perillat (France) 1m 59.93s B,Daniel Daetwyler (Switzerland) 2m 00.32s
1972 G,Bernhard Russi (Switzerland) 1m 51.43s S,Roland Collombin (Switzerland) 1m 52.07s B,Heinrich Messner (Austria) 1m 52.40s
1976 G,F. Klammer (Austria) 1m 45.73s S,B. Russi (Switzerland) 1m 46.06s B,H. Plank (Italy) 1m 46.59s

Alpine Ski-ing (Women)
GIANT SLALOM
1908–48 Event not held
1952 G,Andrea Lawrence-Mead (USA) 2m 06.8s S,Dagmar Rom (Austria) 2m 09.0s B,Annemarie

B,I. Stenmark (Sweden) 3m 27.41s

Buchner (Germany) 2m 10s
1956 G,Ossi Reichert
(Germany) 1m 56.5s S,Josefine
Franal (Austria) 1m 57.8s
B,Dorothea Hochleitner
(Austria) 1m 58.2s
1960 G,Yvonne Rüegg
(Switzerland) 1m 39.9s
S,Penelope Piton (USA)
1m 40.0s B,Giuliana Chenal-
Minuzzo (Italy) 1m 40.2s
1964 G,Marielle Goitschel
(France) 1m 52.24s S,Christine
Goitschel (France) 1m 53.11s
B,Jean Saubert (Austria) 1m 53.11s
1968 G,Nancy Greene
(Canada) 1m 51.97s S,Annie
Famose (France) 1m 54.61s
B,Fernande Bochatay
(Switzerland) 1m 54.74s
1972 G,Marie-Therese Nadig
(Switzerland) 1m 29.90s
S,Annemarie Pröll (Austria)
1m 30.75s B,Wiltrud Drexel
(Austria) 1m 32.35s
1976 G,K. Kreiner (Canada)
1m 29.13s S,R. Mittermaier
(West Germany) 1m 29.25s
B,D. Debernard (France)|1m 29.95s
SLALOM
1908–36 Event not held
1948 G,Gretchen Frazer (USA)
1m 57.2s S,Antoinette Meyer
(Switzerland) 1m 57.7s
B,Erika Mahringer (Austria)|1m 58.0s
1952 G,Andrea Lawrence-
Mead (USA) 2m 10.6s S,Ossi
Reichert (Germany) 2m 11.4s
B,Annemarie Buchner
(Germany) 2m 13.3s
1956 G,Reneé Colliard
(Switzerland) 1m 52.3s
S,Regina Schöpf (Austria)
1m 55.4s B,Jevginija
Sidorova (USSR) 1m 56.7s
1960 G,Anne Heggtveit
(Canada) 1m 49.6s S,Betsy
Snite (USA) 1m 52.9s
B,Barbi Henneberger
(Germany) 1m 56.6s
1964 G,Christine Goitschel
(France) 1m 29.86s S,Marielle
Goitschel (France) 1m 30.77s
B,Jean Saubert (USA) 1m 31.36s
1968 G,Marielle Goitschel
(France) 1m 25.86s S,Nancy
Greene (Canada) 1m 26.15s
B,Annie Famose (France)
1m 27.89s
1972 G,Barbara Cochran
(USA) 1m 31.24s S,Danielle
Debernard (France) 1m 31.26s
B,Florence Steurer (France)
1m 32.69s
1976 G,R. Mittermaier (West
Germany) 1m 30.54s S,C.
Giordani (Italy) 1m 30.87s
B,H. Wenzel (Liechtenstein)
1m 32.20s
DOWNHILL
1908–36 Event not held
1948 G,Hedy Schlernegger
(Switzerland) 2m 28.2s
S,Trude Beiser (Austria)
2m 29.1s B,Resi Hammerer
(Austria) 2m 30.2s
1952 G,Trude Jochum-Beiser
(Austria) 1m 47.1s
S,Annemarie Buchner
(Germany) 1m 48.0s
B,Giuliana Minuzzo (Italy)|1m 49.0s
1956 G,Madeleine Berthod
(Switzerland) 1m 40.7s
S,Frieda Danzer (Switzerland)
1m 45.4s B,Lucile Wheeler
(Canada) 1m 45.9s
1960 G,Heidi Biebl (Germany)
1m 37.6s S,Penelope Piton
(USA) 1m 38.6s B,Traudl
Hecher (Austria) 1m 38.9s
1964 G,Christl Haas (Austria)
1m 55.39s S,Edith Zimmerman

(Austria) 1m 56.42s B,Traudl
Hecher (Austria) 1m 56.66s
1968 G,Olga Pall (Austria)
1m 40.87s S,Isabelle Mir
(France) 1m 41.33s B,Christl
Hass (Austria) 1m 41.41s
1972 G,Marie-Therese Nadig
(Switzerland) 1m 36.68s
S,Annemarie Pröll (Austria)
1m 37.00s B,Susan Corrock
(USA) 1m 37.68s
1976 G,R. Mittermaier (West
Germany) 1m 46.16s S,B.
Totschnig (Austria) 1m 46.68s
B,C. Nelson (USA) 1m 47.50s

Figure Skating (Men)
1908 G,Ulrich Salchow
(Sweden) 1,886.5 pts.
S,Richard Johansson (Sweden)
1,826.0 B,Per Thoren
(Sweden) 1,787.0
1920 G,Gillis Grafström
(Sweden) 2,575.25 pts.
S,Andreas Krogh (Norway)
2,634 B,Martin Stuxrud
(Norway) 2,561
1924 G,Gillis Grafström
(Sweden) 2,575.25 pts.
S,Willy Bockl (Austria)
2,518.75 B,Georges Gautschi
(Switzerland) 2,233.5
1928 G,Gillis Grafström
(Sweden) 2,698.25 pts. S,Willy
Bockl (Austria) 2,682.50
B,Robert van Zeebroeck
(Belgium) 2,578.75
1932 G,Karl Schafer (Austria)
2,602.0 pts. S,Gillis Grafström
(Sweden) 2,514.5
B,Montgomery Wilson
(Canada) 2,448.3
1936 G,Karl Schafer (Austria)
2,959.0 pts. S,Ernst Baier
(Germany) 2,805.3 B,Felix
Kaspar (Austria) 2,801.0
1948 G,Richard Button (USA)
1,720.6 pts. S,Hans
Gerschwiler (Switzerland)
1,630.1 B,Edi Rada (Austria)
1,603.2
1952 G,Richard Button (USA)
1,730.3 pts. S,Helmut Seibt
(Austria) 1,621.3 B,James
Grogan (USA) 1,627.4
1956 G,Hayes Alan Jenkins
(USA) 1,497.95 pts. S,Ronald
Robertson (USA) 1,492.15
B,David Jenkins (USA) 1,465.41
1960 G,David Jenkins (USA)
1,440.2 pts. S,Karol Divin
(Czechoslovakia) 1,414.3
B,Donald Jackson (Canada)
1,401.0
1964 G,Manfred Schnell-
dorfer (Germany) 1,916.9 pts.
S,Alain Calmat (France)
1,876.5 B,Scott Allen (USA)
1,873.6
1968 G,Wolfgang Schwarz
(Austria) 1,904.1 pts.
S,Timothy Wood (USA)
1,891.6 B,Patrick Pera
(France) 1,864.5
1972 G,Ondrej Nepela
(Czechoslovakia) 2,739.1 pts.
S,Sergei Chetverukhim
(USSR) 2,672.4 B,Patrick
Pera (France) 2,653.1
1976 G,J. Curry (Great
Britain) 192.74 pts. S,V.
Kovalev (USSR) 187.64
B,T. Cranston (Canada) 187.38

Figure Skating (Women)
1908 G,Madge Syers (Great
Britain) 1,262.5 pts. S,Elsa
Rendschmidt (Germany)
1,055.0 B,Dorothy
Greenhough-Smith (Great

Britain) 960.5
1920 G,Magda Julin-Mauroy
(Sweden) S,Svea Norén
(Sweden) 887.75 B,Theresa
Weld (USA) 890.0
1924 G,Heima Planck-Szabo
(Austria) 2,094.25 pts.
S,Beatrix Loughran (USA)
1,959.0 B,Ethel Muckelt
(Great Britain) 1,750.50
1928 G,Sonja Henie (Norway)
2,452.25 pts. S,Fritzi Burger
(Austria) 2,248.50 B,Beatrix
Loughran (USA) 2,254.50
1932 G,Sonja Henie (Norway)
2,302.5 pts. S,Fritzi Burger
(Austria) 2,167.1 B,Maribel
Vinson (USA) 2,158.5
1936 G,Sonja Henie (Norway)
2,971.4 pts. S,Cecilia Colledge
(Great Britain) 2,926.8
B,Vivi-Anne Hultén (Sweden)
2,763.2
1948 G,Barbara Scott (Canada)
1,467.7 pts. S,Eva Pawlik
(Austria) 1,418.3 B,Jeanette
Altwegg (Great Britain)
1,405.5
1952 G,Jeanette Altwegg
(Great Britain) 1,455.8 pts.
S,Tenley Albright (USA)
1,432.2 B,Jacqueline du
Bief (France) 1,422.0
1956 G,Tenley Albright (USA)
1,866.39 pts. S,Carol Heiss
(USA) 1,848.24 B,Ingrid
Wendl (Austria) 1,753.91
1960 G,Carol Heiss (USA)
1,490.1 pts. S,Sjoukje Dijkstra
(Netherlands) 1,424.8
B,Barbara Roles (USA)
1,414.8
1964 G,Sjoukje Dijkstra
(Netherlands) 2,018.5 pts.
S,Regine Heitzer (Austria)
1,945.5 B,Petra Burka
(Canada) 1,940.0
1968 G,Peggy Fleming (USA)
1,970.5 pts S,Gabriele Seyfert
(East Germany) 1,882.3
B,Hana Maskova (Czecho-
slovakia) 1,828.8
1972 G,Beatrix Schuba
(Austria) 2,751.5 pts. S,Karen
Magnussen (Canada) 2,673.2
B,Janet Lynn (USA) 2,663.1
1976 G,D. Hamill (USA)
193.80 pts. S,D. De Leeuw
(Holland) 190.24 B,C. Errath
(East Germany) 188.16

Pairs
1908 G,Germany (Anna
Hubler, Heinrich Burger)
56.0 pts. S,Great Britain 51.5
B,Great Britain 48.0
1920 G,Finland (Ludovika
Jakobsson, Wlater Jakobsson)
80.75 pts. S,Norway 72.75
B,Great Britain 66.25
1924 G,Austria (Helene
Engelmann, Alfred Berger)
74.50 pts. S,Finland 71.75
B,France 69.25
1928 G,France (Andrée Joly,
Pierre Brunet) 100.50 pts.
S,Austria 99.25 B,Austria 93.25
1932 G,France (Andrée Brunet,
Pierre Brunet) 78.7 pts. S,USA
77.5 B,Hungary 76.4
1936 G,Germany (Maxi
Herber, Ernst Baier) 103.3 pts.
S,Austria 102.7 B,Hungary
97.6
1948 G,Belgium (Micheline
Lannoy, Pierre Baugniet)
123.5 pts. S,Hungary 122.2
B,Canada 121.0
1952 G,Germany (Ria Falk,
Paul Falk) 102.6 pts. S,USA
100.6 B,Hungary 97.4
1956 G,Austria (Elisabeth

Schwarz, Kurt Oppelt)
101.8 pts. S,Canada 101.7
B,Hungary 99.3
1960 G,Canada (Barbara
Wagner, Robert Paul) 80.2 pts.
S,Germany 76.8 B,USA 76.2
1964 G,USSR (Ludmilla
Belousova, Oleg Protopopov)
104.4 pts. S,Germany 103.6
B,Canada 98.5
1968 G,USSR (Ludmilla
Belousova, Oleg Protopopov)
315.2 pts. S,USSR 312.3
B,Germany 304.4
1972 G,USSR (Irina Rodnina,
Alexei Ulanov) 420.4 pts.
S,USSR 419.4 B,East
Germany 411.8
1976 G,USSR (I. Rodnina,
A. Zaitsev) 140.54 pts.
S,East Germany 136.35
B,East Germany 134.57

Ice Dance
1908–1972 Event not held
1976 G,USSR (L. Pakhomova,
A. Gorshkov) 209.92 pts.
S,USSR 204.88 B,USA
202.64

Speed Skating (Men)
500 METRES
1908-20 Event not held
1924 G,Charles Jewtraw
(USA) 44.0s S,Oskar Olsen
(Norway) 44.2s B, Roald
Larsen (Norway) and Cl s
Thunberg (Finland) 44.8s
1928 G,Clas Thunberg
(Finland) and Bernt Evensen
(Norway) 43.4s B,John
O'Neil Farrell (USA) and Roald
Larsen (Norway) and Jaako
Friman (Finland) 43.6s
1932 G,John A. Shea (USA)
43.4s S,Bernt Evensen
(Norway) B,Alexander
Hurd (Canada)
1936 G,Ivar Ballangrud
(Norway) 43.4s S,Georg
Krog (Norway) 43.5s B, Leo
Freisinger (USA) 44.0s
1948 G,Finn Helgesen
(Norway) 43.1s S,Kenneth
Bartholomew (USA). Thomas
Byberg (Norway) and Robert
Fitzgerald (USA) 43.2s
1952 G,Kenneth Henry (USA)
43.2s S,Donald McDermott
(USA) 43.9s B,Arne Johansen
(Norway) and Gordon Audley
(Canada) 44.0s
1956 G,Yevgeniy Grischin
(USSR) 40.2s S,Rafael
Gratsch (USSR) 40.8s
B,Alv Gjestvang (Norway)
41.0s
1960 G,Yevgeniy Grischin
(USSR) 40.2s S,William
Disney (USA) 40.3s B,Rafael
Gratsch (USSR) 40.4s
1964 G,Richard McDermott
(USA) 40.1s S,Yevgeniy
Grischin (USSR) and Alv
Gjestvang (Norway) 40.6s
1968 G,Erhard Keller (West
Germany) 40.3s S,Magne
Thomassen (Norway) 40.5s
B,Richard McDermott (USA)
40.5s
1972 G,Erhard Keller (West
Germany) 39.44s S,Hasse
Borjes (Sweden) 39.69s
B,Valeriy Muratov (USSR) 39.80s
1976 G,E. Kulikov (USSR)
39.17s S,V. Muratov (USSR)
39.25s B,D. Immerfall (USA)
39.54s

1000 METRES
1908-72 Event not held
1976 G,Peter Mueller (USA)

194

1m 19.32s S,Jorn Didriksen (Norway) 1m 20.45s B,Valeriy Muratov (USSR) 1m 20.57s

1500 METRES
1908-20 Event not held
1924 G,Clas Thunberg .(Finland) 2m 20.8s S,Roald Larsen (Norway) 2m 22.0s B,Sigurd Moen (Norway) 2m 25.6s
1928 G,Clas Thunberg (Finland) 2m 21.1s S,Bernt Evensen (Norway) 2m 21.9s B,Ivar Ballangrud (Norway) 2m 22.6s
1932 G,John A. Shea (USA) 2m 57.5s S,Alexander Hurd (Canada) B,William F. Logan (Canada)
1936 G,Charles Mathiesen (Norway) 2m 19.2s S,Ivar Ballangrud (Norway) 2m 20.2s B,Birger Wasenius (Finland) 2m 20.9s
1948 G,Sverre Farstad (Norway) 2m 17.6s S,Ake Seyffarth (Sweden) 2m 18.1s B,Odd Lundberg (Norway) 2m 18.9s
1952 G,Hjalmar Andersen (Norway) 2m 20.4s S,Willem van der Boort (Netherlands) 2m 20.4s B,Roald Aas (Norway) 2m 21.6s
1956 G,Yevgeniy Grischin (USSR) and Yuriy Michailov (USSR) 2m 08.6s B,Toivo Salonen (Netherlands) 2m 09.4s
1960 G,Roald Aas (Norway) and Yevgeniy Grischin (USSR) 2m 10.4s B,Boris Stenin (USSR) 2m 11.5s
1964 G,Ants Antson (USSR) 2m 10.3s S,Cornelius Verkerk (Netherlands) 2m 10.6s B,V. Haugen (Norway) 2m 11.25s
1968 G,Cornelis Verkerk (Netherlands) 2m 03.4s S,Ard Schenk 2m 05.0s B,Ivar Eriksen (Norway) 2m 05.0s
1972 G,Ard Schenk (Holland) 2m 02.96s S,Roar Gronvold (Norway) 2m 04.26s B,Goran Classon (Sweden) 2m 05.89s
1976 G,J. Storholt (Norway) 1m 59.38s S,J. Kondakov (USSR) 1m 59.97s B,H. Van Helden (Holland) 2m 00.87s

5000 METRES
1908-20 Event not held
1924 G,Clas Thunberg (Finland) 8m 39.0s S,Julius Skutnabb (Finland) 8m 48.4s B,Roald Larsen (Norway) 8m 50.2s
1928 G,Ivar Ballangrud (Norway) 8m 50.5s S,Julius Skutnabb (Finland) 8m 59.1s B,Bernt Evensen (Norway) 9m 10.1s
1932 G,Irving Jaffee (USA) 9m 40.8s S,Edward S. Murphy (USA) B,William F. Logan (Canada)
1936 G,Ivar Ballangrud (Norway) 8m 19.6s S,Birger Wasenius (Finland) 8m 23.3s B,Antero Ojala (Finland) 8m 30.1s
1948 G,Reidar Liaklev (Norway) 8m 29.4s S,Odd Lundberg (Norway) 8m 32.7s B,Göthe Hedlund (Sweden) 8m 34.8s
1952 G,Hjalmar Andersed (Norway) 8m 10.6s S,Kees Broekman (Netherlands) 8m 21.6s B,Sverre Haugli (Norway) 8m 22.4s
1956 G,Boris Schilkov (USSR) 7m 48.7s S,Sigvard Ericsson (Sweden) 7m 56.7s B,Oleg Gontscharenko (USSR) 7m 57.5s
1960 G,Viktor Kositschkin (USSR) 7m 51.3s S,Knut Johannesen (Norway) 8m 00.8s B,Jan Pesman (Netherlands) 8m 05.1s
1964 G,Knut Johannesen (Norway) 7m 38.4s S,P. Moe (Norway) 7m 38.6s B,Anton Maier (Norway) 7m 42.0s
1968 G,Anton Maier (Norway) 7m 22.4s S,Cornelis Verkerk (Netherlands) 7m 23.2s B,Petrus Nottet (Netherlands) 7m 25.5s
1972 G,Ard Schenk (Holland) 7m 23.6s S,Roar Gronvold (Norway) 7m 28.18s B,Sten Stensen (Norway) 7m 33.39s
1976 G,S. Stensen (Norway) 7m 24.48s S,P. Kleine (Holland) 7m 26.47s B,H. Van Helden (Holland) 7m 26.54s

10,000 METRES
1908-20 Event not held
1924 Julius Skutnabb (Finland) 18m 04.8s S,Clas Thunberg (Finland) 18m 07.8s B,Roald Larsen (Norway) 18m 12.2s
1928 Event not held
1932 G,Irving Jaffee (USA) 19m 13.6s S,Ivar Ballangrud (Norway) B,Frank Stack (Canada)
1936 G,Ivar Ballangrud (Norway) 17m 24.3s S,Birger Wasenius (Finland) 17m 28.2s B,Max Stiepl (Austria) 17m 30.0s
1948 G,Ake Seyffarth (Sweden) 17m 26.3s S,Lauri Parkkinen (Finland) 17m 36.0s B,Pentti Lammio (Finland) 17m 42.7s
1952 G,Hjalmar Andersen (Norway) 16m 45.8s S,Kees Broekman (Netherlands) 17m 10.6s B,Carl-Erik Asplund (Sweden) 17m 16.6s
1956 G,Sigvard Ericsson (Sweden) 16m 35.9s S,Knut Johannesen (Norway) 16m 36.9s B,Oleg Gontscharenko (USSR) 16m 42.3s
1960 G,Knut Johannesen (Norway) 15m 46.6s S,Viktor Kositschkin (USSR) 15m 49.2s B,Kjell Bäckman (Sweden) 16m 14.2s
1964 G,Johnny Nilsson (Sweden) 15m 50.1s S,F. Maier (Norway) 16m 06.0s B,Knut Johannesen (Norway) 16m 06.3s
1968 G,Johnny Hoeglin (Sweden) 15m 23.6s S,Anton Maier (Norway) 15m 23.9s B,Oerjan Sandler (Sweden) 15m 31.8s
1972 G,Ard Schenk (Holland) 15m 01.35s S,Cornelis Verkerk (Holland) 15m 04.70s B,Sten Stensen (Norway) 15m 07.08s
1976 G,P. Kleine (Holland) 14m 50.59s S,S. Stensen (Norway) 14m 53.30s B,H. Van Helden (Holland) 15m 02.02s

Speed Skating (Women)
500 METRES
1908-56 Event not held
1960 G,Helga Haase (Germany) 45.9s S,Natalie Dontschenko (USSR) 46.0s B,Jeanne Ashworth (USA) 46.1s
1964 G,Lydia Skoblikova (USSR) 45.0s S,Irina Yegorova (USSR) 45.4s B,Tatyana Sidorova (USSR)
1968 G,Ludmila Titova (USSR) 46.1s S,Mary Meyers (USA) 46.3s B,Dianne Holum (USA) 46.3s
1972 G Anne Henning (USA) 43.33s S,Vera Krasnova (USSR) 44.01s B,Ludmila Titova (USSR) 44.45s
1976 G,S. Young (USA) 42.76s S,C. Priestner (Canada) 43.12s B,T. Averina (USSR) 43.17s

1000 METRES
1908-56 Event not held
1960 G,Klara Guseva (USSR) 1m 34.1s S,Helga Haase (Germany) 1m 34.3s B,Tamara Rylova (USSR) 1m 34.8s
1964 G,Lydia Skoblikova (USSR) 1m 33.2s S,Irina Yegorova (USSR) 1m 34.3s B,Kaija Mustonen (Finland) 1m 34.8s
1968 G,Carolina Geijssen (Netherlands) 1m 32.6s S,Ludmila Titova (USSR) 1m 32.9s B,Dianne Holum (USA) 1m 33.4s
1972 G,Monika Pflug (West Germany) 1m 31.40s S,Atje Keulen-Deelstra (Holland) 1m 31.61s B,Anne Henning (USA) 1m 31.62s
1976 G,T. Averina (USSR) 1m 28.43s S,L.Poulos (USA) 1m 28.57s B,S. Young (USA) 1m 29.14s

1500 METRES
1908-56 Event not held
1960 G,Lydia Skoblikova (USSR) 2m 25.2s S,Elvira Seroczynska (Poland) 2m 25.7s B,Helena Pilejeyk (Poland) 2m 27.1s
1964 G,Lydia Skoblikova (USSR) 2m 22.6s S,Kaija Mustonen (Finland) 2m 25.5s B,B. Kolokoltseva (USSR) 2m 27.1s
1968 G,Kaija Mustonen (Finland) 2m 22.4s S,Carolina Geijssen (Netherlands) 2m 22.7s B,Christina Kaiser (Netherlands) 2m 24.5s
1972 G,Dianne Holum (USA) 2m 20.85s S,Stein Baas-Kaiser (Holland) 2m 21.05s B,Atje Keulen-Deelstra (Holland) 2m 22.05s
1976 G,G. Stepanskaya (USSR) 2m 16.58s S,S. Young (USA) 2m 17.06s B,T. Averina (USSR) 2m 17.96s

3000 METRES
1908-56 Event not held
1960 G,Lydia Skoblikova (USSR) 5m 4.3s S,Valentina Stenina (USSR) 5m 16.9s B,Eevi Huttunen (Finland) 5m 21.0s
1964 G,Lydia Skoblikova (USSR) 5m 14.9s S,Valentina Stenina (USSR) 5m 18.5s B,Pie Hwa (North Korea) 5m 18.5s
1968 G,Johanna Schut (Netherlands) 4m 56.2s S,Kaija Mustonen (Finland) 5m 01.0s B,Christina Kaiser (Netherlands) 5m 01.3s
1972 G,Stein Baas-Kaiser (Holland) 4m 52.14s S,Dianne Holum (USA) 4m 58.67s B,Atje Keulen-Deelstra (Holland) 4m 59.91s
1976 G,T. Averina (USSR) 4m 45.19s S,A. Mitscherlich (East Germany) 4m 45.23s B,L. Korsmo (Norway) 4m 45.24s

Bobsleigh
2-MAN BOB
1908-28 Event not held
1932 G,USA (J. H. Stevens, C. P. Stevens) 8m 14.74s S,Switzerland 8m 16.38s B,USA 8m 29.15s
1936 G,USA (I. Brown, A. Washbond) 5m 29.29s S,Switzerland 5m 30.64s B,USA 5m 33.96s
1948 G,Switzerland (F. Endrich, F. Waller) 5m 29.2s S,Switzerland 5m 30.4s B,USA 5m 35.3s
1952 G,Germany (A. Ostler, L. Nieberl) 5m 24.54s S,USA 5m 26.89s B,Switzerland 5m 27.71s
1956 G,Italy (L. Dalla Costa, G. Conti) 5m 30.14s S,Italy 5m 31.45s B,Switzerland 5m 37.46s
1960 Event not held
1964 G,Great Britain (A. Nash, R. Dixon) 4m 21.90s S,Italy 4m 22.02s B,Italy 4m 22.63s
1968 G,Italy (E. Monti, L. de Paolis) 4m 41.54s S,Germany 4m 41.54s B,Romania 4m 44.46s
1972 G,West Germany (W. Zimmerer, P. Utzschneider) 4m 57.07s S,West Germany 4m 58.84s B,Switzerland 4m 59.33s
1976 G,East Germany (M. Nehmer, B. Germeshausen) 3m 44.42s S,West Germany 3m 44.99s B,Switzerland 3m 45.70s

4-MAN BOB
1908-20 Event not held
1924 G,Switzerland (E. Scherrer, A. Neveu, A. Schläppi, H. Schläppi) 5m 48.54s S,Great Britain 5m 48.83s B,Belgium 6m 02.29s
1928 G,USA (W. Fiske, N. Tocker, C. Mason, C. Gray, R. Parke) 3m 20.5s S,USA 3m 21.0s B,Germany 3m 21.9s
1932 G,USA (W. Fiske, E. Eagan, C. Gray, J. O'Brien) 7m 53.68s S,USA 7m 55.70s B,Germany 8m 00.04s
1936 G,Switzerland (P. Mussy, A. Gartmann, C. Bouvier, J. Beerli) 5m 19.85s S,Switzerland 5m 22.73s B,Great Britain 5m 23.41s
1948 G,USA (F. Tyler, P. Martin, E. Rimkus, W. D'Amico) 5m 20.1s S,Belgium 5m 21.3s B,USA 5m 21.5s
1952 G,Germany (A. Ostler, F. Kuhn, L. Nieberl, F. Kemser) 5m 07.84s S,USA 5m 10.48s B,Switzerland 5m 11.70s
1956 G,Switzerland (F. Kapus, G. Diener, F. Alt, H. Angst) 5m 10.44s S,Italy 5m 12.10s B,USA 5m 12.39s
1960 Event not held
1964 G,Canada (V. Emery, P. Kirby, D. Anakin, J. Emery) 4m 14.46s S,Austria 4m 15.48s B,Italy 4m 15.60s
1968 G,Italy (Eugenio Monti, Luciano de Paolis, Roberto Zandonella, Mario Armano) 2m 17.39s S,Austria 2m 17.48s B,Switzerland 2m 18.04s
1972 G,Switzerland (J. Wicki, E. Hubacher, H. Leutenegger, W. Carmichel) 4m 43.07s S,Italy 4m 43.83s B,West

Germany 4m 43.92s
1976 G,East Germany
(M. Nehmer, J. Babok,
B. Germeshausen, B. Lehmann)
3m 40.43s **S**,Switzerland
3m 40.89s **B**,West Germany
3m 41.37s

Tobogganing
1908-60 Event not held
SINGLE-SEATER—MEN
1964 G,Thomas Koehler
(Germany) 3m 26.77s
S,Klaus Bonsack (Germany)
3m 27.04s **B**,Hans Plenk
(Germany) 3m 30.15s
1968 G,Manfred Schmid
(Austria) 2m 52.48s
S,Thomas Koehler (East
Germany) 2m 52.66s **B**,Klaus
Bonsack (East Germany)
2m 53.33s
1972 G,Wolfgang Scheidel (East
Germany) 3m 27.58s **S**,Harold
Ehrig (East Germany) 3m 28.39s
B,Wolfram Fiedler (East
Germany) 3m 28.73s
1976 G,D. Guenther (East
Germany) 3m 27.688s **S**,J. Fendt
(East Germany) 3m 28.196s
B,H. Rinn (East Germany)
3m 28.574s

2-SEATER—MEN
1964 G,Austria (Josef
Feistmantl, Manfred Stengl)
1m 41.62s **S**,Austria 1m 41.91s
B,Italy 1m 42.87s
1968 G,East Germany (Klaus
Bonsack, Thomas Koehler)
1m 35.85s **S**,Austria
1m 36.34s **B**,West Germany
1m 37.29s
1972 G,Italy (Paul Hildgartner,
Walter Plaikner) 1m 28.35s
S,East Germany (Horst Hornlein,
Reinhard Bredow) 1m 28.35s
B,East Germany 1m 29.16s
1976 G,East Germany (H. Rinn,
N. Hahn) 1m 25.604s **S**,East
Germany 1m 25.889s **B**,Austria
1m 25.919s

SINGLE-SEATER
—WOMEN
1964 G, Otrun Enderlein

(Germany) 3m 24.67s **S**,Ilse
Geisler (Germany) 3m 27.42s
B,Helene Thurner (Austria)
3m 29.06s
1968 G,Erica Lechner (Italy)
2m 28.66s **S**,Christa
Schmuck (West Germany)
2m 29.37s **B**,Angelika
Duenhaupt (West Germany)
2m 29.56s
1972 G,Anna-Maria Muller
(East Germany) 2m 59.18s
S,Ute Ruehrold (East Germany)
2m 59.49s **B**,Margit Schumann
(East Germany) 2m 59.54s
1976 G,M. Schumann (East
Germany) 2m 50.621s **S**,U.
Ruehrold (East Germany)
2m 50.846s **B**,E. Demleitner
(West Germany) 2m 51.056s

Ice Hockey
1920 G,Canada (Robert J.
Benson, Wally Byron, Frank
Frederickson, Chris Fridfinnson,
Mike Goodman, Haldor
Halderson, Konrad Johannesson,
A. "Huck" Woodman) **S**,USA
B,Czechoslovakia
1924 G,Canada (Jack A.
Cameron, Ernest J. Collett,
Albert J. McCaffery, Harold
E. McMunn, Duncan B.
Munro, W. Beattie Ramsay,
Cyril S. Slater, Reginald J.
Smith, Harry E. Watson)
S,USA **B**,Great Britain
1928 G,Canada (Charles
Delahay, Frank Fisher, Dr.
Louis Hudson, Norbert
Mueller, Herbert Plaxton,
Hugh Plaxton, Roger Plaxton,
John G. Porter, Frank
Sullivan, Dr. Joseph
Sullivan, Ross Taylor, David
Trottier) **S**,Sweden
B,Switzerland
1932 G,Canada (William H.
Cockburn, Clifford T. Crowley,
Albert G. Duncanson, George
F. Garbutt, Roy Hinkel,
C. Victor Lindquist, Norman
J. Malloy, Walter Monson,
Kenneth S. Moore,

N. Romeo Rivers, Harold A.
Simpson, Hugh R. Sutherland,
W. Stanley Wagner, J. Aliston
Wise) **S**,USA **B**,Germany
1936 G,Great Britain
(Alexander Archer, James
Borland, Edgar Brenchley,
James Chappell, John
Coward, Gordon Dailley, John
Davey, Carl Erhardt, James
Foster, John Kilpatrick,
Archibald Stinchcombe,
Robert Wyman) **S**, Canada
B,USA
1948 G,Canada (Murray-Alb
Dowey, Bernard Dunster,
Orval Gravelle, Patrick
Guzzo, Walter Halder, Thomas
Hibbert, Ross King, Henri-
Andrel Laperrire, John
Lecompte, George A. Mara,
Albert Renaud, Reginald
Schroeter) **S**,Czechoslovakia
B,Switzerland
1952 G,Canada (George G.
Able, John F. Davies, William
Dawe, Robert B. Dickson,
Donald V. Gauf, William J.
Gibson, Ralph L. Hansch,
Robert R. Meyers, David E.
Miller, Eric E. Paterson,
Thomas A. Pollock, Allan R.
Purvis, Gordon Robertson,
Louis J. Secco, Francis C.
Sullivan, Robert Watt) **S**, USA
B,Sweden
1956 G,USSR (Yevgeniy
Babitsch, Usevolod Bobrov,
Nikolay Chlystov, Aleksey
Guryschev, Juriy Krylov,
Alfred Kutschewskiy, Valentin
Kusin, Grigoriy Mkrttschan,
Viktor Nikiforov, Juriy
Pantjuchov, Nikolay Putschkov,
Viktor Schuwalov, Genrich
Sidorenkov, Nikolay Sologu-
bov, Ivan Tregubov, Dmitriy
Ukolov, Aleksandr Uwarov)
S,USA **B**,Canada
1960 G,USA (Roger A.
Christian, William Christian,
Robert B. Cleary, William J.
Cleary, Eugene Grazia, Paul
Johnson, John Kirrane, John

Mayasich, Jack McCartan,
Robert McVey, Richard
Meredith, Weldon Olson,
Edwyn Owen, Rodney
Paavola, Lawrence Palmer,
Richard Rodenhiser, Thomas
Williams) **S**,Canada **B**,USSR
1964 G,USSR (V. Konova-
lenko, B. Zaitsev, V. Kuzkin,
E. Ivanov, V. Davidov,
A. Ragulin, O. Zaitsev, A.
Almetov, V. Yakushev, V.
Starshinov, K. Loktev,
B. Maiorov, A. Firsov,
S. Pyetukhov, V. Aleksandrov,
E. Maiorov, L. Volkov)
S,Sweden, **B**,Czechoslovakia
1968 G,USSR (V. Zinger,
V. Konovalenko, V. Davidov,
V. Blinov, A. Romishevskiy,
O. Zaitsev, A. Ragulin,
V. Kutzin, B. Mayorov,
A. Firsov, E. Zymin,
V. Polupanov, A. Ionov,
V. Starchinov, E. Michakov,
V. Vikulov, Y. Moiseyev,
V. Aleksandrov)
S,Czechoslovakia **B**,Canada
1972 G,USSR (V. Tretiak,
A. Pachkov, V. Kuzkin,
V. Davidov, Y. Michalkov,
A. Maltsev, A. Iakuchev,
V. Lutchenko, A. Ragulin,
I. Rominchevskiy, G. Tsygankov,
V. Kharlamov, Y. Blinov,
V. Petrov, A. Firsov,
B. Mikhailov, V. Vikulov)
S,USA **B**,Czechoslovakia
1976 G,USSR (A. Sidelnikov,
V. Tretiak, A. Gusev,
V. Lutchenko, S. Babinov,
Y. Liapkin, V. Vasilyev,
G. Tsygankov, S. Kapustin,
V. Shamlimov, A. Maltsev,
B. Alexandrov, B. Mikhailov,
A. Iakuchev, V. Petrov,
V. Kharlamov, V. Shadrin,
V. Jlutkov) **S**,Czechoslovakia
B,West Germany

**Wszola of Poland displaying
perfect high jump technique at
the 1976 Montreal Games.**

196

Discontinued Events

Track and Field (Men)
60 METRES DASH
1900 G,A. Kraenzlein (USA) 7.0s
1904 G,A. Hahn (USA) 7.0s
200 METRES HURDLES
1900 G,A. Kraenzlein (USA) 25.4s
1904 G,H. Hillman (USA) 24.6s
4,000 METRES STEEPLECHASE
1900 G,J. Rimmer (Great Britain) 12m 58.4s
TEAM RACES
1900 G,Great Britain (5,000m)
1904 G,USA (4 miles)
1908 G,Great Britain (3 miles)
3,000 METRES TEAM RACE
1912 G,USK
1920 G,USA
1924 G,Finland
8,000 METRES CROSS-COUNTRY (TEAM)
1912 G,Sweden
8,000 METRES CROSS-COUNTRY (INDIVIDUAL)
1912 G,H. Kolehmainen (Finland) 45m 11.6s
10,000 METRES CROSS-COUNTRY (TEAM)
1920 G,Finland
1924 G,Finland
10,000 METRES CROSS-COUNTRY (INDIVIDUAL)
1920 G,P. Nurmi (Finland) 27m 15s
1924 G,P. Nurmi (Finland) 32m 54.8s
3,000 METRES WALK
1920 G,U. Frigerio (Italy) 13m 14.2s
3,500 METRES WALK
1908 G,G. Larner (Great Britain) 14m 55s
10 MILE WALK
1908 G,G. Larner (Great Britain) 1h 15m 57.4s
10 KM WALK
1912 G,G. Goulding (Canada) 46m 28.4s
1920 G,U. Frigerio (Italy) 48m 6.2s
1924 G,U. Frigerio (Italy) 47m 49s
1948 G,J. Mihaelsson (Sweden) 45m 13.2s
1952 G,J. Mihaelsson (Sweden) 45m 2.8s
STANDING HIGH JUMP
1900 G,R. Ewry (USA) 5 ft. 4 15/16 in.
1904 G,R. Ewry (USA) 4 ft. 10 16/16 in.
1908 G,R. Ewry (USA) 5 ft. 1 13/16 in.
1912 G,P. Adams (USA) 5 ft. 4 3/16 in.
STANDING BROAD JUMP
1900 G,R. Ewry (USA) 10 ft. 6 3/8 in.
1904 G,R. Ewry (USA) 11 ft. 4 7/8 in.
1908 G,R. Ewry (USA) 10 ft. 11 1/16 in.
1912 G,C. Tsiklitiras (Greece) 11 ft. 1/4 in.
STANDING HOP, STEP AND JUMP
1900 G,R. Ewry (USA) 34 ft. 8 1/4 in.
1904 G,R. Ewry (USA) 34 ft. 7 1/16 in.
SPECIAL SHOT PUT
1904 G,E. Desmarteau (Canada)
34 ft. 3 15/16 in.
1912 G,R. Rose (USA) 90 ft. 10 9/16 in.
DISCUS THROW (SPECIAL STYLES)
1908 G,M. Sheridan (USA) 124 ft. 7 11/16 in.
1912 G,A. Taipale (Finland) 271 ft. 10 3/16 in.
56 LB WEIGHT THROW
1920 G,P. MacDonald (USA) 36 ft. 11 1/2 in.
JAVELIN THROW (SPECIAL STYLES)
1908 G,E. Lemming (Sweden) 179 ft. 10 5/8 in.
1912 G,J. Saaristo (Finland) 358 ft. 11 7/8 in.
TUG OF WAR
1900 G,Sweden and Denmark
1904 G,USA
1908 G,Great Britain
1912 G,Sweden
1920 G,Great Britain
PENTATHLON
1912 G,F. Bie (Norway)
1920 G,E. Lehtonen (Finland)
1924 G,E. Lehtonen (Finland)
ALL-ROUND CHAMPIONSHIP
1904 G,T. Kiely (Great Britain)

Track and Field (Women)
80 METRES HURDLES
1932 G,Mildred Didrikson (USA)
1936 G,Trebisonda Valla (Italy)
1948 G,Francina Blankers-Koen (Netherlands)
1952 G,Shirley Strickland (Australia)
1956 G,Shirley Strickland (Australia)
1960 G, Irina Press (USSR)
1964 G,Karin Balzer (Germany)
1968 G,Maureen Caird (Australia)

Swimming (Men)
50 YARDS FREESTYLE
1904 G,Z. Halmay (Hungary) 28s
100 METRES FREESTYLE (SAILORS)
1896 G,J. Malokinis (Greece) 2m 20.4s
500 METRES FREESTYLE
1896 G,P. Neumann (Austria) 8m 12.6s
1,000 METRES FREESTYLE
1900 G,J. Jarvis (Great Britain) 13m 40.2s
1200 METRES FREESTYLE
1896 G A. Hajos Guttmann (Hungary) 18m 22.2s
880 YARDS FREESTYLE
1904 G,E. Rausch (Germany) 13m 11.4s
440 YARDS FREESTYLE
1904 G,C. Daniels (USA)|6m 16.2s
4,000 METRES FREESTYLE
1900 G,J. Jarvis (Great Britain) 58m 24s
100 YARDS BACKSTROKE
1904 G,W. Brack (Germany) 1m 16.8s
440 YARDS BREASTSTROKE
1904 G,G. Zacharias (Germany) 7m 23.6s
400 METRES BREASTSTROKE
1912 G,W. Bathe (Germany) 6m 29.6s
1920 G,H. Malmroth (Sweden) 6m 31.8s
200 METRES OBSTACLE SWIM
1900 G,F. Lane (Australia)|2m 38.4s
4×50 METRES INDIVIDUAL MEDLEY
1968 G,Charles Hickcox
4×100 METRES

FREESTYLE RELAY
1964 G,USA 3m 33.2s
1968 G,USA 3m 31.7s
200 METRES RELAY
1900 G,Germany
200 YARDS RELAY
1904 G,USA 2m 4.6s
60 METRES UNDERWATER SWIM
1900 G,W. de Vaudeville (France) 1m 53.4s
PLUNGE FOR DISTANCE
1904 G,W. Dickey (USA) 62 ft. 6 in.
ARTISTIC DIVING
1920 G,C. Pinkston (USA)
1924 G,A. White (USA)

Swimming (Women)
200 METRES INDIVIDUAL MEDLEY
1968 G,Claudia Kolb (USA)

Greco-Roman Wrestling
NONWEIGHT
1896 G,K. Schuhmann (Germany)

Weight Lifting
ONE HAND
1896 G,L. Elliot (Great Britain)
1904 G,O. Osthoff (USA)
TWO HANDS
1896 G,V. Jensen (Denmark)
1904 G,P. Kakousis (Greece)

Cycling
2,000 METRES TANDEM
1908 G,France (Maurice Schilles, Andre Auffray)
1920 G,Great Britain (Harry Ryan, Thomas Lance)
1924 G,France (Jean Cugnot, Lucien Choury)
1928 G,Netherlands (Bernhard Leene, D. van Dijk)
1932 G,France (Maurice Perrin, Louis Chaillot)
1936 G,Germany (Ernst Ihbe, Carl Lorenz)
1948 G,Italy (Renato Perona, Ferdinando Teruzzi)
1952 G,Australia (Russell Mockridge, Lionel Cox)
1956 G,Australia (Ian Browne, Anthony Marchant)
1960 G,Italy (Sergio Bianchetto, Giuseppe Beghetto)
1964 G,Italy (Sergio Bianchetto, Angelo Damiano)
1968 G,France (Daniel Morelon, Pierre Trentin)
1972 G,USSR (V. Semencks, I. Tselovalnikov)
880 YARDS SCRATCH
1904 G,M. Hurley (USA)
2,000 METRES SCRATCH
1896 G,P. Masson (France)
440 YARD RACE
1904 G,M. Hurley (USA)
THIRD-MILE RACE
1904 G,M. Hurley (USA)
1 MILE RACE
1904 G,M. Hurley (USA)
2 MILE RACE
1904 G,B. Downing (USA)
TEAM PURSUIT (1,500 metres)
1900 G,USA
TEAM PURSUIT (1 1/8 miles)
1908 G,Great Britain
TIME TRIALS
1896 G,P. Masson (France)|333.3m
1900 G,W. Johnson (Great Britain) 3/4 mile
5,000 METRES RACE
1906 G,B. Jones (Great Britain)
10 KM RACE
1896 G,P. Masson (France)
20 KM RACE
1908 G,C. Kingsbury (Great Britain)

50 KM RACE
1920 G,H. George (Belgium)
1924 G,J. Willems (Netherlands)
100 KM RACE
1896 G,L. Flameng (France)
1908 G,C. Bartlett (Great Britain)
5 MILE RACE
1904 G,C. Schlee (USA)
25 MILE RACE
1904 G,B. Downing (USA)
12 HOUR RACE
1896 G,F. Schmal (Austria)

Equestrian Events
20 KM LONG-DISTANCE TEST
1920 G,J. Misonna (Belgium)
50 KM LONG-DISTANCE TEST
1920 G,E. Johansen (Norway)
FIGURE RIDING
1920 G,T. Bonckaert (Belgium)
HIGH JUMP
1900 G,Gardere (France) and G. Trissino (Italy)
LONG JUMP
1900 G,Van Langendonck (Belgium)
3 DAY MILITARY EVENT (INDIVIDUAL)
1912 G,A. Nordlander (Sweden)
3 DAY MILITARY EVENT (TEAM)
1912 G,Sweden

Fencing
FOIL (INDIVIDUAL, PROFESSIONAL)
1896 G,L. Pyrgos (Greece)
1900 G,L. Merignac (France)
FOIL (INDIVIDUAL, JUNIOR)
1904 G,A. Fox (USA)
EPEE (INDIVIDUAL, PROFESSIONAL)
1900 G,A. Ayat (France)
EPEE (INDIVIDUAL, OPEN)
1900 G,A. Ayat (France)
SABRE (INDIVIDUAL, PROFESSIONAL)
1900 G,A. Conte (Italy)
SINGLESTICK
1904 G,A. Van Zo Post (Cuba)

Gymnastics (Men)
TEAM (SWEDISH EXERCISES)
1912 G,Sweden
1920 G,Sweden
TEAM (OPTIONAL EXERCISES)
1912 G,Norway
1920 G,Denmark
1932 G,USA
PARALLEL BARS (TEAM)
1896 G,Germany
HORIZONTAL BAR (TEAM)
1896 G,Germany
MASS EXERCISES
1952 G,Finland
ROPE CLIMBING
1896 G,N. Andriakopoulos (Greece)
1904 G,G. Eyser (USA)
1924 G,B. Supcik (Czechoslovakia)
1932 G,R. Bass (USA)
TUMBLING
1932 G,B. Wolfe (USA)
INDIAN CLUBS
1904 G,E. Hennig (USA)
1932 G,G. Roth (USA)
3 EVENT COMPETITION (INDIVIDUAL)
1904 G,A. Spinnler (Germany)
TRIATHLON
1904 G,M. Emmerich (USA)
7 EVENT COMPETITION (INDIVIDUAL)
1904 G,A. Heida (USA)
TEAM (PRESCRIBED APPARATUS)
1904 G,USA
1908 G,Sweden
1912 G,Italy

Gymnastics (Women)
HAND APPARATUS (TEAM)
1952 G,Sweden
TEAM DRILL
1956 G,Hungary

Canoeing (Men)
SINGLE KAYAK 10,000 METRES
1936 G,E. Krebs (Germany)
1948 G,G. Fredriksson (Sweden)
1952 G,T. Stromberg (Finland)
1956 G,G. Fredriksson (Sweden)
CANADIAN SINGLE 10,000 METRES
1948 G,F. Capek (Czechoslovakia)
1952 G,F. Havens (USA)
1956 G,L. Rottman (Romania)
SINGLE COLLAPSIBLE 10,000 METRES
1936 G,G. Hradeztztky (Austria)
DOUBLE KAYAK 10,000 METRES
1936 G,Germany
1948 G,Sweden
1952 G,Finland
1956 G,Hungary
CANADIAN DOUBLE 10,000 METRES
1936 G,Czechoslovakia
1948 G,USA
1952 G,France
1956 G,USSR
DOUBLE COLLAPSIBLE 10,000 METRES
1936 G,Sweden
SINGLE KAYAK RELAY
1960 G,Germany

Archery
GAME SHOOTING
1900 G,Mackintosh (Australia)
GORDON DORE (50 METRES)
1900 G,Herouin (France)
CHAPALET
1900 G,Mougin (France)
GORDON DORE PERCHE (33 METRES)
1900 G,H. van Innis (Belgium)
A LA PERCHE
1900 G,Foulon (France)
AU CHAPELET (33 METRES)
1900 G,H. van Innis (Belgium)
AMERICAN ROUND (MEN)
1904 G,H. Taylor (USA)
YORK ROUND (MEN)
1904 G,P. Bryant (USA)
1908 G,W. Dod (Great Britain)
TEAM COMPETITION (MEN)
1904 G,USA
CONTINENTAL STYLE (MEN)
1908 G,E. Grizot (France)
COLUMBIA ROUND (WOMEN)
1904 G,M. Howell (USA)
NATIONAL ROUND (WOMEN)
1904 G,M. Howell (USA)
1908 G,Q. Newall (Great Britain)
TEAM COMPETITION (WOMEN)
1904 G,USA
FIXED TARGET (TEAM, 2 EVENTS)
1920 G,Belgium
FIXED TARGET (INDIVIDUAL, SMALL)
1920 G,E. van Meer (Belgium)
FIXED TARGET (INDIVIDUAL, LARGE)
1920 G,E. Clostens (Belgium)
MOVING TARGET (TEAM, 28 METRES)
1920 G,Netherlands
MOVING TARGET (TEAM, 33 METRES)
1920 G,Belgium
MOVING TARGET (TEAM, 50 METRES)
1902 G,Belgium
MOVING TARGET (INDIVIDUAL, 28 METRES)

1920 G,H. van Innis (Belgium)
MOVING TARGET (INDIVIDUAL, 33 METRES)
1920 G,H. van Innis (Belgium)
MOVING TARGET (INDIVIDUAL, 50 METRES)
1920 G,L. Brule (France)
INDIVIDUAL COMPETITION (WOMEN)
1920 G,Q. Newall (Great|Britain)

Tennis and Lawn Tennis
LAWN TENNIS; MEN'S SINGLES
1896 G,J. Boland (Great|Britain)
1900 G,L. Doherty (Great Britain)
1904 G,B. Wright (USA)
1908 G,M. Ritchie (Great|Britain)
1912 G,C. Winslow (South Africa)
1920 G,L. Raymond (South Africa)
1924 G,V. Richards (USA)
LAWN TENNIS; MEN'S DOUBLES
1896 G,J. Boland (Great Britain) and F. Thraun (Germany)
1900 G,R. Doherty and L. Doherty (Great Britain)
1904 G,E. Leonard and B. Wright (USA)
1908 G,G. Hillyard and R. Doherty (Great Britain)
1912 G,H. Kitson and C. Winslow (South Africa)
1920 G,O. Turnbull and M. Woosnam (Great Britain)
1924 G,F. Hunter and V. Richards (USA)
LAWN TENNIS; WOMEN'S SINGLES
1900 G,C. Cooper (Great Britain)
1908 G,D. Chambers-Lambert (Great Britain)
1912 G,M. Broquedis (France)
1920 G,S. Lenglen (France)
1924 G,H. Wills (USA)
LAWN TENNIS; WOMEN'S DOUBLES
1920 G,H. McNair and K. McKane (Great Britain)
1924 G,H. Wightman and H. Wills (USA)
MIXED DOUBLES
1900 G,C. Cooper and R. Doherty (Great Britain)
1912 G,D. Koring and H. Schomburgk (Germany)
1920 G,S. Lenglen and M. Decugis (France)
1924 G,H. Wightman and R. Williams (USA)
TENNIS; MEN'S SINGLES
1908 G,A. Gore (Great Britain)
1912 G,A. Gobert (France)
TENNIS; MEN'S DOUBLES
1908 G,H. Roper-Barrett and A. Gore (Great Britain)
1912 G,M. Germot and A. Gobert (France)
TENNIS; WOMEN'S SINGLES
1908 G,G. Eastlake-Smith (Great Britain)
1912 G,E. Hannam (Great Britain)
TENNIS; MIXED DOUBLES
1912 G,E. Hannam and C. Dixon (Great Britain)
TENNIS; ENGLISH RULES (JEU DE PAUME)
1908 G,J. Gould (USA)

Team Sports
LACROSSE
1904 G,Canada
1908 G,Canada
1948 G,USA and Great Britain

FIELD HANDBALL
1952 G,Sweden
FINNISH BASEBALL
1952 G,Finland
POLO
1908 G,Great Britain
1920 G,Great Britain
1924 G,Argentina
1936 G,Argentina
RUGBY FOOTBALL
1900 G,France
1908 G,Australia and New Zealand
1920 G,USA
1924 G,USA
HANDBALL
1936 G,Germany
BASEBALL
1912 G,USA
1936 G,USA

Miscellaneous Sports
MOUNTAINEERING
1932 G,F. Schmidt (Germany)
GLIDING
1936 G,H. Schreiber (Germany)
SPECIAL FIGURES (SKATING)
1908 G,N. Kolomenkin (Russia)
GOLF (MEN)
1900 G,C. Sands (USA)
1904 G,G. Lyon (Canada)
GOLF (WOMEN)
1900 G,M. Abbot (USA)
ROQUE
1904 G,C. Jacobus (USA)
RACQUETS (SINGLES)
1908 G,E. Noel (Great Britain)
RACQUETS (DOUBLES)
1908 G,V. Pennel (Great Britain)
GLIMA (ICELANDIC WRESTLING)
1912 G,Iceland

Art Contests
ARCHITECTURE
1912 G,H. Monod and A. Laverriere (Switzerland)
1928 G,J. Wils (Netherlands) and A. Hensel (Germany)
1932 G,J. Hughes (Great Britain), G. Saake (France) and P. Bailey (France)
1936 G,W. March (Germany) and H. Kutschera (Austria)
1948 G,Y. Lindegren (Finland) and A. Hoch (Austria)
LITERATURE
1912 G,P. de Coubertin (France) founder of the modern Olympics
1920 G,R. Nicolai (Italy)
1924 G,G. Charles (France)
1928 G,K. Wierzynski (Poland) and F. Mezo (Hungary)
1932 G,P. Bauer (Germany)
1936 G,F. Dhunen (Germany) and U. Karhumaki (Finland)
1948 G,A. Tynni (Finland) and G. Stuparich (Italy)
MUSIC
1912 G,R. Barthelemy (Italy)
1920 G,G. Monier (Belgium)
1936 G,P. Hoffer (Germany)
1948 G,Z. Turski (Poland)
PAINTING & DRAWING
1912 G,C. Pellegrini (Italy)
1924 G,J. Jacoby (Luxemburg)
1928 G,I. Israels (Netherlands)
1932 G,D. Wallin (Sweden)
1936 G,A. Diggelmann|(Switzerland)
1948 G,A. Thomson (Great Britain) and A. Decaris (France)
SCULPTURE
1912 G,W. Winans (USA)
1920 G,A. Collin (Belgium)
1924 G,C. Dimitriadis (Greece)
1928 G,P. Landowski (France) and E. Grienauer (Austria)
1932 G,M. Young (USA) and J. Klukowski (Poland)
1936 G,F. Vignoli (Italy) and E. Sutor (Germany)
1948 G,G. Nordahl (Sweden)

Rowing
SINGLE SCULLS (SENIOR)
1904 G,D. Duffield (USA)
SINGLE SCULLS (INTERMEDIATE)
1904 G,F. Shepherd (USA)

Yachting
OVER 10 METRE CLASS
1900 G,France
1908 G,Great Britain
1912 G,Norway
10 METRE CLASS (OLD)
1900 G,Germany
1912 G,Sweden
1920 G,Norway
8 METRE CLASS (OLD)
1900 G,Great Britain
1908 G,Great Britain
1912 G,Norway
1920 G,Norway
7 METRE CLASS (OLD)
1908 G,Great Britain
1920 G,Great Britain
6 METRE CLASS (OLD)
1900 G,Switzerland
1908 G,Great Britain
1912 G,France
1920 G,Belgium
40 METRE CLASS
1920 G,Sweden
30 METRE CLASS 1920
1920 G,Sweden
12 METRE CLASS (OLD)
1920 G,Norway
12 METRE CLASS (NEW)
1920 G,Norway
10 METRE CLASS (NEW)
1920 G,Norway
8 METRE CLASS (NEW)
1920 G,Norway
1924 G,Norway
1928 G,France
1932 G,USA
1936 G,Italy
6.5 METRE CLASS (NEW)
1920 G,Netherlands
6 METRE CLASS (NEW)
1920 G,Norway
1924 G,Norway
1928 G,Norway
1932 G,Sweden
1936 G,Great Britain
1948 G,USA
1952 G,USA
12 FOOT CENTRE-BOARD BOAT
1920 G,Netherlands
1924 G,Belgium
12 FOOT DINGHY
1928 G,Sweden
18 FOOT CENTRE-BOARD BOAT
1920 G,Great Britain
MONOTYPE CLASS
1932 G,France
1936 G,Netherlands
1952 G,Denmark
1956 G,Denmark
1960 G,Denmark
1964 G,Germany
SWALLOW CLASS
1948 G,Great Britain
FIREFLY CLASS
1948 G,Denmark
SHARPIE CLASS
1956 G,New Zealand
5.5 METRES CLASS
1952 G,USA
1956 G,Sweden
1960 G,USA
1964 G,Australia
1968 G,Sweden
DRAGON CLASS
1948 G,Norway
1952 G,Norway
1956 G,Sweden
1960 G,Greece
1964 G,Denmark
1968 G,USA
STAR CLASS
1932 G,USA

1936 G,Germany
1948 G,USA
1952 G,Italy
1956 G,USA
1960 G,USSR
1964 G,Bahamas
1968 G,USA

Motor Boating
'A' CLASS
1908 G,E. Thubron (France)'
'B' CLASS (UNDER 60 FOOT)
1908 G,T. Thornycroft (Great Britain)
'C' CLASS (6.5–8 METRES)
1908 G,T. Thornycroft (Great|Britain)

Shooting
ARMY GUN (INDIVIDUAL, 200 METRES)
1896 G,P. Karasevdas (Greece)
ARMY GUN (INDIVIDUAL, 300 METRES)
1896 G,G. Orphanidis (Greece)
1900 G,A.Helgerad (USA)
1912 G,S. Prokopp (Hungary)
ARMY GUN (INDIVIDUAL, 600 METRES)
1912 G,P. Colas (France)
ARMY GUN (INDIVIDUAL, 1,000 YARDS)
1908 G,J. Millner (Great Britain)
ARMY GUN (INDIVIDUAL, ALL-ROUND)
1900 G,J. Millner (Great Britain)
ARMY GUN (TEAM, 300 METRES)
1900 G,Norway
ARMY GUN (TEAM, ALL-ROUND)
1900 G,USA
1908 G,USA
FULL-BORE RIFLE (300 METRES KNEELING)
1900 G,K. Staeheli (Switzerland)
FULL-BORE RIFLE (300 METRES STANDING)
1900 G,L. Madsen (Denmark)
FULL-BORE RIFLE (300

METRES PRONE)
1900 G,A. Paroche (France)
FREE RIFLE (TEAM, 300 METRES)
1900 G,Switzerland
1908 G,Norway
6 mm SMALL GUN (OPEN REAR SIGHT)
1900 G,C. Grosett (France)
SMALL-BORE RIFLE (TEAM)
1900 G,Great Britain
1908 G,Great Britain
1912 G,Great Britain
1920 G,USA
1924 G,France
SMALL-BORE RIFLE (VANISHING TARGET)
1900 G,W. Styles (Great Britain)
1908 G,W. Styles (Great Britain)
SMALL-BORE (TEAM, VANISHING TARGET)
1912 G,Sweden
SMALL-BORE RIFLE (MOVING TARGET)
1900 G,A. Fleming (Great|Britain)
1908 G,A. Fleming (Great|Britain)
RIFLE (300 METRES STANDING)
1920 G,C. Osburn (USA)
RIFLE (300 METRES PRONE)
1920 G,O. Olsen (Norway)
RIFLE (600 METRES PRONE)
1920 G,H. Johansson (Sweden)
RIFLE (TEAM, 300 METRES 2 POSITIONS)
1920 G,USA
RIFLE (TEAM, 300 METRES STANDING)
1920 G,Denmark
RIFLE (TEAM, 300 METRES PRONE)
1920 G,USA
RIFLE (TEAM, 600 METRES PRONE)
1920 G,USA
RIFLE (TEAM, ALL-ROUND)
1920 G,USA
1924 G,USA
SMALL-BORE RIFLE (TEAM)

1920 G,USA
1924 G,France
RIFLE
1948 G,E. Grunig (Switzerland)
1952 G,A. Bogdanov (USSR)
1956 G,V. Borissov (USSR)
1960 G,H. Hammerer (Austria)
1964 G,G. Anderson (USA)
FREE RIFLE
1908 G,Albert Helgerud (Norway.)
1912 G,P. Colas (France)
1920 G,Morris Fisher (USA)
1924 G,Morris Fisher (USA)
1948 G,Emil Grunig (Switzerland)
1952 G,Anatoliy Bogdanov (USSR)
1956 G,Vasiliy Borisov (USSR)
1960 G,H. Hammerer (Austria)
1964 G,Gary Anderson (USA)
1968 G,Gary Anderson (USA)
PISTOL (25 METRES)
1896 G,J. Phrangudis (Greece)
PISTOL (TEAM)
1920 G,USA
1924 G,USA
SERVICE REVOLVER
1896 G,J. Paine (USA)
REVOLVER (TEAM)
1900 G,Switzerland
PISTOL AND REVOLVER
1900 G,P. Van Asbrock (Belgium)
1908 G,P. Van Asbrock (Belgium)
1912 G,A. Lane (USA)
PISTOL AND REVOLVER (TEAM)
1900 G,USA
1908 G,USA
1912 G,USA
1920 G,USA
PISTOL OR REVOLVER (INDIVIDUAL)
1920 G,G. Paraense (Brazil)
1932 G,R. Morigi (Italy)
1936 G,T. Ullmann (Sweden)
DUELLING PISTOL

1912 G,A. Lane (USA)
DUELLING PISTOL (TEAM)
1912 G,Sweden
RUNNING DEER (TEAM)
1900 G,Sweden
1908 G,Sweden
1912 G,Sweden
RUNNING DEER (TEAM SINGLE SHOT)
1920 G,Norway
1924 G,Norway
RUNNING DEER (TEAM DOUBLE SHOT)
1920 G,Norway
1924 G,Great Britain
RUNNING DEER
1952 G,J. Larsen (Norway)
1956 G,V. Romanenko (USSR)
RUNNING DEER (SINGLE SHOT)
1900 G,O. Swahn (Sweden)
1908 G,O. Swahn (Sweden)
1912 G,A. Swahn (Sweden)
1920 G,O. Olsen (Norway)
1924 G,J. Boles (USA)
RUNNING DEER (DOUBLE SHOT)
1900 G,W. Winans (USA)
WILD BOAR TARGET (MOVING)
1900 G,L. Debray (France)
LIVE PIGEON
1900 G,L. Bon de Lunden (Belgium)
LIVE PIGEON (HUNTING GUN)
1900 G,R. de Barbarin (France)
CLAY PIGEON (TEAM)
1900 G,Great Britain
1908 G,Great Britain
1912 G,USA
1920 G,USA
1924 G,USA

The East German women won all but two of the 13 Olympic swimming titles at the 1976 Montreal Games.

Additional pictures supplied by:
All Sport 109, 164, 165 (T)
Associated Press 124, 125 (T)
Bavaria Verlag 120 (TL)
Colorsport 11 (TR), 105, 108, 110 (B), 116 (TL), 148-151, 154-155,
   160-163, 165 (B), 196, 199, endpapers
Daily Telegraph 141 (T), 166
Encyclopedia of the Winter Olympic Games 127
Fox photos 126, 130-131
International Newsreel 125 (C)
Keystone Press 132 (BL), 133 (TR), 134 (B), 136 (C), 137, 158-159
Official Report of 1928 Olympics 122-123
Picture Press 132 (TL)
Popperfoto 120 (C), 122 (T), 123 (T), 133 (TL), 134 (C)
Presse Sports 120 (BL), 121 (T), 135 (T), 136
Radio Times Hulton Picture Library 48 (C&B), 120 (TR), 121 (B)
Sport & General 48 (T)
Swedish Olympic Committee 26 (BL)
Syndication International 104, 156-157
UPI 134 (T), 138-139, 141 (B), 144-146
Wide World 125 (BL & BR)

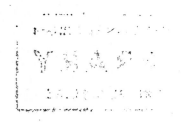